Frommer's®

Maryland & Delaware

10th Edition

by Mary K. Tilghman

John Wiley & Sons, Inc.

ABOUT THE AUTHOR

Maryland native **Mary K. Tilghman** is a journalist and editor and has lived and worked all over the state, from small towns to a farm on the Eastern Shore. She and her family have seen just about every corner of their home state and Delaware, by land and on their sailboat on the Magothy River. She lives in Baltimore.

Published by:

JOHN WILEY & SONS, INC.

111 River St.
Hoboken, NJ 07030-5774

ISBN 978-1-118-25258-1 (paper); ISBN 978-1-118-28333-2 (ebk); ISBN 978-1-118-28448-3 (ebk); ISBN 978-1-118-28714-9 (ebk)

Editor: Kathleen Warnock
Production Editor: Lindsay Beineke
Cartographer: Roberta Stockwell
Photo Editor: Richard Fox
Production by Wiley Indianapolis Composition Services
Front cover photo: Mother and foal wild ponies at Assateague Island National Seashore, Maryland, ©Mary H. Swift / Alamy Images
Back cover photo: Rock Run Mill at Susquehanna State Park Maryland, ©John G. Walter / Alamy Images

For information on our other products and services or to obtain technical support, please contact our Customer Care Department within the U.S. at 877/762-2974, outside the U.S. at 317/572-3993 or fax 317/572-4002.

Wiley also publishes its books in a variety of electronic formats. Some content that appears in print may not be available in electronic formats.

Manufactured in the United States of America

5 4 3 2 1

CONTENTS

5 MARYLAND'S TWO CAPITALS: ANNAPOLIS & ST. MARY'S CITY 100

6 AROUND THE CAPITAL BELTWAY 133

7 THE EASTERN SHORE 143

8 FREDERICK & THE CIVIL WAR CROSSROADS 184

9 WESTERN MARYLAND 206

10 MARYLAND & DELAWARE'S ATLANTIC BEACHES 228

11 WILMINGTON 289

12 THE BRANDYWINE VALLEY & HISTORIC NEW CASTLE 305

13 DOVER & CENTRAL DELAWARE 316

14 PLANNING YOUR TRIP TO MARYLAND & DELAWARE 325

Index 335

LIST OF MAPS

ACKNOWLEDGMENTS

The people I meet as I visit all the wonderful places in Maryland and Delaware make it fun to write this guide. I want to thank the innkeepers, shop owners, chefs, and restaurateurs who kept answering my endless questions, welcoming me into their establishments, and showing me a good time (whether they knew who I represented or not). I'm especially grateful to the many museum and historic site staffers and volunteers who showed me around with such pride and delight. Special thanks to Lyn Lewis of the Greater Wilmington Convention and Visitor Bureau, Sarah Duck from the Garrett County Chamber of Commerce, Joyce Baki from Calvert County, Susan Wilkinson of Historic St. Mary's City, Sara Hisamoto of Visit Baltimore, and Tina Madanat from the Delaware Tourism Office.

My family has given me tremendous support and encouragement. Thanks to my husband Ray and my children Gina, Sean, and Brigid, and my dad Bill Tilghman. I dedicate this book to the memory of my mother Patricia G. Tilghman, often my traveling companion as I researched and wrote previous editions.

—Mary K. Tilghman

HOW TO CONTACT US

In researching this book, we discovered many wonderful places—hotels, restaurants, shops, and more. We're sure you'll find others. Please tell us about them, so we can share the information with your fellow travelers in upcoming editions. If you were disappointed with a recommendation, we'd love to know that, too. Please write to:

Frommer's Maryland & Delaware, 10th Edition
John Wiley & Sons, Inc. • 111 River St. • Hoboken, NJ 07030-5774
frommersfeedback@wiley.com

ADVISORY & DISCLAIMER

Travel information can change quickly and unexpectedly, and we strongly advise you to confirm important details locally before traveling, including information on visas, health and safety, traffic and transport, accommodations, shopping, and eating out. We also encourage you to stay alert while traveling and to remain aware of your surroundings. Avoid civil disturbances, and keep a close eye on cameras, purses, wallets, and other valuables.

While we have endeavored to ensure that the information contained within this guide is accurate and up-to-date at the time of publication, we make no representations or warranties with respect to the accuracy or completeness of the contents of this work and specifically disclaim all warranties, including without limitation warranties of fitness for a particular purpose. We accept no responsibility or liability for any inaccuracy or errors or omissions, or for any inconvenience, loss, damage, costs, or expenses of any nature whatsoever incurred or suffered by anyone as a result of any advice or information contained in this guide.

The inclusion of a company, organization, or website in this guide as a service provider and/or potential source of further information does not mean that we endorse them or the information they provide. Be aware that information provided through some websites may be unreliable and can change without notice. Neither the publisher nor author shall be liable for any damages arising herefrom.

FROMMER'S STAR RATINGS, ICONS & ABBREVIATIONS

Every hotel, restaurant, and attraction listing in this guide has been ranked for quality, value, service, amenities, and special features using a **star-rating system.** In country, state, and regional guides, we also rate towns and regions to help you narrow down your choices and budget your time accordingly. Hotels and restaurants are rated on a scale of zero (recommended) to three stars (exceptional). Attractions, shopping, nightlife, towns, and regions are rated according to the following scale: zero stars (recommended), one star (highly recommended), two stars (very highly recommended), and three stars (must-see).

In addition to the star-rating system, we also use **seven feature icons** that point you to the great deals, in-the-know advice, and unique experiences that separate travelers from tourists. Throughout the book, look for:

special finds—those places only insiders know about

fun facts—details that make travelers more informed and their trips more fun

kids—best bets for kids and advice for the whole family

special moments—those experiences that memories are made of

overrated—places or experiences not worth your time or money

insider tips—great ways to save time and money

great values—where to get the best deals

The following abbreviations are used for credit cards:

AE	American Express	DISC	Discover	V	Visa
DC	Diners Club	MC	MasterCard		

TRAVEL RESOURCES AT FROMMERS.COM

Frommer's travel resources don't end with this guide. Frommer's website, **www.frommers.com** has travel information on more than 4,000 destinations. We update features regularly, giving you access to the most current trip-planning information and the best airfare, lodging, and car-rental bargains. You can also listen to podcasts, connect with other Frommers.com members through our active-reader forums, share your travel photos, read blogs from guidebook editors and fellow travelers, and much more.

THE BEST OF MARYLAND & DELAWARE

1

Maryland and Delaware may be small but don't sell them short. What they lack in acreage they make up in beauty, style, history, and achievement. Thanks to the always-dazzling Chesapeake Bay, ocean beaches, and gently rolling hills and mountains, these two states offer plenty of outdoor charms. The cities of Baltimore, Maryland, and Wilmington, Delaware, are filled with intriguing museums, sophisticated restaurants, and delightful waterfronts that make for a romantic summer evening stroll. Add charming small towns—including Maryland's capital, Annapolis, and Delaware's capital, Dover—friendly people, and a wealth of historic sites, and you've got two states worth a visit whether you have a day, a weekend, or a whole week.

These two states have been shaped by history, from the Colonial days and the American Revolution to the War of 1812 to the Civil War; by industry, from the commercial fisheries of ocean and bay to high-tech banking and information technology; and even by sports—what would NASCAR do without Dover twice a year? And what Baltimoreans don't keep up-to-date with their beloved Orioles, gather for Ravens football, or stop whatever they're doing for the Preakness Stakes?

Every corner of Maryland offers something for those who look. Get off I-95 a little below the Mason-Dixon line and you'll find scenic Havre de Grace. Wander through the Eastern Shore and stop for a tableful of hot steamed crabs. Park the car outside Frederick, and you'll find the leafy glens that surround Cunningham Falls.

And don't be fooled by Delaware's small size. It's got beaches and NASCAR, *and* mansions—castles, really—tucked in the hills of the Brandywine Valley, good food and wine on quiet Wilmington nights, and the charming town of Lewes—where the ocean is just a short walk across a bridge.

Marylanders and Delawareans look toward the future but remember where they've been. They remember their fallen friends with monuments, battlefields, and aging forts that recall battles in 1776, 1812, 1917, and 1945. You can see places where George Washington stood, where brothers died, and where slaves ran for freedom. You can get a glimpse of how people lived when these states were once colonies, or when the Gilded Age made industrialists millionaires.

Whether you visit Maryland and Delaware while on your way to someplace else or because you're drawn to their charm and friendliness, you won't be disappointed.

FROMMER'S favorite MARYLAND & DELAWARE EXPERIENCES

- **Raising the Star-Spangled Banner at Fort McHenry** (Baltimore): Park rangers ask visitors to help with the raising and lowering of the huge flag each day. The nooks and crannies and views keep young ones interested. Outside the fort, the sprawling waterfront park is perfect for families and picnics. See p. 66.
- **Attending the Preakness** (Baltimore): If you're young and want some serious partying, check out the infield. If you actually want to see the horses race for the second jewel in the Triple Crown, head for the grandstand. The race is held the third Saturday in May at **Pimlico Race Course.** Order grandstand tickets up to a year in advance. Infield tickets are available up to the week before. See p. 82.
- **Rafting the Yough:** The Youghiogheny (generally just called the "Yock") is Maryland's great white-water river. Its churning waters race through class III/IV rapids, with such names as Gap Falls, Bastard, Triple Drop, Meatcleaver, Lost and Found, and Backbender. The water levels are controlled by dam release, so the river can be ridden almost year-round. See chapter 9.
- **Kayaking Among the Cypress Trees** (Southern Delaware): A paddle on an early fall day in the cypress swamp of Trap Pond is a peaceful, exhilarating way to get some exercise. The changing leaves are gorgeous, the water is still warm, and most bugs are gone. Coastal Kayak offers tours. See chapter 10.
- **Going to a Baseball Game:** Maryland has baseball's most beautiful stadium—Oriole Park at Camden Yards (p. 82)—and the best team in the world (the Orioles, of course!). The many minor-league teams are also fun, and more affordable. See "The Best Baseball in Maryland," p. 8.
- **Walking through 4 Centuries** (Annapolis, MD): Sailors, statesmen, housewives, and slaves have trod the brick sidewalks of Maryland's capital city since Colonial days. Visit today to see how the city has preserved its memories at the State House and Paca House, while advancing into the modern age at the U.S. Naval Academy and on the water. See chapter 5.
- **Going "Downy Ocean":** Head for the crowded beaches of Ocean City, Maryland (with all those restaurants, shops, and golf courses), or to the quiet public beaches of Rehoboth or Bethany, Delaware. Both have their charms. The sand is white and clean; the waves can be gentle or furious (watch for the red warning flags). The sand crabs are used to being dug up, and the sea gulls will keep an eye on your snacks. (Don't give in and feed them—it can be pretty scary.) See chapter 10.

THE best LODGING BETS

- **Four Seasons Hotel Baltimore:** Stay at the glitzy new-in-2011 Four Seasons in Harbor East, if money's no object. Rooms have floor-to-ceiling views of the harbor, staff couldn't be more accommodating, and amenities include a warm, firelit dining room and spacious spa. Chic style awaits at every turn. See p. 46.

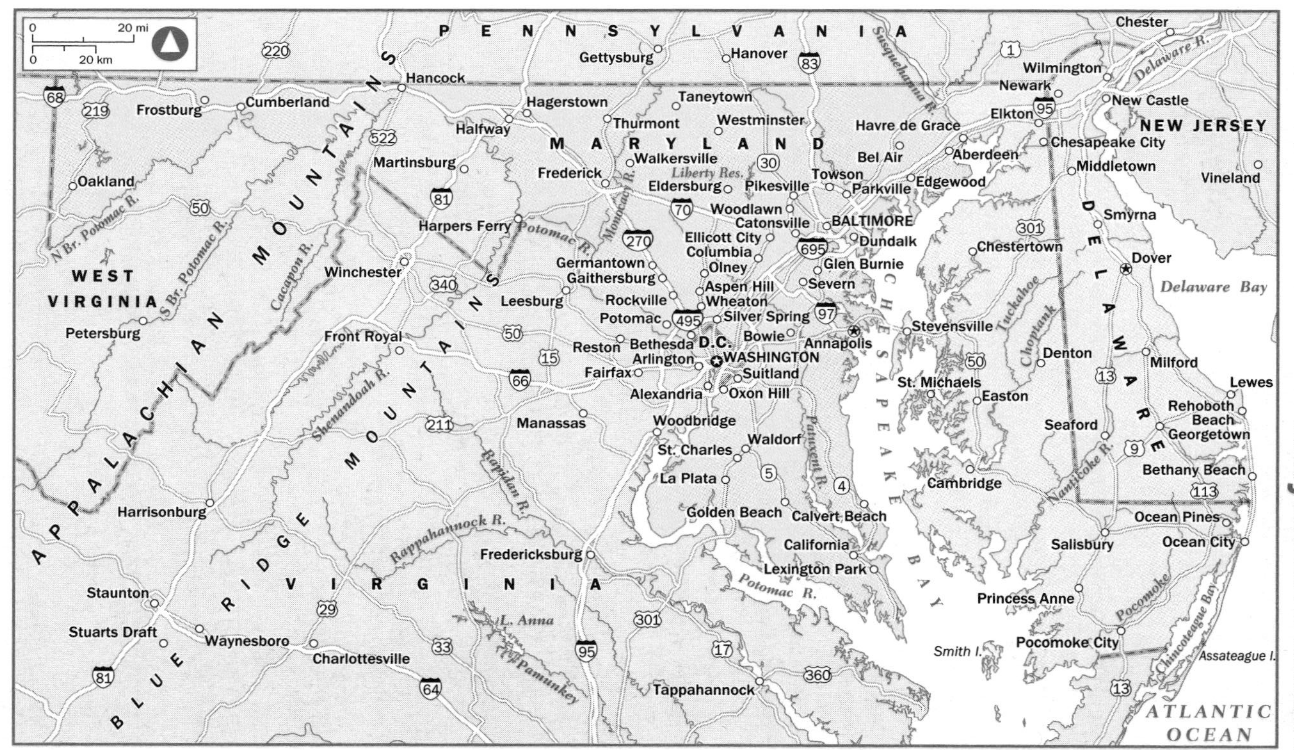
PENNSYLVANIA
NEW JERSEY
DELAWARE
MARYLAND
WEST VIRGINIA
VIRGINIA
APPALACHIAN MOUNTAINS
BLUE RIDGE MOUNTAINS
CHESAPEAKE BAY
ATLANTIC OCEAN
Delaware Bay
Chester
Wilmington
Newark
New Castle
Chesapeake City
Middletown
Vineland
Smyrna
Dover
Milford
Lewes
Rehoboth Beach
Georgetown
Bethany Beach
Ocean Pines
Ocean City
Seaford
Salisbury
Pocomoke City
Princess Anne
Denton
Easton
Cambridge
St. Michaels
Stevensville
Chestertown
Elkton
Aberdeen
Edgewood
Havre de Grace
Bel Air
Towson
Parkville
BALTIMORE
Dundalk
Glen Burnie
Severn
Annapolis
Bowie
Catonsville
Woodlawn
Pikesville
Westminster
Ellicott City
Columbia
Olney
Aspen Hill
Wheaton
Silver Spring
D.C.
WASHINGTON
Suitland
Oxon Hill
Waldorf
St. Charles
La Plata
Golden Beach
Calvert Beach
California
Lexington Park
Bethesda
Arlington
Alexandria
Fairfax
Reston
Potomac
Rockville
Gaithersburg
Germantown
Frederick
Eldersburg
Walkersville
Thurmont
Taneytown
Hanover
Gettysburg
Hagerstown
Halfway
Hancock
Martinsburg
Harpers Ferry
Leesburg
Manassas
Woodbridge
Fredericksburg
Tappahannock
Winchester
Front Royal
Cumberland
Frostburg
Oakland
Petersburg
Harrisonburg
Staunton
Stuarts Draft
Waynesboro
Charlottesville
Susquehanna R.
Delaware R.
Choptank
Tuckahoe
Nanticoke R.
Pocomoke
Chincoteague Bay
Assateague I.
Smith I.
Patuxent R.
Potomac R.
Monocacy R.
Liberty Res.
Rapidan R.
Rappahannock R.
L. Anna
Pamunkey
Shenandoah R.
Cacapon R.
S. Br. Potomac R.
N. Br. Potomac R.
0 20 mi
0 20 km

- **The Annapolis Inn** (Annapolis, MD): This sumptuous Georgian-style house was originally the home of Thomas Jefferson's physician in the 1770s. Selling points include in-room Jacuzzis, a room with its own deck, and experienced, welcoming hosts. See p. 103.
- **The Tilghman Island Inn** (Tilghman, MD): Waterfront rooms take full advantage of the inn's setting on Knapps Narrows on the Eastern Shore. The bedrooms are spacious and comfy, and the welcome is warm. See p. 157.
- **Rock Hall Inns:** The **Osprey Point Inn** (p. 179) and **Inn at Huntingfield Creek** (p. 179), two of the Eastern Shore's most gracious getaway locations, are in tiny Rock Hall, MD. Osprey Point offers rooms with a view. Huntingfield Creek is surrounded by fields with water access. Both are serene and beautifully appointed.
- **The Addy Sea Bed & Breakfast** (Bethany Beach, DE): In a resort filled with condos and rental houses, this B&B offers cozy charm surrounded by beach and surf. It's quiet enough for romance but close enough to beach fun. See p. 255.
- **Lighthouse Club Hotel** (Ocean City, MD): This hotel was designed for romantic beach getaways. Leave the kids at home and come here for secluded luxury with a view of the bay. Some rooms have fireplaces and Jacuzzis, too. See p. 267.
- **Savage River Lodge** (Frostburg, MD): Now this is camping: luxury cabins set in the woods, elegant public spaces, including a gourmet restaurant. There's even room for your dog. See p. 214.
- **Hotel du Pont** (Wilmington, DE): Not only is this a showcase of marble, carved paneling, and DuPont's latest fibers, but it also offers its lucky guests palatial surroundings and amenities, and some of the best dining in town. See p. 292.
- **The Inn at Montchanin Village** (Montchanin, DE): This cluster of buildings was once home for workers of the DuPont powder mills. Now they're charming guest rooms and suites, set in beautiful gardens, located just a few miles from the du Pont homes and gardens. See p. 293.

THE best DINING BETS

- **Charleston** (Baltimore): Southern cuisine takes center stage at this restaurant in the trendy Harbor East neighborhood. Expect to be treated like royalty as the waitstaff serves your grilled yellowfin tuna with andouille sausage and a perfect crème brûlée. See p. 56.
- **Woodberry Kitchen** (Baltimore): Fresh, local ingredients, comfort food with an edge, and dining rooms with rough-hewn wood and a white-cloth look have diners beating their way to this out-of-the-way place. See p. 63.
- **Volt** (Frederick, MD): Chef Bryan Voltaggio became a household name when he competed on *Top Chef* with his brother. But local foodies already knew about his restaurant—all-white and modern inside a Gilded Age mansion—and have long praised the chef's sophisticated way with local ingredients. See p. 189.
- **Carrol's Creek** (Annapolis, MD): The best views of the waterfront and Annapolis's skyline are paired with imaginative food here. Dine indoors or on the porch, from a seasonally changing menu. The cream of crab soup is always a winner. See p. 110.
- **Moro** (Wilmington, DE): Wilmington's Green Room is grand but the low-key Moro is a sophisticated, modern take on Italian food. It's not easy to find but it's delightful from the moment you slide into one of those brown and tangerine booths. See p. 295.

- **Krazy Kat's** (Wilmington, DE): The Brandywine Valley's finest inn also has the finest classic dining. Enjoy a leisurely meal of exceptionally prepared food in the cozy candlelit dining rooms. See p. 297.
- **The Buttery** (Lewes, DE): For sheer romance and excellent French-inspired food and wine, stop at this bistro inside a Victorian mansion. The porch is lovely when the weather's warm; the softly lit dining rooms are warm when it's cold. See p. 234.

THE best AFFORDABLE DINING

- **Tapas Teatro** (Baltimore): Every small plate at this Station North restaurant is a treat. Sangria is flavorful. You never wait once you're finally seated. See p. 62.
- **Celsius** (Rehoboth, DE): Fill your pockets with cash (no credit cards accepted) and come early for Mediterranean-inspired seafood and Asian dishes. Prix-fixe menus and early bird specials make this lovely spot at the beach a good value. See p. 247.
- **Harpoon Hanna's** (Fenwick Island, DE): The food is good; the fresh breads and muffins are outstanding. For a beach restaurant, this one is worth the trip. Set on a canal, its big windows let the sunset in. The fish is fresh, the staff hardworking, and children are welcome. Come early or be prepared for a substantial wait. See p. 257.
- **Mountain State Brewing Company** (McHenry, MD): Enjoy your pizza from a wood-fired oven and locally produced brews, in a relaxed atmosphere with mountain views. See p. 222.

THE best SHOPPING BETS

- **Antique Row** (Baltimore): In a single block of Howard Street, a few blocks north of downtown, serious antiques fans can find old silver, chandeliers, porcelain, and chairs of all sizes and shapes. See p. 85.
- **Downtown Annapolis, MD:** Main Street and Maryland Avenue offer all kinds of choices in little shops. Tuscan kitchenware, Christmas ornaments, antique mirrors, and Navy sweat shirts are only a few of the items on these charming streets. A few are chain stores, but the best shops are locally owned. See p. 121.
- **Tanger Outlets** (Rehoboth Beach, DE): Wear comfortable shoes for this colossal (tax-free) shopping extravaganza. The three centers have everything from Waterford crystal to OshKosh B'Gosh overalls. There's lots of clothing and home decor, as well as books, food, and other stuff. And Delaware has no sales tax! See p. 249.

THE best VIEWS & VISTAS

- **From the Severn River Scenic Overlook** (near Annapolis, MD): On Route 450 outside Annapolis, a stone porch offers stunning views of the Severn River and the U.S. Naval Academy. It's also the site of a memorial, with obelisks bearing the names of Marylanders who gave their lives in World War II. See p. 118.
- **At Great Falls of the Potomac** (near Potomac, MD): Just outside of Potomac, on the C&O Canal, a series of walkways will take you over the Great Falls of the Potomac. Stand above the piles of jagged rocks, the steepest and most spectacular fall-line rapids of any Eastern river, as the Potomac River rushes over them and down to the sea. See p. 207.

- **Atop the Mountain at Wisp Resort** (McHenry, MD): Ride the ski lift to the top, and before you go schussing down, take in the snow-covered slopes, the vast white expanse of Deep Creek Lake lined with the tracks of the occasional snowmobile, and a sky as blue as it can be. See p. 221.
- **From the Brandywine River Museum** (Chadds Ford, PA, in the Brandywine Valley): While the art at this museum is dazzling, take a look out the windows. The view of the river meandering under the canopy of trees is peaceful, though a riot of color in fall. See p. 311.

THE best HIKING

- **Swallow Falls State Park** (Garrett County, MD): A great place for families to hike in Western Maryland, this park's short trails wind through dark, peaty forest and offer relatively easy access to some stunning scenery. There are overlooks to three waterfalls—Swallow Falls, Tolliver Falls, and the 63-foot-high cascading Muddy Creek Falls. See p. 209.
- **Big Savage Trail in Savage River State Forest** (Garrett County, MD): This rugged trail extends 17 miles along the ridge of Big Savage Mountain, passing impressive vistas along the way. A tough hike through almost total wilderness, it's the best choice for serious backpacking in Western Maryland. See p. 209.

THE best FISHING & CRABBING

- **Calvert County Charter Fleets** (Solomons and Chesapeake Beach, MD): For charter fishing on the Chesapeake, Calvert County, south of Annapolis, is the place to go. The small harbor of Chesapeake Beach is home to the largest charter fleet on the bay. Solomons, south of Chesapeake Beach, has a good fleet, too—with over 30 charter boats and a few headboats (charters for individual fishermen, charged by the "head"). From either one, the captains are glad to take you trolling or chumming along the Western and Eastern shores of the Chesapeake. See p. 127.
- **Point Lookout State Park** (St. Mary's County, MD): Location is everything at this peninsular park, with the Chesapeake Bay on one side and the Potomac River on the other. Fish from the pier on the bay, or rent a boat at the camp marina. If they aren't biting in the bay, simply stroll over to the Potomac and try again. See p. 131.
- **Casselman River** (near Grantsville, MD): The beautiful and wild Casselman River, once empty of fish because of acid draining from local mines, is now teeming with trout. Fish tales include catches of up to 40 fish a day—and fly-fishing with the bears. One thing is for certain, though: The Casselman is a great place to fish. See chapter 9.

THE best BIRDING & WILDLIFE-WATCHING

- **Blackwater National Wildlife Refuge** (Eastern Shore, MD): The Delmarva Peninsula is dotted with wildlife refuges and protected lands, havens for migrating waterfowl and other wildlife. Blackwater is the largest of these. During peak migration season, you'll see ducks, tundra and mute swan, and snow geese, as well as the ever-present herons, Canada geese, and osprey, plus the occasional bald eagle. If you explore the wooded areas, you may catch sight of the endangered Delmarva fox squirrel. See p. 167.

- **Butterfly-Watching at Eastern Neck National Wildlife Refuge** (Eastern Shore, MD): The trees here fill up with colorful travelers on their way to South America every fall. Fans of the tundra swan also await the waterfowls' arrival to this resting place. The refuge's website keeps nature lovers up-to-date on the butterflies' arrival. See p. 178.
- **Whale- & Dolphin-Watching on the Mid-Atlantic:** The Atlantic coast of Maryland and Delaware, particularly near Cape Henlopen State Park (DE), is a good place to spot whales and dolphins. The Great Dune at Cape Henlopen is a perfect vantage point (bring binoculars). There are also whale- and dolphin-watching cruises available—even sea kayaking with the dolphins. See chapter 10.
- **Bombay Hook National Wildlife Refuge** (Central Delaware): The largest of Delaware's wildlife refuges, Bombay Hook, northeast of Dover, has nearly 16,000 acres of tidal marsh, freshwater pools, and timbered swamps. You'll see a lot of migratory waterfowl in fall and spring; then the migrant shorebirds and songbirds appear in April, May, and June. See p. 323.

THE best CAMPING

- **Janes Island State Park** (Eastern Shore, MD): For sunset vistas over the Chesapeake Bay, the campsites at this park north of Crisfield can't be beat. Many sites sit on the water's edge, offering unobstructed views and access to the canoe trail. If you prefer less-primitive accommodations, there are a few waterside cabins. See p. 171.
- **New Germany State Park** (Garrett County, MD): It's small, with only 37 well-spaced sites, but they are clean and well kept, with easy access to hiking trails, fishing spots in the park's lake, and facilities of several other state parks and forests. The 11 cabins are great options for winter cross-country skiing trips. See p. 210.
- **Cape Henlopen State Park** (near Lewes, DE): Summer beach camping is always a tenuous venture, with the heat, the bugs, and the sand. But the facilities at Cape Henlopen make for the best beach experience: There are 159 wooded sites, several with full hookups and all with access to bathhouses and running water. You'll also find hiking and biking trails, guarded beaches, and great fishing. See p. 237.

THE best FESTIVALS & EVENTS

- **FlowerMart** (Baltimore): This 2-day festival is held the first weekend in May, around the Washington Monument on Charles Street. You'll see ladies wearing flower-bedecked hats; you can also sample traditional Baltimore foods, such as crab cakes and the lemon stick (halve a lemon, stab it with a peppermint stick, and suck the juice through the candy); and, of course, there are lots of flowers. See p. 22.

- **United States Sailboat Show** (Annapolis, MD): Boat dealers fill the city dock with an array of sailboats, Spartan racing boats, and luxurious floating living rooms. Wear sneakers or boat shoes, and you can climb aboard and dream. It's the first weekend in October. The **Powerboat Show** is the following weekend. See p. 24.
- **Waterfowl Festival** (Easton, MD): This festival, held the second week in November, features paintings of canvasbacks, herons, and Canada geese; decoys both practical and fanciful; and sculptures so lifelike you'll want to smooth their feathers. For fun, stop by the duck-calling contest. See p. 24.
- **NASCAR** (Dover, DE): Twice a year, in June and September, race-car drivers turn their attention to Dover. It's NASCAR 24/7 for 3 noisy, exciting days. See p. 23.

THE best FAMILY ACTIVITIES

- **B&O Railroad Museum** (Baltimore): Kids of all ages are entranced by the gigantic iron horses that fill the roundhouse where American railroading began. See p. 73.
- **Art and Industry** (Baltimore): Baltimore's museums have a few attractions the kids are sure to like. The **Walters Art Museum** (p. 78) has a great armor collection, while the sculpture garden at the **Baltimore Museum of Art** (p. 78) delights even the youngest children. The guides at the **Baltimore Museum of Industry** (p. 66) offer insights on kids' levels and even let them try out some of the machines.

THE best BASEBALL IN MARYLAND

Marylanders *love* baseball. In addition to the American League's Orioles, there are six minor-league teams, two baseball museums, and a monument to a storied slugger.

The **Baltimore Orioles** (✆ **888/848-2473;** http://baltimore.orioles.mlb.com) play at Oriole Park at Camden Yards. The stadium is right off I-95 to I-395 at the bottom of the ramp into town. Parking in lots around the stadium usually runs about $10. The Light Rail also stops here for every game. The ballpark was designed to bring spectators closer to the action, and it does. Watch out for foul balls! There's also a promenade that follows the warehouse building along the outfield wall; stop at the deck overlooking the bullpen to watch the pitchers warm up. You can also take a stadium tour during the season that visits the dugout and the press box.

An Orioles game might be a great place to bring a client (the stands are full of them), but a minor-league game is the place for families. In addition to lower ticket prices (less than $10) and more intimate stadiums, you'll almost always find that minor-league games offer plenty of playgrounds, fireworks, and special family events.

The **Aberdeen IronBirds** (✆ **410/297-9292;** www.ironbirdsbaseball.com), a Class A affiliate of the Orioles, are owned by Aberdeen native and Baseball Hall of Famer Cal Ripken and his brother Billy. Nearby youth-size fields copy the dimensions of famous parks; Cal Sr.'s Yard, for instance, is a miniature replica of Oriole Park at Camden Yards. The "warehouse," like the one at the real Camden Yards, houses a 120-unit Courtyard by Marriott (✆ **410/272-0440**). The Ripken Academy operates a series of baseball clinics, tournaments, and the Cal Ripken World Series.

The **Bowie Baysox** (✆ **301/464-4865;** www.baysox.com), a Class AA Orioles affiliate, play in Prince George's Stadium, in Bowie, northeast of Washington, DC.

The **Delmarva Shorebirds** (✆ **888/BIRDS96** [247-3796] or 410/219-3112;

- **Harbor Queen Boat Ride** (Annapolis, MD): The kids love leaning over the rail as waves hit the boat, and it's a great way to see the bay. There's a little history lesson, but mostly this is a wind-in-your-face, sun-in-your-eyes ride. See p. 119.
- **Delaware Children's Museum** (Wilmington, DE): Don't tell the kids, but they are about to use their brains as they run through this brightly colored museum filled with places to climb and activities and puzzles to play with. See p. 298.
- **Brandywine Gardens** (Wilmington, DE): The Enchanted Woods of **Winterthur** (p. 310) and every acre of **Longwood Gardens** (p. 309), but especially the tree houses and children's garden, make these magical places to bring the whole family.

www.theshorebirds.com), an Orioles affiliate in the Class A South Atlantic League, play near Ocean City, at Arthur W. Perdue Stadium in Salisbury, Maryland. An Eastern Shore Hall of Fame here celebrates Delmarva baseball from amateur to pro.

The **Frederick Keys** (✆ **877/846-5397;** www.frederickkeys.com), a Class A Orioles affiliate, play at Harry Grove Stadium in Frederick, off I-70 and Route 355 (Market St.). The Keys draw fans from Baltimore and Washington, DC.

The **Hagerstown Suns** (✆ **800/538-9967** or 301/791-6266; www.hagerstownsuns.com), a Class A affiliate of the Washington Nationals, play at Municipal Stadium, on Route 40, in Hagerstown, Maryland.

Hall of Famer and former Oriole Brooks Robinson is part-owner of the **Southern Maryland Blue Crabs** (✆ **301/638-9788;** www.somdbluecrabs.com). An independent member of the Atlantic League, the team plays in Regency Furniture Stadium in Waldorf.

Baltimore City has two sports museums celebrating baseball. Yes, the Babe *was* a Yankee, but he was born in Baltimore in the narrow rowhouse that is now the **Babe Ruth Birthplace and Museum,** 216 Emory St. (✆ **410/727-1539;** www.baberuthmuseum.com). Next door to Oriole Park at Camden Yards is **Sports Legends Museum at Camden Yards,** 301 W. Camden St. (✆ **410/727-1539;** www.baberuthmuseum.com), filled with mementos of Orioles history as well as other local sporting memories. For details on these two museums, see p. 73 and 76.

In **Chestertown,** on the Eastern Shore, you'll find the life-size statue of **Bill Nicholson** next to the town hall on Cross Street. In the 1940s, the Chestertown native was a home-run king with the Chicago Cubs. He led the majors in home runs and RBIs in 1943 and 1944. During the 1944 season, the New York Giants intentionally walked him with the bases loaded, rather than risk a grand slam. He died in his hometown, Chestertown, in 1996.

MARYLAND & DELAWARE IN DEPTH

2

Tucked between the Philadelphia–Washington, DC, corridor are two of America's smallest states. But Maryland and Delaware aren't places you want to pass by as you speed down I-95. Nor should you make the mistake of assuming they are two parts of the same geographic location. Far from it . . . read on!

MARYLAND & DELAWARE TODAY

Marylanders consider their state "America in miniature." In the space of 300 miles, a visitor can travel over mountains, past rolling farmlands, and across a mighty body of water to the flat coastal plains that end at the Atlantic Ocean. For every season, there's a pretty-as-a-postcard view: spring tulips in north Baltimore, summer skies over ocean and bay, autumn leaves along the Gunpowder and the Potomac, and snow-topped mountains filled with skiers.

Maryland's First Tourist

"Heaven and earth never agreed better to frame a place for man's habitation."

—Captain John Smith, 1612

Delaware has its own delights. "The First State" revels in its history: Dutch whalers created an outpost along the Delaware Bay; Caesar Rodney raced on horseback to ensure passage of the Declaration of Independence; the state was the first to ratify the U.S. Constitution. And it makes the most of its natural beauty: White sands line its Atlantic Ocean shores; cypress trees wade in the tranquil waters of inland ponds; rolling hills traverse the Brandywine Valley.

As you travel through these two states, you'll have the opportunity to peer into the age of dinosaurs, see where Native Americans made their marks, trace the route of European settlers and runaway slaves, and marvel at the advances of the Industrial Revolution, the Space Age, and the Digital Age.

What's your pleasure? **Food:** You can't beat the seafood restaurants along the Chesapeake Bay or in the ocean resorts. **Wine:** Maryland wineries have produced some pretty decent vintages. **Architecture:** Colonial gems in New Castle, Delaware, and Annapolis, Maryland, are the real deal, protected for more than 200 years; and historic mansions dot the Brandywine. **Music:** Wilmington has both a symphony and an opera company, while Charm City's Baltimore Symphony Orchestra and its musical director Marin Alsop are wowing audiences at home and at Carnegie Hall.

Outdoor adventures: From kayaking and white-water rafting to sailing, fishing, surfing, mountain biking, and camping (and yes, skiing), there is an extreme variety of outdoor activity, from slow to high intensity.

LOOKING BACK: MARYLAND & DELAWARE HISTORY

Maryland

EARLY DAYS

When **Lord Baltimore** and 140 fellow English men and women landed on the shores of the St. Mary's River in 1634, the area was already settled by Native American tribes, including the Yaocomaco people, an Eastern Woodland group, with whom the first colonists traded. Also living in the state were the Algonquin, Leni-Lenape, and Nanticoke. These people are responsible for naming many places whose names are still in use today: the Chesapeake Bay, Potomac River, and Assateague.

Maryland's first capital, **St. Mary's City,** was founded by a Catholic nobleman who enacted the first Freedom of Conscience law in the world. Settlers were free to worship as they saw fit, and to hold office no matter their religion. There were other precedents set here, too. The first man of color held office in Maryland, and the first Catholic church in the English colonies was built here. A woman sought the opportunity to vote here, but, as progressive as the settlers were, they turned her down. The first print shop south of Boston was established here (and run by a woman) in the 1600s.

Meanwhile, 75 miles to the north, in 1631 Englishman William Claiborne established a trading post in the Chesapeake Bay for the colony of Virginia. Now known as Kent Island (the eastern terminus of the Chesapeake Bay Bridge), it became a source of conflict even after it was absorbed into Lord Baltimore's colony.

The colony, centered in St. Mary's City, grew in strength and number. Demand for Maryland tobacco grew in Europe, making the noxious plant the currency of the day. The economy boomed and the town grew with the construction of inns, a statehouse, and a chapel. By the late 1600s, some 20,000 people lived there.

But the days of St. Mary's City were coming to an end. Tensions from an English revolution spilled into the Catholic colony, and disgruntled Protestants led a revolution against Lord Baltimore in 1689. The crown appointed royal governors who moved the capital from St. Mary's City to **Annapolis** in 1695.

The first capital all but disappeared under cornfields and woodlands. Hidden below ground were all sorts of treasures—shards of glass, rosary beads, lead coffins, and shadows of hearths and posts—valuable markings that would enable archaeologists and historians to piece together the design and history of the first capital and rebuild parts of it, now known as Historic St. Mary's City.

REVOLUTION & STATEHOOD

The colony continued to grow. Annapolis became the hub of government and the center for exports, most notably tobacco and for the slave trade, as well. As the home of the state legislature, it attracted the wealthy and the powerful, the trader and the barrister, and the waterman and the farmer.

Farther north, in a deep harbor of the Patapsco River, another city was taking shape. Formed from the shipbuilding center of Fell's Point and the industrial center of Jonestown, the new city, named after the colony's founder, was founded in 1729. **Baltimore** grew quickly as a center of trade and industry. It became the home port of a fleet of speedy trading vessels, the **Baltimore clippers.**

As the colony grew, the desire for independence from England took root, as it did in the other 12 English colonies. Annapolis became a center for revolutionary thought. The tax on tea prompted protest. The *Peggy Stewart,* a ship laden with a ton of tea, was burned when its owner paid the tax. Protesters tossed shipments of tea overboard in the Eastern Shore city of Chestertown, in response to the closing of the Boston harbor.

Marylanders, including three Carrolls—Charles Carroll the barrister, his son Charles Carroll of Carrollton, and Daniel Carroll, the barrister's nephew—and two Chases—Jeremiah and Samuel—took part in the Continental Congresses in Philadelphia. When it was time to sign the Declaration of Independence, Maryland's four delegates stepped up: Charles Carroll of Carrollton, Samuel Chase, William Paca, and Thomas Stone.

As the conflict with England escalated, Annapolis became the United States' first peacetime capital. From November 26, 1783, to August 13, 1784, the legislature met in the State House, where the Maryland General Assembly continues to gather every January through April. This was the site of the ratification of the Treaty of Paris, the document in which Great Britain recognized American independence. It was also here that George Washington resigned his commission as commander in chief of the army.

When the Constitution came before the General Assembly in April 1788, Maryland became the seventh of the original 13 colonies to ratify it. Peace and prosperity continued as the new state grew. Maryland had been virtually untouched during the American Revolution, but this would not be the case when the British Navy returned to reclaim its colonies in 1812. This time, a single flag flying over Baltimore's harbor would become a symbol of America's independence.

The **War of 1812** began with a British blockade of the Chesapeake and Delaware bays. Many small towns along the Chesapeake found themselves facing British warships. The Battle of Baltimore, on the night of September 13, 1814, is remembered every time we sing the national anthem. American forces were ready for the British. Ships were deliberately sunk near **Fort McHenry** to keep the British and their powerful cannons away from Baltimore and its harbor. Instead, the British aimed their guns at the fort through the night. The siege was witnessed by **Francis Scott Key,** a young attorney who had met with the British while seeking the release of a doctor captured during the British march toward Washington. Though the doctor was freed, he and Key were forced to stay aboard the British ship until the battle was over. Seeing the giant flag sewn by Mary Young Pickersgill flying over the fort the following morning inspired Key to write "The Star-Spangled Banner." Set to the tune of a drinking song, it became the national anthem in 1931.

A TIME OF GROWTH

The 19th century was a time of immense growth for Maryland, especially for its most **industrialized** city, Baltimore. The first sugar refinery was built here, and saccharine and Bromo Seltzer antacid were developed here. The first American umbrella factory opened here, as did the first commercial ice-cream factory. Samuel Morse created the first American telegraph line here.

But it was in transportation that Baltimore—and the state—made its mark. The first national road from Baltimore to the frontier began construction in 1806. (Much of it is intact, from Baltimore to Western Maryland, as part of the National Historic Road.)

George Washington envisioned a watery highway between Washington, DC, and the fertile Ohio Valley. The **C&O Canal,** which stretches through the Potomac Valley from Georgetown to Cumberland in Western Maryland, includes a towpath for mules to haul the barges along the canal. A newfangled invention, the railroad, made the canal obsolete before it was even begun. But the towpath has been preserved as a national park and offers visitors 184 miles of trails for biking and hiking from Georgetown to Cumberland.

America's first commercial **railroad,** the Baltimore and Ohio, got its start in Baltimore in 1828. "Tom Thumb," the first steam-burning locomotive, even proved in a race between Baltimore and Ellicott City that it was faster than a horse. (A technical malfunction enabled the horse to win the race, but the point had been made.) Though the Tom Thumb was not preserved, a replica built in 1926 is on display at the B&O Railroad Museum in Baltimore, site of the original B&O headquarters.

CIVIL WAR & THE UNDERGROUND RAILROAD

Baltimore earned its most detested moniker in the opening days of the Civil War. When the Sixth Massachusetts Union Army troops and the Pennsylvania Volunteer Washington brigade passed through Baltimore's President Street Station on their way to Washington, DC, they had to march through the city's streets to reach the Camden Station, a few blocks away. But an angry mob gathered and blocked their passage. The skirmish resulted in the "First Blood of the Civil War." Four soldiers and 12 civilians were killed that day, April 19, 1861, and the city became known as **"Mobtown."**

Maryland was deeply divided during the War Between the States, with many loyal to the South. These divided loyalties caused federal troops to be deployed to Baltimore and martial law enacted. Guns set up on Federal Hill in the Inner Harbor were trained on the city to ensure loyalty to the Union—and guarantee that Washington, DC, would not become surrounded by Confederate states.

Soldiers crisscrossed Maryland several times in the course of the war, including on their way to the July 1863 battle that came to be known as the "high-water mark of the Confederacy" and General Robert E. Lee's final great campaign, Gettysburg. The tiny town of Sharpsburg witnessed the battle at **Antietam,** in September 1862, the bloodiest day of the war—and of any war since, even D-Day. Some 23,000 Americans were killed or wounded that day.

The war touched other Maryland towns, as well. Ransoms were demanded of the citizens of Frederick and Hagerstown to save them from torching. In Southern Maryland, John Wilkes Booth made his way through Waldorf and Clinton both before he assassinated Abraham Lincoln and then as he attempted to escape.

A star-spangled CELEBRATION

The Bicentennial of the **War of 1812,** to be commemorated from 2012 to 2014, will mark the United States' second victory over Great Britain and the writing of "The Star-Spangled Banner." Organizers say they plan the celebration to mark 200 years of peace and friendship with Great Britain.

The War of 1812 touched many parts of Maryland. It was during the Battle of Baltimore in 1814—considered the turning point of the war—that Francis Scott Key wrote the poem that became our national anthem.

The two-year bicentennial begins with a flourish in Baltimore's Inner Harbor June 13 to 19, 2012, with a parade of Tall Ships, naval vessels, and a flyover by the U.S. Navy's Blue Angels.

Other commemorations will be held in places where Marylanders met the British in skirmishes along the shores of the Chesapeake Bay, including St. Michaels, Havre de Grace, and Benedict. In Delaware, Lewes faced the British in April 1813, so look for historical reenactments and other festivities there starting in April 2012. (See p. 23.)

Here is a rundown of places to stop during the bicentennial.

In Baltimore:

- **Fort McHenry** (Baltimore; ✆ **410/963-4290;** www.nps.gov/fomc), site of the battle that inspired Key's poem, has a new visitor center with exhibits about the war.
- **Star Spangled Banner Flag House** (Baltimore; ✆ **410/837-1793;** www.flaghouse.org), the home of Mary Young Pickersgill, has a new exhibition set to open in February 2013.
- **The Maryland Historical Society** (Baltimore; ✆ **410/685-3750;** www.mdhs.org) displays Key's manuscript (p. 77). It opened an exhibit about the Marylanders who repulsed the British forces in 2011, with a larger exhibit set to open in 2012.
- **The Fell's Point Visitor Center** (Baltimore; ✆ **410/675-6750**) offers tours of key waterfront locations of the war.

In Southern Maryland:

- **Sotterley Plantation** (Hollywood; ✆ **800/681-0850** or 301/373-2280; www.sotterley.org) was the target of raids by the British fleet. The British sailors offered slaves their freedom if they would

Though the Civil War never came to the Eastern Shore, the **Underground Railroad** had many routes through the flat farmlands here, where slaves escaped north to freedom. Harriet Tubman was the most famous of the Underground Railroad conductors. A slave in Dorchester County, she escaped to lead several hundred people to freedom. Frederick Douglass, who was enslaved in Talbot County, escaped the bonds of slavery while working in Baltimore and became a renowned abolitionist. Tubman and Douglass are remembered in both counties, as well as other places where they led enslaved people to freedom.

MODERN MARYLAND

Industrial Baltimore continued to grow through the 20th century. It became a major manufacturing city, home to General Motors and Bethlehem Steel plants, Domino Sugar and McCormick Spice, Noxell, and Westinghouse.

join the British in 1814. This is the topic of a living history presentation, "The Choice," offered at Sotterley.

- **Tudor Hall** (41680 Tudor Place, Leonardtown; ✆ **301/475-2467**), the home of Francis Scott Key's cousin, is part of the Star Spangled Banner 200 Trail with a kiosk and special exhibit inside the home of the St. Mary's County Historical Society. A resident of the house, Eliza Key, persuaded British Admiral Cockburn not to burn the county courthouse.
- **Calvert Marine Museum** (Solomons; ✆ **800/735-2258** or 410/326-2042; www.calvertmarinemuseum.com) has an exhibit of artifacts recovered from one of the vessels of the U.S. Chesapeake Flotilla scuttled on August 22, 1814.
- **Jefferson Patterson Park and Museum** (St. Leonard; ✆ **410/586-8501;** www.jefpat.org) offers a cellphone audio tour; call ✆ **410/246-1966** to access the 10 stops. The park also has an exhibit about the Battle of St. Leonard Creek with a reenactment scheduled every September.

A comprehensive map of all the skirmishes in Southern Maryland is available at **www.destinationsouthernmaryland.com/c/326/war-1812**.

On the Eastern Shore:

- **St. Michaels Museum** (St. Michaels; ✆ **410/745-9561;** www.stmichaelsmuseum.org) offers a historical walking tour that includes the Cannonball House and other points of interest from the Battle of 1813. A self-guided tour map is available. Special events are scheduled for August 10, 2012.
- **Historical Society of Talbot County** (Easton; ✆ **410/822-0773;** www.hstc.org) has a small exhibit about the legend of how the citizens of St. Michaels fooled the British.

To see the full scope of how the war came to Maryland's shores, pick up a map of the **Star Spangled Banner Trail** at a visitor center; call ✆ **866/229-9297;** or visit www.visitmaryland.org/pages/star-spangledbannertrail.aspx.

The bicentennial will be marked in other locations around the country. See **www.ourflagwasstillthere.org** for details.

For more on Maryland's commemorations, including schedules, go to **www.starspangled200.com**.

During the world wars, Maryland turned its talents to the creation of military materiel, planes, and ships. Defense contractors built up around Fort Meade, the Patuxent Naval Air Station, and Aberdeen Proving Ground—places that continue to see growth as defense workers relocate from closed military bases.

Modern medicine has made its mark in Baltimore as well, thanks largely to the efforts of health professionals at the Johns Hopkins Hospital and University of Maryland Medical System. These two centers of healthcare attract patients from around the world. The shock trauma center at the University of Maryland, pioneered by Dr. R. Adams Cowley, is a model for emergency rooms around the world.

"The land of pleasant living" was once an advertising slogan, but Marylanders have taken it to heart. **Ocean City** was established as the state's first beach resort in 1875. A year later, a summer resort opened near the B&O railroad line in Garrett County.

The advent of the automobile and new roads, bridges, and other engineering marvels made these attractions popular with the average Joe and Jo. The Chesapeake Bay bridges, built in 1952 and 1973, made the Eastern Shore's delights and the beaches of Ocean City far more accessible to Baltimore and Washington residents. Construction of **Deep Creek Lake** in Western Maryland in 1925 turned that region of the Appalachian Mountains into a family resort. A Pittsburgh resident named Helmuth Heise turned a little hill above the lake into a ski resort he named Wisp. Once I-68 was complete, the trip to Western Maryland got easier and Western Maryland resorts became year-round attractions.

Baltimore, which had seen the rise of industry, a devastating fire in 1905, and civil strife in the 1960s, began to turn around in the 1970s—and continues to do so today. James Rouse's vision of **Harborplace,** a waterfront shopping/dining/entertainment center became a model re-created as far as Sydney, Australia. The immense popularity of Harborplace in 1980 led to further development of the Inner Harbor, including new stadiums for the Baltimore Orioles and the Baltimore Ravens. Harbor East is Baltimore's newest gathering spot, with other neighborhoods around the waterfront showing signs of rebirth. New industries have made Baltimore their headquarters, including Under Armour, a well-regarded maker of sports apparel.

Even St. Mary's City, the state's first city, has experienced a renaissance. Now a living history museum, its State House, print house, taverns and ordinaries, even its Brick Chapel, have been re-created as a testimony of those early days of trial, bravery, and freedom.

Delaware

IN THE BEGINNING

Henry Hudson first saw the Delaware Bay in 1609, but he was discouraged by the dangerous shoals and turned north to discover the Hudson River. Another Englishman, Samuel Argall, came the next year, but decided that he'd made a mistake, named the bay the "Delaware"—after the governor of Virginia, Thomas West, Lord de La Warr—and headed south to his original destination of Virginia.

Dutch fishermen arrived in 1631 to settle on a tiny cape of land lying between the Delaware Bay and the Atlantic Ocean—they called it **Zwaanendael,** the Valley of the Swans. It didn't last. A dispute arose between the settlers and the Leni-Lenape tribes, and the Dutch were massacred.

Swedish settlers came next. In 1637, the *Kalmar Nyckel* and *Vogel Grip* sailed into the Delaware Bay and headed north to a narrow river the settlers called the Christina, after their queen. They built a fortress and log cabins—the first built in the New World—and called their settlement **New Sweden.** The Swedes adapted well to their new home. They raised livestock and grew corn, a staple introduced to them by their Native American neighbors.

The settlement prospered, but it wasn't long before the Dutch returned to claim the land. In 1655, a group of settlers under the leadership of Peter Stuyvesant established **Fort Casimir,** 7 miles south of New Sweden. Hungry for more land, the Dutch sent troops to the Swedish settlement and forced their surrender. The Swedish settlers were allowed to remain in the newly renamed **New Amstel,** under Dutch governance.

Change would come again in 1664 when King Charles II of England granted this land to the duke of York, thus giving England control of most of the Atlantic seaboard. The settlement became known as **New Castle** and became Delaware's first capital and a major Colonial seaport. During this first English rule, a Colonial court was established and the streets were resurveyed. The town developed into a seat of government and Delaware's first capital.

The Dutch returned to power briefly in 1673 but in 1684, William Penn arrived with his Quaker followers to take possession of the Pennsylvania colony granted to him. He arrived first in New Castle before sailing up the Delaware River to establish Philadelphia. Penn, who had been given Delaware as part of Pennsylvania, divided the lands south of Philadelphia into the counties of New Castle, Kent, and Sussex. By 1704, residents of the counties of Delaware became dissatisfied with Pennsylvania, and Penn granted them the right to form their own assembly.

The colony flourished. New colonists arrived to develop **Wilmington** on the site of Fort Christina, and **Dover** was plotted in 1717 according to a street plan of Penn's devising. Sixty years later, the capital was moved to this city in the center of the state.

THE FIRST STATE

Although Delaware is small in size, its people played important roles in the establishment of a free United States. On the Delaware quarter, you'll see an image of a man on horseback. This commemorates the ride of **Caesar Rodney** of Kent County, who broke a deadlock on the vote for independence in 1776 in Philadelphia. Though he was suffering from cancer, he rode 80 miles on horseback through the night to Philadelphia so he could cast his vote in favor of the Declaration of Independence.

To meet the English redcoats in battle, Delaware raised an army of 4,000 soldiers clad in blue coats, who became known for the Kent County Blue Hens they carried with them (fighting roosters favored by Captain John Caldwell).

The Revolution bypassed Delaware except for a skirmish at Cooch's Bridge near Newark. From here, the British would meet George Washington's army at the **Battle of Brandywine,** just north of Delaware, in one of the largest battles of the war.

Delaware had one more crucial role to play in the formation of the new nation: When the Constitution was brought before the state legislature December 7, 1787, Delaware voted aye and became "The First State," the first to ratify the document.

TRANSPORTATION & CHEMICALS

Delaware's location along the Delaware Bay and Atlantic Ocean, downstream from Philadelphia, made it ideal for industrial development, especially with the coming of the railroad and the steamboat to ship these new products as well as crops from Delaware's fertile farmlands. The 1829 construction of the Chesapeake and Delaware Canal offered shippers a shortcut from the Chesapeake Bay (and Baltimore, Washington, and points south) to the Atlantic. Wilmington grew in size and stature.

The arrival of a French aristocrat, **E. I. du Pont,** brought great change to Delaware. He established his black powder mill on the banks of the Brandywine River in 1802. This endeavor grew as the du Pont family extended their research into a wide variety of chemical products used by the military, aerospace industry, and homeowners alike as du Pont became the largest chemical manufacturer in America.

The chemical industries of DuPont continue to pump millions of dollars into the Delaware economy. DuPont money is also responsible for the famous "châteaux" of the Brandywine Valley that visitors flock to each year: Winterthur, Nemours, and Longwood Gardens, as well as Hagley, home of the original powder mill.

With an eye on Baltimore's Inner Harbor, the city planners of Wilmington have developed the **Riverfront** in the past decade in an effort to revive the downtown district. Museums, restaurants, a new stadium, and tall residential buildings have changed the waterfront significantly.

Visitors come to Delaware for many other reasons, as well. Slots at Delaware Park, Harrington, and Dover Downs have made the state a **gambling** mecca. Twice a year,

NASCAR fans descend on Dover by the tens of thousands. **Sales-tax-free shopping** makes the Rehoboth outlets even better. And then there are the **beaches:** The quiet resorts of Fenwick and Bethany, the party known as Dewey, and the towns of Rehoboth and Lewes not only have lovely beaches but attractive small-town charm as well. Add the outdoor delights of a network of great **state parks**—though not even one national park—and you've got lots of fun things to choose from.

ART & ARCHITECTURE

Rowhouses are part of why Baltimore is "Charm City." Low rows of flat-fronted houses have three marble steps leading to the front door. Pink Baltimore brick faces the exterior of many, though you might just see the pink-and-gray fake stone veneer known as **Formstone.** Baltimore's rowhouses have been undergoing a renaissance since the 1970s, when the city sold vacant houses for a buck apiece. You'll find these beauties in Otterbein, near Oriole Park, in Federal Hill, Canton, and Fell's Point. The longest row of rowhouses, at 1,800 feet, is in the 2600 block of Wilkens Avenue in west Baltimore.

Too symmetrical for you? How about a bit of architecture with a European flair? Take a walk up Charles Street and you'll find a row of well-endowed **Beaux Arts** shops and offices along the street, the palatial homes facing the parks around the Washington Monument.

For great **mansions,** the place to go is the Brandywine Valley near Wilmington. Sure, there are great houses in Maryland (the Carroll and Garrett mansions in Baltimore, p. 72 and 79, and the Paca House in Annapolis, p. 117, for example), but the du Pont family has built the most striking examples open to the public. Not only houses, but gardens, too, make Nemours, Winterthur, Longwood Gardens, and Hagley spectacular.

Williamsburg's Colonial streets may be famous but the buildings of **Annapolis** and **New Castle** were built in the 1700s and some even in the 1600s. Carefully preserved Georgian and Federal beauties line the streets of these small towns.

MARYLAND & DELAWARE IN POP CULTURE

Filmed in Maryland

Charm City has had a starring, or at least supporting, role in movies since the early 20th century. Alfred Hitchcock re-created a waterfront street for *Marnie,* and James Bond landed at Friendship Airport (now BWI) with Pussy Galore in *Goldfinger.*

Two Baltimoreans have put their hometown in a variety of movies. John Waters filmed lots of movies in Baltimore from the early *Pink Flamingoes* to the more mainstream *Cry-Baby,* with Johnny Depp, and *Serial Mom,* with Kathleen Turner. *Serial Mom* was a homecoming for Turner, who studied drama at the University of Maryland–Baltimore County.

The musical version of *Hairspray* wasn't filmed in Baltimore—that was Toronto, hon. And that's John Travolta trying to sound like he's really from "Muriland." He'd been to B-more before to film *Ladder 49* in 2004, and we loved him then, too.

Local boy Barry Levinson paid homage to our town in some of his early movies: *Tin Men, Avalon,* and *Liberty Heights,* and of course, *Diner.*

Another local boy, Kevin Clash—you may know his voice as Elmo—was recently the star of a feature film documentary, *Being Elmo: A Puppeteer's Journey.*

We've had our fair share of silver screen beauties. Nicole Kidman was in town to shoot the *Invasion,* released in 2007. Renée Zellweger starred in *He's Just Not That Into You,* with Baltimore stepping into the role of Boston. Diana Ross never actually came to Baltimore when she starred in the 1972 biopic *Lady Sings the Blues,* about Baltimore's Billie Holiday. But that was Whoopi Goldberg in the two-hankie *Clara's Heart.* Elizabeth McGovern came to town twice for *Bedroom Window,* a 1987 murder mystery, and 1991's *He Said, She Said,* which also starred Kevin Bacon, whose six degrees of Baltimore go back to *Diner.*

Thrillers by Marylander Tom Clancy were filmed locally as well. That's the Ravens' stadium being blown up in *The Sum of All Fears* (2002). Annapolis was the setting for Harrison Ford in 1992's *Patriot Games.* Ford had previously been in Baltimore to film the forgettable *Mosquito Coast* in 1986.

Oriole Park at Camden Yards got its star turn, too, in *Major League,* with Charlie Sheen and Tom Berenson; and in *The Babe,* with John Goodman playing Baltimore's Babe Ruth. Kevin Kline came to an Orioles game to throw out the first pitch in *Dave.*

And what better place for a romance than Baltimore, setting for *Sleepless in Seattle* and *The Accidental Tourist* (based on a novel by Baltimorean Anne Tyler). *Step Up* (and *Step Up* 2) showed the grittier side of Baltimore—as well as the refined Baltimore School for the Arts.

The Maryland countryside was the backdrop of a few movies as well. *Wedding Crashers* and *Failure to Launch* are set on the Eastern Shore. Oprah Winfrey starred in *Beloved,* shot in the countryside north of Baltimore in 1988. Sissy Spacek spent time in Ocean City for *Violets Are Blue* in 1986, and then returned to nearby Berlin to film *Tuck Everlasting* in 2002. Little Berlin was turned upside down earlier by Julia Roberts and Richard Gere, when they came to film *Runaway Bride.*

In Robert Redford's film about Mary Surratt, *The Conspiracy,* set in the Civil War era, Georgia stood in for Washington, DC, but some scenes were shot at Mary Surratt's house—and the curator advised the filmmakers.

Another American war fought in Maryland was featured in the PBS documentary *The War of 1812.* Parts were shot in Maryland.

Oh, and one more. The people of suburban Baltimore County and Frederick County would like it if everyone forgot that *The Blair Witch Project* was shot there in 1999.

TV & Books

Baltimoreans remain proud of their town's starring role in *Homicide: Life on the Streets.* HBO's *The Wire,* also by David Simon, was filmed here, as well.

The good-natured folks of Delaware haven't gotten their own dramatic television show, but the Delaware-based *Punkin Chunkin* documentary series has given the state its 15 minutes of fame. It's been featured on ESPN, Discovery, and the Smithsonian Channel among other outlets.

A wide variety of books have local settings. James Michener wrote his historical *Chesapeake* (Random House, 1978) while living on the Eastern Shore. Though it's fiction, the book offers a good history of the area and the watermen who make their living on the Bay.

Several other books celebrate the Chesapeake: William H. Warner's *Beautiful Swimmers* (Little, Brown, 1976), a Pulitzer Prize–winning study of the blue crab; *An Island Out of Time* (Norton, 1996), by Tom Horton, chronicles his 3 years living on remote Smith Island. Cambridge native John Barth set his epic *The Sotweed Factor* (Atlantic Books, 1960) on the Eastern Shore. Children have been reading Katherine Paterson's *Jacob I Have Loved,* a Newbery Medal winner, since Crowell published it in 1980.

MARYLAND beers: MORE THAN NATTY BOH!

There was a time (still is in some parts) when a National Bohemian was the local choice for beer. Times have changed, and instead of reaching for a Natty Boh, beer lovers are crowding into craft breweries for a tour, a tasting—and sometimes a whole meal to go with that brew.

Baltimore's **Clipper City Brewing Company** (✆ **410/247-7822;** www.hsbeer.com) is making waves with its **Heavy Seas** ale brewed in Baltimore County. There are tours and tastings on Saturdays. Look for the Heavy Seas Ale House to open in 2012 in Harbor East.

The Brewer's Art (✆ **410/547-6925;** www.thebrewersart.com) is a restaurant and microbrewery; their regular and seasonal beers are served up in their Mount Vernon restaurant at 1016 N. Charles St. Their "Resurrection" is an Abbey-style ale.

In Frederick, the nationally distributed **Flying Dog Brewery** (✆ **301/694-7899;** www.flyingdogales.com) offers tours of its brewery Thursday and Friday evenings and Saturday afternoon.

On the east side of the Chesapeake, **Dogfish Head Brewery** (✆ **302/684-1000;** www.dogfish.com), with a brewpub in Rehoboth, Delaware, and a brewery (with tours and tastings) in nearby Milton, offers "off-centered" brews—raisin-, and honey- flavored, for instance.

The **Fordham Brewing Company** (✆ **302/678-4810;** fordhambrewing.com) got its start in Annapolis at Rams Head Tavern, where the beer is still served; now brewed in Dover, where tours are offered every day but Sunday.

In Berlin, Maryland, near Ocean City, a new brewery opened in spring 2011 and by fall had to add two new tanks to meet with demand. **Burley Oak** (✆ **443/513-4647;** www.burleyoak.com) serves only beer nightly at the brewery.

Evolution Craft Brewing Company (✆ **443/260-BEER** [2337]; www.evolutioncraftbrewing.com) opened a tasting room in Delmar on the border of Maryland and Delaware, and in 2012 will open a brew pub in Salisbury, Maryland.

As for **Natty Boh,** it's on the menu at Oriole Park at Camden Yards and Boh-logo products are for sale in the Fell's Point shop, **Natty Boh Gear** (✆ **410/276-1038**).

So yeah, Boh-man, we still love ya.

Roots (Doubleday, 1976) opens in Annapolis. Author Alex Haley and his main character Kunta Kinte are remembered at the City Dock there.

The novelist Anne Tyler sets almost all of her books in and around Baltimore. Several have been made into movies, most notably *The Accidental Tourist* (Knopf, 1985). *Ladder of Years* (Knopf, 1995) takes place at the beach.

Nora Roberts, a prolific romance writer, has set several of her books in her adopted state of Maryland. The four-book *Chesapeake Bay* collection is set in St. Michaels and Baltimore.

Baltimore native and sportswriter Frank DeFord based his novel *An American Summer* (Sourcebooks, 2002) in 1954 Baltimore County.

James McBride's *Song Yet Sung,* published in 2008, chronicles a runaway slave's experiences on the Eastern Shore.

Eating & Drinking

If you visit either Maryland or Delaware, you'll want to order seafood. With the Chesapeake Bay and Atlantic Ocean so close, seafood is taken *very* seriously. Crabs used to be available only in the summer, but now you can get crab served any which way year-round. Alas, the crabmeat is often imported from southern waters or, even more shocking, from Asia. It's all blue crab, but it isn't all the same.

Local cooks have come up with the most creative ways to prepare it: soups (white cream of crab or red Maryland crab soups), crab dip, chicken and steak topped with crabmeat, and crab Imperial, a rich crab dish topped with a mayo mixture and broiled.

By far, though, the most popular ways to enjoy crab are **steamed** or as a **crab cake.**

Steamed crabs come piled high under a spicy helping of **Old Bay Seasoning.** Go ahead, grab a mallet and a knife and get your hands dirty. (Someone will show you how to open the crab.) You'll be delighted by the sweet white meat hidden underneath that bright red shell.

If that's too messy, crab cakes, broiled or fried, are the area's most perfect food.

If the month ends in an *r*, it's **oyster** season. Fried, swimming in a milky stew, or raw on the half shell, oysters are a seasonal delight that were the cause of "Oyster Wars" a century ago.

Fish lovers await the short seasons for **roe shad** and **rockfish** (striped bass) every year. They appear as specials on restaurant menus.

WHEN TO GO

The resort towns on the Atlantic, especially Fourth of July through Labor Day, are most popular in summer and usually quite crowded. The shoulder season, May and especially September, is a great time to find cheaper rates, comfortable temperatures, and quieter beaches. Peak season for the Eastern Shore, Annapolis, and Southern Maryland is April through October, when the weather is clear for boating and the fish are biting. Most everything is open in Baltimore year-round, though because of its boating culture and baseball season, summer is the most popular and crowded time to visit. May and fall bring the convention crowds to Baltimore, but the sunny, less humid weather makes a visit more comfortable. Western Maryland attracts visitors year-round, though spring can be too cool and soggy. Fall is magnificent, especially around mid-October; when it snows, winter is beautiful; summers are cooler here than in the rest of the state, a nice respite from the mid-Atlantic heat and humidity. Wilmington and the Brandywine Valley are year-round destinations.

Weather

Maryland and Delaware are blessed with all four seasons. Spring can be wet and soggy with high winds in February and March. But the temperatures can be warm and inviting on the plentiful sunny days. You may even need your shorts if the humidity rises. And rise it will by late May or June. Coupled with temperatures in the 80s, 90s, and lately the 100s, you're going to want to find air-conditioning or at least a waterside retreat where you can catch a cool breeze. We don't have the dry heat of Las Vegas or Phoenix. Fall may be the most beautiful of seasons in Maryland and Delaware. From the shore to the mountains, the temperatures are pleasant, especially on sunny days, and the nights are cool (take a coat if you're headed to Western Maryland). We call snow "the white death from the sky" here and run out for toilet paper and milk at the first warning of snow or ice; and we don't drive in it very well. Luckily, most of the time, the weather is out of the freezing range. Western Marylanders, on the other hand, welcome the snow, hauling out their skis and sleds and reveling in it. Artificial snow makes skiing possible there from about Thanksgiving to President's Day or later.

Baltimore's Average Monthly Temperatures & Precipitation

	JAN	FEB	MAR	APR	MAY	JUNE	JULY	AUG	SEPT	OCT	NOV	DEC
Temp. (°F)	35	37	46	56	66	75	79	77	74	59	49	39
Temp. (°C)	2	3	8	13	19	24	26	25	23	15	9	4
Precip. (in.)	3.1	3.2	3.0	3.7	3.4	3.7	3.5	4.1	3.5	3.5	3	3.3

Deep Creek Lake's Average Monthly Temperatures & Precipitation

	JAN	FEB	MAR	APR	MAY	JUNE	JULY	AUG	SEPT	OCT	NOV	DEC
Temp. (°F)	24	26	36	46	56	64	68	67	61	49	39	29
Temp. (°C)	-4	-3	2	8	13	18	20	19	16	9	4	-2
Precip. (in.)	4.1	3.5	4.4	4.2	4.4	4.3	5.4	4.3	3.7	3.4	4	4.6

Holidays

Banks, government offices, post offices, and many stores, restaurants, and museums are closed on the following legal national holidays: January 1 (New Year's Day), the third Monday in January (Martin Luther King, Jr., Day), the third Monday in February (Presidents' Day), the last Monday in May (Memorial Day), July 4 (Independence Day), the first Monday in September (Labor Day), the second Monday in October (Columbus Day), November 11 (Veterans' Day/Armistice Day), the fourth Thursday in November (Thanksgiving Day), and December 25 (Christmas). In Baltimore, Defenders Day is a city holiday (though it's mostly business as usual); it's September 12. The Tuesday after the first Monday in November is Election Day, a federal government holiday in presidential-election years (every 4 years, next in 2012).

Calendar of Events

For an exhaustive list of events beyond those listed here, check **http://events.frommers.com**, where you'll find a searchable, up-to-the-minute roster of what's happening in cities all over the world.

JANUARY

Chesapeake Bay Boat Show (Baltimore Convention Center, Baltimore; ✆ **617/472-1442;** www.baltimoreboatshow.com): Dream of summer while climbing aboard the boats. Four days in mid-January.

FEBRUARY

American Council Craft Show (Baltimore; http://public.craftcouncil.org/baltimore): Hundreds of the nation's finest crafters bring their wares for this show the last weekend in February. The ACC has shows around the country, but this is the biggest.

MARCH

St. Patrick's Day Parade and Festival (Coastal Hwy., Ocean City, MD; ✆ **800/OC-OCEAN** [626-2326]; www.ococean.com): The second-largest parade in Maryland features floats and live Irish dancing and entertainment. Saturday nearest the actual day.

Maryland Day (Historic St. Mary's City and Annapolis, MD; ✆ **800/762-1634** for St. Mary's, or **410/267-8146** for Annapolis; www.marylandday.org): Tours and ceremonies at historic sites. On or near March 25.

APRIL

My Lady's Manor Steeplechase Races (Ladew Topiary Gardens, Rte. 146 and Pocock Rd., Monkton, MD; ✆ **410/557-9570**): Annual running of the steeplechase. Saturday in mid-April.

MAY

Decoy and Wildlife Art Festival (Havre de Grace Decoy Museum, Havre de Grace, MD; ✆ **410/939-3739;** www.decoymuseum.com): Auctions, retriever demonstrations, and carving competitions. First weekend in May.

FlowerMart (Mount Vernon, Baltimore; ✆ **410/323-0022;** www.flowermart.org): A charming tradition known for its flowers, lemon sticks, and crab cakes. First weekend in May.

U.S. Naval Academy Commissioning Week (Annapolis, MD; ✆ **410/293-8687**): Activities include an air show by the Blue Angels, several dress parades, and graduation. The air show stops traffic near the Severn River and attracts lots of spectators. Other events are closed to the public. Mid-May.

Preakness Week (Baltimore area; ✆ **410/542-9400;** www.preakness.com): The Preakness Stakes, the second jewel of horse racing's Triple Crown, is held at Pimlico Race Course. The celebration begins the previous week with a parade and other events. Third Saturday in May.

Chestertown Tea Party Festival (Chestertown, MD; ✆ **410/778-0416;** www.chestertownteaparty.com): Bostonians weren't the only ones throwing tea overboard in the 1770s. This festival has a reenactment of the 1774 Tea Party, a parade, a crafts show, entertainment, and food. Last weekend in May.

JUNE

"Monster Mile" NASCAR Weekend (Dover, DE; ✆ **800/441-RACE** [7223]; www.doverspeedway.com): This 2-day stock-car race draws top drivers from the circuit to Dover International Speedway. Early June.

Columbia Festival of the Arts (Lake Kittamaqundi, Columbia, MD; ✆ **410/715-3044;** www.columbiafestival.com): Celebration of the arts with local and national stars of theater, music, dance, and visual arts. Ten days in mid-June.

JULY

Salute to Independence (Antietam National Battlefield, Sharpsburg, MD; ✆ **301/432-5124;** www.nps.gov/anti/salute.htm): The Maryland Symphony Orchestra's annual concert, with cannon fire and fireworks. Saturday after July 4th.

Artscape (Baltimore; ✆ **410/837-4636;** www.artscape.org): A weekend festival celebrating the visual and performing arts. Nationally known performers join local artists; children's activities are also offered. About 350,000 attend. Mid-July.

J. Millard Tawes Crab and Clam Bake (Crisfield, MD; ✆ **410/968-2500**): An all-you-can-eat celebration of crabs, clams, and corn. Wednesday in mid-July.

Delaware State Fair (State Fairgrounds, Harrington, DE; ✆ **302/398-3269;** www.delawarestatefair.com): Annual agricultural showcase, as well as stock-car races, a demolition derby, harness racing, rides, games, and live concerts. Third week in July.

AUGUST

Kunta Kinte Celebration (Annapolis, MD; ✆ **443/623-2856**): African-American cultural heritage festival with music, dance, arts, and crafts. Mid-August.

Maryland State Fair (Timonium Fairgrounds, MD; ✆ **410/252-0200;** www.marylandstatefair.com): Eleven days of farm animals, crafts, produce, rides, entertainment, and thoroughbred racing. From the week before Labor Day through the holiday weekend, daily from 10am to 10pm.

SEPTEMBER

The Star-Spangled Banner Weekend (Fort McHenry, Baltimore; ✆ **410/962-4290;** www.nps.gov/fomc): Reenactments of the War of 1812, with musket firing and children's activities. Fall weekend near Defenders Day, September 12 (a Baltimore City holiday).

Maryland Wine Festival (Carroll County Farm Museum, Westminster, MD; ✆ **800/654-4645;** www.marylandwinefestival.com): Maryland wines, food, entertainment, and tours of the farm museum. Mid-September.

Baltimore Book Festival (Baltimore; ✆ **410/837-4636;** www.bop.org): Features local bookstores and publishers, authors and storytellers, art, entertainment, and food. Weekend in mid-September.

"Monster Mile" NASCAR Weekend (Dover, DE; ✆ **800/441-RACE** [7223]; www.doverspeedway.com): This 2-day stock-car race, like June's event, draws dozens of top drivers from around the world. Second or third weekend in September.

Maryland Million (Laurel Park, Laurel, MD; ✆ **410/252-2100;** www.mdhorsebreeders.com): Maryland's own are celebrated in this race of Maryland-bred thoroughbreds. Late September or early October.

OCTOBER

Fell's Point Fun Festival (Baltimore; ✆ **410/675-6756**): Largest urban festival on the East Coast. First weekend in October.

United States Sailboat Show (City Dock, Annapolis, MD; ✆ **410/268-8828;** www.usboat.com): Nation's oldest and largest in-water sailboat show. Columbus Day weekend.

United States Powerboat Show (City Dock, Annapolis, MD; ✆ **410/268-8828;** www.usboat.com): Nation's oldest and largest in-water powerboat show. Weekend after sailboat show.

Autumn Glory Festival (Oakland, MD; ✆ **301/387-4386;** www.autumngloryfestival.com): State banjo and fiddle championship, crafts, and antiques. Second week in October.

Catoctin Colorfest (Thurmont, MD; ✆ **301/271-7533;** www.colorfest.org): Arts and crafts and the beauty of the mountains. Second weekend in October.

Tilghman Day (Tilghman Island, MD; ✆ **410/886-2677**): Local seafood, music, watermen contests, and rides on skipjacks and workboats. Saturday in October.

NOVEMBER

Punkin Chunkin (Bridgeville, DE; www.punkinchunkin.com): Giant pumpkin hurling contest that draws crowds of competitors and spectators. First weekend in November.

Waterfowl Festival (Easton, MD; ✆ **410/822-4567;** www.waterfowlfestival.org): An Eastern Shore celebration of decoys, artwork of waterfowl, duck-calling contests, kids' activities, and food. Second weekend in November.

DECEMBER

Yuletide at Winterthur (Winterthur, DE; ✆ **800/448-3883** or 302/888-4600; www.winterthur.org): Celebrate the holidays in 19th-century style, with a festive program at the Brandywine Valley museum, featuring entertainment and guided tours. Mid-November through early January.

New Year's Eve Spectacular (Inner Harbor, Baltimore; ✆ **410/837-4636;** www.bop.org): Party suitable for families, featuring entertainment, food, and fireworks. December 31.

LAY OF THE LAND

Maryland

WESTERN MARYLAND

Lovers of the outdoors adore this part of Maryland. It has biking and hiking trails, lakes, and white water. It has the Catoctin Mountains and Deep Creek Lake, charming towns, and historic sites. Everything west of Frederick County is considered Western Maryland. Although development has begun, particularly around Hagerstown and Cumberland, the atmosphere is peaceful. You can expect a smile and a welcome from the people you meet.

It used to take hours driving over small winding roads to get to the far reaches of Western Maryland. That's no longer true since the construction of **Route 68,** which continues westward when Route 70 heads north near Hancock. Route 68 bypasses the small towns and slices right through a mountain at Sideling Hill.

Now skiing at Wisp Resort is just a few hours away from the more populous eastern part of the state. Hiking a trail at Swallow Falls can take longer than driving to it. And many visitors frequent Deep Creek Lake and Rocky Gap State Park and Resort.

Summer and winter are the best times to visit. Summer offers hot sunshine and cool shade for outdoor activities. In the winter, state parks offer cross-country skiing, snowshoeing, tobogganing, and rides in horse-drawn sleighs. Spring and fall are the seasons for hiking, biking, horseback riding, fishing, and sometimes boating. Colorful foliage also makes this a popular spot in fall, but sometimes spring can be a little cold and wet for activities other than shopping and limited sightseeing. The Wisp Resort keeps visitors coming year-round, with golf, a white-water course, hiking, and biking, as well as downhill skiing.

THE WASHINGTON, DC, SUBURBS

A lot of territory is dumped into this region. All roads—or at least highways—lead to Washington, DC, and so do many of the people who live in these Maryland counties. But the counties of Frederick, Montgomery, Prince George's, Howard, and Carroll are distinctly different. Frederick's history is tied more to that of Western Maryland, though you'd never know it if you were driving the highways around rush hour. It's part of the Civil War crossroads, so you can't go far without finding another reminder of the War Between the States. The area is also home to **Camp David,** the presidential retreat, and rolling hills covered with orchards and dairy farms. A drive up Route 15 toward Gettysburg offers one of Maryland's best day trips.

The other four counties have mostly given themselves over to urban sprawl. There are still some gems, such as the Great Falls of the Potomac and the home of Clara Barton, the founder of the American Red Cross. Theme-park fans can head for Six Flags America in Prince George's County.

BALTIMORE METROPOLITAN AREA

The heavily populated region around Baltimore and Annapolis is home to most Marylanders. Baltimore keeps attracting more businesses and residents as it continues to transform from aging industrial town to up-to-the-minute cosmopolitan city. Annapolis, 25 miles away, works hard at staying just the way it has always been. That Colonial style, with the U.S. Naval Academy and Chesapeake Bay as charming backdrops, still attracts plenty of visitors.

SOUTHERN MARYLAND

Tobacco once was king in Southern Maryland, and reminders are still evident. As you drive through Charles, Calvert, and St. Mary's counties, you can see tobacco-curing barns with the long narrow slits that open up to the air.

St. Clement's Island, where Maryland's first settlers stepped upon the New World in 1634, is still a remote place. St. Mary's City disappeared after Annapolis became the capital, but archaeologists are rediscovering and rebuilding the 378-year-old village in a fascinating work in progress.

Surrounded by the mouth of the Potomac River and the Atlantic Ocean, this is fishing territory. At Point Lookout State Park, anglers can try their luck in both bodies of water. In Calvert County, both Chesapeake Beach and Solomons offer many a fishing-boat charter.

THE EASTERN SHORE

This is the home of corn, oysters, and geese. On a flat spit of land that stretches up the eastern side of the Chesapeake Bay, the Eastern Shore is different from the rest of Maryland. Natives have their own accent and are sun- and wind-burned from long hours on a tractor or a workboat. Towns are small, and though many are more businesslike than pretty, some have deserved reputations for charm and history. There are rivers for fishing, boating, and swimming. The wide-open spaces attract waterfowl from fall to spring, a delight if you're a hunter or a birder. And the Eastern Shore's flatness makes biking easy.

The Mid-Shore—Talbot, Kent, and Dorchester counties—is the most developed part of the Eastern Shore and the most tourist-friendly. Though fishing and crabbing are important, the main industry here has historically been shipbuilding.

Don't care about any of that? You'll love Route 50, because it will get you "downy ocean" in a hurry, hon.

DOWN THE OCEAN

The Atlantic rules here—sun, beach, and miniature golf as far as the eye can see. Here, too, are the lifesaving stations and concrete watchtowers that once housed those on the lookout for sailors in distress and World War II enemy ships.

Ocean City's condos, shops, and highways dominate the state's coastline; in summer, it's Maryland's second-largest city. South of the inlet is **Assateague Island,** a seashore park renowned for its wild ponies and its pristine landscape.

Delaware

DOWN THE OCEAN, CONT'D

In Delaware, much smaller resorts, such as **Bethany Beach** and **Dewey Beach,** are located between long stretches of public beach and national seashore. **Rehoboth,** Delaware's premier beach, retains its small-town charm in spite of the crowds that can make Route 1 impassable on holidays or summer weekends. (An ever-popular district of outlet stores on Rte. 1 makes the traffic worse—and the bargains more plentiful.) Just north of Rehoboth Beach is Lewes, a quaint Victorian town known as the terminus of the Cape May–Lewes Ferry. It's a nice diversion thanks to its shops, its Delaware Bay beaches, and its many charter fishing boats.

CENTRAL DELAWARE

Kent County, which is primarily farmland, is Delaware's central county and home of **Dover,** the state capital. In striking contrast to Annapolis, Dover is a quiet capital town with charming museums and historic sites—but twice a year on race weekends, it fills up with fans of the big NASCAR auto races. **Bombay Hook National Wildlife Refuge** on the Delaware Bay is a stop along the East Coast for migrating waterfowl and is less developed than Blackwater on Maryland's Eastern Shore.

THE BRANDYWINE VALLEY

This is du Pont country. Their legacy is everywhere, from Longwood Gardens to Winterthur. You could easily spend a week here and not see all the sights. It's not hard to see why the du Ponts, or anyone, would settle here: The rolling hills, fertile land, and the river itself have served as inspiration for the region's other famous family, the Wyeths.

Wilmington lies at the edge of Brandywine Valley. It's a convenient spot for visiting the valley sites, but it's also got interesting restaurants and museums of its own. The city's Riverfront, now lined with office buildings, restaurants, museums, and tall condos, is worth a visit.

SUGGESTED ITINERARIES

3

Two little states. A prospective visitor might think it would be easy to see either one in a few days. But you might want a more leisurely pace here. How much time do you have? How much driving do you want to do? Most visitors do best with a car when exploring Maryland and Delaware. It's the only way to see the Brandywine Valley or Western Maryland.

Civil War buffs will want to include a visit to Baltimore with trips to the battlefields around Frederick. Wine lovers might like to plan a weekend to see local wineries, enjoy the seafood, and experience a little culture. History fans should consider taking a walk on the path to freedom trod by slaves on the Underground Railroad. And outdoorsy types, you're in for a treat: Hiking, skiing, fly-fishing, boating, and kayaking await.

THE BEST OF MARYLAND & DELAWARE IN 2 WEEKS

Annapolis is a good place to start this trip—especially if you're flying into Baltimore/Washington International Thurgood Marshall Airport (BWI). If you're coming from the west, start in Western Maryland and head east. Coming from the south? Take the Chesapeake Bay Bridge Tunnel and visit Delaware and the Eastern Shore before heading across the other Bay Bridge to see the rest of Maryland. Maryland requires a lot of driving to see everything, from the mountains of Western Maryland to the Eastern Shore to the Atlantic Ocean. Delaware's attractions begin at the beach and end in Wilmington. On the way you'll see Civil War battlefields, museums of all sorts, the Chesapeake Bay, waterfalls and mountain trails, historic homes and districts, and veritable castles. I've designed this itinerary for visiting at a quick pace. Feel free to slow down and savor as you are so moved.

Day 1: Annapolis, MD

Annapolis offers a slower pace than big city Baltimore—so you'll feel like you're on vacation. **The Annapolis Historical Museum at the St. Clair Wright Center** is a good first stop for tours and orientation on Maryland's capital. Stop for lunch along the **City Dock,** then visit the **State House,** and spend a leisurely afternoon shopping along Maryland Avenue. Have dinner on Main Street or West Street and finish with a carriage ride through the historic district. Stay at a local B&B or one of the **Historic Inns.** If you want an early start, it's best to stay downtown.

Day 2: U.S. Naval Academy, Historic Homes & Boats

Head to the **Naval Academy** and sign up for a tour at the visitor center—the best one includes a stop at **Bancroft Hall** about the time the midshipmen line up for noon formation. After they march in for lunch, head into the historic district for your own. Near Maryland Avenue are three houses worth a visit: the **Chase-Lloyd House,** the **Paca House and Gardens,** and the **Hammond-Harwood House.** You could see all three or just go to the Hammond-Harwood, and then spend a leisurely time in the Paca Gardens. Or take a boat ride: 2 hours on the schooner ***Woodwind*** or a waterfront tour offered by **Watermark Cruises.** Then catch your breath during dinner in the historic district or across Spa Creek in **Eastport.**

Day 3: Heading "Downy Ocean"

Ocean City is only 2½ hours away but because the Eastern Shore has so many attractions of its own, plan to stop in one of the towns along Route 50. Wander the Colonial streets of **Easton,** or visit Historic High Street and the Richardson Maritime museum in **Cambridge.** Or venture past Easton to the waterfront communities of **Oxford** or **St. Michaels** for a crab cake and quick look. Bird lovers may want to visit the **Blackwater National Wildlife Refuge,** southwest of Cambridge. You'll be at Ocean City (the local lingo is "downy ocean") with time to check in, grab a bite to eat, and walk the **boardwalk** or spend the evening playing **miniature golf;** this town is full of courses.

Day 4: Ocean City, MD

Rent an umbrella and a chair and relax by the surf. Catch a few rays and jump some waves. Or see the wilder side of the Maryland shore at **Assateague Island.** The beaches there attract the famous wild ponies. The state park has only a small stand with restrooms and snacks. The national seashore offers small boat rentals and local companies offer eco-tours around the island.

Day 5: The Delaware Shore

So what do Delaware's beaches offer to make you head north? Rehoboth and Lewes have small-town charm to go with the beach. **Rehoboth** has lots of good restaurants, plus spas, and a plethora of tax-free outlet stores. **Lewes** is the First State's First Town with well-planned museums and historic sites. Choose one and go exploring. Both have inns and boutique hotels to pamper you.

Day 6: Dover, DE

Delaware's capital has a cluster of museums celebrating planes, farms, art, and even Victrolas. Stop at the Delaware Welcome Center to become acquainted with the **First State Heritage Park at Dover,** then the nearby **Biggs Museum of American Art.** These downtown sights, along with the Legislative Hall and state archives, can be seen in a day. Or head to the casinos or horse races at **Dover Downs.** Wildlife fans may prefer to wander **Bombay Hook National Wildlife Refuge** for a little bird-watching. Plan to be there for about 2 hours or more, depending on how much walking you want to do.

The Best of Maryland & Delaware

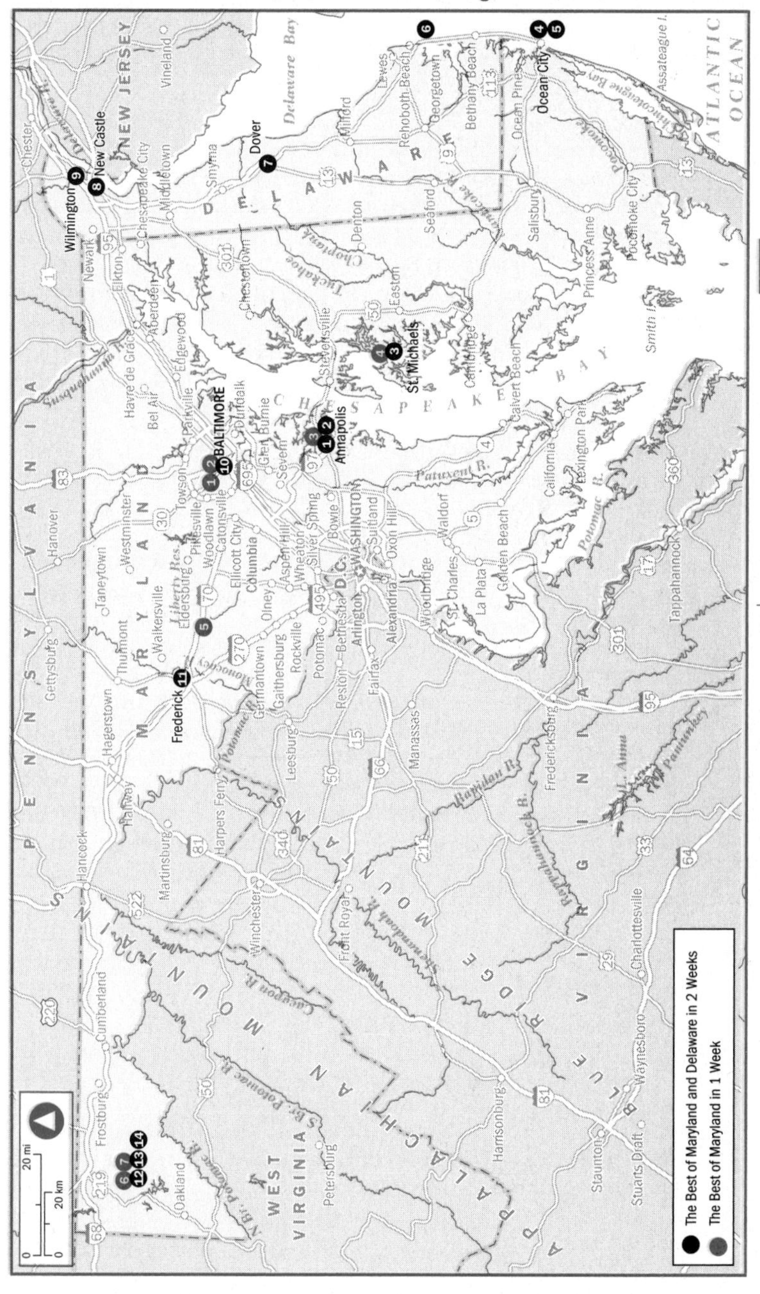

Day 7: Historic New Castle, DE

The original capital of Delaware was the waterfront village of **New Castle.** Its historic sites are still lovingly maintained, including the Federal-style **Read House,** home of the son of a signer of the Declaration of Independence. A number of other Colonial-era homes are open most days (except Mon). Have lunch at a Colonial-era tavern. **Jessop's Tavern** serves traditional dishes from the past.. Spend the night in Wilmington.

Day 8: Wilmington, DE

Make this a base for today's visit to the city and tomorrow's tours of the **Brandywine Valley.** Art-lovers ought to see visit the 12,000 works of art at the **Delaware Art Museum** or the changing exhibits of the **Delaware Center for the Contemporary Arts.** History buffs will want to see the **Delaware History Museum** or visit the ***Kalmar Nyckel*** if it's moored here. Take a walk along the **Riverfront,** home of some good restaurants, a couple of museums, and the **Russell W. Peterson Urban Wildlife Refuge.** Perhaps tonight there's a show at one of Wilmington's many theaters or local watering holes.

Day 9: Brandywine Valley, DE/PA

How do you like your luxury? Today you can see it in many forms at one of the du Pont properties: **Winterthur,** if you love home furnishings; **Nemours,** if you love lavish style; **Longwood Gardens,** if gardening is your passion; or **Hagley,** if you like to learn how things work in a parklike setting. Stop by the Inn at Montchanin for the night or for dinner. It's off to Baltimore tomorrow (a 2-hr. drive).

Day 10: Baltimore

If you have only a day to see Baltimore, first visit **Fort McHenry,** home of the Star-Spangled Banner. Have lunch at **Harborplace** while you consider your next stop. Should it be the **National Aquarium** to see the Australia and rainforest exhibits? The **Reginald F. Lewis Museum of Maryland African American History & Culture**? Art lovers can choose from the **Baltimore Museum of Art,** the **Walters Art Museum,** or the **American Visionary Art Museum.** History buffs can visit the **Maryland Historical Society,** the **Baltimore Museum of Industry,** or sign up for a **Heritage Walk** (at the visitor center in the Inner Harbor). For a view from the top, go to the **Top of the World** observation level in the World Trade Center. Dine in **Little Italy,** tony **Harbor East,** or **Fell's Point.**

Day 11: Frederick, MD

The drive to **Frederick** takes about an hour along I-70. After checking into your hotel or B&B, spend the afternoon at **Antietam Battlefield.** Head to Frederick's historic district for dinner. It's become a foodie heaven.

Days 12–14: Outdoors in Maryland

You have a choice: **Deep Creek Lake** at the western end of Maryland has lots to draw an outdoors enthusiast—skiing, dog-sledding, white-water rafting, hiking, and fly-fishing. Or head north from Frederick to **Cunningham Falls State Park.** Here you can hike to a waterfall and swim or canoe in a nearby lake. Stop for local produce along the way, and have a meal at one of the restaurants along Route 15.

THE BEST OF MARYLAND IN 1 WEEK

If you have only a week, put four places on your itinerary: Baltimore, Annapolis, any place on the Eastern Shore (or Ocean City, on the Atlantic), and Western Maryland. You can slow down long enough to see a Civil War battlefield, too. But hurry: There's lots to do in 7 little days.

Day 1: Baltimore Essentials

See Day 10 of "The Best of Maryland and Delaware in 2 Weeks."

Day 2: Baltimore History & Culture

Spend a second day in Baltimore soaking up the history or the culture. Stop by the visitor center at the Inner Harbor to sign up for a **Heritage Walk.** After lunch in **Little Italy,** take in a museum. Baltimore has plenty to choose from: the **Reginald F. Lewis Museum of Maryland African American History & Culture,** the **Baltimore Museum of Art,** the **Walters Art Museum,** the **American Visionary Art Museum,** or the **Baltimore & Ohio Railroad Museum.** End the day at **Power Plant Live** with dinner and music (or, in season, perhaps an Orioles game).

Day 3: Annapolis

See Day 1 in "The Best of Maryland and Delaware in 2 Weeks." The **State House,** where George Washington resigned as commander in chief, and the **Paca House and Gardens** are also good places to visit. If you haven't clambered aboard a boat yet, make reservations at an **Eastport** restaurant and take the water taxi across the harbor for a good seafood meal.

Day 4: Boat Trip to St. Michaels or Day Trip to Ocean City

Spend the day on Chesapeake Bay. **Watermark Cruises** offers a boat trip to **St. Michaels,** an Eastern Shore village with shops, restaurants, and the **Chesapeake Bay Maritime Museum.** The drive there is about 2 hours; or, if you want to see the ocean, drive to **Ocean City.** It's only 2½ hours from here.

Day 5: Driving to Western Maryland

This is the way settlers headed from the valleys around Baltimore to the hills of Appalachia. The drive to Western Maryland can take up to 4 hours. If you want, stop along I-70. **Ellicott City** has a charming historic district with antiques shops and the oldest railroad station in the world. **New Market** has a street lined with antiques shops. Civil War buffs can stop at **Antietam,** near Frederick. **Frederick** has its own historic district, as does **Cumberland,** a stop along the **C&O Canal.**

Days 6–7: Western Maryland's Great Outdoors

Ski at **Wisp,** if it's wintertime; or head to **Deep Creek Lake** for a swim, if it's warm. Don't miss a chance to hike to Muddy Falls at **Swallow Falls State Park** or enjoy the pristine **Savage River State Forest.** Sign up at one of the outfitters for a white-water rafting trip, fly-fishing, or boat or snowshoe rental. You can even sign up for dog-sledding. Take 2 days. Take 3 if you've got 'em.

THE BEST OF MARYLAND FOR FAMILIES

These two 1-week itineraries both focus on the outdoors. Start in Baltimore with either one so the kids can see Fort McHenry, the National Aquarium, and the Baltimore & Ohio Railroad Museum. Then head east to the Eastern Shore and Ocean City (or a Delaware beach, if you prefer), or head west to the mountains. End in Annapolis with a visit to the Naval Academy and a boat ride.

Days 1–2: Baltimore for Kids

Kids love **Fort McHenry.** The rangers talk on their level, there are lots of cannons to see and nooks and crannies to climb into, and the waterfront lawn outside the fort wall is great for running around or enjoying a picnic. Or have lunch at **Harborplace,** where there's plenty of kid-friendly food. The **National Aquarium** has dolphins and a rainforest, a bit of Australia, and a 4-D movie. You'll probably spend the whole afternoon here. Then head to **Little Italy** for some pasta. Finish with cannoli and gelato at **Vaccaro's.**

On your second day, pick a couple of museums according to your interests—kid-oriented museums are everywhere in Baltimore. **Port Discovery** is a children's museum. The **Baltimore Museum of Industry** has guides who tell great stories and let kids handle some of the artifacts. There are massive locomotives and diminutive model trains at the **Baltimore & Ohio Railroad Museum.** At the **Reginald F. Lewis Museum of Maryland African American History & Culture,** many of the displays tell very personal stories. Sneak a little art education in with a visit to the **Walters Art Museum,** home of some impressive armor, or the **Baltimore Museum of Art,** where kids can enjoy the sculpture garden. Baseball fans can spend the afternoon at **Sports Legends at Camden Yards** or the **Babe Ruth Museum.** Or ditch all that for a fast ride on the ***Seadog,*** a slow harbor cruise, or an adventure with **Urban Pirates.**

Days 3–5, Option A: Ocean City

Throw the bathing suits into the car and head to **Ocean City** for a couple of days of surf and sun. Spend all 3 days building sand castles and bodysurfing during the day and playing miniature golf in the evening. Or book a fishing trip, rent a kayak, or visit **Assateague Island** or **Frontier Town** amusement park. In the evening, take the kids to **Ocean Downs** to watch the harness races. Admission is free, and the lead horse comes up to the fence so children can pet his nose. Or head to Salisbury for a **Delmarva Shorebirds** minor-league baseball game.

Days 3–5, Option B: Western Maryland

Get out your hiking boots, your bathing suit, or your skis—whatever the weather, there's something to do here. Base your family at **Deep Creek Lake** so you can ski at **Wisp Resort,** hike to Muddy Falls at **Swallow Falls State Park,** or enjoy **Savage River State Forest.** Sign up at one of the outfitters for a white-water rafting trip, fly-fishing, dog-sledding or a kennel visit, or boat or snowshoe rental.

Days 6–7: Annapolis

Two days in Annapolis are plenty for children. Just make sure you visit the **Naval Academy** (see suggestions in itineraries above), and then take a ride on the ***Harbor Queen.*** You can easily do this all in a day, with lunch at the **City Dock** in between. Take a carriage ride in the historic district in the evening. Spend your second day hiking or kayaking at **Quiet Waters Park,** or head down Route 2 to **Six Flags America** for some big-time thrills. Children also like the **State House** and the **Annapolis Maritime Museum** in Eastport.

THE BEST OF DELAWARE FOR FAMILIES

Tiny Delaware packs in a lot of fun, history, and culture. This is a 5-day itinerary, but it's easy to pick and choose a couple of days' worth of activity for a long weekend, or stretch out the fun for a whole week's vacation—without getting bored.

Day 1: A Day at the Beach

Unpack your bathing suit or fishing rod and head to **Bethany Beach** or **Fenwick State Park** for a quiet day. By the time you're hungry, you can decide whether you want pizza at **Grotto's** or a heartier dinner at **Frog House** or **Mango Mike's.**

Day 2: Let's Go Shopping

Sales-tax-free Delaware makes shopping even more fun. Head to **Tanger Outlets** in Rehoboth. Or visit the little shops in downtown **Rehoboth Beach** or **Lewes.**

Day 3: Dover

Delaware's capital city has a cluster of unusual museums, and the well-regarded **Biggs Museum of American Art.** The downtown sights, along with the Legislative Hall and state archives, are known as the **First State Heritage Park at Dover.** You could easily see them all in a day. Or head to the casino (adults only, of course) or horse races at **Dover Downs.** Wildlife fans may prefer **Bombay Hook National Wildlife Refuge** for a little bird-watching.

Day 4: Historic New Castle

See "Day 7" in the itinerary "The Best of Maryland and Delaware in 2 Weeks."

Day 5: Wilmington & the Brandywine Valley

The castles of the **Brandywine Valley** beckon, but the exhibits at the **Delaware Art Museum** and the **Delaware History Museum** are hard to pass by. If you've got only a day, you're going to want to see one of the du Pont properties: **Winterthur,** with its Enchanted Gardens; **Nemours,** if you love lavish style; **Longwood Gardens,** with three great tree houses and children's garden; or **Hagley,** for its bucolic setting and displays made for kids. Wilmington's **Delaware History Museum** makes history fun for kids. The new **Delaware Children's Museum** is filled with fun activities (and learning). Climb aboard the ***Kalmar Nyckel*** or walk down to the **Russell W. Peterson Urban Wildlife Refuge** to work up an appetite for dinner along the **Riverfront.**

More Suggested Itineraries

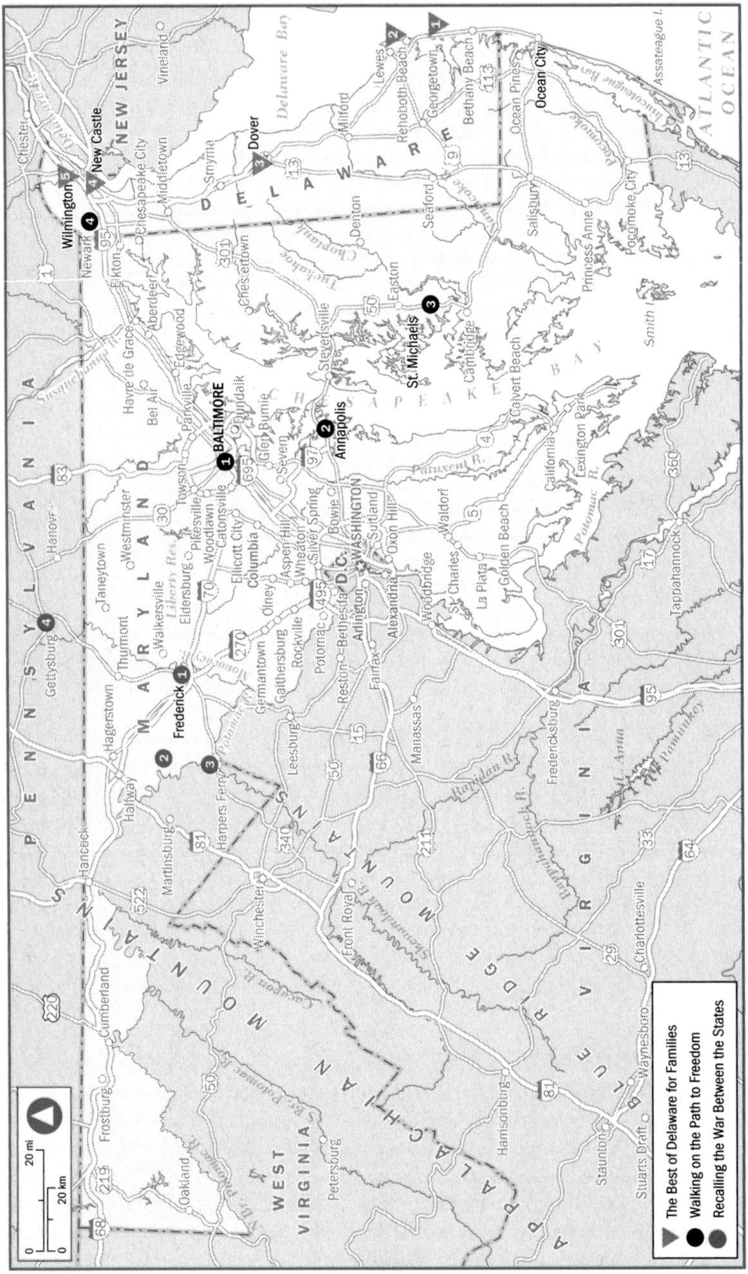

▼ The Best of Delaware for Families
● Walking on the Path to Freedom
● Recalling the War Between the States

FOLLOWING THE PATH TO FREEDOM

African-American history has gotten some well-deserved attention throughout the region. From Baltimore to the Eastern Shore, look for the places where people struggled for freedom and the museums that highlight their courage and faith.

Day 1: Baltimore Museums

Learn about the individuals who found freedom on the Underground Railroad or who made the civil-rights movement their own in three museums here. All eyes are on the **Reginald F. Lewis Museum of Maryland African American History & Culture,** the newest jewel in the city's collection of museums, on the east side of the Inner Harbor. The **National Great Blacks in Wax Museum** is a bit out of the way for downtown visitors, but the figures recall the triumphs and the horrors of slavery in a unique way. The **Eubie Blake Cultural Center** focuses on local musicians, most notably this composer, jazzman Cab Calloway, and others.

Day 2: Annapolis

Alex Haley, author of *Roots,* has a permanent seat at **City Dock,** a place where people were once auctioned off as slaves. The sculpture is only one such tribute. At the **State House,** look for the statue on the lawn of U.S. Supreme Court Justice Thurgood Marshall and the plaque inside honoring North Pole explorer Matthew Henson. Stop in the **Banneker-Douglass Museum** for a look at the lives of other prominent African-American Marylanders. A tour focusing on African-American history is available at the **Historic Annapolis** museum store.

Day 3: Following the Underground Railroad

These roads in Dorchester and Caroline counties on the Eastern Shore, which were traveled by Underground Railroad "conductor" Harriett Tubman, are detailed in the **"Finding a Way to Freedom"** driving-tour brochure and map, available at visitor centers on I-95 and in Cambridge. The roads remain, though most of the buildings, such as Tubman's home, are gone. If you're visiting after 2012, stop by **Harriet Tubman Underground Railroad State Park.** The **Harriet Tubman Museum,** in Cambridge, offers tours to help interpret the places as you go by. The route is about 100 miles long and takes about 4 hours. Most of it goes through farmland, but there are a few places to stop for food and restrooms.

Day 4: Delaware

If you have only a day, be sure to stop in Newark to see the **Paul R. Jones Collection of African American Art**—the largest and most comprehensive collection of 20th-century African-American art in the world. Mr. Jones's collection, which includes works by Jacob Lawrence, Carrie Mae Weems, and Elizabeth Catlett, is on display at the University of Delaware's Mechanical Hall. Stop in nearby **New Castle** and visit the old **Court House** to see the stirring exhibit on the Underground Railroad. If you have time, visit **Wilmington** and walk along the **Riverfront** to see the markers recalling Harriet Tubman's efforts here. The riverside Tubman-Garrett Park is named for her and abolitionist Thomas Garrett.

RECALLING THE WAR BETWEEN THE STATES

Frederick is your base for a 3- or 4-day visit to three major battlefields: Gettysburg, Antietam, and Harpers Ferry. Or you could spend a week and add Baltimore's Civil War Museum (site of the first bloodshed in the Civil War) and Federal Hill (where U.S. cannons were trained on the city), plus Delaware's Fort Delaware, which served as a prisoner-of-war camp for 33,000 Confederate soldiers.

Day 1: Frederick

Begin your day in Frederick at the **National Museum of Civil War Medicine** for a different perspective of the war. Frederick was not only a crossroads for soldiers as they headed off to battle but also where many came to recuperate afterward. Take a walk through the historic district, looking for signs that feature photos of the troops as they marched through town. The confrontation between **Barbara Fritchie** and Stonewall Jackson in 1862 was immortalized in poetry; a reconstruction of her house sits along Carroll Creek.

Day 2: Antietam

More U.S. soldiers were killed, wounded, or missing after the battle here than at any other time in American history. Stop in the visitor center at **Antietam National Battlefield** to see a film about the battle and get a tour map. There are maps for biking and hiking as well. Battlefield guides offer personalized tours. Stop at the **Pry House Field Hospital,** Gen. George McClellan's headquarters prior to the battle and a field hospital afterward. A visit to the battlefield takes a few hours and could be combined with Frederick sightseeing.

Day 3: Harpers Ferry, WV

Abolitionist John Brown's plan to start a rebellion was thwarted here by Lt. Col. Robert E. Lee in 1859. The riverfront town was to see Union and Confederate troops several more times before witnessing the war's largest surrender of Federal troops. It's worth a day trip to visit the **Harpers Ferry National Historical Park,** which still appears much as it did during the war. It's a place of natural beauty, too, so bring your hiking shoes or plan a rafting trip on the Shenandoah-Potomac here.

Day 4: Gettysburg, PA

The 34-mile drive to Gettysburg from Frederick takes you through rolling hills, woodlands, orchards, and farms. If you have just a day, start early so you can fit in the **Gettysburg National Military Park,** including the Gettysburg Cemetery, where President Lincoln delivered his famous address. Driving the battlefield takes a good 2 hours. You'll also want to see the Cyclorama and museum at the visitor center. A number of companies, including the well-regarded **Association of Licensed Battlefield Guides,** offer guided tours with good historical perspective. The town itself, with a charming historic district, has lots of privately owned museums. If you have time, don't miss the **Shriver House Museum** for a view of how citizens fared during the battle here. One day is enough here, but 2 days gives you time to savor your visit, shop, and dine at a historic inn.

BALTIMORE

"Hi, hon!" If you're lucky, you just might hear the old Baltimorean greeting. But so many newcomers have made Charm City their home, the old phrase is disappearing. The "charm" remains every time Baltimore reinvents itself. The city has welcomed newcomers since 1729. Founded as a port and shipbuilding town, its citizens have adapted to constant change. Baltimore Clippers were once cutting-edge technology. Then it was cars and steel. Now the city is on the rise once again with top-notch healthcare, high-tech industries, and nonprofits.

Charm City is a city of neighborhoods, birthplace of the national anthem, and home to a good time. Residents have gathered at the Inner Harbor for over 30 years, for festivals, fireworks, and the arrival of tall ships. Cultural attractions remember the extraordinary—Edgar Allan Poe, Cal Ripken, Jr., Charles Carroll—and the ordinary—boilermakers and oyster shuckers, shipbuilders, and flag makers. Baltimoreans cheer for the Ravens and the Orioles, love college lacrosse, and train for the Baltimore marathon. Parties run late in Fell's Point, Canton, and Federal Hill.

THINGS TO DO The **Inner Harbor** is the heart of downtown Baltimore; it's home to the National Aquarium in Baltimore and a host of boat tours. But don't stop there. Celebrate "The Star-Spangled Banner" at **Fort McHenry.** See the world from an artist's perspective at the **Walters Art Museum** or **American Visionary Art Museum.** Take a walking tour of one of Baltimore's neighborhoods or ride the train at the **B&O Railroad Museum.**

RESTAURANTS AND DINING Locally sourced is the new rage, but Baltimoreans have always loved their Chesapeake Bay crabs and oysters. The **Inner Harbor** is where the tourists eat; locals prefer smaller old favorites along the waterfront of **Fell's Point** and **Canton;** or newer, swanky joints in the glittering towers of **Harbor East;** or more laid-back as well as newer trendy eateries in the hometown neighborhoods of **Hampden** and **Federal Hill.** For pasta and tiramisu, **Little Italy** has no equal. Along **Charles Street,** dinner is served in elegant old town houses.

NIGHTLIFE AND ENTERTAINMENT Baltimore is a theater town. Traveling musicals come to the **Hippodrome. Center Stage** and **Everyman Theatre** boast full seasons of professional (and good) theater. Small companies all over town offer classics and cutting-edge pieces. You'll find great music from the **Baltimore Symphony Orchestra** to opera to local bands playing in the bars of **Fell's Point.** Nationally known musicians get the town rocking at **Pier 6 Pavilion, First Mariner Arena,** and **Rams Head Live.**

ACTIVE PURSUITS Baltimore has become a city for strolling, jogging, and biking. Go on your own, or sign up for a **walking tour** to see the historic neighborhoods around the Inner Harbor. The waterfront **promenade** welcomes bikers and joggers. See the Inner Harbor from the seat of a **paddleboat** or from the top of Federal Hill. Stroll among **Cylburn Arboretum's** gardens or along the rolling hills of the **Maryland Zoo.** Cheer on the Os at **Camden Yards,** or bet on the ponies at **Pimlico.**

ORIENTATION

Arriving

BY PLANE **Baltimore/Washington International Thurgood Marshall Airport** (✆ **800/I-FLY-BWI** [435-9294] or 410/859-7111; www.bwiairport.com) is 10 miles south of downtown Baltimore, off I-295 (the Baltimore-Washington Pkwy.). **Southwest** (✆ 800/435-9792) dominates the market—some 70 percent of BWI's air traffic—along with **AirTran** (now part of Southwest; ✆ 800/247-8726), **American** (✆ 800/433-7300), **Continental** (✆ 800/525-0280), **Delta** (✆ 800/221-1212), **United** (✆ 800/241-6522), and **U.S. Airways** (✆ 800/428-4322).

To get to Baltimore from the airport, take I-195 west to Route 295 north, which will take you into downtown. **SuperShuttle** (✆ **800/622-2089;** www.supershuttle.com) operates vans between the airport and all major downtown hotels. The cost is $22 per person one-way. **Airport Shuttle** (✆ **800/776-0323;** www.theairportshuttle.com) makes connections in the areas from Annapolis to Baltimore to Frederick. The **BayRunner Shuttle** (✆ **855/BAY-RUNR** [229-7867]) takes passengers to the Eastern Shore and Western Maryland. The **Light Rail** connects the airport and Amtrak station at BWI with downtown Baltimore stops at Camden Station and Penn Station.

Plenty of car-rental companies are also available at the nearby car-rental facility, including **Alamo** (✆ 410/859-8092), **Avis** (✆ 410/859-1680), **Budget** (✆ 410/691-2913), **Dollar** (✆ 800/800-8000), **Enterprise** (✆ 800/325-8007), **Hertz** (✆ 410/850-7400), **National** (✆ 410/859-8860), and **Thrifty** (✆ 410/850-7139).

BY CAR **I-95** provides the easiest route to Baltimore from the north and south. From the north, follow I-95 south through the **Fort McHenry Tunnel** ($2 toll) to Exit 53, I-395 north to downtown. Bear left off the exit, and follow signs to the Inner Harbor. From the south, follow I-95 north to Exit 53, I-395 north to downtown. Bear left off the exit, and follow signs to the Inner Harbor.

From the west, take **I-70** east to Exit 91, I-695 south (the **Baltimore Beltway**) heading toward Glen Burnie. Take Exit 11A, I-95, to I-395 north to downtown.

From **I-83** (Pennsylvania to the north), follow I-83 south to where it merges with I-695 (the Baltimore Beltway). Continue on I-83 south for 1 mile to Exit 23A (I-83 south, downtown). The Jones Falls Expressway ends at President Street downtown.

Once you arrive, you'll find parking garages and metered on-street parking downtown. Garages charge up to $30 a day, or $8 to $12 for special events or evening visits. Parking meters must be fed $2 an hour (in quarters only), though most streets now have meters that take both credit cards and change to pay parking fees.

BY TRAIN Baltimore is served by **Amtrak** (✆ **800/872-7245;** www.amtrak.com). Trains on the Northeast Corridor route arrive at and depart from **Pennsylvania Station,** 1500 N. Charles St. (✆ **410/291-4165**), north of the Inner Harbor, and **BWI Marshall Rail Station** (✆ **410/672-6169**), off Route 170 about 1½ miles from the airport.

In addition, you can catch the **MARC** (Maryland Area Rail Commuter) trains on weekdays only from the BWI Marshall Rail Station, with service from Washington, DC, and Baltimore's Penn Station. The MARC fare to the airport is $4 one way.

Another option is the **Light Rail,** which has its BWI stop immediately outside the lower level of the terminal building adjacent to Concourse E. The Light Rail runs Monday through Saturday from 6am to 11pm and Sunday and holidays from 11am to 7pm. The fare to Penn Station is $2 one way. For more information or either MARC or the Light Rail, call © **800/325-RAIL** (7245) or go to **www.mtamaryland.com**.

BY BUS Get to and from Baltimore via **Greyhound** (© **800/231-2222;** www.greyhound.com). Buses stop in South Baltimore near M&T Stadium at 2110 Haines St. (© **410/752-7682**). Two discount bus lines also have stops in Baltimore (or just outside, in White Marsh, where you can pick up a city bus downtown) from major cities in the Northeast. **Bolt Bus** (© **877/265-8287;** www.boltbus.com) stops near Penn Station, 1610 St. Paul St. **Mega Bus** (© **877/462-6342;** http://us.megabus.com) makes stops in White Marsh, on I-95 north of Baltimore City.

Visitor Information

Contact **Visit Baltimore,** 100 Light St., Baltimore, MD 21202 (© **877/BALTIMORE** [225-8466]; www.baltimore.org). It has all sorts of information to help you plan your trip, including maps, brochures, and water taxi schedules. The visitor center is open daily at the Inner Harbor, adjacent to Harborplace, at 401 Light St. Stop by for brochures or advice from one of the knowledgeable staffers. A short film shown several times an hour will introduce you to Baltimore. You can even get tickets for attractions, tours, and boat trips. The **Downtown Partnership,** 217 N. Charles St. (**www.godowntownbaltimore.com**), also has directions, maps, and other information. Downtown Baltimore Guides in the yellow shirts can give directions or provide an escort, © **410/244-8778** (daytime) or 410/802-9631 (nighttime).

SPECIAL EVENTS There are crafts shows, and then there's the **American Craft Council show** (http://public.craftcouncil.org/baltimore) at Baltimore's Convention Center in late February. The horsey set descends on Baltimore and Pimlico Race Course for the **Preakness Stakes** (© **410/542-9400;** www.preakness.com), the second jewel of horse racing's Triple Crown, on the third Saturday in May. The celebrating begins the week before. The park around the Washington Monument becomes a garden party for the **FlowerMart** (www.flowermart.org) the first Friday and Saturday in May. Three days of visual and performing arts make **Artscape** (www.artscape.org) in the Mount Royal/Bolton Hill area one of the largest arts festivals in the nation in mid-July. The **Baltimore Grand Prix** (http://2012baltimoregrandprix.com), on Labor Day weekend, brings Indy Car racing to the Inner Harbor. First run in 2011, the race returns to Baltimore August 31 to September 3 2012. **Defenders Day,** at Fort McHenry (www.nps.gov/fomc), marks the War of 1812's Battle of Baltimore on September 12, a Baltimore City holiday. The commemoration is held the previous weekend. **Free Fall Baltimore** (www.freefallbaltimore.com) is a citywide free celebration of the arts in October.

Baltimore's Neighborhoods in Brief

Baltimore has always been a hardworking town, home to fiercely loyal Orioles fans, with close-knit neighborhoods and families. Below are some neighborhoods you may wish to visit, along with a few of the characteristics that make them unique.

Baltimore Neighborhoods

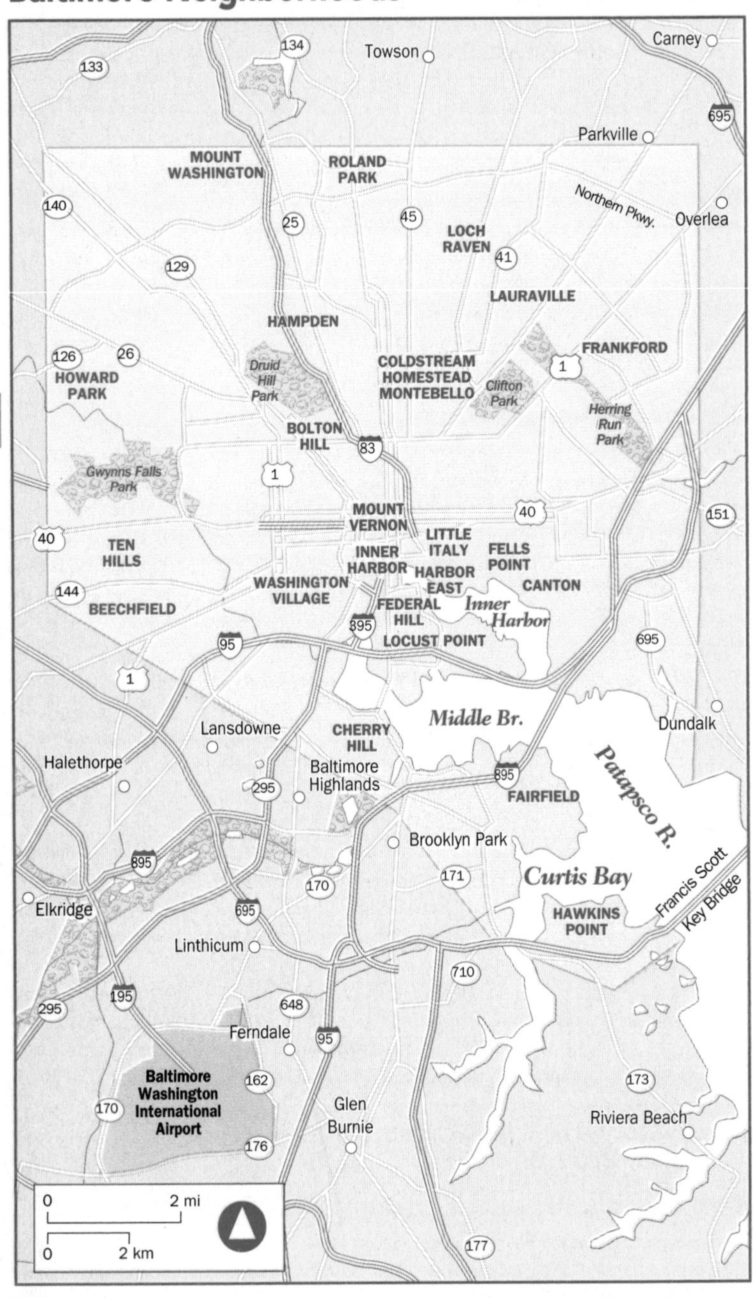

Baltimore's **Inner Harbor** is the obvious starting point for visitors, the focal point of the town's turnaround that began in the late 1970s. Visitors can get a feel for the city's seafaring days through attractions on the Inner Harbor, harbor cruises, and water taxis.

The National Aquarium is home to fish large and small, seagoing mammals like dolphins, and topped with a rainforest. The Maryland Science Center offers an IMAX theater and planetarium. Harborplace and the Gallery are shopping and dining extravaganzas that draw thousands every weekend.

Baltimore has become a destination for pleasure boaters, tall ships, and even high-tech racing sailboats.

Just past the Inner Harbor are some of Baltimore's oldest neighborhoods.

Little Italy has been home to Italian immigrants and their descendants since the mid-1800s, when they first opened the restaurants that continue to anchor the neighborhood. Some of the city's oldest buildings line the charming, narrow streets—these survived the 1905 fire that destroyed downtown. Before or after dinner, take a walk to see the rowhouses and their famous marble steps, which dominate the Baltimore streetscape—and notice the shrines with flowers and statues that grace windows here and there.

Harbor East, once an industrial area, now boasts the city's newest hotels and condos, and some fine restaurants and shops. Young adults moving to Baltimore want to live in this area, which is convenient to the other harborside neighborhoods.

Fell's Point was Baltimore's original seaport and home to the first shipyards. Baltimore clippers, swift and elegant topsail schooners, were made here. For years, immigrants to the U.S. arrived in Fell's Point and settled this area, as well as the surrounding neighborhoods of Highlandtown and Canton.

Fell's Point has long been known as a rowdy part of town. Restaurants and entertainment venues keep this neighborhood hopping all night. But don't miss the history. Walking tours bring the past (and a few ghosts) to life as you pass elegant brick rowhouses.

The Recreation Pier will be familiar to TV viewers as the site of police headquarters in the series *Homicide*.

Canton was once home to families whose breadwinners worked at nearby factories, canneries, and breweries. Today, technology firms rent office space here, while families are moving in to rehab the old brick and Formstone rowhouses. O'Donnell Square is surrounded by bars and eateries, and the Can Company has transformed an abandoned can-making operation into a mixed-use space with offices, a few shops, and restaurants with outdoor patios.

These neighborhoods are connected by a waterfront promenade as well as water taxis.

Federal Hill features not only the grassy hill that overlooks the south side of the Inner Harbor, but a great collection of eateries, watering holes, and boutiques.

Mount Vernon, surrounding the Washington Monument (which, Baltimoreans remind you, predates the one in DC), offers a collection of beautiful buildings from the city's heyday. This tony area is home to the Walters Art Museum and a half-mile walk up Charles Street.

Northern Baltimore City is mostly residential, though **Hampden** and **Mount Washington Village** offer interesting shopping and some good restaurants. If you happen to be in town in December, visit Hampden's **34th Street ★★** to see how the neighbors dress up their rowhouses for the holidays; people come from all over the city to view the lights, model trains, and Santas. Mount Washington Village is a short Light Rail trip from downtown, a good side trip if the glitz of the Inner Harbor is too much for you. It's small but offers a handful of fun eateries, as well as some unique shops, plenty of hair salons, and a pottery studio.

GETTING AROUND

BY CAR If you plan to stay near the harbor, it is easier to walk or take a water taxi than to drive and park. That said, driving in downtown Baltimore is fairly easy. The streets are on a straight grid; many are one-way. The major northbound streets are Howard, Charles, and Calvert. Cathedral and St. Paul are southbound. Lombard and Pratt are the major east and west streets. On the west side, Martin Luther King Boulevard connects the harbor with the cultural district; it runs both north and south.

Need to find an address? Buildings are numbered east and west from Charles Street; 100 E. Lombard is in the first block to the east of Charles. Baltimore Street is the dividing line for north-south addresses; 100 S. Charles is a block below Baltimore.

Car-rental agencies at Baltimore/Washington International Thurgood Marshall Airport include **Alamo** (✆ 410/859-8092), **Avis** (✆ 410/859-1680), **Budget** (✆ 410/691-2913), **Dollar** (✆ 800/800-8000), **Enterprise** (✆ 800/325-8007), **Hertz** (✆ 410/850-7400), **National** (✆ 410/859-8860), and **Thrifty** (✆ 410/850-7139).

BY LIGHT RAIL, SUBWAY & BUS The Maryland Transit Administration (MTA) operates the **Light Rail,** a 27-mile system of aboveground rail lines reminiscent of the city's old streetcars. It travels on one north-south line, from the northern suburb of Timonium to Glen Burnie in the south, with a spur to Penn Station. The key stop within the city is Camden Station, next to the Orioles' ballpark. The Light Rail is the ideal way to get to a game or to travel between Camden Yards and the Inner Harbor, and the train station, the performing-arts district, or Mount Washington. Trains run every 15 to 30 minutes daily between 6am and midnight and Sunday between 11am and 7pm. Tickets, which cost $1.60 one-way, are dispensed from machines at each stop. Better yet, get a day pass for $3.50—it's good on all MTA transportation.

The MTA also operates the **Metro,** a subway system that connects downtown with the northwestern suburbs. Trains run from Johns Hopkins Hospital in East Baltimore through Charles Center and north to the suburb of Owings Mills. Service is available Monday through Friday from 5am to midnight, Saturday and Sunday from 6am to midnight. The fare is $1.60; you can also purchase the aforementioned day pass, which allows unlimited trips on the Light Rail, the Metro, and city buses for $3.50.

A network of **buses,** also operated by the MTA, connects all sections of the city. Service is daily, but hours vary. The base fare is $1.60; exact change is necessary.

The MTA also offers the **Charm Card** for use on all local public transportation—including Washington, DC, public transportation. It's sold online at **www.mtacharm card.com** or at area Giant grocery stores or CVS pharmacies. It costs $2.50 and up to $200 can be added to the cards. In addition to its convenience, if the card is lost, the balance can be returned to its owner.

To get information and schedules for all MTA services, call ✆ **410/539-5000,** or visit **www.mtamaryland.com.**

A terrific way to get around is the new **Charm City Circulator** (www.charmcity circulator.com). This free shuttle with three routes connects city neighborhoods from Penn Station to Federal Hill, from west Baltimore to Harbor East, and City Hall to Johns Hopkins Hospital. Used with the Light Rail, it will get you downtown from the airport and all around town. Buses run every 10 minutes or so, and you can sign up for mobile alerts or use the smartphone app to minimize wait time.

BY TAXI All taxis in the city are metered; two reputable companies are **Yellow Cab** (✆ 410/685-1212) and **Arrow Cab** (✆ 410/358-9697). You can count on a friendly ride from **Wanda Motley,** a longtime cabbie with Checker (✆ 443/600-0606). For airport trips, call **SuperShuttle** (✆ 800/622-2089; www.supershuttle.com).

BY WATER TAXI The water taxi makes for a pleasant way to visit Baltimore's attractions. **Baltimore Water Taxis** (✆ **800/658-8947** or 410/563-3900; www.baltimorewatertaxi.com) run between about a dozen Inner Harbor locations, including Harborplace, Fell's Point, Little Italy, Canton, and Fort McHenry; the main stop at Harborplace is on the corner between the two pavilions. Just tell the mate where you want to go. The cost is $10 for adults and $5 for children 10 and under for a full day's unlimited use. From May through Labor Day weekend, the 16 water taxis generally run about every 15 to 18 minutes, from 10am to 11pm Sunday through Thursday and until midnight Friday and Saturday. From November through March, taxis run from 11am to 6pm, sometimes later. In April, May, and October, Friday and Saturday service runs until 11pm. Service to Fort McHenry runs only April through September. Service is always weather permitting; you can pick up a schedule at the main stop at Harborplace. Tickets are available online; pickup is at the Visitors Center. ***Please note:*** You cannot park your car at Fort McHenry to catch the water taxi. ***Insiders note:*** The map is so good that tour guides use it to get around town.

Note: A free **Water Taxi Harbor Connector** runs between Tide Point, about a mile from Fort McHenry, and Maritime Park in Fell's Point. Water taxis run every 12 minutes 7am to 7pm daily, except in inclement weather. They connect with the Charm City Circulator. A map can be found at **www.charmcitycirculator.com**.

ON FOOT You'll need to know only a few streets to get around. The easiest is the **promenade** around the Inner Harbor, which runs along the water from Federal Hill to Harbor East to Fell's Point and Canton. You can take it to the American Visionary Art Museum, Maryland Science Center, Harborplace, National Aquarium, USS *Constellation,* and Maritime Museum, as well as to shops and restaurants.

Pratt and **Lombard** streets are the two major east-west arteries just above the Inner Harbor. Pratt heads east to Little Italy, while Lombard extends west to the stadiums. **Charles Street** is Baltimore's main route north and home to some good restaurants, Baltimore's Washington Monument, and the Walters Art Museum, all within walking distance of the Inner Harbor. **St. Paul Street** is the major route south.

BY BIKE Biking is permitted from 6 to 10am every day on the promenade, and new bike paths have been painted along many of the city's thoroughfares. There are no published maps yet but the lanes are well marked. (Still, be careful; drivers aren't used to them yet.)

Free bike lockers are available at two stops, the Maritime Park and Canton Waterfront Park. Lock up your bike (bring your own lock) and catch the water taxi here or Charm City Circulator. Buses don't have bike carriers anymore.

[Fast FACTS] BALTIMORE

Area Code The area codes in Baltimore are **410** and **443.**

Car Rentals See "Getting Around" (p. 42) for car-rental agencies at BWI. Two companies have locations at the Inner Harbor: **Avis,** at the Sheraton, 101 W. Fayette St. (✆ **410/685-6405**), and **Enterprise,** at the Sheraton, 300 S. Charles St. (✆ **410/547-1855**).

Emergencies Dial ✆ **911** for fire, police, or ambulance.

Eyeglass Repair Try **For Eyes,** 330 N. Charles St. (✆ **410/727-2027**).

Hospitals Downtown options for emergency rooms include **Johns Hopkins Hospital,** 600 N. Wolfe St. (✆ **410/955-5000**); **University of Maryland Medical Center,** 22 S. Greene St. (✆ **410/328-8667**); and **Mercy Medical Center,** 301 St. Paul Place (✆ **410/332-9000**).

Liquor Laws Restaurants, bars, hotels, and other places serving alcohol may stay open from 6am to 2am. Some opt to close on Sundays and election days. The legal age to buy or consume alcohol is 21.

Newspapers & Magazines The Baltimore ***Sun*** (www.baltimoresun.com) is the city's daily. ***City Paper,*** Baltimore's free weekly, is published Wednesdays and has good activities and entertainment listings. ***Baltimore*** magazine is published monthly.

Pharmacies Two downtown options are **Rite Aid,** 125 E. Baltimore St. (✆ **410/685-4340**), and **Walgreens,** 19 E. Fayette St. (✆ **410/625-1179**). Rite Aid in Mount Vernon, 250 W. Chase St. (✆ **410/752-4473**), and CVS, 1001 York Rd. (✆ **410/823-3900**), in Towson, north of the city, are open 24 hours a day.

Police Dial ✆ **911** for emergencies, ✆ **311** for nonemergencies requiring police attention.

Post Office The main post office is at 900 E. Fayette St. (✆ **410/347-4202**). It's open Monday through Friday from 8:30am to 7pm. Other area post offices are at 111 N. Calvert (✆ **410/539-2335**), and 130 N. Greene St. (✆ **410/244-1981**). Both are open Monday through Friday from 9am to 5pm.

Safety Baltimore has a nagging problem with both property and violent crime. The Inner Harbor and Mount Vernon areas are fairly safe, thanks to a greater number of police officers, along with the Downtown Partnership's safety guides. Still, be alert and follow some common-sense precautions.

Taxes The state sales tax is 6%. The hotel tax is an additional 10%.

Toilets You won't find public toilets or "restrooms" on the streets of Baltimore, but they can be found in hotel lobbies, bars, restaurants, museums, department stores, train and bus stations, and service stations. At the Inner Harbor, you can find public restrooms inside Harborplace and across Pratt Street at the Gallery at Harborplace, as well as at the Baltimore Visitor Center. You could also stop in the markets: Broadway Market at Fell's Point, Cross Street Market in Federal Hill, or at Lexington Market downtown. These aren't open on Sunday.

Transit Information For bus, Light Rail, and Metro info, call the **Maryland Transit Administration (MTA)** at ✆ **866/RIDE-MTA** (743-3682) or 410/539-5000, or go to **www.mtamaryland.com**.

WHERE TO STAY

Baltimore caters to the business traveler but loves families—there are about 9,000 hotel rooms downtown, with all the expected amenities. In 2011, the Four Seasons opened a new hotel on Harbor East's waterfront. Bed-and-breakfasts around town offer unique style and comfort.

Every hotel listed is accessible to travelers with disabilities, although specific amenities vary from place to place. Families with relatives in area hospitals, including Johns Hopkins and the University of Maryland Medical Center, should ask about special room rates and shuttles.

Rates fluctuate with the seasons and with what's going on in town. Prices rise when Yankee or Red Sox fans flock to town, as well as during the Preakness Stakes and other popular events, such as the Grand Prix.

Downtown Baltimore Hotels

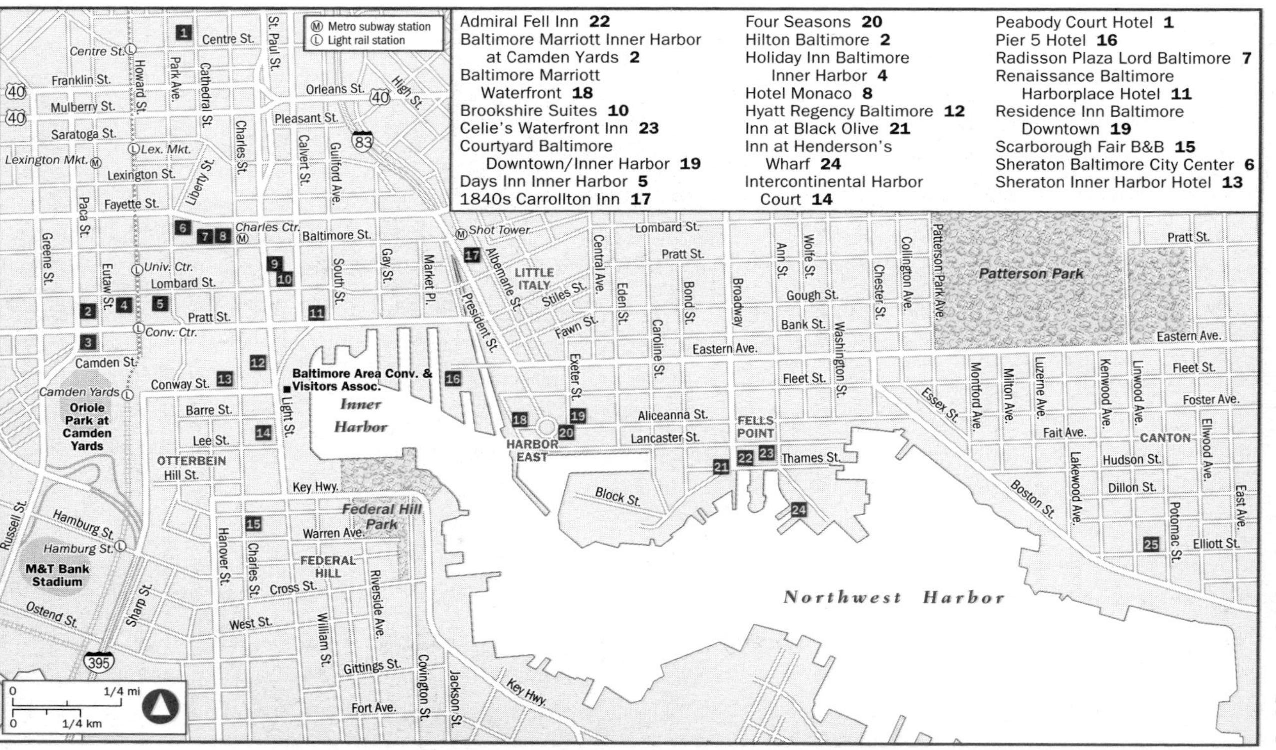

Inner Harbor

Baltimore's waterfront is ringed with tourist attractions, restaurants, and shopping, home to the USS *Constellation,* Harborplace, and several museums.

Best For: Most of the major attractions, tour boats, and restaurants are within walking distance, and the area is the site of many of the city's festivals and celebrations.

Drawbacks: Tourists and conventioneers are everywhere; parking is expensive.

EXPENSIVE

Baltimore Marriott Waterfront ★ ☺ This Marriott dominates a prime piece of Harbor East waterfront—even though it's more than a few steps from the city's best-known attractions and the convention center. As luck would have it, the water taxi stops at a dock outside. The hotel rises 32 floors above the neighborhood. Rooms here, updated in 2008, are standard, with the added pleasures of down duvets and that skyline vista. The 21 suites offer more room. The best views are from the top floors, and cost a bit more.

700 Aliceanna St., Baltimore, MD 21202. www.marriott.com/hotels/travel/bwiwf-baltimore-marriott-waterfront. ✆ **800/228-9290** or 410/385-3000. Fax 410/895-1900. 753 units. $259–$359 double. AE, DC, DISC, MC, V. Valet parking $40; self-parking $26. **Amenities:** Restaurant; coffee shop; lounge; concierge-level rooms; fitness center; indoor pool. *In room:* A/C, flatscreen TV, fridge, hair dryer, MP3 player, Wi-Fi (fee).

Four Seasons ★★★ They thought of everything in planning this waterfront hotel in Harbor East. Luxe finishes such as wood paneling and stone tile floors, a heated infinity pool and hot tub overlooking the harbor, a spacious spa **and** three Michael Mina–led **restaurants**—and all of it takes advantage of the harbor views. The hotel opened in November 2011 with some of the largest guest rooms in the city. A standard king measures 530 square feet. Big flatscreen TVs with Blu-ray DVD players, separate rainforest showers and soaking tubs, and of course that view (in 85% of the rooms) add to all this luxury. Half of the rooms have sofa beds. For some, the real draw may be the two-level pool deck with its curving pool, plenty of chaise longues, and a fireplace overlooking the Inner Harbor.

200 International Dr., Baltimore, MD 21202. www.fourseasons.com/baltimore. ✆ **410/576-5800.** Fax 410/576-5888. 256 units, including 45 suites. $296–$3,000 double. AE, DC, DISC, MC, V. Self-parking $21; valet parking $32. Pets under 40 pounds welcome. **Amenities:** 2 restaurants (Wit & Wisdom Tavern and Pabu); coffee shop; lounge; electric car charging stations in garage; dock space; fitness center; hot tub; pool; sauna; spa. *In room:* A/C, TV, DVD player, hair dryer, minibar, MP3 docking station, Wi-Fi (fee).

Hilton Baltimore ★ It's supposed to be a convention center hotel, but for baseball fans, the Hilton is all about the **stadium-view rooms.** The city's newest and largest hotel has rooms that look right over the outfield wall. Built adjacent to the Baltimore Convention Center, the rooms are standard Hilton comfort. About those ballpark rooms: 10 are suites with balconies. Ask for a south-side room to overlook the stadium. The terrace, outfitted with tables and chairs, off the fitness center looks over the stadium.

401 W. Pratt St., Baltimore, MD 21201. www.baltimore.hilton.com. ✆ **800/HILTONS** (445-8667) or 443/573-8700. Fax 443/683-8841. 757 units. $129–$399. AE, DC, DISC, MC, V. Valet parking $36; self-parking $28. On Light Rail stop. Pets accepted for fee. **Amenities:** Restaurant; lounge; concierge-level rooms; fitness center; indoor pool; sauna; whirlpool. *In room:* A/C, flatscreen TV, hair dryer, MP3 dock-radio, Wi-Fi (fee).

Hotel Monaco ★★★ The marble staircase leading to the lobby may fool you into thinking that you've entered a grand old hotel. The building *is* historic, a 1906 Beaux Arts glamorpuss that once housed the B&O Railroad headquarters—but the Monaco, a Kimpton property, is sleek and modern. Big windows let the light stream into these spacious quarters. Standard rooms are a nice 375 square feet. Majestic suites are the size of a Baltimore rowhouse, at 1,400 square feet. With 12-foot ceilings, tall people should be quite comfortable, but "tall rooms" with special amenities are available. The **B&O Brasserie** restaurant and lounge are worth a trip, even if you don't stay here.

2 N. Charles St., Baltimore, MD 21202. www.monaco-baltimore.com. ✆ **866/973-1904** or 443/692-6170. 202 units. $129–$449 double. Pets accepted. AE, DC, DISC, MC, V. Valet parking $36. **Amenities:** Restaurant; lounge; Kimpton Kids (arranges babysitting, stroller rental); concierge level; fitness center; room service. *In room:* A/C, TV, fridge on request, minibar, MP3 docking station, Wi-Fi (fee).

Hyatt Regency Baltimore ★★★ Location and smart furnishings make this convenient hotel the city's most stylish. Not only is the all-glass facade eye-catching, but you also won't want to miss the distinctive blue and yellow modern decor inside. The most pleasing guest room feature is the chaise longue tucked under the picture window. And the location is still Baltimore's best, with skywalks to the Inner Harbor and the convention center, and a few blocks' walk to the stadiums.

300 Light St., Baltimore, MD 21202. www.baltimore.hyatt.com. ✆ **800/233-1234** or 410/528-1234. Fax 410/685-3362. 488 units. $199–$399 double. Ask about packages and discounts. Children under 18 stay free in parent's room. AE, DC, DISC, MC, V. Self-parking $26; valet parking $37. **Amenities:** Restaurant; bar; executive-level rooms; fitness center; outdoor pool. *In room:* A/C, flatscreen TV, hair dryer, minibar, MP3 docking station, Wi-Fi (fee).

Intercontinental Harbor Court ★★ The glittering chandelier, curving staircase, and paneled walls of the lobby hint at the luxury of this Intercontinental property. Marble bathrooms, traditional furnishing, and plenty of space—even in standard rooms—have made these some of Baltimore's best accommodations for 25 years. A refurb is on the agenda for 2012. Though this lovely hotel shows its age a bit around the edges, you can still count on classic style, luxury bedding, and expert service. The hotel overlooks the harbor, but only a few rooms have a clear harbor view. Breakfast, lunch, afternoon tea on weekends, and dinner are served at cheery **Brighton's,** which offers waterfront views; and the clubby **Explorers Lounge** serves lunch, dinner, and late-night fare, as well as live entertainment every night but Monday.

550 Light St., Baltimore, MD 21202. www.harborcourt.com. ✆ **800/824-0076** or 410/234-0550. Fax 410/659-5925. 195 units, 22 suites. $259–$359 double; $350–$500 suite. AE, DC, DISC, MC, V. Self-parking $21; valet parking $32. **Amenities:** Restaurant; coffee shop; lounge; health club; Jacuzzi; indoor pool; room service; tanning; tennis courts; yoga studio. *In room:* A/C, flatscreen TV, CD player, hair dryer, minibar, Wi-Fi (fee).

Pier 5 Hotel ★ 🎁 Be prepared for something wild when you walk into the lobby of the Pier 5 Hotel. It's bright and airy, with fun, offbeat sofas and a purple, red, and yellow color scheme. The rooms continue the theme, though they're much quieter and more refined urban chic. Standard units are comfortable, with lots of conveniences for both business and leisure travelers. Suites are luxurious, with one, two, or even three tiny balconies overlooking the harbor or the National Aquarium. Just about every room has a water view—and are much closer than at any of the other hotels, as this place is only two stories high and right on the harbor. Ask about their packages for family fun or romance. **McCormick & Schmick's** offers lunch and dinner; and **Ruth's Chris Steak House** serves dinner. Evening activities, such as ghost tours or wine tastings, are offered in the lobby. A destination fee of about $10 covers these activities, as well as a shuttle bus, Wi-Fi, access to a local fitness center, and domestic long-distance calls.

711 Eastern Ave. (at the end of Pier 5), Baltimore, MD 21202. www.harbormagic.com. ✆ **866/583-4162** or 410/539-2000. Fax 410/783-1787. 66 units. $179–$399 double; $250–$850 suite (plus destination fee). AE, DC, DISC, MC, V. Self-parking $22; valet parking $32. Located at a water taxi stop. Pets welcome. **Amenities:** 2 restaurants; lobby cafe/bar; daily activities; day pass to Maryland Athletic Club; shuttle to Admiral Fell Inn, Inn at Henderson's Wharf, and Johns Hopkins Hospital. *In room:* A/C, Wi-Fi (fee).

Renaissance Harborplace Hotel ★★ The Renaissance is in the middle of everything: Business travelers find it convenient to local firms, the convention center, and restaurants, while tourists like its location across the street from Harborplace and the Inner Harbor. The Gallery shopping arcade is on the hotel's lower levels. Guest rooms are among the largest in Baltimore, with comfortable furniture and wide windows (that really open) overlooking the Inner Harbor. The huge rooms on the upper level have the best views. Suites have bedrooms connected to a parlor with living room, dining room, and kitchenette; some have Murphy beds. Public spaces, renovated in 2007, include the contemporary-styled **Watertable** restaurant and lounge.

202 E. Pratt St., Baltimore, MD 21202. www.renaissanceharborplace.com. ✆ **800/HOTELS-1** (468-3571) or 410/547-1200. Fax 410/783-9676. 622 units. $199–$349 double; $300–$449 suite. Children under 17 stay free in parent's room. AE, DC, DISC, MC, V. Valet parking $40; self-parking $34. **Amenities:** Restaurant overlooking harbor; lounge; concierge-level rooms; fitness center with harbor view; indoor pool; sauna; whirlpool. *In room:* A/C, TV, hair dryer, minibar, Wi-Fi (fee).

MODERATE

Baltimore Marriott Inner Harbor at Camden Yards ★ This 10-story hotel is across from Camden Yards and a couple of blocks from the Inner Harbor and the convention center. (Don't confuse it with the Baltimore Marriott Waterfront in Harbor East.) Rooms sport a fresh look with bright colors, white linens, and local art. King and two-queen rooms are the same size; king rooms have a single sleeper chair. Executive kings offer a separate sitting area with sofa bed. A panel on the flatscreen TV allows guests to hook up their laptop, game system, or MP3 to the TV.

110 S. Eutaw St., Baltimore, MD 21202. www.marriott.com/hotels/travel/bwiih. ✆ **800/228-9290** or 410/962-0202. Fax 410/625-7892. 524 units. $179–$389 double. AE, DC, DISC, MC, V. Self-parking $24. **Amenities:** Restaurant; lounge; coffee shop; concierge-level rooms; fitness center; room service. *In room:* A/C, TV, hair dryer, Wi-Fi (fee).

Brookshire Suites ★ ☺ This building was once a parking garage, but only the tallest guests might notice its slightly lower ceilings. Accommodations are comfortable, with room to spread out. Separate sitting rooms have wet bars with fridge. Bedding was updated in 2008. The **Cloud Club** has a terrific view, comfortable seating, and TVs. Families will like the breakfast buffet served every morning. On summer Saturdays, breakfast is hosted by "Bite" the shark. Afternoon receptions on weekdays feature local foods and brews. The hotel is easy to find, a block from the Inner Harbor on one of the city's main arteries—so it's convenient for sightseeing.

120 E. Lombard St., Baltimore, MD 21202. www.brookshiresuites.com. ✆ **866/583-4162** or 410/625-1300. 97 units. $129–$229 double. Ask about packages. Rates include full breakfast in Cloud Club. AE, DC, DISC, MC, V. Valet parking $29. Pets welcome. **Amenities:** Lounge; fitness room; pass to Maryland Athletic Club. *In room:* A/C, flatscreen TV, CD player, fridge, hair dryer, Wi-Fi (fee).

Courtyard Baltimore Downtown/Inner Harbor ★ Set in the middle of trendy Harbor East, the Courtyard offers comfortable accommodations—all immaculate. Even though rooms haven't been renovated since 2007 and redecorating is expected in 2012, these units are spotless, with crisp linens and barely a nick in the furniture. Eight units have jetted tubs and the 10 corner suites feature kitchenettes, pullout sofas, and a curved bank of windows in the bedroom. This hotel is serious enough for business travelers, but casual enough for families on vacation. Though not right at the Inner Harbor, it's an easy walk along the waterfront Promenade to the Inner Harbor or Fell's Point—or catch a cab or water taxi. The exercise room is small but the complimentary access to the nearby Maryland Athletic Club should please serious fitness buffs.

1000 Aliceanna St., Baltimore, MD 21202. www.marriott.com/bwidt. ✆ **443/923-4000.** Fax 443/923-9970. 205 units, including 10 suites. $129–$209 double. AE, DC, DISC, MC, V. Self-parking $23. Water taxi stop nearby. **Amenities:** Breakfast cafe; bar; complimentary coffee in lobby; exercise room; indoor pool; whirlpool. *In room:* A/C, flatscreen TV w/HBO, fridge, hair dryer, microwave, free Wi-Fi.

Days Inn Inner Harbor If you're willing to give up proximity to the harbor (by 2 or 3 blocks), you can get a great deal at this modern nine-story hotel, between the 1st Mariner Arena and the convention center, 3 blocks from Camden Yards. Newly updated in 2011–12, it's got a good setup for conventioneers and business travelers, including rooms with large desks, microwaves, and fridges, and a well-equipped business center. All units have the comfort you expect from this chain but a surprisingly high level of style. In fact, this hotel was chosen as the chain's number one hotel in 2008 and 2009. Most rooms have two double beds, though a few have space for a rollaway cot. Spacious king rooms have a sleeper sofa, as do queen rooms.

100 Hopkins Place (btw. Lombard and Pratt sts.), Baltimore, MD 21202. www.daysinnerharbor.com. ✆ **800/DAYS-INN** (329-7466) or 410/576-1000. Fax 410/576-9437. 249 units. $109–$229 double. Children under 17 stay free in parent's room. AE, DC, DISC, MC, V. Self-parking $23. Pets accepted for fee. **Amenities:** Restaurant; lounge; coffee shop; fitness center; courtyard patio; outdoor pool. *In room:* A/C, flatscreen TV w/pay movies, hair dryer, free Wi-Fi.

Holiday Inn Baltimore Inner Harbor ☺ For value and location, it's hard to beat this old-timer, the first major chain property in Baltimore. It's between the 1st Mariner Arena and the convention center, a block from Camden Yards, and 3 blocks from Harborplace. Guest rooms are a good size with traditional furniture and wide windows with skyline views. Two suites have whirlpool tubs.

301 W. Lombard St., Baltimore, MD 21201. www.holiday-inn.com/bal-downtown. ✆ **800/HOLIDAY** (465-4329) or 410/685-3500. Fax 410/727-6169. 365 units, including 12 suites. $129–$189 double; $40 additional for suite. Children under 18 stay free in parent's room. AE, DC, DISC, MC, V. Self-parking $21. **Amenities:** Restaurant; coffee shop; fitness center; indoor pool; sauna. *In room:* A/C, flatscreen TV w/movies, hair dryer, free Wi-Fi.

Inn at the Black Olive Green meets comfort at this brand new inn, opened in summer 2011. Rooms look a little spartan at first, with their concrete floors and olive-oil-finished plaster walls, but patterned throw rugs, art by local students, cozy organic bedding, and good service soften things up nicely. Best of all, these 800- and 1,000-square-foot suites look out past a vacant lot to the harbor with French doors opening onto balconies. Bathrooms have pipeless whirlpools and plenty of space. Larger fourth-floor rooms also have washer/dryers. An organic **restaurant**—sister to the delicious Black Olive around the corner—sits atop the inn with expansive water views. A cafe and market off the lobby feature Greek foods and fresh-baked olive bread.

803 S. Caroline St., Baltimore, MD 21231. www.theblackolive.com/Inn/index.html. ✆ **443/681-6316.** Fax 410/276-7143. 12 units. $290–$450. Children free. AE, DC, DISC, MC, V. Valet or self-parking $25. **Amenities:** Restaurant; cafe; lounge; market; passes to nearby Maryland Athletic Club fitness room and pool; room service. *In room:* A/C, flatscreen TV w/Netflix, fridge, hair dryer, free Wi-Fi.

Radisson Plaza Lord Baltimore If you love grand old hotels with modern conveniences, this one's for you. The 23-story French Renaissance–style hotel, which opened in 1928, still retains its old-fashioned charm. The grand lobby boasts soaring columns and a glittering chandelier. Those who need extra space should consider a one-bedroom parlor suite or a corner room, which comes with king-size bed and sleeper sofa. Set in the heart of the financial district, the hotel is convenient to Mount Vernon attractions; the Inner Harbor is only 5 blocks away.

20 W. Baltimore St. (btw. Charles and Hanover sts.), Baltimore, MD 21202. www.radisson.com/lordbaltimore. ✆ **888/201-1781** or 410/539-8400. Fax 410/625-1060. 439 units. $99–$279 double. AE, DC, DISC, MC, V. Valet parking $31; self-parking $12. **Amenities:** Restaurant; bar; coffee shop; concierge-level rooms; fitness center; sauna. *In room:* A/C, TV, fridge or microwave upon request, hair dryer, free Wi-Fi.

Residence Inn Baltimore Downtown/Inner Harbor A block from the Inner Harbor and tucked into the financial district is a branch of this family- and business-traveler-friendly chain. The studios, which are comfortable and reasonably priced, fill up quickly. Families may prefer the larger units: One-bedrooms have kitchenettes and pullout sofas, while two-bedroom suites are reserved for extended-stay guests. A hot breakfast is served every morning, with evening receptions Tuesday and Wednesday, all complimentary.

17 Light St., Baltimore, MD 21202. www.marriott.com/bwihb. ✆ **800/331-3131** or 410/962-1220. Fax 410/962-1221. 188 units. $179–$299 double (daily rates decrease for longer stays). Rates include breakfast and Tues and Wed evening refreshments. AE, DC, DISC, MC, V. Valet parking $32. Pets okay for fee. **Amenities:** Restaurant; lounge; snack shop; fitness center; access to pool at nearby Marriott hotels. *In room:* A/C, flatscreen TV w/movies, hair dryer, kitchenette, free Wi-Fi.

Sheraton Baltimore City Center ★ Renovations in 2007 gave the rooms some new polish. The decor features dark wood, taupe, and navy blue, and the rooms, though not large, are comfortable with flatscreen TVs and wide desks. The hotel is one of Baltimore's largest, with two towers; the south tower is said to have slightly bigger rooms, but the amenities are the same everywhere except on the more upscale concierge level. Because this is a big conference hotel, rooms are set up with the business traveler in mind. Tourists will like the outdoor pool and location 5 blocks from the Inner Harbor and next door to the 1st Mariner Arena.

101 W. Fayette St., Baltimore, MD 21202. www.sheraton.com/baltimorecitycenter. ✆ **800/325-3535** or 410/752-1100. Fax 410/385-6865. 706 units. $149–$189 double. Weekend packages available. Children under 18 stay free in parent's room. AE, DC, MC, V. Valet parking $34; self-parking $24. Small pets welcome for fee. **Amenities:** Restaurants; lounge; concierge level; fitness center; outdoor pool; complimentary shuttle to Johns Hopkins Hospital. *In room:* A/C, TV w/movies, fridge in 60% of rooms or available on request, hair dryer, Wi-Fi (fee).

Sheraton Inner Harbor Hotel The Sheraton has a perfect location for conventioneers and Orioles fans (and Red Sox and Yankees fans); the latter will like the location and the packages with tickets to Camden Yards. Furniture and linen upgrades in 2009 made the sleeping rooms bright and more welcoming. The suites are a good idea, set up with Murphy beds so they can be turned into miniconference rooms. The **Orioles Grille** has interesting sports memorabilia. **Morton's, The Steakhouse,** has a restaurant here.

300 S. Charles St., Baltimore, MD 21202. www.sheraton.com/innerharbor. ✆ **410/962-8300.** Fax 410/962-8211. 337 units. $179–$429 double; $550–$1,900 suite. Children under 18 stay free in parent's room. AE, DC, DISC, MC, V. Valet parking $32; self-parking $25. **Amenities:** Restaurant; grill and lounge; club level; fitness center; indoor pool; terrace; free Wi-Fi in lobby. *In room:* A/C, TV, fridge and microwave on request, hair dryer, Wi-Fi (fee).

Fell's Point

Baltimore's original seaport and home to the first shipyards. Now it's known for its nightlife: elegant restaurants and rowdy taverns, as well as trendy hotels and inns. The Recreation Pier served as the police headquarters for the TV series *Homicide*.

Best For: Fun. Baltimoreans and visitors alike mingle here in the mashup of historic taverns, fresh new restaurants, and funky little shops—all on the waterfront.

Drawbacks: Parking's expensive, cobblestone streets that aren't kind to stiletto heels, and early morning drunkenness, and the noise of late night/early morning partying.

Admiral Fell Inn Updated and expanded over the years, this charming inn sits just across Thames Street from the harbor in the heart of the Fell's Point Historic District. It spans eight buildings, built between 1790 and 1996, and blends Victorian and Federal-style architecture. Originally a boardinghouse for sailors, later a YMCA, and then a vinegar bottling plant, the inn now features an antiques-filled lobby and library, along with individually decorated guest rooms with Federal-period furnishings. Some units have four-poster beds with lacy canopies and Jacuzzis, two rooms have balconies, and one suite has a fireplace and Jacuzzi. The loft room is more rustic, with sloping ceilings. But from its three dormer windows, the views are among the best in the inn. Evening activities, such as ghost tours or wine tastings, are offered in the lobby. A destination fee of about $10 covers these activities, the shuttle bus, Wi-Fi, access to a local fitness center, and domestic long-distance calls.

888 S. Broadway, Baltimore, MD 21231. www.harbormagic.com. ✆ **866/583-4162** or 410/522-7377. Fax 410/522-0707. 80 units. $149–$229 double. Pets welcome. AE, DC, DISC, MC, V. Valet parking $29; self-parking $20. Located across the street from a water taxi stop. **Amenities:** 2 restaurants; daily activities; access to Maryland Athletic Club; shuttle to Pier 5 Hotel, Inn at Henderson's Wharf, and Johns Hopkins Hospital. *In room:* A/C, TV, fridge and microwave in double rooms, hair dryer, Wi-Fi.

Inn at Henderson's Wharf ★ From the warm lobby to the courtyard garden, every detail has been chosen for comfort and style. All rooms are on the ground floor (shutters at the windows ensure privacy), with views of the courtyard, the adjacent marina, or the cobblestone streets of Fell's Point. Each is outfitted in neutral colors, with dark mahogany furniture and luxurious marble bathrooms. Evening activities, such as ghost tours or wine tastings, are offered in the lobby. A destination fee of about $10 covers these activities, the shuttle bus, Wi-Fi, access to a local fitness center, and domestic long-distance calls.

1000 Fell St., Baltimore, MD 21231. www.harbormagic.com. ✆ **866/583-4162** or 410/522-7777. Fax 410/522-7087. 38 units. $189–$259 double (plus destination fee). Rates include continental breakfast. AE, DC, MC, V. Free parking. **Amenities:** Daily activities; fitness center plus access to MAC Wellness Center; 256-slip marina; shuttle to Pier 5 Hotel, Admiral Fell Inn, and Johns Hopkins Hospital. *In room:* A/C, TV w/DVD player available, fridge, hair dryer, Wi-Fi.

North of Downtown

A walk up Charles Street toward the Washington Monument is a walk through Beaux Arts beauty. The museums, restaurants, and hotels here came long before the Inner Harbor renaissance and serve as reminders of the city's earlier heyday.

Good For: Quieter than the Inner Harbor, you're also close to the Walters Art Museum, Baltimore Basilica, Peabody Library, and Maryland Historical Society, and there's a good selection of restaurants.

Drawbacks: It's an uphill walk from the harbor; the area has only a few shops, and you'll have to look for them.

Doubletree Inn at the Colonnade ★ If your visit will take you to northern Baltimore, Johns Hopkins University, the Baltimore Museum of Art, or Homeland or Roland Park, this is a stylish choice. Beyond the elegant lobby, rooms are comfortable with Biedermeier-style furnishings. Most standard king rooms have pullout couches. Every room has a separate sitting room and sleeping room. Suites have fridges and microwaves. A new **wellness center** opened in April, 2012, featuring spa treatments and other wellness/health offerings. Self-parking is free for diners at the hotel's **Alizee,** open for breakfast, lunch, and dinner.

4 W. University Pkwy., Baltimore, MD 21218. www.colonnadebaltimore.com. ✆ **800/222-8737** or 410/235-5400. Fax 410/235-5572. 125 units, including 31 suites. $159–$299 double. Pets welcome. AE, DC, DISC, MC, V. Self-parking $20; valet parking $24. **Amenities:** Restaurant; lounge; coffee shop; fitness center; access to nearby jogging track and tennis courts; room service. *In room:* A/C, flatscreen TV w/movies, hair dryer, MP3 docking station, free Wi-Fi.

Peabody Court Hotel ★ This Mount Vernon boutique hotel, a Wyndham property, continues to offer the first-class service that has kept it in business since 1930. The lobby's luxurious, European-style ambience gives way to guest rooms that are some of the most spacious in the city—the light-bathed corner units have upward of 600 square feet. Ask for a room that overlooks Baltimore's most beautiful and historic square. Rooms, already nicely decorated, were upgraded in late 2011 to Wyndham standards. The hotel is close to the Peabody Institute, Walters Art Museum, and Mount Vernon restaurants and shops. The walk to the Inner Harbor takes about 20 minutes—and it's downhill. The low-key, elegant **George's** serves breakfast, lunch, and dinner.

612 Cathedral St., Baltimore, MD 21201. www.peabodycourthotel.com. ✆ **800/292-5500.** Fax 410/727-7101. 104 units. $200–$300 double. AE, DC, DISC, MC, V. Valet parking $29. **Amenities:** Restaurant; lounge; fitness center. *In room:* A/C, flatscreen TV w/movies, fridge, hair dryer, towel warmers, wet bar in some rooms, free Wi-Fi.

Baltimore Bed & Breakfasts

If you prefer accommodations with a bit more individual attention, stop in one of these city bed-and-breakfasts. Located all over town, each has its own style.

Abacrombie Guest performers with the Baltimore Symphony Orchestra often choose this inviting B&B across from the Meyerhoff Symphony Hall. New owners expect to give the eight guest rooms a new "Restoration Hardware" look while maintaining the inn's reputation for personal service. Rooms can be small; singles ($99 a night) are European-hotel-size tiny. For more space, ask for a room at the end of the hall; they have the most square footage and the biggest windows. A restaurant and bar are located on the ground floor.

58 W. Biddle St., Baltimore, MD 21201. www.abacrombieinn.com. ✆ **410/244-7227.** Fax 410/244-8413. 8 units. $125–$159 double. Rates include continental breakfast. AE, DC, DISC, MC, V. Free parking. **Amenities:** Restaurant; bar. *In room:* A/C, TV, hair dryer.

Celie's Waterfront Inn ★ 🎁 Walk down the sally port of this 18th-century town house and enter a quiet refuge in bustling Fell's Point. Two units have fireplaces, whirlpool tubs, and harbor views, while two others—with just as nice city views—have private balconies and whirlpools. Two interior rooms overlooking the flower-filled courtyard are particularly quiet. Two suites (with full kitchens) can accommodate four or six comfortably. Enjoy breakfast in your room, on the deck, or in the garden.

1714 Thames St., Baltimore, MD 21231. www.celiesinn.com. ✆ **800/432-0184.** 9 units. $149–$249 double; $249–$399 suites. Rates include continental breakfast. 2- or 3-night minimum stay may be required on weekends or holidays. AE, DISC, MC, V. Off-street parking $10. Across the street from a water taxi stop. **Amenities:** Roof deck w/harbor views; fridge on request. *In room:* A/C, TV, free Wi-Fi.

1840s Carrollton Inn ★★ Sharing a courtyard with the Carroll Mansion Museum, this 13-room inn offers electric fireplaces, richly carved furniture, whirlpool tubs, and sumptuous bedding, Oriental carpets, and silk drapes in every room. Each room has its own style: The largest is the Carroll Suite, with a separate sitting room and double Jacuzzi in the bathroom. The Scholars Room has a double Jacuzzi and king bed. Light floods the corner Independence Suite. It's convenient to the Reginald Lewis Museum, Star-Spangled Banner Flag House, and Little Italy; the Inner Harbor is a short walk.

50 Albemarle St., Baltimore, MD 21202. www.1840scarrolltoninn.com. ✆ **410/385-1840.** 13 units. $175–$375 double. Rates include full breakfast. AE, DISC, MC, V. Discount parking passes for nearby garages. *In room:* A/C, TV, fridge, hair dryer, microwave, free Wi-Fi.

Inn at 2920 ★ This B&B was made for the youthful guests of the trendy Canton neighborhood. A mix of old Baltimore rowhouse and contemporary style, it features five upscale rooms with Jacuzzi tubs, modern decor, 15-foot ceilings, and windows that open. On a quiet side street, it's a block from the shops and eateries of O'Donnell Square and 2 blocks from the Canton water taxi stop. The Bordello Room features the only king bed (others have queens) and a double whirlpool. The first-floor Gato Casa has a sitting room with kitchenette. Betta fish keep guests company in all rooms.

2920 Elliott St., Baltimore, MD 21224. www.theinnat2920.com. ✆ **877/774-2920** or 410/324-4450. 5 units. $175–$235 double. Rates include full breakfast. 2-night minimum required many weekends. Children over age 12 welcome. AE, DISC, MC, V. On-street parking only. **Amenities:** Concierge services. *In room:* A/C, ceiling fan, flatscreen TV/DVD, CD player, hair dryer, whirlpool tub, free Wi-Fi.

Scarborough Fair ★★ This cozy Federal-style town house on a pretty Federal Hill corner has blossomed into something special. It started with two rooms with whirlpool tubs and five with fireplaces. As we went to press, rooms were getting makeovers one at a time and soon will all have literary themes. The first one finished was the Edgar Allan Poe Suite, a spacious room with fireplace in shades of graphite and lavender with Victorian touches. The Brothers Grimm Room is filled with light. High ceilings in first-floor rooms make them even airier. The first-floor Hickory Vale Room has a canopy bed, fireplace, and en-suite bathroom with double Jacuzzi.

1 E. Montgomery St., Baltimore, MD 21230. www.scarboroughfairbandb.com. ✆ **887/954-2747** or 410/837-0010. 6 units. $224–$259 double. Rates include breakfast. 2-night minimum required many weekends. AE, DISC, MC, V. Off-street parking included. Children welcome. *In room:* A/C, TV/DVD, hair dryer, Wi-Fi.

Near the Airport

An alternative to staying downtown and worrying about parking—especially if you plan to see only the Inner Harbor attractions—is a hotel near Baltimore/Washington International Thurgood Marshall Airport that offers free shuttle service to the North Linthicum Light Rail station. About 15 airport hotels have such shuttles. From North Linthicum, it's a 15-minute ride to the Camden Yards station, which is just 6 blocks from the Inner Harbor. For a train schedule, see **www.mtamaryland.com**.

Closest to the airport are **Four Points by Sheraton BWI Airport,** 7032 Elm Rd. (✆ **800/368-7764** or 410/859-3300; www.bestbwihotel.com)—it's actually on airport property and has an outdoor pool; the **BWI Airport Marriott,** 1743 W. Nursery Rd. (✆ **800/596-2376** or 410/859-8300; www.marriott.com), which has an indoor pool; and **Country Inn & Suites BWI Airport,** 1717 W. Nursery Rd. (✆ **443/577-1036;** www.countryinns.com/bwiairport), with an indoor pool. Situated next to each other at 1110 Old Elkridge Landing Rd., the **Sheraton** (✆ **443/577-2100;** www.sheraton.com/bwi) and the **Westin** (✆ **443/577-2300;** www.westin.com/bwi) both have indoor pools. Among the newest options is the **Aloft,** 1741 W. Nursery Rd. (✆ **410/691-6969;** www.starwoodhotels.com/alofthotels/bwi).

BEST BETS FOR EATING

- **Best Taste of Baltimore: Bo Brooks:** Baltimore is for the crabs, hon. This one is within reach of just about any tourist, has a great view of the Inner Harbor, and has plenty of steamed crabs ready for the picking on a summer afternoon. See p. 59.
- **Best for Families: Little Italy** treats kids like some of their own. **Sabatino's** (p. 58) has classic pasta and a famous Bookmaker Salad. **Amicci's** (p. 59) has a kid-friendly menu and more casual atmosphere. Stop at **Vaccaro's** for gelato and other sweet endings. See p. 59.
- **Best Splurge:** Go out of your way for **Woodberry Kitchen** near Hampden. Everything is local: seafood, bread, vegetables. The menu is filled with delicious surprises. The setting, in a reclaimed mill, is rustic and charming. See p. 63.

WHERE TO EAT

Fine dining is easy to find in Baltimore, but you must look beyond the Inner Harbor—home to chain restaurants serving mediocre fare. Take a walk up charming

PRICE CATEGORIES

Prices are for a three-course dinner (alcoholic beverages and tip not included).

Very Expensive	$70 and up
Expensive	$40–$69
Moderate	$20–$39
Inexpensive	Under $20

Downtown Baltimore Restaurants

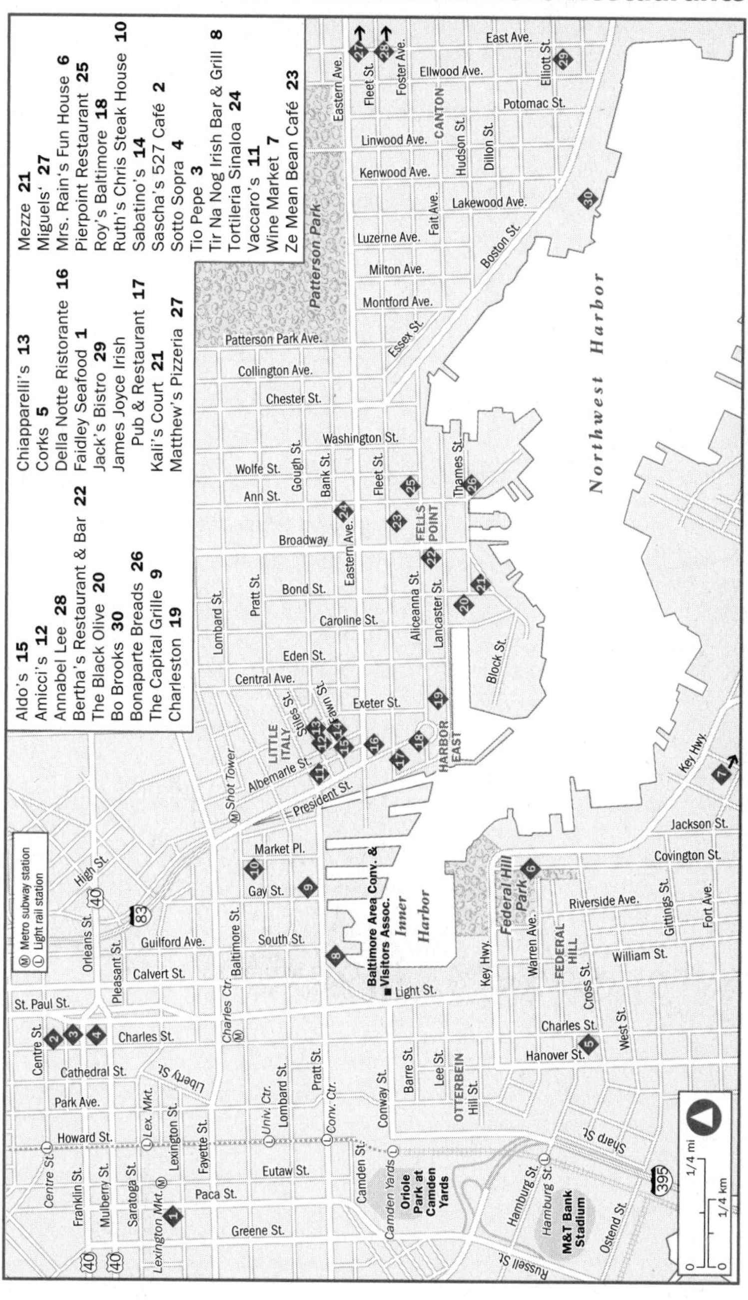

4 BALTIMORE | Where to Eat

Charles Street, head over to Little Italy, Harbor East, or Fell's Point and you'll find a variety of great restaurants, old and new. Or get a cab and make your way to wonderful Dogwood or Woodberry Kitchen in the Hampden area. Lots of restaurants now offer valet parking downtown, in Little Italy, and Harbor East, many for free.

You'll find chefs who know how to make Maryland's famous seafood and produce into culinary works of art—or just darn good crab cakes, steaks and ethnic treats.

Of course if you just want a quick bite, the Inner Harbor has lots of chain favorites, including the Hard Rock Cafe, the Cheesecake Factory, and Johnny Rockets.

Inner Harbor & Harbor East

VERY EXPENSIVE

Charleston ★★★ SOUTHERN The Charleston is Baltimore's special-night-out place. The food here is the undisputed best in Baltimore. Chef Cindy Wolf has turned Southern cooking into an art form. And the menu, with its tasting sizes so you can choose three to six courses (and count on dessert), is oh-so-imaginative. Whether you choose local seafood or beef, you know the food will be fresh, perfectly cooked, with delightful sauces and accompaniments. Service is so smooth, it may be too cool for Baltimore. As waiters glide by, you might get the feeling of being part of a culinary factory. A tiny quibble, perhaps, but with the elegantly appointed dining room and Southern-style dishes, you hope for Southern hospitality, too, as opposed to "cool." A three-course dinner is $74; a six-course meal will run $109 (wine is extra). The co-owner, Tony Foreman, has selected 600 bottles for the restaurant's wine list, which wins accolades. Wolf and Foreman run a virtual chain in Baltimore nowadays—if you like Charleston, try **Pazo,** 1425 Aliceanna St. (✆ **410/534-7296**), for tapas, or **Cinghiale,** 822 Lancaster St. (✆ **410/547-8282**), for its wine bar and modern Italian food. All of them are well worth a visit for food, drink, and ambience.

1000 Lancaster St. ✆ **410/332-7373.** www.charlestonrestaurant.com. Reservations recommended. Prix-fixe dinners $74–$109. AE, DC, DISC, MC, V. Mon–Sat 5:30–10pm. Free valet parking.

EXPENSIVE

The Capital Grille ★★ STEAKHOUSE The Prime Rib is still the king of Baltimore's steakhouses but the Capital Grille, known for its clubby atmosphere, sizzling steaks, and terrific wine list, beats out the rest. The food is expertly prepared and the service solicitous. Lunchtime choices range from sandwiches to salads to steak; at dinner, steak reigns, but there's plenty of seafood, too. All the dishes are flavorful, but the truffle fries may make you forget your steak.

500 E. Pratt St. ✆ **443/703-4064.** www.thecapitalgrille.com. Reservations recommended. Main courses $11–$23 at lunch, $23–$39 at dinner. AE, DC, DISC, MC, V. Mon–Fri 11:30am–3pm; Sun–Thurs 5–10pm; Fri–Sat 5–11pm. Valet parking.

Roy's Baltimore ★★ HAWAIIAN This well-regarded chain restaurant next to the Marriott Waterfront features a menu quite exotic for Baltimore, but it also incorporates Chesapeake ingredients. Known for its blackened ahi tuna, macadamia-encrusted mahimahi, sushi, and other tropical delights, the restaurant also does local seasonal favorites, including crab cakes, oysters, and softshell crabs. Its prix-fixe menu offers an appetizer sampler, entree, and dessert for $36. The sleek bar is a great place to try one of Roy's Hawaiian martinis. Aloha Hour offers discount drinks and apps.

720B Aliceanna St. ✆ **410/659-0099.** www.roysrestaurant.com. Reservations recommended. Entrees $25–$40. AE, DC, DISC, MC, V. Mon–Thurs 5–10pm; Fri–Sat 5–10:30pm; Sun 5–9pm. Valet parking.

BALTIMORE'S best CRAB CAKES

A visit to Baltimore means crab cakes—but what makes a good crab cake is a topic of heated debate. You can expect jumbo lump mixed with a bit of mayo; fried or broiled is often the diner's choice. But each recipe is different. Is Old Bay Seasoning required? How much filler is too much? Should you see a fleck of any plant material besides parsley?

Keep in mind a few things: Crabs run from May to September (more or less), so you have a better chance of getting local crab—not Louisiana or Asia imports—then. You don't have to go to a crab house for a decent crab cake. In fact, the number of crab houses has dwindled in recent years, but you can find good seafood at just about every restaurant around. Expect to pay $12 to $18 for a crab-cake sandwich (served on crackers or a bun). A crab-cake platter will be at least $25 and usually comes with fries, coleslaw, and sliced tomato.

Below is my list of where I think you'll find a good crab cake. Are these the best? Have a marvelous time deciding!

Faidley Seafood, Lexington Market, 400 W. Lexington St. (✆ **410/727-4898;** www.faidleyscrabcakes.com). The Faidley family has been selling seafood from this stall for 120 years, including a great traditional crab cake. Open Monday through Saturday from 9am to 5pm. Carryout only; shipping is available, too.

Gertrude's, at the Baltimore Museum of Art, 10 Art Museum Dr. (✆ **410/889-3399;** www.gertrudesbaltimore.com). Noted chef John Shields offers traditional Baltimore-style cakes as well as a creative chef's special. Open Tuesday through Sunday for lunch and dinner.

Kali's Court, 1606 Thames St., Fell's Point (✆ **410/276-4700;** www.kaliscourt.net). Crab, crab, and not much else. Open daily for dinner.

Nick's Fish House, 2600 Insulator Dr., South Baltimore (✆ **410/347-4123;** www.nicksfishhouse.com). Maybe the old South Baltimore feel of this casual place swayed me, but this is a great traditional crab cake in a traditional crab house. Open every day for lunch and dinner.

Ocean Pride, 1534 York Rd., Lutherville (✆ **410/321-7744;** www.oceanprideseafood.com). This unassuming little restaurant north of Baltimore City never fails to serve a great crab cake at a great price. Open daily for lunch and dinner.

Pierpoint Restaurant, 1822 Aliceanna St., Fell's Point (✆ **410/675-2080;** www.pierpointrestaurant.com). Crab cakes here are smoked—different, but well worth a try. Open Tuesday through Sunday for dinner.

Sunset Restaurant, 625 Greenway Rd. SE, Glen Burnie, MD 21061 (✆ **410/768-1417**; www.sunsetrestaurant.com). Sweet lump crab cooked to a golden brown. Locals know a good thing at this old favorite south of the city.

MODERATE

Tir Na Nog Irish Bar and Grill IRISH This is not your Irish grandmother's Irish pub. Yes, you'll find Guinness on tap and fish and chips. But you'll also find crab cakes, salmon with truffle essence, and fresh fettuccine. The restaurant is a knockout, with two beautifully carved bars and, for diners lucky enough to have window seats, a close-up view of the Inner Harbor. Brunch is served Saturday and Sunday.

Harborplace, 201 E. Pratt St., Level 2. ✆ **410/483-8968.** www.tirnanogbaltimore.com. Reservations recommended. Main courses $11–$16 lunch, $14–$24 dinner. AE, DC, DISC, MC, V. Mon–Fri 11am–2am; Sat–Sun 10am–2am.

INEXPENSIVE

James Joyce Irish Pub & Restaurant IRISH This handsome, wood-paneled pub in Harbor East attracts conventioneers for hearty fare—from Irish stew to potato soup, crab cakes to steak—and beer. It has a musician crooning Thursday to Saturday nights. There's a children's menu and brunch on weekends.

616 President St. ✆ **410/727-5107.** www.thejamesjoycepub.com. Reservations recommended. Main courses $9–$23. AE, DISC, MC, V. Daily 11am–2am. Valet parking available at Roy's next door.

Little Italy

In just a few packed blocks, you'll find all the pasta, cannoli, and Chianti you could want. Make a reservation if you know where you want to eat beforehand. But if you prefer to wander, plan to eat early or late and choose a place as you stroll through the basil-scented streets. If you don't have room for dessert, remember, there's always Vaccaro's to go. ***Tip:*** Parking is fairly easy. Choose the Dodge garage at Pratt and President streets, opt for valet parking at many restaurants, or find a spot on the street.

EXPENSIVE

Aldo's ★★★ SOUTHERN ITALIAN Expect to be treated like royalty. Enjoy your meal in an elegant setting with small, candlelit rooms and an oh-so-grand atrium dining room; there's also a hefty wine list. Plates full of perfectly prepared southern Italian cuisine, such as risotto and heavenly lobster-studded mashed potatoes, are stellar. A bit of seafood, as well as veal saltimbocca and *osso buco* make the grade, too. It's a perfect spot for romance or celebration. They'll even arrange a limo.

306 S. High St. ✆ **410/727-0700.** www.aldositaly.com. Reservations recommended on weekends. Main courses $19–$45. AE, DC, DISC, MC, V. Daily 5–10pm. Valet parking available.

MODERATE

Chiapparelli's SOUTHERN ITALIAN Southern Italian dishes in red sauce are the trademark at this longtime favorite, but try Grandma's *spinache* ravioli in *osso buco* sauce. Pizzas and panini are on the lunch menu, but dinner is the main event, and veal is the star. You'll find tasty chicken dishes and many classics such as chicken Marsala and shrimp Parmigiana. The children's menu includes chicken tenders and pizza bread.

237 S. High St. ✆ **410/837-0309.** www.chiapparellis.com. Reservations recommended. Entrees $7–$14 lunch, $17–$30 dinner. AE, DC, DISC, MC, V. Sun–Thurs 11:30am–9pm; Fri–Sat 11:30am–11pm.

Della Notte Ristorante ★★ ITALIAN Della Notte is noted for its circular main dining room, lined with banquettes and a huge tree in the center. Lunch can be panini, pizza, or pasta. At dinner, choose chicken Marsala, a traditional pasta, or something inventive from the night's specials. Brunch is served on Sunday. The impressive wine list includes 30 wines by the glass. The piano lounge is open from 6 to 10pm nightly. On-site parking is available.

801 Eastern Ave. ✆ **410/837-5500.** www.dellanotte.com. Reservations recommended. Main courses $9–$20 lunch, $24–$39 dinner. AE, MC, V. Sun–Thurs 11am–10pm; Fri–Sat 11am–11pm.

Sabatino's ★★ SOUTHERN ITALIAN For 50 years, Sabatino's has been known for its exceptional cuisine. The house salad with its thick, garlicky dressing is almost as famous as its Bookmaker Salad topped with Italian meats, cheeses, and shrimp—so hearty! Simple pasta dishes come in large portions. The menu also has seafood and meat dishes—*brasciola,* a roll of beef, prosciutto, cheeses, and marinara, is heavenly.

Dining rooms fill three floors of this narrow building. It's worth the wait to be seated upstairs, where it's quieter. This is a good spot for late-night dining and people-watching after the bars have closed.

901 Fawn St. (at High St.). ✆ **410/727-9414.** www.sabatinos.com. Reservations recommended. Main courses $13–$30. AE, DC, DISC, MC, V. Sun–Thurs 11am–midnight; Fri–Sat 11:30am–3am.

INEXPENSIVE

Amicci's ☺ ITALIAN You'll find casual Amicci's crowded with local families and young couples who don't want to spend a lot on good Italian food. Don't be fooled by the small storefront—the restaurant is a maze of dining rooms. If you have to wait, it won't be too long. Start with Amicci's signature *pane rotundo* filled with shrimp scampi. There are pasta choices for traditionalists, seafood lovers, and vegetarians. Desserts come from Vaccaro's. A $5 children's menu is offered all day.

231 S. High St. ✆ **410/528-1096.** www.amiccis.com. Reservations recommended. Main courses $8–$12 lunch, $12–$18 dinner. AE, DISC, MC, V. Mon–Sat 11:30am–midnight.

Vaccaro's ★ ITALIAN DESSERTS To top off the day, stop at the always-busy Vaccaro's for dessert and coffee. The shop's modern Italian design mixes well with the old recipes for cannoli, pastries, and tiramisu. If you love gelato, you'll be thrilled by the huge servings—just one scoop is plenty (really!). If you insist on real food before dessert, Vaccaro's serves breakfast and lunch panini, muffalettas, and salads. There's an outlet in Canton at 2919 O'Donnell St. (✆ **410/276-4744**).

222 Albemarle St. ✆ **410/685-4905.** www.vaccarospastry.com. Reservations not accepted. Desserts $4–$10. AE, MC, V. Mon 9am–10pm; Tues–Thurs and Sun 9am–11pm; Fri–Sat 9am–1am.

Fell's Point & Canton

EXPENSIVE

The Black Olive ★★★ GREEK/SEAFOOD Slip down a quiet residential street and find this taverna, which specializes in fresh, organic Greek treats and an enormous fish selection. The whole-fish preparations are well known among area foodies. Diners can also choose from a variety of small plates and Greek dishes, including chicken souvlaki and village pie. The wine list is hefty, with a lot of options by the glass. Service is smooth but friendly, and the four dining rooms are intimate and comfortable.

814 S. Bond St. ✆ **410/276-7141.** www.theblackolive.com. Reservations required for dinner. Entrees $12–$25 lunch, $27–$40 dinner. AE, MC, V. Daily noon–2pm and 5–10pm. Valet parking for dinner.

Bo Brooks ★ SEAFOOD This is where Baltimoreans take their friends for steamed crabs. It's one of the few places in the city where you can get both a view and a pile of hot, steaming crustaceans. The crabs are fat and spicy. They've got lots of other seafood entrees, as well as sandwiches, salads, and pasta.

2701 Boston St. ✆ **410/558-0202.** www.bobrooks.com. Reservations recommended. Main courses $9–$27. Crabs $50–$96 a dozen. Mon–Thurs 11:30am–10pm; Fri 11:30am–11pm; Sat 12:30–11pm; Sun 12:30–9pm. Parking available on-site.

Kali's Court ★★ GREEK/SEAFOOD This two-story shrine to good food and good times has wonderful crab cakes—giant lump crab held together with little more than a prayer and not even a hint of Old Bay. The place is known for its grilled whole fish; its bouillabaisse comes highly recommended, too. Make a reservation and plan to wait. The bar in the front can be raucous, but upstairs, the mood is more intimate. Once seated, you'll be treated well and your palate will be delighted.

Mezze (✆ **410/563-7600**), right next door, serves Mediterranean-style tapas at affordable prices. It's open Monday to Saturday 4 to 10pm and Sun 11:30am to 4pm. **Meli** (1636 Thames St.; ✆ **410/534-6354**) means *honey,* in Greek so honey-sweetened pastries are featured here. Lunch is served Monday through Friday 11:30am to 2:30pm, with dinner daily 5 to 10pm and dessert served until 1am. Live music on Friday and Saturday and a Sunday jazz brunch are also featured here. **Tapas Adela** (814 S. Broadway; ✆ **410/534-6262**) is the family's newest and hottest venture, with a small-plates menu available 5 to 10pm.

1606 Thames St. ✆ **410/276-4700.** www.kaliscourt.net. Reservations recommended. Main courses $28–$36. AE, DC, MC, V. Daily 5–10pm; brunch Sun 11am–3pm. Free valet parking.

MODERATE

Annabel Lee ★ PUB FARE Baltimore street corners all over the city have these tiny neighborhood taverns. This one is worth going out of the way for. (And you'll have to search for it.) Phrases from Edgar Allan Poe's famous poem are painted on the walls, and the master of horror's portrait is everywhere. But the menu is sheer comfort: crisp salads; upscale appetizers, including a yummy flatbread pizza topped with crab dip; burgers; and sandwiches along with the microbrew beers and fancy cocktails.

601 S. Clinton St. ✆ **410/522-2929.** www.annabelleetavern.com. No reservations, but call ahead to get on the seating list. Main courses and appetizers $9–$17. AE, MC, V. Mon–Sat 4pm–1am.

Bertha's Restaurant & Bar ★ INTERNATIONAL/SEAFOOD This Fell's Point landmark is known for its mussels and music. The decor is shabby chic, with dark walls and plenty of accessories proud of their age. Mussels are famous here, prepared in eight different ways—they're delicious swimming in garlic butter. The entire menu is available all day with a few lunch specials offered daily. It's heavy on seafood. Brunch is served Sundays 11:30am to 2pm. The music starts most evenings after 9pm.

734 S. Broadway, Fell's Point. ✆ **410/327-5795.** www.berthas.com. Reservations accepted only for parties of 6 or more for lunch and dinner. Main courses $6.50–$19 lunch, $12–$22 dinner. MC, V. Sun–Thurs 11:30am–11pm; Fri–Sat 11:30am–midnight. Bar open until 2pm.

Jack's Bistro ★★ INTERNATIONAL Baltimore knows a good thing and Jack's is a very good thing: You'll find plenty of delicious dishes cooked *sous vide,* shrimp and grits luxuriating in a lobster cream, all kinds of meat and seafood dishes taken up a notch with creative seasonings and sauces. Sit in front near the bar, or squeeze in the back dining room and watch the kitchen. A neighborhood gathering spot, Jack's is casual and (get this . . .) it's named for Jack Tripper's place on *Three's Company.*

3123 Elliott St., Canton. ✆ **410/878-6542.** www.jacksbistro.net. Reservations accepted only for parties of 6 or more or on holidays. Main courses $10–$27. AE, MC, V. Wed–Sun 5–10pm.

Pierpoint Restaurant ★ MODERN MARYLAND Chef Nancy Longo has won accolades for her creative American cuisine with its Maryland roots. Smoked crab cakes are a specialty, but you'll also be delighted with the stylish preparations of tenderloin, duck breast, or oysters. Each season brings new dishes. The 44-seat restaurant is a simple little place with a big bar up front. Chef Longo also offers lots of cooking classes on weekends. Check the website for the schedule.

1822 Aliceanna St. ✆ **410/675-2080.** www.pierpointrestaurant.com. Reservations required for lunch, recommended for dinner. Main courses $6–$14 lunch, $18–$27 dinner. AE, DC, DISC, MC, V. Mon 5–9pm; Tue–Thurs 5–9:30pm; Fri–Sat 5:30–10:30pm; Sun 10:30am–1pm and 4:30–9pm.

Ze Mean Bean Cafe EASTERN EUROPEAN At this cozy European-style cafe, you can count on an attentive waitstaff, a menu that maintains its ties to Eastern Europe (this area is rich in Polish and Ukrainian heritage) while trying new things, and food that lives up to its promise. Sample the pierogi or borscht, or try the signature chicken Kiev. Thursday is Slavic night with $14 dinners. The lunch menu includes salads and sandwiches. Brunch is served Saturday and Sunday, with jazz on Sunday. Acoustic music is offered Friday and Saturday nights. Where else can you go for pierogi happy hour every night at the bar from 5 to 7pm?

1739 Fleet St. © **410/675-5999.** www.zemeanbean.com. Reservations recommended. Main courses $10–$24 lunch, $12–$24 dinner. AE, DC, DISC, MC, V. Mon–Thurs 11am–11pm; Fri 11am–1am; Sat 9:30am–1am; Sun 9am–11pm.

INEXPENSIVE

Bonaparte Breads FRENCH/BAKERY This wonderful little spot is part bakery, part cafe, all French. You can take out fresh pastries or bread studded with olives and herbs. Or you can stop in for the breakfast or lunch special. At lunchtime, walk up to the counter and choose from the numerous sandwiches and quiches (the seafood quiche is rich and creamy). Then pull up a leather chair at one of the tables; if you're lucky, you'll sit by the windows looking out at the harbor. After lunch, check out the fresh tarts filled with fruit and sugar, which are all good.

903 S. Ann St. © **410/342-4000.** Breakfast special $7.95; lunch special $15. AE, MC, V. Daily 8am–6pm. Lunch served only until 4pm, but breads and pastries available until 6pm.

Matthew's Pizza PIZZA They know how to make a perfect pizza here: soft, chewy crust, tomato-ey sauce, and the right amount of gooey cheese. They've had some practice—they've been here since 1943.

3131 Eastern Ave. © **410/276-8755.** www.matthewspizza.com. No reservations. Main courses $5–$13. AE, DISC, MC, V. Mon–Thurs 11am–10pm; Fri–Sat 11am–11pm; Sun noon–9pm.

Tortilleria Sinaloa TACOS If you crave a quick bite, something flavorful and cheap, head for this storefront for freshly made tortillas, tacos, quesadillas, and tamales, and sauces with a real kick. If you're starving, order by the pound. Everything is freshly made. You can perch on the high stools around the edge of the shop, or carry out to a spot down by the water.

1716 Eastern Ave., Baltimore, MD 21231. © **410/276-3741.** www.tortilleria-sinaloa.com. No reservations. Main courses $2.85–$8. Cash only. Sun 8am–6pm; Mon–Thurs 8am–7pm; Fri–Sat 8am–8pm.

Mount Vernon

EXPENSIVE

The Prime Rib ★★★ STEAKHOUSE In the heart of Mount Vernon, this restaurant has been dishing out the beef since 1965. The prime rib is the best in town; the Caesar salad is dressed to perfection; and the lobster bisque is rich and creamy. If you want seafood, there are crab cakes and fish. Everything is a la carte. The classic setting—lots of brass, black leather, and flowers—can get noisy when there's a crowd but mostly is a romantic spot for enjoying the food. Music almost every night adds to the ambience.

1101 N. Calvert St. (btw. Biddle and Chase sts.), Baltimore, MD 21202. © **410/539-1804.** www.theprimerib.com. Reservations required. Men are requested to wear jackets on Sat. Main courses $23–$52. AE, DC, MC, V. Mon–Thurs 5–10pm; Fri–Sat 5–11pm; Sun 4–10pm. Bar fare until 1am. Free valet parking.

MODERATE

Mari Luna Bistro MEXICAN An energetic staff works hard to make this a restaurant diners think of coming in on nonconcert nights, and it's worth a visit, even if you're not heading to the Meyerhoff Symphony Hall (where the Baltimore Symphony, led by Marin Alsop, plays). With its brightly painted walls and simple, dark furnishings, Mari Luna has a few features not easy to find in Baltimore: guacamole and sangria bars, weekend Latino music, and even Friday night salsa lessons in the lower lounge. The food, traditional Mexican fare from burritos to ceviche, delivers the spice you expect. A $10 lunch menu is a bargain. As for concertgoers, when the BSO is in, a prix-fixe menu will get them fed and on their way before the maestra raises her baton.

1225 Cathedral St., Baltimore, MD 21201. ✆ **410/637-8013.** www.mariluna.com. Reservations recommended on concert nights. Main courses $9–$28. AE, DISC, MC, V. Tues–Thurs 11am–10pm; Fri 11am–midnight; Sat 4pm–midnight; Sun 11am–9pm.

Sammy's Trattoria ITALIAN Casual enough for a quick bite but pretty enough for a romantic dinner, Sammy's location makes it a great choice for pre-symphony dining. The menu is split between pasta dishes and Italian favorites such as chicken Marsala and shrimp scampi. Panini, salads, and smaller versions of dinner entrees are offered at lunch. Sunday brunch begins at 11am.

1225 N. Charles St., Baltimore, MD 21201. ✆ **410/837-9999.** www.sammystrattoria.com. Reservations recommended. Main courses $10–$17 lunch, $10–$25 dinner. AE, DISC, MC, V. Mon 5–9pm; Tues–Fri 11:30am–11pm; Sat 5–11pm; Sun 5–9pm. Valet parking Thurs–Sun.

Sascha's 527 Café ★ AMERICAN Sascha's has an eclectic menu and a colorful, sophisticated dining room, with high ceilings and velvet banquettes. Dinner choices range from burgers to seafood, but the "taste plates" are where Sascha's shines. These range from a cone of fries to mini bison burgers to tuna roll or fried green tomatoes. At lunch, the restaurant goes buffet style, with salads, panini, and soups.

527 N. Charles St. ✆ **410/539-8880.** www.saschas.com. Reservations recommended on weekends. Main courses $6–$10 lunch, $10–$24 dinner; taste plates $5–$13. AE, DC, MC, V. Mon–Fri 11am–3pm; Mon–Wed 5:30–10pm; Thurs 5:30–11pm; Fri–Sat 5:30pm–midnight.

Sotto Sopra ★★ MODERN ITALIAN One of the best Italian restaurants is outside of Little Italy, tucked in the gilt-edged rooms of an elegant town house. But don't look for the usual marinara and mozzarella here. The pasta (all house-made) may get its color from squid ink; the mussels may swim in coconut milk and curry. Traditional and updated Italian recipes get special treatment here. The wine list, though not huge, has plenty of Italian and non-Italian choices with many offered by the glass.

N. Charles St., Baltimore, MD 21203. ✆ **410/265-0324.** www.sottosoprainc.com. Reservations highly recommended for weekend dinner. Main courses $12–$38; lunch $10–$34. AE, DISC, MC, V. Mon–Sat 11:30am–2pm and 5:30–10pm; Sun 5–9pm. Free valet parking

Tapas Teatro ★★ TAPAS Tapas are big in Baltimore—and as pretty as Sascha's is, the food here is even better. The restaurant, adjacent to the Charles Theatre, is an ode to industrial chic, with exposed-brick walls and metal accents. The refinement is in the food, which changes seasonally: colorful salads, rockfish, country bread rubbed with Maryland tomatoes and Asiago cheese. Need something hearty? Try the paella. Sangria makes a nice accompaniment, or taste one of the 31 wines or 18 beers. The desserts are a delight to the eye and a pleasure to the palate.

1711 N. Charles St. ✆ **410/332-0110.** www.tapasteatro.net. Reservations not accepted. Tapas and main courses $6–$21. AE, DISC, MC, V. Tues–Fri 5pm–2am (tapas served until 11pm); Sat–Sun 4pm–2am (tapas menu served until midnight).

Tío Pepe ★★ SPANISH Walk down the stairs into whitewashed rooms that resemble a wine cellar. Spanish artwork, wrought iron, and pottery decorate the tiny dining rooms that seem to go on and on. An old Baltimore favorite, the place is known for its sangria, roast suckling pig, and a dramatic paella (the best around.) Other menu highlights include shrimp in garlic sauce and sole with bananas and hollandaise sauce. Dessert is a standout: Try the flan, chocolate soufflé, or the roll cakes. Tío Pepe is a special-occasion restaurant, so reservations are a must.

10 E. Franklin St. (off Charles St.). ✆ **410/539-4675.** Reservations recommended (as far as 3 weeks in advance for Sat night). Jackets suggested. Main courses $11–$25 lunch, $18–$35 dinner. AE, DC, DISC, MC, V. Mon–Fri 11:30am–2:30pm; Mon–Thurs 5–10pm; Fri–Sat 5–11:30pm; Sun 4–10pm.

North of Downtown

MODERATE

Dogwood ★★★ ORGANIC/AMERICAN Baltimore's version of Chez Panisse, the Dogwood features organic meats and produce from Maryland and Pennsylvania outlets in an eclectic combination of creative dinner entrees that celebrate the best of each season. Chef Galen Sampson's menu includes vegetarian options along with the meat and seafood. Several of the salads offered at lunch also appear on the dinner menu as casual options. The basement dining room is sleek and dark with a cool vibe.

911 W. 36th St. ✆ **410/889-0952.** www.dogwoodbaltimore.com. Reservations recommended for dinner. Main courses $7–$17 lunch, $17–$30 dinner. AE, DISC, MC, V. Mon–Thurs 11:30am–3pm and 5–10pm; Fri–Sat 11:30am–3pm and 5–11pm.

Gertrude's ★★ 🎁 SEAFOOD Pause at Gertrude's during a visit to the Baltimore Museum of Art. Chef and cookbook author John Shields has created a restaurant filled with local delights and named it for his grandmother—making this place a destination in itself. The sleek space has tall windows overlooking the BMA's sculpture garden, with outdoor seating in warm weather. The menu includes soups (such as rich cream of crab) and sandwiches (with plenty of Old Bay on the shrimp)—and entrees where Chesapeake seafood has a starring role. If you're feeling adventurous, you might like the small plates, such as citrus barbecue shrimp or Portobello crab Imperial. Brunch is served Saturday and Sunday.

At the Baltimore Museum of Art, 10 Art Museum Dr. ✆ **410/889-3399.** www.gertrudesbaltimore.com. Reservations recommended. Main courses $9–$26 lunch, $9–$30 dinner. AE, DC, MC, V. Tues–Fri 11:30am–9pm; Sat 10:30am–3pm and 5–9pm; Sun 10:30am–3pm and 5–8pm.

La Famiglia ★ ITALIAN A neighborhood eatery, La Famiglia makes everyone feel at home with its friendly staff and solid Italian dishes. Owned and managed by a Little Italy veteran, the restaurant features the usual pastas, risotto, and salads, along with some hearty entrees. Mussels are a savory treat, and you can't go wrong with their risotto of the day or pastas, paired with a selection from their Italian-heavy wine list.

105 W. 39th St. ✆ **443/449-5555.** www.lafamigliabaltimore.com. Reservations recommended. Main courses $16–$28 dinner. AE, MC, V. Sun–Mon 5–9pm; Tues–Thurs 5–10pm; Fri–Sat 5–11pm. Free parking across the street.

Woodberry Kitchen ★★★ REGIONAL Fresh, local ingredients, classic culinary techniques, and a generous dash of creativity make this one of Baltimore's hottest restaurants. Set in a reclaimed mill building with rustic touches preserved, Woodberry is casual but refined. The menu, always seasonal, may pair braised beef shanks with mashed celery root or baked rockfish with parsnip cream. Brunch is offered on weekends. You can expect local seafood, fresh baked breads, and cocktails with house-made juices and syrups.

2010 Clipper Park Rd., Baltimore, MD 21211. ✆ **410/464-8000.** www.woodberrykitchen.com. Reservations essential. Main courses $11–$31. AE, MC, V. Mon–Thurs 5–10pm; Fri 5–11pm; Sat 10am–2pm and 5–11pm; Sun 10am–2pm and 5–9pm.

INEXPENSIVE

PaperMoon Diner DINER This funky restaurant is a student favorite, but anyone with a sense of fun will like the toys and knickknacks all around. Open early enough for breakfast and late enough for a snack after a concert, PaperMoon's all-day menu offers burgers, sandwiches, breakfast items, and vegetarian options—all of them good. So is the cake; they have *lots* of cake.

227 W. 29th St. (btw. Remington Ave. and Howard St.). ✆ **410/889-4444.** www.papermoondiner24.com. Reservations not accepted. Main courses $6–$14. MC, V. Sun–Thurs 7am–midnight; Fri–Sat 7am–2am.

Mount Washington Village

MODERATE

Crêpe du Jour FRENCH The bright yellow-and-blue porch may attract your eye, but the huge savory and sweet crepes will thrill your taste buds. Crepes come with all kinds of fillings: ratatouille; walnuts, blue cheese, and mesclun; sugar and lemon. At dinner, the menu expands to include French-flavored steak, chicken, and seafood entrees. Sidewalk tables and a deck increase the dining space in warm months.

1609 Sulgrave Ave. ✆ **410/542-9000.** www.crepedujour.com. Reservations suggested for dinner and weekend brunch. Crepes and sandwiches $4–$16; dinner main courses $10–$26. AE, DISC, MC, V. Mon 11am–3pm and 5–9pm; Tues–Thurs 11am–10pm; Fri 10am–11pm; Sat 10am–11pm; Sun 10am–9pm. Valet parking available.

Ethel and Ramone's ★ CAJUN On a little street in Mount Washington, you'll be confronted with four intriguing restaurants on the same short block. If you crave Cajun, pick Ethel and Ramone's. The folks who run this offbeat eatery know good food. Get the gumbo—it's spicy, filling, and rich with andouille sausage and chicken. Other Louisiana favorites include red beans and rice, jambalaya, and blackened fish. Lunch is mostly overstuffed sandwiches, including po' boys. Breakfast is offered from 7 to 11am. There's seating outdoors in warm weather.

1615 Sulgrave Ave. ✆ **410/664-2971.** www.ethelandramones.com. Reservations recommended for dinner. Main courses $9–$13 lunch, $13–$25 dinner. AE, DISC, MC, V. Tues–Thurs 7am–3pm and 5:30–9pm; Fri–Sat 11am–3pm and 5:30–10pm; Sun 5:30–10pm.

Federal Hill/South Baltimore

MODERATE

Corks ★ WINE BAR Watch the cooks in action in the front room, or head to the back for a cozier, quieter place to savor wine by the glass or the bottle and enjoy a wide variety of choices—eight different steaks, burgers, fish, and crab cakes. The menu looks like plain fare, but the preparations take plain to wow.

1026 S. Charles St. ✆ **410/752-3810.** www.corksrestaurant.com. Reservations recommended for dinner on weekends. Main courses $10–$40. AE, DISC, MD, V. Mon–Sat 5–11pm; Sun 10am–9pm. Bar open until 2am daily. Valet Fri–Sat evenings.

Miguel's Cocina y Cantina ★★ ☺ MEXICAN You may notice that Miguel's is decorated for *El Dia de Los Muertos,* if you can see beyond the terrific margaritas, *fundido,* and other Mexican treats your server will bring you. An added bonus is the great view of Baltimore's outer harbor, the working port of Baltimore City, filled with industrial buildings and ships. Miguel's is located in a rehabbed granary in Locust Point and is a convenient place to stop before or after a visit to Fort McHenry.

1200 Steuart St. (in Silo Point). ✆ **443/438-3139.** www.miguelsbaltimore.com. Reservations recommended on weekends. Main courses $6–$19. AE, DISC, MC, V. Mon and Wed–Thurs 11:30am–10pm; Fri–Sat 11:30am–11pm; Sun 11am–2pm (brunch) and 2:30–10pm (dinner).

Mr. Rain's Fun House NEW AMERICAN This inventive restaurant is a great addition to the eye-catching American Visionary Art Museum. A sleek modern space with zany touches of color and glitter, it has serious food with roots from around the United States. And yes it's fun: pumpkin soup with coconut milk, adobo fried chicken, and even hot dogs with a culinary twist. It's open for lunch, dinner, and weekend brunch, and diners don't have to pay AVAM admission to eat here. (But don't bypass the museum if you have time.) There's street parking as well as a lot across the street.

800 Key Hwy. (next to Federal Hill). ✆ **443/524-7379.** www.mrrainsfunhouse.com. Reservations recommended on weekends, especially brunch. Entrees $9–$12 lunch; $13–$28 dinner; $10–$17 brunch. AE, DISC, MC, V, Sun and Tues–Thurs 11am–3:30pm and 5:30-9pm; Fri–Sat 11am–4pm and 5:30–10pm.

Nick's Fish House 🎁 SEAFOOD Tucked on an old, nonglitzy part of the Patapsco River, Nick's is worth looking for. Once you raise a cold beer or savory crab cake to your lips and look out at the river, you'll know you're in Balmer, hon. Two dining rooms with water views, a bar reminiscent of a beach shack, and waterside dining in summer take full advantage of the location. The menu is Baltimore-style seafood all the way, though you can get a pretty good burger and crab comes on pretzels and grilled cheese. Surprise! Sushi has been added to the menu with quite a selection to choose from. There is live music on weekends. Brunch is served Sunday. Plus you can come by boat; there are slips available.

2600 Insulator Dr. (off Hanover St.). ✆ **410/FISH-123** (347-4123). www.nicksfishhouse.com. Reservations recommended on weekends. Main courses $8–$28 AE, DISC, MC, V. Daily 11am–9pm, until 10pm on summer weekdays and 11pm on summer weekends.

Wine Market ★ WINE BAR Tucked behind a huge wine shop is this casual food-and-wine fan's paradise. The industrial chic dining room in an old foundry is delightful, but in warm weather the patio makes an even better place to sample one of the many wines by the glass and the menu filled with everything from small plates (oysters, flatbread pizza, and cheese) to light fare (sandwiches and salads) to serious entrees such as rib-eye, fish, and braised meat dishes. Order your wine from the wine list or stop in the wine shop to pick out your own bottle.

921 E. Fort Ave. ✆ **410/244-6166.** www.the-wine-market.com. Reservations recommended on weekends. Entrees $10–$14 lunch, $13–$25 dinner. AE, DISC, MC, V. Lunch Tues–Fri 11:30–4pm. Dinner nightly 5–9pm. Sunday brunch 11am–4pm.

EXPLORING BALTIMORE

Inner Harbor ★★★

Although much of Baltimore's business takes place along Charles Street, the city's focal point for tourism is the Inner Harbor, home of the Baltimore Convention Center, Harborplace shopping pavilions, Oriole Park at Camden Yards, M&T Bank Stadium, the National Aquarium in Baltimore, Pier 6 Concert Pavilion, and Reginald F. Lewis Museum of Maryland African American History & Culture. Baltimore is also still a working deepwater port. Boats from all over dock at, and just beyond, the Domino Sugar sign. At the Inner Harbor seawall, it's not unusual to see naval vessels and tall ships and their crews from around the world.

American Visionary Art Museum ★ This curvaceous building is marked by the "Whirligig," a 55-foot wind-powered sculpture at the front. "Visionary" art is created by people who lack artistic training but feel compelled to draw, paint, or build a ship with matchsticks. Everything here is fascinating; some of it can be quite troubling. And the artists' stories in ever-changing exhibitions are as interesting as their art. You'll be entranced from the moment you set your eyes on Emery Blagdon's "Healing Machines" mobile, which hangs down three stories from the ceiling. Some work is too strong for children (the museum will alert you to that); other exhibits are a joy for any age. On summer Thursdays, a free movie is screened on the side of the building. The museum stays open until 9pm on those days. Check the website for film listings.

800 Key Hwy. (take Light St. south, turn left onto Key Hwy. at the Maryland Science Center; museum is about 3 blocks farther on the right). ✆ **410/244-1900.** www.avam.org. Admission $16 adults, $14 seniors, $10 students and children. Tues–Sun 10am–6pm. Closed Thanksgiving and Dec 25.

Baltimore Museum of Industry 🎁 ☺ In a former oyster-packing house on the harbor's southern bank, this museum gives visitors a look at the Baltimore Industrial Revolution that made the city an industrial capital in the 1880s—canning, printing, and garment-making (even umbrellas). Displays are geared toward children, with exhibits set up so kids can get their hands on the oyster-shucking stations, antique irons, and moveable type. Tour guides are sensitive to kids' attention spans and adjust their talks for the younger visitors. When guides aren't available, there are iPod tours that feature stories and video related to the exhibits. Wall-size pictures recall the days before child labor laws, and other displays include a collection of antique delivery trucks and one of only two working steam tugboats in the country. The museum is a few blocks from Fort McHenry; a visit to both (with picnic) could make a great day.

1415 Key Hwy. ✆ **410/727-4808.** www.thebmi.org. Admission $10 adults, $8 seniors, $6 ages 6–18. Tues–Sun 10am–4pm. Closed Memorial Day, Thanksgiving, and Dec 24–25. Water taxis stop nearby. Bus: 1 to Fort Ave., 1 block south of the museum.

Fort McHenry ★★★ 📷 ☺ The flag that flies at Fort McHenry is 30×42 feet, big enough to see "by the dawn's early light." Its 15 stars and stripes still fly as boldly as they did at the Battle of Baltimore in the War of 1812. The star-shaped fort looks much as it did then, and its buildings, repaired in the days following the attack, still stand. The Star-Spangled Banner is central to this fort, a national monument. A talk about the flag is offered every day at noon; Fort McHenry Guardsmen (living-history volunteers) are on duty noon to 4pm on summer weekends. Visitors are invited to take part in the daily changing of the flag (9:30am or 4:30pm, also at7:30pm June–Aug)—in fact, because the flag is so big, around 20 people are needed to keep it off

North Baltimore

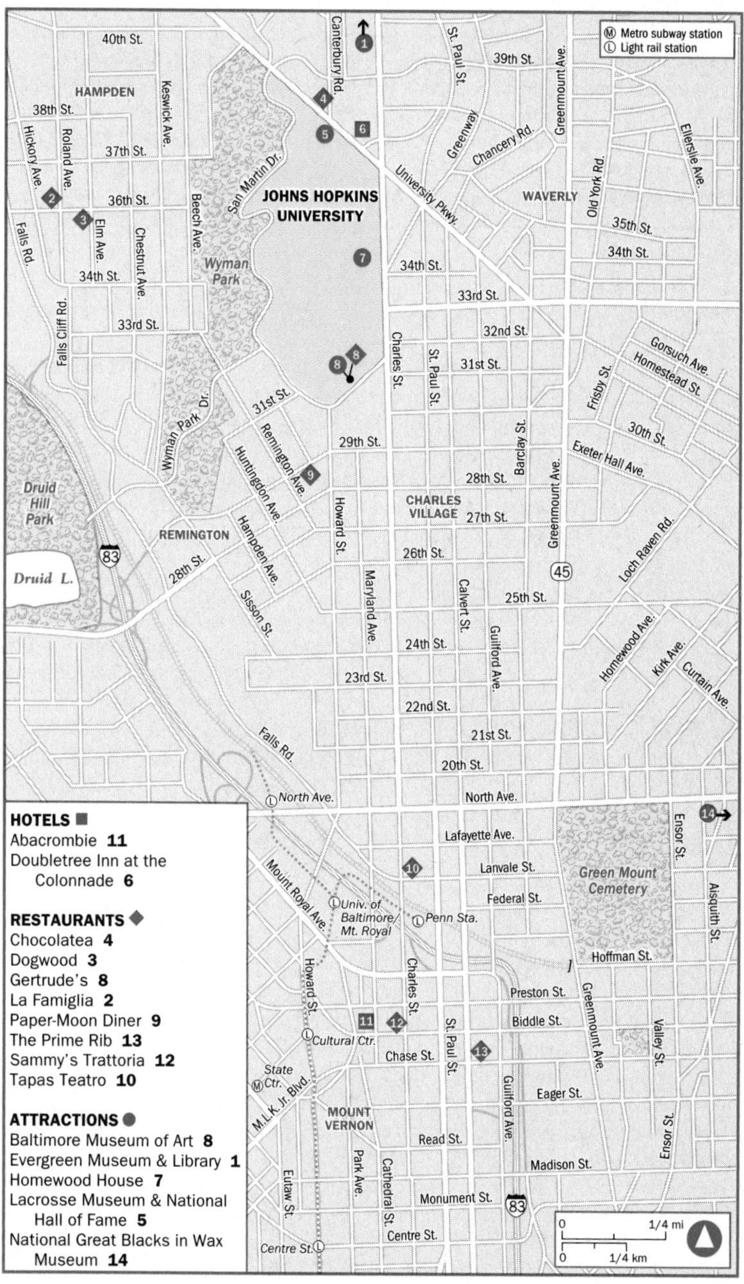

Money-Saving Harbor Pass

Save time and money with a **Harbor Pass.** For $60 for adults, $45 for kids, you can visit the National Aquarium, Maryland Science Center, and the Top of the World Observation Level; choose between Port Discovery or American Visionary Art Museum, and Sports Legends at Camden Yards or the Reginald F. Lewis Museum. A day pass on the Baltimore Water Taxi is included. The passes are valid for 4 consecutive days, but only one visit per location. Order in advance at ✆ **877/BALTIMORE** (225-8466) or **www.baltimore.org**. Or purchase it at the Inner Harbor visitor center.

the ground. The large flag flies only during daylight hours (weather permitting); a smaller flag flies at night.

Exhibits recall Baltimore under siege during the War of 1812 and the fort's service during the Civil War and as a World War I army hospital. Allow at least 90 minutes for a visit. The new **Visitor and Education Center** opened February 3, 2011—80 years after "The Star Spangled Banner" became the national anthem. Its state-of-the-art interactive displays enhance any visit, and the new movie is compelling—and so is the view when the screen rises to reveal a window overlooking the fort. One exhibit plays recordings of some of the many interpretations of the national anthem, including Jimi Hendrix's. Fort McHenry sits on a point in the harbor from which visitors can see the Inner Harbor, the Patapsco River, and down to the Chesapeake Bay. Visits to the park outside the fort are free, and picnicking is allowed.

The **Star-Spangled Banner Weekend,** held in mid-September, recalls the British attack on the fort. Flags are everywhere here on **Flag Day,** June 14. On select Sundays from 6 to 8pm, military bands perform with a color guard, drill teams, and the Fort McHenry Guard dressed in 19th-century uniforms, a ceremony that began in 1803. Admission to this ceremony is free; call or visit the website for a schedule.

Fort McHenry National Monument, E. Fort Ave. ✆ **410/962-4290.** www.nps.gov/fomc. Admission $7 adults, free for children under 16. Sept–May fort and grounds daily 8am–5pm; June to Labor Day grounds remain open daily until 8pm. Closed Thanksgiving, Dec 25, and Jan 1. Bus: 1. Water taxi stop.

Historic Ships in Baltimore ★★ ☺ With the **USS *Constellation*** as its centerpiece, this collection of ships and a lighthouse offers a glimpse at American maritime history. The **Coast Guard Cutter *Taney*** survived the bombing of Pearl Harbor. The submarine **USS *Torsk*** sank the last two Japanese merchant ships of World War II and still holds the record for the most dives and resurfacings of any sub. The lightship ***Chesapeake*** spent 40 years anchored near the mouth of the Chesapeake Bay. The **Seven Foot Knoll Lighthouse** once welcomed immigrants to Baltimore—admission here is always free. Certainly the star of the show is the *Constellation,* docked in front of Harborplace. A triple-masted sloop-of-war launched in 1854, the *Constellation* is the last Civil War–era vessel afloat. It's most notable for its efforts fighting the trans-Atlantic slave trade. Tour her gun decks, visit the wardrooms, see a cannon fired, and learn about a sailor's life. Demonstrations begin with the raising of the colors at 10:30am and continue on the hour. Fourth of July picnics and New Year's Eve receptions end with fireworks (tickets are required). Downtown visitors should note that the ship's cannon is fired daily at noon. "Powder Monkey" tours are

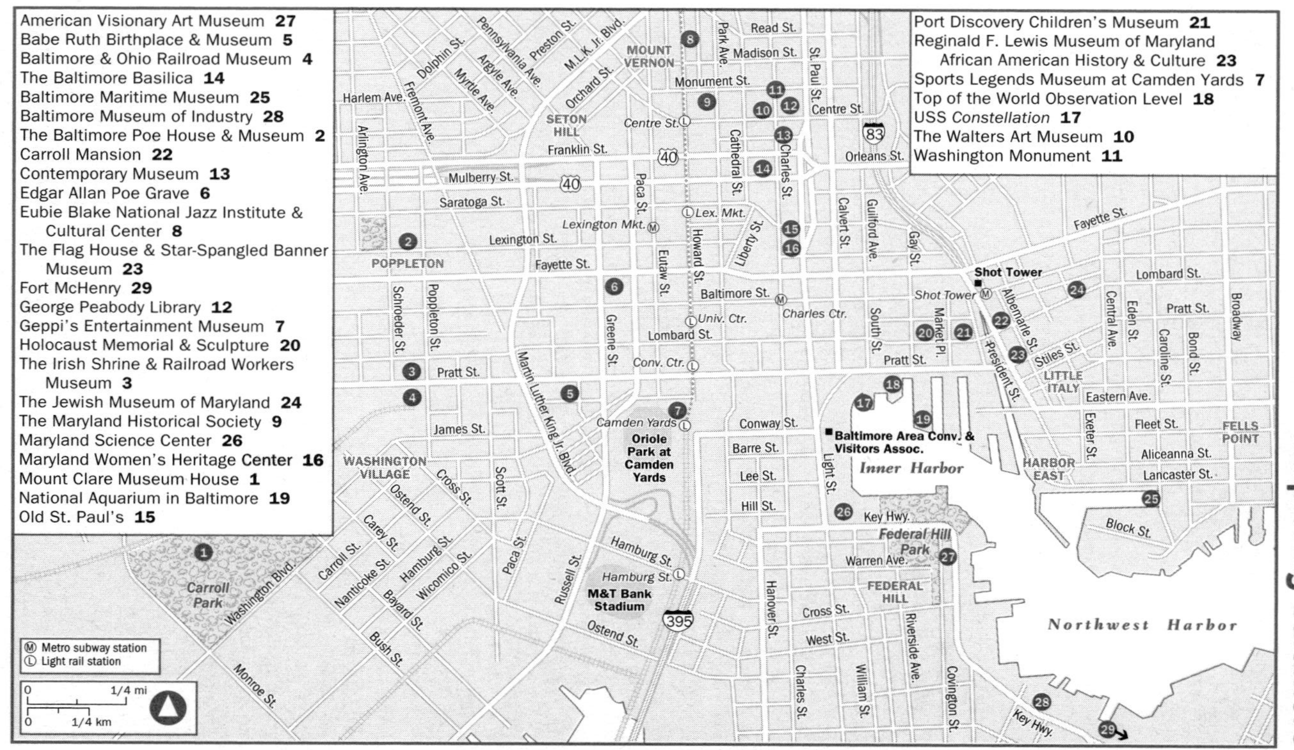
American Visionary Art Museum 27
Babe Ruth Birthplace & Museum 5
Baltimore & Ohio Railroad Museum 4
The Baltimore Basilica 14
Baltimore Maritime Museum 25
Baltimore Museum of Industry 28
The Baltimore Poe House & Museum 2
Carroll Mansion 22
Contemporary Museum 13
Edgar Allan Poe Grave 6
Eubie Blake National Jazz Institute & Cultural Center 8
The Flag House & Star-Spangled Banner Museum 23
Fort McHenry 29
George Peabody Library 12
Geppi's Entertainment Museum 7
Holocaust Memorial & Sculpture 20
The Irish Shrine & Railroad Workers Museum 3
The Jewish Museum of Maryland 24
The Maryland Historical Society 9
Maryland Science Center 26
Maryland Women's Heritage Center 16
Mount Clare Museum House 1
National Aquarium in Baltimore 19
Old St. Paul's 15
Port Discovery Children's Museum 21
Reginald F. Lewis Museum of Maryland African American History & Culture 23
Sports Legends Museum at Camden Yards 7
Top of the World Observation Level 18
USS Constellation 17
The Walters Art Museum 10
Washington Monument 11
Metro subway station
Light rail station
1/4 mi
1/4 km
Inner Harbor
Northwest Harbor
Oriole Park at Camden Yards
M&T Bank Stadium
Baltimore Area Conv. & Visitors Assoc.
Shot Tower
Federal Hill Park
Carroll Park
MOUNT VERNON
SETON HILL
POPPLETON
WASHINGTON VILLAGE
FEDERAL HILL
HARBOR EAST
LITTLE ITALY
FELLS POINT

directed at children 6 and over. A bit of trivia—every one of these ships, even the *Constellation,* played a role in World War II.

Piers 1, 3, and 5, Inner Harbor. ✆ **410/539-1797.** www.historicships.org. Admission for 1 ship: $11 adults, $9 seniors, $5 children 6–14; for 2 ships: $14 adults, $12 seniors, $6 children; for 4 ships: $18 adults, $15 seniors, $7 children. Ticket booths near the National Aquarium or beside the *Constellation.* All ships open Apr–May and Sept–Oct 10am–5pm daily. June–Aug Mon–Thur 10am–6pm, Fri–Sun10am–6pm. Nov–Dec daily 10am–4:30pm. Jan–Mar *Constellation, Torsk* and *Chesapeake* open 10am–4:30m daily; *Taney* open Fri–Sun only 10am–3:30pm and lighthouse open Sat–Sun only 10am–4:30pm Closed Jan–Feb. All ships closed Thanksgiving, Dec 25, and Jan 1.

Holocaust Memorial Park In the heart of downtown near the Inner Harbor, this open-air memorial starkly recalls the six million Jews murdered by the Nazis in Europe between 1933 and 1945.

Corner of Gay and Lombard sts. Free admission. Daily 24 hr.

Maryland Science Center ★ ☺ Three floors of exhibits include **Our Place in Space**—with a huge weather globe display, Hubble Space Telescope pictures, links to NASA and space suits kids can try on—and the towering dinosaurs of **Dino-Quest.** Children get a kick out of the hands-on exhibits of **Newton's Alley** and the **Body Link** and everybody likes the IMAX theater and planetarium. The IMAX movies, which range from *Beauty and the Beast* to *Space Station 3D,* are so popular that extra screenings are held Friday and Saturday evenings, for $8 to $12 per ticket. The stars are on display at the Davis Planetarium and the Crosby Ramsey Observatory; the observatory is free on Friday nights, weather permitting (call for hours). On Friday nights, admission to exhibits, the planetarium, and IMAX is $8 from 5 to 8pm.

601 Light St. (south side of the Inner Harbor). ✆ **410/685-5225.** www.mdsci.org. Admission varies according to exhibits: core experience with planetarium $15 adults, $14 seniors, $12 children 3–12; core experience with planetarium and IMAX film $20 adults, $18 seniors, $15 children 3–12; special exhibits additional charge. Apr–late June Mon–Fri 10am–5pm, Sat 10am–6pm, Sun 11am–5pm; late June–Sept Sun–Thurs 10am–6pm, Fri–Sat 10am–8pm; Oct–Apr Tues–Thurs 10am–5pm, Fri 10am–8pm, Sat 10am–6pm, Sun 11am–5pm. Call ahead, as hours change with some exhibits. Water taxi stop.

National Aquarium in Baltimore ★★★ ☺ Walk into a room surrounded by patrolling sharks, stroll among coral reefs, and visit a rainforest on the roof of one of the best aquariums in the country—no, it's the BEST. **Animal Planet Australia: Wild Extremes,** set in a 120-foot-tall glass cube at the front of the aquarium, takes visitors to the floor of an Australian river gorge. In this immersion exhibit, wander past tanks filled with death adders, pythons, archer fish, and barramundi, while kookaburras, parrots, and lorikeets fly overhead—there are 1,800 animals, as well as plants native to Australia. On a cold day, head for the top of the aquarium and bask in the tropical heat that envelops the brightly colored birds, the shy iguana, and the sloth who reside on this level. (It's best any day to come straight here when the aquarium opens and the animals are most active.) Although you walk in front of most exhibits, you walk *inside* the doughnut-shaped coral reef and shark tanks, getting up close to these exotic creatures. At feeding time, the divers always draw a crowd. The Marine Mammal Pavilion, connected by covered bridge to the main hall, is home to the dolphins. Presentations are offered every hour but visitors can stop by and watch the dolphins swimming and playing any time. 4-D Immersion Theatre shows 3-D movies, with added sensory effect, throughout the day. Admission is an extra $3. ***Tip:*** Crowds are huge in summer. Beat the crush by purchasing timed tickets in advance, in person

Linthicum's Electronics Museum

Galleries on everything from vacuum tubes to cameras used on the moon make the **National Electronics Museum** (1745 W. Nursery Rd., Linthicum, MD 21090; ✆ **410/765-0230;** www.nationalelectronicsmuseum.org) near BWI airport worth a visit—in fact, pilots, flight attendants, and passengers frequently stop in if their flight is delayed or they're early. On display are an Enigma machine, interactive displays like one on infrared light, and a display on radar at Pearl Harbor. Call if you'd like a tour. Admission is $3 adults, $1 students and seniors. Free for children under 6. Monday through Friday 9am to 4pm; Saturday 10am to 2pm. From Baltimore, take Route 295 south, take West Nursery Road exit and turn left at light; go through four lights to museum on left.

or online. Nonpeak visiting hours are weekday mornings, Fridays when the aquarium stays open until 8pm, and after 3pm daily.

501 E. Pratt St. (on the harbor). ✆ **410/576-3800**. www.aqua.org. Admission $30 adults, $27 seniors, $21 children 3–11. Mar–June and Sept–Oct Sat–Thurs 9am–5pm, Fri 9am–8pm; Nov–Feb Mon–Thurs 10am–4pm, Fri 10am–8pm, Sat–Sun 10am–5pm; July–Aug Mon–Thurs 9am–5pm, Fri–Sat 9am–8pm, Sun 9am–6pm. Hours subject to change; call ahead. Exhibits are open 2 hours after last ticket is sold.

Port Discovery Children's Museum ★★ ☺ At this kid-powered museum with three floors of exhibits, children of all ages—though mostly ages 2 to 10—can cross the Nile to explore ancient Egypt, crawl through a kitchen drain to solve a mystery in **Miss Perception's Mystery House,** and climb the three-story-high **Kidworks.** Buy groceries and fill up your car's tank at the convenience store and stop at the diner. **Wonders of Water** is wet, but it sure is fun. Special programs for toddlers are offered Wednesday and Friday at 10:30 and 11:30am and 12:30pm and Sundays at 1:30, 2:30, and 3:30pm. There are also changing exhibits every quarter.

35 Market Place. ✆ **410/727-8120.** www.portdiscovery.org. Admission $14 ages 2 and older. Oct–May Tues–Fri 9:30am–4:30pm, Sat 10am–5pm; Sun noon–5pm; Memorial Day to Labor Day Mon–Sat 10am–5pm; Sun noon–5pm; Sept Fri 9:30am–4:30pm, Sat 10am–5pm; Sun noon–5pm. Bus: 7, 10, 19, or 20. Metro: Shot Tower. Closed Thanksgiving and Dec 25.

Top of the World Observation Level For a 360-degree view of the city, head to the 27th floor of the World Trade Center, the world's tallest pentagonal building, which is next to Harborplace. Take in the view—and look over the exhibits about Baltimore history. A new addition is the September 11 Memorial with a piece of the New York World Trade Center, put on display on the 10th anniversary of the terrorist attacks. The area is accessible to visitors with disabilities.

401 E. Pratt St. (on the harbor). ✆ **410/837-8439.** www.viewbaltimore.org. Admission $5 adults, $4 seniors, $3 children 3–16. Memorial Day to Labor Day, Mon–Thurs 10am–7pm, Sun 11am–6pm; Sept–Dec Wed–Thurs 10am–6pm, Fri–Sat 10am–7pm, Sun 11am–6pm; Jan–Mar Fri–Sat 10am–7pm, Sun 11am–6pm; Apr–May Wed–Thurs 10am–6pm, Fri–Sat 10am–7pm, Sun 11am–6pm. Tickets sold in the lobby up to a half-hour before closing.

Near Little Italy & Fell's Point

Baltimore Civil War Museum Though most of the old President Street train station is gone, the arched entrance hall remains to tell some remarkable history. President

Lincoln sneaked through town from here in 1861. The first blood of the Civil War was shed here on April 19, 1861. It was a real train stop on the Underground Railroad, with Frederick Douglass as one of the passengers. (The story of Henry "Box" Brown is memorable.) The 1800s-era structure is quite a counterpoint to all the 21st-century Harbor East architecture surrounding it.

601 President St. ✆ **443/220-0290.** Free admission. Mon–Sat 10am–5pm; Sun noon–5pm.

Carroll Mansion and Phoenix Shot Tower When Charles Carroll of Carrollton lived in the mansion here, people knocked on his door to meet the last living signer of the Declaration of Independence. After he died in 1832, in a room on the second floor, this stately home became the German Working Man's Club, and then a tenement filled with Russian-born tailors, and finally a recreation center with a basketball court. Slowly, the home is being restored and Carroll's bedroom and his library are now open for visitors on weekends. To visit the iconic **Phoenix Shot Tower,** with its audiovisual exhibits, meet the tour leader at the mansion at 4pm for the short walk to the tower. Inside the 1828 tower, shot was made by dropping lead down the shaft.

4

800 E. Lombard St. ✆ **410/605-2964.** www.carrollmuseums.org. Admission $5 adults; $4 students, seniors, and military with ID. Sat–Sun noon–4pm; last tour at 3pm. Shot tower tours Sat–Sun at 4pm.

Creative Alliance This Highlandtown venue's gallery and performance space celebrate local arts. Contemporary artwork in all media is on display, and the auditorium is the site of classic film showings and events. Though much of the work is edgy, more mainstream works also have their place. It's worth going out of your way for a taste of the Baltimore arts scene. Events are listed online. The Marquee Lounge is open for Friday and Saturday night happy hours and live music on Saturdays.

3134 Eastern Ave. (from downtown, take Pratt St. east, head south around Patterson Park to Eastern Ave., and continue on Eastern Ave. to Highlandtown). ✆ **410/276-1651.** www.creativealliance.org. Free admission to gallery. Tickets for films and performances $5–$60. Gallery Tues–Fri 11am–7pm, Sat 11am–7pm; film and performance times vary.

Fell's Point Visitor Center Home to the Fell's Point Preservation Society, the visitor center has maritime and historical exhibits of the people and places that have made Fell's Point unique. **Walking tours** depart from here (p. 80), and tours of the 1765 Robert Long House around the corner on Ann Street, the oldest residence in Baltimore Town, are offered daily at 1:30pm. There's a gift shop and performance space.

1724 Thames St., Fell's Point. ✆ **410/675-6750,** ext. 16. www.preservationsociety.com. Free admission to gallery. Admission to Long House $5. Dec–Mar Sun, Tues–Fri noon–5pm, Sat 11am–7pm; Apr–Nov Sun, Tues–Thurs 11am–5pm, Fri 11am–8pm, Sat 11am–7pm.

The Jewish Museum of Maryland A visit to this compound offers insight into local Jewish history, a glimpse of Jewish traditions, and a look at the immigration experience. The 1845 Lloyd Street Synagogue is Maryland's oldest (and one of the oldest in the U.S.). It's plainer than the nearby B'nai Israel Synagogue, but it has a matzo oven, a mikvah (ritual bath), and a classroom where the first Hebrew school got its start. The building was restored in 2009 in time for the JMM's 50th anniversary in 2010. The Greek Revival–style B'nai Israel Synagogue, built in 1876, contains what may be the oldest Jewish star in one of its stained-glass windows. Its ark is a hand-carved masterpiece. Take a tour of the synagogues at 1 or 2:30pm for the best experience; the guides are full of stories. Between the two synagogues is exhibit space and a library. The exhibits change often, but always focus on Jewish religion and culture.

15 Lloyd St. ✆ **410/732-6400.** www.jewishmuseummd.org. Admission $8 adults, $4 students, $3 children under 12. Sun and Tues–Thurs noon–4pm. Closed Jewish holidays, Jan 1, Memorial Day, July 4, Labor Day, Thanksgiving Day and Fri after. Travel east on Pratt St.; turn left on Central St., left on Lombard St., and then right onto Lloyd St.

Reginald F. Lewis Museum of Maryland African American History & Culture ★ ☺ 🎁 This striking modern building houses the personal stories of Marylanders great and small who dreamed big and contributed to the state's history: Supreme Court Justice Thurgood Marshall, gymnast Dominique Dawes, musicians Cab Calloway and Billie Holiday, religious leader Mother Mary Elizabeth Lange, as well as nurses, teachers, and others you may never have heard of. Permanent exhibits are on the third floor; changing exhibits are on the second. On-site are a gift shop and cafe.

830 E. Pratt St., Baltimore, MD 21202 ✆ **443/263-1800.** www.africanamericanculture.org. Admission $8 adults; $6 children, students, and seniors. Wed–Sat 10am–5pm; Sun noon–5pm. Closed Thanksgiving, Dec 25, Jan 1, and Easter. Bus: 10. Metro: Shot Tower. Discounted parking available across Pratt St. from museum.

The Star-Spangled Banner Flag House ☺ Everyone remembers Betsy Ross and the first American flag. Baltimoreans recall Mary Pickersgill who stitched the 15-star flag that flew over Fort McHenry during the War of 1812, the flag that inspired Francis Scott Key to write "The Star-Spangled Banner." The flag is now in the Smithsonian, but Pickersgill's 1793 house, open during guided tours seven times a day, has period furniture and artifacts of the war. The modern museum addition, whose glass front is dominated by a giant glass flag, offers additional exhibits, including period uniforms, sheet music for the anthem printed in 1822, and memorabilia of the 1914 centennial commemoration of the Battle of Baltimore. A major exhibition about Mary Pickersgill will open in February 2013. The museum, which is accessible for visitors with disabilities, also has an orientation theater, and children's hands-on room.

844 E. Pratt St., at Albemarle St. ✆ **410/837-1793.** www.flaghouse.org. Admission including house tour $7 adults, $6 seniors, $5 children. Museum and film only $4. Tues–Sat 10am–4pm. Closed major holidays.

West of Downtown

Babe Ruth Birthplace and Museum ★ George Herman "Babe" Ruth was born in this rowhouse, where two rooms have been re-created to look as they would have when the Sultan of Swat was a boy. Other exhibits include a wall enumerating his home runs, plus memorabilia from his major-league career and his days at St. Mary's Industrial School in Baltimore, where he learned to play the game.

216 Emory St. (from Camden Yards, follow the sidewalk baseballs from the Babe Ruth statue at the north end of the warehouse to the house 3 blocks away). ✆ **410/727-1539.** www.baberuthmuseum.com. Admission $6 adults, $4 seniors, $3 children 5–16. Combination ticket with Sports Legends $12 adults, $8 seniors, $5 children 3–12. Daily 10am–5pm. Closed Thanksgiving, Dec 25, and Jan 1.

Baltimore & Ohio (B&O) Railroad Museum ★★ ☺ American railroading got its start here when the B&O was chartered in 1827, and the first locomotive, the *Tom Thumb*, was built here. The remarkable roundhouse, fully accessible for visitors with disabilities and parents with strollers, is filled with an awe-inspiring collection of engines and rolling stock. A car barn has the largest locomotive ever built.

Platforms enable visitors to tour trains outside, including a World War II troop sleeper, a caboose, and a refrigerated car where a train movie runs continuously. A centerpiece during the commemoration of the Civil War sesquicentennial through May 2015 is the exhibit "The War Came By Train," which brings together locomotives and rolling stock used during the war as well as a train ride to the site of Camp Carroll, the largest encampment in Baltimore. Trains depart at 11:30am Wednesday through Friday, three times on Saturday, and twice on Sunday from April through December; weekends only in January.

901 W. Pratt St. ✆ **410/752-2490.** www.borail.org. Admission $14 adults, $12 seniors, $8 children 2–12. Mon–Fri 10am–4pm; Sat 10am–5pm; Sun noon–5pm. Closed Jan 1, Easter, Memorial Day, July 4, Labor Day, Thanksgiving, Dec 24–25 and 31. Free on-site parking. Bus: 31.

The Baltimore Poe House and Museum Edgar Allan Poe composed some of his first works in this tiny West Baltimore rowhouse, which contains five rooms (including the garret where he slept and wrote). Poe lived here from 1833 to 1835 with his grandmother, aunt, and cousin Virginia, whom he later married. You can see portraits, memorabilia, period furniture, changing exhibits, and a video. The house is on a small one-way street heading south; there is no number, but you will see a black antique street lamp out front and two markers on the house. Don't try to walk here from downtown—take a car or cab—and call ahead to verify hours.

203 N. Amity St. ✆ **410/396-7932.** www.eapoe.org. Admission $4 adults, free for children under 13 and military families. Wed–Sat noon–3:30pm. Closed Jan–Mar. Take Charles St. north to Fayette St.; turn left on Fayette and go past Martin Luther King Blvd. to Schroeder St. Turn right on Schroeder; in 2 blocks, turn right on Saratoga St. and continue about a quarter-block to Amity St., the first street on the right. Turn right on Amity and look for the Poe House on the left side, near the end of the block.

Edgar Allan Poe's Grave Three modest memorials in this old graveyard recall the poet who wrote "The Tell-Tale Heart" and "The Raven" (the only poem to inspire an NFL team's name). After his mysterious death in 1849 at age 40, Poe's relatives erected a small gravestone. Before the stone could be installed, however, a train crashed through the monument yard and destroyed it. Since then, the site has been adorned with three newer monuments: the main memorial, which features a bas-relief bust of Poe; a small gravestone adorned with a raven at Poe's original burial lot; and a plaque placed by the French, who, thanks to the poet Baudelaire, enjoy some of the best translations of Poe's works. On the weekend closest to January 19, Poe's birthday, a party is held in his honor. Call ahead for tours offered first and third Fridays and Saturdays April to November.

Westminster Hall and Burying Grounds, southeast corner of Fayette and Greene sts. ✆ **410/706-2072** (answered by a University of Maryland Law School staffer). Daily 8am–dusk. Closed major holidays.

Geppi's Entertainment Museum ★ This stylishly designed museum on the second floor of the historic Camden train station (beside Camden Yards stadium) celebrates the comic book. Its founder, Steve Geppi, made his fortune finding, collecting, and selling this amusing slice of Americana, and some of his favorite pieces are located here along with toys and collectibles associated with *Amazing Stories, Superman,* or *Yellow Kid.* Displays offer a historical look as comics have developed since the 1800s. Other pop culture artifacts, from animation cels and movie posters to TV memorabilia, flesh out the collection. High-tech kiosks allow visitors to thumb through digital comic books. Toys and collectibles—banks,

ONLY in BALTIMORE, HON!

- **Cannoli at Vaccaro's.** All the desserts are divine, but the cannoli is a tradition. Skip dessert wherever you're having dinner and head to Little Italy afterward, or stop by the annex at the Light Street Pavilion.
- **Seventh-Inning Stretch at Camden Yards.** The crowd of up to 45,000 unites for a rousing rendition of John Denver's "Thank God I'm a Country Boy."
- **Spring in Sherwood Gardens.** This community garden at Highfield Road and Greenway Street, in the Guilford neighborhood of northern Baltimore, is out of the way and hard to find—but it's an oasis in May, when the tulips are in bloom. You'll also go through lovely neighborhoods that tourists seldom see.
- **View from the Glass Elevators at the Hyatt.** Short of a harbor-view room, this is the best view in the city, especially at night—and it's free.
- **Water Taxi Ride to Fell's Point and Little Italy.** It's an inexpensive way to see the harbor—and a great way to avoid the hassle of parking.

decoder rings, and lunch boxes—are among the most interesting artifacts. The gift shop stocks lots of cool stuff.

301 W. Camden St. ✆ **410/625-7060.** www.geppismuseum.com. Admission $10 adults, $9 seniors, $7 children 5–18; half-price tickets on Orioles/Ravens game days. Tues–Sun 10am–6pm. Closed Thanksgiving, Dec 25, Jan 1. Light Rail: Camden Yards.

The Irish Shrine and Railroad Workers Museum Two 10-foot-wide 1848 brick rowhouses a block from the B&O Museum have been restored as a monument to the thousands of Irish workers who lived here and worked for the railroad. One house, with the original plaster walls and floors, is sparsely furnished for a family of eight and a boarder. Next door is a museum devoted to Irish Baltimoreans, with photo displays and a video presentation. Volunteer guides are well acquainted with—and may be related to—past residents; their stories are personal and folksy. Because the back wall has been replaced with glass, it is possible to see inside the house any time; volunteers offer house tours most Saturdays. Special events are scheduled on second Tuesdays. Always call ahead.

918–920 Lemmon St. (from the Inner Harbor, go west on Lombard St., turn left on Poppleton St., and turn right on Lemmon St.). ✆ **410/669-8154.** www.irishshrine.org. Free admission. Sat 11am–2pm. Call ahead to confirm opening times.

Mount Clare Museum House This 1760 summer home of barrister Charles Carroll and Margaret Tilghman Carroll is set on a hill with a sweeping view of the Baltimore skyline. Most of the furnishings belonged to the Carroll family, including a Charles Wilson Peale portrait and a fine collection of Chinese and English porcelain. Washington didn't sleep here, but Martha did—and so did the Marquis de Lafayette. Visitors to the B&O Railroad Museum can buy a ticket to this house and ride the train here (tickets are $7 adults, $6 children).

1500 Washington Blvd. (in Carroll Park). ✆ **410/837-3262.** www.mountclare.org. Admission $6 adults, $5 seniors, $4 students. Tues–Sat 10am–4pm (tours on the hour until 3pm). Bus: 11. Closed Jan 1, July 4, Thanksgiving, Dec 24–25 and 31.

Sports Legends Museum at Camden Yards ☺ Two floors of the historic 1856 Camden Station have been developed as a tribute to local sports. The Orioles have their own Hall of Fame here, as do the Baltimore Colts, with special attention given to star quarterback Johnny Unitas. The Ravens, the Blast soccer team, and the Negro Leagues, particularly the Baltimore Elite Giants, also have their own exhibits. But where else can you find high-school and college sports teams represented, along with a history of stadiums in Baltimore? The locker room even has uniforms to try on. The museum is at the baseball stadium, 3 blocks west of the Babe Ruth Museum.

301 W. Camden St. ✆ **410/727-1539.** www.baberuthmuseum.com. Admission $8 adults, $6 seniors, $4 children 3–12. Combination ticket with Babe Ruth Museum $12 adults, $8 seniors, $5 children 3–12. Daily 10am–5pm. Closed Jan 1, Thanksgiving, Dec 25. Light Rail: Camden Yards.

Mount Vernon

The Basilica of the Assumption ★★ Designed by Benjamin Latrobe—who was working on the U.S. Capitol at the same time—this neoclassical basilica is considered one of America's most beautiful. A national shrine and historic landmark, officially the Basilica of the National Shrine of the Assumption of the Blessed Virgin Mary, it was the first cathedral built in the United States and has been a monument to religious freedom since 1806. Notable visitors have included Mother Teresa and Pope John Paul II, both of whom have memorials to their visits. A controversial restoration, including the removal of stained glass and uncovering of 24 skylights in the dome, has resulted in a light-drenched sanctuary filled with glittering details. For natives who remember the dark, solemn space, this was a startling revelation and a welcome one. The project also uncovered balconies once reserved for African-American Catholics and cloistered nuns. A prayer garden dedicated to Blessed Pope John Paul is around the corner on Charles Street. Beginning June 1, 2012, the Basilica will undergo repairs for damage caused by the 2011 earthquake. If you're planning to visit during the week call ahead ✆ 410/ 727-3565 or visit the website www.baltimore basilica.org. The Basilica will remain open weekends during the approximately 8-month repair process. Weekday Masses at 7:30 a.m. and 12:10 p.m. will take place in the chapel in the Basilica undercroft.

400 block of Cathedral St. ✆ **410/727-3565.** www.baltimorebasilica.org. Free admission. Daily 8:30am–4:30pm. Mass Sun 7:30, 9, 10:45am, and 4 and 5:30pm; Mon–Fri 7:15am and 12:10pm.; Sat 7:30am and 5:30pm. Take Charles St. north; turn left on Franklin St. and left again on Cathedral St.

Contemporary Museum 🎁 The Contemporary Museum has expanded to a new space on Charles Street, and that's a good thing for the art—which is distinctly contemporary, ranging from photography and video to paintings and performance art. Rotating exhibits, which last about 3 months, finally have the space they deserve.

505 N. Charles St. ✆ **410/783-5720.** www.contemporary.org. No admission fee; donations suggested: $5 adults, $3 children. Wed–Sun noon–5pm.

Eubie Blake National Jazz Institute and Cultural Center Baltimorean Eubie Blake, the ragtime pianist and Broadway composer, is remembered in this small museum on Howard Street's Antique Row. Exhibits feature local musicians Billie Holiday and Cab Calloway. The Eubie Live! performance space hosts poetry readings and musical performances. Check the website for the events calendar. ***Tip:*** Make sure you talk to the docents—many of them knew Blake or Calloway.

847 N. Howard St. ✆ **410/225-3130.** www.eubieblake.org. Admission $5 adults. Wed–Fri 1–6pm; Sat 11am–3pm.

George Peabody Library ★★★ One of Baltimore's hidden treasures, the 1866 Peabody is an architectural gem with the cast-iron balconies soaring five levels to a shining glass ceiling. It's an academic gem as well—the resting place of 300,000 volumes, mostly rare books, with some dating to when the printing press was new. Philanthropist George Peabody provided the funds to build this magnificent "cathedral of books" and ordered that it be filled with the best works on every subject. Literary exhibits change regularly in an adjacent gallery.

17 E. Mount Vernon Place. ✆ **410/659-8179.** www.library.jhu.edu/collections/specialcollections/rarebooks/peabody. Library Tues–Thurs 9am–5pm, Fri 9am–3pm.

The Maryland Historical Society ★★ ☺ Three floors of historical artifacts offer glimpses of life in Maryland over the centuries. The museum's main exhibit "Looking for Liberty" has Francis Scott Key's manuscript of "The Star-Spangled Banner" as its centerpiece. ***Insiders' note:*** The manuscript most people see is a reproduction. Without any fanfare (although some may be added for the War of 1812 commemoration), the reproduction slides out of the way so visitors may see the real thing. This happens only for 10 minutes on the hour between 11am and 3pm. Other treasures are art by the Peale family painters, Broadway composer Eubie Blake's glasses and baton, Stieff silver, Baltimore furniture, and Baltimore album quilts. Look for expanded exhibits commemorating the Battle for Baltimore (Sept 12–14, 1814) and the Civil War. Civil War tours are offered on the half-hour from 12:30 to 3:30pm. The Maryland Historical Society Players present stories of the Civil War Saturdays and Sunday on the hour from 1 to 4pm. It's easy to spend a couple of hours here, and the society is not far from the Walters Art Museum and the antiques shops of Howard Street.

201 W. Monument St. ✆ **410/685-3750.** www.mdhs.org. Admission $6 adults, $5 seniors, $4 children 3–18, free under age 3. Free admission first Thurs of month. Wed–Sun 10am–5pm. Free parking on-site. Light Rail: Centre St.

Maryland Women's Heritage Center Women from all walks of life are honored in this small museum. Some names are familiar: Billie Holiday, Clara Barton, Rachel Carson. Some ought to be familiar: Henrietta Szold, founder of Hadassah; St. Elizabeth Ann Seton, founder of the U. S. Catholic school system; and Claire McCardell, pioneering fashion designer of women's sportswear. And then there are the "unsung heroines," a small display of names and tributes to women of Maryland who made a difference in someone's life, nominated by their daughters, their patients, their friends. Mostly these are displays of portraits and biographies with a few artifacts and a temporary exhibit—a yearlong exhibit of women of NASA was opened in October 2011, for example. If you are moved by the stories, you could spend more than an hour here.

39 W. Lexington St. ✆ **410/767-0675.** www.mdwomensheritagecenter.org. Free admission. Wed–Sat 10am–4pm.

Old St. Paul's Originally founded in 1692 as one of Maryland's first Anglican parishes, this Italian-Romanesque building dates to 1856 and features Tiffany stained-glass windows and mosaics, notably the Tiffany rose window. In addition, two friezes salvaged from the previous church, which burned in 1817, have been incorporated into the portico. The church is no longer open to the public, though services are, of course.

Charles and Saratoga sts. ✆ **410/685-3404.** www.osp1692.org. Sun services at 8, 9, and 11am.

The Walters Art Museum ★★★ The Walters has always been one of Baltimore's great attractions. Begun with the 22,000-object collection of William and Henry Walters, this gem's ancient and medieval galleries practically sparkle. Walk through the galleries of sculpture, jewelry, mummies, and 19th-century French paintings to see the progress of fine art through the centuries. The Knight's Hall displays tapestries, furnishings, and suits of armor from the Middle Ages. The Egyptian collection is one of the best in the U.S. The original Palazzo building features 1,500 works from mostly the Renaissance and baroque periods. Hackerman House, open Saturday and Sunday, features Asian art. The Palace of Wonders is the imaginary gallery of a 17th-century Flemish nobleman with art, collections from nature, and artifacts from around the world. Docents offer free tours Sunday at 2pm. The cafe serves light fare. An art conservator is available Friday through Sunday 12:30 to 4pm to talk about a work in progress.

600 N. Charles St. ✆ **410/547-9000.** www.thewalters.org. Free admission; admission is charged for special exhibitions. Wed–Sun 11am–5pm. Closed July 4, Thanksgiving, and Dec 24–25. Bus: 3, 11, 31, 61, or 64. Light Rail: Centre St. Take Charles St. north to the Washington Monument.

Washington Monument This 178-foot-tall column, the country's first major architectural memorial to George Washington, was designed in 1815 by Robert Mills, who also designed the *other* Washington Monument (begun in 1848) in Washington, DC. Time has taken its toll, forcing the closure of the interior. Although visitors can no longer climb the 228 steps, the monument is expected to be repaired, perhaps in time for its bicentennial in 2015. News about the restoration of the monument and the pretty park around it is posted at **www.friendsofmountvernonplace.org**.

Mount Vernon Place and Charles St. Park open daily; monument closed to visitors.

North of Downtown

Baltimore Museum of Art ★★★ The largest museum in Maryland, the BMA offers galleries dedicated to modern and contemporary art; European sculpture and painting; American painting and decorative arts; prints and photographs; the arts of Africa, Asia, the Americas, and Oceania; and a 2¾-acre sculpture garden with 35 major works by Alexander Calder, Henry Moore, and others. The BMA is famous for its Matisse collection, assembled by Baltimore sisters Claribel and Etta Cone, who went to Paris in the 1920s and came back with Impressionist and modern art. The $4-million Cone Wing showcases their collection of paintings by Matisse, Cézanne, Gauguin, van Gogh, and Renoir. Visit the special room set up to remember these women, featuring drawers filled with their personal things, pieces of furniture, and a virtual tour of their Baltimore apartments. Other highlights include the 35,000-square-foot West Wing for Contemporary Art, with work by Andy Warhol, Jasper Johns, and Baltimorean Grace Hartigan; early American decorative arts and a gallery of miniature rooms; European art that includes Impressionist paintings by Monet and Degas; and the Jacobs Wing, a collection of 15th- to 19th-century European art displayed in jewel-toned rooms. Younger visitors may like the art packs, Free Family Sundays, or the Family Tours offered the last Sunday of the month. A summer jazz series in the sculpture garden is a delight. ***Please note:*** A major renovation is underway to upgrade infrastructure and amenities of the West Wing. It will remain closed to visitors until Fall 2012.

10 Art Museum Dr. (at N. Charles and 31st sts.; take Howard St. north and bear right onto Art Museum Dr., about 3 miles north of the harbor). ✆ **443/573-1700.** www.artbma.org. Free except for special exhibits. Wed–Fri 10am–5pm; Sat–Sun 11am–6pm. Bus: 3 or 11.

Evergreen Museum & Library What started as a relatively modest Italianate mansion in the mid-1800s became a 48-room marvel of the Gilded Age, with a 23-karat gold-plated bathroom, a theater painted by noted Ballet Russe designer Leon Bakst, and room after room of art, books, and *objets*. Purchased in 1878 by John W. Garrett, president of the B&O railroad, the home grew over the years and became ever more lavish. Its last owners, John and Alice Garrett, turned it into a glittering salon, where they entertained statesmen, authors, artists, and musicians.

The entrance is a porte-cochere topped by a Tiffany glass awning, which leads to a multitude of beautiful rooms, fine arts, and decorative items that reflect the Garretts' travels and interests: a red Asian room displaying Japanese and Chinese items; paintings by Picasso, Modigliani, and Degas; glass by Tiffany; a 30,000-book library; and Dutch marquetry furniture. Tours, offered on the hour, last about an hour. The formal gardens should be visited as well.

4545 N. Charles St. (btw. Loyola College and the College of Notre Dame). ✆ **410/516-0341.** www.museums.jhu.edu. Admission $6 adults, $5 seniors, $3 students. Tues–Fri 11am–4pm; Sat–Sun noon–4pm (last tour at 3pm).

Homewood Museum If you have time, visit both Evergreen (see above) and Homewood (they're a mile apart) to see how differently the rich lived in different centuries. Homewood was designed and built by the son of Charles Carroll of Carrollton, a signer of the Declaration of Independence. Built in 1801, the five-part classic Palladian home is a dazzling example of Federal architecture with superb woodcarving and plaster ornamentation. It's painted in a rainbow of soothing colors and decorated in pieces of the time, some from the Carroll family. Highlights are the main hall, the family sitting room with toys and doll furniture, the music room, the long lemon-yellow hall, and the master bedroom with its high cove ceiling and bookcases tucked into the sides of the fireplace. Tours, offered on the half-hour, last 45 minutes. Changing exhibits in the main hall focus on the decorative arts or architecture.

3400 N. Charles St. (on the campus of Johns Hopkins University). ✆ **410/516-5589.** www.museums.jhu.edu. Admission $6 adults, $5 seniors, $3 students. Tues–Fri 11am–4pm; Sat–Sun noon–4pm (last tour at 3:30pm). Drive to the university's north entrance, on University Pkwy., and follow signs to the parking lot. Press the button at the gate to park. The house is on the other side of a building by the lot.

Lacrosse Museum & National Hall of Fame This museum offers a look at 350 years in the history of lacrosse, America's oldest sport, played with a passion in Maryland. Displays include photographs and murals of athletes at play, sculptures and paintings, vintage equipment and uniforms, a documentary, and a Hall of Fame.

113 W. University Pkwy. ✆ **410/235-6882.** www.uslacrosse.org. Admission $3 adults, $2 children 5–15. Feb–May Tues–Sat 10am–3pm; June–Jan Mon–Fri 10am–3pm; 1st Wed of every month noon–3pm. Hours occasionally change, so call ahead.

The Maryland Zoo in Baltimore ☺ The third-oldest zoo in the U.S. is home to some 2,000 animals, including polar bears, penguins, and chimpanzees. The **Polar Bear Watch** allows visitors a view of Magnet and Alaska. The **Chimpanzee Forest, Leopard Lair,** and **African Watering Hole** are fun, but the best part is the children's zoo, with its lily pads, tree slide, farm animals, and Maryland wilderness exhibit. Feeding time for the African penguins, North America's largest collection, at 11am and 3pm, is a highlight. Tram rides are included with admission.

Druid Hill Park. ✆ **410/366-LION** (5466). www.marylandzoo.org. Admission Mar–Dec $17 adults, $14 seniors, $12 children 2–11; Jan–Feb $9 adults, $7 seniors, $6 children. Mar–Dec daily 10am–4pm; Jan–Feb Fri–Mon 10am–4pm. Closed Thanksgiving and Dec 25. Take Exit 7, Druid Hill Lake Dr., off I-83 and follow signs for the zoo.

National Great Blacks In Wax Museum The first thing you hear when you enter is the sound of moaning, coming from the Slave Ship exhibit. This wax museum doesn't shy away from the tough topics—a lynching exhibit is in the basement—but it revels in the African Americans, and all people of color, who made a difference. Some are expected: Barack Obama, Martin Luther King, Jr., Frederick Douglass, and famous athletes, artists, and entertainers. Some may be people you weren't aware of: rodeo star Bill Pickett, Matthew Henson at the North Pole, and African Americans who made advances in medicine, science, law, and politics.

1601–1603 E. North Ave. ✆ **410/563-3404.** www.greatblacksinwax.org. Admission $12 adults, $11 seniors and students, $10 children 2–11. Feb, July–Aug Mon–Sat 9am–6pm, Sun noon–6pm; Mar–June, Sept 1 Tues–Sat 9am–6pm, Sun noon–6pm; Oct 15–Jan Tues–Sat 9am–5pm, Sun noon–5pm.

ORGANIZED TOURS & CRUISES

Special Interest Tours

A series of guided tours of the Baltimore National Heritage Area takes visitors around and away from the Inner Harbor for a bit of history and culture. The tours last about 90 minutes, and are conducted by Urban Park Rangers. The **Heritage Walk** guides tourists through Baltimore's oldest waterfront neighborhoods, including Little Italy and Jonestown. They are offered weekends in April and in May through October weekdays at 10am and weekends at 10am and 1pm. Tours start from the Inner Harbor Visitor Center, and may vary in content based on season/demand. Private and group tours can also be arranged in advance.

The **Mount Vernon Cultural Walk** goes up Charles Street for a glimpse of Baltimore's financial district and some of its best-known cultural institutions. The tour ends at the iconic Washington Monument in picturesque Mount Vernon. The tour begins at the Visitor Center daily at 1pm May through October.

For a look at Baltimore's African-American heritage, join the tour on the **Pennsylvania Avenue Heritage Trail.** It's offered Sunday mornings May through October to take advantage of a visit to the Arabbers' Market, held only on Sundays, and begins at the State Center Metro Stop.

A nominal fee may be charged, beginning in 2012, for these tours. For information, call ✆ **443/984-2369** or visit www.starspangledtrails.org. The website also outlines a variety of other self-guided tours, both walking and driving, around the city.

The **Fell's Point Visitor Center,** 1724 Thames St. (✆ **410/675-6750,** ext. 16; www.preservationsociety.com), offers tours of some of Baltimore's oldest streets April through November. Walking tours, including the **Immigration Tour** at noon on Saturday and **Secrets of a Seaport,** depart from here at 10am on Saturdays. Authentic Fell's Point **Ghostwalks** are offered Friday and Saturday at 7pm. **African-American History Tours** get underway at 3pm on Sunday. Tickets are $12 for adults, $8 for children 11 and under; reservations are a must. Tours of the 1765 Robert Long House on Ann Street, the oldest residence in Baltimore Town, are offered Tuesday at 1:30pm. Tickets are $5. In addition, Heritage Walks leave from here Tuesdays through Fridays at 11am and 1:30pm. They are $5 for adults, free for children 12 and younger.

African American Cultural Tours and Travel offers tours focusing on contributions of local African Americans, such as Harriet Tubman and Thurgood Marshall, and important landmarks, including filming locations for the TV series *The Wire*. Tours on area movie locations are also available. Call ✆ **410/727-0755;** reservations are essential.

Baltimore Trolley Tours (http://tickets.baltimore.org/eventperformances.asp?evt=144) leave from the Baltimore Visitor Center in the Inner Harbor every day at 11am and 1pm March 15 to November 15. Tickets for the 90-minute look at most of the downtown neighborhoods are $25 for adults, $16 ages 6 to 12, and free for children under 6 (on a lap).

Segs in the City (✆ **410/276-7347;** www.segsinthecity.com) offers City Safaris of Fell's Point and the Inner Harbor. The 2-hour tour costs $70; an hour-long minisafari costs $45. They are offered March to December.

Baseball fans will enjoy the 90-minute tour of **Oriole Park at Camden Yards ★** (✆ **410/547-6234;** http://baltimore.orioles.mlb.com). Well-informed guides fill you in on where Hall of Famer Eddie Murray hit his 500th home run, why there are no bat racks in the dugout, and how many miles of beer lines run under the seats. The tour visits places average fans can't see: the dugouts, scoreboard control room, and the press box. Buy tickets at least 30 minutes beforehand at the box office at the north end of the stadium; prices are $9 for adults and $7 for seniors and children. Tours are conducted four times daily from April through September. No tours are offered on game days. Call ahead to confirm times.

Bring your appetite and sense of adventure for a **Charm City Food Tour ★★** (www.baltimorefoodtours.com). For about $55 you'll cover a good-sized chunk of neighborhood, history, and culture during the 3-hour tour. As you walk through Fell's Point, Little Italy, or Federal Hill, learn a little local history and taste Baltimore's food—from focaccia to crab cakes, pierogies to Berger cookies. Don't make a restaurant reservation afterward. You'll be quite satisfied, thank you.

Zippy Larson Tours (✆ **410/522-7334;** www.zippytours.com) offers specialized tours for groups and individuals, including the filming sites for John Waters's *Hairspray* or the haunts of Wallis Warfield Simpson.

Cruises & Boat Tours

There's no shortage of options for seeing Baltimore from the water. Several touring boats will inevitably be docked at the Inner Harbor during your visit; but the cheapest way to get on the water is to take **Ed Kane's Water Taxi** (✆ **800/658-8947** or 410/563-3901; www.thewatertaxi.com). It provides transportation to various destinations, including Harborplace, Little Italy, Fell's Point, Canton, and Fort McHenry, but you're welcome to stay on for the entire route. See "Getting Around," earlier in this chapter, for details.

Spirit Cruises (✆ **866/312-2469;** www.spiritcruisesbaltimore.com) offers 2-hour lunch, 3-hour dinner, 1-hour sightseeing cruises, and themed and midnight cruises on two 450-passenger ships, which dock by the Light Street Pavilion. The food is passable, but the cruise is worthwhile. Tickets are $20 for sightseeing tours, $35 for lunch cruises, and $70 for dinner cruises. Children's ticket prices begin at $12.

Baltimore Harbor Cruises (✆ **410/268-7601;** www.baltimoreboatcruises.com) offers 45-minute tours of the Inner Harbor five times a day on weekdays and eight times on weekends May through October. Tickets are $17 for adults and $6 for

Bring Your Boat to B'more

On a summer weekend, the Inner Harbor looks like a boat parking lot. So, c'mon, forget the car and sail into town. Inner Harbor docking fees range from $20 for 5 hours or $1.50 a foot for overnight docking. Contact the dockmaster at VHF68 or ✆ **410/396-3174.**

ages 3 to 11. There is also a 90-minute Key Bridge Cruise Friday evening and City Lights Cruise on Saturday evenings mid-April through mid-October.

The ***Black-Eyed Susan,*** a 150-passenger paddle-wheeler, offers Sunday brunch, jazz, sunset, and murder mystery cruises departing from the Broadway Pier in Fell's Point. Cruises cost $30 to $120. Call ✆ **410/342-6960,** or visit www.baltimore paddlewheel.com.

Tired of serious cruises? **Urban Pirates** (✆ **410/327-8378;** www.urbanpirates.com) leaves Fell's Point five times a day in summer and on weekends only in spring and fall on an adventure involving treasure, enemy ships, and swashbuckling. Daytime tours are kid-friendly; evening BYOGrog tours ($25) are best left to the adults. Tickets are $20 for ages 3 and up, $10 for little pirates.

The bright yellow ***Seadog*** (✆ **888/882-5992;** www.seadogcruises.com) combines semi-serious touring with a 20-minute water-in-your-face speedboat cruise. These 90-minute adventures cruise past Fort McHenry and then zoom out to the Key Bridge. The schedule changes according to demand. See the kiosk at the Inner Harbor. Tickets range from $18 to $22 for adults and $11 to $14 for kids. The combination of speed and history makes this my favorite boat tour.

For a tall-ship adventure, plan an autumn trip on a New England schooner that docks in Baltimore for several cruises on the Chesapeake. The 103-foot ***Mystic Whaler*** (✆ **800/697-8420;** www.mysticwhaler.com) offers 3-day Chesapeake Bay cruises from Baltimore. Prices range from $500 to $700.

SPECTATOR SPORTS & OUTDOOR ACTIVITIES

BASEBALL From April to October, you can see the American League's **Baltimore Orioles** play ball. If there's a home game during your visit, try to attend—it's a real Baltimore experience. The team plays at **Oriole Park at Camden Yards,** 333 W. Camden St. (✆ **888/848-BIRD** [2473]; www.oriolepark.com). Afternoon games are usually at 1:35pm; evening games start at 7:05pm. Ticket prices can range from $10 to $65, with bargain night on Tuesday and college-student discounts on Friday, both for the upper deck. Tickets for Yankees or Red Sox games cost more. Tours of the stadium (✆ **410/547-6234**) are available daily, except on home-game days mid-February through mid-December.

FOOTBALL The **Baltimore Ravens** play at M&T Bank Stadium, next to Camden Yards at 1101 Russell St. (✆ **410/261-RAVE** [7283]; www.baltimoreravens.com). About 5,000 tickets are sold per game (the rest are held by season-ticket holders) and cost $80 to $500. You can also check online at venues like StubHub.com.

HORSE RACING Maryland's oldest thoroughbred track and the site of the annual Preakness Stakes is **Pimlico Race Course,** 5241 Park Heights (✆ **410/542-9400;**

www.pimlico.com), on the city's northwest side. (Seabiscuit made history at this track, beating Triple Crown winner War Admiral.) The **Preakness Stakes ★ (www.preakness.com)**, the middle jewel in racing's Triple Crown, is held the third Saturday in May. Clubhouse and grandstand tickets go on sale in October—and go fast. Infield tickets, at $60, are for sale at the box office and online. Post time for regular racing days is 1:10pm; admission is $3 for the grandstand. Self-parking is free; valet parking is $3. Call ahead for opening days.

INDOOR SOCCER The **Baltimore Blast** (✆ **410/732-5278;** www.baltimoreblast.com) have had a loyal following for 30 years. A number of players are local boys. The season lasts November through March; games are played at the 1st Mariner Arena. Tickets cost $16 to $30.

PADDLEBOATS & ELECTRIC BOATS Paddleboats and little electric boats are available for rent at the Inner Harbor, adjacent to the World Trade Center. Hours vary according to season. Paddleboats, some built like dragons, cost $10 to $16 per half-hour per boat, depending on the number of people riding. Not that energetic? A half-hour ride on an electric boat will run $12 for two passengers or $18 for three.

PARTY BOATS In Harbor East, **Duffy Electric Boats** (801 Lancaster St.; ✆ **443/433-2129;** www.experiencetheduffyboat.com) rents 22-foot covered picnic boats. They are quiet and go at a leisurely 6 miles an hour with room for 10. They run $125 an hour or $500 for 5 hours. A Maryland boater license is required, but they'll help tourists obtain one quickly.

Public Parks

Baltimore has many green spaces, including a couple that deserve special mention.

Cylburn Arboretum 📷 Just off Northern Parkway, up the Jones Falls Expressway (I-83), Cylburn is a peaceful collection of gardens and mansion. The 200-plus acres include a formal Victorian garden and gardens devoted to butterflies, shade, roses, and vegetables. Woodland trails wind 2.5 miles through the forests of Cylburn. Among the 161 bird species spotted here have been the Baltimore oriole and bald eagle. Stop inside the stone house with mansard roof and cupola to see its ornate first floor, with inlaid floors, mosaics, and plasterwork. Gardening events are posted on the website.

4915 Greenspring Ave., Mount Washington. ✆ **410/367-2217.** www.cylburnassociation.org. Free admission. Mansion Tues–Sun 10am–4pm. Grounds Tues–Sun 8am–8pm in summer, Tues–Sun 8am–5pm in winter.

Federal Hill ★★★ Get a great view of the city from that big hill overlooking the Inner Harbor. Take the 100 steps on the Battery Avenue side, or enter from Warren Avenue, where you won't have any steps to contend with, except maybe a curbstone. The hill has been valued for its scenic views since the first Baltimoreans came here to watch construction around the harbor. A single cannon recalls the Civil War, when federal guns were trained on the city. Take your dog (on a leash) or your children. Once the kids get tired of the view, they can play in the fenced-in playground.

Federal Hill Park, Battery and Warren aves. Free admission. Best to visit during daylight hours.

SHOPPING

The Inner Harbor is an obvious choice for shopping. But those who like an adventure will find Fell's Point, Hampden, Mount Washington, Antique Row on Howard

SWEET things IN CHARM CITY

Sometimes you just need a sweet—and there are a couple sweet spots around town that shouldn't be missed if you're in the neighborhood.

Charm City Cakes, 2936 Remington Ave. (✆ **410/235-9229**), headquarters for Food Network's *Ace of Cakes* chef Duff Goldman, opens an hour a day for clients to pick up "Cakes for Two"—at $250 each. Otherwise the Remington bakery isn't open to the public.

Charm City Cupcakes, 326 N. Charles St. (✆ **410/244-8790;** www.charmcitycupcakes.com) sells its creative cupcakes downtown. Open Tuesday through Saturday, 10am to 6pm.

Dangerously Delicious Pies, 2839 O'Donnell St., Canton (✆ **410/522-PIES** [7437]; www.dangerouspies.com). No fancy stuff here—just honest, homemade, fresh-out-of-the-oven pies. The rock-'n'-roll guys here make all kinds: fruit, Key (Bridge) lime, derby, and a towering lemon meringue. Open Tuesday through Saturday from 7am to 6pm (or later) and Sunday 8am to 10pm.

Patisserie Poupon, 820 E. Baltimore St. (✆ **410/332-0390;** www.patisseriepoupon.net). You'll find this delightful French pastry shop in the shadow of the Shot Tower and near Port Discovery and Little Italy. (Due to traffic, it's safer to drive here.) Stop for coffee and a croissant or a fabulously decorated pastry. Open Monday through Saturday from 7am to 6pm.

Street, and a lot of fun. If your wallet needs emptying, head over to Cross Keys, near Mount Washington, for designer threads. Harbor East is the newest go-to shopping district.

Inner Harbor

Restaurants and shops fill the two pavilions on Light and Pratt streets that make up **Harborplace** (✆ **410/332-4191;** www.harborplace.com), as well as the Gallery, a vertical mall across the street in the Renaissance Harborplace Hotel. The **Light Street Pavilion** is dominated by the H&M chain store, while the **Pratt Street Pavilion** offers mostly chain restaurants and a few shops. The **Gallery** has three floors of shops, plus a fourth-floor food court. Most of the stores are franchises of national chains, and are open Monday through Saturday from 10am to 9pm and Sunday from noon to 6pm.

The 75 shops in the Gallery (connected via skywalk to the Pratt St. Pavilion) include Banana Republic, Brooks Brothers, Ann Taylor, and Coach. Santa's magical house is located between the Harborplace pavilions from mid-November to Christmas Eve.

Fell's Point

Art Gallery of Fells Point This cooperative gallery features works by regional artists, including paintings, photography, fibers, and jewelry. Open Tuesday through Sunday. 1716 Thames St. ✆ **410/327-1272.** www.fellspointgallery.org.

Brassworks Brass glistens from every shelf here. Fine-quality items include lamps, candlesticks, doorknockers, and more. Open daily. 1641 Thames St. ✆ **410/327-728.** www.baltimorebrassworks.com.

Robert McClintock Baltimore Seen Prints and original works of Baltimore scenes in McClintock's unusual style. Open Tuesday through Sunday. 1809 Thames St. ✆ **410/814-2800.**

Sheep's Clothing Irish woolens and ceramics and Provençal soaps and fragrances. Open Wednesday through Sunday. 1620 Shakespeare St. ✆ **410/327-222.**

The Sound Garden One of the best CD stores around. Also has used CDs and new and used DVDs. It's a good place to check for live music around town. Open daily. 1616 Thames St. ✆ **410/563-9011.** www.cdjoint.com.

Ten Thousand Villages Using the Body Shop model of commissioning handmade products by indigenous peoples, this shop is filled with textiles, pottery, baskets, and coffee, all fairly traded and affordably priced. Open daily. 1621 Thames St. ✆ **410/342-556.** www.baltimore.tenthousandvillages.com.

Harbor East

For a neighborhood that didn't even exist a few years ago, this one's thriving, and the shopping is *très* chic. Most shops are on Exeter or Fleet streets. Look for something hot to carry your stuff in at **Handbags and the City,** 840 Aliceanna St. (✆ **410/528-1443**), or something cool to sit on at **Arhaus Furniture,** 660 S. Exeter St. (✆ **410/244-6376;** www.arhaus.com).

You'll also find plenty of restaurants, including **Mustang Alley's** 10- and duck-pin bowling and sleek eatery, 1300 Bank St. (✆ **410/522-BOWL** [2695]; www.mustangalleys.com). Or stop for a snack or supplies at **Whole Foods,** 1001 Fleet St. (✆ **410/528-1640**), or for wine at **Bin 604,** 604 S. Exeter St. (✆ **410/576-0444;** www.bin604.com), which has wine classes on Saturdays and tastings on Thursdays.

BALTIMORE'S antique ROW

On a single block in Mount Vernon—the 800 block of North Howard Street—is an amazing string of antique shops. The first antique stores opened here in the 1840s—they were furniture resellers, really—making this the oldest antiques district in the U.S. Most of the shops are open from 11am or noon to 5pm. Street parking is metered—bring quarters, or take the Light Rail, which runs up Howard.

The 20 dealers at **Antique Row Stalls** (✆ **410/728-6363**), an 8,000-square-foot co-op, sell just about everything. They're closed Tuesdays. **Drusilla's Books** (✆ **410/225-0277**) stocks all kinds of old and rare books.

Dubey's Art and Antiques (✆ **410/383-2881**) boasts a wealth of Chinese export porcelain and other American, English, and Asian treasures. For antiquities from Europe and Asia, see **Richard Sindler** (✆ **410/225-2727**).

Check out the old silver at **Imperial Half Bushel** (✆ **410/462-1192**)—the shop fairly glitters with flatware and hollowware. The **20th Century Gallery** (✆ **410/728-3800**) stocks American and European art pottery, as well as prints and paintings. **Crosskeys** (✆ **410/728-0101**), which specializes in English, continental, and American furnishings, is open only Saturday and Sunday.

Mount Vernon

A People United This nonprofit shop features goods made by women who are part of development cooperatives in India, Guatemala, Kenya, and other lands. You'll find clothing, jewelry, and accessories; sweaters here are not your average pullovers. Open daily. 516 N. Charles St. ✆ **410/727-447.** www.apeopleunited.com.

Beadazzled Be dazzled by the array of beads, which come from everywhere and in every color. Jewelry-making classes are available. Open daily. 501 N. Charles St. ✆ **410/837-232.** www.beadazzled.net.

C. Grimaldis Gallery Contemporary art is the focus here, with new exhibitions 11 times a year. Open Tuesday through Saturday. 523 N. Charles St. ✆ **410/539-109.** www.cgrimaldisgallery.com.

The Woman's Industrial Exchange Founded in 1880, this shop's mission has always been to help women by selling their handiwork, originally as part of a national movement after the Civil War. The work here is finely done: smocked dresses and handmade afghans, quilts, and other wares. Open Monday through Saturday. 333 N. Charles St. ✆ **410/685-438.** www.womansindustrialexchange.org.

Hampden

Antreasian Gallery Antreasian Gallery features the works of 50 regional artists, from painting to jewelry to ceramics. Open Wednesday through Sunday. 1111 W. 36th St. ✆ **410/235-442.** www.antreasiangallery.com.

Charlotte Elliott Three levels of antiques, vintage clothing, Thai silks, and the like. Open daily. 837 W. 36th St. ✆ **410/243-099.**

HONtown The spot for a real Baltimore souvenir, hon. The shop's soda fountain opens at noon. Open daily. 1001 W. 36th St. ✆ **410/662-443.** www.celebratebaltimore.com.

Ma Petite Shoe Splurge on two indulgences—eye-catching footwear and gourmet chocolates—in one shop. Local chocolatiers Cacao Lorenzo and Mouth Party are featured. Open daily. 832 W. 36th St. ✆ **410/235-344.** www.mapetiteshoe.com.

Mud and Metal This shop specializes in functional art—lamps, tables, business-card holders, and jewelry—often created from recycled materials by local artists. Open daily. 1121 W. 36th St. ✆ **410/467-869.** www.mudandmetal.com.

Wild Yam Pottery The pottery (think lamps, baking dishes, vases) made on these premises is mostly practical, in soothing earth tones. Special orders and handcrafted jewelry are available. Open daily. 863 W. 36th St. ✆ **410/662-112.** www.wildyampottery.com.

The Wine Source The friendliest wine people staff this big store a block from "the Avenue." Besides a wealth of wine, they stock beer, spirits, and cheeses. Open daily. 3601 Elm St. ✆ **410/467-777.** www.the-wine-source.com.

Mount Washington Village

Baltimore Clayworks This nonprofit center holds classes, rents studio space, and runs a gallery and shop. The main building has a warren of little gallery rooms where exhibits of art pieces change frequently. The shop has functional pottery, made by local potters. Open daily. 5707 Smith Ave. ✆ **410/578-191.** www.baltimoreclayworks.org.

O'Malley Antiques This spacious and sunny shop gleams from wall to wall with silver, mirrors, walnut, and mahogany. If you're looking for authentic 18th-, 19th- and early-20th-century furnishings and accessories, don't miss it. 1501 Sulgrave Ave. ✆ **410/466-060.** www.omalleyantiques.com.

Something Else You won't find the clothing here in a department store. Flowing dresses, exotic jewelry, and South American sweaters are made of flax, wool, and cotton. Open Monday through Saturday. 1611 Sulgrave Ave. ✆ **410/542-044.**

Sunnyfields Traditional girls will like this shop's Williamsburg reproduction furniture and accessories, porcelain, crystal, and party furnishings. Open Tuesday through Saturday. 6305 Falls Rd. ✆ **410/823-666.**

Village of Cross Keys

This upscale shopping center, at 5100 Falls Rd. in north Baltimore, has local stores, plus a few chains such as Talbots and Williams-Sonoma. Hours are from 10am to 6pm or later. From downtown, take the Jones Falls Expressway north to the Northern Parkway East exit. Turn right at the light at Falls Road; the center is on the right.

The Pied Piper Spoil your children with these luxurious clothes, everything from christening dresses to bibs. Open Monday through Saturday. ✆ **410/435-267.**

Ruth Shaw You need designer clothes, you come here. Where else are you going to get your Jimmy Choo shoes? Open Monday through Saturday. ✆ **410/532-7886.**

The Store Ltd. Pared down to their simplest form, these home furnishings and personal accessories are contemporary and always fresh. Jewelry here is designed by the store's owner. Open Monday through Saturday. ✆ **410/323-2350.**

Markets & Malls

Baltimore still has several old-fashioned covered markets with vendors selling seafood, baked goods, produce, and sweets. The outdoor farmers' market held under the Jones Falls viaduct is a Sunday tradition for many people.

Arundel Mills South of Baltimore, this theme-park-like mall is *huge,* with some 200 shops. Larger retailers, such as Off 5th Saks Fifth Avenue Outlet, Neiman Marcus Last Call, and Bass Pro Shops Outdoor World, are joined by smaller shops, a 24-screen movie theater, and lots of restaurants. The combination of games and food at Dave & Buster's is an afternoon's diversion, and Medieval Times offers dinner and a show. Open daily. ✆ **410/540-511.** www.arundelmills.com. Off Rte. 295, 10 miles south of Baltimore. Take Rte. 295 south; pass BWI exit to Exit 10 for Arundel Mills.

Baltimore Farmers' Market For a look at Old Baltimore, stop at this weekly outdoor gathering—a great source for crafts, herbs, jams, jellies, baked goods, smoked meats, cheeses, local produce, and flowers. It has expanded with its popularity, opening crafts stalls, closing streets, and adding free parking in a nearby lot. Open May to mid-December, Sunday from 7am to noon. Saratoga St., btw. Holliday and Gay sts. (under JFX). ✆ **410/752-863** (for office at 200 W. Lombard St.).

Belvedere Square If you're in northern Baltimore, near Hopkins or Loyola universities, this market is a great place to stop. A cluster of takeout counters and retail shops offer mouthwatering choices: sushi, fresh fruits and vegetables, baked goods, and organic items. Atwater's soups, breads, and desserts should never be passed up. Open daily; store hours vary. 540 E. Belvedere Ave. (just south of Northern Pkwy.), Roland Park. ✆ **410/464-977.** www.belvederesquare.com.

Broadway Market This 200-year-old market, with two large covered buildings, is staffed by local vendors selling produce and ethnic and raw-bar foods (ideal for a quick lunch). Open Monday through Saturday from 7am to 6pm. S. Broadway, btw. Fleet and Lancaster sts., Fell's Point. No phone. www.bpmarkets.com.

Cross Street Market First opened in 1846, Cross Street Market is one of Baltimore's public markets. Local vendors offer produce, seafood, meats, candy, baked goods, and much more. Open Monday through Saturday from 7am to 7pm. 1065 S. Charles St., at Cross St., Federal Hill. No phone. www.bpmarkets.com.

Lexington Market Established in 1782, this Baltimore landmark claims to be the oldest continuously operating market in the U.S. Some 140 merchants sell prepared foods (for eat-in or takeaway), seafood, produce, meats, baked goods, and sweets. A parking garage is attached to the market. Open Monday through Saturday from 8:30am to 6pm. 400 W. Lexington St. ✆ **410/685-616.** www.lexingtonmarket.com.

BALTIMORE AFTER DARK

Baltimore, once a sleepy town at night, is now jumping when the sun sets: The Inner Harbor, Federal Hill, Canton, and Mount Vernon have all developed lives after dark.

For major events, check the arts and entertainment sections of the Baltimore *Sun* and the *Washington Post*. The free weekly *City Paper* has very complete listings, down to the smallest bars and clubs. On the Web, try **www.baltimorefunguide.com**.

Tickets for most major venues are available at the individual box offices or through **Ticketmaster** (✆ **410/547-SEAT** [7328]; www.ticketmaster.com).

The Performing Arts

Baltimore has a solid range of resident companies, including a nationally recognized symphony, an opera company, a major regional theater, and several local professional theater companies.

CLASSICAL MUSIC

The world-class **Baltimore Symphony Orchestra** ★★★ (✆ **877/BSO-1444** [276-1444] or 410/783-8000; www.bsomusic.org) is led by Marin Alsop. The BSO performs classical and pops concerts at the Meyerhoff Symphony Hall, 1212 Cathedral St. In summer, you'll also find the BSO at Oregon Ridge Park, north of the city off I-83. Its Fourth of July concerts with fireworks are terrific fun. Tickets are $25 to $75.

The **Peabody Symphony Orchestra** (✆ **410/234-4800;** www.peabody.jhu.edu/pso) is one of several performing units of the Peabody Institute of Music; concerts are held in Friedberg Hall, at 1 E. Mount Vernon Place.

Lyric Opera Baltimore (✆ **410/900-1150;** www.lyricoperahouse.com) presents three operas a season at the Patricia and Arthur Modell Performing Arts Center at the Lyric. Their inaugural 2011–12 season was very well received.

THEATER

Baltimore has an active independent theater scene, as well as hosting a major regional theater and touring shows. For entertainment by local professional actors at affordable prices, the **Vagabond Players,** in Fell's Point at 806 S. Broadway (✆ **410/563-9135;** www.vagabondplayers.org), stage a variety of classics, contemporary comedies, and dramas. The **Fells Point Corner Theater,** 251 S. Ann St. (✆ **410/276-7837;** www.fpct.org), presents seven productions a year.

The city's prominent African-American theater company, **Arena Players,** 801 McCulloh St., off Martin Luther King Boulevard (✆ **410/728-6500**), presents contemporary plays and romantic comedies in weekend performances year-round.

Everyman Theatre, 1727 N. Charles St. (✆ **410/752-2208;** www.everyman theatre.org), earns rave reviews for its productions of classics and new works. If everything goes as planned, the company will move to a theater at 315 W. Fayette St. for the 2012 season. The **Theatre Project ★**, 45 W. Preston St. (✆ **410/752-8558;** www.theatreproject.org), presents experimental and avant-garde work. Theatre Project is often the site for plays by a new Baltimore company, **Iron Crow Theatre** (✆ **443/468-4837;** www.ironcrowtheatre.com), which stages works primarily by lesbian, gay, bisexual, and transgender artists. The **Single Carrot Theatre Company,** 120 W. North Ave. (✆ **443/844-9253;** www.singlecarrot.com), is also making a name for itself by offering innovative work at affordable prices.

The **Baltimore Playwrights Festival** (www.baltimoreplaywrightsfestival.org) offers new works at theaters around town June through September.

CenterStage ★★ Many major American plays—including works by August Wilson and Eric Overmyer—have been developed at Maryland's state theater, which has presented new and classic work since 1963. A new artistic director, London-born playwright Kwame Kwei-Armah, took the reins in 2011. Center Stage offers child care at several matinees and "Nights Out" for its gay and lesbian fans. Two theaters offer both traditional seating and a more flexible black-box experience. 700 N. Calvert St. ✆ **410/332-003.** www.centerstage.org.

Hippodrome Theatre ★ At the France-Merrick Performing Arts Center, this restored former vaudeville venue, built in 1914, now offers touring Broadway shows and musical acts. Orchestra seats and front balcony seats are good, but pass up the back rows of the balcony, unless it's a show you absolutely have to see. A cafe serves light fare, but it's usually crowded; it now takes reservations (✆ **410/625-7850**). 10 N. Eutaw St. ✆ **410/837-740.** or 410/547-SEAT (7328) for tickets. www.france-merrickpac.com.

The Club & Music Scene

Baltimore has a variety of live-performance venues. Major national acts come to the **1st Mariner Arena Baltimore** near the Inner Harbor, 201 W. Baltimore St. (✆ **410/347-2020;** www.baltimorearena.com), **Pier Six Concert Pavilion** at the Inner Harbor, 731 Eastern Ave. (✆ **410/783-4189;** www.piersixpavilion.com), and **Rams Head Live** at Power Plant Live, 20 Market Place (✆ **410/244-1131;** www.ramsheadlive.com). Get tickets at **www.ticketmaster.com** for 1st Mariner Arena and at Rams Head Live for Pier Six and Rams Head.

Power Plant Live, 34 Market Place (✆ **410/752-5483;** www.powerplantlive.com), a mix of restaurants and bars, is a short walk from the Inner Harbor, at Water Street and Market Place. It packs in young singles, especially on weekend nights, who frequent gigantic **Luckie's Tavern,** a sports bar/rock bar; **Havana Club,** a cigar bar; **Howl at the Moon,** a rock-'n'-roll piano bar; as well as Rams Head Live. **Leinenkugel's Beer Garden** is set in a glass pavilion.

A number of clubs welcome smaller touring acts and local performers, from rock to jazz to folk. These are listed below.

COMEDY & MAGIC

Comedy Factory The Comedy Factory has relocated to Power Plant Live and presents live comedy Thursday at 8pm, Friday at 8 and 10pm, and Saturday at 7, 9, and 11pm. 6 Market Place. ✆ **410/547-779.** www.baltimorecomedy.com. Cover varies.

Illusions Bar and Theater Magic, sleight of hand, and Houdini-like escapes are part of the show at this Federal Hill bar. Shows begin at 9pm on Friday and Saturday, usually featuring the magic of local illusionist Spencer Horsman. Reservations are a good idea. 1025 S. Charles St. ✆ **410/727-5811.** www.illusionsmagicbar.com. Bar open Wed–Sat 5pm–1am.

FOLK & TRADITIONAL

Cat's Eye Pub A Fell's Point bar with an Irish feel, Cat's Eye is known for its traditional Irish music, but you'll often hear blues, bluegrass, zydeco, and jazz as well. In addition to the nightly live music at 9pm, there's a back room with chessboards and game tables. Open daily from noon to 2am. 1730 Thames St. ✆ **410/276-986.** www.catseyepub.com. Occasional $5 cover, mostly free.

J. Patrick's Locust Point's gathering spot for Irish music most nights of the week. Musicians welcome. 1371 Andre St. ✆ **410/244-8613.**

Mick O'Shea's One of Baltimore's centers for traditional Irish music, there's live music Thursday through Saturday nights, and food (sandwiches, soups, and Irish specialties) starting at 11:30am. 328 N. Charles St. ✆ **410/539-7504.** www.mickosheas.com. Cover about $3.

JAZZ & BLUES

An Die Musik Live! ★ Jazz and classical performances are held on the second floor of this Mount Vernon music shop a couple times a week. Grab yourself an armchair and relax for an hour or so of good music. Calendar is online. 409 N. Charles St. ✆ **888/221-617** or 410/385-2638. www.andiemusiklive.com. Cover varies.

Bertha's Restaurant & Bar The Fell's Point bar/restaurant is a great venue for live jazz and blues nearly every day of the week. 734 S. Broadway. ✆ **410/327-5795.** www.berthas.com.

Germano's Trattoria An upper room at this Little Italy restaurant becomes a jazz cabaret Thursday through Sunday. 300 S. High St. ✆ **410/752-4515.** www.germanostrattoria.com. Cover $10–$20.

The Baltimore Jazz Alliance has a website listing local shows: **www.baltimorejazz.com**.

ROCK

The 8×10 This longtime favorite in Federal Hill has room for 350 on two floors. The focus is live music—from rock to blues to funk. The schedule is on their website. 10 E. Cross St. ✆ **410/625-200.** www.the8x10.com. Cover varies.

The Horse You Came In On This Fell's Point bar has been pouring drinks since 1775. Popular with the local college and post-collegiate crowds, the Horse features live rock or acoustic music almost every night. 1626 Thames St. ✆ **410/327-811.** www.thehorsebaltimore.com. Cover varies.

The Ottobar Classic indie-rock club with shows nightly upstairs and down. 2549 N. Howard St. ✆ **410/662-006.** www.theottobar.com. Cover varies.

Fueling Up While You're Barhopping

Hungry Andy's, 629 S. Broadway (✆ **410/558-1869;** www.hungryandys.com), has quickly grown into the place to stop while barhopping in Fell's Point. Just a little carryout with a handful of tables, this place sells 50 pounds of french fries between 11pm and 3am. These are hand-cut quality fries and the pit beef (Maryland's answer to barbecue) with homemade sauce is rich, meaty goodness.

The Recher Theatre North of town in Towson, this former movie theater has become a magnet for local and national musicians, mostly rock but also some ska, reggae, and blues. 512 York Rd., Towson. ✆ **410/337-717.** www.rechertheatre.com. Cover varies; music lovers under 21 admitted.

Sonar Sonar has a DJ or concerts most nights, with an emphasis on techno and house music. There are three rooms; the Main Stage room holds 1,000 people. 407 E. Saratoga St. ✆ **410/783-788.** www.sonarbaltimore.com. Cover varies.

Beloved Hangouts

Bad Decisions Bacon happy hour and creative alcoholic concoctions make this a popular spot. 1928 Fleet St. ✆ **410/979-516.** www.makeabaddecision.com.

Havana Club 🎁 Upstairs from Ruth's Chris Steak House is this sophisticated little spot offering cocktails, appetizers, desserts, but no cigars due to the antismoking laws. A DJ spins tunes beginning at 9pm. Salsa music and even dance lessons on Thursdays. Closed Sunday through Wednesday. 600 Water St. ✆ **410/468-002.** www.havanaclub-baltimore.com.

Max's Taphouse Max's is a Baltimore institution known for its tremendous beer selection: 140 rotating drafts and 1,200 bottles. 737 S. Broadway. ✆ **410/675-MAXS (6297).** www.maxs.com.

The GLBT Scene

For a complete listing of nightspots and events, check out *Gay Life,* published by the **Gay, Lesbian, Bisexual & Transgender Community Center of Baltimore** (✆ **410/837-5445;** www.baltimoregaylife.com). The city's tourism website (www.baltimore.org) publishes LGBT community information, including a newsletter, *The Rainbow Roundup*. Below are some longtime community favorites.

The Creative Alliance This performance space hosts the Charm City Kitty Club, an LGBT cabaret. See the website for a schedule and ticket prices. 3134 Eastern Ave., Highlandtown. ✆ **410/276-165.** www.charmcitykittyclub.com.

Grand Central This Mount Vernon pub has six bars, a video bar, and pool tables. Sappho's is a ladies' lounge. The high-tech industrial dance floor is open Wednesday through Sunday, 9pm to 2am. 1001–1003 N. Charles St. ✆ **410/752-713.** www.centralstationpub.com.

The Hippo ★ This longtime classic has three large rooms with pool, videos, and a dance floor that attracts a primarily GLBT clientele, but all are welcome. The music is mostly house and techno. Happy hour is 4 to 8pm. Wednesday bingo is a smash hit among both gay and straight players, raising funds and fun, too. 1 W. Eager St. (at Charles St.). ✆ **410/547-006.** www.clubhippo.com. Cover varies.

Leon's Baltimore's oldest gay bar. Leon's also operates **Leon's Leather Lounge,** entrance around the corner at 227 W. Chase St. (✆ **410/539-4850**), offering live entertainment and karaoke. 870 Park Ave. ✆ **410/539-499.**

Station North Arts Cafe Gallery The only gay-owned and gay-operated cafe in the city's Station North arts and entertainment district serves breakfast and lunch until 3pm and hangs local art on the walls. 1816 N. Charles St. ✆ **410/625-644.** www.stationnortharts.com.

Film

The Charles The Charles, in a historic industrial building, offers first-run independent and foreign films, as well as classics. It has five comfortable auditoriums with stadium seating. The Charles is also a venue of the annual Maryland Film Festival, held in the spring. 1711 N. Charles St. ✆ **410/727-345.** www.thecharles.com.

IMAX Theater/Maryland Science Center Even if you aren't visiting the science center, you can still see the IMAX movies. In addition to regular daytime features, there are evening screenings on weekends on the theater's five-story-high, 75-foot-wide screen. 601 Light St. (on the harbor). ✆ **410/685-522.** www.mdsci.org.

Landmark Theatres Movies returned to downtown with the opening of this new seven-screen cinema in Harbor East. They'll even validate parking for a reasonable $5. 645 S. President St. ✆ **410/624-262.** www.landmarktheatres.com.

Little Italy Open-Air Film Festival On summer Fridays, you can catch a free movie. Bring a lawn chair, or use the ones already set up, to see films with an Italian accent, such as *Cinema Paradiso* and *Spartacus*. The movies are projected from the bedroom window of a nearby house. High and Stiles sts. www.littleitalymd.com.

Gaming

Interested in a bit of gambling? Get out of town! At least for the moment. Maryland recently legalized slot machines, and the slots parlors are beginning to come on board.

Hollywood Casino Perryville Situated on I-95, about an hour north of Baltimore, the Hollywood has 1,500 gaming machines, two restaurants, and a lounge. 1201 Chesapeake Overlook Pkwy. (1 Turnpike Dr.), Perryville, MD 21903. ✆ **410/378-850.** Sun–Thurs 8am–2am; Fri–Sat 8am–4am.

Maryland Live! Scheduled to open adjacent to Arundel Mills megamall (about a half-hour south of the city) in June 2012, this will be the state's largest gaming facility with 4,750 slot and electric table games, restaurants, and a live music venue. There's talk of a Bobby Flay–led restaurant, too. Construction was well underway in the fall of 2011, so it should open sometime in 2012—updated info should be on the website. Arundel Mills Circle, Hanover, MD 21076. ✆ **410/572-544.** www.marylandlivecasino.com.

SIDE TRIPS AROUND BALTIMORE

Ellicott City

Visitors have been coming to this tiny Patapsco River town, 14 miles west of Baltimore, for 230 years. The town was built to support the Ellicott brothers' mill, the largest flour-milling center in Colonial America. In 1831, America's first railroad terminal was constructed and still stands today. It was also here that the *Tom Thumb,* Peter Cooper's steam engine, raced and beat a horse-drawn vehicle. The country's first national road also ran through Ellicott City and gave farmers a route to the Atlantic.

Step back and look at the solid stone buildings still lining Main Street. The inns built in the 1800s remain—even the Colonial Inn and Opera House (now the Forget-Me-Not Factory), where John Wilkes Booth, it is said, got his start as an actor. Over the years, the town has endured fires, floods, and hurricanes. Through it all, it has survived, and its history and charm continue to draw visitors.

ESSENTIALS

GETTING THERE From Route 70, take Route 29 South to Route 40 East. Turn right on Rogers Avenue and right again on Courthouse Drive, which ends at Main Street (Rte. 144). Turn left into the historic district. From the Beltway (Rte. 695), either take Route 70 West and follow the above directions or take Route 40 West and turn left on Rogers Avenue, right on Courthouse Drive, and left on Main Street.

VISITOR INFORMATION The visitor center, at 8267 Main St. (✆ **410/313-1900**), is open Monday through Saturday from 10am to 5pm, Sunday from noon to 5pm. Look for the side entrance on Hamilton Street. You'll find a great self-guided walking tour brochure that offers some insight into the buildings' history. A new visitor center (in the same building) is expected to be open by summer 2012.

PARKING If you look hard, you can find parking spaces in lots marked with blue "P" signs. There are metered lots off Main Street near the visitor center, down a driveway under the railroad bridge, and on Maryland Avenue near the Ellicott City B&O Railroad Museum. You can get change for the meters at the visitor center or the railroad museum. (If the parking space is lined in yellow, you have to pay; it's free if the space is white.) ***Warning:*** On-street parking, though not metered, has a 1- or 2-hour limit between 10am and 6pm—and cars are ticketed for staying too long.

Some lots are free: Try the Oella lot across the Patapsco River Bridge near the Trolley Stop restaurant. Another free lot is down a driveway on Ellicott Mills Drive. Finally, the two lots at the courthouse, 2 blocks from the historic district, have 200 free spaces. The walk is short, though uphill on the way back to your car. A good brochure from the visitor center explains where and how to park.

WHERE TO EAT

Ellicott City has 17 restaurants along its narrow streets. For traditional French, don't miss wonderful **Tersiguel's French Country Restaurant,** 8293 Main St. (✆ **410/465-4004;** www.tersiguels.com). **La Palapa,** 8307 Main St. (✆ **410/465-0070;** www.lapalapagrill.com), serves Mexican in a gaily decorated atmosphere. **Cacao Lane Restaurant,** 8066 Main St. (✆ **410/461-1378;** www.cacaolane.net), is a casual spot with a Continental menu. Light-rock musicians perform Friday and Saturday evenings. The **Ellicott Mills Brewing Company,** 8308 Main St. (✆ **410/313-8141;** www.ellicottmillsbrewing.com), brews its own beer to accompany the German and pub-style entrees. Tea is served at **Tea on the Tiber,** 8081 Main St. (✆ **410/480-8000;** www.teaonthetiber.com), Thursday through Sunday afternoon.

WHAT TO SEE & DO

Ghost Tours of Ellicott City are offered April through November, Friday and Saturday at 8:30pm. Reservations are a must; call ✆ **800/288-8747** or 410/313-1900.

The **Ellicott City B&O Railroad Station,** 2711 Maryland Ave. (✆ **410/313-1413;** www.ecborail.org), America's oldest train station, houses artifacts and model trains. Annie Oakley and Charles Dickens once passed through. Hours are Wednesday through Sunday from 11am to 4pm. Admission is $5 adults, $4 seniors, $3 for children.

The Thomas Isaac Log Cabin, 8398 Main St. (www.thomasisaaclogcabin.net), a settler's cabin, was built about 1780—making it the town's oldest residence (Fri–Sat and Mon 1–6pm and Sun noon–5pm). It's decorated to look like a way station on the national road. (Not that it was ever used that way, but it's interesting.)

The yellow 1889 **Howard County Firehouse Museum** sits perched above the historic district at 3829 Church Rd. It's the town's oldest firehouse and is open Saturday and Sunday, 1 to 4pm.

The town also features the 1879 **Colored School,** Howard County's oldest publicly funded school for African-American children. Because it isn't within walking distance—it's just past the historic district at 8683 Frederick Rd.—it only opens at 3pm on Saturday and Sunday when there are visitors. Or call ✆ **410/313-1428** to make an appointment. All three historic buildings are closed November until April.

Head east on Frederick Road—called Main Street in the historic district—where you'll find the **Benjamin Banneker Historical Park and Museum,** 300 Oella Ave. (✆ **410/887-1081**). Dedicated to the first African-American "man of science," the modern museum has interactive exhibits about Banneker, who surveyed the land for construction of Washington, DC. The park has a log cabin, simulating Banneker's house, lots of green space, and nature trails. It's open Tuesday through Saturday from 10am to 4pm; a $3 donation is suggested. The 138-acre park is open dusk to dawn. Take Frederick Road east across Patapsco River Bridge; turn left at Oella Avenue.

SHOPPING

Shopping is the thing to do here among the antiques and gift shops on Main Street and the side streets. Hours are usually 10am to 6pm; stores close on Monday or Tuesday.

For home decor, stop at **Cottage Antiques,** 8181 Main St. (✆ **410/465-1412**); **Joan Eve,** 8018 Main St. (✆ **410/750-1210**); **Taylor's Antique Mall,** 8197 Main St. (✆ **410/465-4444**), and **Su Casa,** 8307 Main St. (✆ **410/465-4100**).

Ellicott's Country Store, 8180 Main St. (✆ **410/465-4482**), is worth a visit for the architecture—it's considered the oldest duplex in the country. Handcrafted gifts are featured at **Discoveries,** 8055 Main St. (✆ **410/461-9600**).

The **Forget-Me-Not Factory,** 8044 Main St. (✆ **410/465-7355**), stocks magic wands and fairy wings. **The Wine Bin,** 8390 Main St. (✆ **410/465-7802**), stocks a wide array of modestly priced wines.

Havre de Grace

Havre de Grace—tucked up near the Mason-Dixon line, 28 miles northeast of Baltimore—is primarily a sailing town now, though it was once an important Colonial crossroads. In fact, it is said that a single vote kept it from becoming the new nation's capital. Today, it makes an excellent stop either to or from Baltimore. It's known for good restaurants, charming shops, a lighthouse, and stunning views of the spot where the Susquehanna River becomes the Chesapeake Bay.

The area was originally home to the Susquehannocks, with the first European settlers arriving in 1658. First called Harmer's Town, it soon became the location of a river ferry, which operated for 170 years. After the Revolutionary War, it adopted its current name from a suggestion by French soldiers who lovingly compared it to La Havre back home. This was a popular destination in the early 20th century, when a famous racetrack drew the likes of the legendary Seabiscuit, Man o' War, and Citation. Today, the town is much quieter, but it remains a crossroads—for trains racing across the river, for barges carrying stone down the bay, and for people speeding along I-95.

ESSENTIALS

GETTING THERE You could sail into Havre de Grace from the lower Chesapeake Bay. Most people, however, drive. It's only 4 minutes off I-95 at Exit 89 (Rte. 155). Take Route 155 east and go under the Route 40 bridge. Turn right on Juniata Street, left on Otsego Street, and right on Water Street, and you'll be heading into town along the water's edge. Parking is available on the street, at the parks and museums, and at each end of the promenade.

VISITOR INFORMATION The **Havre de Grace Tourism Commission** is at 450 Pennington Ave., between Union Avenue and Market Street (✆ **800/851-7756** or 410/939-2100; www.hdgtourism.com). Check the website for maps and sightseeing information. Pick up a walking-tour guide and the handy museum guide.

SPECIAL EVENTS In early May, the **reenactment of the attack on Havre de Grace** in the War of 1812 (✆ **410/939-5780**) takes place on the Lock House grounds. Mid-August brings the **Havre de Grace Seafood Festival** (✆ **410/939-1525**) to Tydings Park, with auctions and a crab-calling contest. On the weekend after Labor Day, the **Duck Fair** (✆ **410/939-3739**) celebrates wildlife art at the Havre de Grace Decoy Museum and grounds. **First Fridays,** from May to December, feature street performances and specials at restaurants and shops.

WHERE TO STAY

Because Havre de Grace is up Route 40 from Aberdeen Proving Ground, a military installation, there are plenty of chain hotels nearby, such as **Days Inn** (✆ **410/272-8500**), **Courtyard by Marriott, Aberdeen at Ripken Stadium** (✆ **410/272-0440**), and the **Holiday Inn** (✆ **410/272-8100**).

Currier House Bed & Breakfast This B&B is a few steps from the promenade, lighthouse, and several museums. The 1790 farmhouse is filled with antiques reflecting the days when Havre de Grace attracted hunters and racing fans. It's a homey place with a wide front porch, cozy parlor, and quiet backyard. The rooms are small and simply but comfortably furnished; two have balconies with water views.

800 S. Market St., Havre de Grace, MD 21078. www.currierhouse.com. ✆ **800/827-2889** or 410/939-7886. 4 units. $95–$135 double. Rates include full breakfast. AE, DISC, MC, V. Free parking. *In room:* A/C, TV/VCR, hair dryer, no phone, free Wi-Fi.

The Old Chesapeake Hotel ★★ The owners have converted several buildings near their original inn into guest suites. The historic building houses a restaurant, **Chiapparelli's,** and four suites. Two Victorian homes, the O'Neil and the Hitchcock, and three brick apartment buildings offer spacious surroundings popular with business travelers. Though there's a nod to local history, the operative word here is comfort.

400 N. Union Ave., Havre de Grace, MD 21078. www.oldchesapeakehotel.com. ✆ **410/939-5440.** Fax 410/939-8020. 30 units. $99–$159 double. AE, MC, V. Free parking. **Amenities:** Restaurant. *In room:* A/C, TV, fridge, hair dryer, Internet.

The Spencer Silver Mansion ★★★ This granite grande dame will take you back to Havre de Grace's gay '90s. From the wraparound porch to the 12-foot ceilings, the 1896 B&B offers an elegant yet warm welcome. All that heavy furniture and Victorian-style decor could be intimidating, but the innkeeper works hard to keep it cozy. Big windows give the bedrooms an airy feel; the Iris Room even has a whirlpool tub. A carriage house just past the garden has a sitting room, kitchenette, large bedroom with two window seats, and bathroom with whirlpool; it sleeps four.

200 S. Union Ave., Havre de Grace, MD 21078. www.spencersilvermansion.com. ✆ **800/780-1485** or 410/939-1485. 5 units, 2 with shared bathroom. $85–$160 double. Rates include full breakfast. AE, DC, DISC, MC, V. Free parking. Children and pets welcome. **Amenities:** Fridge and microwave; tea service. *In room:* A/C, TV/DVD, free Wi-Fi.

Vandiver Inn This sprawling Victorian mansion, built in 1886, is on the National Register of Historic Places. It's on tree-lined Union Avenue, 2 blocks from the water. Bedrooms come in all sizes—some can be connected to create a suite. A spacious honeymoon suite has a gas fireplace, four-poster bed, and whirlpool tub. Two guesthouses offer a little more privacy. ***Note:*** This is a popular wedding venue with music and dancing many weekends. Monday night supper is open to the public.

301 S. Union Ave., Havre de Grace, MD 21078. www.vandiverinn.com. ✆ **800/245-1655** or 410/939-5200. Fax 410/939-5202. 17 units. $129–$159 double. Rates include full breakfast. AE, DISC, MC, V. Free parking. *In room:* A/C, TV, fridge, hair dryer, free Wi-Fi.

WHERE TO EAT

The Laurrapin AMERICAN Here is where Chesapeake cuisine meets the rest of the world. Lobster is added into the crab cake; gazpacho is seasoned with Old Bay. Salmon is served *piccata,* with a lemon caper sauce, or Chesapeake-style with crab. Try cioppino from the west coast or mahimahi caught off Ocean City. Brunch is served Sundays only.

209 N. Washington St. ✆ **410/939-4956.** www.laurrapin.com. Reservations recommended on weekends. Main courses $7–$14 lunch, $13–$25 dinner. MC, V. Tues–Thurs 11am–10pm; Fri–Sat 11am–2am; Sun noon–6pm.

MacGregor's Restaurant ★★ SEAFOOD High above the water, MacGregor's boasts a view from every table. Food is served on the deck and in the two-tiered dining room at lunch, dinner, Sunday brunch, and weekday happy hour. The menu is heavy on seafood items like crab dip, crab cakes, and lobster fettuccine; the Dijon-encrusted rockfish filet has won awards. This casual spot with brick walls is a place for fun—there's live music on Fridays and Saturdays, as well as Sundays in summer.

331 St. John St. ✆ **800/300-6319** or 410/939-3003. www.macgregorsrestaurant.com. Reservations suggested for dinner. Main courses $9–$15 lunch, $18–$26 dinner. AE, MC, V. Mon–Thurs 11am–10pm; Fri–Sat 11am–11pm; Sun 10am–9pm.

Tidewater Grille ★★★ SEAFOOD/STEAKS Here you might get so caught up in the action on the river and beyond, you could forget to eat. Trains race past on the nearby bridge; sailboats and barges skim across the water. The food is worth paying attention to: everything from delicately seasoned crab cakes, burgers, soups, salads, and sandwiches to pasta, prime rib, lamb chops, and fresh fish, all served all day. In pretty weather, eat on the deck—it's heaven. There are transient slips for hungry boaters, a children's menu, and entertainment on weekends.

300 Franklin St. ✆ **410/939-3313** or 410/575-7045. www.thetidewatergrille.com. Reservations required for parties of 6 or more. Main courses $8–$34. AE, DC, MC, V. Sun–Thurs 11am–10pm; Fri–Sat 11am–11pm.

WHAT TO SEE & DO

Lots of visitors come for the water views—which you can see from the **promenade ★★★**, the parks, and several restaurants. The **Millard E. Tydings Memorial Park** has room for a picnic, or you can bring your fishing rod to the **Frank J. Hutchins Memorial Park.** The half-mile promenade takes pedestrians (and bikers before 10am) along the southeast edge of town. It starts (or ends) at the Concord Point Lighthouse and winds through wetlands and along the shore to Tydings Park. Along the way, stop at the Havre de Grace Decoy Museum or the Havre de Grace Maritime Museum.

The town boasts six small museums and historic sites: four in town and two on the outskirts. They take only an hour or two to walk through, and admission is downright cheap: An adult can visit all six for less than $20. Hours are limited to the weekends, except the decoy and maritime museums, which are open daily.

Concord Point Lighthouse ★★★ This stout 36-foot-tall lighthouse at the headwaters of the bay has been watching over sailors since 1827—it's one of the oldest continuously operating lighthouses on the East Coast.

Concord and Lafayette sts., at north edge of promenade. ✆ **410/939-3213.** www.concordpointlighthouse.org. Free admission. Apr–Oct Sat–Sun 1–5pm. Closed major holidays.

Havre de Grace Decoy Museum ★★ Decoys are the star here, where the carved geese and ducks range from purely functional to fine art. The first-floor exhibits look at decoys as tools, while the second-floor decoys are exhibited as folk and fine art. Don't miss the full-size figure of R. Madison Mitchell, one of the best-known carvers in this decoy-carving capital. The museum has re-created in 3-D a photo of Mitchell by the famous Baltimore photographer Aubrey Bodine.

215 Giles St. ✆ **410/939-3739.** www.decoymuseum.com. Admission $6 adults, $5 seniors, $2 children 9–18. Mon–Sat 11am–4:30pm; Sun noon–4pm. Closed Jan 1, Easter, Thanksgiving, and Dec 25.

Havre de Grace Maritime Museum Exhibits tell the story of Havre de Grace's maritime commerce, with most of the items donated by local residents—including a replica of a shad shack and artifacts from 400 years of fishing and crabbing. Expansion in 2009 added exhibit space and provided ground-floor homes for the Susquehanna Flats Environmental Center's ecology programs and the Chesapeake Wooden Boat Builders School. Stop here to see boats, from sailboats to canoes, under construction.

100 Lafayette St. ✆ **410/939-4800.** www.hdgmaritimemuseum.org. Free admission. June–Aug daily 10am–5pm; Sept–May Wed and Fri–Mon 10am–5pm.

Mount Felix Winery Wines produced at this family-owned establishment pay homage to historical figures from the area, including John Adlum, the father of American viticulture.

2000 Level Rd. (off Rte.155). ✆ **410/939-0913.** www.mountfelix.com. Tasting room Wed–Sun 11am–5pm, Sun noon–5pm.

Rock Run Historic Area at Susquehanna State Park Sure, this is a great park for hiking along the Susquehanna River, climbing the hills, and riding a bike or horse along the miles of paths through the forest—but the historic area is worth a visit as well. Start at the Jersey Toll House (now an information center for the park) for maps and to see if there are any closings. Also in this area are the Rock Run Grist Mill, built in 1794, the Rock Run Mansion which was under repairs at press time, and the Steppingstone Museum (described below).

Off Rte. 155, 3 miles northwest of Havre de Grace. ✆ **410/734-9035.** Free admission. Park daily 9am–sunset; historic buildings Sat–Sun 1–5pm Memorial Day to Labor Day.

Steppingstone Museum ★ Steppingstone, in Susquehanna State Park, celebrates the area's agricultural history with demonstrations of the rural arts. Visitors can see the 1772 farmhouse, blacksmith forge, a 1900-era general store, veterinary office from the 1800s, and cannery. The farm is the site of a Civil War encampment in May, Scottish Festival in June, and Fall Harvest Festival in September. Of special note are the collections of quilts, toys, and hats.

461 Quaker Bottom Rd., off Rte. 155. ✆ **410/939-2299.** Admission $2 adults, free for children under 13. May–Sept Sat–Sun 1–5pm.

Susquehanna Museum of Havre de Grace ★ ☺ This restored 1840 lock tender's home, listed on the National Register of Historic Places, sat at the end of the Susquehanna and Tidewater Canal, where the canal emptied into the river. The canal is no longer used, but the pivot bridge has been reconstructed so visitors can see how it worked. Inside the house are kitchen gadgets (which the kids can touch), a massive Steinway piano, a century-old bicycle with canvas tires, and even the last lock tender's wedding coat. You can also see changing exhibits and a video on the town's history. In early December, don't miss the candlelight boutique with gifts, wreaths, and food; it's part of the town's Christmas Candlelight Tour, held the second Sunday in December.

817 Conesteo St., at northern edge of town. ✆ **410/939-5780.** www.thelockhousemuseum.org. Free admission. Sat–Sun 1–5pm.

TOURS & BOAT RIDES

The ***Martha Lewis*** ★ (✆ **410/939-4078;** www.chesapeakeheritage.org), docked at Tydings Park, offers cruises on most weekends from May to mid-October. Summer visitors can learn about sailing one of the last skipjacks on the bay—the 1955 boat is still a working girl, spending her winters dredging for oysters in the Chesapeake Bay. Oyster dredging trips are available in November. Call for reservations. The Mississippi riverboat ***Lantern Queen*** (✆ **410/939-1468;** www.lanternqueen.com) offers dinner and sunset cruises from its dock at Hutchins Park, at the foot of Congress Avenue. Call for reservations and sailing schedule.

SHOPPING

Havre de Grace's shops are about 7 blocks north of the promenade. Though it can be a pleasant walk along tree-lined Union Avenue or Market Street, it might be worth driving the short distance if it's a sultry day. Parking is free but limited to 2 hours.

Antiques shops dot Franklin and Washington streets. For furniture, stop at **Bayside Antiques,** 232 N. Washington St. (✆ **410/939-9397**). Decoy fans will want to stop at **Vincenti Decoys,** 353 Pennington Ave. (✆ **410/734-7709**). Chocolates are made on the premises at family-owned **Bomboy's,** 329 Market St. (✆ **410/939-2924;** www.bomboyscandy.com), and ice cream is served in their shop across the street.

OUTDOOR ACTIVITIES

BIKING **Biller's Bikes,** 450 Franklin St. (✆ **443/502-2377**), rents bikes for about $25 a day. Take them along Havre de Grace's quiet back lanes or head over to the trails in nearby Susquehanna State Park. They also offer a bridge crossing service for those who want to cross the Susquehanna to continue biking up the East Coast

Greenway; make arrangements 48 hours in advance. It's open Tuesday to Sunday in warm weather, more limited the rest of the year.

BOATING Boat ramps are at Millard E. Tydings Memorial Park, Frank J. Hutchins Memorial Park, and Jean Roberts Memorial Park. The launching fee is $8. **Tidewater Marina,** 100 Bourbon St. (✆ **410/939-0950**), has transient boat slips. Experienced sailors can charter a yacht from **BaySail** (✆ **410/939-2869;** www.baysail.net). It also has 1- to 5-day courses for everyone from beginners to advanced sailors.

GOLFING **Bulle Rock,** 320 Blenheim Lane (✆ **410/939-8887;** www.bullerockgolf.com), home of several LPGA tournaments, is open to the public. Be warned; it has a reputation not only for its good looks but its challenging holes.

HIKING Trails through **Susquehanna State Park** offer pretty views of the Susquehanna River, and are open to hikers, bikers, horses, and cross-country skiers. If you go by way of the **Lower Susquehanna Heritage Greenway,** it's possible to walk to the dam—which is quite a sight. The huge concrete dam holds back the mighty river, reducing it to a shallow rocky bed.

KAYAKING **Old Town Parasail,** 211 Congress Ave. (✆ **410/688-2397**), rents kayaks at Hutchins Park for $15 an hour or $50 for half a day mid-May to September. They also rent canoes and pedal boats.

PARASAILING **Old Town Parasail,** 211 Congress Ave. (✆ **410/688-2397**), offers flights for $30 to $70 mid-May to September. Ride along for $15.

MARYLAND'S TWO CAPITALS: ANNAPOLIS & ST. MARY'S CITY

5

Maryland's two capitals, present-day Annapolis and the state's first capital, St. Mary's City, are 86 miles—and 3 centuries—apart. Annapolis thrives today, while St. Mary's City has disappeared. But St. Mary's is reemerging, with archaeological digs and reconstruction of the colony's first town.

Annapolis retains much of its Colonial heritage. The State House is where George Washington resigned as commander-in-chief and Congress ratified the treaty to end the Revolutionary War. More than 1,500 Colonial buildings are scattered along the narrow brick streets—more than in any other town in the country. Annapolis is also a college town, home to the United States Naval Academy and to St. John's College, known for its "Great Books" curriculum.

Get out your boat shoes (no socks, please; this is Annapolis) and you'll be appropriately dressed for a visit to Maryland's capital. Annapolitans cherish their place in history and on the water. This is a perfect place for strolling, taking in some history, having a bite of local seafood and getting a little Chesapeake Bay spray in your face.

THINGS TO DO You can visit the same sights George Washington saw on his way between the **Charles Carroll House** and the **State House.** If you prefer, look to the future with a tour of the **U.S. Naval Academy.** The **Chesapeake Bay** beckons whether you climb aboard a tour boat, a schooner, or a kayak.

SHOPPING Unique shops in the **Historic District,** mostly on Main Street and Maryland Avenue, offer good souvenirs: handmade pottery, antiques and T-shirts, a good bottle of wine, or a book of poetry.

EATING & DRINKING Give Annapolitans a crab cake and a beer or glass of wine, sit them by the water or at a sidewalk table, and they'll be happy. Choose from Colonial taverns, casual eateries, or sidewalk tables in the **Historic District.** Across Spa Creek, **Eastport's** Restaurant Row offers seafood and steak with water views. **City Dock** shops and the **Market House** have snacks perfect for a dockside picnic. Along **West Street** restaurants feature fusion, tapas, or whatever's the new thing.

NIGHTLIFE & ENTERTAINMENT Sailors head to **Ego Alley** and **Eastport.** Music lovers seek out live acts at small spots on **West Street.** Local talent fills the stages of several theatres in the **Historic District.** The **Maryland Hall for the Creative Arts** is home to local opera, ballet, and classical music.

ORIENTATION

Arriving

BY PLANE **Baltimore/Washington International Thurgood Marshall Airport** (✆ **800/I-FLY-BWI** [435-9294] or 410/859-7111; www.bwiairport.com) is 24 miles north of Annapolis, off I-295 (the Baltimore-Washington Pkwy.). Domestic airlines serving BWI include **American** (✆ 800/433-7300), **Continental** (✆ 800/525-0280), **Delta** (✆ 800/221-1212), **Southwest** (✆ 800/435-9792), **United** (✆ 800/241-6522), and **U.S. Airways** (✆ 800/428-4322).

To get to Annapolis from the airport, follow I-97 south to U.S. Route 50. Various exits will take you into town (although many chain hotels are right off Rte. 50). The Rowe Boulevard exit is the most direct one to the Historic District. **SuperShuttle** (✆ **800/258-3826;** www.supershuttle.com) charges about $30 between BWI and Annapolis. A taxi is about $45 one-way; call **BWI Airport Taxi** at ✆ **410/859-1103.**

BY TRAIN Train passengers can get from the BWI station to Annapolis with airport shuttles, including SuperShuttle (see above) and **Airport Shuttle** (✆ **800/776-0323;** theairportshuttle.com). The cost is about $40 one-way.

BY CAR From Baltimore and points north, take I-695 (the Baltimore Beltway) to I-97 south to U.S. Route 50 east. Rowe Boulevard from U.S. Route 50 will take you into downtown. From Washington, DC, take U.S. Route 50 east off the Washington Beltway (I-495) to Rowe Boulevard.

BY BOAT Docking at the Annapolis City Dock or moorings in the harbor are available on a first-come, first-served basis. Moorings cost $30 for boats under 45 feet. Dock fees are $7 an hour for boats up to 50 feet, $15 for bigger vessels. Electric is extra. Pay fees at the Harbormaster's Office on the City Dock. For information, call ✆ **410/263-7973,** or e-mail harbormaster@ci.annapolis.md.us.

BY BUS **Greyhound** (✆ **800/231-2222** or 410/263-7964; www.greyhound.com) offers service to 308 Chinquapin Round Rd. **Dillon's Bus Service** (✆ **800/827-3490** or 410/647-2321; www.dillonbus.com) runs commuter buses to DC, with stops at the Navy/Marine Corps Stadium, Harry S. Truman Park & Ride, and West Street. It costs $4.25 one-way. The **Maryland Transit Administration** (✆ **866/743-3682** or 410/539-5000; www.mtamaryland.com) provides commuter bus service between Annapolis and Baltimore, as well as Washington, DC, connecting to some of the MTA's Light Rail stops.

Visitor Information

The **Annapolis and Anne Arundel Conference and Visitors Bureau** (✆ **410/280-0445;** www.visit-annapolis.org) runs a visitor center at 26 West St., just west of Church Circle. Trolley and walking tours (p. 117) depart from here daily. The volunteers will make recommendations and reservations for tours, dinner, and accommodations. A continuously running film gives visitors a taste of Annapolis's charms (daily

9am–5pm, except Jan 1, Thanksgiving, and Dec 25). The bureau also runs an information booth at the City Dock during warm weather.

City Layout

The streets of downtown Annapolis radiate from two circles: **State Circle** and **Church Circle.** The three main streets of the Historic District are Main, Maryland, and West. Main Street leads from Church Circle to the City Dock. Maryland Avenue stretches from State Circle to the walls of the U.S. Naval Academy. West Street runs from Church Circle to Westgate Circle and out to Routes 2 and 50. The U.S. Naval Academy, surrounded by a high gray wall, is in its own enclave, east of downtown.

GETTING AROUND

BY ANNAPOLIS CIRCULATOR Park in one of the four city garages and ride the **Annapolis Circulator** (✆ **410/263-7964;** www.annapolis.gov/transport) for free all over the Historic District by showing your garage parking stub. It's free to ride between stops in the Historic District. A ride from the parking lot at the Navy/Marine Corps Stadium into downtown costs $2. Hail the circulator bus as you would a cab. The Circulator operates 6:30am to midnight Sunday through Thursday and until 2:30am on Friday and Saturday. The buses run about 10 minutes apart in a loop from the Marriott Waterfront to the City Dock to Church Circle out West Street to Westgate Circle.

BY BUS Regular Annapolis bus service can get visitors all around town, from the Historic District to West Annapolis and the shopping centers near Route 50. (The Brown route shuttles between the City Dock and Westfield Annapolis Mall. Base fare is $1.50; exact change is required.) Buses run every 45 minutes, Monday through Saturday, from 6am to 7pm, Sunday from 8am to 7pm. Get a schedule at **www.annapolis.gov/transport**.

BY CAR Car-rental firms in Annapolis include **Budget,** 2002 West St. (✆ **410/266-5225**); **Discount,** 1032 West St. (✆ **410/269-6645**); and **Enterprise,** 1023 Spa Rd. (✆ **410/268-7751**).

Parking is limited in the Historic District, where streets are narrow and much of the 18th-century layout is intact. Visitors are encouraged to leave their cars in a park-and-ride lot on the edge of town, off Rowe Boulevard just west of the Navy/Marine Corps Stadium for $5, and then take the Circulator downtown (see above). This is an especially good idea on festival days, such as one of the boat shows.

Parking garages can be found behind the visitor center off Northwest Street ($12 a day), on Duke of Gloucester Street behind City Hall ($16 a day), and two on West Street. These two, the Knighton and Park Place, only cost $5 a day. You can also try your luck at metered parking at the City Dock or on the street. If you park on a side street, look for parking restriction signs; without a permit, parking is limited to 2 hours. If you come on a summer weekend, look for the parking valet near the City Dock.

Cars with handicapped tags can park at meters for twice the time limit at no charge. In residential districts, they may park 4 hours.

BY TAXI Call **Annapolis Cab** (✆ **410/268-0022**) or **Yellow Cab** (✆ **410/268-1212**) for taxi service.

BY WATER TAXI The **Water Taxi** (✆ **410/263-0033**) operates from the City Dock to restaurants and other destinations along Spa and Back creeks. You can also call for a water taxi, just as you would a land taxi, and get picked up from your boat or waterfront location. If you're at a restaurant, ask the waiter to call for a ride back. It's a handy way to avoid the parking hassle as well as a pleasant sightseeing experience. Fares range from $2 to $6. Hours from May to October are Monday through Thursday from 10am to 11pm, Friday from 10am to 1am, Saturday from 9am to 1am, and Sunday from 9am to 11pm. In the off season, the shuttle operates Friday 4 to 11pm, Saturday 10am to 11pm, and Sunday 10am to 7pm.

[Fast FACTS] ANNAPOLIS

Area Code The area codes in Annapolis are **410** and **443.**

Emergencies Dial ✆ **911** for fire, police, or ambulance.

Hospital Go to **Anne Arundel Medical Center,** 2001 Medical Pkwy., Jennifer Road off Route 50 (✆ **443/481-1000**).

Liquor Laws Places serving alcoholic beverages may stay open from 6am to 2am, except on Sunday and election days. The minimum age for buying or consuming alcohol is 21.

Newspapers & Magazines The local daily newspaper is the Annapolis ***Capital.*** The Baltimore ***Sun*** and the ***Washington Post*** are also widely available. The leading monthly magazine is ***What's Up? Annapolis.***

Pharmacies Try **CVS,** 123 Main St. (✆ **410/295-3061**).

Post Office The main branch is at 1 Church Circle (✆ **410/263-1083**), open Monday through Friday from 9am to 5pm.

Taxes The local sales tax is 6%. The local hotel tax is an additional 7%.

WHERE TO STAY

Downtown Annapolis offers a mix of big hotels, historic inns, and bed-and-breakfasts, while Eastport has several good B&Bs. Accommodations in the Historic District are convenient but pricey. ***Note:*** All major hotels have rooms accessible for travelers with disabilities, but most inns and bed-and-breakfasts do not. Also keep in mind that special events—the Naval Academy's Parents' Weekend in late summer, Commissioning Week in May, Army-Navy games, and the two Annapolis Boat Shows in October, to name a few—send hotel prices skyrocketing.

A number of more affordable chain hotels are on Route 50, a 15-minute ride from the Historic District. These generally cost less and offer pools and larger rooms; some offer shuttle service to downtown and Eastport. The **Country Inn and Suites by Carlson,** 2600 Housley Rd. (✆ **800/830-5222** or 410/571-6700; www.countryinns.com), is across from Westfield Annapolis and has an indoor pool and a shuttle into downtown. The **Courtyard Annapolis,** 2559 Riva Rd. (✆ **800/392-5407** or 410/266-1555; www.marriott.com/bwian), has an indoor pool. **Sheraton Annapolis Hotel,** 173 Jennifer Rd. (✆ **800/325-3535** or 410/266-3131; www.sheraton.com/annapolis), has a shuttle and indoor pool.

Expensive

The Annapolis Inn ★★★ This Georgian-themed inn was good enough for Thomas Jefferson's doctor in the 18th century, and it's perfect for a romantic getaway today. The three bedrooms on separate levels are shrines to comfort, with plush beds,

Annapolis

HOTELS ■

The Annapolis Inn **28**
Annapolis Marriott Waterfront **36**
Eastport House **42**
Flag House Inn **27**
Gatehouse of Annapolis B&B **24**
Georgian House B&B **10**
Governor Calvert House **19**
The Inn at 30 Maryland **21**
Inn at Horn Point **43**
Loews Annapolis Hotel **4**
Maryland Inn **9**
O'Callaghan Annapolis Hotel **2**
Robert Johnson House **17**
Scotlaur Inn **11**
Westin Annapolis **1**

RESTAURANTS ◆

Annapolis Ice Cream Company **15**
Aqua Terra **12**
Boatyard Bar & Grill **39**
Cafe Normandie **13**
Carrol's Creek **38**
Castlebay Irish Pub **14**
Chick & Ruth's Delly **11**
Federal House Bar & Grille **31**
Leeward Market **44**
Lemongrass **3**
Lewnes Steak House **40**
Level Small Plates Lounge **5**
Market House **32**
McGarvey's Saloon & Oyster Bar **30**
Middleton Tavern **29**
O'Leary's Seafood Restaurant **41**
Piccola Roma **16**
Rams Head Tavern & Fordham Brewing Co. **6**
Reynolds Tavern **8**
The Rockfish **37**
Treaty of Paris **9**

ATTRACTIONS ●

The Annapolis Maritime Museum **45**
The Banneker-Douglass Museum **7**
Charles Carroll House of Annapolis **35**
Chase-Lloyd House **23**
Hammond-Harwood House **22**
Historic Annapolis Museum at the St. Clair Wright Center **34**
The Kunta Kinte-Alex Haley Memorial **33**
Maryland State House **18**
St. John's College **20**
The Wiliam Paca House & Garden **25**
U.S. Naval Academy **26**

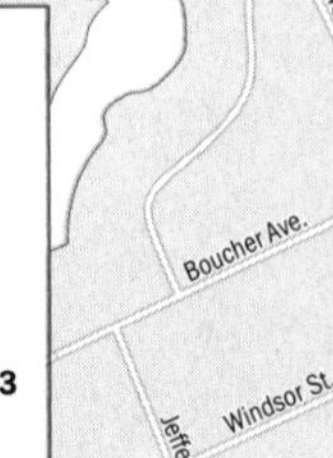

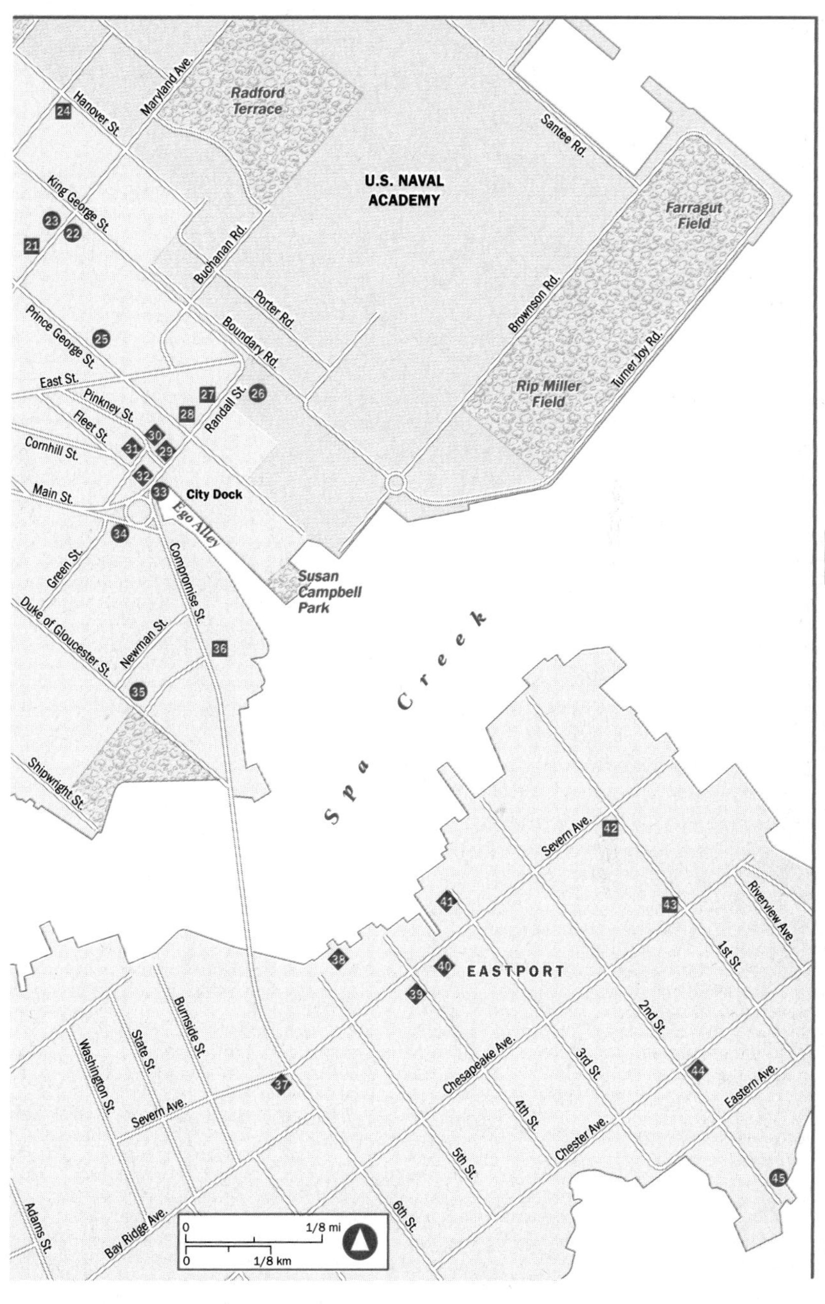

Radford Terrace
U.S. NAVAL ACADEMY
Farragut Field
Rip Miller Field
City Dock
Ego Alley
Susan Campbell Park
Spa Creek
EASTPORT
Hanover St.
Maryland Ave.
King George St.
Buchanan Rd.
Porter Rd.
Boundary Rd.
Santee Rd.
Brownson Rd.
Turner Joy Rd.
Prince George St.
East St.
Pinkney St.
Randall St.
Fleet St.
Cornhill St.
Main St.
Green St.
Compromise St.
Duke of Gloucester St.
Newman St.
Shipwright St.
Severn Ave.
Riverview Ave.
1st St.
2nd St.
3rd St.
4th St.
5th St.
6th St.
Chesapeake Ave.
Chester Ave.
Eastern Ave.
Burnside St.
State St.
Washington St.
Adams St.
Bay Ridge Ave.
0 1/8 mi
0 1/8 km
21
22
23
24
25
26
27
28
29
30
31
32
33
34
35
36
37
38
39
40
41
42
43
44
45

lush seating, and bathrooms with Jacuzzis and heated marble floors. There are no phones, televisions if you must, and wireless Internet access only if absolutely necessary. The Murray suite is roomiest with a separate sitting room. Up under the eaves, the Rutland with its rustic fireplace is coziest. A three-course breakfast is served on china and crystal in the dining room and, in warm weather, on the patio. Annapolis attractions are all close by. Want a boat charter, in-room massage, string quartet, or cooking lessons? The innkeepers do what they can to make your stay exactly as you want it.

144 Prince George St., Annapolis, MD 21401. www.annapolisinn.com. ✆ **410/295-5200.** Fax 410/295-5201. 3 units. $259–$479 double. Rates include full breakfast. AE, MC, V. Street parking only. *In room:* A/C, TV upon request, free Wi-Fi.

Annapolis Marriott Waterfront ★★ The only waterfront hotel in Annapolis, and the only one with boat docks for guest use, this six-story property attracts the nautical crowd. It sits in the middle of all the action, beside the City Dock overlooking Ego Alley and Spa Creek. Guest rooms have floor-to-ceiling windows; about three-quarters of the rooms have water views or waterfront balconies, while 20 look right out over the water. Two rooms have Jacuzzis. Most rooms have pullout chair beds. "Pure" rooms have special bedding, air filters, and are treated to reduce allergens. Historic photographs and ship models, including *Old Ironsides* and Hollywood's *African Queen,* adorn the public spaces.

80 Compromise St., Annapolis, MD 21401. www.annapolismarriott.com. ✆ **800/393-0047** or 410/268-7555. Fax 410/269-5864. 150 units. $269–$389 double; $349–$479 waterfront view. AE, DC, DISC, MC, V. Valet parking $22. **Amenities:** Indoor/outdoor restaurant and lounge; boat dock; fitness center; room service. *In room:* A/C, TV w/HBO, fridge and microwave on request, hair dryer, Wi-Fi (fee).

The Inn at 30 Maryland ★ The 1886 Queen Anne Victorian in the middle of Maryland Avenue is architecturally unusual. Its owners, a former chef and his wife, have outfitted their B&B with style and comfort. Rooms are large enough to stretch out in, especially two suites. These are more like double-sized rooms with sofas and refrigerators in a sitting area. The back suite has a porch overlooking the neighboring Chase-Lloyd House's gardens. Breakfast is cooked to order and served in the dining room, "cafe" room, or outside in warm weather. Children over age 12 are welcome.

30 Maryland Ave., Annapolis, MD 21401. www.30maryland.com. ✆ **410/263-9797.** 5 units. $169–$239 double; $219 –$269 suites. Rates include breakfast. AE, MC, V. On-street parking. **Amenities:** Refrigerator and microwave; snacks and drinks in cafe. *In room:* AC, TV w/FiOS and HBO, fridge, hair dryer, MP3 docking station, Wi-Fi.

Loews Annapolis Hotel ★★★ ☺ The Loews Annapolis is loaded with amenities (though they don't have a pool) and a friendly staff. Near Church Circle, within walking distance of the Historic District, this modern brick hotel has a tree-shaded courtyard entrance and sky-lit public areas. Guest rooms, in nautical colors, offer views of the skyline and historic area. Ask about packages for kids, grandparents traveling with children, or spa packages. A shuttle to the Historic District attractions is available.

126 West St., Annapolis, MD 21401. www.loewshotels.com. ✆ **800/526-2593** or 410/263-7777. Fax 410/263-0084. 215 units. $99–$329 double; $149–$379 suite. AE, DC, DISC, MC, V. Valet parking $22; self-parking $18. Pets accepted for a fee. **Amenities:** Restaurant; bar; coffee shop; concierge-level rooms; fitness center; spa. *In room:* A/C, TV, hair dryer, fridge and microwave upon request, umbrellas, Wi-Fi (fee).

O'Callaghan Annapolis Hotel ★★ This stylish Irish-owned hotel, sporting a contemporary Euro-style furniture in its spacious guest rooms, whispers low-key luxury—it would be vulgar to shout. New duvets and other enhancements, including fridges in most rooms, freshened the look in 2009. Eight units have balconies, some with table and chairs. Two suites are roomier, situated in the back of the hotel away from West Street traffic noise. If you're here on business, note the large desks, Internet access, and extensive 24-hour business center. The hotel provides free transportation in the Historic District. ***Eco-note:*** Rooms are outfitted with recycling bins.

174 West St., Annapolis, MD 21401. www.ocallaghanhotels-us.com. ✆ **410/263-7700.** Fax 410/990-1400. 120 units. $99–$289 double; $249–$439 suite. Higher on summer weekends and during special events. AE, DC, DISC, MC, V. Valet parking $18. **Amenities:** Restaurant; lounge; fitness center; room service. *In room:* A/C, TV w/pay movies and video games, fridge, hair dryer, Wi-Fi.

The Westin Annapolis ★★★ Annapolis' newest hotel anchors the west end of the town's redevelopment of West Street—and its sleek contemporary styling is a breath of fresh air. The tea-scented lobby houses a lounge with fireplace, and there's a **restaurant** that serves breakfast, lunch, and dinner. A shuttle bus will get you to and from the Historic District. The rooms feature big windows (great light but no great views), fluffy bedding, neutral colors, and the usual amenities. Three restaurants are nearby. The pool and fitness center are nicely outfitted. Packages include one with the nearby Aveda spa. Free "unwind" events are offered Monday to Friday 5 to 8pm.

100 Westgate Circle (corner of Taylor Ave. and West St.), Annapolis, MD 21401. www.westin.com/annapolis. ✆ **410/972-4300** or 800/937-8461. 225 units. $159–$409 double; $209–$509 suite. Small dogs accepted for a fee. AE, DC, DISC, MC, V. Valet parking $23; self-parking $5. **Amenities:** Restaurant; lounge; fitness center; room service; indoor pool; outdoor pool; whirlpool. *In room:* A/C, TV w/pay movies and video games, fridge, hair dryer, Wi-Fi (fee).

Moderate

Flag House Inn The flags waving from the front porch offer a hint of who's staying here: The innkeepers fly the flags of their guests' home states or nations. This 1870s Victorian beauty, down the street from the Naval Academy's main gate, offers good-size rooms with either one king-size or two twin beds. Accommodations are well kept and bright, with a nice mix of modern and antique pieces. Every unit has a ceiling fan; front rooms have sound machines to soften the traffic noise outside. One room, decorated in lavender toile, is downright spacious. The innkeepers are proud parents of a 1999 USNA graduate, and the house is well located for visitors to the Naval Academy and the town itself. When you arrive, knock on the right-hand door.

26 Randall St., Annapolis, MD 21401. www.flaghouseinn.com. ✆ **800/437-4825** or 410/280-2721. 5 units (shower only). $160–$300 double. Rates include full breakfast. MC, V. Free off-street parking. No children 12 and under. *In room:* A/C, ceiling fan, TV, free Wi-Fi.

The Gatehouse of Annapolis Bed & Breakfast In the shadow of the Naval Academy, this brick town house combines Colonial style with modern convenience. Often filled with USNA relatives, it is convenient to the Naval Academy and a short walk from the Historic District—and far enough out of the way to be quieter than places near Main Street. The best units are the two minisuites, each with a four-poster or sleigh bed, private sitting area, and bathroom. The fifth unit is available only as a two-room package with shared bathroom for $330. All come with fresh flowers, robes, and special soaps. The deck offers a quiet place to relax in the sun or under the stars.

249 Hanover St., Annapolis, MD 21401. www.gatehousebb.com. ✆ **888/254-7576** or 410/280-0024. 5 units. $200–$230 double. Rates include full breakfast. 2-night minimum stay and higher rates required some weekends. MC, V. Street parking only. *In room:* A/C, TV, free Wi-Fi.

Georgian House Bed & Breakfast ★ This B&B is one of the oldest structures in Annapolis. Its charm is enhanced by the modern conveniences and the location. Walk through the back gate, and you're on your way down Main Street. One room has a deck, one has a working fireplace, and another has a double shower.

170 Duke of Gloucester St., Annapolis, MD 21401. www.georgianhouse.com. © **800/557-2068** or 410/263-5618. 4 units. $189–$225 double. Rates include full breakfast. Rates higher on event weekends. AE, MC, V. Street parking only. **Amenities:** Fridge on 2nd floor; video/book library; microwave. *In room:* TV/VCR, free Wi-Fi.

Inexpensive

Gibson's Lodgings of Annapolis On a side street, this three-building complex is a quiet choice, yet it's only a few steps from the City Dock and Naval Academy. Two of the buildings are historic town houses: the Patterson (a 1760s Federal Georgian with five bedrooms) and the Berman (an 1890s house with a porch and nine bedrooms, one equipped for travelers with disabilities). Behind them is Lauer House, a 1988 addition with six suites, a full kitchen, and a sitting room that can serve as a conference room. The bedrooms are of varying sizes, and decorated with antiques and reproductions. A central garden and courtyard serve as a common area.

110 Prince George St., Annapolis, MD 21401. www.gibsonslodgings.com. © **877/330-0057** or 410/268-5555. Fax 410/268-2775. 21 units, 2 with shared bathroom. $129–$149 double with shared bathroom; $169–$259 double with private bathroom. Rates include continental breakfast. AE, MC, V. Free courtyard parking. Kids and pets welcome. *In room:* A/C, TV, hair dryer, free Wi-Fi.

Scotlaur Inn Bed & Breakfast The Scotlaur is the best value in the Historic District. It's housed in the top two floors of a three-story brick building; the ground floor belongs to Chick & Ruth's Delly (see "Where to Eat," below). Rooms are various sizes, with larger ones in front. Room 301 has the disadvantage of two flights of steep stairs, but it's large, bright, and has the best view, looking out on Main Street. A parking garage behind the inn is convenient but makes the back rooms a bit noisy.

165 Main St., Annapolis, MD 21401. www.scotlaurinn.com. © **410/268-5665.** 10 units. $95–$180 double. Rates include discounts on breakfast at Chick & Ruth's and parking. MC, V. 2-night minimum on weekends. *In room:* A/C, TV, hair dryer, free Wi-Fi.

Historic Hostelries

Historic Inns of Annapolis ★★ Clustered around the city's two key traffic circles, these hotels offer a taste of the historic. The buildings may date from colonial days but amenities such as flatscreen TVs and Wi-Fi are pure 21st century. Two buildings are on State Circle (location of the State House) and the third building fronts on Main Street at Church Circle. And each has its own personality. The Governor Calvert House serves as the check-in point and has the most conference and party space. The restaurant, lounge, and coffee shop are at the Maryland Inn—with the fitness center. The "RJ" has only sleeping rooms and so is the quietest.

Governor Calvert House, 58 State Circle, combines the 1727 house with a modern addition and has 51 rooms. Even if you are staying in the Maryland Inn or Robert Johnson, stop here to check in and the valet will take you and your luggage to your hotel. A continental breakfast is served every morning in a room with a glass floor. The floor covers the "hypocaust" used in the 1700s to keep Governor Calvert's house and his citrus trees warm. The reception desk is staffed 24/7. Rooms here look like typical hotel rooms, except for the nine Historic Queens, with nonworking fireplaces, hardwood floors, thick drapes, and crystal sconces. Accessible rooms are available for travelers with disabilities.

Renting a Home Away from Home

During U.S. Naval Academy's Parents' Weekend or Commissioning Week, many Annapolis homeowners rent their houses to the families of midshipmen. **Annapolis Accommodations** (✆ **410/ 263-3262;** www.stayannapolis.com) offers dozens of homes in the Historic District and on the waterfront, within about 12 miles of downtown, for rent during Commissioning Week, and on Boat Show weekends or for vacation rentals. Corporate rentals are also available. Homes range from one to five bedrooms. All are fully furnished, including linens and well-equipped kitchens; some have pools. Rates range from $250 a night for small rentals to up to $10,000 for Commissioning Week. House rentals are popular, with some dates very much in demand, so if you're interested, book well in advance.

The flatiron-shaped **Maryland Inn,** 16 Church Circle (at Main St.), has been operating as an inn since the 1770s. The location and helpful staff make it a good choice. The 44 rooms vary widely in size and layout although you can count on Colonial-style furnishings. Some rooms are cramped but others have fireplaces and extra room. The Hyde Suite (no. 217) is located in the narrow "tip" of the inn: The bath is wedged in the narrowest section while the sitting and sleeping rooms are spacious. Access is from a second-story porch. In winter, the aroma of wood smoke wafts through the building in keeping with its Colonial heritage.

The **Robert Johnson House,** 23 State Circle (btw. School and Francis sts.), overlooks the governor's mansion and the State House and has 30 rooms over four floors. The 29 artfully restored rooms have four-poster beds and antiques; each unit also has a private bathroom. The Peg Bednarsky Suite, honoring the longtime innkeeper, spreads over two levels and has access to the hotel's porch.

Historic Inns of Annapolis, 58 State Circle, Annapolis, MD 21401. www.historicinnsofannapolis.com. ✆ **800/847-8882** or 410/263-2641. Fax 410/268-3613. 124 units in 3 properties. $119–$399 double; rates may be higher on holiday weekends. AE, DC, DISC, MC, V. Valet parking $24. Check-in at the Governor Calvert House. **Amenities:** Restaurant; coffee shop; tavern; complimentary coffee and tea; fitness center, local shuttle. *In room:* A/C, flatscreen TV, hair dryer, free Wi-Fi.

Across the Spa Creek Bridge

Eastport is gaining interest as a place to live and a place to play. For centuries, it was home to Annapolis's working people: watermen, boat builders, and those who worked downtown or at the Naval Academy. Sailing schools and marinas, a handful of comfortable B&Bs, and Restaurant Row—down Severn Avenue—make this an attractive part of town for tourists. It's easy and friendly and can be a lot of fun.

Eastport House ★ This is the oldest standing house in Eastport, but it's been lovingly maintained. The owner had fun decorating the bedrooms, but she hasn't forgotten any necessities, like robes, fluffy bedding, even Sleep Number beds in two rooms. Breakfast is served in the dining room, or guests can sit on the broad side porch.

101 Severn Ave., Annapolis, MD 21403. www.eastporthouse.com. ✆ **410/295-9180.** 4 units. $150–$200 double. Rates include full breakfast. MC, V. Free parking. **Amenities:** Free use of bicycles; fridge. *In room:* A/C, TV, Wi-Fi.

Inn at Horn Point ★★ A 1902 house with a wraparound porch has been turned into a stylish B&B, filled with bright colors and bay windows. Rooms in the eco-friendly

B&B are named for Eastport's own Trumpy Yachts. While all are spacious, the Sequoia king suite on the second floor is luxurious with its own private porch, two-story-high sitting area with gas fireplace, and bathroom with claw-foot tub. Enchantress, the first-floor room, with roll-in shower, and its own private entrance, was specifically designed to be wheelchair accessible.

100 Chesapeake Ave., Annapolis, MD 21403. www.innathornpoint.com. © **410/268-1126.** 5 units. $169–$219 double; $239–$269 suite. Rates include breakfast. MC, V required to guarantee room; check or cash only for final payment. Free parking. **Amenities:** A room for those w/limited mobility. *In room:* A/C, TV on request, Internet.

WHERE TO EAT

In Annapolis you can eat at Colonial dining rooms, taverns, bistros, and waterside seafood houses. For families and travelers on the go, a wide selection of fast-food and family-style eateries are clustered at the intersection of Routes 50, 301, and 450, about 4 miles from downtown, near the Annapolis Shopping Plaza.

Expensive

Carrol's Creek ★★★ SEAFOOD For the best views of the waterfront and Annapolis skyline, along with imaginative food, head for this sleek waterfront spot in Eastport. Seating is available in a windowed dining room and on an umbrella-shaded porch. Start with the cream of crab soup—it's one of Maryland's best. Definitely a seafood place, the chef is quite creative, serving scallops tequila or herb-encrusted rockfish, for instance. Arrive by water taxi for the full waterfront experience. Come at lunch for a sunny view and the same delicious food at a fraction of the price.

410 Severn Ave., Eastport, MD 21403. © **410/263-8102.** www.carrolscreek.com. Reservations recommended. Main courses $8–$18 lunch, $21–$30 dinner; $24 Sun brunch buffet. AE, DC, DISC, MC, V. Mon–Thurs 11:30am–9pm; Fri–Sat 11:30am–10pm; Sun 10am–1:30pm and 3–9pm.

Lewnes Steakhouse ★ STEAKHOUSE In a clubby atmosphere of burgundy beadboard walls and leatherette booths with touches of brass, the Lewnes family serves up carefully chosen, carefully prepared prime steaks. The simple menu features steak, steak, steak, a couple of fish dishes, and crab cakes, with only a few appetizers and side dishes. The wine list—a veritable tome—is complicated enough. But if it's steak you want, served in a quiet atmosphere, this Eastport establishment is the place for you.

401 4th St., Eastport, MD 21403. © **410/263-1617.** www.lewnessteakhouse.com. Reservations recommended on weekends. Main courses $20–$40. AE, DC, DISC, MC, V. Mon–Sat 5–10pm; Sun 4–10pm.

Middleton Tavern ★ AMERICAN/SEAFOOD Established in 1750 as an inn for seafaring men, this restaurant also drew the likes of Washington, Jefferson, and Franklin. Restored and expanded, the City Dock landmark offers many seafood entrees, as well as steaks and chateaubriand for two. It's a nice mix of historic location and good food. At lunch, the menu includes pasta, sandwiches, and a few entrees. A drink on the tavern's front porch is a favorite summer activity for locals and visitors. There is piano music upstairs on weekends and other entertainment downstairs nightly.

2 Market Space (at Randall St.). © **410/263-3323.** www.middletontavern.com. Call ahead for priority seating. Main courses $10–$30 lunch, $16–$37 dinner. AE, DC, DISC, MC, V. Mon–Fri 11:30am–1:30am; Sat 11am–1:30am; Sun 10am–1:30am.

O'Learys Seafood Restaurant ★★ SEAFOOD Just over the Spa Creek Bridge, this Eastport spot has been a local favorite for over 20 years. Come here for the freshest seafood, including the chef's famous swordfish au poivre, served in a dining room awash in dark, warm tones. The menu lists other options such as duck, pork, and filet mignon. The wine list changes regularly and includes bottles from smaller vintners. Some find the main dining room noisy on weekends. The back room can be quieter.

310 3rd St., Eastport. ✆ **410/263-0884.** www.olearysseafood.com. Reservations strongly recommended. Main courses $29–$35. AE, DC, MC, V. Mon–Sat 5–10pm; Sun 5–9pm.

Moderate

Aqua Terra ★ GLOBAL Tucked into a storefront on Main Street, this restaurant offers a sleek, modern atmosphere, with adventurous food to match. Expect the fresh and inventive, small plates of jambalaya or sushi such as the surf and turf roll or a traditional entree. There are plenty of salads and flatbread pizzas, as well as a menu until 1am for weekend night owls.

164 Main St. ✆ **410/263-1985.** www.aquaterraofannapolis.com. Reservations recommended. Main courses $12–$30. AE, MC, V. Tues 4:30–10pm; Wed–Sat 11:30am–2pm and 4:30–10pm; Sun 11:30am–2:30pm and 4:30–9pm. Lounge open until 1am Fri and Sat.

Boatyard Bar & Grill ★★ AMERICAN/SEAFOOD Big and airy by day, crowded and fun by night, locals love the Boatyard—and so do visitors. You can count on the old reliables, such as crab dip and garlic mussels, as well as burgers and a delightful crab cake. The Caribbean/Chesapeake sailing atmosphere brings a little summer even to a wintry day. The lunch/dinner menu offers everything from sandwiches to steak and crab. There's live music on Thursdays. A market on the side offers prepared foods and box lunches (for picnics or boat rides). Breakfast is served Monday through Friday with brunch on weekends. The Boatyard is a member of the environmental group One Percent for the Planet.

Severn Ave. and 4th St., Eastport. ✆ **410/216-6206.** www.boatyardbarandgrill.com. Reservations not accepted. Main courses $5–$9 breakfast, lunch/dinner $9–$24 AE, DISC, MC, V. Daily 8am–midnight.

Café Normandie ★ FRENCH This rustic storefront in the heart of the Historic District offers the tastes and atmosphere of a French country restaurant. From its hearty onion soup to the delicate baked Brie, every starter is a hit. Entrees include such classics as crepes, chateaubriand for two, and breast of chicken Normandie. The chef uses locally produced foods and the house emphasizes sustainable practices. Breakfast is served weekends from 9am to noon.

185 Main St. ✆ **410/263-3382.** www.cafenormandie.com. Reservations recommended for dinner on weekends. Main courses $8–$15 breakfast, $12–$18 lunch, $14–$30 dinner. AE, DC, DISC, MC, V. Mon–Fri 11am–3:30pm and 5–10pm; Sat 9am–3:30pm and 5–10:30pm; Sun 9am–3:30pm and 5–10pm.

Castlebay Irish Pub IRISH In a town full of Irish pubs, here's one that stands out. The specialties are shepherd's pie, fish and chips, and corned beef and cabbage; the beef and lamb stews are exceptional. The lunch menu is lighter, with burgers and corned beef. A children's menu lists smaller portions of the traditional fare. Sunday brunch includes a full Irish breakfast. Irish and pop bands play Wednesday through Saturday nights.

193A Main St. ✆ **410/626-0165.** www.castlebayirishpub.com. Reservations advised for dinner. Main courses $9–$22 lunch, $12–$29 dinner. AE, DISC, MC, V. Mon–Sat 11am–midnight; Sun 10am–midnight.

Federal House Bar & Grille AMERICAN This 1813 building, with its exposed brick, old well-used bar, and dark wood furnishings has been drawing crowds for nearly 2 centuries. In its current incarnation, it has an all-day menu that mixes old (crab cakes and burgers) with new (macadamia-nut tilapia or seafood symphony with lemon butter sauce and Old Bay). Service is attentive, portions are generous, salads are crisp, and the cream of crab soup is rich with sherry. There's live music Wednesday through Friday, DJ on Saturday. Brunch is served at 10am on Sunday.

22 Market Space, City Dock. ✆ **410/268-2576.** www.federalhouserestaurant.com. Reservations recommended on weekends; none taken on holidays. Main courses $8–$25. AE, DISC, MC, V. Mon–Sat 11am–2am; Sun 10am–2am.

Level Small Plates Lounge SMALL PLATES One of West Street's newest eateries, Level focuses on locally sourced foods for its small-plates menu. You can find classics—crab dip, clams in a white wine and Pernod broth, grilled rockfish, and rockfish fish sticks—but if you're looking for excitement rather than comfort, they've got a few twists: bison satay or carpaccio, scallops with dinosaur kale, or pizza topped with duck. Portions are small, but the flavor is big. When there's a crowd, the noise level can be high. Most bottles of wine are offered for $38; pricier bottles are charged at the wholesale level plus a $38 corkage fee.

69 West St., Annapolis, MD 21401. ✆ **410/268-0003.** www.levelsmallplateslounge.com. Reservations strongly encouraged. Main courses $7–$12. AE, DISC, MC, V. Daily 4pm–1am.

McGarvey's Saloon & Oyster Bar PUB FARE/SEAFOOD When you need a good sandwich, cup of chowder, or burger to go with your beer, you can't beat McGarvey's. Two narrow rooms, both dominated by bars, are set with tiny marble-topped tables. Chicken- or crab-cake–topped Caesar salads, filet Béarnaise, and oyster stew, as well as heartier entrees, are available all the time—along with 30 craft beers. The specials are usually top-notch and a good value. Brunch is served on Sunday.

8 Market Space, City Dock. ✆ **410/263-5700.** www.mcgarveyssaloon.com. Reservations accepted Mon–Thurs only. Main courses $6–$13 lunch, $19–$27 dinner. AE, MC, V. Mon–Sat 11:30am–1am; Sun 10am–1am.

Piccola Roma ITALIAN The menu is bursting with Italian favorites—pasta, risotti, antipasti—at lunch and dinner. Dinnertime is romantic in small dining rooms. But stopping here for lunch will soothe your palate without hurting your wallet. Add a hefty wine list filled with Italian vintages and great bread baked by the restaurant's original owner. An Italian respite in the midst of Colonial America is most enjoyable.

200 Main St. ✆ **410/268-7898.** www.piccolaromaannapolis.com. Reservations recommended Fri–Sat nights. Main courses $10–$16 lunch, $16–$30 dinner. AE, DC, DISC, MC, V. Lunch daily 11:30am–3pm. Dinner Mon–Thurs 5:30–10pm; Fri–Sat 5–11pm; Sun 5–9pm.

Rams Head Tavern & Fordham Brewing Co. ★★ INTERNATIONAL Come for dinner in one of the cozy, brick-walled dining rooms, or for a drink and appetizers on the wisteria-covered heated patio. On a summer evening, the front sidewalk is the place to be. The all-day menu includes regional favorites, from the Chesapeake's own crab to Cajun jambalaya; and steaks are available at dinner. The storefront pub serves more than 170 beers, including seasonal selections from its microbrewery, the Fordham Brewing Company. Get a sampler to try them all. The Rams Head is also a favorite venue for live entertainment (p. 123).

33 West St. ✆ **410/268-4545.** www.ramsheadtavern.com. Reservations recommended for dinner. Main courses $8–$30. AE, DISC, MC, V. Mon–Sat 11am–2am; Sun 10am–2am. Meals served until 11pm; light fare until midnight.

Reynolds Tavern ★ TEA After a day of visiting historic sites, why not enjoy teatime in a Colonial-era tavern? It's a genteel affair, with aromatic pots of loose tea, scones piled high with jam and cream, tea sandwiches, and sweets. Afternoon tea is served from 11am to 5pm. Need something more filling? Hearty sandwiches, salads, and cream of crab soup are also on the lunch menu and dinner, with seafood and English favorites, served after 5pm.

7 Church Circle. ✆ **410/295-9555.** www.reynoldstavern.org. Reservations recommended. Main courses $9–$12 lunch, $14–$30 dinner; tea $17. AE, DISC, MC, V. Daily 11am–5pm; Wed–Sun 5–9pm.

The Rockfish ★ SEAFOOD Step out of Colonial days and into this contemporary restaurant—a "certified environmental steward"—serving an all-day menu of fresh seafood obtained from sustainable sources, as well as a few pasta dishes, stone-hearth pizzas, and chicken and ribs. The crab soup is done right, seasoned with herbs other than the standard Old Bay and studded with lump crab. Softshell crabs are a golden delight, and fish is accompanied by creative side dishes. A jazz brunch is served on Sunday 10am to 2pm. From downtown, the restaurant is an easy walk across the Spa Creek Bridge. The Rockfish has its own parking lot. There's a children's menu, too.

400 6th St., Eastport. ✆ **410/267-1800.** www.rockfishmd.com. Reservations strongly recommended. Main courses $10–$34. AE, DC, DISC, MC, V. Mon–Thurs 4:30–10pm; Fri–Sat 11:30am–11pm; Sun 10am–2pm and 4–9pm. Lounge stays open later.

Treaty of Paris AMERICAN In the Maryland Inn, this cozy dining room exudes an 18th-century ambience with its brick walls, Colonial-style furnishings, candlelight, and open fireplace. The menu combines fresh seafood and meat with French-style sauces, such as salmon with Dijon cream sauce or rack of lamb with mint demi-glace.

At the Maryland Inn, 16 Church Circle. ✆ **410/216-6340.** www.historicinnsofannapolis.com. Reservations recommended for dinner. Main courses $10–$16 breakfast, $8–$13 lunch, $17–$26 dinner. AE, DC, DISC, MC, V. Thurs–Fri 5:30–9:30pm; Sat 8am–2pm and 5:30–9:30pm; Sun 8am–2pm.

Inexpensive

Annapolis Ice Cream Company ICE CREAM Superpremium ice cream stars at this little shop on Main Street. It's all made on the premises, with flavors such as Maple Walnut, Key Lime Pie, and Blackberry Cobbler. The cobblers and pies are made here and then smashed into ice cream. Sundaes and shakes are also available.

196 Main St. ✆ **443/482-3895.** www.annapolisicecream.com. Reservations not accepted. Ice cream $3.50–$8 AE, DC, DISC, MC, V. Summer Sun–Thurs 11am–10pm, Fri–Sat 11am–11pm; shorter hours off-season.

Chick & Ruth's Delly AMERICAN An Annapolis tradition, this ma-and-pa establishment has been run by the Levitt family for 40 years. Sit wherever you like, and a waiter will take your order in the friendly deli/restaurant, famous for its sandwiches named after political figures and local attractions. Platters, pizzas, salads, sundaes, and shakes are also available. Breakfast is served all day.

165 Main St. ✆ **410/269-6737.** www.chickandruths.com. Reservations not accepted. Main courses and lunch items $4–$10. No credit cards. Sun–Thurs 6:30am–11:30pm; Fri–Sat 6:30am–12:30am.

Leeward Market CAFE Eat in at this Eastport eatery or carry out breakfast or lunch—from sandwiches to pizza. Get crew lunches for your sailboat races here, too.

601 2nd St., Eastport. ✆ **443/837-6122.** www.leewardmarket.com. Reservations not accepted. Main courses $4.50–$19. V. Mon 6:30am–3pm; Tues–Thurs 6:30am–5pm; Fri 6:30am–3pm and 6–9pm; Sat 8:30am–6pm; Sun 8:30am–3pm.

Lemongrass ★ THAI Locals clamor for a seat at Lemongrass—such a tiny space but so much flavor in these spicy dishes. Arrive early or be patient for that order of hot and sweet crispy string beans, pad Thai, and tiger crying salad; and bring an appetite—plates are piled high with spicy goodness. The menu offers lunch- and dinner-size portions, both available all day. (They also have takeout.)

167 West St. ✆ **410/280-0086.** www.kapowgroup.com/lemongrass. Reservations for dinner recommended. Main courses $8–$12 lunch, $10–$15 dinner. MC, V. Mon–Fri 11:30am–3pm and 5–10pm; Sat noon–4pm and 5–11pm; Sun 4–10pm.

Market House AMERICAN The historic Market House, site of a market since the 1690s, offers carryout—burgers, local produce, gelato, coffee, and a raw bar. Tables are set outside the market, though a seat by the City Dock is a popular spot for an impromptu picnic. There's also a bank and ATM.

25 Market Place, City Dock. No phone. www.annapolismarkethouse.com. Mon–Fri 11am–6pm; Sat–Sun 9am–6pm. Hours, credit cards, and prices vary by stall. (It's always open for breakfast and lunch.)

HISTORIC ANNAPOLIS

Annapolis's National Historic District has more than 1,500 restored and preserved buildings, and its narrow streets are best seen on foot. If your visit is short, make sure to see the **U.S. Naval Academy,** the **Maryland State House,** the **William Paca House & Garden,** the **Hammond-Harwood House,** and the **Chase-Lloyd House.** Enjoy the stroll down pretty Prince George Street on your way to the Paca House—it's packed with striking homes from Annapolis's 4 centuries. Tours are offered from the visitor center.

The **City Dock,** once the destination of merchant sailing ships, now attracts pleasure boats from near and far. Sightseeing boats, both gas- and wind-powered, offer cruises from spring to fall. The area around the City Dock has plenty of good restaurants, bars, shops, and a summer theater. As if frozen in time, a **sculpture of Alex Haley** reaches out toward the Chesapeake Bay to tell the story of *Roots,* his best-selling novel, to a group of children sitting on the City Dock. This display not only memorializes Haley and his African ancestor Kunta Kinte, but also recalls an actual place where enslaved Africans arrived in the New World. The sculpture is accompanied by a series of engraved plaques that complete the story and the memorial.

The Annapolis Maritime Museum This Eastport riverfront museum, headquartered in the old McNasby Oyster Company building, celebrates the waterman, the oyster and the terrapin, and other Chesapeake treasures. Even the arts are on exhibit with a gallery of regional art work and a Thursday concert series of traditional Chesapeake music. Educational activities for kids and adults are scheduled throughout the summer. In summer, boat tours of the picturesque **Thomas Point Lighthouse,** at $70 a person, include a half-hour boat ride to the Chesapeake Bay lighthouse and a tour of the 1875 screw-pile lighthouse—the last one left in its original location and still a navigational aid. Reservations are required; see the website for details.

723 2nd St. and Back Creek, Annapolis, MD 21403. ✆ **410/295-0104.** www.amaritime.org. Free admission; donation suggested. Thurs–Sun noon–4pm.

The Banneker-Douglass Museum This museum focuses on African Americans of the Chesapeake region from 1633 to the civil-rights movement. Named after two prominent local residents, astronomer/inventor Benjamin Banneker and abolitionist Frederick Douglass, continuously changing temporary exhibits join the museum's permanent exhibit on local African-American history, "Deep Roots, Rising Water."

84 Franklin St. (off south side of Church Circle). ✆ **410/216-6180.** www.bdmuseum.com. Free admission. Tues–Sat 10am–4pm. In July, also open Sun 1–5pm and until 7pm on Thurs.

Charles Carroll House of Annapolis This is the birthplace and home of Charles Carroll of Carrollton, the only Catholic to sign the Declaration of Independence. With sections built in 4 centuries, it sits on high ground overlooking Spa Creek, a block from City Dock. Visitors can tour the house, which is still undergoing restoration. Some features are original, including the walnut staircase, floors, and woodwork. Also take a look at the waterfront gardens and the 18th-century wine cellar. There is an elevator.

107 Duke of Gloucester St. (behind St. Mary's Church at Spa Creek). ✆ **410/269-1737.** www.charlescarrollhouse.org. Free admission. Private tours may be arranged; $5 per person. May–Oct Sat–Sun noon–4pm and by appointment. Closed Nov–Apr.

Chase-Lloyd House ★★ Home of Samuel Chase, a signer of the Declaration of Independence, this historic home (built from 1769–74) is outstanding for its brilliant interior design, exquisite hanging staircase, and intricate moldings. It was designed by William Buckland, architect for the Hammond-Harwood House across the street. Only the first-floor rooms are on view, as the house continues to be a home for retired women. It's well worth the charge to see the house and formal gardens. Hours are quite limited and docents are sometimes unavailable, so call ahead.

22 Maryland Ave. (at King George St.). ✆ **410/263-2723.** Admission $4. Mon–Sat 2–4pm.

Hammond-Harwood House ★★★ If you see only one historic house in Annapolis, make it this one. A five-part classic Georgian home quite unlike the Paca mansion, with semi-octagonal wings and carved moldings, it is considered one of the 18th century's most noteworthy. The architecture, by William Buckland, is stunning. On exhibit are decorative arts from the last 3 centuries and paintings including works by the various Peales, among Maryland's finest. The collection of 18th-century items, including furniture by John Shaw, handicrafts, and textiles, is not to be missed. There are some children's things and a few "modern conveniences" of the Colonial period.

19 Maryland Ave. (northeast of State Circle, at the corner of King George St.). ✆ **410/263-4683.** www.hammondharwoodhouse.org. Admission $6 adults, $3 children 6–17. 50-min. tours Apr–Oct Tues–Sun noon–5pm on the hour (last tour 4pm); Nov–Dec Tues–Sat noon–4pm (last tour 3pm). Closed Jan–Mar. Closed Easter, Memorial Day, Labor Day. Schedule may change for special events during Christmas season; see website for schedule.

Historic Annapolis Museum at the St. Clair Wright Center The Historic Annapolis Foundation's orientation center, at the foot of Main Street, is a restored 1790s building that once housed a bakery. Exhibits are designed to help visitors understand the state capital's history, architecture, and culture. It's a great place to get oriented for a tour of Annapolis, the "museum without walls." The center rents audio walking tours for $5.

99 Main St. ✆ **410/267-6656.** www.annapolis.org. Free admission. Mon–Sat 10am–5pm, Sun 11am–5pm.

Maryland State House ★★★ This is the oldest state house in continuous use in the nation. Constructed between 1772 and 1779, it served as the U.S. Capitol from

1783–84. George Washington came to the Old Senate Chamber to resign his commission as commander-in-chief of the Continental Army in December 1783 and the Treaty of Paris, ending the Revolutionary War, was ratified here in January 1784. Restoration of the Old Senate Chamber is expected to continue until 2014 but is open to visitors. The Old House of Delegates chamber has been restored to its 19th century appearance and is open to the public when not being used for official business as is the newly restored State House Caucus Room, which has the *USS Maryland* silver service on display. Visitors may also visit the contemporary Senate and House of Delegate chambers built in 1906 where Maryland's General Assembly meets from January to mid-April. Pick up a self-guided tour brochure. The grounds, overlooking the city and shaded by magnolias and evergreens, are a lovely spot for a break. Enter through the Rowe Boulevard entrances, up the steps or on the ground level.

State Circle. ✆ **410/974-3400.** www.msa.md.gov. Free admission; ID required for visitors over 16. Building daily 9am–5pm. Closed Dec 25.

St. John's College One of the oldest U.S. colleges, St. John's started in 1696 as a prep school but was chartered as a college in 1784. A good self-guided walking tour brochure is available online. Mellon Hall is home to the **Mitchell Gallery** (✆ **410/626-2556**) and—for a completely different style of architecture—was designed by a student of Frank Lloyd Wright. Two buildings are named for Maryland's signers of the Declaration of Independence, the Chase-Stone House and the Paca-Carroll House, both built in 1857. Don't miss the Carroll Barrister House, built about 1724 for Charles Carroll the barrister, a member of the prominent Maryland family.

60 College Ave. ✆ **410/626-2539.** www.sjca.edu. Campus open for visits during daylight hours. Gallery Tues–Sun noon–5pm.

U.S. Naval Academy ★★★ Tucked behind Annapolis's Historic District, standing proudly on the Severn River, the U.S. Naval Academy (USNA) has been educating future naval officers for more than 160 years.

For the full USNA experience, enter the Naval Academy at the pedestrian entrance near Gate 1, at Randall and King George streets, or at the other entrance closer to the City Dock at Craig Street. (The only cars allowed in the yard are those with handicapped or DOD stickers.) Start your visit at the **Armel-Leftwich Visitor Center,** just beyond the Halsey Field House, to see exhibits about midshipman life and browse the gift shop. Space fans will want to see the Freedom 7 capsule, flown by Alan Shepard (a USNA grad).Then, sign up for a tour to see Bancroft Hall, the world's largest dorm, and walk through the grounds.

The **Chapel** displays Bibles belonging to Commodore John Barry and Admiral David Farragut. In the undercroft is the marble **Crypt of John Paul Jones,** along with his swords and many medals. During the American Revolution, the commodore was the first to hoist the colors of the new nation over a flagship. The chapel is open Monday through Saturday 9am to 4pm and Sunday 1 to 5pm, except during weddings or funerals. Worshipers are also welcome to attend Sunday services.

The **USNA Museum** (✆ **410/293-5256;** www.usna.edu/museum) in Preble Hall features displays of naval officers' swords, medals, and other artifacts, as well as stunning ship models from the 16th to the 19th century. Famous admirals, astronauts, and one president (Jimmy Carter) have memorable exhibits. The War of 1812 flag proclaiming "Don't Give Up the Ship," which hung for decades in Bancroft Hall, is shown here. The museum is open Monday through Saturday 9am to 5pm, Sunday

The Colors of Annapolis

The Historic Annapolis Foundation has spent years identifying historic buildings throughout Annapolis. When a house meets the criteria, it receives a marker decorated with the Liberty Tree, a 400-year-old tree that once graced the grounds of St. John's College. Marker colors indicate the house's style:

Green 17th-century "vernacular," built 1681 to 1708

Terra cotta 18th-century "vernacular," or Georgian, built 1715 to 1800

Bronze Georgian of national importance, built 1730 to 1800

Blue Federal-style, built 1784 to 1840

Verdigris Greek Revival, built 1820 to 1860

Aubergine Victorian, built 1869 to 1901

Gray 19th- or 20-century Annapolis "vernacular," built 1837 to 1921

Ocher Distinctive homes of all styles, built in the 20th century

11am to 5pm. Admission is free. ***Insider's note:*** Bring your government-issued ID to Gate 3 at the end of Maryland Avenue; the Chapel is to your right and the Museum is to your left. The Severn River is straight ahead.

At 12:05pm Monday through Friday, weather permitting, see the midshipmen line up in **noon formation** in front of Bancroft Hall before the midday meal. **Commissioning Week,** usually held the third week in May, is a colorful time of full-dress parades, parties, and an air show by the Blue Angels.

Armel-Leftwich Visitor Center, 52 King George St. ✆ **410/293-TOUR** (8687). www.navyonline.com. Free admission to grounds and visitor center (photo ID required for those over 16). Tours $9.50 adults, $8.50 seniors, $7.50 students. Visitor center Mar–Dec daily 9am–5pm, Jan–Feb daily 9am–4pm. Closed Jan 1, Easter, Thanksgiving, and Dec 25. Tours offered daily, usually 10am–2:30pm; schedules vary by day and season, so call ahead or check website before coming.

The William Paca House & Garden ★★★ The home of William Paca, a signer of the Declaration of Independence and a governor of Maryland, this estate was built between 1763 and 1765 and restored by Historic Annapolis. It's one of two such houses in town (another, the Brice House, is around the corner but isn't open to the public). The five-part structure is composed of a central block, flanked symmetrically with hyphens and wings. The 45-minute house tour offers a glimpse of life during Annapolis's "golden age." One exhibit focuses on a child's sick room; another features Colonial leisure activities. The 2 acres of formal gardens feature a pond crossed by a Chinese Chippendale bridge and a two-story summer house. Climb to the top for a bird's-eye view of your surroundings. If your time is limited, at least see the gardens.

186 Prince George St. ✆ **410/267-7619.** www.annapolis.org. House and garden tours $8 adults, $7 seniors, $5 children 6–17. Garden only $5. Apr–Dec Mon–Sat 10am–5pm, Sun noon–5pm; call for hours for mid-Jan to Mar. Tours offered every half-hour; last is at 3:30pm. Closed Thanksgiving and Dec 24–25.

ORGANIZED TOURS & CRUISES

Walking Tours

Most tour operators in Annapolis take reservations for their tours—historical highlights, carriage or trolley tours, food or ghost tours—at the **Historic Annapolis Museum Store,** 77 Main St. (✆ **410/268-5576;** www.annapolis.org). This makes it easy to decide what tours visitors are interested in and which are available. They are also outlined on Historic Annapolis's website.

To hit the high points, take a **Historic Annapolis Walk.** Visitors carry digital audio wands and follow a map to go to places of the most personal interest. Tours focus on African-American heritage, the Civil War, the Revolution, and Annapolis Highlights. They're available at the Historic Annapolis Museum Store, 77 Main St. (✆ **410/268-5576;** www.annapolis.org). Tours take about 2 hours and cost $5.

Annapolis Tours by Watermark (✆ **410/268-7601;** www.annapolistours.com) are led by guides in Colonial costume. Tours of the Historic District, which include the Naval Academy, last 2 hours and don't require reservations. From April through October, they depart daily at 10:30am from the visitor center at 26 West St., and at 1:30pm from the City Dock information booth. (If you take a morning tour, guides try to get you to the Naval Academy in time for the midshipmen's noon formation.) From November through March, there is only one tour a week, Saturday at 1:30pm, departing from the City Dock information booth. The price is $16 for adults and $10 for children under 18. (***Note:*** Picture ID is required for those over 16 to gain access to the Naval Academy and State House.) Other options include African-American heritage tours, ghost tours on October evenings, and candlelight strolls on December evenings; check the website for a schedule.

U.S. Naval Academy Walking Tours depart from the Armel-Leftwich Visitor Center of the U.S. Naval Academy at Gate 1 on King George and Randall streets (✆ **410/293-8687;** www.navyonline.com) daily except Thanksgiving, Christmas, and New Year's Day. In July and August, tours depart every half-hour. From September through November and April through June, tours depart every hour Monday through Friday, and every half-hour Saturday and Sunday. From December through March, tours are offered as needed. The schedule varies a lot, so call ahead or check the website—or sign up when you get to the visitor center. The price is $9.50 for adults, $8.50 for seniors, and $7.50 for students. Those ages 16 and up should bring picture ID.

Annapolis Food Tours (✆ **800/979-3370;** www.annapolisfoodtours.com) mixes bits of history and bites of local dishes during a stroll of the historic capital. There are also Evening Dine Around, War of 1812, and Civil War tours. Reservations are recommended; tickets are $55.

Capital City Colonials (✆ **800/979-3370;** www.capitalcitycolonials.com), which offers the food tours, offers a variety of theme tours, including Annapolis in an Hour, Women of Annapolis, Colonial Gossip, and Grand Houses.

Tours by Bus, Trolley, Carriage & Segway

Discover Annapolis Tours, 31 Decatur Ave. (✆ **410/626-6000;** www.discover-annapolis.com), offers 1-hour trolley or minibus tours of the city and outlying areas. An air-conditioned 25-passenger trolley takes visitors through the Historic District—by the State House, Chase-Lloyd House, Hammond-Harwood House, and St. John's College—and areas not covered by the walking tours: Eastport, the Charles Carroll House, and the **Severn River Scenic Overlook ★**. Tours operate daily April through November, departing from the lot behind the visitor center at 26 West St. Saturday tours are available December through March. The cost is $18 for adults, $9 for children 11 to 15, and $3 for children 10 and under (free for preschoolers). A 40-minute tour is also available, leaving from the Historic Annapolis Museum, 99 Main St. Tickets are $15 for adults, $7.25 for ages 11 to15 and military, and $3 for children under 11.

Annapolis Carriage (www.annapoliscarriage.com) offers 20-minute carriage rides throughout the day. The coachman points out areas of interest and gives a brief history for up to four riders (six with kids). Reserve online, by phone, or in person at the Historic Annapolis Museum, 99 Main St. (✆ **410/267-6656;** www.annapolis.org). Tours cost $35 for adults, $15 for children for the 50-minute tour. Private tours are available. Hours vary by season; check the website for a schedule.

Segs in the City, 42 Randall St. (✆ **800/SEGS-393** [734-7393]; www.segsinthecity.net), lets visitors explore the Historic District on Segways. Guided 90-minute tours cost $60.

Cruises & Boat Tours

Watermark Cruises ★, at the City Dock (✆ **410/268-7601;** www.watermarkcruises.com), offers excursions along Annapolis Harbor and beyond. Choices include a 40-minute kid-friendly narrated cruise aboard the *Harbor Queen* that covers the highlights of Annapolis Harbor, the U.S. Naval Academy, and the Severn River; a 40-minute tour aboard the *Miss Anne* of the Eastport waterfront along Spa Creek and the Naval Academy shore; a 90-minute Thomas Point Lighthouse Cruise on the Severn River; and a Day-on-the-Bay excursion to St. Michaels. The *Lady Sarah* offers bay lighthouse cruises. In summer, catch a ride on a pirate ship. Prices range from $12 to $25 for adults, $5 to $10 for children 3 to 11. Sailings are daily from Memorial Day to Labor Day, with abbreviated schedules in spring and fall. Boats are accessible for visitors with disabilities. Dogs on leashes are welcome.

Pirate tours seem to be all the rage and you can find them in Eastport. **Pirate Adventures on the Chesapeake,** 311 Third St. (✆ **410/263-0002**), goes out six times a day at the height of the season. Cruises aimed at 2- to 9-year-olds last 75 minutes. Kids get "tattoos," wear pirate clothes, find treasure, and engage in water gun battles. Reservations for weekend cruises are recommended. Tickets are $19.

OUTDOOR ACTIVITIES

With the Chesapeake Bay and Severn River at its doorstep, Annapolis is the pleasure-boating capital of the eastern U.S. The city offers many opportunities to enjoy sailing and watersports, as well as other outdoor activities.

BIKING **Free Wheelin',** an Annapolis Transit program, rents bikes to riders ages 18 and older for $5, daily from 9am to 8pm, June through August. Bring a photo ID and credit card to the Harbormaster's Office on the City Dock and have the bike back by 8pm. Helmets are recommended and required on USNA grounds. Riders also get a pass to ride city buses, which have bike racks. For information, call ✆ **410/263-7973.**

If the streets are too crowded for a leisurely excursion, try one of the parks and paths outside of town. The **Baltimore and Annapolis Trail** (✆ **410/222-6244**) is a smooth 13-mile asphalt route from Annapolis north into the suburbs. Formerly a rail corridor, it's ideal for biking or walking. The trail, which connects with the waterfront **Jonas Green Park,** under the Route 450 bridge, runs parallel to Ritchie Highway and ends on Dorsey Road at Route 648 in Glen Burnie, where it connects with the 12.5-mile BWI Trail. The trail is open daily from sunrise to sunset.

Outside the city, on the South River and Harness Creek, **Quiet Waters Park** (✆ **410/222-1777**) has 6 miles of biking and hiking trails with an overlook along the South River. Dogs have their own park and beach. The park is open Wednesday through Monday, 7am to dusk; you'll pay $6 per vehicle, $5 per vehicle for the physically challenged. You'll find a map of the trails at www.annapolis.gov/Government/Departments/Transit/BikeAnnapolis/EcoTour.pdf.

ICE-SKATING A pond at **Quiet Waters Park,** 600 Quiet Waters Park Rd. (✆ **410/222-1711**), is turned into a popular skating rink November to February (depending on temperature). Admission is $6 for adults, $5 for children under 13, plus the park's $6 vehicle entry fee. Rentals are also available; Monday mornings, skating is free.

KAYAKING **Paddle or Pedal** (✆ **410/271-7007;** www.paddleorpedal.com) offers 3-hour sunset kayak tours in the South River on Fridays at 6pm. It also offers trips in creeks on both sides of the bay, as well as instruction and kayak rentals at Quiet Waters Park south of Annapolis. Preregistration is necessary for sunset paddles. Admission to Quiet Waters is $6 per vehicle; walk-ins and bike-ins are free. **Annapolis Canoe and Kayak** (✆ **443/949-0773;** www.kayakannapolistours.com) rents boats from its Eastport shop by Spa Creek and guides tours from nearby Truxtun Park.

LACROSSE Major League Lacrosse's **Chesapeake Bayhawks** (✆ **866/994-2957;** www.thebayhawks.com) play home games at Navy/Marine Corps Stadium on Rowe Boulevard. The season runs May through August.

SAILING SCHOOLS & SAILING TRIPS The sailing capital of the world has lots of schools that will get you at the helm for a few days. Learn to sail at the oldest sailing school in America: the **Annapolis Sailing School,** 601 Sixth St. (✆ **800/638-9192;** www.annapolissailing.com). With more than 50 boats and a huge support staff, this school offers programs for novices and veterans, including **KidShip** for children 5 to 15. Options range from a weekend beginner course for $495 to a 5-day vacation sailing course for $900 a person. Grads may rent the 24-foot *Rainbows* or the 36-foot *Hunter.* Hotel packages are also available.

Womanship, 137 Conduit St. (✆ **800/342-9295** or 410/267-6661; www.womanship.com), is an outstanding sailing program for women. Instruction levels range from "Chicken of the Sea" to advanced, in daytime or live-aboard settings. Learning cruises range from 2-day weekend lessons for $645 to a 5-day live-aboard program for $2,579. Other options are available, including lessons for couples.

There are many other sailing schools in the area, so call around for one that best suits your needs. Try **JWorld Annapolis** (✆ **800/966-2038** or 410/280-2040; www.jworldannapolis.com), which uses the wicked fast J-boats, or **Chesapeake Sailing School** (✆ **800/966-0032** or 410/295-0555; www.sailingclasses.com), which offers courses on Back Creek.

The 74-foot schooner ***Woodwind,*** 80 Compromise St. (✆ **410/263-7837;** www.schoonerwoodwind.com), departs from the Marriott side of the City Dock for 2-hour sailing trips four times daily, April to November. Departure times vary, so call or check the website. If you like sailboat racing, you can watch the Wednesday night races aboard the *Woodwind.* Prices are $36 to $39 for adults, $34 to $37 for seniors, and $25 for children under 12. Special destination cruises, overnight trips, and bed-and-breakfast sails are also available.

SWIMMING Visitors don't have to go too far to find a Chesapeake beach. Beaches at **Sandy Point State Park,** 1100 E. College Pkwy. (✆ **410/974-2149**), are guarded Memorial Day to Labor Day, 11am to 6pm. There are concessions stands, boat rentals, picnic areas, marina, and hiking paths, too. Admission is $6 for nonresidents. The park is open dawn to dusk. The park is located by the Bay Bridge, Route 50 off Exit 32.

WATERSPORT RENTALS & CHARTERS To charter a sailboat, contact one of the sailing schools or call **South River Boat Rentals** (✆ **410/956-9729;** www.southriverboatrentals.com), which rents both sail- and powerboats; it's south of Annapolis by the South River Bridge on Route 2.

SHOPPING

Shops in Annapolis's Historic District are filled with all kinds of gifts and nautical-themed merchandise. Navy T-shirts, the classic souvenir, are everywhere. You could redecorate your house from the shops on Maryland Avenue. This town is picturesque in December—with greenery draped around every window and white lights on the trees, it's a delightful, old-fashioned place to buy those last-minute items. Finish your day with a drink at McGarvey's (p. 112) or a meal at one of the downtown restaurants.

In the Historic District, the main shopping streets are: **Main Street,** which runs from Church Circle to the City Dock, has many apparel and gift shops; **Maryland Avenue** has shops in the block just below the State House and State Circle, where you might find home accessories and antiques; **West Street** has added lots of new shops and restaurants; and the shops around the **City Dock** itself are mostly nautical in nature. Most stores are open Monday through Saturday from 10 or 11am to 5 or 6pm, Sunday from noon to 5pm. Many stay open until 8 or 9pm on Friday and Saturday.

At **Plat du Jour,** 220 Main St. (✆ **410/269-1499;** www.platdujour.net), you'll be convinced you've walked into Tuscany or Provence. It's filled with tableware, linens, toiletries, and a cookbook or two.

Handmade arts and crafts are available in several places. **Annapolis Pottery,** 40 State Circle (✆ **410/268-6153**), sells wares made on the premises; you can watch the stock being made. **Easy Street,** 8 Francis St. (✆ **410/263-5556**), focuses on art glass.

For home furnishings, head for Maryland Avenue. **Peake House,** 76 Maryland Ave. (✆ **410/280-0410**), sells new stuff, including Mottahedeh, Quimper, and Herend. Interior designers display their finds at **Be Home,** 82 Maryland Ave. (✆ **410/280-8616**).

For artwork, check out **McBride Gallery,** 215 Main St. (✆ **410/267-7077;** www.mcbridegallery.com), or the juried exhibits at the Maryland Federation of Art's **Circle Gallery,** 18 State Circle (✆ **410/268-4566;** www.mdfedart.org). For something nautical, check out **Annapolis Marine Art Gallery,** 110 Dock St. (✆ **410/263-4100;** www.annapolismarineart.com). For gifts and collectibles, stop by the **Annapolis Country Store,** 53 Maryland Ave. (✆ **410/269-6773;** www.annapoliscountrystore.com): It has Pooh, Raggedy Ann, and Curious George items. Pick up your Navy T-shirt at **Peppers,** 133 Main St. (✆ **410/267-8722;** www.navygear.com). For gifts for your favorite teen, see **Brown Eyed Girl,** 234 Main St. (✆ **410/990-4475**). Get something stylish at **Diva,** 30 Market Space (✆ **410/280-9198;** www.modadiva.com). **Re-Sails,** 42 Randall St. (✆ **410/263-4982;** www.resails.com), stocks bags, jackets, and sofa pillows refashioned from old sails.

You'll find a few treasures in Eastport. Marylanders have long admired the photos of Marion E. Warren: find them at the **Eastport Gallery,** 419 Fourth St. (✆ **410/268-2898;** www.theeastportgallery.com). Liz Lind sells her sailboat prints at **Liz Lind Editions,** 423 Fourth St. (✆ **410/295-6880;** www.lizlindeditions.com).

Howard L. Rogers carves teak boat signs and displays his marine paintings at **Raven Maritime Studio,** 130 Severn Ave. (✆ **410/268-8639;** www.azinet.com/raven).

Malls & Markets

Annapolis Harbour Center West of downtown, at the junction of Routes 2 and 665, this shopping center is laid out like a maritime village, with more than 40 stores, services, and fast-food eateries, as well as nine movie theaters. Open daily. 2512A Solomons Island Rd. ✆ **410/266-5857.** www.annapolisharbourcenter.com.

Pennsylvania Dutch Farmers' Market This market is run by Amish and Mennonite families from Lancaster County, Pennsylvania. Wares range from sausages and pickles to organic produce, as well as homemade jams, fudge, and baked goods. Handmade quilts are available in a crafts section. Open Thursday and Friday from 9am to 6pm and Saturday from 8:30am to 3pm. 2472 Solomons Island Rd. (opposite Annapolis Harbour Center). ✆ **410/573-0770.** www.padutchfarmmarket.com.

Westfield Annapolis Situated off Route 50 between West Street and Bestgate Road, this mall has five department stores (including Nordstrom and Lord & Taylor), more than 330 specialty shops, food court, and 11 movie theaters. Open daily. 2002 Annapolis Mall. ✆ **410/266-5432.** www.westfield.com/annapolis.

ANNAPOLIS AFTER DARK

Annapolis is a town of small venues. Most local bars feature live music on weekends—everything from pop to classic rock to blues and funk—and there are a few good theater companies. For up-to-date listings, check the Friday "Entertainment" section of the *Capital* newspaper. The visitor center gives out event calendars as well.

Bars & Clubs

Armadillo's This place offers a variety of live entertainment—jazz, blues, funk, classic rock, acoustic rock, and oldies—Thursday through Saturday. Music usually starts at 10pm. 132 Dock St. ✆ **410/280-0028.** Cover varies.

49 West Coffeehouse, Winebar & Gallery ★ A welcome addition to Annapolis nightlife, 49 West is located a block west of Rams Head Tavern. This coffeehouse/wine bar features live classical, jazz, and folk music every night. 49 West St. ✆ **410/626-9796.** www.49westcoffeehouse.com. Cover none–$20.

McGarvey's Saloon & Oyster Bar McGarvey's, O'Brien's, and the Federal House (see p. 112 for a review), all near the City Dock, make up Annapolis's most happening nightspot. McGarvey's doesn't have live music, but draws a crowd for its oysters and beer (p. 112). It even has its own Aviator Lager. The place is loud, friendly, and fun. 8 Market Space. ✆ **410/263-5700.** www.mcgarveyssaloon.com.

O'Brien's Oyster Bar & Restaurant O'Brien's, near the City Dock, has entertainment almost every night, from live bands to DJs to open-mic. 113 Main St. ✆ **410/268-6288.** www.obriensoysterbar.com. No cover.

Pusser's Caribbean Grille The entertainment here is the boat traffic: Boaters motor up "Ego Alley" to show off their craft at the City Dock, only to turn around and head back into the harbor. Spend a summer evening on the deck with one of the specialty rum drinks. Pusser's also serves meals all day. At the Annapolis Marriott Waterfront, 80 Compromise St. ✆ **410/626-0004.** www.pussersusa.com.

Rams Head Tavern On Stage ★★★ The Rams Head has become the top nightspot in town, hosting acts ranging from Kenny "Babyface" Edmonds to Paula Poundstone to Buckwheat Zydeco. The audience usually ranges from young adult to middle-aged; you must be 21 or over for most shows. Thursdays are devoted to local talent. 33 West St. ✆ **410/268-4545.** www.ramsheadtavern.com. Cover varies; advance ticket purchase recommended.

The Performing Arts

The town's largest venue, the **Maryland Hall for the Creative Arts ★**, 801 Chase St. (✆ **866/438-3808** or 410/263-5544; www.mdhallarts.org), presents performances by the Annapolis Symphony Orchestra, Annapolis Opera, Annapolis Chorale, and the Ballet Theater of Maryland, as well as national acts. Check out the calendar of events online. Tickets are $10 to $50.

The **Colonial Players,** 108 East St. (✆ **410/268-7373;** www.cplayers.com), stage five plays per year in a 180-seat theater-in-the-round. Shows are Thursday through Saturday at 8pm, Sunday at 2:30 or 7:30pm. Ticket prices are $10 to $15.

Since 1966, the **Annapolis Summer Garden Theatre ★★**, 143 Compromise St., across from the City Dock (✆ **410/268-9212;** www.summergarden.com), produces three shows a summer. Reservations are encouraged; tickets cost $18.

A Side Trip to Historic London Town & Gardens ★

There are three reasons to set aside half a day to visit the remnants of London Town, one of Maryland's oldest towns: the 1760 house set high above the South River, the lush 8 acres of gardens surrounding the property, and the ongoing archaeological research to uncover the lost buildings of this once thriving seaport. Although it was central to the state's trade, with a busy ferry landing in the 1600s and 1700s, by the 1800s it was just a memory. Today, only the William Brown House remains.

The three-story brick mansion, now a National Historic Landmark, is worth a look for its 18th-century furnishings and its tavern, which covers much of the first floor. Don't miss the antique clock (with only an hour hand), leather water buckets, and prints by Elizabeth Blackwell. Children will like the basement, with its toys, clothes, and hats to help them "get into" the 18th century. Knowledgeable docents lead tours on the hour of either the historic area or the Brown house, tailoring their presentations to the ages of their guests. Stop first at the new visitor center to get oriented.

In the gardens, native plants, wildflowers, camellias, and hollies cover 8 acres overlooking Almshouse Creek and the South River. The mile-long trail is delightful when the azaleas in spring or 200 camellias in fall are in bloom.

The historic area that has been re-created represents activities that would have happened here: rope-making, tradesmen's houses, a carpenter shop.

Historic London Town & Gardens (✆ **410/222-1919;** www.historiclondontown.org) is open year-round, except major holidays, Wednesday through Saturday 10am to 4pm and Sunday noon to 4pm. Admission is $10 for adults, $9 for seniors, and $5 for children 7 to 18. Between January and March, the Brown House is closed and the property is open Wednesday to Friday 10am to 4pm.

To get here, take U.S. 50/Md. 301 to Exit 22, Aris T. Allen Boulevard. Exit onto Route 2 south, go over the South River Bridge, and continue one-half mile. Turn left onto Mayo Road, go ¾ mile, and turn left onto Londontown Road. Go 1 mile to the end of the road and enter the site through the gates.

SOLOMONS ★

55 miles S of Annapolis; 80 miles S of Baltimore; 60 miles SE of Washington, DC; 150 miles SW of Wilmington, DE

For more than 100 years, Calvert County—with Solomons as its centerpiece—has been a Baltimore-Washington playground. Largely agricultural, the area is becoming much more a Washington suburb, but its nearby parks, local history, outdoor activities, and marine sports continue to attract visitors.

Solomons, also known as "Solomons Island" for the island that makes up its center, is dominated by water. The island sits at the end of two peninsulas formed by the Patuxent River, Back Creek, and Mill Creek (the Patuxent's mouth into the Chesapeake is visible from the town's southern end). The island is connected to land by a bridge so short that if you blink, you'll miss it, but you'll still feel surrounded by water. A walk through town will take you past sailboats and charter fishing boats, as well as watermen's homes, the century-old Drum Point Lighthouse, and Solomons' wide public pier, the place to see beautiful sunsets over the Patuxent.

Essentials

GETTING THERE Solomons is at the southern tip of Calvert County. Maryland Routes 2 and 4 merge and run north-south across the county. To reach Solomons from Washington, DC, and points south, take I-95 to the exit for Route 4 south; follow Route 4 all the way to Solomons. From Annapolis and points north, take the exit for Route 4 south off U.S. Route 50; follow Route 2–4 to Solomons.

VISITOR INFORMATION Contact the **Calvert County Department of Economic Development,** in the Courthouse, Prince Frederick (✆ **800/331-9771** or 410/535-4583; www.ecalvert.com). In Solomons, stop by the information center at the base of the Gov. Thomas Johnson Bridge, on Route 2–4 (✆ **410/326-6027**).

Where to Stay

Back Creek Inn ★★ In a blue 1880 waterman's house, this inn offers travelers a relaxing stay in a waterfront setting. The innkeepers have decorated the place with antiques, quilts, flowers, and original paintings. From the cozy sitting room, or from a chair in the garden, you can watch boats drift by on the Back Creek. The Lavender Room is a small cottage with a Jacuzzi, fireplace, and screened porch overlooking the creek. The Tansy, Chamomile, and Peppermint rooms also enjoy water views.

210 Alexander Lane (at Calvert St.; P.O. Box 520), Solomons, MD 20688. www.backcreekinnbnb.com. ✆ **410/326-2022.** Fax 410/326-2946. 7 units. $110–$125 double; $160–$170 suite; $225 cottage. Additional guests $25. Rates include full breakfast. MC, V. Off-street parking. No children under 12. **Amenities:** Bikes; boat slips. *In room:* A/C, flatscreen TV, hair dryer, free Wi-Fi.

Comfort Inn Beacon Marina This two-story hotel is geared toward boat enthusiasts as well as tourists. The complex includes a 187-slip marina with 40 covered slips. Guest rooms are clean, comfortable, and modern; 10 have Jacuzzis. Best of all, guests can open the windows to enjoy the breezes off Back Creek.

255 Lore Rd. (P.O. Box 869), Solomons, MD 20688. www.comfortinn.com. ✆ **800/228-5150** or 410/326-6303. Fax 410/326-9492. 60 units. $109–$150 double. AE, DC, DISC, MC, V. Rates include continental breakfast. Off-street parking. **Amenities:** Waterfront restaurant and bar on-site; 187-slip marina; outdoor pool. *In room:* A/C, fridge, hair dryer, microwave, free Wi-Fi.

Hilton Garden Inn Solomons The only thing this hotel doesn't have is a water view. It's tucked beside a wooded lot. (Ask for an even-numbered room if you prefer a view of trees.) All the other amenities are covered: a lobby with plenty of seating, indoor and outdoor pools, free Wi-Fi, and rooms with the level of comfort you would expect. Most rooms feature two queen beds, but there are king rooms, two-room suites, and six rooms with whirlpools. A free shuttle takes guests to Solomons' waterfront.

13100 Dowell Rd., Dowell, MD 20629. www.solomons.stayhgi.com. ✆ **410/326-0303.** 100 units. $149–$229. Children 17 and under stay free in parent's room. AE, MC, V. Free self-parking. **Amenities:** Restaurant; lounge; fitness center; hot tub; indoor and outdoor pools. *In room:* A/C, flatscreen TV w/movies, hair dryer, MP3 docking station, free Wi-Fi.

Holiday Inn Conference Center and Marina The biggest hotel in Solomons is a standard Holiday Inn with comfortable, good-sized rooms. Many units have views of the marina, particularly on the second floor or above and on the southern ends of the hotel's guest wings. Suites have balconies. There are packages that include boat slips.

155 Holiday Dr. (off Rte. 4; P.O. Box 1099), Solomons, MD 20688. www.solomonsmd.hiselect.com. ✆ **410/326-6311.** Fax 410/326-1069. 326 units. $129–$159 double; $169–$239 suite. AE, DISC, MC, V. Free parking. **Amenities:** Water-view restaurant; dockside bar; fitness center; 90-slip marina; outdoor pool; sauna; weekend shuttle $5 a trip; tennis courts. *In room:* A/C, hair dryer, free Wi-Fi.

Solomons Victorian Inn Bed & Breakfast ★ This Victorian inn is decorated with antiques and reproductions and sits near the water. It has four public spaces, including a glassed-in porch (where breakfast is served). All but one of the bedrooms enjoy a view of Back Creek Harbor or the Patuxent River. The third-floor Solomons Sunset suite features a king-size bed, microwave and galley area, whirlpool tub, and great views of the harbor on two sides. Two luxurious suites in the Carriage House have private entrances, whirlpool tubs, and harbor views.

125 Charles St. (P.O. Box 759), Solomons, MD 20688. www.solomonsvictorianinn.com. ✆ **410/326-4811.** Fax 410/326-0133. 7 units. $110–$240 double. Rates include full breakfast. 2-night minimum stay required Apr–Oct. AE, DISC, MC, V. Free off-street parking. No children under 13. *In room:* A/C, TV, hair dryer, microwave in some rooms, free Wi-Fi.

Where to Eat

The CD Cafe AMERICAN People crowd into this bright, cozy spot for an assortment of dishes such as shepherd's pie and breast of chicken topped with pecans, apples, and an apple-schnapps glaze. Lunchtime salads are creative and tasty—try the curried chicken—and wraps and burgers are generous. Behind the cafe is the **Next Door Lounge,** a laid-back place for light fare and drinks (Tues–Sat 4:30–11pm). A light fare menu is offered weekdays between 2:30 and 4:30pm.

14350 Solomons Island Rd., Solomons, MD 20688. ✆ **410/326-3877.** www.cdcafe.info. Reservations not accepted. Main courses $11–$22 lunch, $11–$26 dinner. MC, V. Daily 11:30am–2pm and 5:30–9:30pm (until 9pm Sun).

The Dry Dock SEAFOOD You've got to walk through a gravelly marina parking lot and up steps to the waterfront restaurant. Once inside, the atmosphere is about Solomons' most formal. The seasonal menu, though filled with seafood choices, includes some creative options (creative for Solomons). Dress up in your cleanest boating togs and get ready to dig into surf and turf, the inevitable crab cakes, or ahi tuna. With 10 tables, reservations are a must. Deck dining is available in summer.

14575 Solomons Island Rd., Solomons, MD 20688. ✆ **410/326-4817.** www.zahnisers.com/drydock.htm. Reservations recommended. Main courses $19–$30. DISC, MC, V. Summer Sun 10am–2pm and 5–9:30pm; Mon–Thurs 5–9:30pm; Fri–Sat 5–9:30pm. Winter Tues–Sat 5–9pm; Sun 10am–2pm.

Solomons Pier SEAFOOD This casual restaurant jutting out into the water has views of the soaring bridge and Patuxent River to accompany its fresh seafood. The gazebo on the dock has panoramic views, cool breezes to go with your drink and crab cake. The all-day menu offers lots of casual fare: soups, salads, sandwiches, and plenty of appetizers, including a gooey crab pretzel. Entrees run from the expected crab cake to a rockfish dinner. If you're not hungry, get a drink to toast the sunset.

14575 Solomons Island Rd., Solomons, MD 20688. ✆ **410/326-2424.** www.stoneysseafoodhouse.com. Reservations accepted only for large parties. Main courses $12–$30. DISC, MC, V. Memorial Day to Labor Day daily 11:30am–10pm. Other times Sun–Thurs 11:30am–9pm; Fri–Sat 11:30am–10pm. Closes 2 weeks in Jan.

Stoney's Kingfishers SEAFOOD Casual, with a crab-house atmosphere, Stoney's emphasizes seafood. Its half-pound crab cake is renowned, but the "baby" version is available, too. Lunch ranges from sandwiches to soups; at dinner look for softshell crabs, steaks, and filet mignon stuffed with crab imperial. Eat in the dining rooms with picture windows overlooking the water or sit out on the deck.

14442 Solomons Island Rd., Solomons, MD 20688. ✆ **410/394-0236.** www.stoneysseafoodhouse.com. Reservations not accepted. Main courses $11–$19 lunch, $25–$36 dinner. AE, DISC, MC, V. Memorial Day to Labor Day daily 11:30am–10pm. Other times Sun–Thurs 11:30am–9pm; Fri–Sat 11:30am–10pm.

Exploring Solomons

Annmarie Sculpture Garden and Arts Center Where else can you go for sculpture, sylvan solitude, and art-filled bathrooms? This 30-acre retreat, affiliated with the Smithsonian Institution, features some 20 pieces of sculpture on loan from the Hirshhorn Museum. The Arts Center houses exhibit galleries, studios, gift shop, and cafe. Visitors are welcomed by the *Tribute to the Oyster Tonger,* with other sculptures installed along the quarter-mile walking path. Rest on one of the benches designed by local children, enjoy the 113 varieties of azaleas, and don't miss those bathrooms.

13480 Dowell Rd. (off Rte. 4), Solomons, MD 20688. ✆ **410/326-4640.** www.annmariegarden.org. Admission $3 adults, $2 seniors and children. Garden daily 9am–5pm; arts center 10am–5pm.

Calvert Marine Museum and Drum Point Lighthouse ★★★ ☺ In a state brimming with maritime museums, this is the best. It has exhibits on local industry and the environment, fossils from nearby Calvert Cliffs, a lighthouse, and even an otter to visit. The sea-horse exhibit is intriguing—who knew they lived in the bay? The Discovery Room will have kids learning a little history while digging for fossils. Then there's the Drum Point Lighthouse, one of three remaining screw-pile lighthouses on the Chesapeake. (Thomas Point Lighthouse still operates near Annapolis, and the Hooper Strait Light is the centerpiece of the Chesapeake Bay Maritime Museum on the Eastern Shore.) You can build a little boat or take a cruise on the 1899 bugeye *Wm. B. Tennison.*

Nearby is the J. C. Lore and Sons Oyster House, which has exhibits on Patuxent watermen and "deadrise" workboat-building. Admission is free; it's open June through August, daily from 1 to 4pm, plus the same hours on May and September weekends.

WINE tasting IN SOLOMONS

Just north of Solomons are two tiny wineries. Those interested in the winemaking process will enjoy tasting the wares and talking to the winemakers.

Solomons Island Winery, 515 Garner Lane (off Monticello Drive), Lusby (✆ **410/394-1933;** www.solomonsislandwinery.com), offers tastings Tuesday through Sunday noon to 5pm. From Route 4, turn left on Monticello Lane and left on Garner Lane; the winery will be on the right.

Cove Point Winery, 755 Cove Point Rd., Lusby (✆ **410/326-0949;** www.covepointwinery.com), has tastings every Saturday and Sunday from noon to 5:30pm, or by appointment. From Route 4, turn right on Cove Point Road.

North of Solomons, Cove Point Lighthouse, the oldest continuously operating lighthouse in the state, is open for tours 1 to 4pm daily in summer.

14200 Solomons Island Rd., Solomons, MD 20688. ✆ **800/735-2258** or 410/326-2042. www.calvertmarinemuseum.com. Admission $7 adults, $6 seniors, $4 children 5–12. Cruise tickets $7 adults, $6 seniors, $2 children 5–12. Daily 10am–5pm. Closed Jan 1, Thanksgiving, and Dec 25. Limited docking available for visitors.

Outdoor Activities

CHARTER FISHING ★

Fishing is one of Calvert County's biggest draws. And for good reason: The bay waters here are filled seasonally with rockfish (striped bass), bluefish, Spanish mackerel, white perch, spot, croaker, flounder, sea trout, and black drum. Before you head out to sea, check with your charter-boat captain to find out what's in season.

Charter fishing is available in two ways: through organized operations and through loose affiliations of captains. It's easy to charter a boat either way. In the case of an organized operation, call the office, which will supply a boat. If all its boats are full, the company will contact a local captain and have him run the charter.

It works a little differently with captains' associations. In this case, you call a contact person for the association, usually one of the captains. If that captain has an opening, he will take you out on his boat. If he doesn't, he will arrange for another captain to take you out or give you the names of captains who might be available.

Remember to ask what you'll need to bring. Most charters include fishing gear; some supply bait for free and some don't. Bring a cooler to take your catch home. The mates on charter boats work for cash tips, which should be at least 15%.

In Solomons

Bunky's Charter Boats Bunky's operates out of a well-stocked bait-and-tackle shop across from the walking pier on Solomons Island. It has a fleet of 10 charter boats, including one 47-foot headboat, the *Marchelle.* Charter rates for up to six passengers on all boats except the *Marchelle* are $575 per half-day (6 hr.) and $685 per full day (8 hr.). Rates for six on the *Marchelle* are $675 per half-day and $785 per full day. There's a per-person charge of $70 for extra passengers. Fishing on a headboat costs $45 a person for 6 hours. Bunky's also rents 16-foot motorboats, but if you're not on a charter boat, you'll need a license to fish—which you can get here, too.

14448 Solomons Island Rd. S. ✆ **410/326-3241.** www.bunkyscharterboats.com.

Solomons Charter Captains Association (SCCA) The association runs many of its 40 boats out of the Calvert Marina Charter Dock, on Dowell Road. Eleven of the SCCA's boats can carry more than six people; some can carry as many as 40. Standard association rates are $400 to $575 for six people; additional fishermen cost about $75 each. Cruise tours and packages are also available.

Solomons. ✆ **410/808-3832.** www.fishsolomons.com.

Fin Finder Charters The *Fin Finder,* a 46-foot Chesapeake-style workboat, carries up to 30 passengers. Rates for a full day start at $840; half-day rates for the first six passengers range from $660 to $760. Cruise tours and packages are also available.

14485 Dowell Rd., Solomons, MD 20629. ✆ **240/925-9598.** www.finfinder.com.

In Chesapeake Beach

Chesapeake Beach charters are popular, with a fleet that takes passengers to waters filled with rockfish, blues, and flounder. To get here from Annapolis, take Route 2 south to Maryland Route 260 west, which ends just north of the harbor at Maryland Route 261. From Washington, DC, take Route 4 west to Route 260 west and follow the directions above. It's about an hour north of Solomons.

Chesapeake Beach Fishing Charters This association of charter captains has a dozen boats that can accommodate a half-dozen or 30. A half-day for six people costs $550; a full day goes for $700.

Chesapeake Beach. ✆ **301/855-4665** or 866/532-9246. www.chesapeakefishingcharters.com.

Rod 'N' Reel Charter Fishing Rod 'N' Reel has a huge share of the charter-fishing operation in Maryland's portion of the Chesapeake. Charter rates for up to six people are $600 per 6-hour trip, $750 per 8-hour trip. Or get on a headboat for $65 per person; rod rentals are $5. Trips leave in the morning as well as Sunday afternoon.

4160 Mears Ave., Chesapeake Beach. ✆ **800/233-2080.** www.chesapeakebeachresortspa.com.

SPORTFISHING

Although charter fishing is this area's forte, there are also several choice locations for sportfishing, including **Bay Front Park,** in Chesapeake Beach; and **Solomons Fishing Pier,** under the Gov. Thomas Johnson Bridge (Rte. 4) in Solomons.

Bait and tackle are available at **Bunky's Charter Boats,** in Solomons (✆ **410/326-3241**), and **Rod 'N' Reel Dock,** in Chesapeake Beach (✆ **866/312-5596**).

BIKE & KAYAK RENTALS

If you just want to meander around Solomons, **Patuxent Adventure Center,** 11380 Solomons Island Rd. (✆ **410/394-2770;** www.paxadventure.com), rents bikes and kayaks and can arrange for tours of nearby waterways. Reserve online.

EXCURSION TO SMITH ISLAND

Smith Island Cruises (www.smithislandcruises.com, ✆ **410/425-2771**) offers day trips from Point Lookout to Smith Island, a 1½ hour trip across the Chesapeake Bay, on the twin-hulled *Chelsea Lane Tyler*. From Memorial Day to Labor Day, boats depart most Wednesdays through Sundays at 10am, returning to Point Lookout at 4pm. Cruises also depart on weekends only from September through mid-October. Check the website before you go; actual cruise dates are listed there. Round trip fare is $40 for adults and $ 20 for children 3 to 11. The company also offers overnight packages from Point Lookout and Solomons to Crisfield; they are listed on the website. For details on Smith Island, and more ways of getting there, visit **www.visitsmithisland.com/gettinghere.html**.

ST. MARY'S CITY

86 miles S of Annapolis; 101 miles S of Baltimore; 69 miles SE of Washington, DC; 173 miles SW of Wilmington, DE

The Free State got its start here, where the Potomac River meets the Chesapeake Bay, in 1634. The settlers came here to start a colony based on freedom of conscience, and a sense of democracy that welcomed people of other faiths, other nations. It was here that the first man of color was able to participate in representative government.

St. Mary's City is on a lovely but remote peninsula, in a county dotted with aging tobacco barns and laced with rivers and creeks. Nearby Lexington Park, the county's biggest town, is the home of the Patuxent River Naval Air Station. It's a quick hop from Annapolis, Washington, or Baltimore. Or combine a visit with a stay in Solomons for a quintessential Chesapeake Bay vacation.

Essentials

GETTING THERE St. Mary's City is on Route 5. From Washington, take the Route 5 exit from I-495 (the Capital Beltway). Or from Annapolis, take Maryland Route 50 to Route 301 to Route 4 to Solomons and across the Gov. Thomas Johnson Bridge. Turn left a few miles past the bridge onto Route 235, right on Route 489, and left onto Route 5 into St. Mary's City. For a more scenic drive, take Route 50 to Route 301 to Route 5 all the way to St. Mary's City—a slow and meandering route.

VISITOR INFORMATION See the **St. Mary's County Tourism Office,** 23115 Leonard Hall Dr., Leonardtown (✆ **800/327-9023** or 301/475-4200, ext. 1404).

Discovering Maryland's First Capital

Historic St. Mary's City ★★★ History happened here. Though most of the 17th-century buildings of Maryland's first capital city are gone, it was here that Cecil Calvert enacted laws that permitted anyone to vote and participate in government, regardless of their faith. This freedom drew a wide variety of settlers. The first Catholic chapel in English America was established here at a time when they were forbidden elsewhere. The first African American voted in the legislature here. A woman demanded the right to vote here. (Nothing's perfect: Her request was denied.)

St. Mary's City was founded in 1634 and was home in its heyday to 20,000 people. Laid out in a traditional grid pattern, the state house was at one end of the town with the church at the other end. Taverns, shops, and homes once filled the spaces in between. But by the end of the 17th century, the capital had moved to Annapolis, and St. Mary's City disappeared.

Through careful digs and painstaking research, some of the buildings have been reconstructed; and, in the summer, visitors can watch the St. Mary's College field school conduct new searches for bits of old buildings, artifacts, and even the marks left in the dirt that recall the buildings and the people who once lived in the early Colonial town.

In the town center, visits can see mostly small, simple buildings, like an inn and an early print shop, the grander State House and the Brick Chapel, and climb aboard a reproduction of a ship like one that brought the first Marylanders here. Nearby are an early plantation and Indian woodland village. An archaeological museum has been built over the site of the building where the legislature sat. Allow at least 4 hours for your visit, wear comfortable shoes, and bring water, as it can get very hot and humid in summer. Guides will help you get a feel for 17th-century Maryland.

At the **visitor center,** get the gear for the state-of-the-art audio tour, watch the introductory video, and see an exhibit chronicling the rise and fall of St. Mary's City. It's the only building open year-round. Other exhibits close between Thanksgiving and Maryland Day (Mar 25).

Don't miss the **State House** or **Godiah Spray's 17th-century tobacco plantation.** While the public building is formal, the plantation shows how hard life was for the early colonists. The house is simple, the fields rough.

The reconstructed **Print Shop,** Maryland's first, was run by a woman, and was the first one south of Boston in the 17th century.

Smith's Ordinary, a reconstructed 17th-century inn, features a medieval-style fireplace and tiled inglenook. A second inn, **Farthing's Ordinary,** built in the 1600s, has a good gift shop with out of the ordinary merchandise.

The **St. John's Site Museum** features modern galleries atop a glass floor over the original home's foundation. At this site, Margaret Brent asked to vote and Matthias DeSousa was the first black man to participate in the legislature. The building is open year-round and there's no admission charge. The 1667 **Brick Chapel** has been rebuilt but is still empty. Originally built by the Jesuits who accompanied the settlers, it is perhaps the grandest of the buildings so far reconstructed. It is expected to be furnished in the next few years—once the historians figure out how it would have looked.

Walk to the water to see the 76-foot ***Dove,*** a reproduction of a mid-17th-century square-rigged merchant ship similar to the ships that brought Maryland's first settlers in 1634. Children love to board the boat and talk with the costumed sailors.

A bonus is the waterfront setting. Walking trails through woodlands and near the water stretch 3.5 miles and recall how this area must have looked to early settlers.

Special programs are offered on **Maryland Day,** March 25; **Community and Trail Day,** in June (free admission); **Tidewater Archaeology Dig Day,** in late June (join the archaeologists); **Woodland Indian Discovery Day,** the weekend after Labor Day (with storytelling, Native American crafts, and exhibits); and **Grand Militia Muster Day,** in October (a gathering of 17th-c. reenactment units). Leashed dogs are welcome.

St. Mary's City. ✆ **800/SMC-1634** (762-1634). www.stmaryscity.org. Admission $10 adults, $8 seniors, $6 students 6–18. Admission in off season $2 adults, $1 children 6–12. Audio guides $3. Mid-Mar to mid-June Wed–Sat 10am–5pm; mid-June to Sept Wed–Sun 10am–5pm; Oct–Nov Tues–Sat 10am–5pm. Dec to mid-Mar Wed–Sun 10am–5pm (only visitor center, grounds are open). Because the staff is small, it's best to call ahead to confirm hours. From Rte. 4, turn left on Rte. 235 and right on Mattapany Rd. St. Mary's City will be ahead, across Rte. 5. From Washington, take Rte. 5 to St. Mary's.

Another Historic Site in St. Mary's County

Sotterley Plantation ★ This 1703 house is the only Tidewater-style tobacco plantation house open to the public. The 1760 Chinese Chippendale railing is a marvel, as is the withdrawing room's intricate carving, which was done over a period of 20 years by enslaved African Americans. An 1830s slave cottage is open for visits. Restoration is ongoing at this National Historic Landmark, but the house is fully furnished. The grounds are open year-round for self-guided visits and walks through the formal gardens and trails to the Patuxent River. Check the website for special events, from wine festivals to ghost tours. Commemorations are taking place for one of the battles of the War of 1812 that took place nearby. ***Note:*** A dock is available; call ahead for a slip. It's a 20-minute walk from the dock to the house.

44300 Sotterley Lane (off Rte. 245), Hollywood, MD 20636. ✆ **800/681-0850** or 301/373-2280. www.sotterley.org. House tours $10 adults, $8 seniors, $5 children 6–12. Grounds and self-tour admission $3. House tours May–Oct Tues–Sat 10:30am–4pm; Sun noon–4pm. Grounds and self-tour available year-round Mon–Sat 10am–4pm; Sun noon–4pm. Site closed Jan 1, Martin Luther King Day, Presidents' Day, Easter, Memorial Day, July 4, Labor Day, Thanksgiving weekend, and Dec 24–Jan 3.

Outdoor Activities

POINT LOOKOUT STATE PARK ★

At the tip of St. Mary's County, at the confluence of the Potomac River and the Chesapeake Bay, **Point Lookout State Park** (✆ **301/872-5688;** www.dnr.state.md.us/publiclands/southern/pointlookout.asp) offers visitors a chance to see both bodies of water. The park's 1,046 acres offer a swimming beach on the Potomac, a fishing pier on the Chesapeake, Civil War–era prisoner-of-war camp Fort Lincoln, docks for boating, and campsites and cabins. The lighthouse at the tip of the peninsula, built in 1830, is now dark but open to visitors one weekend in November. Day use of the park is $5 for state residents and $6 for nonresidents on weekends and holidays, May through September. On weekdays and out of season, the fee is $3 or $4 per vehicle. The boat-launch fee is $10. ***Note:*** The park is popular on summer and holiday weekends and can fill up; call before heading down and finding out it's full.

Day-use facilities with a guarded beach for swimming are on the Potomac side, past the fishing pier. There's a pet beach north of the causeway, too.

Visitors interested in **fishing** can cast their lines just about anywhere except the beach swimming area. Favorite areas are the pier on the bay side and the point on the bay or riverside. The pier is closed mid-December through March. Night fishing is the only activity allowed in the park (except camping) after sunset. Campers can also fish at designated piers near campsites. A fishing license is required and available at the park office. Boat and canoe rentals are available at the camp store off Route 5.

The park offers 143 **campsites** (26 with full hookups). The cost is $25 to $40 per site. Cabins sleeping four cost $50 a night. Reservations can be made up to a year in advance by calling ✆ **888/432-CAMP** (2267). The office (✆ **301/872-5688**) is open from 8am to 4pm in summer.

FISHING CHARTERS

Several dozen charter boats, accommodating 6 to 60 passengers, head out of the creeks and rivers of St. Mary's County. The St. Mary's County tourism office has a comprehensive list of about 30 boat captains online at **www.visitstmarysmd.com/Charter%20Boats.asp**.

Where to Stay

St. Mary's City has only one lodging option, but nearby Lexington Park has some chain hotels, including the **Hampton Inn** (✆ **301/863-3200**) and the **Fairfield Inn** (✆ **301/863-0203**).

The Inn at Brome Howard New management took over here in late 2011 with an eye towards keeping the old vibe but modernizing amenities. The inn is right on the St. Mary's River within walking distance of the historic site. The bedrooms vary in decor; three have fireplaces (decorative only) and the third-floor suite has a queen bed in each room. New paint and some modern touches were being put in place in early 2012.

18281 Rosecroft Rd. (P.O. Box 476), St Mary's City, MD 20686. www.bromehoward.com. ✆ **240/434-3209** or 301/866-0656. Fax 240/895-4968. 4 units. $125–$185 double on weekends; $140 all rooms weekdays. Rates include breakfast. AE, MC, V. Off-street parking. **Amenities:** Coffee and tea; free Wi-Fi hotspot. *In room:* A/C, flatscreen TV/DVD, fridge, hair dryer.

Where to Eat

Visitors to St. Mary's City have only a few options. Bring a picnic lunch or buy a snack in Farthing's Ordinary. Visitors can grab a bite at the Student Center at St. Mary's College, across Route 5 from the Visitor Center parking lot. There's a coffee shop on the ground floor and a dining hall serving three meals Monday through Friday and brunch and dinner on the weekends. Call ✆ **240/395-3963** to confirm the dining hall is open. A couple of restaurants are down Route 252 (Wynne Rd.) in Ridge near the water; seafood is the specialty.

Courtney's Restaurant SEAFOOD Nothing's fancy in here. It's a cinder-block building with a simple dining room and a bar with the TV going. But after a day outdoors, you'll be hungry for home cooking—and that's what Courtney's does best. You can get steamed crabs, crab cakes, or softshells. Want fresh fish? Courtney's husband comes home every morning with the day's catch. Carryout is available.

48290 Wynne Rd., Ridge. ✆ **301/872-4403.** Reservations not necessary. Main courses $8–$10 lunch, $19–$22 dinner. MC, V. Daily 7am–9pm.

Scheible's Marina SEAFOOD Simple seafood is served in a wood-paneled dining room across from the marina. Choose from seafood and chicken, with club sandwiches at lunch and steaks and pasta at dinner. Portions are generous. Picture windows offer views of Smith Creek. Karaoke on Friday nights keeps the place hopping until midnight.

48342 Wynne Rd., Ridge. ✆ **301/872-0025.** Reservations recommended. Main courses $5–$12 lunch, $9–$27 dinner AE, DISC, MC, V. Apr–Nov Tues–Sun 6am–9pm; Dec–Mar Sat–Sun 6am–9pm, Thurs–Fri 11am–9pm.

AROUND THE CAPITAL BELTWAY

6

The suburbs of Washington, DC, are jammed with housing developments, shopping centers, and highways. But there are also some delightful sights. They're easy to get to from Baltimore or Annapolis and accessible from the Capital Beltway. Among the gems are several historical homes. You can visit farms and gardens, see spaceships, shop for antiques, and ride a roller coaster.

NORTHWEST

40 miles W of Annapolis; 40 miles SW of Baltimore; 8 miles NW of Washington, DC; 110 miles SW of Wilmington

The northwest section of the Capital Beltway is accessible by I-270, which connects to Frederick. **Bethesda** is home to the Discovery Channel, the National Institutes of Health, and the Bethesda Naval Hospital. It's also home to the Music Center at the Strathmore. Bethesda also has a fine collection of restaurants along Woodmont Avenue including **Jaleo** (✆ **301/913-0003;** www.jaleo.com), a stylish tapas bar owned by TV chef Jose Andres, and **Mon Ami Gabi** (✆ **301/654-1234;** www.monamigabi.com), a terrific French bistro far better than its sister restaurant in the Paris Las Vegas resort. The C&O Canal Historical Park, Clara Barton's home, and Glen Echo Park are close enough to each other to plan a day's outing. Brookside Gardens offers another respite for the weary. Prefer shopping? Get new stuff at White Flint Mall or old stuff on Howard Avenue (see Antique Row listing) in Kensington.

Attractions

American Film Institute Silver Theatre and Cultural Center Something wonderful is always on the screen at this restored 1938 movie palace. In addition to showing new and classic pictures at two stadium-seating theaters, the theater hosts a series of festivals, including the SilverDocs international documentary series each June. Movie tickets can be reserved online. Several parking garages are within walking distance.

8633 Colesville Rd., Silver Spring, MD 20910. ✆ **301/495-6720** or 495-6700 for recorded film information. www.afi.com/silver. $11 adults, $9 seniors, $7 children, $8.50 matinees. Movies daily noon–9pm. Box office opens 30 min. before screening. Parking in nearby Wayne St. Garage is free after 6pm.

Washington, DC, Suburbs

Antique Row You've got two choices for the antiques shops in Kensington. Go east for 80 shops filled with knickknacks, silver, old books, and china. Or head west for the warehouses with antique European furniture, chandeliers, and objets d'art. (Connecticut Ave. divides the two areas by more than traffic.) If you enjoy a day of poking around little shops, turn right off Connecticut Avenue (Rte. 185) to Kensington's Antique Row, 3786 Howard Ave. (www.kensingtonantiquerow.com). You'll find 5 blocks of little shops, including **Antiques and Uniques** (✆ **301/942-3324**); **Pritchard's** (✆ **301/942-1661**), which also sells new decorative tiles and lighting; and the multidealer **Antique Village** (✆ **301/949-5333**), which has a small tea room. **Goldsborough Glynn** (✆ **301/933-4460**) has wonderful tableware and **Sally Shaffer Interiors** (✆ **301/933-3750**) has furniture and decorative items. For serious shopping, decorators (and homeowners) head to West Howard Avenue for their large pieces. There, among the car repair shops and warehouses, are more than a dozen dealers who import their wares from overseas. The mahogany gleams at crowded **Acanthus** (✆ **301/530-9600**). The **Great British Pine Mine** (✆ **301/493-2565**) imports both antique and reproduction furniture with a decidedly country feel. **Hollis and Knight** (✆ **202/333-6999**) offers antiques as well as modern reproductions to go with them. Most of these showrooms are open Thursday through Sunday.

From I-495, take Exit 33 north to Rte. 185, Connecticut Ave. Turn left at Howard for the historic district. For W. Howard, turn left at the Knowles Ave. traffic light, right on Summit Ave., left on W. Howard.

Brookside Gardens ★ It's just 50 acres, but it's a gem. The top draws are the conservatories with their tropical plantings and the summertime butterfly show, but don't overlook the rose and aquatic gardens or the children's garden. Enjoy the serenity of the Japanese Tea House. From May to September, **Wings of Fancy** puts butterflies on display. Between Thanksgiving and early January, a million lights twinkle in displays open at night. **Amy's Garden** honors cancer patients with tulips. Paths are accessible for wheelchairs and strollers, and some wheelchairs are available at the visitor center. The gardens' green practices have won it local honors. There's no picnicking, but take your lunch to neighboring **Wheaton Regional Park,** 2000 Shorefield Rd. (✆ **301/680-3803**), which has lots of trees, playgrounds, and also a miniature train and carousel to ride.

1800 Glenallan Ave., Wheaton. ✆ **301/962-1400.** www.brooksidegardens.org. Free admission. Gardens daily dawn–dusk; conservatories daily 10am–5pm; visitor center daily 9am–5pm. Closed Dec 25. From I-270 and points west, take Exit 4A, Montrose Rd. east, which turns into Randolph Rd. Go 7 miles and turn right onto Glenallan Ave. From I-495, the Capital Beltway, take Exit 31A (north on Georgia Ave./Rte. 97) toward Wheaton. Drive 3 miles north on Georgia Ave. to Randolph Rd. and turn right. At the 2nd light, turn right onto Glenallan Ave. Park at the visitor center at 1800 Glenallan Ave. or at the conservatories at 1500 Glenallan Ave.

Chesapeake & Ohio Canal National Historical Park ★★★ This is *the* stop on the Chesapeake & Ohio Canal. The wheelchair-accessible **Olmsted Island Boardwalk** runs through woods to a bridge overlooking one branch of the falls, then to the overlook where the falls crash over the rocks. The boardwalk is crowded on nice days, but when you get to the falls, you'll have plenty of space to take in the view. The strenuous Billy Goat Trail is a first-rate hike. The mule-drawn canal boat *Charles F. Mercer* takes visitors for an hourlong ride Wednesday through Sunday spring through fall. The 1831 lockhouse, the **Great Falls Tavern,** serves as a visitor center. And, you can spend the night in a historic lockhouse: rustic **Lockhouse 22,** Pennyfields, is 4 miles from Great Falls and sleeps four. Reservations ($70–$100 a night) are available at **www.canaltrust.org**. A website for the park's 40th anniversary, **www.canaldiscoveries.org**, offers information on points along the whole towpath.

11710 MacArthur Blvd., near Falls Rd. (Md. Rte. 189), Potomac. ✆ **301/767-3714** or 299-3613. www.nps.gov/choh or www.canaldiscoveries.org. Park entry fee $5 per vehicle, $3 for walk-ins. Admission valid for 3 days. Boat rides $8 adults, $6 seniors, $5 children. Daily park dawn–dusk, visitor center 9am–4:30pm. Visitor center closed Jan 1, Thanksgiving, and Dec 25. Take Exit 41W off I-495.

Clara Barton National Historic Site ★ The Red Cross was everything to its founder, Clara Barton. At her Glen Echo home, closets, filled with blankets, lanterns, and other supplies for disaster relief, line the walls. Her office is no-nonsense, including her chair: It's said she cut off the back so she wouldn't rest while working. The 1891 home is a quirky thing, its design unusual, but as you wander through the rooms that sheltered Clara and her staff, you'll get to know more about the woman who made this her mission and her life. It was here that she came up with disaster relief and first aid kits. You can see it all in 45 minutes. The guides are great with kids.

5801 Oxford Rd. (at MacArthur Blvd.), Glen Echo. ✆ **301/320-1410.** www.nps.gov/clba. Free admission. Daily 10am–5pm; by guided tour only (given on the hour; last tour at 4pm). Closed Jan 1, Thanksgiving, and Dec 25. From I-495, take Exit 40, Cabin John Pkwy., which merges with the Clara Barton Pkwy. Follow signs to Glen Echo and MacArthur Blvd. Left lane turns off with small spur to the right. Take right spur up ramp to MacArthur Blvd. Turn left to Oxford Rd.

The Fillmore Silver Spring A new home for live entertainment in the DC suburbs, it's across the street from AFI in a bustling restaurant and shopping district. The venue is huge, with seating for 2,000. Schedule and tickets are available on its website.

8656 Colesville Rd., Silver Spring, MD 20910. ✆ **301/960-9999.** www.fillmoresilverspring.com. Nearby garages charge no admission after 6pm.

Glen Echo Park Combine a visit to Clara Barton's house with a trip to this cultural arts park—it's just across a parking lot. First a Chautauqua meeting ground established in 1891, its emphasis on culture continues today. Call ahead or go to the website for a schedule of ballroom dancing events, puppet shows, and plays. You can stop here to picnic or to ride on the 1921 hand-carved Dentzel carousel for $1.25.

7300 MacArthur Blvd., Glen Echo. ✆ **301/492-6229.** www.nps.gov/glec. Free admission; tickets required for carousel; event ticket prices vary. Carousel May–June Wed–Thurs 10am–2pm, Sat–Sun noon–6pm; July–Aug Wed–Fri 10am–2pm, Sat–Sun noon–6pm; Sept Sat–Sun noon–6pm. See directions to Clara Barton site above.

Gravesite of F. Scott and Zelda Fitzgerald A simple gravestone marks the final resting place of the great American novelist and his wife, as well as their daughter. Listed on the National Register of Historic Places, the white-painted brick 1817 St. Mary's Church and graveyard were built when this was the countryside; now it's on a busy thoroughfare. Fans leave tokens of affection on Fitzgerald's gravestone, which is engraved with a quote from *The Great Gatsby.*

520 Veirs Mill Rd., Rockville, MD 20852. ✆ **301/424-5550.** www.stmarysrockville.org. Free admission. Cemetery open during daylight hours. Directions on church website; parking available at church—parking may be difficult during worship on Sun.

The Music Center at Strathmore ★ The architecture of this music hall is striking, with an undulating roofline, picture windows letting in the light and the leafy scenery, and warm maple and birch wrapped around curved walls and floors. The sound will wow you. Every note is unmistakably clear. Nearly 2,000 seats surround the stage, which has featured everyone from the Baltimore Symphony Orchestra—this is its DC-area headquarters—and National Philharmonic to Queen Latifah to Patti LuPone. It's just off the Capital Beltway and I-270; during ticketed events, there's free parking in the adjacent Metro garage and valet parking for $15. This is also home to a busy arts school that stages its performances here.

5301 Tuckerman Lane, North Bethesda, MD 20852. ✆ **301/581-5100.** www.strathmore.org. From I-495, take Exit 34 north, Wisconsin Ave. (Rte. 355) to Tuckerman Lane.

White Flint Mall Four floors of shopping—including Bloomingdale's, Lord & Taylor, Pottery Barn, AMC Lowes Theatres, and a Dave & Buster's restaurant—offer plenty of outlets for both necessities and luxuries.

11301 Rockville Pike, North Bethesda, MD 20895. ✆ **301/231-7467.** www.shopwhiteflint.com. From I-495, take Exit 34 north, Wisconsin Ave. (Rte. 355), to mall. Free valet parking.

NORTHEAST

30 miles W of Annapolis; 30 miles SW of Baltimore; 9 miles NE of Washington, DC; 100 miles SW of Wilmington

Connected to Baltimore by Routes 29 and 1, and I-95, this section is dominated by the University of Maryland's main campus in College Park, as well as Fort Meade. Laurel is home to a mill-turned-antiques center, and a resting place of George Washington. The science-minded may be interested in the Goddard Space Flight Center, while Muppet fans may want to homage to their creator (see Jim Henson Memorial listing, below). Prefer a picnic or roller-coaster ride? This area's got them, too.

Attractions

College Park Aviation Museum ☺ The oldest continuously operating airport in the world is next to the University of Maryland. The museum next to the airport, a Smithsonian Institution affiliate, celebrates milestones of aviation, including a visit by Wilbur Wright in 1909, and has 10 aircraft from the airplane's early days. For kids, there are props to spin and a wind tunnel. You can also try a flight simulation station.

1985 Cpl. Frank Scott Dr., College Park, MD 20740. ✆ **301/864-6029.** www.collegeparkaviationmuseum.com. Admission $4 adults, $3 seniors, $2 children. Daily 10am–5pm. Closed major holidays. From I-495, take Exit 23 south to Paint Branch Pkwy., to Cpl. Frank Scott Dr.

Dinosaur Park Twice a month, dinosaur fans have an opportunity to walk through this fossil treasure-trove, looking for fossils as small as a shell fragment or as large as a dinosaur bone. There's no digging allowed. Paleontologists give presentations and identify what visitors find. The 1-acre site is one of the East Coast's only intact deposits of fossils from the Early Cretaceous Period, 110 million years ago. You can't take your finds (if any) with you; they go to the Smithsonian. The park is at the end of a cul-de-sac in an industrial park. When it's closed, you can see the garden with plants from dinosaur times and there are informational signs about fossils and local history. Plans to add an accessible path, playground, shelter, and visitor center are in the works.

13201 Midatlantic Blvd., Laurel, MD 20708. ✆ **301/627-7755.** Free admission. 1st and 3rd Sat of the month noon–4pm; garden daily dawn–dusk.

Goddard Space Flight Center Just up the road (Rte. 295) from the aviation museum, Goddard celebrates flight into space. Exhibits focus on the beginning of space exploration (there's one on rocket pioneer Robert Goddard), the present (the latest discoveries of the Hubble Space Telescope and the latest Mars expedition Curiosity), and the future (scientists' predictions about global warming, pollution, and other earth and space issues). While the Hubble is the centerpiece of the visitor center, "Science on a Sphere" may be as fascinating to your inner geek. A ball-shaped screen shows the earth in 3-D, and you can watch weather, see the planet light up at night, or follow winds as they spread sand from China to California. The Rocket Garden features a 1960 Delta rocket, an Apollo model, and small rockets. Groups can tour the research facilities (call for reservations), including the world's largest "clean room," where scientists work on innovations for the telescope or new satellites. The website lists science nights, model-rocket launches, and experiments. Many of the exhibits require lots of reading and the help of an adult will make it more interesting for kids.

8800 Greenbelt Rd., Greenbelt, MD 20771. ✆ **301/286-9041.** Fax 301/286-1781. www.nasa.gov/centers/goddard. Free admission. Sept–June Tues–Fri 10am–3pm, Sat–Sun noon–4pm; July–Aug Tues–Fri 10am–5pm, Sat noon–4pm. Open some federal holidays, including MLK Day, Presidents' Day, Memorial Day, Columbus Day, and Veterans Day. Take Rte. 295 north from Capital Beltway to E. Greenbelt Rd. (Rte. 193). Turn left onto IceSat Rd. and left to visitor center.

Greenbelt Park This national park is like the DC suburbanites' backyard. With picnic tables, playground equipment, and walking trails, it's a nice getaway from the traffic and noise. The campground is open year-round. Reservations are taken (and recommended) for summer.

6565 Greenbelt Rd., Greenbelt, MD 20770. ✆ **301/344-3948.** www.nps.gov/gree. Free admission; camping $16. Daily dawn–dusk. Take Rte. 295 north from Capital Beltway to W. Greenbelt Rd. (Rte. 193). Park will be on the left.

Historic Savage Mill This restored 1822 cotton mill has antiques shops, galleries, boutiques, and a couple of places to stop for refreshment. It's an interesting place that keeps its heritage alive by using the names of the buildings' original purposes in signs and maps. You have only to follow your nose to **Bonaparte Breads** (✆ **410/880-0858**), in the Spinning Building, where you'll find coffee, French pastries, sandwiches, soup, and other treats. In the Carding Building is the **Rams Head Tavern** (✆ **301/604-3454**), a brewpub with hearty fare. In the Carding Building and Old Weave Building, you can find antiques, handmade sweaters, and needlework supplies.

8600 Foundry St., Savage, MD 20763. ✆ **800/788-6455.** www.savagemill.com. Free admission. Mon–Wed 10am–6pm; Thurs–Sat 10am–9pm; Sun 11am–6pm. Closed Easter, Thanksgiving, and Dec 25. Take Rte. 32 to Rte. 1 south. Turn right at Howard St. and follow the signs.

Jim Henson Memorial Those who love the Muppets may want to take a detour while in College Park to see the bronze-and-granite memorial to one of the University of Maryland's own, Jim Henson. Henson created the first Muppets while he was a student in the 1950s. Jay Hall Carpenter, a nationally known sculptor, created the work, which was cast in a Baltimore foundry. Alumni raised the funds for the memorial built in 2003. You'll find Jim and Kermit sitting on a bench outside the student union.

Stamp Student Union, University of Maryland, College Park, MD 20742. No phone. Free admission. From I-495, take Exit 27 and follow signs to Exit 25, U.S. 1 S., College Park. Right on Campus Dr., go around circle, pass Hornbake Library, and Stamp Student Union will be on right. Visitors may park during the school day at the nearby Union Lane Garage or Stadium Dr. Garage. Other lots require parking permits before 4pm. They are open to the public on evenings and weekends (except during football and basketball games) and in the summer.

Walking History's Trails

Montgomery County offers two hiking trails that allow walkers to stretch their minds as well as their legs. **Underground Railroad Experience Hikes ★** are offered Saturdays at 10am April through November, beginning at Woodlawn Manor, 16501 Norwood Rd., Sandy Spring. For directions and information, call ✆ **301/650-4373.** The 2-mile hikes are free. You can hike on your own, too. The trail is part of the **Rachel Carson Conservation Park Trails** that honor the memory of the author of *Silent Spring.* The environmental activist was also a Montgomery County resident. This 650-acre park has more than 6 miles of trails for hiking and horseback riding. (Bring your own horse.) To reach the park, go to 22201 Mt. Zion Rd., in Olney. For information, call ✆ **301/948-3471. Trail maps** for both hikes are available online at **www.montgomeryparks.org/PPSD/ParkTrails/trails_MAPS/Rural_legacy.shtm.**

Montpelier Mansion ☺ This 1780s five-part Georgian mansion, which once sat on 9,000 acres, was built by the grandson of an indentured servant and was grand enough for George and Martha Washington and Abigail Adams to spend the night. Now part of Prince George's County Parks, it has been restored to what historians think it looked like in the 1830s. The setting, now just 90 acres, is an idyllic green spot—which blazes orange and red in autumn. Christmas candlelight tours with rooms decorated by local garden clubs make the place festive. Children's hands-on programs and a boxwood maze keep kids occupied. Also on the property is the **Montpelier Arts Center** (✆ **301/377-7800**), which offers art exhibitions and performing arts events.

9650 Muirkirk Rd., Laurel, MD 20708. ✆ **301/377-7817.** www.pgparks.com/places/eleganthistoric/montpelier_intro.html. Admission $3 adults, $2 seniors, $1 children. Mar–Nov Mon–Thurs self-guided tours 11am–3pm, Sun guided tours on the hour noon–3pm; Dec–Feb Mon–Thurs self-guided tours 11am–3pm, Sun guided tours 1 and 2pm. Grounds daily dawn–dusk. From I-295, take exit to Rte. 197 W., left on Muirkirk Rd.

Where to Eat

On Route 29 in Silver Spring is the historic **Mrs. K's Tollhouse Restaurant,** 9201 Colesville Rd. (✆ **301/589-3500;** www.mrsks.com). The home of the last operating tollhouse in Montgomery County, the building has been a restaurant since 1930. Surrounded by gardens and expanded over the years, it remains an elegant, old-fashioned establishment, serving lunch and dinner Tuesday through Saturday, brunch and dinner on Sunday. It is closed Mondays. They also have tollhouse cookies to go!

SOUTHEAST

40 miles SW of Annapolis; 50 miles SW of Baltimore; 15 miles SE of Washington, DC; 115 miles SW of Wilmington

These sites are accessible from Exit 7A, Route 5 South. This section of the Washington suburbs is the least congested. Although more housing developments are popping up on farmland, you can still see vestiges of the agricultural past, perhaps even a tobacco farm or two and the fields John Wilkes Booth rode through to make his getaway. Six Flags is the exception. It is accessible from Route 214, off of I-495 or Route 301.

Attractions

Dr. Samuel A. Mudd House Dr. Mudd set John Wilkes Booth's broken leg after Booth shot Lincoln. For that action, he was incarcerated on a Caribbean island prison. The house hasn't changed much since those days. It remained the Mudd home until it was turned into a privately owned museum. In fact, Mudd family members still volunteer here. The 1830 house, surrounded by 200 acres, is filled with medical implements from Dr. Mudd's office and several items he made while in prison, including a checkerboard tabletop, a desk, and several shell-encrusted boxes. Also on the property are a farm museum and Mudd's original tombstone.

3725 Dr. Samuel Mudd Rd., Waldorf, MD 20601. ✆ **301/645-6870.** www.somd.lib.md.us/MUSEUMS/Mudd.htm. $6 adults, $2 ages 6–16. Wed and Sat 11am–4pm; Sun noon–4pm. Last tour at 3:30pm. Closed Dec–Mar. Parking on-site.

National Colonial Farm ★ ☺ The sheep will greet you as you walk up the path, and maybe the barn cat will insist you rub its ears at this modest two-room farmhouse surrounded by tobacco and other crops. The house's architecture is unique to this part of Prince George's County: With two fireplaces and a few luxuries (at least for colonists) this may seem a fairly well-to-do place. But this house actually recalls a middling family of the 1770s. The farm is part of the larger **Piscataway Park.** Its hiking trails lead to the Potomac River, where you can get a great view of George Washington's Mount Vernon directly across the river. Fishing is permitted here, too.

3400 Bryan Point Rd., Accokeek, MD 20607. ✆ **301/283-2113,** ext. 15. www.nps.gov/pisc/planyourvisit/ncf.htm. Park admission free; Colonial farm admission $2 adults, 50¢ children. Park daily dawn–dusk. Colonial farm mid-Mar to mid-Dec Tues–Sun 10am–4pm; mid-Dec to mid-Mar Sat–Sun 10am–4pm. Parking on-site.

Six Flags America ☺ Six Flags has some awesome coasters: Joker's Jinx, Superman, and Batwing. Unfortunately, the lines are awesome, too. During peak times, waits can be as long as an hour. Take a break and go to **Hurricane Harbor Water Park** to cool off in the wave pool, water slides, and Bahama Blast inner-tube ride. ***Note:*** The park requires visitors to go through metal detectors. Don't bring valuables—you'll have to put down your bags for some of the rides and to go in the water. A $15 **Flash Pass** allows holders to shoot to the front of the line.

13710 Central Ave., Bowie, MD 20721. ✆ **301/249-1500.** www.sixflags.com/america. Admission $60 adults, $40 children (48 in. and shorter), free for kids 3 and under. Parking $15. AE, DISC, MC, V. Apr–May and Sept Sat 10:30am–6pm; Memorial Day to Labor Day daily 10:30am–6pm or later; Mid-Oct Sat–Sun noon–9pm. Closed Nov–Mar. From Washington, DC, take I-495/I-95 to Exit 15A to Rte. 214 east; the park will be on the left in 5 miles. From Baltimore and points north, take I-695 to Exit 7, I-97 south, then Rte. 3/301 south to Rte. 214 west to the park, 3 miles on the right. From Annapolis, go south on Rte. 3/301 to Rte. 214 west to the park.

Surratt House Museum John Wilkes Booth slept here as he planned to kidnap and kill President Abraham Lincoln. The home's owner Mary Surratt was hanged for her part, although how much she knew is still hotly debated—it is the topic of Robert Redford's 2010 film "The Conspirator." Visitors can see the tavern and family's rooms in this 1852 house, including original furnishings, such as Mary's desk. Additional Surratt family items are displayed in the visitor center next door. During the 45-minute tour, costumed volunteer guides tell how Mary got entangled in this black period of history. The house, once part of a farm, now sits on a suburban road.

9118 Brandywine Rd., Clinton. ✆ **301/868-1121.** www.surratt.org. $3 for adults, $2 seniors, $1 ages 5–18. Wed–Fri 11am–3pm; Sat–Sun noon–4pm. Closed mid-Dec to mid-Jan. Parking on-site.

Thomas Stone National Historical Site The youngest Marylander to sign the Declaration of Independence made his home in this unusual hyphen house (a house built to connect two other houses). Called Haberdeventure, the home was restored by the National Park Service after the main section burned in 1977. Visitors can see exhibits in the two kitchens, the first-floor bedroom and the beautifully paneled East Room, which still holds Stone's desk. Because as many as 35 people lived here, George Washington probably didn't sleep here—but, because Stone was a friend, he probably visited. Special programs are scheduled for the Fourth of July and there's a December candlelight tour. Stone and his wife Margaret are buried here. There are 322 acres of trails around the property.

6655 Rose Hill Rd., Port Tobacco, MD 20677. ✆ **301/392-1776.** www.nps.gov/thst. Free admission. Summer daily 9am–5pm; Labor Day to Memorial Day Wed–Sun 9am–5pm. 30-min. tours offered 10am–4pm. Closed Jan 1, Thanksgiving, and Dec 25. Parking on-site.

NATIONAL HARBOR

47 miles SW of Annapolis; 10 miles SE of Washington, DC; 55 miles SW of Baltimore; 115 miles SW of Wilmington

On the banks of the Potomac River, downstream from the nation's capital, a brand-new 300-acre development offers a weekend getaway with restaurants, nightclubs, and waterfront activities. A short drive over the Woodrow Wilson Bridge or a water taxi ride will take you to Georgetown, George Washington's Mount Vernon, or Union Station, where you can catch a subway to anywhere in Washington.

Essentials

GETTING HERE National Harbor is accessible with its own ramps off I-95/495 and I-295 on the Maryland side of the Potomac.

Metrobus (✆ **202/637-7000;** www.metroopensdoors.com) service will take visitors from bus stops at the Oxon Hill Park and Ride Lot off Route 210. Buses run 20 to 30 minutes every day on the NH1 Line. Fare is $1.35 one-way.

The **Water Taxi,** operated by Potomac Riverboat Company (✆ **703/684-0580;** www.potomacriverboatco.com), takes passengers between the Gaylord complex, the main National Harbor dock, and Old Town Alexandria. A separate taxi goes to Washington Nationals baseball games. Boats depart about every hour May through October with abbreviated schedules November and December. The fare is $8. Additional taxis go on from Alexandria to Georgetown, daily May through October and weekends off-season. The fare is $16.

GETTING AROUND National Harbor is designed for walking. Park your car in one of the garages or paid lots. Garages are clearly marked with entrances on Fleet Street and Mariner Passage. Other parking is available on the fringes of the development.

What to See & Do

The Awakening Don't be startled by the face and arms reaching out from the riverbank at National Harbor's waterfront. The cast-iron sculpture created by J. Seward Johnson depicts the arousing of a bearded giant.

On the waterfront.

National Children's Museum Scheduled to open in 2013, this museum will explore environmental and sustainable practices. Even its building on St. George Boulevard will be eco-friendly. Until the new space is completed, visit the **Launch Zone,** a storefront filled with children's activities with a green theme. Visitors can also offer their own ideas for the new museum's exhibits.

112 Waterfront St. ✆ **301/686-0225.** www.ncm.museum. Free admission. Apr–May and Sept–Oct Mon–Sat 10am–5pm, Sun 11am–5pm; June to Labor Day Mon–Wed 10am–5pm, Thurs–Sat 10am–7pm, Sun 11am–7pm; Nov–Mar Mon–Fri 11am–3pm, Sat 10am–5pm, Sun 11am–5pm.

Potomac Cruises George Washington's home in Mount Vernon is a short boat ride away from National Harbor. The Potomac Riverboat Company gives 40-minute narrated cruises three times a day as well as daylong trips to Mount Vernon, which include a tour of Washington's home. Also available are dog-friendly, pirate, and monument cruises, as well as 90-minute rides on a Chesapeake skipjack, the *Minnie V.* Boats depart from the commercial pier and the pier at the Gaylord. Call for a reservation. Ticket prices range from $12 to $40 for adults, $6 to $20 for children.

At the pier. ✆ **877/511-2628** or 703/684-0580. www.potomacriverboatco.com. Closed Nov–Mar.

Where to Stay & Eat

National Harbor has 3,000 hotel rooms—and plenty are on the waterfront. The biggest is the **Gaylord National** (www.gaylordhotels.com; ✆ 301/965-2000), a mini-version of its Opryland in Nashville, with 2,000 rooms and a convention center. The **Westin National Harbor** on the waterfront (www.starwoodhotels.com/westin; ✆ 301/567-3999) has some of the best views. Cool, sophisticated rooms highlight **Aloft** (www.aloftnationalharbor.com; ✆ 301/749-9000). There are also a **Marriott Residence Inn** (www.marriott.com/residenceinn; ✆ 301/749-4755) and **Hampton Inn and Suites** (www.hamptoninn.hilton.com; ✆ 301/567-3531). If you want to come by boat, transient slips up to 120 feet are available on the Potomac River at **National Harbor Marina** (✆ 301/749-1582).

National Harbor has 24 eateries from a coffee shop to a posh lounge to several seafood restaurants. Most are chains, including the upscale **Ketchup** (✆ **301/749-7099**), Ashton Kutcher's place; **McCormick and Schmick's** (✆ **301/567-6224**); and the casual **Elevation Burger** (✆ **301/749-4014**). **Grace's Mandarin** (✆ **301/839-3788**) is a local entry and well worth a visit for Asian atmosphere and delicious foods.

Shopping

National chains occupy most of the glitzy shopping arcade with everything from Swarovski crystal to Godiva chocolate. **America!,** 154 National Plaza (✆ **301/686-0413**), has National Harbor and DC-themed souvenirs. **CakeLove,** 160 National Plaza (✆ **301/686-0340**), is owned by a local baker and Food Network host Warren Brown. National Harbor has a local outlets of the DC-area gallery **ArtWhino,** 120 American Way (✆ **301/567-8210**), an Alexandria gallery featuring pop-surrealism. **Tanger Outlets** plans to build a center here on 40 acres sometime in 2013.

THE EASTERN SHORE

7

Across the Chesapeake Bay Bridge, life slows down. Turn off Route 50 or Highway 301 and go down a country road past cornfields. Pause by rivers and marshes where birds and rustling grass are the only sounds. Stop in small towns where mom-and-pop shops still thrive. If you love to watch trees light up with fireflies on a summer night, or cycle down a country lane, or let the breeze take your boat past farms as old as America, you'll love the Eastern Shore.

Easton is the Eastern Shore's Colonial capital—its roots are evident on every picturesque street. It's the main town of Talbot County, home to three waterfront communities within driving distance. Waterfront **St. Michaels** has the most shops, and the Chesapeake Bay Maritime Museum. Boaters clog the harbor on summer weekends, but in spring and fall or midweek in summer, its charms are more accessible. **Oxford** is quieter, with a slower pace, waterfront park, and garden-bedecked streets. **Tilghman** (my favorite place!) hasn't bothered to beautify for the tourists—but its unique waterman's lifestyle is enough to draw them.

Cambridge, on the Choptank River, is beginning to capture the attention it deserves with the introduction of new lodging and the early stages of a downtown renaissance. Its history and outdoor activities make it worthwhile.

The southern areas of the Eastern Shore, including **Smith Island** and **Crisfield,** are the ultimate in waterman villages. Change comes slowly to these remote places, and residents like it that way. That attitude draws visitors to these hard-to-reach spots.

North of the Bay Bridge, **Chestertown** is not only a Colonial town with leafy streets and elegant homes, it's also a college town. George Washington permitted the college founders to use his name for Washington College. A dozen miles away is **Rock Hall,** a waterfront village with marinas and seafood restaurants.

Farther north is **Chesapeake City,** on the Chesapeake & Delaware Canal, which remains a crossroads for the marine traffic using the canal every day.

TALBOT COUNTY ★★★

40 miles SE of Annapolis; 60 miles SE of Baltimore; 71 miles SE of Washington, DC; 110 miles SW of Wilmington

In the middle of the Eastern Shore, Talbot (pronounced *Tall*-but) County has the most popular tourist towns north of Ocean City. Easton, the

THE ultimate CRAB CAKE, EASTERN SHORE STYLE

Finding a good crab cake on the Eastern Shore is easy, especially in warm months when crabs are in season. Even making a list can start an argument, since everybody has his or her favorite spot. Below are two good bets—just to get the discussion going.

Ruke's Seafood Deck (Main St., Ewell, Smith Island; ✆ **410/425-2311**): You've got to get on a boat and go to Smith Island to get these old-fashioned, deep-fried gems. If you find yourself on the other Smith Island in Tylerton instead, you can't go wrong with a crab cake from **Drum Point Market** (✆ **410/425-2108**). It's the local sweet crab that makes the difference.

Jimmie & Sook's (421 Race St., Cambridge; ✆ **443/225-4115**): No tomato or lettuce, just a crab cake on an ordinary roll. Delicate and sweet, this crab cake is filled with lump crab and little else. The homemade tartar and cocktail sauce are good, too.

Snappers (112 Commerce St., Cambridge; ✆ **410/228-0112**): Not satisfied with just a crab cake? Stop here for a crab cake club—local crab formed into a big flat cake and sandwiched in between toast with lettuce, tomato, and bacon.

county seat, is filled with Colonial buildings. St. Michaels clings to its maritime tradition, and lots of visitors arrive by boat at one of the town's many marinas on the Miles River. Continue down Route 33 to charming and remote Tilghman, where watermen and fresh seafood reign. Oxford was once a busy seaport, home of Revolutionary War financier Robert Morris.

Essentials

GETTING THERE The best way to get to Easton is by car, via U.S. Route 50 from all directions. Follow the signs on Route 50 near Easton to get to St. Michaels, Tilghman, and Oxford. All are reachable by boat as well, with plenty of dock space.

Easton Airport, on U.S. Route 50 (✆ **410/770-8055**), serves local planes and runs a charter with three- and eight-passenger planes. **Greyhound** (✆ **800/231-2222** or 410/822-3333; www.greyhound.com) offers bus service to the Fast Stop Convenience Store, 9543 Ocean Gateway (Rte. 50), across from the airport.

VISITOR INFORMATION Contact the **Talbot County Visitors Center,** 11 S. Harrison St., Easton (✆ **410/770-8000;** www.tourtalbot.org). The ***Tidewater Times,*** a free pocket magazine with good maps, is available in many shops.

GETTING AROUND You're going to have to drive to reach Talbot's quaint towns, though boats are a great option for St. Michaels, Oxford, and Tilghman Island. Maryland Route 33 from Easton will take you to St. Michaels and Tilghman; Maryland Route 333 goes to Oxford.

The shortest (in miles, not time) and most scenic route from Oxford to St. Michaels is via the **Oxford-Bellevue Ferry** (✆ **410/745-9023;** www.oxfordferry.com), across the Tred Avon River. Established in 1683, this is the country's oldest privately operated ferry. The ¾-mile trip takes 7 minutes. You can catch the nine-vehicle ferry from Bellevue, off Routes 33 and 329, 7 miles from St. Michaels, or from Oxford, off Route 333. From April through October, the ferry runs every 20 minutes, Monday through Friday from 7am to sunset, Saturday and Sunday from

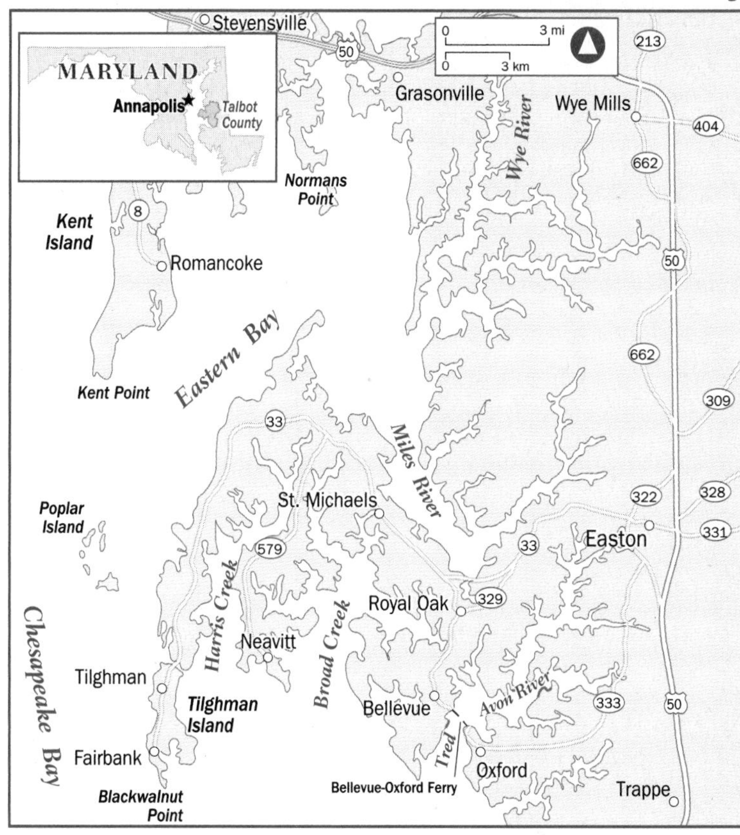

9am to sunset. There's no service December through March. It runs Saturday and Sunday only in November. Rates for a car and driver are $10 one-way and $18 round-trip; vehicle passengers pay $1 one-way; walk-on passengers $3; bicyclists $4; and motorcycles $6. Trailers and RVs can be accommodated, but call first. This tiny ferry offers a short, fun ride to a long country road leading to either St. Michaels or Easton.

To rent a car, call **Enterprise,** Route 50 and Dover Road (✆ **410/822-3260**). For cab service, try **Scotty's Taxi** (✆ **410/822-1475**).

SPECIAL EVENTS The **Waterfowl Festival ★★★** (✆ **410/822-4567;** www.waterfowlfestival.org), held the second week in November, turns Easton into a celebration of ducks, geese, and other birds. The 3-day festival draws some 20,000 visitors. You don't have to like hunting to attend. Some 400 artists' works are displayed, and venues around town display Federal Duck Stamp paintings, duck decoys, and carvings so realistic you'll want to smooth those ruffled feathers. Admission is $10 for adults and free for children under 12, with free shuttle buses running from site to site. If you visit wildlife refuges around Maryland, you'll see where the proceeds of

GETTING away FROM IT ALL, EASTERN SHORE STYLE

Why not make yourself at home? If you're looking for a waterfront view, a place that will take your dog, a pool, or dock, you might want to consider renting a house. Try **Eastern Shore Vacation Rentals,** 21 S. Harrison St., Easton (© **410/770-9093;** www.easternshorevacations.com), with properties of two to eight bedrooms all over Talbot and Dorchester counties; **Tidewater Vacations,** 300 N. Talbot St., St. Michaels (© **410/745-5255;** www.tidewatervacations.com); and **Chesapeake Bay Real Estate Plus** (tel **410/745-6702;** www.cbreplus.com/vacation_rentals.htm).

this event are used—about $5 million has been raised over the years to protect and conserve wildlife habitats.

Oxford Day (www.oxfordday.org), held the last Saturday in April, is a fun local fest, with music, entertainment, and crab races. Log canoes (small, fast, old-fashioned sailboats with lots of canvas) race in the **Oxford Regatta** (www.blogcanoe.com) the second weekend in August.

Tilghman Island Day (www.tilghmanmd.com), held the third Saturday in October, celebrates boats, crabs, and oysters and benefits the local fire department.

Easton

Visitors to the Eastern Shore usually start at Easton. Called the "Colonial Capital of the Eastern Shore," this town values its visitors. Route 50 is filled with reasonably priced chain hotels, and the downtown district has many worthy restaurants.

WHERE TO STAY

Accommodations range from chain hotels on Route 50 to high style and luxury downtown. You'll pay for the luxury, especially on busy weekends during the Waterfowl Festival or hunting season.

National chains include **Comfort Inn,** 8523 Ocean Gateway/Route 50 (www.comfortinn.com; © **800/228-5150** or 410/820-8333), and **Days Inn,** 7018 Ocean Gateway/Route 50 (www.daysinn.com; © **410/822-4600**).

Bartlett Pear Inn ★★ New owners, both Talbot natives, have put their mark on this 2-centuries-old building. Sophisticated colors, art by the owner's aunt, a first-floor bar, and a restyled dinner menu offer a warm welcome to guests. Rooms are named for pear varieties and feature luxurious bedding and big windows. Some bathrooms have claw-foot tubs. Everyone is welcome to sit on the second-floor porch. Two king suites are especially spacious. The 30-seat **restaurant** is open to the public for dinner 5:30 to 10pm every day but Tuesday.

28 S. Harrison St., Easton, MD 21601. www.bartlettpearinn.com. © **410/770-3300.** 7 units. $149–$279 double Rates include breakfast. AE, DISC, MC, V. Children- and pet-friendly. **Amenities:** Restaurant; lounge. *In room:* A/C, flatscreen TV, hair dryer, MP3 docking station, free Wi-Fi.

Inn at 202 Dover ★★★ This stately 1874 home downtown has been restored to show off its elegant beginnings. Accommodations are appointed with elegant decor and bathrooms fitted with steam or rain showers and jetted tubs. The Asian suite and the manly Safari suite have gas fireplaces. The chintz-upholstered English suite has

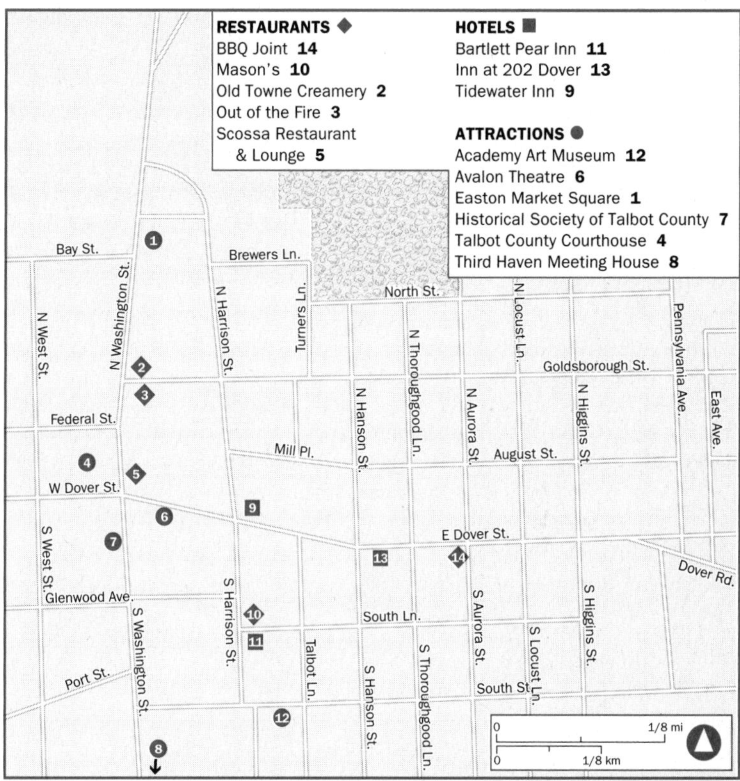

the most space. **Peacock,** the inn's fine-dining restaurant, serves dinner and afternoon tea on Thursdays; reservations are required. (You don't have to be a guest to eat here.)

202 E. Dover St., Easton, MD 21601. www.innat202dover.com. ✆ **866/450-7600.** 5 units. $275–$475 double. Rates include full breakfast. AE, DISC, MC, V. Pets welcome. No children under 15. **Amenities:** Restaurant. *In room:* A/C, TV w/DVD, hair dryer, free Wi-Fi.

The Tidewater Inn ★ This 200-year-old hotel hardly looks its age. Remodeled a few years ago and still being upgraded, it continues to be the model of Eastern Shore hospitality it has been for decades. Rooms may be smallish but guests can expect crisp white linens, softly colored walls, and white-tiled bathrooms. Suites offer a smidge more room; Room 231 has great space and a view of the courtyard. **Hunters' Tavern** has a traditional feel. Make reservations a year ahead to stay here for the Waterfowl Festival.

101 E. Dover St., Easton, MD 21601. www.tidewaterinn.com. ✆ **800/237-8775** or 410/822-1300. Fax 410/820-8847. 98 units, including 11 suites. $229–$259 double; $270–$450 suites. Golf and waterfront hunting packages available. AE, DC, DISC, MC, V. Valet parking $10. Pets accepted. **Amenities:** Restaurant; bar; fitness center. *In room:* A/C, TV w/movies, fridge (in suites), hair dryer (on request), high-speed Internet.

WHERE TO EAT

Seafood lovers, rejoice: Crabs, oysters, and fish are star attractions at restaurants all around Easton. If you're in the mood for something else, Easton is blessed with some sophisticated restaurants with creative menus.

BBQ Joint BARBEQUE Totally casual, totally delicious, this new eatery is set in the elegant surroundings of a former Thai restaurant—with sawdust on the floor. The food is all-American: barbequed meat, fries and great country sides, beer, and a couple of simple desserts. Stay here for lunch or call ahead and have your order (family portions or individual sandwiches) ready to-go when you arrive. Stopping here on the way to your vacation destination (assuming it isn't Easton) is a good idea.

216 E. Dover St., Easton, MD 21601. ✆ **410/690-3641.** www.andrewevansbbqjoint.com. Reservations not accepted. Call ahead for carryout. Main courses $4–$16. AE, MC, V. Mon–Sat 11am–9pm.

Mason's AMERICAN The menu changes often at this delightful little place, where you can sit on the porch, on the terrace, or in the more formal dining room. Get a sandwich to go or stay for a full meal. Lunchtime choices range from sandwiches and salads to some hearty entrees from quiche to steak frites. At dinner, look for fresh seafood and roasted meats with rich sides. An in-between light fare menu is served 2:30 to 5:30pm. A coffee bar is open Monday through Saturday 9am to 5pm.

22 S. Harrison St., Easton, MD 21601. ✆ **410/822-3204.** www.masonsgourmet.com. Reservations recommended for dinner. Main courses $7–$17 lunch, $19–$30 dinner. AE, DC, MC, V. Mon 11:30am–2:30pm; Tues–Sat 11:30am–9:30pm.

Old Towne Creamery ICE CREAM Sometimes you just need an ice-cream cone. Here's a cheery place with tiny tables, pink walls, and all kinds of cones and sundaes.

9B Goldsborough St., Easton, MD 21601. ✆ **410/820-5223.** Reservations not accepted. Ice-cream desserts $2–$6. No credit cards. Summer Mon–Thurs 1–9pm, Fri–Sat noon–9pm, Sun noon–8pm; hours may be shortened in cooler months.

Out of the Fire ★★ MEDITERRANEAN Trendy food flavored with seasonings from around the world has made it to Easton. This chic dining room is dominated by a wood-fired oven. Lunch means soups, pizzas, and salads. Dinner choices include pasta, meats, and poultry, all with international zing; pizza, too. The whole menu is good but whatever you choose, get at least a sliver of their crispy-crust pizza with either traditional or exotic toppings. Pizza doesn't get any better than this. It's even tastier because of the owners' commitment to supporting local farms and eco-friendly practices.

22 Goldsborough St., Easton, MD 21601. ✆ **410/770-4777.** www.outofthefire.com. Reservations recommended for dinner. Main courses $8–$18 lunch, $15–$26 dinner. AE, MC, V. Mon–Fri 11:30am–2pm; Mon–Thurs 5–9pm; Fri–Sat 5–10pm.

Scossa Restaurant & Lounge ★★★ NORTHERN ITALIAN With doors that fold away to reveal the rich, sleek interior, you'll be drawn by this restaurant's long banquettes and sepia-toned photos of Venice. But Scossa's real appeal is its northern Italian dishes, which feature fresh, simple ingredients. Pureed vegetables transform into velvety soups. Crusty bread is topped with olive butter. The fresh-made pastas and risottos are the star. Lunchtime salads and sandwiches have Italian style, too. Daily specials and prix-fixe menus, as well as the creative bar menu, are easier on the wallet. The wine list features Italian and California vintages with some French champagnes.

8 N. Washington St., Easton, MD 21601. ✆ **410/822-2202.** www.scossarestaurant.com. Reservations recommended for dinner. Main courses $7.50–$24 lunch, $17–$30 dinner. AE, DC, DISC, MC, V. Sun 11:30am–8pm; Tues–Thurs 11:30am–9pm; Fri–Sat 11:30am–10pm; Mon 4–9pm.

Hunting Season on the Eastern Shore

Maryland's Eastern Shore has long been considered the finest duck- and goose-hunting region on the Atlantic Flyway, with hundreds of thousands of migratory game birds passing through. Over 20 local organizations conduct guided waterfowl hunts for Canada geese (2 weeks in Nov and mid-Dec to late Jan), ducks (late Nov to mid-Jan), and sea ducks (early Oct to mid-Jan). Quail and pheasant hunting are also available. White-tailed and sika deer may also be hunted (Sept–Dec). The **Department of Natural Resources** (✆ **877/620-8DNR** [8367]; www.dnr.state.md.us/huntersguide) publishes an annual guide with hunting regulations, including bag limits, season dates, and licensing. **Albright's Gun Shop,** 36 E. Dover St., Easton (✆ **800/474-5502** or 410/820-8811; www.albrightsgunshop.com), can help plan your hunting trip, with or without guides.

WHAT TO SEE AND DO

A walk through Easton's historic district will take you past buildings that witnessed the birth of the United States and have stood through 2 centuries. The **Talbot County Courthouse,** for instance, at 11 N. Washington St., was built in 1710.

The museum of the **Historical Society of Talbot County ★**, 25 S. Washington St. (✆ **410/822-0773;** www.hstc.org), offers an intimate look at life in the county and Talbot's industries, such as boat-building and duck-decoy carving. The museum is open Monday through Saturday from 10am to 4pm; admission is free. It also offers guided tours of historic Easton and of local historic houses. Don't miss the Federal-style gardens behind the museum, a quiet haven for a spot of relaxation. It is surrounded by three fascinating houses, which are open Fridays at 11:30am April to November, or by appointment: a humble 1795 home of a Quaker cabinetmaker, the grander 1805 Federal home of his brother, and a replica Colonial home built as a studio by a noted Easton architect.

The **Academy Art Museum,** 106 South St., at Harrison Street (✆ **410/822-2787;** www.art-academy.org), a light-filled gallery transformed from 18th-century buildings, has exhibits by regional and national artists, and a performing-arts series. Admission is $3 for visitors over 11. Hours are Monday through Friday 10am to 4pm, and until 7pm Wednesday and Thursday; Saturday 10am to 3pm.

The restored Art Deco **Avalon Theatre,** 40 E. Dover St. (✆ **410/822-7299;** www.avalontheatre.com), has been providing entertainment since 1921. Its performing-arts series draws local and national acts, as well as films such as the Metropolitan Opera in HD. For tickets, call the box office or buy online.

Farther from downtown is **Third Haven Meeting House,** 405 S. Washington St. (✆ **410/822-0293**). Opened in 1684, this Quaker house of worship once hosted William Penn, who preached to Lord Baltimore. It is the oldest religious building in use in the U.S. Admission is free, donations are welcome. It's open daily from 9am to 5pm (meetings for worship are Sun at 10am and Wed at 5:30pm).

SHOPPING

Easton's main shopping is along Washington, Dover, and Harrison streets. You'll find a number of galleries, as well as antiques, clothing, and gift shops. Hours are generally daily from 9am to 5pm; some shops close midweek and have shorter hours in winter.

 A drive TO WYE MILLS

Three things in the hamlet of Wye Mills make the detour from Easton worthwhile: a pre-Revolutionary War flour mill, the remains of a 400-year-old tree, and beaten biscuits. This could be one of those trips the kids talk about for a long time.

From Route 50, go west on Route 404 or Route 213, about 13 miles north of Easton or 14 miles southeast from Kent Island. This burg is a mile off Route 50.

Flour ground at **Wye Grist Mill ★**, Old Wye Mills Road (Rte. 662), off Route 50, in Wye Mills (✆ **410/827-6909;** www.historicqac.org/sites/WMgristmill.htm), was sent to George Washington's troops at Valley Forge during the Revolutionary War. The mill has been in operation since 1682. Visitors can watch the wheat-grinding on the first and third Saturdays of the month, 10am to 4pm. With volunteers in short supply, call ahead to be sure there will be staff. During the week, the mill is open but not operating Monday to Friday 10am to 4pm and most weekends 10am to 4pm on Saturday and 1 to 4pm on Sunday. Guides are good at explaining the gear that makes the water wheel and grinding stones turn. It's worth a visit to see the exhibits and machinery and buy a bag of flour or cornmeal. There's no admission fee, but a $2 donation is requested.

The 450-year-old **Wye Oak** fell in a 2002 storm—but the stump of the largest white oak in the country and Maryland's official state tree remains, now surrounded by a fence. An enormous chunk of the historic tree has been put on display and a sapling cloned from the original grows in the old tree's place. Next door, take a look inside the tiny brick **Wye Oak House,** Talbot County's oldest school building.

You can't leave Wye Mills without getting a taste of an old Maryland tradition. **Orrell's Maryland Beaten Biscuits ★**, 124 Old Wye Mill Rd. (Rte. 662), Wye Mills (✆ **410/827-6244**), in business since 1935, has limited hours, but try to schedule a stop. The dough really is beaten—usually with a hammer, though the back of an ax works, too—to get the biscuits to rise. The method was used in a time when leavening was in short supply. You can try the finished product or buy some to bring home. Free admission. Open Wednesday (baking day) from 9am until baking is done, usually about 3pm. Call ahead (✆ **443/454-4361**) to visit.

If you bring your fishing rod, you can try your luck in the **Wye Mills Community Lake** which feeds the mill across the street. This 50-acre lake is home to bass, bluegill, and who knows what else. A non-tidal-waters fishing license is required. There are lots of grassy spots for a picnic, too.

Albright's Gun Shop This shop stocks guns and accessories, sport clothing, watches, canvas goods, and tackle. It's an authorized Orvis dealer. Custom gunsmithing is done on the premises. 36 E. Dover St. ✆ **800/474-550** or 410/820-8811. www.albrightsgunshop.com.

Crackerjacks Stop by this children's store for books, toys, games, dolls, stuffed animals, pinwheels, crafts, and more. 7 S. Washington St. ✆ **410/822-771.**

Easton Market Square Local produce, gourmet shops, Jean McHale Antiques, as well as a French bistro, **Brasserie Brightwell,** and a great coffee shop, **Coffee for a Cause,** are clustered in this European-style market. The produce market and bistro are open Wednesday through Sunday; other shops are open throughout the week. The coffee shop is open daily 6am to 6pm. 137 N. Harrison St. www.eastonmarketsquare.com.

Tharpe Antiques and Decorative Arts Proceeds from this consignment shop benefit the Historical Society of Talbot County. It's open Tuesday to Saturday 10am to 5pm, Sunday 11am to 4pm. It is in a restored 1788 house. 30 S. Washington St. ✆ **410/822-077.**

Troika Gallery The artist-owners present their own work, as well as pieces by local and national artists. 9 S. Harrison St. ✆ **410/770-919.** www.troikagallery.com.

St. Michaels

Since its founding in the late 1700s, St. Michaels has looked to the water for its livelihood. Shipbuilding made it famous. Log canoes were first workboats and then became better known as racing boats. Bugeyes and Baltimore clippers were built here. Watermen came to sell their catch, and canneries and oyster-packing plants sprang up. Local residents are proud of the legend (true or not) when residents here fooled the British and saved their town during the War of 1812.

Today, St. Michaels is a popular destination for boaters, who are crammed into the harbor on sunny weekends. It's also bed-and-breakfast heaven; many have views of the beautiful Miles River. Make time for the Chesapeake Bay Maritime Museum, where the history of the whole Chesapeake Bay is celebrated. The town's streets also offer a variety of shops and restaurants.

WHERE TO STAY

Aida's Victoriana Inn On the harbor, this 1875 home offers comfortable rooms, many with water views. Three rooms have fireplaces. Porches and Adirondack chairs on the lawn invite guests to stop if only for a minute. Rooms are of varying sizes. The junior suite has its own deck and fireplace. The Sharp Room has only a garden view but, with its fireplace and canopy bed, is quite romantic.

205 Cherry St., St. Michaels, MD 21663. www.victorianainn.com. ✆ **410/745-3368.** 7 units. $149–$339 double. Rates include breakfast. MC, V. Free parking. Pets accepted for fee. Children over 5 welcome. **Amenities:** Deck; fax; sunroom. *In room:* A/C, TV/DVD, CD player, hair dryer, MP3 docking station, whirlpool tub, free Wi-Fi.

Bob Pascal's St. Michaels Harbour Inn, Marina & Spa ★ Here are all the mod cons in the heart of St. Michaels. The Harbour Inn has kept up with the times, replacing its kitchenettes with Jacuzzis and adding an outdoor grill to the marina deck. All but four rooms—38 are suites—have a water view, most have terraces, and third-floor rooms have cathedral ceilings. On-site are a waterfront **restaurant** and a casual eatery.

101 N. Harbor Rd., St. Michaels, MD 21663. www.harbourinn.com. ✆ **800/955-9001** or 410/745-9001. Fax 410/745-9150. 46 units. $189–$525 double. DISC, MC, V. **Amenities:** 2 restaurants; bikes; concierge; fitness room; marina; outdoor pool; resort shuttle; spa; watersports equipment; water taxi stop. *In room:* A/C, TV w/movies, fridge in most rooms, hair dryer, free Wi-Fi.

Five Gables Inn & Spa Get pampered at this combination B&B and spa, which spreads over four buildings on the main street. Every room has a fireplace, whirlpool tub, and, since it's a spa, Aveda toiletries. Most have private porches. A small pool, sun deck, sauna, and steam room—as well as six treatment rooms for hydrotherapy, scrubs, and massages (one is for couples)—add to the pampering. A sailing or girls' getaway package can add to the spa experience.

209 N. Talbot St., St. Michaels, MD 21663. www.fivegables.com. ✆ **877/466-0100** or 410/745-0100. Fax 410/745-2903. 20 units. $99–$425 double. Rates include continental breakfast. 2-night minimum stay required weekends. AE, MC, V. Pets accepted for fee. **Amenities:** Indoor pool; sauna; spa treatments; steam room. *In room:* A/C, TV/VCR, CD player, hair dryer, whirlpool tub, free Wi-Fi.

Hambleton Inn Set right on the harbor but steps from the shopping district, every room at this Victorian-style B&B has a water view and antique furnishings. A suite has room for six and families are welcome. An open second-floor porch, enclosed lower porch, and harborside deck provide three more spots to view the boats docked at St. Michaels. Tell the innkeeper of special needs, especially dietary, in advance.

202 Cherry St., St. Michaels, MD 21663. www.hambletoninn.com. ✆ **866/745-3350** or 410/745-3350. Fax 410/745-5709. 8 units. $155–$285 double; $375–$625 suite. Rates include breakfast. 2-night minimum stay required on most weekends in high season. MC, V. No children under 13. *In room:* A/C, TV w/movies in some rooms, free Wi-Fi.

Harris Cove Cottages Bed 'n Boat ☺ Harris Cove is a throwback to a simpler time. Though these cottages were built in the 1930s, they've been updated with new furniture, floors, and appliances. They remain unfussy but comfortable with full kitchens, sitting areas, and nice-sized sleeping areas. Each cottage sleeps four. A one-room "stateroom" is also available. Their setting beside a quiet shallow cove—with gazebos, lounge chairs, and hammocks—makes them an old-fashioned getaway. There's also a 65-foot pier, and kayaks and paddle boats to rent.

8070 Bozman-Neavitt Rd., St. Michaels, MD 21663. www.bednboat.com. ✆ **410/745-9701.** 6 cottages, 2 units in main house. $150–$230 per cottage; $150 "stateroom" unit. Week-long rentals available. No credit cards. Open late Apr to Oct. **Amenities:** Boats; boat ramp; dockage for guests' boats; crabbing equipment; gazebos; charcoal grills. *In room:* A/C, TV w/VCR or DVD, kitchen.

The Inn at Perry Cabin ★★ Part of the Orient Express chain, this English country–style inn on the Miles River is richly appointed and designed for comfort. There are seven tiers of rooms, from standard to master suite. At every level, you'll find plenty of space, river views, and luxurious linens. Units of the historic building and the lobby underwent complete renovation in early 2012, bringing their style into the 21st century. Some units have gas fireplaces. Amenities, such as the **Linden Spa,** are fabulous, although some may find service a bit cool for the Eastern Shore. It's a short walk from downtown, though right next to the maritime museum.

308 Watkins Lane, St. Michaels, MD 21663. www.perrycabin.com. ✆ **800/722-2949** or 410/745-2200. Fax 410/745-3348. 76 units. $445–$780 double. Ask about winter or B&B packages. AE, DISC, DC, MC, V. Pets accepted for a fee. **Amenities:** Restaurant; bar; poolside lounge; babysitting; bikes; complimentary docks for restaurant or hotel guests' boats; fitness center; outdoor pool; spa; steam room. *In room:* A/C, flatscreen TV/DVD, fridge (upon request), hair dryer, free Wi-Fi.

Parsonage Inn ★ This redbrick Victorian home, built in 1883, is a beauty. It served as the parsonage to the United Methodist Church from 1924 to 1985. Today, it's a respite for travelers willing to exchange a water view for a delicious breakfast, cozy decor, and creature comforts. All rooms have brass beds, three have fireplaces, and many have ceiling fans and access to a sun deck. The first-floor room has a wood-burning fireplace. Packages combine a stay with a skipjack ride, dinner at a local restaurant, or visits to the maritime museum.

210 N. Talbot St., St. Michaels, MD 21663. www.parsonage-inn.com. ✆ **800/394-5519** or 410/745-5519. Fax 410/745-6869. 8 units. $110–$160 double. Rates include gourmet breakfast. 2-night

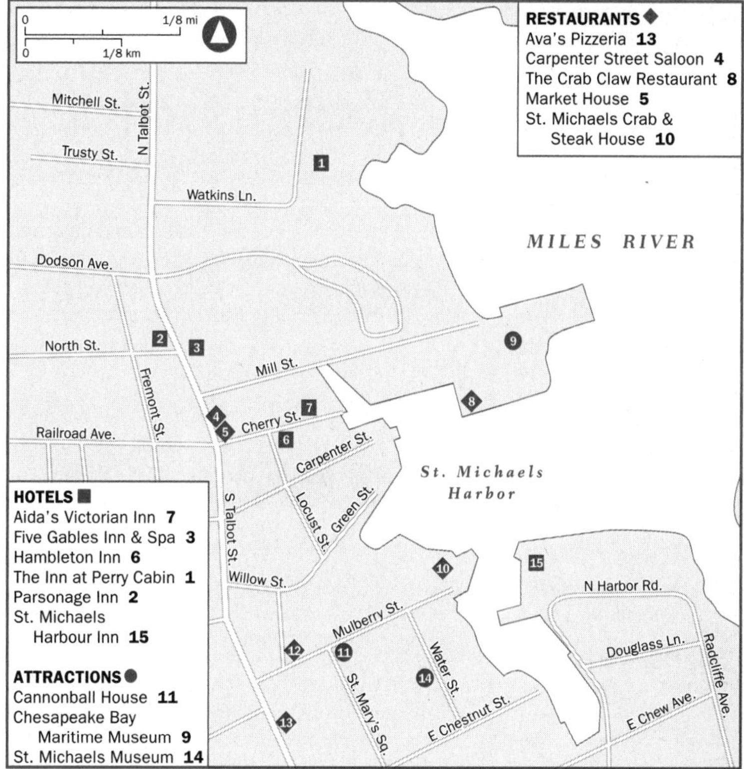

minimum stay required most weekends. DISC, MC, V. Children welcome with prior approval. **Amenities:** Complimentary bikes; concierge service. *In room:* A/C, TV w/DVD (in 6 rooms), free Wi-Fi.

Wades Point Inn on the Bay ★★ Set on a peninsula in the bay, Wades Point Inn offers an old-fashioned vacation outside St. Michaels. The sprawling house, built in 1819 by Thomas Kemp (designer of the famous Baltimore clipper ship), has been host to many a summer holiday over the past century. The main house and Kemp Guest House next door have spacious bedrooms decorated with period furniture. The Kemp rooms have porches or balconies; some have kitchenettes. A separate farmhouse is available for groups of up to 13. The 1890 Victorian Summer Wing, open seasonally, has cottage-style rooms with screen doors. Breakfast includes eggs and produce from the inn's organic farm. Kayaks, a floating dock, a swim dock, and fishing rods (the fishing's great in Eastern Bay) help guests take full advantage of the waterfront.

Wades Point Rd. (P.O. Box 7), St. Michaels, MD 21663. www.wadespoint.com. ✆ **888/923-3466** or 410/745-2500. Fax 410/745-3444. 24 units. $159–$270 double. Rates include full breakfast on weekdays, continental breakfast on weekends. Children under 12 stay free in parent's room. 2-night minimum stay required on weekends and holidays. Discounts available for seniors and for stays of 3 days or more. MC, V. Located 5 miles west of St. Michaels, off Rte. 33, at end of Wades

Point Rd. **Amenities:** Bike rentals; canoe/kayak launch; dock; executive-level rooms; walking trails; watersports equipment/rentals. *In room:* A/C, hair dryer (upon request), Wi-Fi available.

WHERE TO DOCK

St. Michaels Marina Coming to St. Michaels by boat? Make a reservation for one of the marina's 54 transient slips. Rates are determined by season and boat length.

301 Mulberry St., St. Michaels, MD 21663. ✆ **800/678-8980.** 54 slips, $1.50 per ft.–$4.25 per ft. Reservations required. AE, DC, DISC, MC, V. **Amenities:** Fuel dock; marine store; outdoor pool; pump-out station; showers; TV; Wi-Fi.

WHERE TO EAT

Ava's Pizzeria PIZZA A wood-fired oven and house-made dough and mozzarella gives these pizzas their pizzazz. If you opt for a sandwich, it comes with fresh-made potato chips. At dinner, entrees range from short ribs to fish and chips. And pizza, of course. Wine is offered by the glass or the bottle, with nearly 50 beers available.

409 S. Talbot St. ✆ **410/745-3081.** www.avaspizzeria.com. Reservations accepted. Main courses $11–$17 lunch, $11–$27 dinner. AE, DC, MC, V. Daily 11:30am–10pm.

Carpenter Street Saloon SEAFOOD/PUB FARE A noisy, casual pub with a bar in one room and a dining room next door, this place makes a good stop for a beer and a burger—and for a family outing, too. It's got a little of everything: crab soup and crab cakes, rockfish and chips, prime rib. Locals come for their steaks. It offers a kid's menu, a few games and pool tables upstairs, live music on Wednesday through Saturday, late-night pizza, and breakfast.

113 Talbot St., at Carpenter St., St. Michaels, MD 21663. ✆ **410/745-5111.** Main courses $6–$13 lunch, $9–$24 dinner. DISC, MC, V. Daily 8am–9pm. Bar open until 2am.

The Crab Claw Restaurant ★ SEAFOOD Many Marylanders consider this a destination restaurant. They come by the busloads for the fresh seafood, steamed crabs, and river breezes. It's casual and fun—and it's right beside the Chesapeake Bay Maritime Museum. The emphasis is crabs, served every way possible. Platters of chicken, oysters, sandwiches, and a raw bar are also available.

Navy Point, Mill St., St. Michaels, MD 21663. ✆ **410/745-2900.** www.thecrabclaw.com. Reservations recommended for dinner. Main courses $18–$27. No credit cards. Mar–Nov daily 11am–9pm. Closed Dec–Feb.

St. Michaels Crab and Steak House ☺ SEAFOOD Located on the marina, this casual, family-friendly crab house offers a choice of indoor seating in a nautical setting or outdoors under an umbrella. The building is an 1830s oyster-shucking shed. The menu, which includes a children's section, features steamed crabs, crab cakes, softshells, and crab Benedict, as well other seafood, steaks, and chicken. A raw bar has everything from oysters to shrimp to steamed crabs.

305 Mulberry St., St. Michaels, MD 21663. ✆ **410/745-3737.** www.stmichaelscrabhouse.com. Reservations recommended for dinner. Main courses $7.50–$16 lunch, $13–$25 dinner. DISC, MC, V. Mid-Mar to mid-Dec Thurs–Tues 11am–10pm. Closed mid-Dec until last weekend in Mar.

WHAT TO SEE & DO

The **Chesapeake Bay Log Sailing Canoe Association** sponsors log canoe races—just about the oldest class of boat still sailing around here. Usually races are more exciting for the sailor than for the spectator. But these boats—big on sail, small on hull—have to be seen to be appreciated. Races are usually held on weekends from

June to September. For information, contact the **Miles River Yacht Club** (✆ **410/745-9511;** www.milesriveryc.org or www.blogcanoe.com).

The **Cannonball House,** on Mulberry Street at St. Mary's Square, may look like an ordinary Colonial-style house—but it was witness to the day the town outsmarted the British. According to legend, now in serious dispute, when the British attempted to shell St. Michaels during the War of 1812, the townspeople blacked out the town and hung lanterns high in the trees, causing the British to overshoot the houses. Only one cannonball hit the town August 10, 1813, striking the chimney of this house. The town was saved, and the "blackout strategy" was born. The house is privately owned and not open to the public, but it's a good place to retell this old tale.

Chesapeake Bay Maritime Museum ★★★ Celebrate the way people work and play Chesapeake Bay at this unusual museum. You'll know you're in for something different when you enter the driveway—under the old Knapps Narrows Bridge. The centerpiece of this 18-acre waterfront site is the picturesque 1879 Hooper Strait Lighthouse, and all around are fascinating exhibits about boat-building, fishing, oystering, and the people who earn their livelihood on the water. Climb aboard the skipjack installed in the Oystering Building or stop by the boatyard where expert builders work year-round to restore historic boats. Go ahead and talk to them. They're delighted to talk about their work. A new tugboat exhibit, including the Delaware (which once graced the *Frommer's Maryland & Delaware* cover), goes on display in 2012. Look for War of 1812 commemorations, too. The grounds are open as a waterfront park after the buildings close for the day; no admission is charged then.

Navy Point, Mill St. ✆ **410/745-2916.** www.cbmm.org. Admission $13 adults, $10 seniors, $6 children 6–17; 2-day passes $18 adults, $13 seniors, $10 children. Summer daily 10am–6pm; spring and fall daily 10am–5pm; winter daily 10am–4pm. Closed Jan 1, Thanksgiving, and Dec 25. Take Rte. 33 to St. Michaels; turn right at driveway with drawbridge.

St. Michaels Museum ★ Two 19th-century buildings have been joined together to create a gallery of old photos and artifacts in one while maintaining the Sewell House as it was when the Sewells and their six children lived here. Needlework samplers and a fine collection of quilts and toys are interesting. The gallery's photos, produced by a Sewell descendant, and the changing exhibits highlight the town's history as a waterman's town. Tours highlighting the waterfront and the early life of Frederick Douglass begin here. They are $10 for adults and $5 for children.

St. Mary's Square. P.O. Box 714, St. Michaels, MD 21663. ✆ **410/745-9561.** www.stmichaelsmuseum.org. Admission $3 adults, $1 ages 6–17. May–Oct Mon 10am–1pm, Fri 1–4pm, Sat 10am–4pm, Sun 1–4pm.

OUTDOOR ACTIVITIES

BIKING Rent bikes at **St. Michael's Marina,** 305 Mulberry St. (✆ **800/678-8980**).

BOAT RIDES ★ All this water, and you don't have your own boat? Not to worry: There are all kinds of ways to get on the water here. Take a ride on the ***H.M. Krentz*** (✆ **410/745-6080;** www.oystercatcher.com), a skipjack that dredges oysters in winter and earns its keep with sailboat rides from April to October. It's docked by the maritime museum. Or perhaps you'd like a slightly more modern sailboat? The 41-foot 1926 gaff-rigged ***Selina II*** (✆ **410/726-9400;** www.sailselina.com), captained by the boat's original owners' granddaughter Iris Clarke, with room for just six passengers, offers more intimate 2-hour sails.

Go in air-conditioned comfort with **Patriot Cruises,** by the Chesapeake Bay Maritime Museum (✆ **410/745-3100;** www.patriotcruises.com), which offers 1-hour and 90-minute narrated cruises on a 65-foot tour boat April through November.

St. Michaels Harbor Tours & Water Taxi (✆ **410/924-2198**), berthed at the foot of Mulberry Street, offers daily 30-minute tours in season every half-hour. It also serves as water taxi service, with stops at the Crab Claw, St. Michaels Marina, St. Michaels Harbour Inn, and St. Michaels Crab & Steak House.

SHOPPING

The best shops are concentrated along Talbot Street. They're usually open from 10am to 6pm on weekends and most weekdays, with shorter hours in winter. Look for the St. Michaels/Tilghman Island visitors' guide at the visitor center, at North Talbot and Mill streets. There's a parking lot at that corner as well.

Need a gift to take home? Stop by **A Wish Called Wanda,** 110 N. Talbot St. (✆ **410/745-6763**), for American crafts, or **Keepers,** 300 S. Talbot St. (✆ **800/549-1872** or 410/745-6388), for Orvis clothes or antique waterfowl decoys. For older treasures, stop by **Antiques on Talbot,** 211 N. Talbot St. (✆ **410/745-5208**).

For the palate, get some locally produced wines at **St. Michael's Winery,** 605 S. Talbot St. (✆ **410/745-0808;** www.st-michaels-winery.com), or chocolates at the **St. Michaels Candy and Gifts,** 216 S. Talbot St. (✆ **888/570-6050** or 410/745-6060; www.candyisdandy.com). Or stop and have a flight of the handcrafted beer at **Eastern Shore Brewing Company,** 605 S. Talbot St. (✆ **410/745-8010**).

Tilghman Island

Keep driving southeast on Route 33, the road from Easton to St. Michaels, for about 8 miles. Cross the Knapps Narrows Bridge, and you'll find yourself on Tilghman Island. Though some development has filled a cornfield here and there—especially at the waterfront—this is the place for true Eastern Shore living: ospreys to wake you, stars to light the night, skipjacks and crabbing boats bobbing in the harbor or slicing through the bay. Come for fresh seafood, quiet roads, and water views. Tilghman is a good place to spend a day with a camera, a bike, or a kayak. Bring your fishing pole, as there are plenty of places off the island—not to mention charter boats for hire—to cast your line. The few hotels and B&Bs are welcoming places. Tilghman celebrates its food and culture on **Tilghman Island Day** in mid-October **(www.tilghmanisland.com).**

WHERE TO STAY

Black Walnut Point Inn ★ Drive down the main road to the very end and keep going. You'll find yourself on the southern point of Tilghman Island, with views of water on three sides, huge trees, and an 1845 house with wide porch to call home, at least for a while. Every room has a view of the water, and they are all furnished simply in a country style. The Tilghman Room has windows on three sides, while the Attic Hideaway is quaint but best suited for shorter people. Knotty-pine-paneled luxury cabins are compact, with living rooms, kitchens, fireplaces, and screened porches a few feet from the water. Nature lovers take note: Fishing is great here from the pier or your boat, and the whole 57-acre site is a bird sanctuary and home to bald eagles.

Black Walnut Rd. (P.O. Box 308), Tilghman, MD 21671. www.blackwalnutpointinn.com. ✆ **410/886-2452.** 4 rooms in main house, 3 cabins. $125–$225 double; $325 cabin. Rates include hot breakfast. DC, DISC, MC, V. No children under 12. **Amenities:** Hammocks; hot tub; kayak launch; pier; pool. *In room:* A/C, TVs in cottages, hair dryer, free Wi-Fi.

Harrison's Chesapeake House Nothing about Harrison's is fancy. Rooms are clean. Half have a water view. There's a pool, a sun porch, and a restaurant downstairs. But the real attraction is the proximity to the fishing and hunting charters run by Buddy Harrison—ask about the many packages. An on-site gift shop, Island Treasures, sells apparel and Tilghman Island souvenirs.

21551 Chesapeake House Dr., Tilghman, MD 21671. www.chesapeakehouse.com. ✆ **410/886-2121.** 56 units, 4 rental houses. $75–$125 double. MC, V. **Amenities:** Restaurant; lounge; pool. *In room:* A/C, TV.

Knapps Narrows Marina and Inn Every room here has a view of the Knapps Narrows. They're simple, fresh, and spacious—and a good value. Third-floor units have cathedral ceilings and Internet access. One suite can be turned into a meeting space. Hammocks under the trees beckon. A full-service facility, boaters will find their vessels as welcome as they are.

Knapps Narrows (P.O. Box 277), Tilghman, MD 21671. www.knappsnarrowsmarina.com. ✆ **410/886-2720.** 20 units. $120–$170 double; $240–$260 suite. Rates include continental breakfast. DISC, MC, V. **Amenities:** Restaurant; bike rentals; boat-repair services; boat slips; marina; pool. *In room:* A/C, TV, free Wi-Fi.

The Lazyjack Inn ★★ Water views, romance, and gourmet breakfasts make this a Tilghman Island delight. The Nellie Byrd Suite, with its king-size brass bed, fireplace, whirlpool tub, and harbor view, is hard to beat. But the other rooms are bright and comfortable, too. The first-floor Garden Suite has a fireplace that opens onto the bedroom and the sitting room, as well as a whirlpool. The innkeepers will accommodate any dietary needs and use organic food whenever possible.

5907 Tilghman Island Rd. (P.O. Box 248), Tilghman, MD 21671. www.lazyjackinn.com. ✆ **800/690-5080** or 410/886-2215. 4 units. $159–$289 double. Includes full breakfast. 2- or 3-night minimum stay may be required on weekends or holidays. MC, V. No children under 12. **Amenities:** Library. *In room:* A/C, hair dryer, free Wi-Fi.

The Tilghman Island Inn ★★ Here's a modern inn with old-fashioned Eastern Shore hospitality. Set on Knapps Narrows across from a bird-filled marsh, the waterfront rooms take full advantage of the lovely setting, with French doors and balconies or patios. Decor varies from room to room, but five have gas fireplaces and most have "ultra spa baths." The inn has a cozy lounge, two dining rooms with great reputations, and a waterfront bar. There's piano music in the lounge every Saturday. The staff is ready to help you find all the treasures Tilghman has to offer.

21384 Coopertown Rd. (P.O. Box B), Tilghman, MD 21671. www.tilghmanislandinn.com. ✆ **800/866-2141** or 410/886-2141. 20 units. $175–$300 double. Rates include continental breakfast. AE, DISC, MC, V. Pets accepted. **Amenities:** Restaurant (closed Wed); lounge; 9 boat slips; waterside deck; outdoor pool; tennis court. *In room:* A/C, TV, VCR on request, hair dryer, Wi-Fi.

WHERE TO EAT

For a quick bite, stop by the **Island Deli and Grill,** 6030 Tilghman Island Rd. (✆ **410/866-1000**). Open every day but Sunday, this lunch counter has lots of sandwiches, pizza, and kids' items.

Bay Hundred Restaurant SEAFOOD Just before you reach the Knapps Narrows Bridge on your way to Tilghman, turn right to find this restaurant overlooking the marina and the bridge. In this scenic spot, you can expect to find great local seafood from crabs to fish to oysters. Slips are available for boating diners.

6178 Tilghman Island Rd., Tilghman MD 21671 (Knapps Narrows Marina). ✆ **410/886-2126.** www.bayhundredrestaurant.net. Reservations recommended for dinner. Main courses $6–$11 lunch,

$14–$22 dinner. AE, DISC, MC, V. Mon 11am–8:30pm; Tues–Thurs and Sun 11am–4pm and 5–8:30pm; Sat 11am–4pm and 5–9pm. Tavern stays open later on weekends. Hours may vary in winter, so call ahead.

Grassini's Bridge Restaurant ☺ SEAFOOD Overlooking the Knapps Narrows Bridge, this place serves traditional Eastern Shore fare along with steaks, rack of lamb, and nightly specials. Expect fresh seafood and a professional, friendly staff. It's casual, but good enough for a special occasion. A children's menu is available. Lunch choices include subs and pizza. Boat docking is available for diners at no charge. Entertainment is featured at the tiki bar on summer evenings, and the tavern is warm in winter, with pool table and darts.

6136 Tilghman Rd. ✆ **410/886-2330.** www.grassinisbridgerestaurant.com. Reservations recommended for dinner. Main courses $5–$14 lunch, $16–$19 dinner. AE, DC, DISC, MC, V. Summer daily 11am–10pm; winter Thurs–Tues 11am–8pm.

Harrison's Chesapeake House ☺ SEAFOOD This may be the best known of the Tilghman Island restaurants, because of its hearty Eastern Shore seafood served by a friendly staff. The house special combines two local favorites, fried chicken and crab cakes. But you can get anything from crab to prime rib here, served family style with plates of vegetables and homemade bread and a view of the water. Look for crab feasts in summer and an oyster buffet in winter. Breakfast, lunch, and dinner are served daily.

21551 Chesapeake House Dr. ✆ **410/886-2121.** www.chesapeakehouse.com. Reservations recommended for dinner. Main courses $3.95–$16 lunch, $12–$25 dinner. AE, MC, V. Hours vary according to season, but always open Sat–Sun; call ahead to confirm.

WHAT TO SEE AND DO

The **Tilghman Watermen's Museum,** 5778 Tilghman Island Rd. (✆ **410/886-2830;** www.tilghmanmuseum.org), is housed in a former barbershop but is expected to move to a traditional Tilghman Island home in the future. With photos, boat models, and memorabilia donated by residents, this small display tells the story of life on the Chesapeake. It's open Saturday and Sunday 10am to 3pm or by appointment.

Get your hands on a horseshoe crab or other local wildlife at the **Phillips Wharf Environmental Center,** 21604 Chicken Point Rd. (✆ **410/886-9200;** www.pwec.org). Exhibits and touch tanks are open mid-April to mid-October Thursdays through Mondays 10am to 4pm.

OUTDOOR ACTIVITIES

Rent a bike and take a long ride on flat, fairly quiet roads. Board a skipjack for a ride into history, or see what's biting from a fishing boat. Rent a kayak and poke around the many coves. Whatever you do, slow down.

BIKING Get a bike or a motor scooter or moped (no motorcycle license required) from **Tilghman Island Marina** (✆ **410/886-2500;** www.tilghmanmarina.com). Rent for an hour or a full day. (St. Michaels is a half-hour scooter ride away.)

BOATING **Tilghman Island Marina** (✆ **410/886-2500;** www.tilghmanmarina.com) offers kayaks, pontoon boats, skiffs with outboard motors, sailboats, and personal watercraft, as well as fishing and crabbing gear, by the hour, half-day, day, or week. Or sign up for the Poplar Island excursion: They'll tow your kayak to this small group of islands for a 4-hour expedition, box lunch included. Reservations are required for the Poplar Island excursion, and suggested for others. If you prefer others to drive, sign up for a pontoon cruise.

Look for the **Tilghman Island Water Trail** map, available at the Talbot County visitor center in Easton (✆ **410/770-8000;** www.tourtalbot.org).

CRUISING Captain Wade Murphy will take you on a 2-hour tour on his skipjack, the ***Rebecca T. Ruark*** (✆ **410/886-2176** or 410/829-3976; www.skipjack.org), docked at Dogwood Harbor. As he sails the oldest working sailboat in the country, the captain talks about the history of his boat and tells tales about crabs and oysters.

Dockside Express (✆ **888/312-7847;** www.docksidexpress.com) offers sunset tours, crabbing cruises, and eco-tours.

The ***Lady Patty*** (✆ **888/250-3030;** www. ladypatty.com), a 45-foot ketch, docked at Knapps Narrows, sails the Choptank on 2-hour, sunset, half-, or full-day trips.

Tour the **Chesapeake Lights** aboard the MV *Sharp's Island,* a former U.S. Navy special operations vessel. Take a 3-hour cruise and see three lighthouses up close, or spend the whole day and see 10 lighthouses (✆ **800/690-5080** or 410/886-2215; www.chesapeakelights.com).

FISHING & CRABBING **Harrison's Sport Fishing Center** (✆ **410/886-2121;** www.chesapeakehouse.com) is the best known of the charters here. Captain Buddy Harrison has 20 charter boats and room for 1 or 100. Half-day charters are available April through December, as well as packages with breakfast and lunch or even overnight lodging. Or be a waterman for a day: Captain Wade Murphy takes tourists out on his work boat the ***Miss Kim*** (✆ **410/886-2176** or 410/829-3976; www.skipjack.org) for a half-day of crabbing or fishing. Other charters are available at **Knapp's Narrows Marina** (✆ **410/886-2720;** www.knappsnarrowsmarina.com) and **Tilghman Island Marina** (✆ **410/886-2500;** www.tilghmanmarina.com). If these aren't enough, there's plenty more listed by the **Maryland Charter Boat Association** at www.marylandcharterboats.com/area10.htm.

Oxford

Oxford is a refined place, with a shady park and beach in the center of town. It wasn't always so quiet, though. One of the state's oldest towns, it was the Eastern Shore's first port of entry in the 1700s. It was home to many of Maryland's prominent citizens, including Robert Morris, a shipping agent, and his son Robert Morris, "financier of the Revolution," and Tench Tilghman, George Washington's aide who carried the news of Cornwallis's surrender to the Continental Congress. Tilghman is remembered with a monument in Oxford Cemetery. Although Oxford is quieter than St. Michaels, the peace is a big part of its charm. There aren't many tourists, but there is a leafy park set on a narrow beach and charming old streets that are best seen at a slow pace.

You can also arrive or depart via the tiny **Oxford-Bellevue Ferry ★**, one of the oldest in the country (see p. 144 for details).

WHERE TO STAY

Combsberry Inn ★★ Down a country lane, this 1730 manor house offers elegant, luxurious comfort. The main house, known for its fireplaces, staircase, and brickwork, has three units, while the two cottages offer kitchen areas and fireplaces. Every room has a water view. The carriage house features a living room with fireplace, a kitchen, and two master bedrooms. For a fireplace in the main house, ask for the Magnolia Suite (which also has a balcony under the shade of a magnolia) or Waterford Room. Some rooms have whirlpool tubs. Gardens dotted with trees surround the house, and a dock awaits boaters. Canoes are available for exploring the cove.

4837 Evergreen Rd., Oxford, MD 21654. www.combsberryinn.com. ✆ **410/226-5353.** 6 units. $250–$395 double. Rates include full breakfast. AE, MC, V. Pets accepted in Oxford Cottage. No children under 12. **Amenities:** Bikes; canoes; boat dock. *In room:* A/C, hair dryer, Wi-Fi.

Mears Yacht Haven So you want to stay in Oxford but you're bringing your boat? Mears has 95 boat slips on an hourly, daily, weekly, or monthly basis. They can accommodate boats 20 to 130 feet. They've got the things a boater needs, including fuel pumps, showers, and laundry, and things a boater wants, including cable TV, a pool, and bikes for rental.

502 E. Strand (P.O. Box 130), Oxford, MD 21654. ✆ **410/226-5450,** or call on VHF Channel 16 as you approach Oxford. Rates vary by boat size and season. Weekend rates include continental breakfast. AE, DISC, MC, V. **Amenities:** Rental bikes; fuel dock; pool; picnic area; marine pumpout; showers; free Wi-Fi.

Oxford Inn The owners have put a lot of TLC into this well-established inn, located beside Town Creek and close to everything. It remains a good value. All rooms are decorated in French-country style, and many have window seats and views of the water. Two rooms can be combined as a family suite. Guests can relax in the cozy library with fireplace. **Pope's Tavern,** a local favorite, serves dinner Thursday through Monday, beginning at 5pm. Make reservations.

504 S. Morris St. (P.O. Box 627), Oxford, MD 21654. www.oxfordinn.net. ✆ **410/226-5220.** 7 units. $110–$175 double. Rates include continental breakfast, plus hot dishes on weekends. AE, DISC, MC, V. **Amenities:** Restaurant; lounge. *In room:* A/C.

Robert Morris Inn ★ Ships' carpenters built this house in 1710 for Robert Morris, Jr., a financier of the American Revolution. It retains its Colonial (and romantic) character with wide floorboards, the original staircase, and traditional furnishings. Rooms differ in size and appointments; one has a four-poster bed and fireplace. Four of the original rooms face the water. Some bathrooms have claw-foot tubs and river views. Author James Michener spent time here while writing his novel *Chesapeake.* The restaurant, **Salter's Tavern,** is a delight whether in the paneled tavern room, the elegant living room, or outside the inn.

314 N. Morris St. (P.O. Box 70), Oxford, MD 21654. www.robertmorrisinn.com. ✆ **888/823-4012** or 410/226-5111. Fax 410/226-5744. 15 units. $120–$240 double. MC, V. Rates include hot breakfast. Pets accepted for a fee. **Amenities:** Restaurant; lounge; beach at Sandaway; bike; canoe and fishing equipment rentals; free Wi-Fi on ground floor. *In room:* A/C, no phone.

Sandaway This Victorian country home built on a point jutting into the river offers spacious rooms, including a second-floor suite with a king-size bed that looks through French doors to the river beyond. The thoroughly modern Sandaway Suite has a sitting room on the beach, a fireplace, TV/VCR, and lots of windows. Lots of porches at the Sandaway, trees, and chaise longues make this a comfortable retreat.

103 W. Strand Rd. (also known as Lovers Lane), Oxford, MD 21654. www.sandaway.com. ✆ **888/SANDAWAY** (726-2929) or 410/226-5111. 18 units. $200–$370 double. Rates include continental breakfast. MC, V. Closed Dec–Mar. **Amenities:** Beach; bike and kayak rentals; free Wi-Fi. *In room:* A/C, no phone.

WHERE TO EAT

Latitude 38° Bistro & Spirits INTERNATIONAL/SEAFOOD You'll forget you saw gas pumps out front once you walk into this white-tablecloth dining room—and the creative cuisine will take you far, far away. The menu—which changes every few weeks—takes advantage of the area's bounty and mixes in an international style. Lunch is served only in winter, but Sunday brunch is offered year-round. Half portions are available at dinner for smaller appetites. The bar separates the formal dining room from the more casual side. But both sides choose from the same menu, which recently featured rack of lamb, rockfish with leek sauce, and crab cakes. The bar has its own special item each night, including $13 burgers.

26342 Oxford Rd. ✆ **410/226-5303.** www.latitude38.org. Reservations recommended for dinner; none taken for bar area. Main courses $8–$13 lunch, $13–$30 dinner. DISC, MC, V. Dinner Tues–Sun 5:30–9pm; brunch Sun 11am–2pm; lunch winter months only Tues–Sat 11:30am–2pm.

The Masthead at Pier Street Marina SEAFOOD It looks a little ramshackle, but it's a truism that good seafood is often best at a place like this. (The owners also run Latitude 38°, so you know it's good.) Views of the Tred Avon River are incredible, especially from the covered deck. And so many choices: sandwiches and salads for lunch, seafood platters for dinner. Slips are available for boaters.

104 W. Pier St. ✆ **410/226-5171.** Reservations required for dinner. Main courses $10–$16 lunch, $18–$26 dinner. MC, V. Daily 11:30am–9pm. Closed mid-Oct to Apr 1.

Salter's at the Robert Morris Inn ★★★ SEAFOOD Oh happy days: The restaurant at this historic inn has reopened. And it's wonderful! The crab cake is one of Maryland's best, with all that beautiful crabmeat bound together with a slightly citrus-y dressing. The emphasis is on fresh seafood, crabs, oysters, and fish. The dining room offers a more formal menu, while the paneled tavern is more of an open-collar place, with sandwiches, fish and chips, and some dining-room-level entrees. In summer, sit on the porch or the brick patio and enjoy the view of the Tred Avon River. Breakfast is served daily 7:30 to 10am. Afternoon tea is served 3 to 5pm. The bar is open between meals.

314 N. Morris St. (P.O. Box 70), Oxford, MD 21654. ✆ **888/823-4012** or 410/226-5111. www.robertmorrisinn.com. Reservations required for dinner. Main courses $21–$34 dinner, $15–$29 lunch or tavern dinner. MC, V. Daily 7:30–10am, noon–2:30pm, 5:30–9:30pm.

Schooner's SEAFOOD This informal spot is on a marina with great views of the water and deck seating in season. Schooner's all-day menu offers prime rib, crab, oyster, shrimp, sandwiches, soups, and a catch of the day. It's a good place for lunch or for a boisterous evening of sailing stories, aided by several draft beer options. Bands play some summer nights. There's a kids' menu, too.

314 Tilghman St. ✆ **410/226-0160.** Reservations accepted for dining room only. Main courses $6–$24. AE, MC, V. Thurs–Tues 11:30am–9pm. Closed Oct–Mar.

OUTDOOR ACTIVITIES

Surrounded by all that water, you just might want to charter a boat yourself. **Choptank Charters,** 102 S. Morris St. (✆ **410/226-5000;** www.tays.com), offers sailing yachts for 2 days to a week and a motor yacht for 5 to 7 days. Captains are extra. Rates begin at $1,300 for 2 days on a 34-foot Sabre.

SHOPPING

Oxford shops are usually open Saturday and Sunday from 10am to 6pm; many close midweek when the town's pretty quiet. Hours may be cut back in winter, too.

Americana Antiques Old treasures for sale on weekends only. 111 S. Morris St. ✆ **410/226-5677.**

Hinckley Yacht Services The wares here range from nautical necessities and yachting apparel to gifts and games. Transient slips and boat repair are available, too. 202 Banks St. ✆ **410/226-5113.** www.hinckleyyachts.com.

PLAYING A round ON THE EASTERN SHORE

Lots of flat land, terrific water views, and beautiful weather make the Mid-Shore an up-and-coming golf destination.

The **Hog Neck Golf Course,** 10142 Old Cordova Rd., Easton (✆ **410/822-6079;** www.hogneck.com), has been rated among the top 25 U.S. public courses by *Golf Digest*. This par-72, 18-hole course and par-32, 9-hole executive course is north of town, off Route 50. Rates are $57 Monday through Thursday, $67 Friday through Sunday, carts included.

The Easton Club, 28449 Clubhouse Dr., Easton (✆ **800/277-9800;** www.eastonclub.com), has a par-72 course on Route 333 open to the public. Greens fees, including cart, are $59 on weekends and $49 on weekdays in season.

Harbourtowne Golf Resort, in St. Michaels (✆ **800/446-9066;** www.harbourtowne.com), is a par-70 course designed by Pete Dye. Greens fees are $70 for Harbourtowne hotel guests and $85 for nonguests, including cart. Harbourtowne offers 1- and 2-night golf packages, too. Fees go down in winter.

Mystery Loves Company Everybody needs a good read on vacation. Nautical books and local authors' works are for sale here, too. 202 S. Morris St. ✆ **410/226-0010.**

Oxford Market Essentials are sold here: groceries, deli goods, ice cream, coffee, and wine. Open 7am to 8pm daily, even in winter. 203 S. Morris St. ✆ **410/226-0015.**

The Scottish Highland Creamery Tasty ice cream is made here from an old family recipe. There's a dock available, if you want to stop by boat. 314 Tilghman St. ✆ **410/924-6298.** www.scottishhighlandcreamery.com.

CAMBRIDGE

58 miles SE of Annapolis; 85 miles SE of Baltimore; 86 miles SE of Washington, DC; 99 miles S of Wilmington, DE

Since its founding in 1684, Cambridge has drawn those who love the water. Once it harbored ships taking tobacco to England, later it became a deepwater port for 20th-century freighters, and it was also a shipbuilding town. The town still draws boaters—but now they're pleasure boaters.

Cambridge lies just across the Choptank River Bridge from Talbot. Still more of a commercial center than a tourist town, it has its charms. High Street leads to the Choptank—a lovely stroll with a great view at the end. History buffs, especially those interested in the Civil War era, may explore the town's connections with Harriet Tubman and the Underground Railroad. Nature lovers find it a nice stop on their way to Blackwater Refuge or to a hunting or fishing trip. Visitors planning a Mid-Shore visit to Easton or St. Michaels may prefer this quiet place as a base.

In its prosperity in Colonial times and again in the early 20th century, Cambridge became the home of governors, lawyers, and landowners. Their beautiful homes line High Street, Water Street, Mill Street, and Hambrooks Boulevard. Sharpshooter Annie Oakley built her house at 28 Bellevue Ave., on Hambrooks Bay. The roofline was altered so Oakley could step outside her second-story windows and shoot waterfowl coming in over the bay. The house is now privately owned, but the owners have erected a small sign in Annie's memory.

Harriet Tubman's home no longer exists, but she often walked the streets and country roads around here as she led more than 300 slaves to freedom on the Underground Railroad. She is remembered in monuments, markers, a museum in Cambridge, and a driving tour.

If you read James Michener's *Chesapeake* or John Barth's *The Sot-Weed Factor* you may recognize some places—this is one of the towns that inspired the novels.

Essentials

GETTING THERE Come by boat (your own; there aren't any ferries)—from the Chesapeake Bay east on the Choptank River—or come by car. Cambridge is on Route 50, about 15 miles south of Easton. Once you cross the Sen. Frederick Malkus Bridge over the Choptank, you're here. The historic district is west of the highway, which is called Ocean Gateway here.

Boat slips are available at the city marina and in front of the county offices, both on the Choptank. Boats can tie up for free for 48 hours in front of the county office building but need permission to stay longer. The city marina has slips for larger boats; reservations are required. Call © **410/228-4031** for reservations or information.

VISITOR INFORMATION The **Dorchester Visitor Center at Sailwinds Park,** 2 Rose Hill Place, just east of the bridge in Cambridge (© **800/522-8687** or 410/228-1000; www.tourdorchester.org), is full of information about Cambridge, Harriet Tubman, and the nearby Blackwater National Wildlife Refuge. The center has restrooms, a waterfront playground, and picnic tables, too. It's open daily 8:30am to 5pm.

GETTING AROUND The quickest way to get around is by car, but since the area is so flat, many prefer bicycle. Roads are fairly quiet, making it a pleasure to drive or bike. Be sure to stop at the visitor center for brochures and maps for walking, biking, and boating. They've got some really useful ones.

Where to Stay

Cambridge House Bed and Breakfast ★ This Queen Anne–style sea captain's mansion, next to Long Wharf, puts visitors in the middle of Cambridge's most beautiful street. Watch the tourists go by as you sit on the front porch, or get away from it all in the Victorian gardens. The elegant rooms, most with fireplaces, feature queen- and king-size beds. A breakfast buffet is served each morning in the dining room or on the porch. A hot tub on the back deck overlooks the garden.

112 High St., Cambridge, MD 21613. www.cambridgehousebandb.com. © **410/221-7700.** 6 units. $140–$225 double. Rates include breakfast and refreshments. 2-night minimum stay required some weekends. AE, DISC, MC, V. No children under 8. *In room:* A/C, TV/DVD, CD player, hair dryer, free Wi-Fi.

Holiday Inn Express Cambridge Eastern Shore hospitality and location near downtown Cambridge and Blackwater Wildlife Refuge make this a chain hotel worth mentioning. Bedding, including duvets, was updated in 2008.

2715 Ocean Gateway, Cambridge, MD 21613. www.hiexpress.com. © **410/221-9900.** 86 units. $84–$174 double. Rates include continental breakfast. AE, DC, DISC, MC, V. Free baby cribs; rollaway cots available. **Amenities:** Hot tub; indoor pool. *In room:* A/C, TV, fridge, hair dryer, microwave available, free Wi-Fi.

Hyatt Regency Chesapeake Bay ★★ This resort, on 342 acres on the Choptank River, has facilities beyond any other property in the area, with enough amenities to keep families busy without leaving the grounds—as well as a variety of packages that take advantage of the countryside. Most rooms have balconies of varying size (if you want one big enough to sit on, ask for it). Corner rooms seem a little bigger. Rocking chairs and hammocks invite visitors to watch the river roll by. The spa, marina, and 18-hole par-5 golf course are open to the public. Have your heart set on a massage? Make a reservation before you arrive.

100 Heron Blvd., Cambridge, MD 21613. www.chesapeakebay.hyatt.com. ✆ **800/233-1234** or 410/901-1234. 400 units, including 18 suites. $139–$400 double. AE, DC, DISC, MC, V. Pets accepted for a fee. **Amenities:** 4 restaurants; 2 bars; beach; bike rentals; Camp Hyatt children's program; general store; golf course; health club; jogging trails; 150-slip marina; indoor pool; 2 outdoor pools; room service; spa; 4 tennis courts; watersports equipment/rentals. *In room:* A/C, TV w/pay movies and games, fridge, hair dryer, Wi-Fi (fee).

Kindred Spirits Family Massage & Cottage Retreat This one-room bed-and-breakfast offers a real sense of getting away from it all, with a massage thrown in. Run by a licensed massage therapist, the guest room is in a converted workshop behind the main house. It's a 500-square-foot room decorated with comfort in mind, with a jetted tub, a sleeper sofa, and a king bed. The patio has a view of the Choptank River and the massage room is adjacent to the guest room. Massage packages are offered. In keeping with the retreat idea, continental breakfast items are left in the kitchen, so guests can count on total privacy. Walk to Cambridge's historic district via a riverside walkway.

102 Hiawatha Rd., Cambridge, MD 21613. www.kindredspiritscottageretreat.com. ✆ **410/221-7575** or 410/725-9364. 1 unit. $125–$150 double. Rate includes continental breakfast. No credit cards; PayPal accepted. *In room:* A/C, TV w/DVD, fridge, hair dryer, Wi-Fi.

Lodgecliffe on the Choptank ★★★ Come for the views of the Choptank River at Cambridge's only waterfront B&B. Enjoy tranquil views from every public room, the deck, the broad lawn, and three of the guest rooms. Guest rooms are spacious; the best has its own door to the waterfront deck. All four rooms in this 1898 home offer a mix of modern luxury and antique charm. Three rooms are on the first floor; one is on the second. Downtown restaurants, attractions, and shops are a few blocks away, but when you're sitting on the deck with a glass of wine at sunset, it feels like you've gotten away from it all. The B&B has adopted eco-friendly standards, including using locally sourced ingredients and fair-trade coffee.

103 Choptank Terrace, Cambridge, MD 21613. www.lodgecliffeonthechoptankbandb.com. ✆ **866/273-3830.** 4 units. $150–$200 double. Rates include full breakfast. AE, DISC, MC, V. **Amenities:** Bikes. *In room:* A/C, hair dryer, free Wi-Fi.

Mill Street Inn Bed & Breakfast ★★ This 1894 Victorian combines the charm of antique style with the convenience of modern technology. Breezes off the Choptank River cool the screened porch and air-conditioning cools the guest rooms. Visitors can choose from relaxing in a TV room with cable and a DVD player or at the chess table in a turret nook. Innkeepers here aren't afraid of color, and each en-suite sleeping room is ablaze with hues like cornflower blue or marigold yellow. The Cambridge Suite boasts a separate sitting room, and an enormous bathroom with air-jetted tub.

114 Mill St., Cambridge, MD 21613. www.millstinn.com. ✆ **410/901-9144.** 3 units. $135–$200 double. Rate includes breakfast. DISC, MC, V. 2-night minimum may be required some weekends and holidays. **Amenities:** Bikes. *In room:* A/C, TV/DVD, hair dryer, free Wi-Fi.

Where to Eat

Bistro Poplar ★★ FRENCH Classic French food in a classy bistro setting has come to Cambridge. Steak frites, croque-monsieur, and onion soup share the menu with salads, including a poached lobster salad, crepes and coq au vin. The menu, which changes seasonally, is offered from noon until the last diner heads home after 9pm. A tapas menu is available for Sunday dinner. The chef here has trained with the best, including Thomas Keller and Baltimore's Cindy Wolf. Desserts are made in house.

Poplar St., Cambridge. ✆ **410/228-4884.** www.bistropoplar.com. Reservations recommended during the summer and on weekends. Main courses $12–$14 lunch, $22–$30 dinner. AE, MC, V. Thurs–Mon noon–9pm (or later).

Jimmie & Sook's Raw Bar and Grill ★★ SEAFOOD The big open dining room is dominated by the bar on one side with an open kitchen and a gorgeous mural of Chesapeake watermen on the other. The food is Chesapeake perfection: simple, golden brown crab cakes with homemade tartar and cocktail sauces, sweet tender oysters, fresh fish, and crisp salads. This is the place if you like your seafood simple, fresh, and local. Bands play Thursday through Saturday nights. (BTW—if you need to use the bathrooms, you should know that Jimmies are boy crabs and Sooks are girls.)

421 Race St., Cambridge. ✆ **443/225-4115.** www.jimmieandsooks.com. Reservations accepted for parties of 5 or more. Main courses $6–$16 lunch, $14–$25 dinner. AE, DC, DISC, MC, V. Mon–Wed 11am–10pm; Thurs–Sat 11am–11pm; Sun 11am–9pm.

Kay's at the Airport HOME COOKING Locals fill the place for old-fashioned favorites: fried shrimp or chicken tender baskets, roast beef, pork chops, and crab imperial for lunch or dinner. Breakfast is quite a production, too, with everything from pancakes in several flavors to breakfast wraps and full country breakfasts. Leave room for the homemade cakes and pies. A young pilot's menu is available. And it's really at the airport. Two-story windows overlook the private plane runways.

5263 Bucktown Rd., Cambridge. ✆ **410/901-8844.** No reservations. Main courses $6–$9 breakfast, $6-$10 lunch, $11–$20 dinner. MC, V. Sun 8am–3pm; Mon–Tues and Thurs–Sat 8am–8pm.

Snappers Waterfront Cafe ★ ☺ SEAFOOD/INTERNATIONAL We end up here a lot because we know it's going to be fun, the view of Cambridge Creek is a winner, and the food is reliably good. It's very casual and looks a little worn, but the crab is local—picked next door—the fajitas are sizzling and the rest of the menu is going to have something to please everybody at your table. You can't miss with the crab dip, served in a crusty French loaf. Brunch is served on weekends.

112 Commerce St., Cambridge. ✆ **410/228-0112.** www.snapperswaterfrontcafe.com. Reservations recommended Fri–Sat. Main courses $8–$25. AE, DC, DISC, MC, V. Mon–Thurs 11am–9pm; Fri 11am–10pm; Sat 8am–10pm; Sun 8am–9pm.

Suicide Bridge Restaurant ★ SEAFOOD This is the place to be on a Saturday night, when you'll see people waiting up to 45 minutes for the seafood and crab cakes. Chicken and steak dishes are offered, but the very fresh seafood is cooked simply and well. A lunchtime menu of panini, sandwiches, and wraps is available Tuesday through Saturday. The restaurant overlooks the Suicide Bridge—whose sad history is printed on the menu—and has a marina for boating diners. Boats must be less than 50 feet tall to fit under the Choptank River Bridge.

The restaurant operates two paddle-wheelers, the *Dorothy-Megan* and the *Choptank River Queen*. Lunch cruises are $35, dinner cruises $48, and sightseeing cruises $15. Call ✆ **410/943-4775** for a schedule.

6304 Suicide Bridge Rd., Hurlock, MD 21643. ✆ **410/943-4689.** www.suicide-bridge-restaurant.com. Reservations not accepted; call ahead for priority seating list. Main courses $9–$36; kids' menu $6–$7. MC, V. Apr–Dec Tues–Thurs 11am–9pm, Fri–Sat 11am–10pm, Sun noon–9pm; Jan 15–Mar 30 Thurs–Sat 11am–10pm, Sun noon–9pm. Closed Jan 1–15.

What to See & Do

Historic High Street ★, which ends at Long Wharf, is lined with 19th-century homes from a variety of periods, including French Second Empire, Queen Anne, and Federal. Take a look on your own or take the 1-hour tour offered every Saturday April through October, offered by the **West End Citizens Association** (✆ **410/901-1000**). The tours begin at 11am at the Wallace Office Building, 301 Gay St.

Stop in the **Dorchester Center for the Arts,** 321 High St. (✆ **410/228-7782;** www.dorchesterarts.org), to see locally produced arts and crafts, which change every month, and browse the gift shop. It's open Monday through Thursday from 10am to 5pm, Friday and Saturday 10am to 4pm.

At Long Wharf, the ***Nathan of Dorchester*** (✆ **410/228-7141;** www.skipjack-nathan.org), a living museum built by local volunteers, offers tours on Saturdays May through October. Shorter Sunday sails are offered monthly. Visitors can climb aboard the 63-foot skipjack for a 2-hour cruise on the Choptank River, with oyster dredging demonstration. Book ahead online or call for a same-day reservation.

Dorchester County Historical Society The society operates several museums, including the Neild Museum (which focuses on industrial and agricultural history), the 1760s Meredith House, the 1790 Goldsborough Stables, and a Colonial-style herb garden. The Robbins Heritage Center presents exhibits on watermen, sharpshooter Annie Oakley (who used to live in town), and the canning and seafood industries. A porch overlooks Shoal Creek and a path leads to the water. A new self-guided tour launches in mid-2012.

LaGrange Plantation, 902 LaGrange Ave. ✆ **410/228-7953.** www.dorchesterhistory.org. Free admission to all the buildings. Mon–Fri 10am–4pm, Sat 10am–2pm in summer; off-season Mon–Fri 10am–4pm.

Harriet Tubman Museum A tribute to Harriet Tubman, a former slave and conductor in the Underground Railroad, this small museum has exhibits on Tubman's life, her work on the Underground Railroad, and her efforts during the Civil War and later. The center also offers tours of places in Dorchester County where Tubman lived, prayed, and worked. Only a few of the actual buildings still stand, but guides use the locations to tell stories about her life. A new theater shows films about Tubman.

424 Race St. ✆ **410/228-0401.** Free admission. Tues–Fri 10am–3pm; Sat noon–4pm. Call ahead to ensure museum opening, as staff are few.

Richardson Maritime Museum Come here to find out what a bugeye is, how a log canoe sails, or what a skipjack was built to do. With builders' models, hand tools, and building plans, the museum focuses on all the boats used on the Chesapeake Bay for fishing, oystering, and trading.

401 High St. ✆ **410/221-1871.** www.richardsonmuseum.org. $3 donation suggested. Wed and Sun 1–4pm; Sat 10am–4pm. Closed Jan 1, Easter, July 4, Thanksgiving, and Dec 25.

Ruark Boatworks Old wooden boats get a new lease on life at this wood-chip-filled workshop on Cambridge Creek. Visitors are welcome to take a look, talk to the workers restoring historic vessels, or take up some tools and join in a boat-building project Monday, Wednesday, and Friday morning. A docent is there Saturday 1 to 4pm.

103 Maryland Ave., at Hayward St. ✆ **410/221-1871.** www.richardsonmuseum.org. Free admission. Mon, Wed, Fri 9am–2pm; Sat 1–4pm. Closed Jan 1, Easter, July 4, Thanksgiving, and Dec 25.

Outside of Town

Three tributes to the Underground Railroad and its most famous conductor, Harriet Tubman, will open to the public sometime in late 2013 or 2014.

A 17.4-acre parcel near Blackwater Wildlife Refuge is being developed as the **Harriet Tubman Underground Railroad State Park.** The park is due to open in mid-2013 with a visitor center exhibiting artifacts about Tubman and the Underground Railroad, as well as hiking and biking paths, a picnic pavilion, and spots for paddling and viewing wildlife. This is Dorchester's first state park.

The Harriet Tubman Underground Railroad National Historical Park will protect 6,750 acres of farmland, forest, and wetlands over which Tubman and fleeing slaves found their way to freedom. These landscapes won't really be available for the public's use but will be preserved. The state park land, which is included in this national park, will, of course, be accessible. That will be important for those who want to drive on the **Harriet Tubman Underground Railroad All American Road.** Maps for this 125-mile byway through Dorchester and Caroline counties are available at the visitor center. New interpretative signs will be added by 2013.

For a worthwhile side trip, visit the **Spocott Windmill ★★** (**www.spocottwindmill.org**), 7 miles west of Cambridge on Route 343 at 1663 Hudson St. The only existing post windmill for grinding grain in Maryland, it's still operated at least twice a year, mid-April and mid-October. It's not the original—three others have been on this site since the 1700s. Also on the site are a **tenant house,** a humble 1½-story wood dwelling built around 1800; a one-room **schoolhouse,** built in 1870; and a **country museum store,** which evokes an old-time feeling with its potbellied stove and World War II–era merchandise (open only on special occasions). The sites stay open dawn to dusk daily so visitors are free to wander among the desks in the school and peek in the upstairs bedroom of the tenant house. Admission is free.

A Visit to a Natural Refuge

Blackwater National Wildlife Refuge ★★★, 12 miles south of Cambridge, gives waterfowl a place to land, provides a safe haven for bald eagles and endangered Delmarva fox squirrels, and lets humans stand in awe of nature. Some 25,000 acres of marsh, freshwater ponds, river, forest, and field were set aside in 1933 for the migratory birds that use the Atlantic Flyway.

The most popular time to visit is during the fall migration, which peaks in November. Some 35,000 geese and 15,000 ducks fill the refuge. Blackwater's free open house, held the first weekend in October, is a great time to see some of the refuge residents up close.

Winter is the best time to see bald eagles. As many as 200 eagles have been seen at Blackwater, and some 18 nesting pairs have set up homes high in the trees—the greatest breeding population of bald eagles on the East Coast north of Florida.

Visitors in spring will see lots of birds headed north. Marsh and shorebirds arrive, as do the ospreys who set up house for their new families. The ospreys build huge nests on platforms in the middle of the marsh. They swoop and dive into the water for fish, and then fly back to feed their noisy offspring. The refuge hosts an Eagle Festival in March, and a youth fishing derby is held the first weekend in June.

In summer, birders can find warblers, orioles, blue herons, and even wild turkeys. ***Be prepared:*** Mosquitoes and flies can be fierce here in summer. Wear a hat and be on the lookout for ticks in early summer.

GETTING THERE From Route 50, take Route 16 southwest from Cambridge; turn south on Route 335, then left on Key Wallace Drive and right to the visitor center.

VISITOR CENTER The visitor center, rebuilt and expanded in early 2012, is on Key Wallace Drive (✆ **410/228-2677;** www.fws.gov/blackwater). It's open year-round, Monday through Friday from 8am to 4pm, Saturday and Sunday from 9am to 5pm. Staff members can provide maps, bird lists, and calendars of events. Exhibits explain who lives at the refuge, while an observation deck gives visitors a view of the waterfowl browsing in nearby fields. Look for the real-time cameras trained on the osprey and eagle nests. (The nest cams are on the Friends of Blackwater website, too—go to www.friendsofblackwater.org.)

FEES & REGULATIONS The entry fee for the wildlife drive (see below) is $3 per vehicle, $1 per pedestrian or bicyclist. It's free to anyone holding a Federal Duck Stamp, Interagency Pass, Senior Pass, Access Pass, or Blackwater National Wildlife Refuge Pass. Pets are not permitted on trails but are allowed in vehicles on the drive.

WILDLIFE DRIVE Though the refuge belongs to the wildlife, the park has set aside hiking paths and a short drive for cars and bicycles so visitors may see and hear these amazing crowds of birds. These are open from dawn to dusk.

After paying the entry fee at a self-service pay station, visitors will reach a fork in the road about one-third mile into the drive. Turn left for the Marsh Edge Trail and Observation Site. Then head back up the road for the rest of the drive.

The 5-mile ride meanders through woodlands and marshes that stretch to the horizon. It's quiet, except for the insects and calling birds. Bring your binoculars and camera: You might see any number of birds, deer, or the rare Delmarva fox squirrel.

Insider's note: An alternate and much longer way to get an idea of how big Blackwater really is, ask for the **Bike and Canoe Map**—it shows a 25-mile loop that will take you out beyond the edges of the refuge and into the countryside.

Want to stretch your legs and see everything a little more closely? You can park at one of the four walking trails. The **Woods Trail** is .5 miles long and runs through a mature forest. The 2.7-mile **Key Wallace Trail** centers on forest interior birds and forest management. For a look at how Mother Nature recovers after a tornado, take a walk on the 2-mile **Tubman Road Trail.**

The .3-mile **Marsh Edge Trail** begins in the woods and ends with an 80-foot boardwalk extending into Little Blackwater River. If you visit in spring or summer, look for the osprey. In fall, you'll see waterfowl. An observation site has been set up at the end of this part of the drive, with an information kiosk. The view over the Blackwater River, with all the sights and sounds of thousands of migrating waterfowl, can be awe-inspiring. A photo blind is at the edge of a pond and connected by a boardwalk to the drive overlooking the Little Blackwater River.

Other Outdoor Activities

BIKING The 5-mile wildlife drive is an easy ride on flat, mostly quiet roads. If you plan to bike from Cambridge (about 10 miles) or Vienna (about 15 miles), bring

A Bike Ride Through Historic Landscapes

The bike ride along Blackwater Wildlife Refuge's 7-mile **Wildlife Drive** offers effortless pedaling along wooded paths and breathtaking water vistas. It only gets better if you start at the Bucktown Store, 4.5 miles away at 4303 Bucktown Rd. It was here, many say, that Harriet Tubman got her start assisting slaves when she defied an overseer chasing a slave. At this store, he struck her and fractured her skull. The store now houses **Blackwater Paddle and Pedal** (✆ **410/901-9255**). Then on the way to Blackwater—through landscapes that were once part of the Underground Railroad—stop at the site where Tubman was born and at the Native American longhouse once used as a freed slaves' church in the 1800s. Two hours of pedaling, hundreds of years of history.

water—there aren't many places to get it between Cambridge and Blackwater. Before you go, get the "Cycling Trails of Dorchester County" map (available at the visitor center in Cambridge or at **www.tourdorchester.org**). In addition, Blackwater has its own bike map with two suggested loops: a 20-mile loop from Cambridge's public high school into the refuge and a 5-mile loop crossing the refuge in two locations and winding through beautiful country roads. Ask about it at the visitor center.

BIRDING Refuge volunteers offer bird walks on various weekend mornings in spring and fall. These meet at the visitor center and last about 2 hours. Call ✆ **410/228-2677** for a schedule. The visitor center also has a bird list.

BOATING & FISHING Launching ramps for canoes and kayaks are available year-round. ***Caution:*** Before you start paddling in fall and winter, check the waterfowl-hunting schedule. Refuge staff advises against getting between a hunter and a goose.

To rent a kayak, motorboat, or bike, try **Blackwater Paddle and Pedal Adventures** (✆ **410/901-9255;** www.blackwaterpaddleandpedal.com), on the road to Blackwater. They also give kayak tours. Contact **'Peake Paddle Tours** (✆ **410/829-7342;** www.paddletours.com) for information on kayaking tours with knowledgeable guides.

Fishing and crabbing are permitted from April 1 to September 30 from small boats and bridges, but note that state laws apply here. A state sportfishing license is required for fishing in the Blackwater and Little Blackwater rivers. No fishing is allowed from the shores. A **Water Trails Guide** with maps is available at the visitor center.

CRISFIELD & SMITH ISLAND ★★

126 miles SE of Annapolis; 153 miles SE of Baltimore; 155 miles SE of Washington, DC; 142 miles S of Wilmington, DE

The remote town of Crisfield, on the extreme southern end of the Eastern Shore, offers an insider's look at the lives of the watermen and the seafood industry. Crisfield, built on acres of oyster shells, was once known as the seafood capital of the world. Even though the industry has shrunk over time, crab and oyster packing, along with services for pleasure boaters, remain major businesses here. Indeed, the crab-packing houses now share the waterfront with marina slips for yachts and new condominiums. For visitors, Crisfield and its neighbor, Smith Island, make a great launching point for fishing and boating trips on the deep waters of the southern Chesapeake.

Essentials

GETTING THERE Crisfield is accessible by car via Maryland Route 413 from Route 50 or U.S. Route 13. You can also take your boat to Crisfield past Smith Island. (Before heading into shallow Tangier Sound, check your charts.)

VISITOR INFORMATION For helpful information about Crisfield and the surrounding countryside, contact **Somerset County Tourism** (✆ **800/521-9189** or 410/651-2968; www.visitsomerset.com). In town, stop at the visitor center, 1003 W. Main St. (✆ **410/968-1543**).

SPECIAL EVENTS The **National Hard Crab Derby and Fair** ★ is a 3-day event with a crab-cooking contest, a crab-picking contest, country music, and, of course, the crab race. It's held Labor Day weekend at Somers Cove Marina; admission is about $4. Make hotel reservations well in advance. The **J. Millard Tawes Crab and Clam Bake,** held the third Wednesday in July from 1 to 5pm, is an all-you-can-eat affair; buy tickets in advance. For either event, call ✆ **800/782-3913** or 410/968-2500 for information.

Where to Stay

Most people come to Crisfield by boat or drive here for a day visit or to catch a boat to Smith Island. Accommodations are simple. You can choose from the well-kept **Captain Tyler Motel** (✆ **410/968-2220**), run by the family of the Smith Island cruise boat, or the **Somers Cove Motel** (✆ **410/968-1900**) near the marina. A third choice is the pretty B&B on a quiet side street, listed below.

My Fair Lady ★ Painted blue with a wraparound porch, this 1900 B&B is within walking distance of the waterfront but set in a residential area. Rooms are filled with antiques and collectibles. A three-room suite in the attic has space for a small family. Other rooms are small but comfortable. Some have walk-in closets and all feature beautifully carved woodwork and 12-foot ceilings. All rooms have bathrooms en suite except one, and that one uses the hall bathroom with the house's original claw-foot tub.

38 W. Main St., Crisfield, MD 21817. www.myfairladybandb.com. ✆ **410/968-0352.** 6 units. $140–$380 double. MC, V. *In room:* A/C, TV, hair dryer upon request.

Where to Eat

Olde Crisfield Crab and Steak House SEAFOOD You can't miss this citrus-colored eatery that features, no surprise, crab and steak. The owners have pretty good credentials—they also own the venerable Middleton Tavern in Annapolis. Outside seating is available on patios and decks by Tangier Sound. **The Tiki Bar** next door has live entertainment on summer weekends with light fare and drinks after 3pm.

204 S. 10th St., Crisfield. ✆ **410/968-2722.** No reservations accepted. Main courses $6–$15 dinner. AE, DC, DISC, MC, V. Mar–Oct Thurs–Sun noon–9pm.

Watermen's Inn AMERICAN Although this well-designed eatery does not boast water views, the food is the prime attraction, with an adventurous menu that ranges from the expected softshell crabs and crab cakes to seafood pastry or rib-eye topped with red onion and black olive marmalade. In summer, there's alfresco dining.

901 W. Main St., Crisfield. ✆ **410/968-2119.** www.crisfield.com/watermens. Reservations recommended for dinner. Main courses $5–$16 lunch, $15–$25 dinner. AE, DISC, MC, V. Summer Thurs–Sat 11am–9pm, Sun 8am–8:30pm; winter Thurs 11am–8:30pm, Fri–Sat 11am–9pm, Sun 8am–8:30pm.

What to See & Do

The **J. Millard Tawes Historical Museum,** Somers Cove Marina, 3 Ninth St. (✆ **410/968-2501;** www.crisfieldheritagefoundation.org), was founded in 1982 to honor the Crisfield-born former governor of Maryland. Exhibits detail the town's history as well as its boat-building and seafood industries. The museum and gift shop are open year-round, in summer Monday through Saturday, from 10am to 4pm and Thursday through Saturday 10am to 2pm in winter. Admission is $3 for adults, $1 for children 6 to 12. A combined tour and museum admission ticket is $5. This is also the starting point for the **Port of Crisfield Escorted Walking Tour ★★**, offered from Memorial Day to Labor Day, Monday through Saturday at 10am. The tour winds around town and through the crab-packing plant.

While you are in the area, take a detour to **Princess Anne,** a small country town on the National Register of Historic Places about 15 miles north of Crisfield on U.S. Route 13. The town's many historic homes here are privately owned, except for the grand neoclassical **Teackle Mansion ★**, 11736 Mansion St. (✆ **410/651-2238;** www.teacklemansion.org). Built in 1801 by Littleton Dennis Teackle, a shipping magnate and an associate of Thomas Jefferson, it's undergoing careful restoration and is open for guided tours April through mid-December, Wednesday, Saturday, and Sunday from 1 to 3pm. Inside, you'll see elaborate plaster ceilings, a 7-foot fireplace, a beehive oven, American Chippendale furniture, a Tudor-Gothic pipe organ, and an 1806 silk world map. Admission is $5 for adults, free for ages under 12.

Outdoor Activities

The 515-slip **Somers Cove Marina,** 715 Broadway (✆ **800/967-3474** or 410/968-0925; www.somerscovemarina.com), is one of Maryland's largest, able to accommodate both sailboat and motor yachts from 10 to 150 feet. Facilities include boat ramps, showers, a laundry room, a pool, boat storage, electricity, water, a fuel dock, and Wi-Fi.

Fishing trips leave from the marina and the town dock each day for flounder, trout, spot, drum, blues, and rock. To book a headboat or charter, talk with the captains along the waterfront, or call any of the following: **Captain Keith Ward** (✆ **800/791-1470** or 410/968-0074; www.crisfield.com/prim), **Captain Charlie Corio** (✆ **410/957-2151**), or **Captain Larry Laird** (✆ **443/235-6282**). Charters cost $70 to $120 per person.

Janes Island State Park, 26280 Alfred Lawson Dr. (✆ **410/968-1565;** www.dnr.state.md.us), has 2,900 acres of wilderness for hiking, camping, canoeing, and

Wildfowl Counterfeiters in Wood

Walk inside the two-room shack where Lem and Steve Ward fashioned their 25,000 world-famous waterfowl decoys and you'll swear they've just stepped out for a moment. Lovingly restored by fans, **The Ward Brothers Workshop ★★** is outfitted with the carvers' tools and paints. Sawdust covers the floors; cigarettes sit in the ashtrays; and notes the men scribbled on the walls have been carefully preserved. A comprehensive story emerges of two "wildfowl counterfeiters in wood," as they called themselves, who were country gentlemen and humble artists. To visit, you must make an appointment. Call the Crisfield visitor center at ✆ **410/968-2501.**

boating. On the edge of Tangier Sound, Janes Island has miles of isolated beaches, 25 boat slips, and 30 miles of canoe/boat trails, the only way to see the island portion of the park. In warm weather, the park rents canoes and kayaks. There are 104 campsites, 49 with electricity, and three backcountry sites; they go for $25 to $90 a night. Most are closed in winter, but four modern waterfront cabins can be rented year-round. Pets are allowed in the park, except the cabins.

An Excursion to Smith Island ★

Isolated, quiet, friendly Smith Island is set apart from the rest of the Eastern Shore. No bridge connects it to the mainland; residents rely on boats to get to the doctors, the malls, even schools. And they rely on one another as they share the bonds of island living: the seafood industry, hard winters, church suppers.

But they're delighted to see visitors, offering a warm welcome in the distinct Smith Island accent. So hop aboard one of the boats that leaves around lunchtime from Crisfield or Point Lookout.

Walk the modest streets with only a few cars, long shacks where "peelers" doff their shells to become the highly prized softshell crab, to see the vistas of bay and wetlands.

Go for the food: crabs steamed the minute they land on the dock and multilayered Smith Island cake, the official state dessert.

Meet the Smith Islanders and hear the lyrical twist they put on their English. Listen to their stories about life in this out-of-the-way place.

Located 12 miles west of Crisfield, at the edge of Tangier Sound, Smith Island is a cluster of islands making up Maryland's largest inhabited offshore community. There are three towns. On one island is Ewell, where the cruise boats land, and Rhodes Point. Pretty Tylerton is on a second island; Martin National Wildlife Refuge is on the third.

You're going to have to decide whether to go to Ewell or Tylerton. For your first trip, go to Ewell for a pick of restaurants, to see the museum, and see more people. Want to get away from everything? Go to tiny Tylerton. There's nothing to do there; and that's the reason to go. You'll stop for a crab cake at Drum Point Market and take a walk and set a spell. Captain Terry Laird called it the most remote place in Maryland.

A few notes: You can't bring a car. Plan on a stroll, or rent a bike or golf cart. There are no bars, as it's a "dry" island, but you can BYOB. Shops are few, but make sure to stop for a piece of cake or a jar of preserves made from the island's pomegranate, pear, or fig trees. Remember your bug repellent and sunscreen—black flies and mosquitoes are sure to plague you, and although the streets are shady, the sun can be fierce.

One thing's for sure: If you take the ferry for a day trip, you're going to leave wishing you had at least a few more hours here.

ESSENTIALS

GETTING THERE The excursion boats come only in summer, but you can catch the mail boat or residents' ferry (which leave promptly at 12:30pm) if you want to visit off-season. Passenger ferry boats leave from Crisfield and from Point Lookout State Park on Maryland's Western Shore. Or you can bring your own boat.

From Somers Cove Marina in Crisfield, **Smith Island Cruises** (✆ **410/425-2771**) sails at 12:30pm and docks at the Bayside Inn about 40 minutes later. The boat leaves for Crisfield at 3:45pm. Service runs daily Memorial Day Weekend through October 15. Round-trip fare is $25 for adults and $12 for children 3 to 11. Reservations are required. This boat is biggest and most comfortable.

Two ferries go to Ewell. **Captain Otis Ray Taylor** (✆ **410/968-2428**) goes year-round. His ***Island Belle II*** is the mail boat; it leaves Crisfield's City Dock at 12:30pm and departs Ewell at 4pm. **Terry Laird's *Captain Jason*** (✆ **410/422-0620**) leaves from Crisfield for Ewell at 12:30 and 4pm and returns at 7:30am and 3:30pm.

To get to Tylerton, call **Larry Laird** (✆ **410/425-4471** or 410/251-4951) whose ***Captain Jason II*** goes to both Tylerton and Ewell from Crisfield's City Dock. The boat departs Crisfield at 12:30 and 5pm, and leaves Smith Island at 7:30am and 3:30pm.

None of these three boats requires reservations. Fare is $25 for a same-day round-trip, $40 on separate days. The *Captain Jason I* and *II* also take kayaks for a fee.

You can bring your own boat, but check the charts for shallow spots: Smith Island Harbor at Ewell can be 4½ feet at low tide. Water is deeper if you come from Tangier Sound via Big Thorofare. Smith Island Marina is beside the county dock and Bayside Restaurant. The gas dock in Ewell is open Monday through Saturday from 8am to 5pm. (Avoid gassing up in late afternoon, as the watermen use the pumps then.) **Smith Island Marina** (✆ **410/425-4220**) has transient slips, $1 a foot for overnight, $10 for daytime docking. (It is said that Ernest Hemingway once docked his boat here.)

VISITOR INFORMATION While you are in Crisfield, stop at the visitor center at 1103 W. Main St. (✆ **410/968-1543**) or visit the **Tawes Museum** at Somers Cove Marina, 3 Ninth St. (✆ **410/968-2501**), for information.

Once in Ewell, the island's largest town (pop. 100), visit the **Smith Island Center** ★ (✆ **410/425-3351**), up Smith Island Road from the Bayside Inn, to get a sense of how the island is laid out, learn a little history, and see exhibits about the island. Admission is $2; from May through October, it's open daily from noon to 4pm.

GETTING AROUND No cars are permitted on the island. Everything is within walking distance. You can bring your bike on the ferry or rent a bike or a golf cart next to the Bayside Inn.

ORIENTATION **Ewell** is the largest town. It's where most cruise boats dock and has most of the island's seafood-packing houses. **Rhodes Point,** a mile south of Ewell and the island's center for boat repair, was once called Rogues Point because of pirates who stopped here. A marshy place, it's reachable via a wooden bridge from Smith Island or March roads. **Tylerton** may be the most remote place in Maryland, accessible by only one boat. The state's last one-room school was here until it closed in 1996.

Where to Stay & Eat

Ewell has two major restaurants. **Bayside Inn** (✆ **410/425-2771**), with its white siding and red roof, is the first spot most visitors see. Food is hearty and served family style. For my money, the best crab cakes in the state come from **Ruke's Seafood Deck** (✆ **410/425-2311**), down the road in a shabby brown building. If you don't want to eat with a crowd, bypass the restaurants and pop into **Harbor Side Groceries** (✆ **410/425-2525**) for a snack or carryout. In Tylerton, the only place to eat is the **Drum Point Market** (✆ **410/425-2108**). It isn't pretty, but the crab cakes are terrific and inexpensive ($8.95) and it's fun to talk with customers stopping by. These places are open daily in season, but may close from 3 to 6pm.

If you want to take home a multilayered Smith Island cake, stop by **Smith Island Baking Company,** 20926 Caleb Jones Road (✆ **410/425-2253**), across from the post office. They are open every afternoon in season.

B&Bs in Ewell and Tylerton offer the only overnight accommodations.

Ewell Tide Bed & Breakfast This 100-year-old country house offers three simple but comfortable rooms. A first-floor room has an en suite bathroom. Upstairs, a room with two double beds has great water views.

20926 Tyler Rd., Ewell, MD 21824. www.smithisland.net. ✆ **888/699-2141** or 410/425-2141. 4 units, 2 with shared bathroom. $55–$105 double. 25% discount off-season. Rates include hot breakfast. Rollaway beds available for small charge. MC, V. **Amenities:** Use of bicycles and kayaks; dock. *In room:* A/C, TV.

Inn of Silent Music Visitors can find respite in this 1913 farmhouse surrounded on three sides by water. All bedrooms have water views. The hospitable innkeepers pick up guests by golf cart at the Tylerton dock. They'll arrange for a crabbing trip and steam your catch; even order a Smith Island cake you can take when you go. Dinner is available on the screened-in porch or in the newly redesigned kitchen for $25 a person.

2955 Tylerton Rd., Tylerton, MD 21866. www.innofsilentmusic.com. ✆ **410/425-3541.** 3 units. $110–$130 double. Rates include gourmet breakfast. 2-night minimum on weekends. No credit cards. Closed Nov–Apr. No children under 12. **Amenities:** Dinner available; use of bikes, canoes, and kayak. *In room:* A/C, fridge.

Susan's on Smith Island Both rooms offer views of the harbor. The Somerset has the better view; the Golden Pond the bigger bed. Dinner can be arranged, and Susan will also arrange for boating excursions and other activities on the island.

20759 Caleb Jones Rd., Ewell, MD 21824. www.susansonsmithisland.com. ✆ **410/425-2403.** 2 units. $100–$150 double. Rates include hot breakfast. MC, V. **Amenities:** Dinner available; use of bicycles, kayaks. *In room:* A/C.

CHESTERTOWN

48 miles NE of Annapolis; 55 miles E of Baltimore; 70 miles NE of Washington, DC; 50 miles SW of Wilmington, DE

Chestertown, north of the Bay Bridge, looks terrific for her age. Built in 1706 on the Chester River, this was once a thriving seaport. Residents showed their revolutionary leanings when they tossed English tea into the harbor, just as Boston's patriots did. The sea captains' homes, many built in the mid-1700s, still line Water Street—an elegant sight to see as you cross the Chester River Bridge. As you cross, look for the yellow reproduction of the schooner *Sultana*. Chestertown is also home to Washington College. This riverside town makes for a good day trip or a leisurely weekend visit.

Essentials

GETTING THERE From Easton, take U.S. Route 50 north to Route 213; then follow Route 213 north into Chestertown. From I-95 and U.S. Route 40, take the Elkton exit and follow Route 213 south into Chestertown.

VISITOR INFORMATION For a map and brochures about Chestertown and the surrounding area, contact the **Kent County Office of Tourism,** 400 High St., Chestertown (✆ **410/778-0416;** www.kentcounty.com). In town, stop at the visitor center at 122 N. Cross St. (✆ **410/778-9737**). It's open year-round, Monday through Friday from 9am to 5pm, Saturday and Sunday from 10am to 4pm (2pm in winter).

GETTING AROUND With no public transportation in Chestertown, touring by car or walking through the historic streets are the best ways to see the sights. High Street is Chestertown's main thoroughfare. Stop by the visitor center for brochures on a self-guided driving tour and a walking tour.

SPECIAL EVENTS On Memorial Day weekend, the town reenacts the tea-tossing from the decks of brigantine *Geddes* at the **Chestertown Tea Party Festival ★★**. On May 23, 1774, after hearing of the closing of the port of Boston, local citizens boarded the British ship in the harbor and tossed its tea overboard. The festival includes boat rides, Colonial costume parades, crafts, buggy rides, and bands. For information, go to **www.chestertownteaparty.com**. On **First Fridays** of the month, shops and galleries are open until 8pm with special activities.

Where to Stay

Brampton Bed & Breakfast Inn ★★ A curving, tree-lined driveway leads to this Greek Revival plantation house, a mile southwest of town. Built in 1860 and listed on the National Register of Historic Places, it sits on 20 acres of hills and farmland. Guests enjoy the use of two sitting rooms, a wide front porch, and spruce-shaded grounds with lawn furniture. Seven rooms are furnished with period antiques; all units have working gas or log fireplaces and bathrooms have air-jetted tubs, body-jet or steam showers. The amenities of the Mulberry and Olivia's cottages (privacy, soaking tub, screened porch, to name a few) along with their comfortable style make these the ones to choose. Three other cottage units offer space and privacy; Russell's Cottage welcomes dogs.

25227 Chestertown Rd. (off Rte. 20), Chestertown, MD 21620. www.bramptoninn.com. ✆ **866/305-1860** or 410/778-1860. 12 units. $199–$299 double; $219–$419 cottage. Rates include full breakfast and afternoon tea. 2- or 3-night minimum stay required on weekends. DISC, MC, V. *In room:* A/C, flatscreen TV w/DVD, hair dryer, free Wi-Fi.

The Imperial Hotel ★★ With a gingerbread-trimmed triple-porch facade, this three-story brick building is a focal point along Chestertown's main street. Inside you'll find a restaurant, parlor, and lounge/bar, with a courtyard garden in back. Guest rooms are furnished with antiques. The third-floor suite has a private porch overlooking High Street. The Carriage House Suite has a porch overlooking the courtyard.

208 High St., Chestertown, MD 21620. www.imperialchestertown.com. ✆ **410/778-5000.** Fax 410/778-9662. 13 units. $125–$135 double; $160–$175 suite. Rates include continental breakfast. AE, DISC, MC, V. No children 12 and under. **Amenities:** Restaurant (see "Where to Eat"); bar. *In room:* A/C, TV, hair dryer, free Wi-Fi.

The Inn at Mitchell House ★★ 📷 If you're looking for a quiet old-world retreat surrounded by farmland and habitats for birds, geese, white-tailed deer, and red fox, try this three-story 1743 manor house with a screened-in porch. Nestled on 10 acres overlooking Stoneybrook Pond, it sits midway between Chestertown and Rock Hall off Routes 21 and 445. If you come by boat, they'll pick you up at the Tolchester Marina. Guest rooms are furnished with four-poster beds, hooked rugs, and antiques; most have a fireplace or sitting area. The very private "Stones Throw Cottage" offers a bedroom, bathroom, and sitting area with fireplace and kitchen. The inn is Maryland's first member of the Green Hotels Association for its eco-friendly practices.

8796 Maryland Pkwy., Chestertown, MD 21620. www.innatmitchellhouse.com. ✆ **410/778-6500.** 6 units. $109–$149 double; $239 cottage. Rates include full country breakfast. 2-night minimum stay required on most weekends. MC, V. Hunters' kenneled dogs welcome. **Amenities:** Video library. *In room:* A/C, TV/VCR, free Wi-Fi.

Lauretum Bed & Breakfast Inn Crowning a 6-acre spot on a shady knoll outside of town, this three-story 1870 Queen Anne Victorian (listed on the National Register of Historic Places) was named Lauretum ("laurel grove" in Latin) by its first owner, Harrison Vickers. The inn has a formal parlor with fireplace, reading room, screened porch, and sitting room. Hammocks hang under the trees. Bedrooms are bright and large; the third floor has two suites.

954 High St. (Rte. 20), Chestertown, MD 21620. www.lauretuminn.com. ✆ **800/742-3236.** 5 units. $130–$140 double; $160 suite. Rates include hot breakfast. 2-night minimum stay required on weekends in high season. AE, DISC, MC, V. Closed Nov–Apr. **Amenities:** Bike rental; golf and pool privileges at Chester River Yacht Club; TV w/satellite service in library. *In room:* A/C, hair dryer, free Wi-Fi.

The White Swan Tavern ★★ Washington may have only had a drink at this tavern, but now *you* can sleep here. This 1730 inn has six comfortable Colonial guest rooms. You can choose the former kitchen, which dates to 1706, and features brick floors and an open-beam ceiling. The Thomas Peacock Room has luxurious furnishings and a garden view. A two-room suite is so plush you may never leave. The Bittersweet Guest Suites, two apartments next door, each sleep three. Even if you don't stay here, stop for afternoon tea, served from 3 to 5pm, for a civilized break in the day.

231 High St., Chestertown, MD 21620. www.whiteswantavern.com. ✆ **410/778-2300.** 6 units. $150–$190 double; $220–$250 suite. Rates include continental breakfast and afternoon tea. MC, V. No children 12 and under. **Amenities:** Fridge; TV in sitting room. *In room:* A/C, free Wi-Fi.

Widow's Walk Inn In the middle of all that Colonial grandeur sits this Victorian lady, an 1877 beauty with five guest rooms, all with king- or queen-size beds. A first-floor room with private bathroom is spacious, with big windows and fireplace. Another, with a private bathroom, has a claw-foot tub original to the house.

402 High St., Chestertown, MD 21620. www.chestertown.com/widow. ✆ **888/778-6455** or 410/778-6455. 5 units, 2 with shared bathroom. $100–$165 double. Rates include continental breakfast. MC, V. **Amenities:** Fridge; TV in parlor. *In room:* A/C.

Where to Eat

A delicious way to start your day in Chestertown is at **Against the Grain Bread Company,** 203 High St. (✆ **410/778-3333;** www.atgbreadco.com). It's open every day except Monday until 2pm.

Blue Heron Cafe AMERICAN Two cheerful rooms in a low building on a side street offer diners a retreat where they can find a glass of wine, a crab cake with lemon *beurre blanc,* or even veal sweetbreads. For 10 years, this cafe has been serving seafood dishes, such as oyster fritters and seafood pasta, and American favorites such as rack of lamb and chicken potpie. Because it's a street off the main drag, we'll join the locals and keep this our little secret.

236 Cannon St., Chestertown, MD 21620. ✆ **410/778-0188.** www.blueheroncafe.com. Dinner reservations recommended on weekends. Main courses $16–$28 dinner. AE, DISC, MC, V. Mon–Sat 5–8:30pm.

Fish Whistle AMERICAN There's only one place for waterfront dining and that's the casual Fish Whistle. Admire the view with a drink and some drunken mussels, maybe a plate of fried oysters, chicken and mashed potatoes, or surf and turf. There's live music or karaoke in the bar on weekends. A children's menu is available.

98 Cannon St., Chestertown, MD 21620. ✆ **410/778-3566.** www.fishandwhistle.com. Dinner reservations recommended on weekends. Main courses $8–$14 lunch, $12–$28 dinner. AE, DISC, MC, V. Mon–Thurs 11am–8pm; Fri–Sat 11am–9pm; Sun 11am–7pm.

The Front Room ★★ AMERICAN This restaurant at the Imperial Hotel offers fine cuisine and an elegant ambience in intimate dining rooms and on the patio in summer. The menu changes seasonally, but house favorites include fresh fish and beef, all accompanied by vegetables just delivered from local farms. When it's in season, the rockfish is delectable. Brunch on Saturday and Sunday offers crab cake Benedict, softshell crabs or oysters (depending on the season), and sandwiches.

208 High St., Chestertown, MD 21620. ✆ **410/778-5000.** www.imperialchestertown.com. Reservations recommended. Main courses $8–$17 lunch, $10–$35 dinner. AE, MC, V. Mon 11:30am–3pm and 4–8pm; Tues–Fri 11:30am–3pm and 4–9pm; Sat 9am–3pm and 4–9pm; Sun 9am–3pm and 4–8pm.

Lemon Leaf Cafe ★ AMERICAN This cheerful dining room painted in lemon and lime hues offers home-style fare that will stick to your ribs. We're talking about flannel cakes for breakfast, pastry puffs filled with shrimp or chicken salad at lunch, and chicken and dumplings for dinner. Seafood, naturally, is on the menu, too. Bring your own bottle and hope the lemon meringue pie is on the dessert table when you get here.

117 S. Cross St., Chestertown, MD 21620. ✆ **443/282-0004.** Reservations for dinner recommended. Main courses $5–$11 breakfast, $6–$16 lunch, $11–$26 dinner. AE, DISC, MC, V. Sun–Wed 7:30am–3pm; Thurs–Sat 7:30am–8pm.

What to See & Do

Take a walk down the shady streets of Chestertown. **High Street,** the main thoroughfare, takes visitors past shops, restaurants, and inns down to the river. **Water Street** is lined with the brick homes built by shipbuilders, lawyers, and merchants. In midtown is the **Courthouse,** on Cross Street, the site of a 1706 court and jail. Get a walking tour map from the visitor center or at the Geddes Piper House (see below).

Behind the courthouse is the **Geddes Piper House ★**, 101 Church Alley (✆ **410/778-3499;** www.kentcountyhistory.org/geddes.php), home of the Kent County Historical Society and a delightful small-town museum. The house is open Tuesday through Friday 11am to 4pm and also from May through September Saturdays from 1 to 4pm. Wander through this tall 1784 three-story charmer built by James Piper to see fans, quilts, clothing, and toys from the 1880s.

Washington College offers a free iPod tour, **History on the Waterfront: A Journey into Chestertown's Past,** beginning at the Custom House on the Chester River, 101 S. Water St. (www.starrcenter.washcoll.edu/thecustomhouse.html). In addition to the 1745 house, visitors see the basement archaeology exhibit and take a walk along the waterfront. It's open Friday, noon to 4pm, and Saturday, 11am to 4pm.

How big are the trees in this old town? A giant American basswood, the state champion with a circumference of almost 17 feet and height of 108 feet, is on High Street, about a block from the river. For more foliage, check out the **Virginia Gent Decker Arboretum** at Washington College (✆ **800/422-1782,** ext. 7726; www.arboretum.washcoll.edu). A wide variety of trees—from Japanese pagoda to American lindens—grow around these historic college buildings.

About halfway between Chestertown and Rock Hall is **St. Paul's Church,** off Route 20, erected in 1713, one of Maryland's oldest in continuous use. It's open daily from 9am to 5pm; donations are welcome. The church served as a barracks for British soldiers during the War of 1812. Actress Tallulah Bankhead is buried in the church cemetery.

Outdoor Activities

Just south of Rock Hall, **Eastern Neck National Wildlife Refuge,** 1730 Eastern Neck Rd. (© **410/639-7056;** www.fws.gov/northeast/easternneck), is well known to nature lovers, who flock to see migrating waterfowl all winter and the arrival of butterflies heading to South America in August and September. Like Blackwater National Wildlife Refuge near Cambridge, this 2,286-acre wooded island, a "globally significant birding area," is a winter haven for migratory birds, including Canada geese and tundra swan. A water trail circles the island. The refuge has 6 miles of walking trails, an accessible boardwalk, and an accessible trail with platform. At least part of the refuge is open every day dawn to dusk (sections are closed during hunting season in the fall; check the website for closures). There's no entry fee.

BIKING Rent a bike for $6 an hour or $30 a day from **Bikework,** 208 S. Cross St. (© **410/778-6940**). Discounts for multiday rentals are available. The shop also does bike repairs and sells kayaks.

BOATING If the ***Sultana*** (© **410/778-5954;** www.sultanaprojects.org), a reproduction 1768 schooner, is in town, call or check the website for a schedule of cruises. Two-hour cruises cost about $30, $15 for children 5 to 11. Ecology or music sails cost $35. Reservations are recommended.

HUNTING A couple of area properties welcome visitors who want to take their guns for a walk. **Fair Winds Gun Club** (© **410/778-5363**) has 2,200 acres around Chestertown and trained guides available for waterfowl hunting. **Hopkins Game Farm** (© **410/348-5287**) has 600 acres, a lodge open year-round, and can provide guides and dogs. Shooting lessons are also available.

PICNICKING Go down Water Street to find Wilmer Park, a wide-open waterfront park with gazebos, shade trees, and picnic tables.

Shopping

High, Cross, and Cannon streets are lined with shops. Most stores are open Tuesday through Saturday from 9 or 10am to 5pm. Many have Sunday afternoon hours, too.

Village House, 103 S. Cross St. (© **410/788-5766**), stocks eye-catching wares for the home, including lamps, pillows, and knickknacks.

Twigs and Teacups, 111 S. Cross St. (© **410/778-1708**), carries a huge assortment of gifts, including stationery, soaps, toys, joke items, and teacups. Have a cup of tea or fair-trade coffee and a bite to eat across the street at **Play It Again Sam,** 108 S. Cross St. (© **410/778-2688**).

Robert Ortiz Studio, 207 S. Cross St. (© **410/810-1400;** www.ortizstudios.com), sells the craftsman's high-end Shaker and Japanese-inspired furniture in a little showroom by the workshop.

The **Compleat Bookseller,** 301 High St. (© **410/778-1480**), stocks everything from classics to bestsellers, plus *Chesapeake* and other Eastern Shore favorites.

The **Artists Gallery,** 239 High St. (© **410/778-2425**), displays contemporary prints, clocks, lamps, jewelry, and accessories.

A Side Trip to Rock Hall ★

This sleepy fishing village was once a major crossroads: In Colonial times, travelers had to stop here on their way to Philadelphia. George Washington, Thomas Jefferson, and James Madison all really did sleep here. Now Rock Hall, on a peninsula between the Chesapeake and Swan Creek, is better known for its marinas, fishing charters, and some good restaurants. Water's everywhere, so pleasure boaters consider this a good destination for dinner. It's an enjoyable day trip, too.

WHERE TO STAY

Inn at Huntingfield Creek ★★★ Lucky Rock Hall: Two of the state's finest bed-and-breakfasts are in Rock Hall. This is one of them. (The Osprey Point Inn is the other.) The property, 70 acres of soybean, sunflower, and lavender fields, fronts the peaceful undeveloped creek. Walk down to the dock to watch the sun set and see the lights come on over Baltimore across the Chesapeake Bay. Bedrooms, which have private bathrooms, are spacious, with king-size beds. There's a saltwater pool just beyond the kitchen garden. Cottages behind the main house offer more privacy with sitting rooms with pullout couches, TVs, two-sided fireplaces, and bedrooms with king-size beds. These are also kid- and pet-friendly. Three lovable dogs greet you when you arrive.

4928 Eastern Neck Rd., Rock Hall, MD 21661. www.huntingfield.com. ✆ **410/639-7779.** 4 units, 4 cottage units. $179–$199 double; $260–$285 cottage. Rates include gourmet breakfast. DISC, MC, V. Pets welcome for a fee. **Amenities:** Dock; pool. *In room:* A/C, flatscreen TV/DVD, hair dryer, free Wi-Fi.

Osprey Point Inn ★★★ One of the loveliest inns on the Eastern Shore, this place has the charm of a waterfront Colonial home and the space and necessities required by modern travelers. Designed to look vintage, it's less than 20 years old. There are high ceilings, fireplaces, and lots of windows. Each bedroom has its own ambience: Bolero has a fireplace and window seats overlooking the water, while the waterfront Escapade suite has a whirlpool tub in its black-marble bathroom. In addition, the farmhouse on the property may be rented as a whole or by the room. Five units, most with water views, are available at nearby Gratitude Marina.

20786 Rock Hall Ave., Rock Hall, MD 21661. www.ospreypoint.com. ✆ **410/639-2194.** 15 units. $135–$280 double. Rates include continental breakfast. DISC, MC, V. **Amenities:** Restaurant (see "Where to Eat," below); bar; bikes; children's play area; 160-slip marina; pool. *In room:* A/C, TV, hair dryer, free Wi-Fi.

Tallullah's on Main An old apartment building on Rock Hall's Main Street has been turned into this simple but comfortable hotel. Rooms are furnished in a retro style, each with some reference to the town's famous resident Tallulah Bankhead. All have galley kitchens, private bathrooms, and access to a shady deck. Three rooms can be combined into a suite. A two-bedroom cottage, which sleeps six and has a TV, offers views of Rock Hall's tiny bayfront beach.

5750 Main St., Rock Hall, MD 21661. www.tallulahsonmain.com. ✆ **410/639-2596.** 5 units and beach cottage. $125–$145 double; $250 cottage. AE, MC, V. *In room:* A/C, TV, hair dryer (on request), free Wi-Fi (not at cottage).

WHERE TO EAT

Bay WolfAUSTRIAN/SEAFOOD The owners offer their Austrian cuisine—Wiener schnitzel, Black Forest cake—as well as traditional Eastern Shore fare. Salads, soups, and sandwiches (including a $10 crab cake) are featured at lunch. At dinner, you can choose between roast pork napped in a rich brown gravy with a caraway seeded dumpling and sauerkraut and a perfectly seasoned crab cake. The setting is more Bavarian than Eastern Shore, with watercolors of Salzburg and the Alps and stained-glass windows. There's also a bar and sidewalk dining in summer.

Rock Hall Ave. ✆ **410/639-2000.** Reservations recommended on summer weekends. Main courses $5–$8 lunch, $17–$19 dinner. AE, DISC, MC, V. Daily noon–9pm. Closed Sun in winter.

Java Rock COFFEE This slice of the 21st century serves coffee drinks, offers wireless Internet service, and a small collection of gourmet foods perfect for a picnic or stocking the boat's pantry. There's a tempting assortment of bagels, pastries, soups, and sandwiches. Eat in the airy little dining room or out on the deck, find a spot in the wireless nook, or take your goodies to go.

21309 Sharp St., at Main St. ✆ **410/639-9909.** Reservations not accepted. Coffee and pastry $2–$7. AE, DISC, MC, V. Mon–Fri 7am–5pm Sat 7am–7pm; Sun 7am–3pm.

Osprey Point Restaurant AMERICAN In a small but elegant Colonial-style dining room, diners have their choice of crab cakes, fresh fish, and maybe duck or lamb, all served with creative sauces and seasonal vegetables. A recent menu offered rockfish with pistachio dust and butter basted scallops. For all the formal elegance of the setting and the food, this is a place to relax and enjoy. Brunch is served on Sundays.

At the Osprey Point Inn, 20786 Rock Hall Ave. ✆ **410/639-2194.** www.ospreypoint.com. Reservations recommended. Main courses $25–$34. DISC, MC, V. Wed–Sat 5–9pm; Sun 10:30am–2pm and 5–8pm. Closed Jan.

Waterman's Crab House Restaurant & Dock Bar ★ SEAFOOD The dining room is a nice enough place for cracking steamed crabs, but the deck is made for it. Water views, bay breezes, and trays filled with the little gems make a picnic table the perfect dining spot. Waterman's has earned its reputation for good fresh seafood, seafood pasta, and prime rib. Save room for an ice-cream sundae or adult ice-cream drink. There's music on weekends in warm weather. Boat docking is available.

Rock Hall Harbor, end of Sharp St. ✆ **410/639-2261.** www.watermanscrabhouse.com. Reservations recommended on weekends. Main courses $8–$15 lunch, $9–$35 dinner. AE, DISC, MC, V. Sun–Thurs 11am–8:30pm; Fri–Sat 11am–9:30pm. Free docking while you dine; directions by water on website.

WHAT TO SEE & DO

Several evenings a month, the **Mainstay** ("the Home of Musical Magic") on Main Street (✆ **410/639-9133;** www.mainstayrockhall.org) presents a wide assortment of acts, including jazz, traditional, and classical, for $10 to $25 a ticket. It's intimate, with 120 seats. Buy tickets in cash at the door.

Rock Hall also has three museums, all with a focus on local history. **Tolchester Beach Revisited ★**, Main and Sharp streets (✆ **410/778-5347;** www.rockhallmd.com/tolchester), is a two-room museum at the end of the Oyster Court shopping area. Anyone who has ever taken the ferry to the Eastern Shore beaches or heard stories from a grandparent will appreciate this collection of memorabilia, photos, and trinkets—all given by people who remember Tolchester Beach, the Ocean City of its day. From the 19th century until construction of the first Bay Bridge, thousands of people escaped the city heat by heading to Tolchester's beach, amusement-park rides, and hotel. The museum is free and open March through December Saturday and Sunday from 11am to 3pm, and by appointment.

The **Waterman's Museum,** Haven Harbour Marina, 20880 Rock Hall Ave. (✆ **410/778-6697;** www.havenharbour.com/destination/rock-hall), focuses on the people who harvest the bay. The reproduction shanty house has three rooms of photographs, carvings, and tools of the trade. There's free admission, and it's open daily from 10am to 4pm. Get the key from the Ditty Bag Store at nearby Haven Harbour Marina.

The **Rock Hall Museum,** in the Municipal Building at 5585 Main St. (✆ **410/639-7611;** www.rockhallmd.com/museum), features the usual small-town exhibits: boat models, old tools, a sleigh, and photos of all the Chesapeake Bay ferries. What makes it worthwhile is a tiny vignette in the corner, a creative display of a duck-decoy carver's studio. Admission is free, and it's open Saturday, Sunday 11am to 3pm, and by appointment.

OUTDOOR ACTIVITIES

BIKING This is easy biking territory, flat and quiet. Rent a bike from **Haven Harbour Marina** (✆ **800/506-6697** or 410/778-6697; www.havenharbour.com).

BOATING **Blue Crab Chesapeake Charters** (✆ **410/708-1803;** www.bluecrabcharters.com) has room for six on its 36-foot *Crab Imperial*. The 90-minute sail costs $50 a person; overnight charters start at $300. The 48-foot *Jennifer Ann II* (✆ **410/708-7751;** www.fishfearus.com) takes six fishermen out twice a day. **Haven Harbour Marina** (✆ **800/506-6697** or 410/778-6697; www.havenharbour.com) has slips that can accommodate boats of up to 50 feet as well. Don't know the difference between tack and jibe? Learn to sail at the **Maryland School of Sailing & Seamanship** (✆ **410/639-7030;** www.mdschool.com). It offers 5-, 6-, and 8-day live-aboard cruises for both new and experienced sailors. **Rock Hall Yacht Club** hosts a variety of regattas and sailing competitions throughout the warm weather; see **www.rockhallyachtclub.org** for their calendar.

If you like your boats smaller, see **Chester River Kayak Adventures,** 5758 Main St. (✆ **410/639-2001;** www.crkayakadventures.com), for kayak rentals and tours. Or go to **Haven Harbour Marina** (✆ **800/506-6697** or 410/778-6697; www.havenharbour.com).

SHOPPING

Barely a block of downtown is devoted to shops. Most are open only on weekends. The shops of **Oyster Court** (✆ **410/708-0057**), just off Main Street, are open 10am to 5pm Saturday and Sunday. Stop by for gifts from gardening treasures to hot sauce. **Smilin' Jake's,** at 5745 Main St. (✆ **410/639-7280**), sells Hawaiian-inspired garb and is open daily. Get your Vera Bradley fix at the **Hickory Stick,** 5761 Main St. (✆ **410/639-7980**), which is open daily, or local arts and crafts at the **Rock Hall Gallery,** 5764 Main St. (✆ **410/639-2494**), open Friday through Sunday. If you see something you like in **Tallullah's** window (Murano glass jewelry and gifts, mostly), call ✆ **410/639-2596** and the innkeepers will open the shop at 5750 Main St. for you. For ice cream, stop by the 1930s-era soda counter at **Durding's Store,** at Main and Sharp streets (✆ **410/778-7957**).

CHESAPEAKE CITY

75 miles NE of Annapolis; 54 miles NE of Baltimore; 40 miles SW of Wilmington, DE; 25 miles NE of Chestertown

Chesapeake City, on the Chesapeake & Delaware Canal, remains a crossroads for the maritime traffic using the canal every day. Technically an Eastern Shore town, it is easily accessible via I-95, and thus makes an easier Eastern Shore visit than some of the other places discussed in this chapter.

The first thing you notice when driving over the 800-foot Chesapeake & Delaware (C&D) Canal Bridge is the view of the canal. Both private boats and commercial ships use this connection between the Chesapeake Bay and Delaware River. Construction of the canal brought prosperity to this town, which changed its name from the Village of Bohemia to Chesapeake City in 1839. Its inhabitants built beautiful homes, most of which still survive. Several restored Victorians now house shops and B&Bs. Boaters find it a great destination or place to stop on a cruise along the Inland Waterway.

Essentials

GETTING THERE From Easton and other points south, take Route 301 northeast to Route 213, which leads into Chesapeake City. From Baltimore, take I-95 to the Elkton exit (Rte. 279); follow Route 213 south. Or sail into town via the canal.

VISITOR INFORMATION For brochures, contact the **Cecil County Tourism Office,** 68 Heather Lane, Ste. 43, Perryville (✆ **800/232-4595** or 410/996-6292; www.seececil.org).

GETTING AROUND Although downtown Chesapeake City lends itself to walking, the best way to see the surrounding sights is by **car.** There is also a free seasonal passenger **ferry** service, operated by the ***Miss Clare,*** connecting the north and south sides of the canal. It runs Wednesday through Sunday in summer, weekends only in spring and fall. The schedule is posted on a kiosk in Pell Gardens.

ORIENTATION The C&D Canal divides the city into north and south sides. The main commercial and historic area is on the south side of the canal. South Chesapeake City is pedestrian-friendly; its one main street, Bohemia Avenue, has stores and businesses. Look for free walking and shopping brochures in any shop. Free parking areas under the bridge and farther in town are clearly marked.

Where to Stay

The Blue Max Inn ★ Built in 1844, this house was once occupied by author Jack Hunter while writing his book *The Blue Max.* The large bedrooms are decorated in period style. Thoughtful touches include chocolates, flowers, and complimentary beverages. Guests can enjoy a cozy parlor (with fireplace), dining room, gazebo, and, best of all, first- and second-floor porches overlooking the historic district.

300 Bohemia Ave., Chesapeake City, MD 21915. www.bluemaxinn.com. ✆ **877/725-8362** or 410/885-2781. Fax 410/885-2809. 9 units. $105–$265 double. Rates include full breakfast and afternoon tea. 2-night minimum stay required on some weekends and holidays. AE, DISC, MC, V. No children 10 and under. **Amenities:** Bikes. *In room:* A/C, TV/VCR, CD player, hair dryer, free Wi-Fi.

Inn at the Canal ★ The high painted ceilings in the public areas of this inn will remind visitors of the grand old post–Civil War days. Though the guest rooms are smaller, that style continues up to the third-floor suite. Decorated with antiques, soft colors, and embroidered bedding, the 1868 house is welcoming and comfortable. Windows look out over the Back River Basin. The Upper Bay Suite fills the third floor with its own kitchenette, sitting area with a trundle daybed, and water-view deck. The Greenbriar Point Room has a good-size sitting area and windows on two sides.

104 Bohemia Ave. (P.O. Box 187), Chesapeake City, MD 21915. www.innatthecanal.com. ✆ **410/885-5995.** 7 units. $105–$250 double. Rates include breakfast and afternoon refreshments. 2-night minimum stay required on weekends in high season. AE, DC, DISC, MC, V. *In room:* A/C, TV (most w/VCR or DVD player), hair dryer, free Wi-Fi.

Where to Eat

Bayard House ★★★ AMERICAN This 1780s house overlooking the canal has two cozy dining rooms, but who could resist the water views from the porch or brick patio? Then there's the food, artfully presented and creatively prepared. Don't miss the tournedos Baltimore: twin petite filets topped with crab and lobster, napped in Madeira cream. Other options include oysters in season, steak, and lobster ravioli. Lunchtime brings salads, sandwiches, a $10 burger, and smaller portions of the dinner entrees. The historic Hole-in-the-Wall bar has its own bar menu. Brunch is served on Sunday.

11 Bohemia Ave. ✆ **887/582-4049** or 410/885-5040. www.bayardhouse.com. Reservations recommended for dinner. Main courses $10–$16 lunch, $16–$27 dinner. AE, DC, DISC, MC, V. Sun–Thurs 11am–9pm, Fri–Sat 11am–10pm in summer; Mon–Sat 11am–9pm, Sun 11am–8pm off-season.

Chesapeake Inn Restaurant & Marina SEAFOOD Walk or sail to this modern building with its own boat slips for fine or casual dining, all with waterfront views. The deck's light-fare menu (from appetizers to sandwiches to mahimahi quesadillas) and live entertainment are offered daily in summer, weekends off-season. The upper-level dining room features a well-rounded wine list and a fine-dining menu of seafood, steak, veal, chicken, and pasta. Lunch features sandwiches, salads, and smaller entrees. Sunday brunch is served 10am to 2pm.

605 2nd St. ✆ **410/885-2040.** www.chesapeakeinn.com. Reservations recommended for dinner. Main courses $12–$16 lunch, $18–$33 dinner. AE, DC, DISC, MC, V. Mon–Thurs 11am–10pm; Fri–Sat 11am–11pm; Sun 10am–10pm. Deck May–Oct Mon–Thurs noon–10pm, Fri–Sat noon–1am; Nov–Apr Fri–Sun noon–1am.

What to See & Do

On the waterfront, the **C&D Canal Museum ★**, 815 Bethel Rd., at Second Street (✆ **410/885-5622**), tells the story of the giant waterway running through town. The 1829 pump house (now the museum) features the largest water wheel built in the U.S. The admission is free; it's open Monday through Friday from 9am to 4pm.

At the water's edge is **Pell Gardens,** a grassy park with a gazebo next to the town wharf. It's a good place to enjoy an ice-cream cone from the **Canal Creamery,** 9 Bohemia Ave. (✆ **410/885-3314**), across the street (May–Oct).

Take a cruise aboard the ***Miss Clare*** (✆ **410/885-5088**), captained by a fifth-generation resident who has plenty of stories and historical photos to share. Cruises are scheduled April through October on Saturday and Sunday.

Shopping

Shopping is one of the main attractions in Chesapeake City; most stores are open from 10am until 9 or 10pm on Friday and Saturday, and until 5pm on Sunday. Winter hours tend to be more limited.

Bohemia Avenue, the major thoroughfare, begins at the waterfront with a collection of galleries offering original and local art, as well as limited-edition prints. The oldest of these, **Firefly Glass Studio,** 1709 Bohemia Ave. (✆ **410/504-9357**), stocks stained glass in an old bank building.

Back Creek General Store, 100 Bohemia Ave. (✆ **410/885-5377**), is housed in an 1861 building that's packed with gifts and a large collection of Sheila and Byers Choice items, including ones of Chesapeake City. Artist and printmaker Neil Snodgrass sells his own works at **Neil's Artwork,** 226 George St. (✆ **410/885-5094**). His shop is open April through December.

FREDERICK & THE CIVIL WAR CROSSROADS

8

Frederick, in our country's early years, was, and still is, an important crossroads. With the building of the National Pike in the 1700s, it was linked with the port of Baltimore and became a major stop on the road west. Francis Scott Key grew up and practiced law here before writing the poem that would become our national anthem. When Elizabeth Ann Seton sought a place for her community of religious women, she found a home just north of the city in Emmitsburg.

During the Civil War, thousands of wounded soldiers arrived here to recover. The first wave came in August 1862, following the Battle of South Mountain. More arrived the next month after the battle at Antietam, the bloodiest day of the Civil War. So many wounded arrived, they outnumbered Frederick's own citizens.

In 1862, Barbara Fritchie confronted General Stonewall Jackson and was immortalized in poetry: "'Shoot if you must this old gray head, but spare your country's flag,' she said."

Two years later, Confederate General Jubal Early demanded ransom that saved the town from destruction. Battles at Harpers Ferry and Gettysburg brought more wounded before the Battle of Monocacy was waged to the southeast.

Reminders of these sad days remain in the area's historic sites, museums, and the battlefields of **Antietam, Gettysburg, Harpers Ferry,** and **Monocacy,** maintained by the National Park Service. These battlefields and memorials are part of the ongoing sesquicentennial commemorations of the War Between the States through 2015. West Virginia is also marking its 150th anniversary June 20, 2013.

Today Frederick is Maryland's second-largest city, its suburbs extending down toward Washington, DC. Downtown is a popular spot for shopping and dining, while outside town are rolling fields and orchards, the foothills of the Catoctin Mountains, and green space for picnicking and hiking.

FREDERICK ★

46 miles W of Baltimore; 45 miles NW of Washington, DC; 33 miles S of Gettysburg

Once a largely agricultural community, Frederick is now a busy small city with a population of 65,000. Though its downtown district is surrounded by housing developments, the 33-block historic area maintains its small-town charm. The 18th- and 19th-century buildings and cluster of church spires that make up Frederick's skyline are still a main attraction. Antiques and crafts shops dominate the shopping area, and there's a vibrant restaurant and bar scene. Frederick also lies at the junction of two national scenic byways, the Historic National Road (alternate U.S. 40) and the Catoctin Mountain Scenic Byway (Rte. 15). North and west of the city, the agricultural community still thrives, with produce stands popping up among the fields.

Essentials

GETTING THERE From Washington, DC, take I-270 to Frederick, where it becomes U.S. 15 and continues north to Gettysburg. From Baltimore, take I-70 west. From points west, take I-68 east to I-70. To get to the historic district, take Route 15 to the Rosemont Avenue exit to Second Street, across the street from the exit ramp.

Greyhound (✆ **800/231-2222;** www.greyhound.com) operates daily **bus** service to Frederick's MARC train station, 100 S. East St. (✆ **301/663-3311**).

The MTA's **MARC** train runs between Frederick and Washington, DC, with service Monday through Friday. Call ✆ **866/RIDE-MTA** (743-3682), or go to **www.mtamaryland.com** for schedule and fare information.

The **BayRunner Shuttle** (✆ **301/898-2571;** www.bayrunnershuttle.com) operates a regular schedule from a variety of Maryland destinations, including Baltimore/Washington International Thurgood Marshall Airport, and Amtrak and Greyhound stations. Call for reservations.

VISITOR INFORMATION The **Tourism Council of Frederick County** operates a visitor center at 151 S. East St. (✆ **800/999-3613** or 301/600-4047; www.fredericktourism.org). This office, open daily, supplies maps, brochures, and listings of accommodations and restaurants. It has a good 14-minute film to introduce you to the town and its history. There are brochures for a variety of self-guided tours of the historic district, African-American sites, wineries, breweries, and covered bridges.

GETTING AROUND The best way to get around Frederick's historic district is on foot. So park your car. It's a buck an hour at the meters and free for 3 hours at the five town garages. These are at 17 E. Church St., 44 E. Patrick St., 2 S. Court St., 125 E. All Saints St. (the one closest to the visitor center), and 138 W. Patrick St. Stop at the visitor center to have your ticket validated for free parking before you leave. If you park in a residential district, check for the signs that restrict nonresident parking.

Frederick County operates **TransIT** (✆ **301/600-2065;** www.frederickcountymd.gov/transit), a **bus** service that connects outlying hotels, malls, and colleges with the historic district and Frederick-area train stations.

SPECIAL EVENTS Fall colors are at their peak in mid- to late October, which is also the peak time for special events. Thurmont's **Catoctin Colorfest** (✆ **301/271-7533;** www.colorfest.org), a crafts show of enormous proportions, is held in mid-October. **First Saturday Gallery Walks** are held monthly in Frederick. Shops, galleries, and restaurants stay open until 9pm. Call ✆ **301/698-8118** for details.

A couple of events mark the anniversaries of Civil War battles. The commemoration of the 1864 **Battle of Monocacy,** the "battle that saved Washington," is held the weekend closest to the July 9 anniversary (✆ **301/662-3515** for information). Its 150th anniversary will be marked with great ceremony in 2014.

Historic Frederick

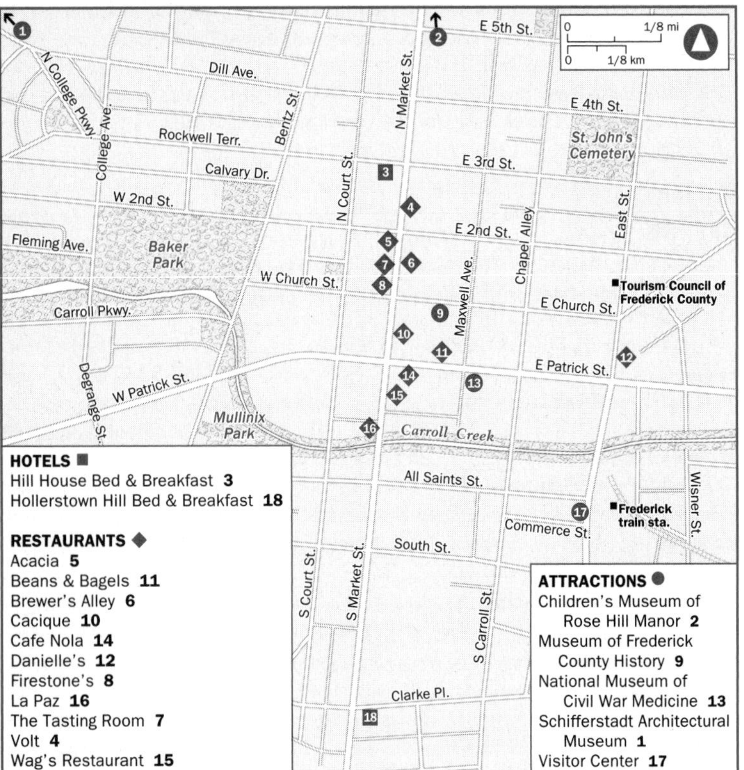

The 1862 **Battle of Antietam** is recalled in September (✆ **301/432-5124** for information). Its 150th anniversary commemoration will take place in 2012.

Where to Stay

There are B&Bs in the historic district, and charming inns in the countryside. A number of chain hotels are along the city's edges, many north on Route 15.

Hampton Inn Frederick Located 2 miles south of downtown Frederick, this modern six-story hotel is standard Hampton style, updated in early 2012. What makes it different is the bar housed in a lighthouse replica nestled beside an artificial lake and connected by footbridge to the hotel. Many guest rooms overlook the lake.

5311 Buckeystown Pike, Frederick, MD 21704 (take Exit 31B off I-270 at Rte. 85). www.hamptoninn.hilton.com. ✆ **800/HAMPTON** (426-7866) or 301/698-2500. Fax 301/695-8735. 160 units. $109–$159 double. Rates include hot breakfast. AE, DC, DISC, MC, V. Pets accepted for a fee. **Amenities:** Restaurant; fitness center; outdoor pool. *In room:* A/C, flatscreen TV w/movies, fridge, hair dryer, microwave, free Wi-Fi.

Hill House Bed & Breakfast ★★ This 1870s town house is in the historic district—off the beaten track enough to be quiet, but within walking distance to everything. Accommodations are cheery and comfortable; two units have TVs. The grand canopy bed in the Victorian Room takes up most of the space, but the bathroom is enormous. The Mexican Room has twin beds in a gaily painted setting, plus a huge plant-filled bathroom with chaise longue and access to the balcony. The Chesapeake Room also has balcony access. The Steeple Suite has a sitting room with TV and fridge.

12 W. 3rd St., Frederick, MD 21705. www.hillhousefrederick.com. ✆ **301/682-4111.** 4 units. $125–$145 double; $175 suite. Rates include full breakfast. MC, V. *In room:* CD player, hair dryer, free Wi-Fi.

Holiday Inn Frederick ☺ This modern two-story hotel is a popular conference center, its public areas often bustling with activity. However, except for the handful of guest rooms overlooking the courtyard or pool, most are separated from common areas and are relatively quiet. Its indoor pool, miniature golf course, and game tables make it a great place for kids. Expect standard Holiday Inn size and decor. Studio suites offer sleeper sofa, fridge, and microwave. The hotel is adjacent to the Francis Scott Key Mall, and it's a short drive from the historic district.

5400 Holiday Dr. (I-270 at Rte. 85), Frederick, MD 21703. www.hifrederick.com. ✆ **888/465-4329** or 301/694-7500. Fax 301/694-0589. 155 units. $139–$169 double. Children 18 and under stay free in parent's room; children 12 and under eat free. AE, DC, DISC, MC, V. Pets accepted for a fee. **Amenities:** Restaurant; lounge; fitness center; indoor pool; recreation area w/indoor miniature golf course, table tennis, and foosball; sauna; whirlpool. *In room:* A/C, TV/VCR w/pay movies, fridge and microwave in some rooms, hair dryer, free Wi-Fi.

Hollerstown Hill Bed & Breakfast This rose-and-gray 1901 Victorian beauty is on a quiet lane at the southern end of the historic district. Guest rooms have small sitting areas and Victorian furnishings (some antiques, some reproductions—but all designed for comfort). One room has twin beds; the Dutrow has a king-size bed and huge bathroom; the Cottage Garden room has a balcony nestled in the branches of an old tree. The game room has a pool table and Civil War–soldier chess set.

4 Clarke Place, Frederick, MD 21701. www.hollerstownhill.com. ✆ **301/228-3630.** 4 units. $135–$145 double. Rates include full breakfast and afternoon tea. AE, MC, V. No children 15 and under. **Amenities:** Sitting area w/TV. *In room:* A/C, TV, free Wi-Fi.

The Inn at Buckeystown ★★ Set in a quiet country village on the Monocacy River, this 1897 mansion is rich in Italianate Victorian details, with a wraparound porch, widow's walk, and ornate trim. The interior boasts antiques, Oriental rugs, chandeliers, and five working fireplaces. Sleeping rooms have unique touches including fireplaces, chandeliers, or Civil War decor. The Victoriana's bed is tucked into the curve of a turret. Third-floor rooms, which have shared bathrooms, can be combined with the game room for a family or bridal party. Lunch, Sunday brunch, dinner, and high tea are served on Victorian china with period silver and glassware (reservations required for all meals). Check the website for murder-mystery dinners. Guests rave about the food.

3521 Buckeystown Pike (Rte. 85), Buckeystown, MD 21717. www.innatbuckeystown.com. ✆ **800/272-1190** or 301/874-5755. Fax 301/831-1355. 9 units. $115–$175 double. Rates include breakfast. AE, DISC, MC, V. **Amenities:** Restaurant. *In room:* A/C, TV/VCR in most rooms, hair dryer, free Wi-Fi.

Where to Eat

Get coffee and a bagel at the cozy **Beans & Bagels,** 49 E. Patrick St. (✆ **301/620-2165**). **Cafe Nola,** 4 E. Patrick St. (✆ **301/694-6652**), serves coffee and breakfast all day, as well as salads, sandwiches, and entrees later in the day.

Acacia ★★ NEW AMERICAN Fill up on the $11 plate of Asian-inspired appetizers at lunch or Asian dishes, steak, or seafood at dinner. Most entrees have at least a smidge of Asian spiciness, but if your tastes lean more to the West, you'll find something you like, too. Locally sourced ingredients are featured. The back dining rooms are refined with white tablecloths and warm colors.

129 N. Market St., Frederick, MD 21701. ✆ **301/694-3015.** www.acacia129.com. Reservations recommended on Fri–Sat. Main courses $8–$10 lunch, $11–$31 dinner. AE, DC, MC, V. Sun–Thurs 11:30am–10pm; Fri–Sat 11:30am–11:30pm.

Brewer's Alley BREWPUB Regular pub fare here is good, but the specialty wood-fired pizzas are especially creative—try one topped with barbecued chicken. Beer is brewed on the premises, including the 1634 Ale designed for Maryland's 375th anniversary in 2009. It's a very popular place; on busy weekends, the wait for a table can be long. In warm weather, the sidewalk patio is delightful.

124 N. Market St., Frederick, MD 21701. ✆ **301/631-0089.** www.brewers-alley.com. Reservations recommended on Fri–Sat. Main courses $9–$21 all-day menu. AE, DC, MC, V. Mon–Thurs 11:30am–11:30pm; Fri–Sat 11:30am–12:30pm; Sun noon–11:30pm.

Cacique Restaurant SPANISH/MEXICAN Diners can sit in one of the cozy rooms with white tablecloths and Latino music piped in, or outside on the sidewalk patio. The Tex-Mex and Spanish favorites include paella, fajitas, and quesadillas, with a side of undeniably fresh *pico de gallo,* sharp with lime and cilantro. The food is good, if not surprising, and the service is as friendly as you'd expect in Frederick.

26 N. Market St., Frederick, MD 21701. ✆ **301/695-2756.** www.caciquefrederick.com. Reservations recommended for dinner. Main courses $11–$30. AE, DISC, MC, V. Sun–Thurs 11:30am–10pm; Fri–Sat 11am–11:30pm.

Danielle's ★ AMERICAN/ITALIAN With three settings—a more formal dining room, an outdoor patio, and a casual pub—and an extensive menu with Italian dishes and American favorites, Danielle's has something for everybody. Danielle's gained its reputation as Tauraso's and the quality has remained. For lunch, you'll find sandwiches, pastas, and salads. Pizzas made in a wood-burning oven are also featured.

Everedy Sq., 6 N. East St., Frederick, MD 21701. ✆ **301/663-6600.** www.danielles-restaurant.com. Reservations recommended for dinner on Fri–Sat. Main courses $9–$21 lunch, $14–$29 dinner. AE, DC, DISC, MC, V. Sun 11:30am–9pm; Tues–Thurs 11:30am–10pm; Fri–Sat 11:30am–11pm.

Firestone's ★ AMERICAN Fish and beef are lifted to a new level through their artful preparation. Deviled eggs with caviar, anyone? A fish sandwich napped in orange aioli at lunch is a tasty sensation. That doesn't mean you can't get a good burger or cowboy steak served by a thoughtful waiter. The wine list is long and the beer menu is extensive, too. Ask for a table by the window up on the mezzanine. Jazz brunch is served on Sundays.

105 N. Market St., Frederick, MD 21701. ✆ **301/663-0330.** www.firestonesrestaurant.com. Reservations recommended on weekends. Main courses $8–$16 lunch, $21–$37 dinner. AE, DC, DISC, MC. Tues–Sat 11am–1:30am; Sun 10am–1am.

La Paz Mexican Restaurant MEXICAN Two floors of dining rooms, plus a waterfront patio overlook Carroll Creek. The menu offers good Mexican food—fajitas, flautas, and burritos—and good margaritas. There's also a children's menu.

51 S. Market St., Frederick, MD 21701. ✆ **301/694-8980.** www.lapazmex.com. Reservations accepted for parties of 6 or more except Fri and Sat evenings. Main courses $4–$17. AE, DC, DISC, MC, V. Mon–Thurs 11am–10pm; Fri 11am–11pm; Sat 11:30am–11pm; Sun 3:30–11pm.

The Tasting Room NEW AMERICAN After a day of visiting museums and quaint shops on charming little streets, this minimalist cream-and-black restaurant is a breath of fresh air. Its menu is as up to the minute as the decor, with the trendiest of ingredients, such as salmon cakes, *osso buco,* or seared tuna. Choose from the 200-bottle wine list or martini specials.

101 N. Market St. ✆ **240/379-7772.** www.tastetr.com. Reservations recommended for dinner. Main courses $10–$18 lunch, $26–$36 dinner. AE, DC, DISC, MC, V. Mon–Sat 11am–3pm and 5–10pm (until 11pm Fri–Sat).

Volt ★★★ AMERICAN Bryan Voltaggio's modern take on American cuisine using fresh local ingredients is extremely popular (and even more so after his appearance on TV's *Top Chef*). Dinner reservations can be difficult to obtain. Lunch is a little easier; if there's space in the lounge, take it. The restaurant—set in a grand old stone mansion with all-white interior—offers tasting menus at lunch and dinner. Or order individual courses. Another option (even harder to get) is the 21-course **Table 21,** the kitchen table. Quiet dining rooms, flawless service, and imaginative food await. Is it worth it? Fans are voting with their feet and forks (including ours, when we can get in). Voltaggio opened **Lunchbox** (✆ **301/360-0580;** www.voltlunchbox.com) in late 2011 along Carroll Creek, serving gourmet sandwiches, soups, and salads.

228 N. Market St. ✆ **301/696-VOLT** (8658). www.voltrestaurant.com. Reservations essential for dinner. Main courses $35–$55 3- and 5-course prix-fixe lunch, dinner $80–$150. AE, DISC, MC, V. Lounge: Tues–Sun 3pm–close, Sat–Sun 11:30am–close. Main & Chef's Dining Room: Tues–Sun 5:30–10pm; brunch, Sat–Sun 11:30am–2pm; Table 21, Tues–Sun, 7pm seating.

Wag's Restaurant 🎁 BURGERS This basement bar is the smallest of Frederick's favorite nightspots. People come for burgers. Dripping with Wag's special sauce, they continue to be voted the best in town. There are other equally artery-clogging and wonderful sandwiches, including the Reuben and steak-and-cheese.

24 S. Market St. ✆ **301/694-8451.** www.eatatwags.com. Reservations not accepted. Main courses $6–$9. AE, DISC, MC, V. Mon–Sat 11am–2am.

What to See & Do

The **Frederick Visitor Center,** 151 S. East St. (✆ **301/600-2888;** www.frederick tourism.org), is the place to stop for maps, information, and, if you parked in one of the four city garages, validation of your ticket for 3 hours of free parking. **Guided walking tours** of the historic district depart from the Museum of Frederick County History on weekends in spring and summer. The cost is $7 for adults, $6 for seniors, and $5 for children 12 and under. If **wineries** or **breweries** are more your thing, or if you'd like a candlelight ghost tour, the staff can suggest plenty of options. **Covered bridges** fans should ask for the directions to three in Frederick County. **Ghost tour** fans, call ✆ **301/668-8922** for one of the Saturday evening tours offered June through November.

Frederick's 33-block historic district was honored in 2005 as a **Great American Main Street** by the National Trust for Historic Preservation. This area features shops, a handful of museums, and lots of good restaurants. Some streets are filled with tiny town houses; others are lined with one mansion after another. And you can't miss the church spires: Not only is Frederick is known for them, the town's seal features them. (Look for a pair of ornate gray spires to find a conveniently located parking garage.)

Kids can let loose at **Carroll Creek Park,** which runs east-west through the historic district between Patrick and Bentz streets. Redevelopment has added new bridges, walkways, water features, and an amphitheater. Cross Bentz Street to get to the playground and picnic tables at Baker Park. You'll find Barbara Fritchie's tiny house in the park on Patrick Street. Alas, the house is no longer open to the public.

Keep an eye out for the **"Angels in the Architecture" ★★★**: Local artist William Cochran painted fantastic *trompe l'oeil* angels, birds, and other objects on walls around town. "Earthbound," at the corner of West Church and North Market streets, and the Community Bridge, part of Carroll Creek Park, should not be missed.

DOWNTOWN MUSEUMS & HISTORIC SITES

Rose Hill Manor Park & Children's Museum ★ ☺ Adults will enjoy seeing the grand architecture and decorative arts of this 1790s manor house. Kids will love looking at old-fashioned toys, trying on bonnets and hats, learning how a spinning wheel works, working a loom, and touching all the labor-saving kitchen gadgets of that era. Also in the 43-acre park are an icehouse, garden, log cabin, blacksmith shop, farm museum, and carriage museum. The lawns invite picnickers to set a spell. The house tour takes about 1½ hours. Lots of events focus on kids' fun.

1611 N. Market St., Frederick, MD 21701. ✆ **301/600-1650.** www.rosehillmuseum.com. Admission $5 adults, $4 children and seniors. House tours Apr–Sept Mon–Sat 11am–4pm, Sun 1–4pm; Oct–Nov Sat 11am–4pm, Sun 1–4pm. No tours Dec–Mar. Park is open daily 8am–8pm Apr–Oct.

Museum of Frederick County History ★ Nobody famous lived here, the guides at this 1820s Federal-style house will tell you. But, at various times, it was home to a doctor and his family; it witnessed the Civil War, with Union and Confederate troops passing through the streets just outside; and more than 100 orphaned girls called it home. Look for portraits of Roger B. Taney, chief justice of the U.S. Supreme Court and author of the *Dred Scott* decision, and Francis Scott Key, author of "The Star-Spangled Banner." There's also a formal garden. The Historical Society of Frederick County also conducts tours of the **Roger B. Taney House** at 121 S. Bentz St. It is open on Saturday 10am to 4pm and Sunday noon to 4pm. Admission is $3. The Historical Society also offers walking tours in season; they are listed on their website.

24 E. Church St., Frederick, MD 21701. ✆ **301/663-1188.** www.hsfcinfo.org. Admission $7 adults, $3 for children 12–18, and free under 12. Tues–Sat 10am–4pm; Sun 1–4pm.

National Museum of Civil War Medicine Using display cases, wall exhibits, and particularly touching life-size dioramas with wax figures and sound effects, this museum brings to life the suffering and healing of the Civil War soldier. Exhibits focus on Civil War medicine from the initial treatment on the battlefield to the hospitals, hospital trains, operating rooms, evacuation of the wounded, and, finally, embalming practices used during that time—all telling the story of developments and discoveries in a way that changed medicine forever. The building itself is where several thousand dead from the Battle of Antietam were housed and embalmed. The museum also operates **Pry House Field Hospital Museum** at Antietam Battlefield (p. 194).

48 E. Patrick St., Frederick, MD 21701. ✆ **800/564-1864** or 301/695-1864. www.civilwarmed.org. Admission $7.50 adults, $7 seniors, $5.50 children 10–16. Mon–Sat 10am–5pm; Sun 11am–5pm. Closed Jan 1, Easter, Thanksgiving, and Dec 24–25.

Schifferstadt Architectural Museum Frederick's oldest standing house, one of America's finest examples of German Colonial architecture, is listed on the National Register of Historic Places. Built in 1756 by the Brunner family, who named it for their homeland in Germany, it has stone walls more than 2 feet thick, hand-hewn beams of native oak pinned together with wooden pegs, a vaulted cellar and "wishbone" chimney, and a perfectly preserved five-plate jamb stove—the only one left in the world. Guided tours are given throughout the day.

1110 Rosemont Ave. (on the western edge of town), Frederick, MD 21701. ✆ **301/663-3885.** www.frederickcountylandmarksfoundation.org. Suggested donation $3. Apr–early Oct Sat noon–4pm. Closed mid-Oct to Mar.

NEARBY CIVIL WAR & OTHER HISTORIC SITES

Fort Frederick State Park If you're driving through the area, take a look at this 1756 stone fort. Its primary role in Civil War history was as a post for Union troops, though it faced Confederate raiders once in December 1861. During the French and Indian War, it served as a supply base for English campaigns; during the Revolutionary War, it was a refuge for settlers and a prison for Hessian and British soldiers. Daily in summer and on weekends in spring and fall, living-history reenactors show visitors about frontier life. The park has campsites for $15 a night (✆ **888/432-2267**), two hiking trails through woods and wetlands, and boat rentals. Nearby, the 23-mile **Western Maryland Rail Trail** runs along an old train line. The Rails to Trails Conservancy named this one of the top 12 U.S. trails for viewing fall foliage. Pets are welcome in campground and picnic areas.

11100 Fort Frederick Rd. (40 miles west of Frederick, off I-70), Big Pool, MD 21719. ✆ **301/842-2155.** www.dnr.maryland.gov. Admission $4 adults ($1 discount for MD residents). Fort exhibits mid-May to mid-Sept daily 9:30am–5:30pm; Apr to mid-May and mid-Sept to mid-Nov Sat–Sun 9:30am–5:30pm. Park open Apr to mid 8am–sunset, Nov–Mar 10am–sunset. Fort closed Nov to Mar.

Monocacy National Battlefield This stretch of farmland was the site of a little-known but important Civil War encounter. General Jubal Early led 15,000 Confederates against a Union force of 5,800 under General Lew Wallace in July 1864. Though the Confederates won, their forces were so weakened that Union troops at Fort Stevens pushed them back from Washington and saved the nation's capital from capture. Today, the battlefield remains mostly unchanged. The new visitor center has an expanded display of uniforms (even one kids can try on), swords and medals, and a fiber-optic map that relates the battle story. An **auto tour** is 6 miles round-trip; five **walking trails** offer historic and scenic vistas. The short **Gambrill Mill Trail** offers a view of the railroad bridge Union troops were forced to use to retreat. From May through August, events are scheduled the first weekend of the month; a commemoration of the battle is held on a weekend near July 9—look for a grand 150th anniversary commemoration in 2014. Pets on a leash are welcome.

5201 Urbana Pike, Frederick MD 21704. ✆ **301/662-3515.** www.nps.gov/mono. Free admission. Daily 8:30am–5pm. Closed Jan 1, Thanksgiving, and Dec 25. From the north, east, or west, use I-70; take Exit 54 and proceed south on Rte. 355 to the visitor center. From the south, use I-270; take Exit 26 and turn left onto Rte. 80; then turn left onto Rte. 355 north.

Spectator Sports & Outdoor Activities

BASEBALL The (Class A) Carolina League **Frederick Keys** (✆ **877/8GO-KEYS** [846-5397]; www.frederickkeys.com), an Orioles farm team, play at Harry Grove Stadium, off I-70, from May to September. General admission is $8 to $11.

BIKING Bikers and hikers can access the towpath of the **Chesapeake & Ohio (C&O) Canal** at Point of Rocks, off Route 15 South; Brunswick, Route 79 off Maryland Route 340; or Sandy Hook, left off Route 340, before you cross the Potomac River. The canal runs along the Potomac for 185 miles from Georgetown to Cumberland. Bicycle bells are required on the towpath. The **Western Maryland Railway trail,** a 23-mile paved path, is accessible off I-70 at Exit 12, Big Pool.

Nearby, both Antietam National Battlefield and Gettysburg National Military Park are terrific sites to tour on bike. Rent a bike at **Wheel Base,** 229 N. Market St., Frederick (✆ **301/663-9288**). They sell and service bikes, too. Prices vary.

HIKING The **Appalachian Trail** (www.appalachiantrail.org) runs along the border of Frederick and Washington counties, through Washington Monument State Park, South Mountain State Park, Greenbrier State Park, and Gathland State Park. You can hike the Maryland portion in 3 or 4 days, but any section makes a great 1-day excursion. North of Frederick, off Route 15, **Catoctin Mountain Park,** 6602 Foxville Rd., Thurmont, MD 21788 (✆ **301/663-9388**), and **Cunningham Falls State Park,** 14039 Catoctin Hollow Rd., Thurmont, MD 21788 (✆ **301/271-7574**), offer several miles of hiking trails. (See "Serenity & Apples on Route 15," p. 201.)

Shopping

If you want antiques, vintage clothing, eye-popping jewelry, handcrafted gifts, or something that's just different, you're going to love Frederick's shopping. The historic district has plenty of interesting shops, mostly on Patrick, Market, Church, and North East streets. They're usually open from 10am to 5pm, though many close on Mondays. Lots of shops and restaurants with sidewalk dining welcome your canine companions.

For **First Saturday Downtown Frederick,** shops stay open until 9pm; some offer trunk shows or special merchandise, and some serve refreshments.

Everedy Square/Shab Row, around North East Street, is a cluster of shops and restaurants. Everedy Square is housed in modern buildings, while Shab Row shops are in historic town houses—even a log cabin. They stay open late every Friday night.

Antiques lovers should check out **Heritage Antiques,** 39 E. Patrick St. (✆ **301/668-0299**), for china, crystal, and mahogany furniture. **Little's** two shops at 15 and 55 E. Patrick St. (✆ **301/620-0517**) also have handmade reproductions; they're closed Tuesday and Wednesday. **Emporium Antiques,** 112 E. Patrick St. (✆ **301/662-7099**), has more than 130 dealers crammed into an old car dealership. You'll also find antiques dealers on East, Patrick, and Carroll streets.

On Market Street, girlfriends shop at **Molly's Meanderings,** 17 N. Market St. (✆ **301/668-8075**), and **Tiara Day,** 153 N. Market St. (✆ **301/694-4911**). Need a gift? Go for chocolate from **Candy Kitchen,** 52 N. Market St. (✆ **301/698-0442**); jewelry or animation cels from **McGuire Fine Arts,** at 110 N. Market St. (✆ **301/695-6567**); or fun tableware and crafts from the **Muse,** 19 N. Market St. (✆ **301/663-3632**). Teenagers love the clothes at **Velvet Lounge,** 203 N. Market St. (✆ **301/695-5700**). **Potters' Guild of Frederick** at 15 N. Market St. (www.pottersguildoffrederick.com) markets local handicrafts.

Just off Market, **Savage Soaps,** 10 E. Church St. (✆ **301/694-5002**), stocks homemade soaps and lotions. Near Everedy Square, **Frederick Cellars,** 221 N. East St. (✆ **301/668-0311**), sells local wines; or treat yourself at the **Perfect Truffle,** 16A N. East St. (✆ **301/620-2448**). For jams and apple butter, visit **McCutcheon's** at 13 S. Wisner St. (✆ **800/875-3451**).

Serious antiques shoppers may want to visit nearby **New Market,** which calls itself "the antiques capital of Maryland" and is itself registered on the National Register of Historic Places. Shops line Main Street (Rte. 144) with everything from furniture to estate jewelry. Shops are open on weekends, most 10am to 5pm. Several are open on most weekdays, as well. The **New Market Antique Dealers Association** (✆ **301/831-6755**) publishes a free guide available in town. To reach the town, 6 miles east of Frederick, go east on I-70 and take Exit 62.

Frederick After Dark

BARS & LIVE MUSIC

Most of Frederick's nightspots are on or near Market Street. **Olde Town Tavern,** 325 N. Market St. (✆ **301/695-1454**), has live music and darts for its young crowd. Heading south on Market, **Bushwallers,** 209 N. Market St. (✆ **301/695-6988**), hosts Irish music on Sunday and Wednesday, and live bands on Friday and Saturday. **Firestone's,** 105 N. Market St. (✆ **301/663-0330;** www.firestonesrestaurant.com), has acoustic music on Thursday and jazz with their Sunday brunch, described on p. 188. If you just need a place to hang out, go to **Brewer's Alley,** 124 N. Market St. (✆ **301/631-0089**), described on p. 188, or **Wag's,** 24 S. Market St. (✆ **301/694-8451**), described on p. 189. The **Bentz Street Sports Bar,** 6 S. Bentz St. (✆ **301/620-2222;** www.bentzstreetsportsbar.com), has 30 TVs tuned to sports, live entertainment on weekends, and trivia night is Thursday.

THE PERFORMING ARTS

All kinds of events, including dance, music, theater, classic movies, and family entertainment, are staged year-round at the **Weinberg Center for the Arts,** 20 W. Patrick St. (✆ **301/600-2828;** www.weinbergcenter.org), a 1926 movie theater.

The **Fredericktowne Players** (✆ **240/315-3855;** www.fredericktowneplayers.org) perform at several venues. The **Maryland Shakespeare Festival Theatre** (✆ **301/668-4090;** www.mdshakes.org) offers works by the Bard at All Saints Episcopal Church, 106 W. Church St. The **Maryland Ensemble Theatre** (✆ **301/694-4744**) performs at 31 W. Patrick St.

ANTIETAM NATIONAL BATTLEFIELD ★★

22 miles W of Frederick; 10 miles S of Hagerstown; 57 miles SW of Gettysburg, PA

Antietam (or Sharpsburg to Southerners) is perhaps the saddest place you can visit in Maryland. A walk down Bloody Lane will send shivers up your spine—especially after you've seen the photographs of the corpses piled up on this road. (Photos at Antietam were the first taken of a battlefield before the bodies were buried.) More than 23,000 men were killed or wounded here when Union forces met and stopped the first attempted Southern invasion of the North in September 1862. It is the site of the bloodiest day of the Civil War—with more Americans killed or wounded than on any other single day of combat, including D-Day. President Lincoln made a battlefield appearance shortly after the battle at Antietam to confront the Union's Gen. George McClellan over his unwillingness to pursue the retreating Confederate army. Clara Barton, who founded the American Red Cross 19 years later, nursed the wounded here.

Today, the battlefield is marked by rolling hills and farmland and attended by a visitor center, a cemetery, modest monuments, and the gentle waters of Antietam Creek. The mood is somber. Gettysburg has all the monuments and displays, but this is the place to come to consider the tragedy, rather than the triumph, of war. The battle's 150th anniversary will be commemorated in 2012.

FEES Admission to the battlefield is $4 for adults, $6 per family, and free for children 17 and under. It's good for 3 days.

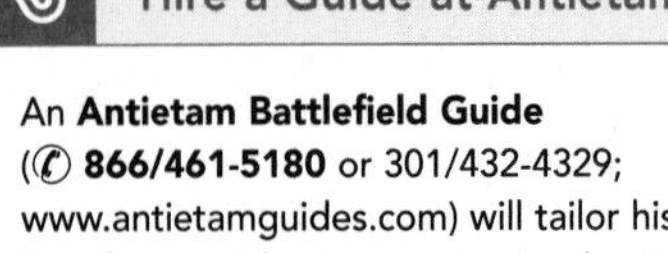

Hire a Guide at Antietam

An **Antietam Battlefield Guide** (✆ **866/461-5180** or 301/432-4329; www.antietamguides.com) will tailor his tour for you. They're passionate about their Civil War history—they've studied and passed tests to qualify. They'll drive you around the battlefields and tell you stories about all the regiments, generals, and soldiers. Guides charge $75 for a 2-hour tour for up to six people. Reservations are recommended, but if you come without one, ask at the gift shop and you may be able to book one on the spot.

VISITOR CENTER Begin your trip at the **visitor center,** 1 mile north of Sharpsburg on Route 65 (✆ **301/432-5124;** www.nps.gov/anti). It has exhibits, documentaries, a museum, a gift shop, and an observation room overlooking the battlefield. The staff provides maps, literature, and suggestions for routes to explore the battlefield and cemetery. A film narrated by James Earl Jones is shown daily at noon. It's open June through August daily from 8:30am to 6pm, September through May daily from 8:30am to 5pm; closed Thanksgiving, December 25, and January 1. ***Note:*** The battlefield officially closes 20 minutes after sunset.

Seeing the Highlights

Antietam's quiet hills and limited number of monuments make it a stark and silent contrast to the massive memorials of Gettysburg. The park service offers an 8½-mile self-guided auto tour that can also be walked or bicycled. Maps, as well as tours on audiotape and CD, are also available at the visitor center. **Battlefield Guides** (✆ **866/461-5180** or 301/432-4329; www.antietamguides.com) take groups or families for a 2-hour tour; reservations are required. Park rangers offer free battlefield walks and talks and give an orientation talk at the visitor center several times a day.

Burnside Bridge crosses Antietam Creek near the southern end of the battlefield. Georgia snipers stalled 4,000 Union soldiers for over 3 hours as the Union tried to secure this stone arch bridge. Another must-see is the observation tower over a country lane near the center of the battlefield. This road, now known as **Bloody Lane,** was the scene of a 4-hour encounter that ended with no decisive winner and 4,000 casualties. And don't miss **Dunker Church,** which figures in a number of Civil War photos. These locations are among the most memorable, graceful, and harrowing.

The **Pry House Field Hospital Museum** (✆ **301/416-2395;** www.civilwarmed.org), a 5-minute drive off the battlefield, served as General George McClellan's headquarters during the battle. Several generals were treated here; the barn was also used as a field hospital. Admission to Pry House is by $2 donation. It's open daily 11am to 5pm Memorial Day to October 31 and in May and November, Saturday and Sunday, 11am to 5pm. It's closed December through April. Check with the visitor center to confirm opening hours.

Every year on September 17, and on the weekend closest to the date, the anniversary of the battle is remembered with ranger-led hikes and special events. An Independence Day concert, featuring the Maryland Symphony Orchestra and fireworks, is held on the Saturday closest to the Fourth of July.

A Candlelight Remembrance

On the first Saturday of December, Antietam National Battlefield is illuminated with 23,000 **luminaria,** one for each of those killed, wounded, or missing in the battle. People come from everywhere, willing to wait up to 3 hours or more, for the chance to drive past this sad but beautiful sight. Cars start moving through the park at about 6pm and continue until midnight or until all the cars have passed. The slow, respectful drive through the route takes about an hour. The only entrance is on Route 34. The visitor center closes at 3pm on this day.

Outdoor Activities

BIKING & HIKING The wide-open fields of Antietam Battlefield beckon hikers and bikers with 9 miles of paved roads good for bicycling. Some 10 miles of hiking trails, including the **Final Attack Trail,** have been marked with trail maps to give visitors a chance to trek into history. For maps, stop by the visitor center. Or download one or more of the three trail guide podcasts on the website.

WATERSPORTS Antietam Creek, which flows the length of the park to the Potomac, is an excellent novice-to-intermediate canoe and kayak run offering views of a waterfall, Burnside Bridge, the ruins of Antietam Furnace, and the C&O Canal aqueduct. **River & Trail Outfitters,** 604 Valley Rd., Knoxville (✆ **301/695-5177;** www.rivertrail.com), leads guided trips down the creek, and rents canoes and kayaks.

Where to Eat

Sharpsburg has only a few options for hungry visitors, but one place popular with locals and visitors is **Nutter's Ice Cream,** 100 E. Main St. (✆ **301/432-5809**).

For fine dining, go to Shepherdstown, West Virginia, across the Potomac on State Route 64. The small college town has coffee shops and cafes along its main drag, East German Street. The **Yellow Brick Bank Restaurant,** 201 E. German St. (✆ **304/876-2208**), serves lunch and dinner. The **Bavarian Inn** ★, 164 Shepherd Grade Rd. (✆ **304/876-2551;** www.bavarianinnwv.com), serves hearty German fare in its Alpine-style dining room and on the terrace. Breakfast, lunch, and dinner are available.

Another option is **Old South Mountain Inn,** 6132 Old National Pike, Boonsboro (✆ **301/432-6155;** www.oldsouthmountaininn.com), located at the top of South Mountain ridge on Alternate Route 40 between Antietam and Frederick. It serves Saturday lunch, Sunday brunch, and dinner Tuesday through Sunday.

HARPERS FERRY (WV) NATIONAL HISTORICAL PARK

22 miles SW of Frederick; 54 miles W of Baltimore; 55 miles S of Gettysburg, PA

Harpers Ferry, West Virginia, was a bustling industrial center from the 1700s until the 1930s, when it was hit by both the Depression and a flood. It's perhaps best known for abolitionist John Brown's rebellion and the town's part in the Civil War.

On October 16, 1859, Brown—already notorious from a bloody raid against slaveholders in Kansas—enlisted 19 men to raid the federal arsenal at Harpers Ferry, intent on arming the nation's slaves and starting a rebellion. Frederick Douglass warned Brown that the arsenal, in a town wedged between mountains and the Shenandoah and Potomac rivers, would be impossible to hold with so few men, and the raid failed. Brown and his men captured the arsenal but were unable to raise any significant number of slaves into rebellion. They were soon pinned in the arsenal's firehouse (later known as John Brown's Fort), and Brown was captured when U.S. Marines, under Lt. Col. Robert E. Lee, stormed the building. Brown was tried and convicted of "conspiring with slaves to commit treason and murder," for which he was hanged. His action polarized the nation and was one of the sparks that ignited the war. Harpers Ferry later witnessed the largest surrender of Federal troops during the Civil War; it also opened one of the earliest integrated schools in the U.S.

Today, Harpers Ferry National Historical Park is a delightful place to spend a day or weekend. Its narrow streets are lined with historic homes and shops that sell antiques and handicrafts. The National Park Service administers much of the town. Exhibits focus on John Brown's raid, the town's industry, Storer College (an early African-American college), and the town's role in the Civil War, when it changed hands between the Union and the Confederacy eight times. Hills soar overhead and plunge down into the waters of the Shenandoah and Potomac rivers. There are 4 miles of trails for a stroll or a strenuous hike. You can also take a rafting or kayaking run. Pets on a leash are allowed in the park but not in the buses or visitor center.

A number of commemorations of the 150th Anniversary of the Civil War are underway and are scheduled through 2015, from reenactments of battle to exhibits focusing on the Emancipation Proclamation. Details are on the park service website.

ACCESS POINTS To get here, take Route 340 west from Frederick, Maryland. You will cross the Potomac River Bridge (the town is to your right) into Virginia, and then about ¾ mile later cross the Shenandoah River into West Virginia. The park's parking lot is about a mile past the Shenandoah Bridge, on the left.

FEES Park admission is $6 per vehicle, $4 per pedestrian or cyclist. The fee includes the shuttle bus and is good for 3 days.

VISITOR CENTER Start at the **Cavalier Heights Visitor Center,** 1 mile west of Shenandoah Bridge, off Route 340 (✆ **304/535-6029**). Leave your car in this parking lot (the park service has removed almost all parking from the lower town) and catch the shuttle here. The staff provides free maps and information on ranger-led tours (available in spring, summer, and fall). The visitor center is open daily from 8am to 4pm, except January 1, Thanksgiving, and December 25. The park stays open until 5pm. Shuttles run about every 12 to 15 minutes from 8am to 5:45pm (later in summer).

Seeing the Highlights

Skip the hassles of parking and take the 6-minute shuttle ride from the visitor center. Once in the lower town, stop first at the information center on Shenandoah Street (if you didn't already get brochures and trail maps at the Cavalier Heights visitor center).

The **John Brown Museum,** on Shenandoah Street, offers exhibits and displays on the abolitionist and tracks the course of his raid, capture, and conviction. Hours for the museum are the same as the park's hours, and admission is included in the park entry fee. The **Harper House** is a restored dwelling that sits at the top of the stone stairs, above High Street. The oldest remaining structure in Harpers Ferry, it was built between 1775 and 1782 and served as a tavern for such notable guests as Thomas Jefferson and George Washington.

Walking, Hiking & White-Water Rafting

Remember to wear sturdy shoes for the short but moderately strenuous climb farther up the stone stairs, past **St. Peter's Church,** to **Jefferson Rock ★**. At this spot, looking over the confluence of the Shenandoah and Potomac rivers, President Jefferson called the view "stupendous," and said it was worth crossing the Atlantic to see.

If you don't feel like climbing the stairs to Jefferson Rock, you might enjoy a stroll over the walking/railroad bridge across the Potomac for a view of the mighty river. On the way, you'll pass the old armory fire house, known as **John Brown's Fort,** where Brown and his men took their last stand. On the other side, you'll find the bottom of Maryland Heights (see below) and the ruins of **Lock No. 33** on the C&O Canal.

Virginius Island, a long curl of land along the Shenandoah, offers visitors an easy stroll among trees and stone ruins. This was once a booming industrial center with a rifle factory, iron foundry, cotton mill, granary, and lumberyard. It's a silent reminder of what once was. The short history trail, about a mile long, offers some explanation of what remains, and the lovely flat site is a great place to rest or let the children run.

If you're ready for a more strenuous hike, head over the railroad bridge to walk up the cliffs of **Maryland Heights** to one of the most spectacular views in the state. The hike can take 3 to 5 hours, but the view of Harpers Ferry and the confluence of the two rivers makes the effort worthwhile. The park service provides trail maps for the hike to Maryland Heights as well as to **Weverton Cliffs,** which also boast a good view. The **Appalachian Trail** and the **C&O Canal** join briefly and pass right by Harpers Ferry, on the opposite side of the Potomac, making the town a great stop on either route.

River & Trail Outfitters, 604 Valley Rd., Knoxville, MD (✆ **301/695-5177;** www.rivertrail.com), offers half-day white-water rafting trips down the Shenandoah and Potomac. Although this can be quite an adventure during high-water season (Feb to mid-Apr), most of the time it's a fun raft trip through beautiful scenery and a few rapids—suitable for families. Guides share local history, legends, and jokes. Prices depend on the season but generally run $60 to $95 per person. River & Trail also offers guided hikes up Maryland Heights, C&O bike trips, cross-country ski trips in winter, and Monocacy River paddle trips. Experienced paddlers can rent a canoe or kayak; lessons are available for every level.

Fishing is permitted in both the Potomac and Shenandoah rivers, but adults may require licenses; check with the visitor center.

Where to Stay

Harpers Ferry is about 22 miles from Frederick (p. 184). Closer to the historical park, the 50-room **Econo Lodge,** 25 Union St., off Route 340 (✆ **800/521-2121** or 304/535-6391; www.choicehotels.com), is about a mile from the visitor center.

Where to Eat

Dining options are limited. There are cafes and sandwich shops along Potomac and High streets. Stop early for breakfast or wait until later in the day to eat. There are also plenty of places to stop for a drink or an ice cream—and the wait isn't as long.

GETTYSBURG (PA) NATIONAL MILITARY PARK ★★★

34 miles N of Frederick; 50 miles NW of Baltimore

Here on the rolling green hills just north of the Maryland-Pennsylvania line, and in the streets of a tiny town that was home to just 2,400 people, some 160,000 soldiers met in battle. For 3 days in July 1863, the 70,000 men of the Confederate Army faced the 93,000 Union soldiers under the command of General George Meade. When the 3 days of fighting ended, the rebels had been driven back; some 51,000 were killed, wounded, or captured; and General Robert E. Lee would never mount another campaign of such magnitude again. Most important, the tide of the war had changed. The battle would become known as the "high water mark of the Confederacy."

Today, the 20,000-acre battlefield is one of the most famous in the world, drawing people to its hills and valleys, beckoning them to pause for a moment before the long rows of graves in the cemeteries and monuments in the fields. They stop, too, to recall the 272 words of Abraham Lincoln as he dedicated the cemetery on November 19, 1863. All of these events will be commemorated through 2015 as the town and the country mark the Civil War's sesquicentennial.

The park surrounds the small town of Gettysburg, which still bears war wounds of its own. Plenty of small privately owned museums display collections of firearms, uniforms, and other memorabilia of those dark days.

The busiest time to visit is during the 3-day reenactment held every July 1 to July 3, when 350,000 people descend on Gettysburg. If you plan to come, make hotel reservations at least 8 months in advance—and make dinner reservations before arriving. It's a good idea to come before the reenactment to get a look around, take a tour, and gain some historical perspective. Bring a lawn chair and comfortable shoes. In 2012, the 150th anniversary commemoration is expected to be grander than ever.

Another popular event is Remembrance Day, held the Saturday closest to November 19, the anniversary of the Gettysburg Address. Weekends in spring and fall are perhaps the most pleasant times to visit. Schoolchildren flow in during the school year, and families keep the attractions filled all summer.

GETTING THERE Take U.S. Route 15 north from Frederick and I-70. After about 30 miles, you'll cross into Pennsylvania; then take the first exit and turn left on Business U.S. Route 15 north. The visitor center is 6 miles ahead on your right; the town is just past the visitor center.

Parking garages or lots are on Race Horse Alley, at Middle and Stratton streets, and on Baltimore Street between the Jennie Wade House and the Tour Center. On-street parking is available most weekends. Museums and the battlefield have their own lots.

FEES & HOURS Admission to Gettysburg National Military Park is free. The battlefield is open daily year-round: from 6am to 10pm April through October, and from 6am to 7pm November through March. The visitor center is open daily from 8am to 5pm (until 6pm in summer), except January 1, Thanksgiving, and December 25. The cemetery is open from dawn to dusk.

VISITOR CENTER Stop first at the **Gettysburg National Military Park Visitor Center** (✆ **717/334-1124;** www.nps.gov/gett). The new 139,000-square-foot headquarters off the battlefield, at 1195 Baltimore Pike (Rte. 97), has a museum focusing on Gettysburg in the Civil War, a bookstore, and Cyclorama. It is also the starting point for tours and ranger walks (see "Organized Tours," below). Rangers are glad to answer questions and provide maps of hiking trails and the 18-mile self-guided auto tour. Backpacks and large parcels are not allowed in the visitor center.

Seeing the Highlights

Admission to the **Visitor Center** is free, so be sure to stop here for a map, schedule of free ranger talks and tours, and to browse the well-stocked shop and bookstore. There's also a short film and display of Civil War artifacts, as well as a large food court. The Visitor Center is open daily 8am to 5pm, and until 6pm April through October.

The major exhibits here, however, come at a price. A ticket for a movie narrated by Morgan Freeman, the collections of the **Gettysburg Museum of the Civil War,** and the **Cyclorama** is $11 for adults, $9.50 for seniors, and $6.50 for children.

The film is a good introduction to the Civil War and the museum displays a good collection of weaponry and uniforms from both sides. Look for the things the soldiers carried, including musical instruments, medical supplies, and personal effects.

But it's the newly restored **Cyclorama ★★★**, a 360-degree depiction of Pickett's Charge—the climactic battle of the Gettysburg campaign—that is worth the price of admission. Brilliantly colored with gripping scenes of battle, the 1884 painting by Paul Dominique Philippoteaux is enhanced by its display, the dramatic narration, and the accompanying light-and-sound show.

The battlefield and cemetery are the main reasons for a visit. The **Gettysburg National Cemetery** gate is on Taneytown Road. Get a map at the visitor center, walk among the gravestones, and learn about the Union and Confederate soldiers now united in this place. Graves encircle the spot where Abraham Lincoln gave the Gettysburg Address, at the Soldiers' National Monument. The cemetery is open dawn to dusk.

The battlefield is so large, you must see it by car, bike, or bus. Along the ridges and valleys of the park are more than 100 monuments, dedicated by various states to their military units who fought here. The largest and most often visited is the granite-domed **Pennsylvania Memorial.** Constructed of nearly 3,000 tons of cut granite, raw stone, and cement, the monument consists of a dome supported by four arched columns, topped by a statue depicting the winged goddess of victory and peace. Other monuments recall the bravery of the troops on both sides of the battle. Of the Southern states, Virginia was the first to build a monument here. The **Virginia State Memorial,** dedicated in 1917, is topped by a brass sculpture of General Lee mounted on a horse. It's located where Pickett's Charge took place.

As you're visiting the monuments, look for the **John Burns Portrait Statue.** At over 70 years of age, this local constable and veteran of the War of 1812 asked Colonel Langhorn Wister for permission to fight with the Union troops. Although initially mocked, he earned the soldiers' respect, fighting alongside Union regiments at Gettysburg before being wounded and carried from the field.

Other Attractions

The **David Wills House,** 8 Lincoln Sq. (✆ **866/486-5735;** www.davidwillshouse.org), on Gettysburg's town square, is part of the Gettysburg National Military Park but has a separate admission. Its exhibits focus on the man who organized the dedication of the Soldiers' National Cemetery and invited the president to speak. Lincoln spent the night here before delivering the Gettysburg Address on November 19, 1863. The bed where he slept and some of his things are on display—really the best reason to pay the $6.50 admission ($5.50 seniors, $4 children 6–18). The house is open May to August daily 10am to 6pm; spring and fall Wednesday to Monday 10am to 5pm; winter Thursday to Monday 10am to 5pm.

Eisenhower National Historic Site ★ (www.nps.gov/eise), President Eisenhower's farm, overlooks the Gettysburg Battlefield. Eisenhower first came to Gettysburg as a West Point cadet, to study the battlefields. He and his wife Mamie bought their 189-acre farm south of town; as president, he entertained world leaders here. Today, visitors can catch a shuttle at the battlefield visitor center to tour the home and walk the grounds. Admission is $7.50 for adults and $5 for children 6 to 12.

Gettysburg is dotted with small, privately owned museums filled with Civil War memorabilia. The best is the **Shriver House Museum,** 309 Baltimore St. (✆ **717/337-2800;** www.shriverhouse.org), which relates the story of a civilian family caught up in the terror of the battle. Visitors can tour the home, including the attic where sharpshooters were holed up. (If you're in town for the reenactment, stop here on Sat evening for a compelling living history tour.) Admission is $7.50 for adults, $7.25 for seniors, and $5 for children 6 to 12. It's closed January and February.

Organized Tours

The best battlefield tours are offered by the **Association of Licensed Battlefield Guides** (✆ **877/594-3162** or 717/334-1124), which was set up in 1915 by Civil War veterans to ensure that visitors received accurate information about the battle. These guides can tell you about everything from troop movements to who built the Pennsylvania Memorial and how much it cost. A licensed guide will ride in your vehicle—and even drive—to give a customized tour. It's best to reserve a guide at least 3 days ahead of your visit, but guides are also assigned at the visitor center on a first-come, first-served basis. A 2-hour tour costs $55 to $75 for 1 to 15 people.

Gettysburg Battlefield Bus Tours, 778 Baltimore St. (✆ **717/334-6296;** www.gettysburgbattlefieldtours.com), gives battlefield tours in either air-conditioned or double-decker buses. Recorded, dramatized tours cost $25 for adults and $15 for children. Licensed battlefield guides lead some tours. Buses leave from the visitor center; you can buy tickets there or at numerous locations around town.

There are plenty of free tours offered by the **National Park Service.** In fact, in warm weather, up to 34 presentations are given in the cemetery and battlefield each day. These rangers' walks, talks, and tours vary—some are brief; others include up to a 3-mile hike with lots of detail about the battles. Contact the visitor center for details.

Where to Stay

With several hotels in town and more along the main routes, visitors have plenty of options—and Frederick lodgings are close enough, too. If you plan to attend the reenactment in July, reserve at least 8 months in advance.

In town, the 109-room **Quality Inn Gettysburg Motor Lodge,** 380 Steinwehr Ave. (✆ **800/228-5151** or 717/334-1103; www.gettysburgqualityinn.com), has outdoor and indoor pools and an exercise room. The **Best Western Gettysburg Hotel,** 1 Lincoln Sq. (✆ **800/528-1234** or 717/337-2000; www.gettysburg-hotel.com), is on the town square. Down the street is the **James Gettys Hotel,** 27 Chambersburg St. (✆ **888/900-5275** or 717/337-1334; www.jamesgettyshotel.com), with 12 suites.

Two hotels are at the Gettysburg Gateway complex northwest of the battlefield on Route 15. The **Wyndham Gettysburg ★**, 95 Presidential Circle (✆ **717/339-0020**), has 248 rooms, indoor and outdoor pools, and a contemporary style. The

Courtyard by Marriott, 115 Presidential Circle (✆ **717/334-5600**), is slightly more casual with 152 rooms and an indoor pool. The location of these hotels is ideal for families. About 5 minutes from downtown, they offer four restaurants, a lounge, and free parking. Also here is the eight-screen **Gateway Theatres** (✆ **717/334-5575,** or 334-5577 for movie schedule), which shows the 30-minute "Fields of Freedom" film about Gettysburg all day long in summer (afternoons only other times).

Outside of town, the **Quality Inn at General Lee's Headquarters,** 401 Buford Ave. (✆ **800/228-5151** or 717/334-3141; www.thegettysburgaddress.com), overlooks the battlefield of Seminary Ridge, and has an outdoor pool. The **Hilton Garden Inn Gettysburg,** 1061 York Rd. (✆ **877/782-9444** or 717/334-2040; www.gettysburg.gardeninn.com), has an indoor pool.

Where to Eat

Gettysburg is dotted with little restaurants and fast-food joints. To start your day with coffee and a pastry, visit **Seasons Bakery,** 100 Chambersburg St. (✆ **717/334-0377**). It's open for breakfast and lunch. Closed Mondays.

Two historic taverns are experiences in themselves. The **Dobbin House,** 89 Steinwehr Ave. (✆ **717/334-2100;** www.dobbinhouse.com), serves lunch and casual dinner daily in the Springhouse Tavern. Dinner is served in the Alexander Dobbin Dining Rooms, one of which is a bedroom (you actually eat in bed!). It's open daily at 5pm. The **Farnsworth House,** 401 Baltimore St. (✆ **717/334-8838**), serves dinner in the bullet hole–covered 1863 inn. Or have a casual meal in the adjacent garden. Lunch begins at 11am. Dinner is daily at 5pm.

SERENITY & APPLES ON ROUTE 15

20 miles N of Frederick; 60 miles W of Baltimore; 15 miles SW of Gettysburg, PA

When planning a trip to Frederick or a drive through the Civil War sites and on to Gettysburg, reserve some time for the treasures of Route 15, the **Catoctin Mountain National Scenic Byway.** Along the way, stop in **Thurmont,** known for its two main parks, and **Emmitsburg,** the home of St. Elizabeth Ann Seton and Mount St. Mary's University, where there's a replica of the Grotto of Lourdes.

What to See & Do

Catoctin Mountain Park (✆ **301/663-9343;** www.nps.gov/cato), a national park, has several good trails and is the home of presidential retreat Camp David—whose precise location is top secret. The park's entrance is on Route 77 west of Route 15. Admission is free. Tent camping here is $30 a night; cabin rentals are $75 to $185. Reserve at **www.recreation.gov**.

Cunningham Falls State Park ★★ (✆ **301/271-7574;** www.dnr.maryland.gov) has as its centerpiece a 78-foot-high waterfall, set in a canopy of 100-year-old oaks and hickories. The park is also the site of 43-acre **Hunting Creek Lake,** which offers swimming, canoe rentals, and picnic areas. Get a guide to the many park trails at the Manor Area visitor center, off Route 15, or at Park Central, on Route 77. Four short trails will take you to the base of Cunningham Falls. Three are in the William Houck Area, off Route 77. They range from moderate to strenuous and from .5 to 2.8

miles. The fourth trail is wheelchair accessible, with a handicapped-only parking lot on Route 77 and a .3-mile boardwalk to the falls. Another trail ends at the **Catoctin Iron Furnace,** the remains of a Revolutionary War–era iron-making complex. The park is open daily from 8am to sunset. In peak season, fees run $3 to $4 per person; at other times they're $3 to $4 per car. Campsites cost about $25 a night, $30 with electric hookup; cabins run about $60 April through November.

National Fallen Firefighters Memorial This site, at the National Fire Academy, holds special significance since September 11, 2001: The firefighters who died at the World Trade Center have their own memorial here. The service in tribute to firefighters killed in the line of duty is held during Fire Prevention Week, in October.

16825 S. Seton Ave., Emmitsburg, MD 21727. © **301/447-1365.** www.firehero.org. Free admission. Bring photo ID to visit, as this is a federal site. Daily dawn–dusk.

National Shrine Grotto of Our Lady of Lourdes If you know the story of St. Bernadette—the French peasant girl who saw Mary, mother of Jesus, in a grotto—but aren't planning a trip to Lourdes, you might want to stop here. The site has been re-created on a mountain overlooking Mount St. Mary's University. The spot is marked with a 95-foot-tall campanile topped with a golden statue of Mary. As you stroll on wooded paths, you'll see other shrines and the Stations of the Cross. Mass is offered in the glass and stone Chapel of St. Mary on the Hill at noon on Saturday and Sunday.

Mount St. Mary's University & Seminary, 16300 Old Emmitsburg Rd., Emmitsburg, MD 21727. © **301/447-5318.** www.msmary.edu/grotto. Free admission. Mar–Sept daily 7:30am–7:30pm; Oct–Feb daily 7:30am–5:30pm.

National Shrine of Saint Elizabeth Ann Seton ★★★ This shrine honors the first American-born saint canonized in the Roman Catholic Church. A young widow who converted to Catholicism, Mother Seton lived here with her children as she began the Catholic parochial school system and a new order of religious women. The church, a minor basilica, is a beautiful monument with Italian stained glass and mosaics. The nearby houses—the **Stone House** (built about 1750) and the **White House** (built for her in 1810)—offer a glimpse of the saint's life. The guides are patient with children.

333 S. Seton Ave., Emmitsburg, MD 21727. © **301/447-6606.** www.setonshrine.org. Free admission; donations welcome. Basilica daily 10am–4:30pm; other sites Tues–Sun 10am–4:30pm. Closed Jan 1, 2nd week of Jan, Easter, July 4, Thanksgiving, and Dec 24–25 and 31. From Rte. 15, turn left on S. Seton Ave. The shrine is ¾ mile on the right.

Shopping

Don't miss the orchard stands along your drive. There are several, all selling fruit and vegetables grown right in these foothills.

Catoctin Mountain Orchard, 15036 N. Franklinville Rd. (Rte. 15), Thurmont (© **301/271-2737;** www.catoctinmountainorchard.com), has locally baked pastries and McCutcheon's preserves, as well as fresh produce. Pick your own berries in June and July, pumpkins and apples in fall. Open May through January, daily 9am to 5pm.

Gateway Farm Market and Candyland, 14802 N. Franklinville Rd. (Rte. 15), Thurmont (© **301/271-2322**), has not only produce and fresh cider in season but also long tables filled with boxes of penny candy (really about $4 a pound). Open Monday through Thursday from 8am to 9pm, Friday and Saturday from 8am to 10pm, and Sunday from 10am to 7pm.

Scenic View Orchards, 16239 Sabillasville Rd. (Rte. 550), Sabillasville, MD 21780 (✆ **301/271-2149**), offers valley views along with fresh produce, preserves, and breads. It's open daily from 10am to 6pm, June through Thanksgiving.

Where to Stay

Cozy Country Inn The Cozy Inn has a certain charm, with premium rooms named after presidents and decorated in their style. The Reagan Cottage features a portrait of the president and horse decor, while the Roosevelt Room has a king-size bed in a style used by FDR. Every premium room has two TVs, a fireplace, and a Jacuzzi garden tub. Call ahead to reserve, especially if the president will be at Camp David—the press corps and president's staff often fill up the rooms. Shops here carry antiques, vintage clothing, and small specialties. The Churchill Cottage accommodates six.

103 Frederick Rd. (Rte. 806), Thurmont, MD 21788. www.cozyvillage.com. ✆ **301/271-4301.** 21 units, including 5 cottages. $62–$120 double; $117–$169 premium rooms. Rates include continental breakfast. Children 12 and under stay free in rooms with 2 beds. AE, DISC, MC, V. **Amenities:** Restaurant (see "Where to Eat," below). *In room:* A/C, fridge, hair dryer, microwave (some rooms).

Sleep Inn & Suites Emmitsburg ☺ Emmitsburg's first and (so far) only hotel offers standard rooms but with a detail kids will like: Nintendo. One room of note is the fireplace suite, with a gas fireplace and a Jacuzzi for two. Call ahead for reservations, as the place can fill up with families and athletic teams visiting nearby Mount St. Mary's University.

501 Silo Hill Pkwy., off Rte. 15, Emmitsburg, MD 21727. www.sleepinn.com. ✆ **800/SLEEP-INN** (753-3746) or 301/447-0044. Fax 301/447-3144. 79 units. $90–$159 double. Rates include continental breakfast. Children stay free in parent's room. AE, DC, DISC, MC, V. Pets accepted for fee. **Amenities:** Fitness room; indoor pool. *In room:* A/C, TV w/movies and Nintendo, hair dryer, free Wi-Fi.

Where to Eat

Carriage House Inn ☺ AMERICAN Plenty of people, including presidents, come to this 1857 inn for the crab cakes or hearty American fare. A stone fireplace dominates the dining room, which has wide plank floors and Early American–style furniture. It's a good place for children, whose menus are pasted inside picture books. There's a brunch buffet on Sundays 10am to1pm.

200 S. Seton Ave., Emmitsburg, MD 21727. ✆ **301/447-2366.** www.carriagehouseinn.info. Reservations recommended. Main courses $8–$17 lunch, $18–$35 dinner. AE, DISC, MC, V. Sun 10am–8pm; Mon–Thurs 11am–8pm; Fri–Sat 11am–9pm.

Cozy Restaurant 🎁 AMERICAN Just by looking at the photos and memorabilia on the walls, you can tell the Cozy's been around a long time. It features hearty buffets as well as simple fare served in the dining rooms and on the deck in summer. Afternoon tea and special fondue suppers are other options, by reservation only. If you're a root beer fan, try the house brew. Stop by the Camp David Museum for a glimpse of all the presidents who've stayed at the presidential retreat nearby.

103 Frederick Rd. (Rte. 806), Thurmont, MD 21788. ✆ **301/271-7373.** www.cozyvillage.com. Reservations recommended on Fri–Sat, required for candlelight fondue hideaway. Main courses $8–$16; buffet $8–$24. AE, MC, V. Mon–Fri 11am–9pm; Sat–Sun 8am–9pm.

Fitzgerald's Shamrock Restaurant SEAFOOD/STEAKS This homey, friendly restaurant proudly proclaims its Irish roots. Get a Harp or Guinness to wash down onion rings, shad in season, Angus beef, crab cakes, or chicken Chesapeake (a popular combination of chicken and crab). Sandwiches are available all day. No room for dessert? Take a pie with you.

7701 Fitzgerald Rd., Thurmont, MD 21788. ✆ **301/271-2912.** www.shamrockrestaurant.info. Reservations recommended on Fri–Sat. Main courses $7–$26. AE, MC, V. Sun noon–9pm; Mon–Sat 11am–10pm.

HAGERSTOWN

25 miles W of Frederick; 20 miles N of Antietam

Once a frontier town where Jonathan Hager built a fort to protect against Indian attack, Hagerstown is now best known for its charming city park, home to graceful swans and the remarkable Washington County Museum of Fine Arts, and perhaps for the factory outlet stores near I-70. Hagerstown's location also makes it a convenient place to stop while visiting Civil War sites—have a picnic in City Park, visit the museum or Hager's house, or have a bite to eat in the town's arts-and-entertainment district.

What to See & Do

City Park Swans on the lake, plenty of tree-shaded places, and playground equipment make this a charming spot to stop. The town began developing the 50-acre park in 1914 and Anna and William Singer chose it as the site of their art museum.

501 Virginia Ave., Hagerstown. No phone. Free admission. Daily dawn–dusk.

Discovery Station at Hagerstown This children's museum, in a mid-20th-century bank, has some interesting items, but it's not a place where you can just let the kids loose. Instead, it offers adults the opportunity to wander through some dusty old memories and share them with the younger generation. These include a 15-foot model of the *Titanic,* a Cessna 150, and a diesel engine built in Hagerstown's Mack factory. Other exhibits focus on rocks, space, health, and agriculture. Several play areas, with blocks and toys and giant storybooks, are totally kid-friendly.

101 W. Washington St., Hagerstown, MD 21741. ✆ **877/790-0076** or 301/790-0076. www.discoverystation.org. $7 adults, $5 seniors, $6 children 3–17. Tues–Sat 10am–4pm; Sun 2–5pm. Closed Sun May–Jan; also Jan 1–2, Easter, Mother's Day, Father's Day, July 4, Thanksgiving and Dec 24–26.

The Hager House This 1740 stone house recalls when this was America's frontier. Jonathan Hager, a fur trader and gunsmith, designed the house to be impregnable in case of attack (which never came). Its modest collection of 17th- and 18th-century artifacts, including spinning wheels and a rare German clavichord (an early piano), makes it an interesting stop, especially for those visiting the park or art museum.

110 Key St., City Park, Hagerstown, MD 21741. ✆ **301/739-8393.** www.hagerhouse.org. $3 adults, $2 seniors, $1 children 6–12. Thurs–Sat 10am–4pm. Closed Jan–Mar.

Hagerstown Roundhouse Museum There's nothing fancy about the design here, and the exhibitions are amateurish. But what makes this museum worth a look are the model train layouts. If you love O-gauge trains and marvel at cute little houses, you're going to enjoy yourself. Certainly the **Trains of Christmas** layout, open November through March, is the big draw, but during the rest of the year, two other train layouts feature local sites and topography. Artifacts from Hagerstown's history as a "hub city" and a Brio train layout for kids to play with round out the visit.

Outside, the CSX trains rumble by local tracks holding decommissioned trains owned by the museum. The cabooses are open for visits in spring and fall.

300 S. Burhans Blvd., Hagerstown. ✆ **301/739-4665.** www.roundhouse.org. $3.50 adults, 50¢ ages 4–12. Fri–Sun 1–5pm.

Washington County Museum of Fine Arts Rodin's sculptures are here, as are paintings by Whistler, Courbet, seven members of Charles Wilson Peale's family, and Joshua Johnson. The museum, overlooking the City Park's Lower Lake, was built in 1931 thanks to the generosity of local girl Anna Brugh and William Henry Singer, a steel heir and painter. The eclectic 7,000-piece collection has pieces from Europe, America, and Asia, most from the 18th to the 20th centuries. One gallery focuses on the Singers with their portraits, landscapes painted by Singer, and other works from their friends. With only 13% of the collection on the walls at a time, exhibits change regularly.

401 Museum Dr., City Park, Hagerstown, MD 21740. ✆ **301/739-5727.** www.wcmfa.org. Free admission. Tues–Fri 9am–5pm; Sat 9am–4pm; Sun 1–5pm. Closed Jan 1, Good Friday, July 4, Thanksgiving, Dec 24–25 and 31.

Where to Stay & Eat

Hagerstown's Potomac Street has a couple of good restaurants. Local favorites are the **Rhubarb House,** 12 Public Sq. (✆ **301/733-4399;** www.rhubarbhouse.com), with sandwiches and burgers, and the charming **Schmankerl Stube Bavarian Restaurants,** 58 S. Potomac St. (✆ **301/797-3354;** www.schmankerlstube.com), serving Bavarian favorites such as sauerbraten and Wiener schnitzel.

Chain hotels line Route 40. For more interesting options, these two inns are a short drive from the Antietam battlefield as well as Hagerstown.

Inn BoonsBoro ★ Novelist Nora Roberts mixes old-fashioned romance with up-to-the-minute luxury in the B&B she opened in 2008 in a 1798 stone structure in tiny Boonsboro, 10 miles from Antietam. Rooms have their own ambience and are named for literary romantic couples. The "Jane and Rochester" room boasts an enormous canopy bed while "Nick and Nora" is Art Deco chic. All the rooms are spacious with flatscreen TVs and DVD players, and have access to a small porch; some rooms have private entrances and two have gas fireplaces. Bathrooms are spacious with separate showers and tubs. The penthouse has a whirlpool tub (guests enter by the back door).

1 N. Main St., Boonsboro, MD 21713. www.innboonsboro.com. ✆ **301/432-1188.** 8 units. $220–$300 double. Rates include full breakfast. AE, DISC, MC, V. No children 12 and under. **Amenities:** Library w/high-speed Internet access. *In room:* A/C, TV/VCR, hair dryer.

Jacob Rohrbach Inn ★ Inhabitants of this three-story stone house, built at the turn of the 19th century, once heard the gunfire of the Battle of Antietam. Confederate soldiers woke the house's namesake and shot him dead. Today, the home is an elegant inn. The four largest rooms have private entrances. One is located in a spacious separate cottage with sitting room and private porch.

7138 W. Main St., Sharpsburg, MD 21782. www.jacob-rohrbach-inn.com. ✆ **877/839-4242** or 301/432-5079. 5 units. $104–$195 double. Rates include full breakfast. 2-night minimum stay required on weekends and holidays. AE, DISC, MC, V. No children 10 and under. **Amenities:** Bike rentals. *In room:* A/C, TV w/VCR or DVD, hair dryer, free Wi-Fi.

WESTERN MARYLAND

9

Western Maryland is a haven for lovers of the outdoors. Garrett and Allegany counties offer a wide variety of outside activities any season. More than 100,000 acres of parkland stretch over peaks and valleys. Gently rolling mountain slopes draw visitors to their hiking and biking paths and ski slopes. Rivers and streams, particularly the Youghiogheny and the Savage, attract fly-fishermen and white-water rafters. The centerpiece is Deep Creek Lake.

Western Maryland, which begins at the state's skinniest section at Hancock and ends at the West Virginia border, is easy to reach. From Baltimore, take I-70. Washingtonians can connect with I-70 from I-270. When I-70 turns north into Pennsylvania near Hancock, it connects to I-68, which heads into West Virginia. I-81 joins I-70 near Hagerstown from Pennsylvania and Virginia. U.S. Route 219 intersects I-68 and heads south to Deep Creek Lake.

For a more scenic route, old U.S. Route 40, the nation's first national pike, connects Frederick to Cumberland and other points west and east. It's slower going but much more interesting.

THE GREAT OUTDOORS IN WESTERN MARYLAND

Western Maryland's gently rolling mountains are part of the Appalachians, with **Backbone Mountain** (elevation 3,360 ft.) marking the eastern Continental Divide. Outdoors enthusiasts can find forests, mountain lakes, and miles of streams and rivers. White-water rafters come to meet the challenges of the Youghiogheny (pronounced Yok-a-*gain*-ee; or just the "Yough"). Boaters flock to Garrett's seven lakes. Skiers head for the hills of Wisp Resort, and cross-country skiers glide along the state parks' trails. There are also plenty of opportunities for windsurfing, snowmobiling, fly-fishing, mountain biking, golfing, hunting, hiking, and camping.

Of the 100,000 acres of protected wilderness in Western Maryland, 40,000 are part of **Green Ridge State Forest,** east of Cumberland, while 53,000 are in the **Savage River State Forest,** near Deep Creek Lake. The area is great for wildlife-watching and fishing: Some species, notably hawks and black bears, had begun to disappear, but they are returning to the region's parks and forests. And although mining runoff once threatened Garrett County's water, the Casselman, North Branch Potomac, and Youghiogheny rivers now boast some of the best fly-fishing around.

In other chapters of this book, the sections on outdoor pursuits are organized by activities such as biking and camping. This chapter instead has a rundown of each of the parks—except Deep Creek Lake State Park, which is described in the section about the lake itself—and some of their individual offerings to help you decide where you want to go and what you want to do. For more information, call for brochures and maps (see numbers below), or go to **www.dnr.maryland.gov.** To reserve a campsite, call ✆ **888/432-2267,** or reserve online at **http://reservations.dnr.state.md.us.** The DNR has a "Your Free Guide to Camping in Maryland" brochure that lists state parks and private campgrounds. ***Note:*** It is illegal to consume or possess liquor in a state park, except in motor homes and full-service cabins.

Allegany County

Allegany has two outstanding state parks, plus the terminus of the C&O Canal, which is popular with bikers, hikers, and history buffs.

The **Chesapeake & Ohio Canal National Historical Park** (✆ **301/722-8226;** www.nps.gov/choh) is an ideal place for a trek on the flat, wide canal towpath. Cyclists and hikers alike enjoy all or part of the 184-mile route along the Potomac River, all the way from Cumberland to Georgetown, in DC. Any portion can make a great 1-day biking trip. The canal passes by numerous sites, including Paw Paw Tunnel, Fort Frederick, Harpers Ferry, and **Great Falls ★**. The trip from Cumberland is almost all gently downhill. Because flooding can make some of the towpath impassable, check with the park service to see if the route you intend to bike is clear.

Green Ridge State Forest, Exit 64 off I-68 (✆ **301/478-3124**), is home to 46,000 acres of abundant wildlife and scenic vistas over the Potomac River. Adirondack-style shelters are placed along the 24-mile backpacking trail. Mountain bikers have access to the park's roads, most of the 43 miles of hiking trails, and a separate bike trail and racecourse. At the oak-hickory forest's southern end, you'll find the Paw

THE great ALLEGHENY PASSAGE

The **Great Allegheny Passage** makes it possible to walk or cycle 335 miles from Pittsburgh to Washington, DC. The Passage and the C&O Canal towpath come together in Cumberland, and Maryland's section of the trail, the **Allegheny Highlands Trail** (www.atatrail.org), stretches from Cumberland to Frostburg. Enthusiasts see this as a trail to conquer, but it's actually the fulfillment of George Washington's dream to connect the Chesapeake Bay to the Ohio River.

This 141-mile path through mountain vistas all the way to Pittsburgh is an opportunity to test your endurance up hills and over miles. The climb from Cumberland to the Eastern Continental Divide marker is 1,700 feet. Riders go through three tunnels in Maryland, including the 3,294-foot-long Big Savage Tunnel (closed late Nov to early Apr). Along the trail you'll find lodging, camping areas, restrooms, and restaurants. There's also the possibility of meeting up with bears, turkeys, and copperhead snakes. And at one point, the trail parallels the Western Maryland Scenic Railway tracks.

Local bicycle shops provide rentals, equipment, and repairs, and some will shuttle cyclists to various trail heads. (See "Suppliers & Guides" listings for both Allegany and Garrett counties, below.) For a map, go to **www.atatrail.org**. For information, call ✆ **888/282-2453.**

Western Maryland

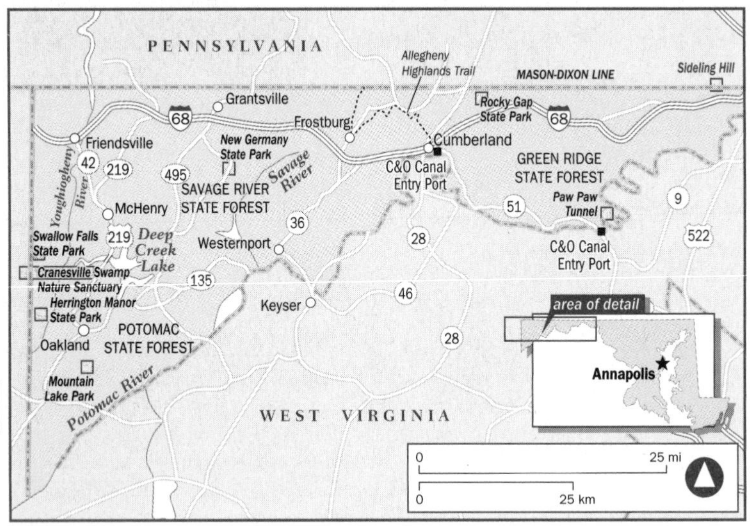

Paw Tunnel on the C&O Canal (p. 215). Primitive camping is available at 100 sites ($10 per night). The park's activities include off-road driving, hunting, canoeing, kayaking, and fishing. The shooting range is open Wednesday through Saturday and Monday from 10am to sunset, Sunday from noon to sunset.

Rocky Gap State Park ★, Exit 50 off I-68 (✆ **301/722-1480**), has great trails with views of 243-acre Lake Habeeb, mountain overlooks, and a stout 5-mile trail up Evitts Mountain to the remains of a 1784 homestead. Walk along Rocky Gap Run to see the mile-long gorge and hemlock forest. The lake has three swimming beaches; two boat ramps; and boat, canoe, kayak, and paddleboat rentals. Boats are permitted on the lake 24 hours a day. Fishing licenses are required. The park has 278 campsites, including 14 minicabins ($50–$65 per night). Reservations here are recommended.

SUPPLIERS & GUIDES IN ALLEGANY COUNTY

C&O Bicycle, 9 S. Pennsylvania Ave., Hancock (✆ **301/678-6665;** www.cando bicycle.com), rents and sells bikes in its shop, located between the C&O Canal towpath and the 20-mile Western Maryland Rail Trail. C&O also repairs bikes and operates a general store with lodging in the bunkhouse (reservations are a good idea). Shuttle service available. Closed Tuesday through Thursday in cold weather.

Adventure Sports, 113 E. Main St., Frostburg (✆ **301/689-0345**), rents, sells, and services bikes, skis, and canoes.

The staff at **Cumberland Trail Connection,** Canal Place, Cumberland (✆ **301/777-8724;** www.ctcbikes.com), right on the C&O towpath, know both the towpath and the Allegheny Highlands Trail. They rent and sell bikes, cycling equipment, and camping gear.

Allegany Expeditions (✆ **800/819-5170** or 301/722-5170) rents canoes, kayaks, cross-country skis, and camping equipment. It offers guided trips for hiking, rock climbing and rappelling, cave exploration, and canoeing. Call to inquire about cross-country ski packages as well as fly-fishing and bass-fishing expeditions.

Garrett County

Garrett County is covered by state forests and parks. It's the home of swimming holes, the state's highest waterfall, and an intriguing preserve owned by the Nature Conservancy. To find a park that best suits you, visit **www.dnr.maryland.gov**.

The day-use fee at state parks for Marylanders is $2 on weekends and holidays, $3 during ski season. Nonresidents pay $1 more.

Note: Visitors planning to stay a few days may want to get a **Garrett County Weekly Fun Pass,** valid for up to 10 people in one vehicle. It's good for all Garrett state parks for 7 days, including unlimited boat launching. It's $30 for Marylanders, $31 for out-of-state visitors.

Swallow Falls State Park ★★★, c/o 222 Herrington Lane, Oakland, MD 21550 (✆ **301/387-6938;** www.dnr.state.md.us/publiclands/western/swallowfalls.asp), has 10 miles of hiking trails. Follow the Youghiogheny River for views of Swallow Falls and even more spectacular Muddy Falls, which drops 63 feet. The walk through one of Maryland's last virgin forests of giant pines and hemlocks shouldn't be missed. The park has the area's largest camping facility, with 65 improved sites and modern bathhouses with showers and laundry tubs. Camping costs $25 to $50 per night; reservations can be made up to a year in advance. Pets are permitted on leashes in designated camping areas and in day-use areas in the off season. A 5.5-mile trail good, for hiking or cross-country skiing, connects the park with Herrington Manor.

Herrington Manor State Park, 222 Herrington Lane, Oakland, MD 21550 (✆ **301/334-9180**), draws cross-country skiers to its 10 miles of groomed trails. It offers ski and snowshoe rentals ($15 a day), sled rentals ($6 a day), 20 furnished cabins, and stone warming rooms. Trails and rental facilities are open from 8:30am to 4pm during good skiing conditions. In summer, the park's trails draw hikers and bikers. The 53-acre Herrington Lake has guarded beaches and canoes, rowboats, and paddleboats to rent from May through September. Bring your tennis racquet or volleyball: Courts are waiting. Campers can reserve 1 of 20 furnished log cabins year-round; book as much as a year ahead. Rentals range from $20 to $100 for a full-service cabin. Pets are allowed only in day-use areas.

Savage River State Forest, 127 Headquarters Lane, Grantsville, MD 21536 (✆ **301/895-5759**), which surrounds New Germany and Big Run, is the largest of Maryland's state forests, at more than 54,000 acres, 11,000 as state wildlands. It features miles of hiking trails. It's also home to many bears, so plan accordingly. The longest trail, Big Savage, follows a 17-mile path along the ridge of Big Savage Mountain at an average elevation of 2,500 feet. Also popular is **Monroe Run,** which traverses the forest between New Germany and Big Run. Mountain bikers may use all trails except Big Savage and Monroe Run. Snowmobiles and off-road vehicles have one trail; permits are required and available at park headquarters. Stop by for trail maps, including one delineating 10 miles of cross-country-ski trails. Savage River Lake was the site of the 1989 world white-water championships; only nonpowered watercraft are allowed on the water. Fifty-two primitive campsites are spread throughout the forest—you may not see another camper while you're here. Backwoods camping is also permitted, but fires are not allowed at some sites. Camping is available year-round at $5 per night, with sites offered on a first-come, first-served basis with self-registration. Pets are permitted on leashes. If you don't have the time or the inclination to stay for a while, at least drive through the park, as many motorcyclists do on weekends. The roads are public, and the feeling of escape that comes from all those acres of trees is worth the ride.

New Germany State Park ★★, 349 Headquarters Lane, Grantsville, MD 21536 (✆ **301/895-5453**), has 12 miles of trails, well marked for cross-country skiing. It also offers equipment rentals, cabins, and large stone warming rooms where skiers can stop and get a snack. Trails and rental facilities are open from 8am to 4pm during good skiing conditions. The park has 39 improved campsites with clean bathhouses and hot showers. All sites are large, private, and located in a wooded glen; the cost is $20 per night. These can be rented up to a year in advance for visits between April and Labor Day; September through October, the sites are offered on a first-come, first-served basis. Available year-round are 11 furnished cabins—with electricity, fireplaces, and room for two to eight persons—for $90 to $120 a night, with a 2-night minimum required. You can reserve cabins up to a year in advance. The park also has a 13-acre lake, popular for swimming and boating, with boat rentals available. A nature center has a snack bar and free Wi-Fi. Pets are not permitted.

Big Run State Park, 10368 Savage River Rd., Swanton, MD 21561 (✆ **301/895-5453**), just down the road, offers fishing and hiking along Monroe Run and Big Run. You can launch your boat at Savage River Reservoir. The 300-acre park has 30 rustic campsites with chemical toilets and running water. Some are in wooded areas along Monroe Run and Big Run, others on the shore of the Savage River Reservoir. Sites at Big Run are open year-round and cost $15 per night (available on a first-come, first-served basis). Pets are permitted on leashes.

Potomac-Garrett State Forest, 1431 Potomac Camp Rd., Oakland, MD 21550 (✆ **301/334-2038**), is spread over 11,000 acres in two separate tracts in the lower westernmost corner of the county. With plenty of streams, beaver ponds, and cranberry bogs, it offers beautiful scenery, including the highest point in any Maryland state forest: Backbone Mountain, in Garrett State Forest near Route 135 and Walnut Bottom Road. There are 8 miles of mountain-biking trails, as well as trails for snowmobiles, dirt bikes, and ATVs. Off-road-vehicle permits are required and can be obtained at each park's headquarters. Hikers can choose from 30 miles of trails, many easy enough for day hikes and many with mountain views that can only be seen off the road. Geocaching is also big here. The fishing here is some of the best in Western Maryland, with 21 miles of first-class trout streams, including 9 miles of the North Branch of the Potomac River. Here's the place to catch the Maryland Grand Slam: brook, brown, 'bo, and cutthroat trout. A 3-D archery range is open April through September. Potomac-Garrett offers five primitive camping areas, open year-round. Getting to them may take some effort, however: The sites are beautiful and generously spaced, and a few have three-sided wooden shelters, but the roads to the sites are not well maintained. The cost is $10 for regular sites, $15 for a site with a shelter. Pets are permitted off-leash, if they're under control.

Youghiogheny NRMA, 898 State Park Rd., Swanton, MD 21561 (✆ **301/387-5563**), offers Class IV and V whitewater rapids as well as hiking and catch-and-release fly-fishing. Much of the area is remote and rugged with rare species of flora and fauna. Access the river through Swallow Falls' Sang Run Area for hiking and in the Hoyes Run Area for fly-fishing. Rafters usually stop at an access point near Friendsville.

Jennings Randolph Lake (✆ **301/359-3861**) covers 952 acres and has 13 miles of shoreline. It straddles the Maryland–West Virginia line. On the Maryland side, there's a boat ramp at Mt. Zion Road via Route 135 and a scenic overlook at Walnut Bottom Road. The lake is open for boating, fishing, and water-skiing. Hiking trails on the Maryland side start at one of the overlooks. White-water rafting is available in spring. For the dam release schedule, see **www.nab.usace.army.mil/Recreation/jenran/recinfo.htm**. Call ✆ **304/355-2890** for lake conditions. Pets on leashes are permitted in some areas.

Broadford Lake, near Oakland (✆ **301/334-9222**), is open from March 31 to early November during daylight hours. The 140-acre park has a guarded beach as well as a boat launch and rentals. Electric boat motors only are permitted. There are picnic pavilions, playgrounds, and ball fields. Pets on leashes are permitted in some areas. Admission is $2 per car on weekdays and $3 per car on weekends.

Cranesville Swamp Preserve ★ (✆ **301/897-8570;** www.nature.org) is a vestige of the last ice age. Operated by the Nature Conservancy, it's a 1,600-acre peat bog home to sedges, cranberry, sphagnum moss, and tamarack trees—a species usually not found south of Alaska. Quiet and wild, the four trails lead through a cathedral of pine forests and cross a 1,500-foot boardwalk to see the unusual plants, some carnivorous. To get to the entrance (which is in West Virginia), go south on U.S. Route 219; turn right on Mayhew Inn Road, left on Bray School Road, right on Oakland Sang Run Road, left on Swallow Falls Road, and right on Cranesville Road at the fork. Turn left on Lake Ford Road, right at the next fork. It's about a fifth of a mile on the right. The preserve is open dawn to dusk year-round. Admission is free. Pets are not allowed. Wear boots and bring water and bug repellent. There are no restrooms.

THE WILD RIVERS OF GARRETT COUNTY

The "three sisters"—the Youghiogheny, Casselman, and North Branch Potomac rivers—have become so popular that the area is often featured on national fly-fishing shows. The Casselman is a fertile catch-and-release river; anglers here have been known to catch 40 fish a day. The Youghiogheny supports a strong population of brown and rainbow trout, but be aware that dam releases cause substantial increases in the water level below the Deep Creek Lake power plant. Call ✆ **315/413-2823** or visit **www.deepcreekhydro.com** for a dam-release schedule.

Garrett County offers myriad opportunities for white-water rafting, kayaking, and canoeing. The Youghiogheny, the North Branch Potomac, and the Savage are the area's best-known runs. Although they can be challenging all year, they're at their fiercest in the spring after snowmelt. In 1976, the Youghiogheny River between Millers Run and Friendsville became Maryland's first officially designated Wild and Scenic River. This portion, known as the **Upper Yough,** contains approximately 20 Class IV and V rapids. Fortunately for the inexperienced paddler, outfitters have sprung up all over the area to take people down this exciting river. If you'd prefer a little less excitement, the Middle Yough offers Class I and II rapids, and the Lower Yough is a Class III run. There are also several rivers just across the border in West Virginia—the Cheat, Gauley, Big Sandy, and Russell Fork—that are rated Class IV or higher.

Kayakers hoping to avoid raft traffic would do well to visit the North Branch Potomac and Savage rivers (both Class III/IV); however, they can only be run after heavy rains or snowmelt. For open canoeing, the Casselman River (Class II) to the west is good in winter and spring.

Most outfitters run raft trips on several or all of these rivers; see below for options.

SUPPLIERS & GUIDES IN GARRETT COUNTY

Guided rafting trips cost $100 to $140 per person for an (expert) Upper Yough trip. Middle Yough (novice) trips cost about $60; Lower Yough (intermediate) trips are $75 to $135 depending on the level of service. Family float trips cost around $30. ***Note:*** Remember to tip your guide—$3 to $5 per person is appropriate.

Friendsville, located on the Upper Youghiogheny, has become a white-water center. Friendsville is at the intersection of I-68, Maryland Route 42, and the Yough; from Deep Creek Lake, take U.S. Route 219 north to Maryland Route 42 into town.

Precision Rafting, in Friendsville (✆ **800/477-3723;** www.precisionrafting.com), and **Cheat River Outfitters** (✆ **888/99-RIVER** [997-4837]; www.cheatriveroutfitters.com) offer trips in the Upper Yough's Class V waters (depending on the dam release schedule). Precision also offers raft trips down all of the rivers and paddling lessons. Cheat River offers trips on the Class II, III, and IV Cheat River in West Virginia, about 45 minutes from Deep Creek.

Several outfitters based in nearby Ohiopyle, Pennsylvania, offer similar trips. Try **Laurel Highlands River Tours** (✆ **800/4-RAFTIN** [472-3846]; www.laurelhighlands.com). To get to Ohiopyle from Deep Creek Lake, take U.S. Route 219 north to U.S. Route 40 west (just past the intersection with I-68). Go into Pennsylvania and turn north onto State Route 381 to Ohiopyle. It's about an hour from Deep Creek Lake.

All Earth Eco Tours (✆ **301/746-4083**) offers kayak tours in the Savage River Reservoir and hiking tours along the Yough.

Allegany Expeditions (✆ **301/722-5170**) offers equipment rentals and various guided excursions. See "Suppliers & Guides in Allegany County," above, for details.

For tackle and bait, stop by **Bill's Outdoor Center,** 20768 Garrett Hwy. (U.S. Rte. 219), McHenry (✆ **301/387-FISH** [3474]).

High Mountain Sports, 21327 Garrett Hwy., Oakland, MD 21550 (✆ **301/387-4199;** www.highmountainsports.com), sells, rents, and services bicycles, stand-up paddleboards, and kayaks. It also offers water-ski and kayak lessons and tours, and mountain-bike tours, from this location. At its location next to Wisp Resort, 7827 Sang Run Rd., McHenry, MD 21541 (✆ **301/387-2113**), it rents skis, snowshoes, and snowboards. It can also handle repairs on bikes, skis, and snowboards.

Rent pontoon boats from **Deep Creek Marina,** 1899 Deep Creek Dr. (✆ **301/387-6977**).

Snowshoes can be rented at **Herrington Manor State Park** (✆ **301/334-9180**) and **Deep Creek State Park** (✆ **301/387-5563**) for $15 for a full day.

CUMBERLAND & ALLEGANY COUNTY

140 miles W of Baltimore; 140 miles NW of Washington, DC; 113 miles SE of Pittsburgh, PA

The city of Cumberland sits on a tight bend of the Potomac River in the heart of the Allegheny Mountains, with a portion of the C&O Canal as its centerpiece. Once a large industrial city, it is now quieter, though tourism is a growing industry. Visitors come to see the canal, George Washington's headquarters, and the surrounding mountains.

At the turn of the 20th century, Cumberland was Maryland's "Queen City," second in size only to Baltimore. Many reminders of those days remain: a long street of Victorian mansions, the ornate storefronts of the rejuvenated shopping district, the black smoke of the *Mountain Thunder* coal-powered train.

Since the construction of I-68 cut right through—you might say right on top of—Cumberland, the city has become more accessible to the rest of the state. People come to see not only Cumberland, but also Rocky Gap State Park (known for Lake Habeeb) with its resort, golf course, and area parks.

The Allegheny Mountains are particularly beautiful in autumn, and the area is popular with bikers and hikers who find Cumberland and nearby Frostburg cheaper and closer to home than Deep Creek Lake to the west.

Essentials

GETTING THERE I-68, which runs through the center of Cumberland, is the fastest route by car from east or west. From the east and north, I-70 will take you to I-68. For a more scenic drive, get off I-70 or I-68 onto the Old National Pike (U.S. Rte. 40).

Amtrak (✆ **800/872-7245;** www.amtrak.com) serves Cumberland on its *Capitol Limited* train route from Washington, DC, to Chicago. It stops at the station at 301 E. Harrison St.

The **Greater Cumberland Regional Airport** (✆ **304/738-0002;** www.cumberlandairport.com) is actually in Wiley Ford, West Virginia, 2½ miles off Route 68 at Exit 43B. It serves only private planes.

VISITOR INFORMATION Walking-tour brochures, maps, and information about the Cumberland are available at the visitor center operated by **Allegany County Tourism** (www.mdmountainside.com) at the **Western Maryland Railway Station,** 13 Canal St., Cumberland (✆ **800/425-2067**), open daily from 9am to 5pm.

SPECIAL EVENTS The **Heritage Days Festival** (✆ **301/722-0037**), held in mid-June in Cumberland, fills the streets with arts and crafts, entertainment, and train rides. **Fridays after Five** (✆ **800/425-2067**) brings live entertainment to the streets of downtown Cumberland on summer Fridays.

Where to Stay

The Cumberland-Frostburg area offers an inviting blend of modern and old-fashioned lodging. Most are moderately priced and offer very good value. All have free parking.

Failinger's Hotel Gunter ★ This 1897 landmark hotel boasts guest rooms and public areas, particularly the centerpiece oak staircase, that are a work of Victorian charm. Modern conveniences are plentiful, but original oak doors, brass fixtures, claw-foot tubs, and sconces remain. Rooms are individually furnished, with canopy or four-poster beds, armoires, and pastel fabrics; several of them were redecorated in 2009. Room no. 307, the Roy Clark Room, named after the country singer who stayed here in 1990, is the most masculine of the rooms with black-and-white Victorian trimmings.

11 W. Main St., Frostburg, MD 21532. www.failingershotelgunter.com. ✆ **301/689-6511.** Fax 301/689-6034. 11 units. $88–$100 double; from $110 suites. Rates include continental breakfast. AE, DC, DISC, MC, V. Off-street parking. **Amenities:** Free Wi-Fi. *In room:* A/C, TV, fridge and microwave available.

Holiday Inn Cumberland This modern six-story hotel sits at the east end of Cumberland's shopping promenade, providing easy walking access to the downtown area. King and double rooms are clean and comfortable, as you would expect from a Holiday Inn. Railroad enthusiasts might like a room overlooking the nearby tracks (the trains aren't too loud); everyone else will prefer the town side, where there's less noise.

100 S. George St., Cumberland, MD 21502. www.hicumberland.com. ✆ **833/465-4329** or 301/724-8800. Fax 301/724-4001. 130 units. $119–$209 double. Children 19 and under stay free in parent's room; children 12 and under eat free with parent. AE, DC, DISC, MC, V. Pets accepted for a

fee. **Amenities:** Restaurant; lounge; billiards; fitness center; outdoor pool. *In room:* A/C, flatscreen TV, fridge and microwave available on request, free Wi-Fi.

Rocky Gap Lodge & Golf Resort Beside Lake Habeeb and the rolling hills of Rocky Gap State Park, Rocky Gap Lodge mixes luxury accommodations with a challenging 18-hole Jack Nicklaus golf course—populated by wild critters unafraid of flying golf balls—and the beauty of the Appalachian mountains. Golf-package guests should check with the manager to extend their checkout time (as tee times and golf clinics can run later than the usual checkout time). Rocky Gap also offers a year-round program of outdoor activities, including rappelling, rock climbing, caving, kayaking, horseback riding, fly-fishing, biking, horse-drawn carriage or sleigh tours, cross-country skiing, and boating. Or you can just pull up a lounge chair beside the lake, or choose from the many treatments offered at the **Garden Spa.**

16701 Lakeview Rd. NE, Flintstone, MD 21530. www.rockygapresort.com. ✆ **800/724-0828** or 301/784-8400. Fax 301/784-8408. 216 units. $119–$239 double; $199–$619 suite. Children 18 and under stay free in parent's room. AE, DC, MC, V. Pets welcome but reservation by phone required. **Amenities:** 2 restaurants (3 in summer); lounge; golf; health club; indoor pool; spa; tennis courts. *In room:* A/C, flatscreen TV, hair dryer, free Wi-Fi.

Savage River Lodge ★★★ Tucked in the woods of the Savage River State Forest down a winding 1½-mile road, this lodge will take you away. Cellphone reception is spotty but the scenery is a sure bet. Eighteen log cabins with front porches, spacious but simple, combined with an elegant restaurant (see "Where to Eat," below) and plenty of outdoor activities make this a spot you won't want to leave. Pets are welcome in most of the cabins; several are pet-free to accommodate those with allergies.

1600 Mt. Aetna Rd., Frostburg, MD 21532 (about 5 miles off I-68). www.savageriverlodge.com. ✆ **301/689-3200.** 18 cabins (sleep 4). $185–$240; higher in Oct and Dec. Rates include continental breakfast. AE, DISC, MC, V. **Amenities:** Restaurant; lounge; 10 miles of hiking trails; outdoor activities; TV in lodge; Wi-Fi in lodge. *In room:* A/C, gas fireplace, fridge, hair dryer, high-speed Internet.

Where to Eat

CUMBERLAND

Queen City Creamery Coffee Bar & Deli COFFEE/ICE CREAM Mix nostalgia with your ice cream at this soda fountain, which has a counter, booths, and a 1952 jukebox. Three flavors of frozen custard are made fresh every day. Coffee drinks, soups, and sandwiches are available. A shop at Canal Place is open summer weekends.

108 Harrison St., Cumberland, MD 21501. ✆ **240/979-4125.** www.queencitycreamery.com. Reservations not accepted. Sandwiches $3–$9. MC, V. Mon–Thurs 7am–8pm; Fri 7am–9pm; Sat 8am–9pm; Sun 8am–8pm. Open later in summer.

Ristorante Ottaviani ★ ☺ ITALIAN Sit up front for a quieter, more intimate dinner. If you sit in back, you just might feel you've become part of a big Italian family (one in which children 7 and under get a complimentary beverage and bowl of pasta). Everybody greets everybody else, music blares from the sound system, and the mood is jovial as waitresses pass by with plates of great pasta.

25 N. Centre St., Cumberland, MD 21501. ✆ **301/722-0052.** www.ristoranteottaviani.com. Reservations recommended on Fri–Sat. Main courses $13–$27. MC, V. Tues–Sat 5–10pm.

FROSTBURG

Start your day with a cup of joe at **Mountain City Coffeehouse and Creamery,** 60 E. Main St. (✆ **301/687-0808**). They've got Deep Creek Lake's famous Lakeside Creamery ice cream and Wi-Fi, too. They are open every morning but Monday.

Au Petit Paris Restaurant Français ★ FRENCH Au Petit Paris is a find—a fine, intimate French restaurant, worth the drive from Cumberland or Deep Creek Lake. The interior has a Parisian feel, with French posters and bistro-style furnishings. The restaurant, which celebrated its 50th anniversary in 2010, is a favorite for classic French fare, such as chateaubriand (order 24 hr. in advance) and coq au vin.

86 E. Main St., Frostburg, MD 21532. ✆ **301/689-8946.** Reservations recommended. Main courses $20–$35. AE, DISC, MC, V. Tues–Sat 5:30–9:30pm.

Giuseppe's Italian Restaurant ITALIAN In the heart of town and a block from the Frostburg State University campus, this spot is popular with the college community and locals. It offers first-rate food and cozy atmosphere. The pizzas are great and you can't beat the usual Italian favorites, such as pasta, shrimp scampi, veal Parmigiana, and the antipasti, as well as a few unusual dishes such as crab carbonara.

11 Bowery St., Frostburg, MD 21532. ✆ **301/689-2220.** www.giuseppes.net. Reservations recommended on Fri–Sat. Main courses $13–$27. AE, DISC, MC, V. Tues–Sun 4:30–11pm.

The Savage River Lodge ★★★ AMERICAN Even if you don't stay here, it's worth the drive down the long road to sit in the rustic dining room or out on the porch. You'll eat well, whether it's the weekend breakfast with omelets, crab Benedict, and rich French toast or a simple lunch of soup, salad, or a sandwich. For dinner, choose from steak, seafood, or maybe a stuffed portobello mushroom or vegetable lasagna.

1600 Mt. Aetna Rd. (about 5 miles off I-68), Frostburg, MD 21532. ✆ **301/689-3200.** www.savageriverlodge.com. Reservations required. Main courses $8–$12 breakfast, $9–$13 lunch, $18–$35 dinner. AE, DISC, MC, V. Mon–Fri 11:30am–1:30pm and 5–8:30pm; Sat–Sun 9am–2pm and 5–8:30pm.

What to See & Do

One of the highlights of a visit to Cumberland is a stroll through the **Victorian Historic District** ★★★ along Washington Street on the western side of town. This area includes the site of the original Fort Cumberland (now the Emmanuel Episcopal Church) and more than 50 residential and public buildings built in the 1800s, when Cumberland was at its peak. Listed on the National Register of Historic Places, Washington showcases homes with stained-glass windows, cupolas, and mansard roofs. You'll see architectural styles ranging from Federal, Queen Anne, Empire, Colonial Revival, Italianate, and English Country Gothic to Georgian Revival, Gothic Revival, and Greek Revival. A self-guided walking tour available from the visitor center offers a glimpse into their history. Two homes are open for tours (see below).

Canal Place (Chesapeake & Ohio Canal National Historical Park/Cumberland Visitor Center) The C&O Canal opened here in 1850. For more than 75 years, it was an important transport line and had a major impact on the development of the town. Visit the Western Maryland Station Center at track level, check out the exhibits on the history of the canal (including a model of the Paw Paw Tunnel), and pick up a brochure. Then explore the towpath, a nearly level trail for walkers, hikers, and bikers. There are remnants of locks, dams, lockhouses, and other features along the way.

13 Canal St. ✆ **301/722-8226.** www.nps.gov/choh. Free admission. Daily 9am–5pm.

C&O Canal Paw Paw Tunnel ★ Construction on the Paw Paw Tunnel, part of the C&O Canal National Historical Park, started in 1836 when engineers decided to build the canal right through, rather than around, an intervening mountain. The result was an engineering marvel lined with more than six million bricks passing ¾ mile through the hill. Today, the tunnel is open to walkers, who can make the one-way trip in 20 minutes. This is not for the claustrophobic or those afraid of the dark (you must walk down a narrow towpath bounded by a guardrail, with the canal on one side and a sloping brick wall on the other). If you're up for it, pass through the massive brick arch into the darkness, then head for the light at the end of the tunnel. A flashlight is a must.

Rte. 51 and the Potomac River, south of Cumberland. ✆ **301/722-8226.** www.nps.gov/choh. Free admission. Daily dawn–dusk.

Emmanuel Episcopal Church This church, in Cumberland's historic district, is built on the 1755 foundations of Fort Cumberland, where George Washington began his military career. Although the Emmanuel parish dates from 1803, the cornerstone of the current building was laid in 1849. The church contains original Tiffany stained-glass windows and a scale model of Fort Cumberland. The grounds are part of the Fort Cumberland Walking Trail.

16 Washington St. ✆ **301/777-3364.** www.emmanuelparish.ang-md.org. Free admission. Mon–Fri 9am–5pm, except during services. Services Wed 5:30pm; Thurs 10:30am; Sun 8 and 10am, 6pm.

F. Brooke Whiting House of Art Whiting, a curator of rare books for UCLA, bequeathed his 1911 bungalow and collection to the Allegany County Historical Society, which has opened the house for tours. Memorabilia from his world travels, including paintings, Asian ceramics, and Murano and Tiffany glass, are on display.

632 Washington St. ✆ **301/777-7782.** www.thewhitinghouse.org. Admission $5. May–Oct. 2nd and 4th Fri and Sat with tours at 1, 2, and 3pm, and by appointment.

George Washington's Headquarters This log cabin, believed to be the only remaining structure from the original Fort Cumberland, was used by then-Col. George Washington as his official quarters during the French and Indian War. The one-room cabin is not open to the public but has a window with an audio description.

In Riverside Park, Greene St. (at the junction of Wills Creek and the Potomac River). ✆ **301/777-5132.** Free admission. Daily 24 hr.; exterior viewing only.

Gordon-Roberts House Built as a private residence in 1867 for the president of the C&O Canal, this fascinating 18-room Second Empire home is now in the hands of the Allegany County Historical Society. It's filled with antiques, such as a Victorian courting couch and an 1840 square grand piano. Other features include a research room, a walled garden, and a basement kitchen with antique utensils and fireplace.

218 Washington St. ✆ **301/777-8678.** www.gordon-robertshouse.com. Admission $7 adults, $6 seniors, $5 children 12 and under. Wed–Sat 10am–5pm. Last tour at 4pm.

Thrasher Carriage Museum ★ In a renovated train warehouse opposite the Western Maryland Railroad depot in Frostburg, this museum houses an extensive collection of late-19th- and early-20th-century horse-drawn carriages, featuring more than 50 vehicles from the collection of the late James R. Thrasher. Highlights include the inaugural coach used by Teddy Roosevelt, several Vanderbilt sleighs, elaborate funeral wagons, formal closed vehicles, surreys, and open sleighs.

Depot Center, 19 Depot St., Frostburg. ✆ **301/689-3380.** www.thethrashercarriagemuseum.com. Admission $4 adults, $2 children 6 and over. May–Oct Thurs–Sun 10am–2pm; Nov to mid-Dec Sat–Sun 10am–2pm; late Dec to Apr by appointment.

The Western Maryland Scenic Railroad ★★ ☺ The 32-mile round-trip between Cumberland and Frostburg—enhanced by live commentary—follows a mountain valley route through the Cumberland Narrows, with panoramic vistas and a 1,300-foot elevation change. All trains depart from and return to Cumberland. The trip takes 3½ hours, including a 1½-hour layover in Frostburg, where you can visit the Thrasher Carriage Museum or get a snack. The railroad also offers weekend murder-mystery dining excursions. The website lists dates and times. Diesel trains are used May through August and in October. Santa Express trips, offered Thanksgiving weekend through December, are aboard the steam train.

Western Maryland Station Center, 13 Canal St. ✆ **800/872-4650** or 301/759-4400. www.wmsr.com. Tickets $30 adults, $28 seniors, $16 children 12 and under; first-class tickets that include lunch $55 adults, $53 seniors, $35 children 12 and under. Reservations required. Excursions generally leave at 11:30am; special excursions leave at 6pm; 4:30pm departures added in Oct. From I-68, take downtown Cumberland exit 43C (westbound) or Johnson St. exit 43A (eastbound) and follow signs.

Shopping

Cumberland's pedestrian mall along Baltimore Street is worth a stroll. Most shops are open every day. **Monkey Business,** 62 Baltimore St. (✆ **301/724-2050**), features upscale women's fashions. The **Saville Gallery,** 9 N. Centre St. (✆ **301/777-2787;** www.alleganyartscouncil.org), is operated by the Allegany Arts Council and features the work of Western Marylanders. Just off the pedestrian mall is the **Book Center,** 15 N. Centre St. (✆ **301/722-2284**), where you'll find a large selection of books on Maryland, local history, railroading, and canals.

Canal Place, adjacent to the Western Maryland Railway Station (✆ 800/989-9394; www.canalplace.org), is home to **Arts at Canal Place** (✆ 301/777-8199) and **Cumberland Trail Connection Bicycle Shop.** For a bite to eat, options include the **Crabby Pig** (✆ 301/724-7472), **Queen City Creamery** (✆ 301/777-2552, closed in winter), and **Roman's** (✆ 301/876-9211).

Cumberland After Dark

There's an active arts scene at three area theaters and nearby Frostburg State University's **Performing Arts Center** (www.frostburg.edu). Check with the **Allegany Arts Council,** 9 N. Centre St. (✆ **301/777-ARTS** [2787]; www.alleganyartscouncil.org), for a schedule of concerts and cultural events.

The **Cumberland Theatre,** 101 N. Johnson St., Cumberland (✆ **301/759-4990;** www.cumberlandtheatre.com), in a renovated church, presents a professional program of everything from musicals to Shakespeare. **New Embassy Theatre,** 49 Baltimore St., Cumberland (✆ **301/722-4692;** www.newembassy.org), a 1931 Art Deco movie theater, hosts classic films, live music, theater, and dance. Its restoration was featured on Bob Vila's *Restore America.* Call for a schedule and tickets. **Windsor Hall,** 37 Baltimore St., Cumberland (✆ **301/724-6800;** www.windsorhall.org), offers live music with blues, jazz, rock, and occasionally, stand-up comics.

DEEP CREEK LAKE ★★★ & GARRETT COUNTY ★

50 miles SW of Cumberland; 190 miles W of Baltimore; 120 miles SE of Pittsburgh, PA

Garrett County's mountain scenery has beckoned visitors for centuries. Native American hunters combed these hills a thousand years ago looking for game. In

Colonial days, this was the American frontier, populated mostly by Indians and trappers. Few settled here until the coming of the Baltimore & Ohio Railroad in the 1850s. Farmers, coal miners, and loggers were the first to arrive. During the Civil War, the railroad provided a needed supply link, and Garrett towns became the targets of Confederate attack. Once peace returned to the country, Garrett became a vacation destination. Three presidents—Grant, Cleveland, and Harrison—vacationed here.

You Can Get There . . . by Boat!

Skip the car and head to lakeside establishments by boat in summer. Businesses have added piers so visitors can get to the store, the movies, and even church by boat. The visitor center has a "Travel by Boat" map listing all the places with docks. Call ✆ **301/387-4386** for information.

When Deep Creek Lake was created in the 1920s and the Wisp Resort built in 1944, leisure travelers had even more reasons to make the trip to Garrett County. Deep Creek Lake is now the state's largest freshwater lake, nearly 12 miles in length, with 65 miles of shoreline occupied by private vacation homes and chalets. The northern end is where the action is—the commercial centers, the Wisp Resort, and the waterfront hotels and inns. Summer temperatures, averaging a comfortable 66°F (19°C), draw visitors escaping the heat and humidity of the big cities. In winter, Deep Creek Lake is Maryland's premier ski resort, with an average temperature of 28°F (2°C) and a yearly snowfall of more than 100 inches.

In recent years, Garrett County has become a four-season destination as well as *the* place for mid-Atlantic residents to buy a second home. It's centrally located between Pittsburgh, Baltimore, and Washington, and eastern Ohio cities, a 3- to 4-hour drive from each. Visitors can hike or bike the scenic trails; go skiing, snowtubing, or snowshoeing; take to the waters and try boating, fly-fishing, kayaking, or white-water rafting; and visit antiques and crafts stores. Or they can do nothing but sit back and enjoy the old-time charm that this region has long been known for.

Essentials

GETTING THERE From the east or west, take I-68 to Exit 14 and drive south on U.S. Route 219.

VISITOR INFORMATION The visitor center is at 15 Visitors Center Dr., McHenry, MD 21541—on U.S. Route 219, near the bottom of the Wisp Resort's ski runs. It's open daily from 9am to 5pm. Ask for a vacation guide, which contains a calendar of events and information on local history, restaurants, hotels, and shopping. For information, call ✆ **301/387-4386** or go to **www.visitdeepcreek.com**.

For **ski conditions,** call ✆ **301/387-4911** or visit **www.wispresort.com**.

GETTING AROUND Businesses in Deep Creek Lake sometimes have mailing addresses in McHenry or Oakland. Deep Creek Lake and McHenry are, for all intents and purposes, the same place, and you can count on those addresses to be on the lake or close by. Oakland, the county seat of Garrett County, is several miles south of Deep Creek Lake. Some businesses maintain mailing addresses there; others are actually just off the lake, outside the Deep Creek Lake/McHenry postal zone. Proximity to the lake resort areas is indicated in the listings in this section.

U.S. Route 219 runs beside the northern half of Deep Creek Lake and swings south toward Oakland. The Glendale Road Bridge crosses the middle of the lake and leads to Deep Creek Lake State Park (where you'll find the best public beach and a nature center). North of this bridge is where all the action is. South of this bridge, it's quieter and more remote. Most sailors sail their boats here; look for the weekend regattas.

SPECIAL EVENTS Garrett County celebrates fall's colors with a 5-day **Autumn Glory Festival** (✆ **301/387-4386**), usually held the second weekend in October. In early June, Scottish pride shows during the **McHenry Highland Festival** (✆ **800/313-0811**)—come for the sounds of bagpipe, harp, and fiddle, plus dance and athletic competitions, bluegrass music, crafts, and food. The **Garrett Lakes Arts Festival** (✆ **301/387-3082;** www.artsandentertainment.org), a year-round series of performances, includes a sampling of music and drama.

Where to Stay

VACATION RENTALS

The Deep Creek Lake area offers plenty of vacation properties—cabins, town homes, and mountain chalets—for rent by the week or in 2- and 3-day intervals. They come in all sizes, from a two-bedroom lakeside cottage or slopeside town house to eight-bedroom behemoths with extra everything (fireplaces, pools, hot tubs, decks, boat slips, and even ski-in/ski-outs are available). Many allow pets. They generally come with all the linens, appliances, and tools you'll need. Most homes are individually owned and rented through agencies. Reputable ones are **Railey Mountain Lake Vacations** (✆ **866/544-3223;** www.deepcreek.com), **Long & Foster Resort Vacation Rentals** (✆ **800/336-7303;** www.deepcreekresort.com), and **Coldwell Banker Deep Creek Realty** (✆ **800/769-5300;** www.deepcreekrealty.com).

HOTELS, MOTELS & B&BS

Carmel Cove Inn ★★ You'll notice this little B&B, with its steeples and clock tower, looks a bit like a monastery—and it was once a Carmelite priory. Tucked in a wooded area off Glendale Road, you'll feel the serenity of the place as you stroll its 2 acres down to the cove and dock. Inside, these are no monks' cells. The comfortable guest rooms offer a variety of amenities. Some units have hot tubs; others have private decks or fireplaces. Breakfast is delivered to premier and terrace rooms; appetizers are offered in the evening. The parlor has a striking stone fireplace and a billiards table.

105 Monastery Way, Swanton, MD 21561. www.carmelcoveinn.com. ✆ **301/387-0067.** 11 units. $175–$195 double. Rates include full breakfast and snacks. DISC, MC, V. No children 12 and under. **Amenities:** Billiards table; DVD library; fishing dock; snow- and watersports equipment; tennis court; Wi-Fi w/laptop available for guests' use. *In room:* A/C, flatscreen TV/DVD, hair dryer.

Haley Farm Bed & Breakfast ★★ If you dream of a country vacation, surrounded by orchards, wildflowers, and horses, this could be your spot. Set on 65 acres, Haley Farm offers country living in luxurious accommodations. Rooms range from spacious to cavernous; most are suites with fireplaces, Jacuzzis, and traditional furnishings. Three units have kitchenettes. More private (and huge) accommodations are available in the carriage house and barn. The lakeside cottage offers the amenities of an entire house with boat dock and hot tub. The inn offers spa treatments, such as massages and facials (reservations required). Ask about packages and group retreat programs.

16766 Garrett Hwy., Oakland, MD 21550. www.haleyfarm.com. ✆ **888/231-FARM** (3276) or 301/387-9050. Fax 301/387-9050. 10 units. $150–$245 double; $425 cottage. Rates include full breakfast.

2-night minimum stay required on weekends. DISC, MC, V. No children 12 and under. **Amenities:** Sauna; snow- and watersports equipment. *In room:* A/C, TV/VCR, free Wi-Fi.

Inn at Deep Creek ☺ New owners have brought this old 1961 hotel back to life. Those of us who've been coming to Deep Creek for, well, decades are delighted. The best rooms are at the A-frame points along the top level. These eight have fireplaces, cathedral ceilings, and kitchenettes. Most have views of the lake. (If a view is important, ask for Rooms 216 to 220—Room 220 has the best view.) The rest are similar but without the cathedral ceiling. Executive king rooms on the lower level have sleeper sofas and full kitchens. The deck on the lakeview side has chairs and picnic tables and snowdrifts in winter, making the opposite side more popular in winter.

6766 Garrett Hwy., Oakland, MD 21550. www.innatdeepcreek.com. ✆ **877/853-6932** or 301/387-5534. Fax 301/387-9050. 29 units. $89–$129 winter; $119–$199 summer. Rates include continental breakfast on weekends. 2-night minimum required Memorial Day through Autumn Glory Weekend. AE, DISC, MC, V. Pets welcome for a fee. **Amenities:** 7 boat slips; fire pits; gas and charcoal grills; outdoor pool; sun deck. *In room:* AC, flatscreen TV w/movies, hair dryer, MP3 docking station, free Wi-Fi.

Lake Pointe Inn ★★ Built in the 1800s, this mission-style inn has a variety of accommodations. Room sizes vary, from small to spacious enough for three. Expect dreamy beds, earth tones, and arts-and-crafts-style furnishings. All units have gas fireplaces, most have Jacuzzis, some have steam showers, and you can count on a view of the lake. A couple units, including the spacious McCann, have balconies. South-facing rooms offer the best views, but all have comfortable amenities. The blazing fire in the living room may keep you from heading outdoors—but the lake and the ski slopes, both within walking distance, are bound to beckon. If you're allergic to down pillows and comforters, alternatives are available. Reserve ahead for spa treatments.

174 Lake Pointe Dr., McHenry, MD 21541. www.deepcreekinns.com. ✆ **800/523-LAKE** (5253) or 301/387-0111. 10 units. $232–$292 double. Rates include full breakfast. 2-night minimum stay required on weekends. DISC, MC, V. No children 16 and under. **Amenities:** Bikes; massage room; sauna; steam room; tennis court; video library; watersports equipment. *In room:* A/C, TV/VCR, hair dryer, MP3 docking station, free Wi-Fi.

Oak & Apple B&B The O&A meets all the requirements of a cozy, country B&B: charming historic Victorian, comfortable rooms, scrumptious breakfast, good location in town but near the state parks, hosts that know and love their community and will steer you in the right direction for whatever you want to do. Rooms on the second and third floor are decorated with antique family photos and heirlooms—but furnishings are of homey stock rather than delicate showpieces. It's easy to relax here.

208 N. 2nd St., Oakland, MD 21550. www.oakandappleinn.com. ✆ **301/334-9265.** 4 units. $100–$130. Rates include full breakfast. No minimum stay required. Cash and check only. No children 12 and under or pets. **Amenities:** TV room; porch. *In room:* AC, hair dryer, free Wi-Fi.

Riverside Hotel Set on a quiet section of the Youghiogheny River, this 1889 inn offers eco-friendly lodgings and a hearty vegetarian dinner popular with hungry kayakers. Though thoroughly modern, the hotel contains some of the original hotel's beds. Room no. 5, really a suite with separate sitting room, has river views. Room no. 2, the only room that's air-conditioned, also has a fireplace. Dinner, served 4 to 8pm Friday to Monday, is open to the public. Other days, dinner is available by reservation for groups of six or more. Though breakfast isn't served here, the accurately named **Friendly Cup,** 641 Water St. (✆ **410/859-3608**), next door, opens at 7am

Friday through Tuesday May to September with fair-trade coffee, sweet treats, and free Wi-Fi.

609 Water St., Friendsville, MD 21531. www.riversidehotel.us. ✆ **301/746-5253.** 3 units. $69–$109 double. DC, DISC, MC, V. Closed Nov–Mar. **Amenities:** Free Wi-Fi. *In room:* Fridge, microwave.

Suites at Silver Tree Privately owned condominium units overlooking the lake are rented out in this hotel-like enterprise. Each unit is furnished according to the owners' tastes, with a variety of one-bedroom, one-bedroom-with-loft, and studio apartments. All have kitchenettes, gas fireplaces, and TVs. The majority of units have lakeview balconies and most will accommodate four people. Silver Tree takes advantage of its picturesque cove location with a gigantic deck and plenty of Adirondack chairs. Two massive stone fireplaces dominate the lobby overlooking the lake.

565 Glendale Rd., Oakland, MD 21550. www.suitesatsilvertree.com. ✆ **800/711-1719.** 51 units. $149–$319 in season; $109–$266 off-season. AE, DISC, MC, V. **Amenities:** Restaurant; lounge; fitness center; marina; sauna. *In room:* A/C, TV, hair dryer, kitchenette, Wi-Fi (fee).

Will O' the Wisp ☺ Variety makes this a place to consider. Room layouts vary from a one-room efficiency to a two-story, three-bedroom apartment. For example, unit no. 308 adjoins unit no. 408 for a two-story unit. All have decks or balconies with views of the swimming beach and lake. Units are individually owned with varying levels of furnishings, though everything is clean and well kept. When you call to book, ask how long ago the units were updated. If you want a clearer view of the lake in summer, ask for a unit ending in 01 to 05. There's maid service every day. An indoor pool, game room, and great restaurant—**Four Seasons**—make this a great spot.

20160 Garrett Hwy., Oakland, MD 21550. www.willothewisp.com. ✆ **888/590-7283** or 301/387-5506. 55 units. $145–$400 in season; $105–$235 off-season. AE, DC, DISC, MC, V. **Amenities:** Restaurant; lounge; beach; dock; fitness center; indoor pool; sauna. *In room:* A/C, TV, hair dryer, free Wi-Fi.

Wisp Resort ★★ ☺ You'll find accommodations overlooking the slopes and ski lockers just inside the door. Recently refurbished, Wisp offers two-room suites in the tower or standard rooms or efficiencies with kitchenettes in the Lodge; all have queen-size beds and sofa beds. Two rooms have fireplaces, and the tower suites have Murphy beds in the sitting room. A center for kids 3 to 14 offers half- and full-day skiing and snowboarding classes. The resort offers a variety of outdoor activities year-round, including mountain biking, boat tours, and off-road vehicles.

290 Marsh Hill Rd. (off U.S. Rte. 219, on north side of Deep Creek Lake), McHenry, MD 21541. www.wispresort.com. ✆ **800/462-9477** or 301/387-5581. Fax 301/387-4127. 169 units. $79–$229 double. AE, DC, DISC, MC, V. Pets accepted for a fee. **Amenities:** Restaurant; coffee shop/pizzeria; 2 lounges; warm-weather mountain biking; scenic chairlift rides; children's center; concierge; fitness center; 18-hole golf course; hot tub; paintball; indoor pool; skate park; ski shop; ski/snowboard program for children 3–14; spa; tennis court. *In room:* A/C, fridge, hair dryer, Wi-Fi (fee).

Where to Eat

Note: Garrett County liquor regulations prohibit alcohol sales on Sunday, except when served with a meal. No alcohol can be served before 1pm.

Canoe on the Run DELI This unpretentious sandwich shop serves gourmet sandwiches, coffee, and pastries; there are even a few vegetarian options, a rarity in these parts. The dining area is spare but quiet and cozy, with a gas fireplace. In warm weather, you can eat on the outdoor deck. Beer and wine are sold here.

2622 Deep Creek Dr., McHenry. ✆ **301/387-5933.** Reservations not accepted. Sandwiches and salads $5–$8. AE, DISC, MC, V. Mon–Fri 8am–2:30pm; Sat–Sun 8am–3:30pm.

The Deer Park Inn ★★ FRENCH For fine dining in a turn-of-the-20th-century atmosphere, head for this lovely 1889 inn, built deep in the country as a summer home for Baltimore architect Josiah Pennington. The restored 17-room "cottage" is listed on the National Register of Historic Places. Furnished with Victorian antiques, it is a romantic setting for candlelit French cuisine with an American flair. The menu recently included confit of duck with braised red cabbage, heavenly crab strudel, and filet with dried cherry sauce. The inn also offers three guest rooms upstairs ($145–$165 double).

65 Hotel Rd., Deer Park, MD 21550. ✆ **301/334-2308.** www.deerparkinn.com. Reservations recommended. Main courses $20–$29. DISC, MC, V. May–Nov Mon–Sat 5:30–9:30pm; Dec–Apr Thurs–Sat 5:30–9:30pm. Located 9 miles southeast of the Deep Creek Lake Bridge, off Sand Flat Rd. and Rte. 135; look for signs.

Four Seasons ★ AMERICAN Four Seasons is more formal than many of the other eateries in Deep Creek, with lots of polished wood, stone trim, and picture windows overlooking the lake. Dinner choices range from a simple filet mignon or hearty entree salad to salmon atop a pool of *beurre blanc* or tuna with berry Port sauce. Diners may also choose their own sauce, if they prefer. There's also a children's menu. Boat docking is available.

At Will O' the Wisp, 20160 Garrett Hwy. (U.S. Rte. 219), Oakland. ✆ **301/387-5503,** ext. 2201. Reservations recommended for dinner. Main courses $15–$39. AE, DISC, MC, V. Daily 5–9:30pm. Just south of the Deep Creek Lake Bridge.

Lakeside Creamery ICE CREAM If you see a crowd outside the Lakeside Creamery in the morning, you know it must be close to opening time. The homemade ice cream draws people by car, on foot, and even by boat. It offers at least 22 flavors. Try the handmade waffle cones, too.

20282 Garrett Hwy. (U.S. Rte. 219), Oakland, MD 21550. ✆ **301/387-2580.** www.lakesidecreamery.com. Reservations not accepted. Most items $2–$6. MC, V. Summer daily 11am–11pm; off-season Mon–Fri 11am–9pm, Sat–Sun 11am–10pm. Closed mid-Oct to May.

Mountain State Brewing Company ★ BREWPUB Two standouts here are beer and flatbread pizza. Brewed in nearby Thomas, West Virginia, the beers range from the lightest Cold Trail Ale to the deepest oatmeal stout. Flatbread pizza is baked in a wood-fired oven. Play a game or sit on the deck and watch the sun set over the mountains. Listen to the live music on summer weekends. Takeout pizza and beer (no beer sales on Sun, though) are available.

6690 Sang Run Rd., McHenry, MD 21541. ✆ **301/387-3360.** www.mountainstatebrewing.com. Reservations recommended. Main courses $6–$21. DISC, MC, V. Mon–Thurs 11am–10pm; Fri–Sat 11am–11pm; Sun noon–10pm.

Uno Chicago Grill ☺ PIZZA Everybody comes here. It's a family place, with a playground and wide lawn by the lake so the kids can wear themselves out while waiting for a table. (And there *can* be a wait, especially on weekends.) A central fireplace dominates the dining room, covered outside seating overlooks the lake, and a deck at the **Honi-Honi Bar** has entertainment Friday and Saturday evenings. The food is the usual for Uno's: pizza, pastas, sandwiches, soups, salads, and a children's menu. Bake-it-yourself pizzas are available, too.

19746 Garrett Hwy., Oakland, MD 21550. ✆ **301/387-4866.** www.deepcreekuno.com. Reservations not accepted. Main courses $9–$20. AE, DC, DISC, MC, V. Mon–Sat 11am–midnight (Mon–Thurs until 11pm in winter); Sun 11am–11pm.

Wendy's Towne Restaurant CAFE Wendy took over this Oakland restaurant in the midst of a recession after waitressing for 27 years. She collected recipes from friends and family and turned a rundown space into a charming cafe. Wendy serves good home cooking for breakfast, lunch, and dinner in a congenial atmosphere. Try Logan's chocolate chip pancakes, or maybe Collin's fried pickles. Sandwiches at lunch, including old-time favorites such as liver and onions and honey-dipped chicken, keep people coming back. Breakfast, including a local favorite, buckwheat cakes, is served all day. Wi-Fi is available, too.

230 E. Alder St., Oakland, MD 21550. © **301/334-3300.** Reservations not accepted. Main courses $3–$15. DISC, MC, V. Mon–Sat 6am–8pm (until 11pm in winter); Sun 7am–2pm.

Outdoor Activities

BOATING You can rent just about any kind of powerboat, from a ski boat to a pontoon boat. Paddleboats, canoes, and fishing boats are also available at marinas around the lake. A water-ski boat costs about $300 a day, fishing boats are about $50 for a half-day to $75 a day, and a pontoon boat runs around $300 a day. Jet skis can be rented by the half-hour for about $50 to $100. Some of the leading firms along U.S. Route 219 at Deep Creek Lake are **Aquatic Center** (© 301/387-8233), **Bill's Outdoor Center** (© 301/387-3474), **Bill's Marine Service** (© 301/387-5536), **Crystal Waters** (© 301/387-5515), and **Deep Creek Marina** (© 301/387-0732).

If you don't want to rent a boat, **Wisp Resort** (© **301/387-4911**) offers pontoon and kayak tours of the lake and Savage River Reservoir kayak tours.

If you want to sail, you'll have to bring your own boat, as none are available for rent. Or you can learn to sail at **Deep Creek Sailing School** (© **301/387-4497;** www.deepcreeksailingschool.com). Courses run 5 days and cost $250 to $275. Private lessons may also be arranged.

CAMPING **Deep Creek Lake State Park** (© **301/387-5563**) offers 112 improved campsites (26 with electric hookups) plus a yurt, Adirondack-style cabin, and two minicamper cabins. Facilities include bathhouses with showers. Rentals are $25 to $65 a night. Reservations are recommended; call © **888/432-2267.** Pets are permitted in designated loops. See the Garrett County section of "The Great Outdoors in Western Maryland," earlier in this chapter, for other camping options.

CROSS-COUNTRY SKIING Cross-country skiing is available at **Herrington Manor State Park** (© 301/334-9180) and **New Germany State Park** (© 301/895-5453), both described in "The Great Outdoors in Western Maryland," earlier in this chapter. **Deep Creek Outfitters** (© 301/387-2200), **Allegany Expeditions** (© 800/819-5170), and **High Mountain Sports** (© 301/387-4199; www.highmountainsports.com) rent cross-country skis. **All Earth Eco-Tours** (© 301/746-4083) offers lessons at Herrington Manor.

DOG-SLEDDING **Husky Power Dogsledding** (© **301/746-7200;** www.huskypowerdogsledding.com) offers dog-sledding in area parks. The weather must be cool enough for the dogs (50°F/10°C or lower). If there's no snow, sleds on wheels are available. Reservations are required. They even have kennel visits ($100 for groups of up to five) if you want to get to know one of these Siberian or Alaskan beauties. It also offers dog-sled rides and learn-to-mush tours for $200 to $245.

DOWNHILL SKIING & SNOWBOARDING Deep Creek Lake is the home of Maryland's only ski area. With an elevation of 3,115 feet and a vertical drop of 700 feet, the **Wisp Resort** ★★, 296 Marsh Hill Rd., McHenry (© **301/387-4911;**

White-Water Rafting Without Fear

A white-water course at the top of Marsh Hill enables rafting wannabes the chance to get their feet wet before venturing over to the Yough. **Adventure Sports Center International** (© **301/387-3250;** www.adventuresportscenter.com) offers 2-hour sessions with lessons for beginners. Or bring your own raft or kayak. The course can be changed to accommodate the rafters' abilities, from easy for first-timers to Class IV for a white-knuckle thrill. ASCI will host the ICF Canoe Slalom World Championships in September 2014.

www.skiwisp.com), offers 32 ski runs and trails. Beginners can ski or ride on several of the long, scenic trails, while black-diamond skiers can head for the face, which is straight down the front of the mountain with lots of moguls. Trails through the forest can be fast enough for intermediates and experts alike. Lift tickets range from $39 on weekdays to $57 on weekends, with reduced rates for night skiing, 2-day tickets, early- or late-season skiing, and children. Kids 6 and under ski free. The ski season runs from early December (sometimes Thanksgiving weekend) to March. Wisp also operates a ski school for kids 3 to 14, child-care facility, rental service, and ski shop.

ECO-TOURS Deep Creek Lake State Park's **Discovery Center** (© **301/387-7067**) houses an exhibit on local geology, fauna, and flora. It's also the starting point for fun (and educational) outdoor adventures. Interpretive programs, campfires, hikes, and stargazing are among the possibilities throughout the year. Activity schedules are available here and at the visitor center on U.S. Route 219. It's open daily in summer 10am to 5pm, and other times 10am to 4pm Friday to Sunday.

All Earth Eco Tours (© **800/446-7554** or 301/746-4083; www.alleartheco tours.com) offers adventure tours, from Savage Reservoir kayaking and photography workshops to cross-country skiing and hikes. Toddler Tuesdays at the Discovery Center are a big draw.

FISHING Deep Creek Lake is home to about 22 species of fish, including yellow perch, bass, bluegill, catfish, crappie, chain pickerel, northern pike, walleye, and trout. Four world-class rivers in the area make this fly-fishing heaven. Come for the cutthroat, rainbow, brown, and brook (wild) trout. Fishing is best April through June, but ice fishing in January and February is becoming popular. The state of Maryland requires a fishing license, which can be bought at most tackle shops.

The Casselman, North Branch of the Potomac, and Yough rivers are good trout areas, too, of course. The Casselman is home to brook and brown, the North Branch has rainbow, and the Yough has rainbow and brown. A trout stamp is required if you intend to remove trout from nontidal waters.

Try **Bill's Outdoor Center** (© **301/387-3474**), **Deep Creek Outfitters** (© **301/387-2200**), or **Deep Creek Marina** (© **301/387-0732**) for tours, equipment, and boat rentals. The **Orvis** fly-fishing shop at Wisp (© **301/387-4911**) offers tours, too.

GOLF The **Golf Club at Wisp,** Wisp Resort Golf Course, 296 Marsh Hill Rd., McHenry (© **301/387-4911;** www.wispresort.com), has an 18-hole, par-72 championship facility built beside (and on) the ski slopes. It's open daily from April to mid-October. Fees for 18 holes are $40 to $65. A pro shop and driving range are on the grounds. The **Oakland Golf Club,** 433 N. Bradley Lane, Oakland

(✆ **301/334-3883;** www.golfatoakland.com), has an 18-hole, par-71 championship course and driving range, open April through October. Fees range from $25 to $54.

HIKING Five trails ranging from easy to challenging are in **Deep Creek Lake State Park,** south of McHenry on State Park Road (✆ **301/387-5563**). The most scenic is Indian Turnip Trail, which is approximately 2.5 miles and winds along Meadow Mountain and across the ridge top. Entry fee is $2 per vehicle; the park is open daily from 8am until sunset in summer, until 4pm in winter. **Wisp Resort** (✆ **301/387-4911**) offers scenic chairlift rides after the snow melts for a mountain-top view and a downhill hike. See the Garrett County section of "The Great Outdoors in Western Maryland," earlier in this chapter, for other hiking options.

ICE-SKATING **Wisp Resort** (✆ **301/387-4911**) opens its rink daily from 10am to 4pm November to March (depending on weather) with ice-skate rentals and lessons. A 90-minute session costs $10, $12 with a skate rental.

MOUNTAIN COASTER Downhill thrills without snow! **Wisp Resort** (✆ **301/387-4911**) has erected this roller-coaster-style ride on its slopes. Riders fly down the 5,000-foot track at a speed they are comfortable with—these coasters for one or two people have brakes. Take it slow and the ride lasts about 5 minutes. Forgo the brakes and you'll be down in a minute and a half. It's $10 a ride.

MOUNTAIN TOURS There are other ways to get around Marsh Mountain. How about a Segway tour, chairlift ride, or mountain buggy tour? (Go with the Segway for a less strenuous but challenging adventure.) Prefer to fly? The Flying Squirrel Canopy Tour will have you soaring through the trees on zip lines up to 400 feet above the slope. All of these are at **Wisp Resort** (✆ **301/387-4911**).

SLEIGH RIDES **Pleasant Valley Dream Rides** (✆ **301/334-1688;** www.pleasantvalleydreamrides.com) offers horse-drawn sleigh and carriage rides on the hour, from 10am to 10pm; $14 for adults and $10 children 3 to 10.

SNOW TUBING **Wisp Resort** offers the Bear Claw Snow Tubing Park (✆ **301/387-4911**), a fast dash down a 750-foot groomed run on a big inflatable tube and a tow back to the top. Two-hour sessions cost $15 to $29. Reservations are a must.

SWIMMING **Deep Creek Lake State Park** (✆ **301/387-5563**) features an 800-foot guarded sandy beach with bathhouses and lockers nearby. It's one of the only public places for swimming. Entry fees to the park are $3 to $4 a person in season. Off-season fees are $3 to $4 per vehicle, with free admission for seniors and children in restraint seats. The park is open from 8am until sunset. Lifeguards are on duty from Memorial Day to Labor Day, Thursday through Sunday from 10am to 6pm.

Other Attractions in Garrett County

Church of the Presidents Presidents Grant, Harrison, and Cleveland attended services here, as did Chester Arthur (before he took office). Built in 1868 as a Presbyterian church, it's made of the same sandstone used for B&O railroad bridges.

St. Matthew's Episcopal Church, 126 E. Liberty St., Oakland. ✆ **301/334-2510.** Sun services at 8 and 10:45am.

Deep Creek Cellars Paul Roberts and Nadine Grabania built this little winery in their home in the northwest corner of Maryland. It produces 14,000 bottles of some of Maryland's best wine every year, and the owners take great pride in their

Farm Tours

If you want your kids to see a real farm, stop by the Deep Creek visitor center for the brochure called *Visit Our Working Farms, Share Our Heritage,* which lists farms that welcome visitors.

At **Cove-Run Farms,** 596 Griffith Rd., Accident (✆ **301/746-6111**), there's a corn maze built into 10 acres—Maryland's largest. The corn is tall and the paths are tricky, but it's fun to hear the kids squeal as they make their way through. It's open mid-August through October, Friday from noon to 10pm, Saturday from noon to 9pm, and Sunday from 2 to 6pm.

Duntrussen Holstein Farms, 1689 Pleasant Valley Road, Oakland (✆ **301/334-1688**), offers farm tours by reservation. You can even come for milking at 4am or 4pm.

Another pleasant way to appreciate the farming community is to take the **Barn Quilt driving tour.** A dozen or so farmers have mounted colorful oversized quilt squares to their barns and the tour through the countryside is easy to follow using the map and directions available online. Cellphone commentary is also available. Go to www.garrettbarnquilts.com, or call ✆ **877/577-BARN** (2276).

work. (You can find their wines throughout Maryland and Washington, DC.) Wander through the vineyard. At harvest time, you can see the juice as it's pressed from the fruit. Best of all, try the final product in the tasting room. Even the trip up Route 42 is scenic.

177 Frazee Ridge Rd., Friendsville, MD 21531. ✆ **301/746-4349.** www.deepcreekcellars.com. Tasting room Apr 20–Nov 20 Wed–Sat 11am–6pm; call ahead for winter and holiday hours.

Garrett County Historical Society Museum This quaint museum staffed by friendly volunteers has a pioneer cabin and rooms focusing on local history (the B&O Railroad, military life, and so on). There's an amazing array of local artifacts, including those of the famous hunter Meshach Browning.

107 S. 2nd St., Oakland, MD 21550. ✆ **301/334-3226.** www.garrettcountymuseums.com/historicalmuseum.html. Free admission; donations accepted. May–Dec Mon–Sat 11am–4pm; Jan–Apr Thurs–Sat 11am–4pm.

Garrett County Museum of Transportation ★ An antique ski-mobile, the Deer Park Hotel's omnibus from the 1870s, fire trucks, and plenty of automobiles make this a welcome addition to Oakland. Two floors of exhibits also include a locally produced Flying Scot sailboat, sleigh, and Amish buggy. The facade pays tribute to local businesses in a creative way. The museum is across the street from the Queen Anne–style train station.

117 E. Liberty St., Oakland, MD 21550. ✆ **301/334-2569.** www.garrettcountymuseums.com/transportationmuseum.html. Free admission; donations accepted. May 1–Dec 31 Mon–Sat 10am–3pm; Jan–Apr Fri–Sat 10am–3pm.

Oakland Train Station The restored Queen Anne–style station is striking, with its bell-shaped turret and stained glass. Built in 1884 for the growing resort clientele, it is closed to the public while it awaits necessary upgrades to reopen as a museum. It's still pretty enough to take a peek while you're visiting town. Group tours are available by appointment (there's nothing inside, but people still like to visit).

117 E. Liberty St., Oakland, MD 21550. ✆ **301/334-2569.** Free admission.

Our Town Theatre Throughout the year, this community theater puts on a variety of shows, a little Neil Simon or Steve Martin, a bit of Shakespeare and Lillian Hellman. The shows are kid-friendly but there are programs just for children, too. Upcoming productions are listed online.

121 E. Center St., Oakland, MD 21550. ✆ **301/334-5640.** www.ourtowntheatre.org. Tickets $8–$10.

Simon Pearce ★ Cross the catwalk over the furnaces and workbenches of glass artisans as they create the crystal-clear pieces for which Simon Pearce is famous. Most artisans work until 3pm, but there's usually at least one team working until 5pm and on weekends. The showroom is filled with the elegant, modern wares created here and at the other Simon Pearce factories around the country.

265 Glass Dr., Mountain Lake Park, MD 21550. ✆ **301/334-5277.** www.simonpearce.com. Daily 10am–5pm. Located south of Deep Creek Lake and Oakland: Take Rte. 219 south to Rte. 135; turn left and then turn right on Glass Dr.; the factory is on the left.

Shopping

Around the lake you'll find a few shops for clothing and souvenirs. New on the scene is **Deep Creek Sweets,** 1550 Deep Creek Dr., at the fort in McHenry (✆ **301/387-7979;** www.deepcreeksweets.com), stocked with locally made chocolates and fudge.

A few places in outlying areas of Deep Creek Lake are worth a stop. **Schoolhouse Earth,** 1224 Friendsville Rd., north of the lake off Route 42 (✆ **301/746-8603;** www.schoolhouseearth.com), specializes in country accessories, gourmet food, jewelry, and home and garden decor. It's open daily from 10am to 6pm.

In Oakland, the **Book Mark'et & Antique Mezzanine,** 111 S. Second St. (✆ **301/334-8778;** www.thebookmkt.com), has children's books, fiction, history, and biography, as well as antiques and collectibles. It's open Monday through Saturday from 9:30am to 5:30 or 6pm, Sunday from 11am to 4pm. **Englander's,** 205 E. Alder St. (✆ **301/553-0000**), is filled with antiques but it's okay to stop in for a milkshake or meal at **Dottie's Fountain & Grill** in the back. The shop and grill open at 8:30am every day. **Rudy's,** 115 S. Second St. (✆ **301/334-2654**), has the clothes you wished you packed.

Located 8 miles south of Oakland on U.S. Route 219, just past the intersection of U.S. Route 50, is the 1,200-square-foot **Red House School Antiques** (✆ **301/334-2800;** www.redhouseschoolantiques.com). It carries antiques and crafts. It's open Monday through Saturday from 10am to 5pm, Sunday from 11am to 5pm in season. Closed Monday to Wednesday in spring.

MARYLAND & DELAWARE'S ATLANTIC BEACHES

10

A trip to the beach, or "downy ocean" in local parlance, is the favorite vacation for many Marylanders and Delawareans. There are several communities to visit and enjoy: Bethany's vacationers can't keep away from Rehoboth's shops and restaurants or Ocean City's amusements. Anglers head to Ocean City and Lewes for the charter boats. The beaches of Delaware Seashore State Park are the quietest. If you want to party, head for Delaware's Dewey Beach or the boardwalk of Ocean City, Maryland.

Delaware beaches are different from Maryland's. For one thing, all Maryland beaches are public, whereas Delaware has private beaches. In this chapter, I give you a snapshot of each, starting at the north end of Delaware and heading south to Maryland.

THE BEACHES IN BRIEF

Delaware Beaches

Stretched along 25 miles of ocean and bay shoreline, Delaware's five beach towns—Lewes, Rehoboth Beach, Dewey Beach, Bethany Beach, and Fenwick Island—have their own personalities and ambience.

For information on dinner specials, coupons, and local news, grab one of the free publications piled up in restaurants and hotels. Look for ***The Wave, Sunny Day,*** and ***Southern Delaware Explorer.***

LEWES With such a quaint little town to explore, you might forget there's a beach on the other side of the canal. Metered parking at the beach is available. There are also bathhouses and lifeguards in season. The water is calm and the sand white. The best beach is at **Cape Henlopen State Park** (✆ **302/645-8983;** www.destateparks.com/park/cape%2Dhenlopen), 1 mile east of Lewes. Admission is $8 per out-of-state car—and worth it. The beaches are never wall-to-wall with bodies as they can be in Rehoboth or Ocean City. Even the water at the confluence of Delaware Bay and the ocean seems calmer. You can take a walk or ride a bike on a nature trail here and look for shorebirds.

REHOBOTH & DEWEY Swimming at Rehoboth's and Dewey's wide sandy beaches is one of the area's top activities. All the beaches have public access and are guarded, but there are no bathhouses.

At Rehoboth, look for the NO SWIMMING signs between Brooklyn Avenue and Laurel Street that warn against swimming near two sunken ships. Though the ships have been cut down to the waterline, it's best to avoid this spot. ***Tip:*** Rehoboth offers complimentary "Beach Wheels," wheelchairs for beach use, at the boardwalk and Maryland Avenue or Laurel Street. They're available first-come/first-served. Call **© 302/227-2400** for details. Two strips of beach draw the LGBT crowd. Poodle Beach south of the boardwalk draws gay men, while lesbian sunseekers prefer North Shores Beach.

Just south of Dewey is perhaps Delaware's finest, quietest beach. A narrow strip of land between the ocean and Rehoboth and Indian River bays, **Delaware Seashore State Park ★** (**© 302/227-2800;** www.destateparks.com/park/delaware-seashore) offers ocean waves and quiet bay waters. Besides 6 miles of beach—two of them guarded from 9am to 5pm in summer—there's a 310-slip full-service marina and boat ramp, plus 500 sites for RVs and campers. Part of the beach is set aside for surfing. Unguarded beach is available for surf fishing. With a yearly license, you can drive onto the beach. With a day pass, you can walk on. Concessions are available at the guarded beaches. Admission is $4 for Delaware cars, $8 for out-of-state vehicles. ***Note:*** Construction of the Indian River Inlet Bridge was due to be completed by press time; if it is delayed, expect travel lane closures and some detours. For updates, see **www.deldot.gov/information/projects/indian_river_bridge/whn.shtml**.

BETHANY & FENWICK Bethany's public beach is small and can be very crowded. Visitors staying in oceanside houses and condos have their own private beaches, in most cases, and don't have to worry about crowds as much. You'll hear about dolphin sightings all around the Delaware beaches, but they're quite common here. The beach in front of the boardwalk is free and open to the public. It is guarded from Memorial Day weekend to Labor Day, Monday through Friday from 10am to 5pm, weekends and holidays from 9:30am to 5:30pm. There are large, clean bathhouses. **Bethany Resort Rental** (**© 800/321-1592** or 302/539-6244) operates a rental concession on the beach, with umbrellas, surf mats, boogie boards, chairs, and more.

Fenwick, on the border with Maryland, has more public beaches than Bethany. It's slightly more relaxed than Ocean City, but not as quiet as Bethany. Its claim to fame is the very narrow but long **Fenwick Island State Park** (**© 302/227-2800**), where you can watch the sun rise over the ocean and later watch the sun set over Assawoman Bay. The 3-mile beach offers public space for swimming, sunbathing, surf fishing, and surfing. Guards watch the beach daily 9am to 5pm in season. Facilities include showers, changing rooms, a first-aid room, lifeguards, a gift shop, picnic tables, nonmotorized boat rentals, and refreshments. Admission is $4 for Delaware cars, $8 for out-of-state cars. Entry is free weekdays in spring and fall and all week in winter. Hours are 8am to sunset year-round.

Maryland Beaches

Ocean City has the most public beaches—and some of the most crowded. The beach near the southern tip of O.C. is the widest and usually least crowded; a huge parking lot makes this convenient for day-trippers. The beach along the boardwalk gets quite narrow in a few places. Still, for those who love the boardwalk and its shops and restaurants, this is the best beach. In northern Ocean City, land of high-rise

Delaware Beaches

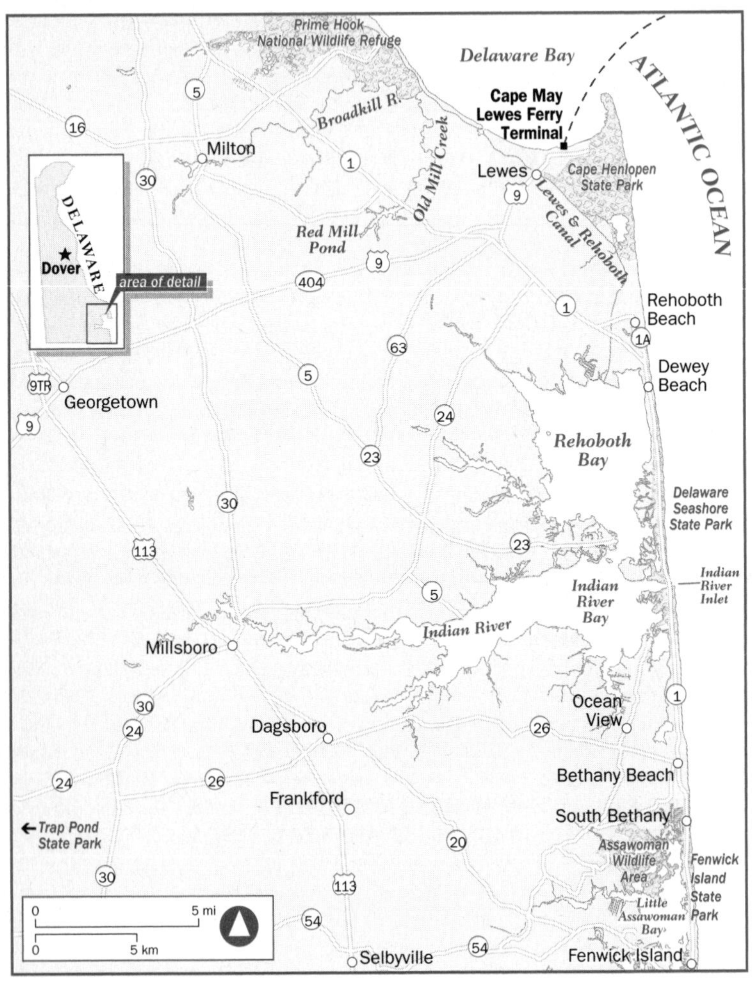

condos, the beach widens. Crowds depend on the size of the building, but it's easy to find a place for your blanket.

The inlet at Ocean City's southern end divides touristy O.C. from the wild and pristine beaches of **Assateague Island,** which doesn't have a single restaurant, gas station, or hotel. Although you can see it across the inlet from Ocean City, it's about an 11-mile drive to the visitor center and parking lots. Most of the 30-mile strip of barrier island is not open to vehicles. It's home to an enormous number of shorebirds, sika deer, and the wild ponies made famous by Marguerite Henry's *Misty of Chincoteague* books. The visitor center and campgrounds are the only buildings here.

The entire 10-mile stretch of Ocean City beach is open to the public free of charge. Lifeguards are on duty from 10am to 5:30pm all summer and weekends in

September. Beach chairs, umbrellas, and boogie boards can be rented by the day or week. Attendants will position your umbrella and, if you rent for the week, have your umbrella and chairs ready when you arrive each day. They usually accept cash only.

Wicomico Street Bathhouse is at Wicomico and Philadelphia streets, near the southern end of O.C. It's privately operated and charges a fee. Find public restrooms along the boardwalk at Worcester, Caroline, 9th, and 27th streets.

The beach at the inlet at the southern end of the island is set aside for surfers on weekdays in summer. Look for the yellow stands that mark the limits. Elsewhere in Ocean City, surfing beaches rotate among designated "surf beaches" at the north and south end of O.C. You can check where surfing is permitted at **www.oceancitysurfreport.com**.

Surf fishing is not permitted within 50 yards of swimmers between 9am and 6pm, so the big poles usually come out in the evening or early morning. When the swimmers go home in the fall, the surf fishermen take over.

LEWES, DE

86 miles SE of Wilmington; 34 miles N of Ocean City; 107 miles SE of Baltimore; 121 miles E of Washington, DC

Delaware's northernmost and oldest beach resort, Lewes (pronounced *Loo*-is) is also its oldest town, founded in 1681 as a Dutch whaling station named Zwaanendael. The community maintains strong ties to its Dutch heritage, which you can learn about at the Zwaanendael Museum, and to the sea—as a beach resort, a marina, and port for fishing fleets. The town, which was attacked during the War of 1812 will mark the bicentennial with exhibitions, reenactments, and other events from 2012 through 2014. See p. 236.

Though Lewes is where the Delaware Bay meets the Atlantic Ocean, the town has grown up west of the Lewes-Rehoboth Canal, turning away from the water. Here you'll find the historic sites, small shops, restaurants, and inns. The result is a quaint, friendly little town that also happens to have a beach.

Beach fans must take an easy walk across the Savannah Road Bridge to the water. Parking is available in a paid lot. And lots of Lewes vacationers head to nearby Cape Henlopen State Park for the wide, sandy beaches there.

Lewes seems more like a Cape Cod resort than a Delmarva beach resort. With its small-town atmosphere and proximity to beaches, it's a good choice for anybody tired of the bustle of the other resorts.

Essentials

GETTING HERE **By Car** From points north, take routes 113 and 13 to Route 1 and then to Route 9 (Savannah Rd.) into town. From the south, take Route 113 to Georgetown, and then take Route 9 east to Lewes. From Ocean City or Rehoboth, take Route 1 to Route 9. From the west, take Route 50 across the Bay Bridge to Route 404 east, and then to Route 9.

BY FERRY Many visitors from the north arrive via the **Cape May–Lewes Ferry,** an 80-minute Delaware Bay minicruise that connects southern New Jersey to mid-Delaware and saves considerable driving for north- or southbound passengers along the Atlantic coast. In operation since 1964, this ferry service maintains five vessels, each holding up to 800 passengers and 100 cars. Departures are daily year-round, with almost hourly service in the summer from 7:30am to 9pm. Rates for passengers (and passengers with bikes) are $8 one-way off season, $10 in high season; the charge for vehicles ranges from $26 to $44, with reduced prices for motorcycles. Reservations are required for vehicles. In New Jersey, the **Cape May Terminal** is at the end of the Garden State Parkway. The **Lewes Terminal** is by the Cape Henlopen State Park entrance, about a mile from the center of town. For reservations and information, call ✆ **800/64-FERRY** (643-3779) or see **www.cmlf.com**. Shuttle service is available to Cape May and Lewes every day in summer and weekends in spring and fall for an extra $4, under 6 free.

BY PLANE Visitors arriving by plane should fly into the **Salisbury–Ocean City–Wicomico Regional Airport.** See p. 261 for details.

VISITOR INFORMATION Contact the **Lewes Chamber of Commerce and Visitors Bureau** (✆ **877/465-3937** or 302/645-8073; www.leweschamber.com). The chamber's office is in the Fisher-Martin House at 120 Kings Hwy., next to the Zwaanendael Museum. It's open year-round, Monday through Friday from 10am to 4pm. In summer, it's also open Saturday from 9am to 3pm and Sunday from 10am to 2pm. Restrooms are located in the park behind the house. You can also get a visitors' guide from the **Southern Delaware Tourism Office** (✆ **800/357-1818;** www.visitsoutherndelaware.com).

GETTING AROUND The **Seaport Taxi of Lewes,** 306 Savannah Rd. (✆ **302/645-6800**), operates a taxi service from the terminal to downtown, as well as local service. Ferry passengers can call from the ferry terminal.

SPECIAL EVENTS The first weekend in October brings the Boast the Coast/Coast Day weekend. **Boast the Coast,** sponsored by the Lewes Chamber of Commerce, celebrates the town's nautical history. The highlight is the boat parade in the canal. **Coast Day** (✆ **302/831-8083;** www.decoastday.org) is sponsored by and held at the University of Delaware College of Marine Studies in Lewes. The fair includes lectures, ship tours, aquariums, and a crab-cake cook-off. The events are free except for parking.

The **Great Delaware Kite Festival** (✆ **302/645-8073**) is held at Cape Henlopen State Park on Good Friday.

The **World Championship Punkin Chunkin** ★ (✆ **302/684-8196;** www.punkinchunkin.com), held the first weekend in November, is held in a field near Bridgeville, off Route 404. Directions are on the website. Contestants enter their own mechanical contraptions (no explosives allowed) to see which can hurl a pumpkin the farthest—and that can be 4,000 feet or more. In addition, there are food and crafts vendors, live bands, and entertainment for kids. RV and tent camping is allowed. It's silly, rowdy, and a lot of fun—and up to 35,000 people attend. Admission is $10.

Where to Stay

Lodging options in Lewes range from handsome inns to traditional motels. Prices range from moderate to expensive in summer—and can be a bargain in the off season. Some places require minimum stays. Reservations are mandatory in summer months and recommended at other times. Parking is at a premium; metered parking on the street may be necessary at some local inns.

For vacation rentals, call a real-estate agent. One reputable company is **Jack Lingo,** 1240 Kings Hwy. (✆ **800/331-4241** or 302/645-2207; www.jacklingo.com). Most rentals are houses or town houses in Lewes, some with views of or frontage on Delaware Bay.

MODERATE

The Blue Water House ★★ Stay at this brightly colored inn, tucked between town and beach, closer to the beach, though a bit off the beaten track. Its charm lies in its feeling of seclusion and its beautiful rooms. Accommodations are spacious, decorated with a sense of island fun, and look out on a balcony hung with hammocks. The sitting room has a flatscreen TV and game tables, while a lookout provides panoramic views and a place to relax.

407 E. Market St. (across the canal on the bay side of town), Lewes, DE 19958. www.lewes-beach.com. ✆ **800/493-2080** for reservations, or 302/645-7832 for information. 9 units. $140–$180 double. Rates include hot buffet breakfast. 2- or 3-night minimum stay required in high season, on spring and fall weekends, and on holidays. AE, MC, V. Free parking. No children. **Amenities:** Free use of bikes, beach chairs, towels, and umbrellas; movie library; watersports equipment rentals. *In room:* A/C, TV/VCR, fridge, hair dryer, free Wi-Fi.

Hotel Blue ★★ The Blue is all about fun for adults only. The bathroom basins glow with a blue light. Every room has a fireplace and balcony. There are pillows that look like beach balls, a rooftop pool with a fireplace and seating area off to the side, and tower suite rooms with the queen bed tucked into a curved wall of windows. And the style is colorful and contemporary. The hotel is a short walk to the beach or the historic district and rooms look over the canal's marinas or the wetlands behind it. If you get a ground-level room, your balcony will look over a koi pond.

110 Anglers Rd., Lewes, DE 19958. www.hotelblue.info. ✆ **800/935-1145** or 302/645-4880. 16 units. $150–$320 double. Minimum stays on weekends required. AE, MC, V. Free parking. Children 17 and under are not allowed. **Amenities:** Rooftop deck w/fireplace; fitness room; fresh fruit and coffee all day in lobby; pool. *In room:* A/C, flatscreen TV, fridge, hair dryer, microwave, robes, free Wi-Fi.

Hotel Rodney ★ Modern styling covers the elegant old bones of this 1926 hotel in the historic district. Now a boutique-style hotel, it boasts antique furnishings with modern headboards, custom fabrics, and flatscreen TVs. The sleek lobby is comfortable and hints at the decor throughout. Corner rooms with bright windows are a delight. Master suites have extra room and a pullout couch. Computers and bikes are available. A fitness center is on the lower level next to a cozy lounge.

142 2nd St. (at Market St.), Lewes, DE 19958. www.hotelrodneydelaware.com. ✆ **800/824-8754** or 302/645-6466. 23 units. $90–$250 double; $130–$300 suite. Weekly rates available. 2-night minimum stay required on weekends in high season. AE, DISC, MC, V. Pets welcome. **Amenities:** Bikes; fitness room; free Wi-Fi in lobby. *In room:* A/C, TV, fridge (in suites), hair dryer, MP3 docking station, wet bar (in suites).

The Inn at Canal Square ★ This four-story property overlooking the canal has a casual country-inn atmosphere with the amenities of a full-service hotel. Its traditionally styled rooms come in every size, from a standard unit with two queen-size beds to a full apartment. Most have views of the canal, though two parlor suites overlook Lewes. Fourth-floor rooms have extra comforts, like honor bars, CD players, robes, and oversize balconies. The Commodore Suite and Admiral's Quarters come with kitchen, fireplace, and sun deck. A massage studio is available; make an appointment at the front desk.

122 Market St., Lewes, DE 19958. www.theinnatcanalsquare.com. ✆ **888/644-1911** or 302/644-3377. 25 units. $125–$310 double; $525–$625 cottage suite. Rates include European-style breakfast. Children 4 and under stay free in parent's room. Seasonal getaway packages. AE, MC, V. Free parking. Pets welcome in courtyard room for a fee. **Amenities:** Fitness center. *In room:* A/C, TV, hair dryer, free Wi-Fi.

FROM farm TO ICE-CREAM CONE

Local farms have been selling their corn, tomatoes, and cantaloupes along the roads to the beach for years, but now the dairy farms are getting into the act.

Near Lewes, stop by **Hopkins Farm Creamery,** 18186 Dairy Farm Rd. (on Rte. 9), Lewes, DE 19958 (✆ **302/645-7163;** www.hopkinsfarmcreamery.com), for ice cream—you can thank the cow who gave the milk. She "works" on the premises.

Near Ocean City, **Chesapeake Bay Farms,** 8905 Logtown Rd. (on Rte. 50), Berlin MD 21811 (✆ **410/629-1997;** www.chesapeakebaycheese.com), sells ice cream, cheese, and butter made from their own cows' milk. Local seafood also available.

The John Penrose Virden House ★ This 1888 ship's pilot's house has the best location of the B&Bs in Lewes, in the heart of the business district. With a mix of antique and modern furnishings, it's gracious and comfortable. Breakfast is served in the dining room, where an old ship's bar serves as a buffet, and on the patio in summer. In winter, dining by the fireplace of the sitting room is cozy. Two well-appointed guest rooms offer views of the town or the canal. A cottage off the garden offers privacy.

217 2nd St., Lewes, DE 19958. www.virdenhouse.com. ✆ **302/644-0217** or 644-4401. 3 units. $150–$240 double. Rates include full breakfast and afternoon refreshments. No credit cards. Free parking. Children are not accepted. **Amenities:** Beach equipment; bikes; garden. *In room:* A/C, TV, fridge, free Wi-Fi.

INEXPENSIVE

Beacon Motel This motel near Fisherman's Wharf, opened in 1989, occupies the top two floors of a three-story property, with the ground level devoted to shops and a reception area. Guests can spread out in the large rooms, which feature bamboo furnishings; suites have trundle twin beds.

514 E. Savannah Rd. (P.O. Box 609), Lewes, DE 19958. www.beaconmotel.com. ✆ **800/735-4888** or 302/645-4888. 66 units. $95–$220 double. Rates include morning coffee and tea. Children 11 and under stay free in parent's room. AE, DISC, MC, V. Free parking. Closed Nov–May. **Amenities:** Outdoor pool; sun deck. *In room:* A/C, TV w/free movies, fridge, hair dryer, free Wi-Fi.

Where to Eat

EXPENSIVE

The Buttery ★★★ NOUVEAU FRENCH This is as close as you'll get to a Paris bistro on the Delaware shore: a restored Victorian mansion with candlelit dining rooms, a bar, and an extensive wine list. It may well be the most romantic restaurant at the beach. In warm weather, the veranda is a lovely spot. The menu takes advantage of local seafood (crab cakes, pan-seared yellowfin tuna, bouillabaisse), with a few beef and poultry options. Sunday champagne brunch is delightful. The best deal is the elegant $30 prix-fixe dinner served nightly from 5 to 7pm. Casual diners may prefer the light fare menu offered in the bar and on the veranda 2:30 to 5pm every day.

102 2nd St. ✆ **302/645-7755.** www.butteryrestaurant.com. Reservations recommended. Main courses $11–$20 lunch, $22–$38 dinner. MC, V. Sun–Thurs 11am–8pm; Fri–Sat 11am–9pm.

Jerry's Seafood SEAFOOD Washingtonians may feel at home at this beach outlet of a DC institution. It's the home of the "crab bomb" (a 10-oz. crab cake), as well as a raw bar, a few salads and sandwiches at lunch, and filet mignon and chicken dishes at dinner. The reputation for crab cakes—they're jumbo lump meat bound with a whisper of filler—is well earned.

108 2nd St., Lewes, DE 19958. © **302/645-6611.** www.jerrys-seafood.com. Reservations recommended for dinner. Main courses $8–$34 lunch, $11–$34 dinner. AE, MC, V. Daily 11am–3:30pm and 4:30–10pm (Sun until 8pm).

MODERATE

Notting Hill Coffee, 124 Second St. (© **302/645-0733**), roasts its fair-trade coffee and bakes its pastries right there.

Café Azafrán MEDITERRANEAN Order your lunch at the counter at this little cafe; waiters will come to your table at dinner. Sandwiches, soups, and salads taste of olives and Manchego and Serrano ham. At dinner, choose from traditional tapas or a small variety of "large plates" such as tuna with Moroccan marinade, veal tenderloin, or a vegetarian platter. Desserts have a Mediterranean accent, too. Thursday is paella night (reservations are a must). The cafe opens for coffee and pastries daily at 7am. Takeout is available.

109 Market St., Lewes, DE 19958. © **302/644-4446.** www.cafeazafran.com. Reservations recommended for dinner. Main courses $6–$9 lunch, $19–$29 dinner. AE (at dinner only), MC, V. Thurs–Tues 7am–3:30pm and 5:30–9pm; Wed 7am–3:30pm.

Gilligan's ★ SEAFOOD Gilligan's menu includes a variety of straightforward seafood dishes, with a zing here or there. The heft of the 8-ounce crab cakes, which have earned honors as the "best in Delaware," make them a great option. Try the softshell crab or salmon BLT. The menu is offered all day with a few specials in the evening. A children's menu is available. The look is more upscale than deserted island, with a casual, tropical vibe. An outdoor bar overlooking the canal serves food until 1am.

134 Market St. (at Front St.), Lewes, DE 19958. © **302/644-7230.** www.gilliganswaterfront.com. Reservations accepted only for parties of 5 or more. Main courses $9–$19. AE, DISC, MC, V. Late May–Sept daily 11am–9pm; Apr to mid-May and Oct–1st week of Dec Tues–Sun 11am–9pm. Call for weekend hours Dec–Mar.

Half Full WINE AND PIZZA How can you go wrong with creative personal pizzas paired with a glass of wine or beer? Pull up a bar stool, put your elbows on the table, and enjoy the Margherita, black-and-white (with truffles), or spinach salad pizzas. Pizzas are about 8 inches by 12 inches, big enough for most people to share. The owners of this tiny marvel also run Striper Bites (see below) so I'm sure they know what they're doing.

113 Market St., Lewes, DE 19958. © **302/645-8877.** www.halffulllewes.com. No reservations accepted. Main courses $8–$13. AE, DISC, MC, V. Tues–Thurs 4–10pm; Fri–Sat 4–11pm.

Striper Bites Bistro ★★ SEAFOOD Bright and airy, this casual spot celebrates seafood. Sure, you can find steak or chicken on the intriguing menu here, but seafood reigns. You can't go wrong with the sherry-laced crab bisque or the melt-in-your-mouth pan-seared tuna. Grilled salmon, blackened-tuna pasta, and lump crab cake are all fresh and served by a friendly waitstaff. Fifteen wines are available by the glass.

107 Savannah Rd., Lewes, DE 19958. © **302/645-4657.** www.striperbites.com. Reservations not accepted. Main courses $9–$14 lunch, $16–$25 dinner. AE, DISC, MC, V. Mon–Sat 11:30am–9pm.

What to See & Do

Pretty Lewes is more than a beach and shopping town. The First City in the First State shows off its roots in the eye-catching Zwaanendael Museum and in a complex of buildings that are part of the Lewes Historical Society.

Fort Miles Bit by bit, this World War II army outpost on Cape Henlopen is being restored to its 1942 appearance. Tour guides dressed in war-era uniforms take visitors around the low, beige buildings and talk about how this base was built early in the 20th century to defend the Delaware Bay (and thus the cities of Wilmington and Philadelphia) from naval attack. It remained on active duty until 1958. Tours are offered three times a week. There are also lantern tours at dusk and a firepower tour focusing on artillery. One of the concrete towers that line Delaware's beaches is open to visitors here. Climb the 100-plus steps of the spiral staircase for bird's-eye views of Lewes and the beach. A visit to the tower is worth the price of admission.

Cape Henlopen State Park, 15099 Cape Henlopen Dr., Lewes. ✆ **302/644-5007.** www.destateparks.com or www.fortmiles.org. Admission included with park fee: $4 Delaware-registered vehicle per day, $8 out-of-state vehicle per day Mar 1–Nov 30. Free Dec–Feb. Daily 8am–sunset. Fort orientation building Tues–Sat 10am–4pm Apr–Oct; Fri–Sat 10am–4pm Nov–Mar.

Lewes Historical Society ★★ This collection of 12 historic buildings includes the **Ryves-Holt House,** built about 1665 and the oldest house in Delaware, and the Dr. Hiram Burton House. Tours are offered in the summer at 11:30am, 1 and 2:30pm. Get tickets at the Ryves-Holt House at 218 Second St. Separate admission is required for the **Cannonball House Lewes Maritime Museum** at Front and Bank and the **Lewes Life-Saving Station** at Shipcarpenter and Front streets. Both are open Monday through Saturday 11am to 4pm and admission to each is $5 for adults. Both got new exhibits in 2011. The society also hosts **Trolley Tours** (see below) and the **Haunted Lewes Tour.** These ghostly tours are offered summer Saturday evenings for $5 for ages over 12. They sell out so get your tickets early if you dare.

110 Shipcarpenter St. ✆ **302/645-7670.** www.historiclewes.org. $5 mid-June to mid-Sept Mon–Sat 11am–4pm.

WHEN THE war CAME TO LEWES

For 2 days in April 1813, British ships trained their cannons on the town of Lewes. The Cannonball House, now the maritime museum for the Lewes Historical Society, was nearly lost when it was bombarded. But the 1765 house with a cannonball still in it still stands. The house, which Delaware Bay pilots called home, has had new exhibits installed and will be, along with the War of 1812 Park across the street, part of the town's commemorations in 2013. On April 6–7, 2013, some historical and just-plain-fun activities are scheduled, including an encampment and reenactment of the battle and a War of 1812 Pub Night with period food and drink. Look for special exhibits about the war and a scholarly symposium, as well. Most events will be scheduled for April 2013. Check the **Lewes Historical Society** website for details: www.historiclewes.org. The **Zwaanendael Museum** (www.history.delaware.gov/museums/zm/zm_main.shtml) expects to host an exhibit beginning in the fall of 2012.

Trolley Tours The Lewes Historical Society offers 45-minute tours of the town's historic sites twice a day midweek mid-June through mid-September. Learn the town's story in air-conditioned comfort.

Tour pickup at corner of 2nd and Market sts. ✆ **302/645-7670.** www.historiclewes.org. $7 ages 13 and over, $3 ages 3–12, free 2 and under.

Zwaanendael Museum This red Dutch-style building is unlike anything else in Lewes. Built for the town's 300th anniversary in 1931, it resembles the city hall of Hoorn, in the Netherlands. Exhibits celebrate Delaware's "First Town in the First State"; maritime archaeology, including artifacts (even a ketchup bottle) from the sunken ship the HMS *DeBraak*; and local, maritime, and military history. Look for a War of 1812 exhibit here by fall 2012.

102 Kings Hwy. at Savannah Rd. ✆ **302/645-1148.** Free admission. Apr–Oct Tues–Sat 10am–4:30pm, Sun 1:30–4:30pm; Nov–Mar Wed–Sat 10am–4:30pm. Also Memorial Day, July 4, and Labor Day.

Outdoor Activities

Cape Henlopen State Park ★ (✆ **302/645-8983;** www.destateparks.com/chsp/chsp.htm), with its 3,143 acres bordered on one side by the Atlantic and on another by Delaware Bay, offers beach swimming, tennis, picnicking, nature trails, crabbing, and pier fishing, accessible from all the Delaware beach resorts. It's also the home of the 80-foot **Great Dune,** the highest sand dune between Cape Hatteras and Cape Cod. For those who enjoy a good climb, a refurbished World War II observation tower (115 steps) offers some of the best coastal views for miles. Walking with kids? Ask for the *Seaside Interpretive Trail Guide;* it tells about things you'd probably just walk by without noticing. The park is open year-round from 8am to sunset. Entry fee to the park is $4 for Delaware residents and $8 for out-of-state visitors from May through October; it's free the rest of the year.

BIKING Even if you're not a serious cyclist, it's good to bring a bike to Lewes: The historic streets and shoreline paths are ideal for cycling, and it's a great way to avoid the parking problem in the shopping district. All of Southern Delaware is easy to bike with flat terrain and pleasant views of farmland, villages, and wetlands; and most roads are wide, with good shoulders. The **Delaware Bicycle Council** (✆ **302/760-BIKE** [2453]; www.deldot.gov) produces *Delaware Maps for Bicycle Users.* All roads are marked and color-coded according to their suitability for cyclists, so there's no guesswork involved in planning your route. Maps can be obtained online.

Bicycling on your own near the beaches is a breeze thanks to the level terrain and wide back roads. Even a trip up Route 1 from Bethany to the Indian River Inlet is easy. For family excursions, biking is a great way to see **Cape Henlopen State Park** (✆ **302/645-8983;** www.destateparks.com). Paved bike routes run through the park and take you places that cars can't go. The terrain is mostly flat, with just a few hills on routes to overlooks. Or head to **Trap Pond State Park** (see below), which has 5 miles of trails for cyclists, hikers, or equestrians, or to the 6-mile **Junction and Breakwater Trail** that connects Lewes and Rehoboth Beach via a crushed-stone trail suitable for walkers, joggers, bikers, and wheelchairs. Motorized vehicles are prohibited. To access the wooded trail, find the trail head off Wolf Neck Road off Route 1, where there's a parking lot and visitors' services. A map is available at **www.destateparks.com/Activities/trails.j-and-b-trail.pdf**.

Delaware state law requires that children under 16 wear helmets.

You can rent bikes from **Lewes Cycle Sports,** in the Beacon Motel, Savannah Road (✆ **888/800-BIKE** [2453] or 302/645-4544). The shop also has a bike rental stand at the Lewes–Cape May Ferry terminal.

BIRD- & WILDLIFE-WATCHING Lewes, between Cape Henlopen and Prime Hook, is the best base for birders on the Delaware coast. **Cape Henlopen State Park** (✆ **302/645-8983;** www.destateparks.com) is prime breeding ground for the endangered piping plover. (Access is restricted certain times to protect the nesting grounds.) Whales and dolphins appear regularly off the coast of Cape Henlopen, usually a little farther south. About 10 miles north of Lewes, **Prime Hook National Wildlife Refuge,** 11978 Turkle Pond Rd., Milton, DE 19968, off Route 16 (✆ **302/684-8419;** www.fws.gov/northeast/primehook), is the best place for birding and wildlife photography. The refuge has two hiking trails and a 7-mile self-guided canoe trail (bring your own canoe); they're great places to view migrating waterfowl in spring and fall, plus shorebirds, warblers, amphibians, and reptiles in spring. Admission is free; the refuge is open daily from 30 minutes before sunrise to 30 minutes after sunset. The visitor center is open Monday through Friday from 7:30am to 4pm, plus Saturdays and Sundays between April and November from 9am to 4pm. ***Note:*** Bring bug repellent, especially in summer.

CAMPING Campgrounds at **Cape Henlopen State Park** are open March 1 to November 30. Reservations must be made at least 24 hours in advance. Call ✆ **877/987-2757.** Two sites are accessible for those with disabilities, and 12 are set aside for tent camping only. It's an inexpensive option in a resort area. The 152 sites sit on pine-covered dunes, with water hookup and access to clean bathhouses with showers. The sites are all fairly spacious, but the ones in the center loops are not terribly private. The largest and most private are located in the back loop, but they aren't well suited for trailers or motor homes. Rates are $28 to $32 per night. As with all camping on the Atlantic coast, mosquitoes can be a problem, so bring bug repellent.

Another option is the 142 campsites, including eight rustic cabins overlooking the pond at **Trap Pond State Park,** 33587 Baldcypress Lane, Laurel, DE 19956. Call ✆ **877/987-2757** for reservations; www.destateparks.com/camping/trap-pond/index.asp. Rates for out-of-state campers are $19 for tent sites, $28 for electric and water sites, $49 for one of the two yurts, and $59 for a cabin. The park also has boat rentals and pontoon boat tours in the summer.

DISC GOLF Did you know there were disc golf stars? They get together at **Trap Pond State Park,** 33587 Baldcypress Lane, Laurel, DE 19956 (✆ **302/875-5153;** www.destateparks.com/tpsp/tpsp.htm), for a series of tournaments held on a course that winds through the wooded areas of the park. The course is available for amateurs, too.

FISHING With easy access to both Delaware Bay and the Atlantic, Lewes offers a wide variety of sportfishing opportunities. The fishing season starts when the ocean fills with huge schools of mackerel in late March through April. Large sea trout (weakfish) arrive in early May and June; flounder arrive in May and remain throughout the summer, as do bluefish and shark. As the ocean warms up in June, offshore species such as tuna and marlin begin roaming the waters. Bottom fishing in the bay for trout, flounder, sea bass, and blues continues all summer, with late August through September often providing the largest catches. October and November bring porgies, shad, and blackfish. Delaware now requires licenses for all fishermen ages 16 to 64.

Arrange headboat ocean and bay fishing excursions and cruises at **Fisherman's Wharf,** Anglers Road (✆ **302/645-8862**), or at **Angler's Fishing Center,** Anglers Road (✆ **302/644-4533;** www.anglersfishingcenter.com). Call for full-day, half-day, or nighttime excursions. There are even family shark-fishing excursions.

Cape Henlopen is great for shore and surf fishing. In Lewes, try the **Lewes Harbor Fishing and Boating Outfitters,** 217 Anglers Rd. (✆ **302/645-6227**), for supplies.

HORSEBACK RIDING **Winswept Stables** (✆ **302/645-1651;** www.winsweptstables.net) offers rides along trails or the beach in summer.

PADDLING The creeks and ponds of Sussex County make for lovely canoe excursions. A 5-mile canoe trail along the Hitch Pond and James branches of the Nanticoke River will take you past the two largest trees in Delaware, one of which is estimated to be 750 years old. The wide, glassy pond is surrounded by the northernmost stand of naturally planted bald cypress trees, one some 300 years old. The trail begins at **Trap Pond State Park,** 33587 Baldcypress Lane, Laurel, DE 19956 (✆ **302/875-5153;** www.destateparks.com/tpsp/tpsp.htm), where you can rent canoes or kayaks for $6 to $8 an hour.

Nearby in Laurel is the smaller, wilder **Trussum Pond,** which looks and feels more like the Florida Everglades or a bayou than southern Delaware. From Route 24, take Route 449, which goes by the entrance to Trap Pond State Park, to Road 72 (Trussum Pond Rd.). A small park and parking area are located next to the pond, where you can paddle among abundant lily pads and the last graceful trees from a prehistoric bald cypress stand. You'll have to do the navigating yourself; there aren't any trail markers.

Prime Hook National Wildlife Refuge, 11978 Turkle Rd., Milton (✆ **302/684-8419;** www.fws.gov/northeast/primehook), offers 15 miles of streams and ditches, including a 7-mile canoe trail. Electric-powered boats can also use the waterways. There are no rentals at the 10,000-acre refuge. You can launch your boat at the ramp behind the visitor center for $1. Admission is free.

Quest Kayak (✆ **302/745-2925;** www.questfitnesskayak.com) offers excellent tours to watch the sunset, look for dolphins, or pass by lighthouses. The Pints and Paddles tour is for the beer enthusiast. Rentals are available.

Shopping

Lewes has the most interesting collection of arts, crafts, and antiques shops at the beach. Most shops are open daily from 10 or 11am to 5 or 6pm, with extended hours in summer.

Auntie M's Emporium Head here for lots of old stuff: kitchenware, books, furniture, and garden sculptures. 116 W. 3rd St. ✆ **302/644-1804.**

Cape Artists Gallery Local artists bring their original works to display here. 110 3rd St. ✆ **302/644-7733.**

Deanna's/Piccolino Need a new sundress, a new bag, or a whole new look? Here's one of the great clothing shops in town. 113 2nd St. ✆ **302/644-1112.**

Kids' Ketch Get your beach toys here—or perhaps something to while away those rainy days. 132 2nd St. ✆ **302/645-8448.** www.kidsketch.com.

Lewes Gourmet This gourmet shop has international goodies, as well as Food Network cooks' wares. 110 Front St. ✆ **302/645-1661.**

A DELAWARE brewery & WINERY

Nassau Valley Vineyards, 32165 Winery Way (just off Rte. 1, on Rte. 14B), Lewes, DE 19958 (✆ **302/645-WINE** [9463]; www.nassauvalley.com), offers self-guided tours and tastings Monday through Saturday from 11am to 5pm, Sunday from noon to 5pm. You can see where the wine ferments; look at displays on viniculture, viticulture, coopering, and bottling; and taste their chardonnay, cabernet, and rosé. It won't take long, but it's a nice break from the beach.

If you feel like a brew, try the **Dogfish Head Craft Brewery,** 3 miles west of Lewes, 6 Cannery Village Center, Milton, DE 19968 (✆ **888/8DOGFISH** [364-3474]; www.dogfish.com). Locals are big fans of Dogfish Head's quirky brews, which sell in 27 states and four countries. Free tours are offered Tuesday through Saturday 11am to 5pm year-round. Reservations are required.

Peninsula Gallery Across the canal below the Beacon Hotel, this gallery displays mainly works by regional artists. Closed Mondays January through March. 520 E. Savannah Rd. ✆ **302/645-0551.** www.peninsula-gallery.com.

Puzzles Exercise your brain with the games and puzzles here, including jigsaws, crosswords, and brainteasers. 108 Front St. ✆ **302/645-8013.**

Sand N Stones Jewelry from sea glass and shells, as well as photos, books, and gifts with a beachy look. 112 Front St. ✆ **302/645-0576.** www.gemwrap.com.

Shorebreak Casual clothes and accessories for men. 107 Savannah Rd. ✆ **302/645-8488.**

Stepping Stone Look for American crafts here, with something new every visit. Front and Market sts. ✆ **302/645-1254.**

Two Friends Pretty gifts for your best bud or her home, with wares from Mariposa and Vera Bradley. 205 2nd St. ✆ **302/644-0477.**

Organized Cruises

A good way to see the Delaware Bay and the Lewes Canal harbor is by sea. You can pick up a self-guided tour brochure from the visitor center in the Fisher-Martin House, on Kings Highway. It covers more than 40 sites with brief descriptions of each one. For sightseeing cruises from Lewes, call **Fisherman's Wharf Cruises,** 217 Anglers Rd. (✆ **302/645-8862;** www.fishlewes.com), which operates narrated excursions around the harbor of Lewes and the Delaware breakwater areas. Trips include a 2-hour dolphin-watching cruise, a 3-hour whale- and dolphin-watching cruise, and a 2-hour sunset cruise. Prices are $15 to $35. Most tours are offered June through September; call for details and departure times.

REHOBOTH & DEWEY BEACHES, DE ★★★

88 miles SE of Wilmington; 27 miles N of Ocean City; 110 miles SE of Baltimore; 124 miles SE of Washington, DC

Rehoboth is the most popular of the Delaware beaches: It's small-town friendly and beach-resort casual, yet has a touch of style. Visitors can choose from beachfront condominiums, boardwalk hotels, and old-fashioned cottages. On the south side of town, grand homes overlook Silver Lake. The town's shops offer a lovely diversion, with everything from home fashions to hippie accessories. Just outside town on Route 1, Rehoboth has become synonymous with outlet shopping—and Delaware has no sales tax.

Rehoboth is also a popular destination for gay and lesbian travelers, a mid-Atlantic alternative to Provincetown or Fire Island, with a number of gay-owned and predominantly gay venues.

Head south from Rehoboth and you come to Dewey Beach. It's a more casual suburb of Rehoboth, with a trolley connecting the towns in summer. Dewey is noted for its nightspots. The beach is good, and Rehoboth Bay is only a couple of blocks from the ocean.

Essentials

GETTING THERE **By Car** From the north, take Routes 113 and 13 to Route 1, and then Route 1A into Rehoboth. From the south, take Route 113 north to Route 26 east to Bethany Beach, and take Route 1 north to Rehoboth. From the west, take Route 50 across the Bay Bridge to Route 404 east; then take Route 9 east to Route 1 south. From Ocean City, continue up Coastal Highway as it turns into Route 1 to Dewey.

By Plane For visitors arriving by plane, the nearest airport is **Salisbury–Ocean City–Wicomico Regional Airport.** See p. 261 for details.

VISITOR INFORMATION The **Rehoboth Beach–Dewey Beach Chamber of Commerce,** 501 Rehoboth Ave. (✆ **800/441-1329,** ext. 12, or 302/227-2233; www.beach-fun.com), is open year-round Monday through Friday from 9am to 5pm and Saturday from 9am to 1pm. (Stop here for quarters for the parking meters.) The **Welcome Grove** has a playground, and farmers' market in summer, as well as the visitor center. Gay and lesbian travelers should visit **www.camprehoboth.com** or look for the *Letters from Camp Rehoboth* newsletter around town.

GETTING AROUND **By Public Transportation** From mid-May to mid-September, **DART First State** (✆ **800/355-8080** or 302/739-3278; www.dartfirststate.com) operates a daily shuttle service down Route 9 from Georgetown to Lewes, and down Route 1 to Rehoboth and on to the border with Ocean City. Buses go down Savannah Road in Lewes and travel along Rehoboth Avenue to the Rehoboth boardwalk, the park-and-ride lot, and the shopping outlets. They stop at Ocean City, where passengers can catch the Ocean City bus. A daily pass is $2.40 per person—or $7 per carload when parking at the park-and-ride lot on Shuttle Road off Delaware Route 1. Your pass is also good for one ride on Ocean City's bus; likewise, an Ocean City pass is good for one ride in Delaware.

The **Jolly Trolley of Rehoboth Beach** (✆ **302/227-1197;** www.jollytrolley.com) operates a shuttle between Rehoboth Beach and south Dewey Beach. Buses run Memorial Day through Labor Day, daily every half-hour from 8am to 2am; limited service is available in May and September. The fare is $2.50 for adults, $1 for children under 6. Bus stops are posted. Call for guided tours of Dewey and Rehoboth.

By Car Parking in Rehoboth Beach can be difficult. Metered parking at $1.50 an hour is in effect from Memorial Day weekend to mid-September, daily from 10am to midnight. The meters take only quarters but electronic meters also take credit and debit cards. There are change machines in the first and second blocks of Rehoboth Avenue.

Rehoboth Beach

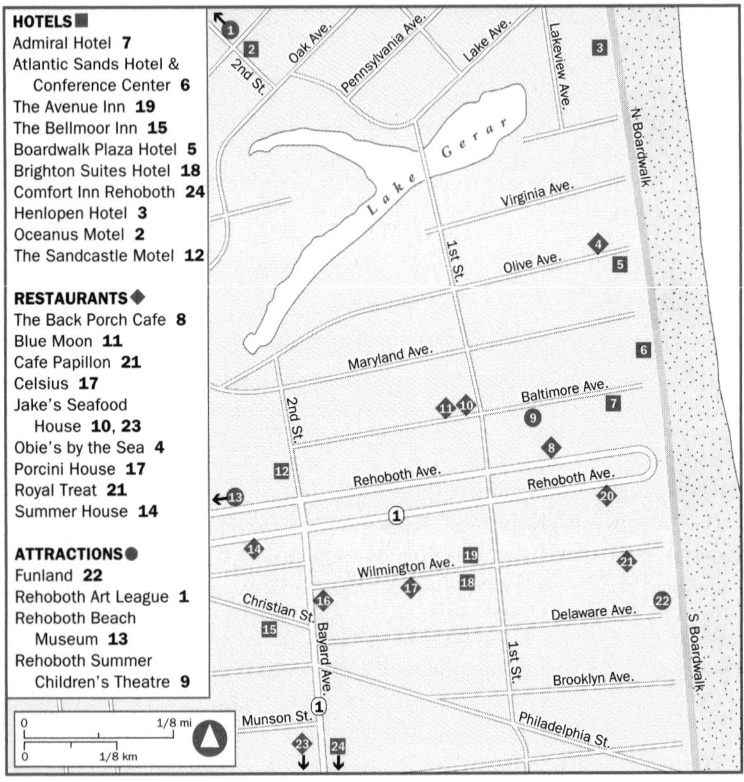

To park in a nonmetered area Memorial Day to Labor Day, get a **parking permit.** Permits for daily, weekly, or seasonal parking are available from the Parking Meter Division, 30½ Lake Dr. (behind City Hall), City Hall, the Visitor Center at 501 Rehoboth Ave., and various real-estate offices. They cost $45 for a week, $30 for a 3-day weekend, $13 for a weekend day, and $8 for a weekday. The police will explain the rules and help you get change. Call ✆ **302/227-6184** for information. Once you've parked, you can leave it. Almost everything you'll need is within walking distance.

SPECIAL EVENTS Once the sunbathers go home, it's festival time at the beach. Greyhound lovers converge on Dewey and Rehoboth beaches on Columbus Day weekend for the **Greyhounds Reach the Beach Weekend** ★ (www.greyhoundsreachthebeach.com). This social gathering was started in 1995 and now some 3,500 ex-racers and their humans usually take part. It's fun to see and meet these graceful animals and their gracious owners.

The 3-day **Sea Witch Halloween and Fiddler's Festival** at the end of October features a costume parade, trick-or-treating, a 5K race, and a fiddling contest. For information, contact the Rehoboth Beach–Dewey Beach Chamber of Commerce (✆ **800/441-1329** or 302/227-2233).

The **Rehoboth Beach Independent Film Festival** (✆ **302/645-9095** or www.rehobothfilm.com) takes place the first weekend in November.

Where to Stay

Most accommodations in Rehoboth and Dewey are moderately priced. In July and August, however, you may encounter difficulty finding any room near the beach for under $200 a night. Even though Rehoboth and Dewey are seasonal destinations, don't expect dramatic off-season discounts like those you'll find in Ocean City. The outlets are a huge attraction for holiday shoppers, so the shoulder season extends through December (but ask your hotel about weekday packages). There are sometimes significant discounts in January, February, and March. In any case, reservations are always necessary in summer and strongly recommended through the holiday shopping season.

House rentals are popular, so they can be tough to get. For families, they can be a good idea: lots of space, kitchens, and maybe two bathrooms for about $1,000 per week and up—way up. Larger houses go for up to $5,000 a week, but a condo is considerably more reasonable. **Crowley Associates Realty** (✆ **800/242-4213** or 302/227-6131; www.crowleyrealestate.com) is a popular rental agent in the Rehoboth/Dewey area. Reservations should be made as early as possible—there's so much return business, families often put in their request when they return the keys at the end of their vacation. If you'd like to rent a house or condo, be sure to call soon after Labor Day. Then again, something, probably older or farther from the beach, could be available in spring. As with other beach resorts, most condos come well equipped, except for linens, towels, and paper products; plan to bring those.

You could "rough it" and rent a cottage at the **Indian River Inlet Marina,** at the Delaware State Seashore Park. There are only 12 available—and with the amenities they offer, they're popular. Each has two bedrooms and a loft (sleeping six people comfortably), kitchen, fireplace, satellite TV, washer/dryer, and screened porch. In summer, they can be rented for $1,800 a week. Off-season rates run $280 to $460 for 2 nights. Two-night minimums are required off season; weekly rentals are required in summer.

Reserve online at **http://delawarestateparks.reserveamerica.com** or call ✆ **877/98-PARKS** (987-2757).

REHOBOTH BEACH

Very Expensive

Atlantic Sands Hotel & Conference Center ★ The Atlantic Sands, on the boardwalk, is Rehoboth's largest hotel. Sun worshipers love it for its spacious deck and pool on the oceanfront. Guest rooms feature dark-wood furniture and balconies with a water view. Some units have a whirlpool, wet bar, or microwave.

101 N. Boardwalk (btw. Baltimore and Maryland aves.), Rehoboth Beach, DE 19971. www.atlanticsandshotel.com. ✆ **800/422-0600** or 302/227-2511. 182 units. $185–$445 double. AE, DC, DISC, MC, V. Free parking. **Amenities:** Restaurant; poolside bar; health club; outdoor pool; spa; rooftop sun deck. *In room:* A/C, fridge, hair dryer, free Wi-Fi.

The Bellmoor Inn ★★★ This family-run establishment doesn't skimp anywhere. The lobby and library—with English-country decor, fireplace, and sumptuous furnishings—offer the first clue. Accommodations, though standard in layout, are richly furnished with thoughtful touches. Some units are part of a 1960s-era motel, but they are cleverly disguised and set in a soothing garden. Rooms in the newer section are equally well appointed and somewhat larger. Choose from standard rooms, junior suites, king rooms (with fireplace and whirlpool tub), or full apartments. One pool is for adults only; a second one is for families. A full-service spa completes the luxury.

6 Christian St., Rehoboth Beach, DE 19971. www.thebellmoor.com. ✆ **302/227-5800.** Fax 302/227-0323. 78 units. $109–$499 double; $269–$589 suite. Rates include full breakfast and afternoon tea. 2- or 3-night minimum stay required on weekends and holidays. AE, DISC, MC, V. Free parking. **Amenities:** Concierge-level suites; health club; indoor hot tub (adults only); 2 outdoor pools and sun deck; spa. *In room:* A/C, fridge, hair dryer, free Wi-Fi.

Boardwalk Plaza Hotel ★★ Step into the dark, ornate Victorian parlor of a lobby—complete with two tropical birds—and enjoy the old-fashioned hospitality of this friendly staff, who go out of their way to serve you in style. The fourth-floor concierge level is decorated with Victorian antiques, while the lower floors have pretty good reproductions. Most rooms are oceanfront or oceanview suites; a few have whirlpools. There are also a few standard rooms in the back of the hotel plus a spacious corner apartment. The pool is quite small but has an abundance of whirlpool jets. Two restaurants are on the premises, **Victoria's** and the more casual **Plaza Pub.**

Olive Ave. and the boardwalk, Rehoboth Beach, DE 19971. www.boardwalkplaza.com. ✆ **800/33-BEACH** (332-3224) or 302/227-7169. Fax 302/227-0561. 84 units. $269–$599 double in summer; $119–$339 double off season. Children 6 and under stay free in parent's room. AE, DC, DISC, MC, V. Free parking. **Amenities:** Restaurant; pub; concierge-level rooms; fitness center; indoor/outdoor pool. *In room:* A/C, flatscreen TV/DVD, hair dryer, free Wi-Fi.

Expensive

Avenue Inn & Spa You might have trouble finding this place if you're on Rehoboth Avenue—step back and then you'll see it. Shops on the ground floor obscure it (the entrance is on Wilmington). Inside, you'll find a country-inn kind of place. There are 13 floor plans. Some rooms have TV/DVDs, fireplaces (electric), and Jacuzzis. The inn is filled with English-country style furniture and burgundy fabrics.

33 Wilmington Ave., Rehoboth Beach, DE 19971. www.avenueinn.com. ✆ **800/433-5870** or 302/226-2900. Fax 302/226-7549. 48 units. $124–$330 double. Rates include continental breakfast, afternoon wine and cheese, and cookies served by the lobby fireplace. 2-night minimum stay required on some weekends. AE, DISC, MC, V. Free parking. **Amenities:** Fitness center; outdoor hot tub; indoor pool and deck; spa. *In room:* A/C, fridge, hair dryer, microwave, free Wi-Fi.

Brighton Suites Hotel ★ For families, this all-suite hotel a short walk from the beach is a good choice. The sandy-pink, four-story property's bedrooms have one king-size or two double beds, a large bathroom, and a separate living room with pull-out sofa, newly renovated in early 2012. The hotel's DVD library, with about 250 choices, is popular on rainy days.

34 Wilmington Ave., Rehoboth Beach, DE 19971. www.brightonsuites.com. ✆ **800/227-5788** or 302/227-5780. Fax 302/227-6815. 66 units. $269–$649 suite. Rates drop precipitously off season. Ask about packages. 2- or 3-night minimum stay required on summer weekends and holidays. AE, DISC, MC, V. Free parking. **Amenities:** Beach equipment; DVD library; fitness center; indoor pool; rooftop sun deck. *In room:* A/C, TV/DVD, fridge, hair dryer, microwave, wet bar, free Wi-Fi.

Henlopen Hotel ★ On the north end of the boardwalk, this beachfront lodging is a tradition dating from 1879, when the first Henlopen Hotel was built here. Recently modernized, the rooms are simple. All 12 oceanfront rooms and 80 oceanview rooms have balconies. Families will like the suites.

511 N. Boardwalk, Rehoboth Beach, DE 19971. www.henlopenhotel.com. ✆ **800/441-8450** or 302/227-2551. Fax 302/227-8147. 92 units. $199–$399 double oceanfront; $69–$269 double oceanview. 2- or 3-night minimum stay required on summer weekends and holidays. AE, DISC, MC, V. Free parking. Closed Nov–Mar. *In room:* A/C, fridge, hair dryer, Wi-Fi (for fee).

Hotel Rehoboth ★ This stylish inn offers a few welcome amenities. Besides the well-appointed rooms, there are the outdoor heated pool (big enough for a dip, but forget laps), continental breakfast, evening reception, and the jaunty shuttle to the ocean 3 blocks away. The best rooms are perhaps the second-floor rooms with balconies overlooking the action on Rehoboth Avenue.

247 Rehoboth Ave., Rehoboth Beach, DE 19971. www.hotelrehoboth.com. ✆ **877/247-7346** or 302/227-4300. Fax 302/227-1200. 52 units. $129–$399 double. AE, DISC, MC, V. Free parking. *In room:* A/C, TV/DVD, fridge, hair dryer, MP3 docking station, free Wi-Fi.

Moderate

Admiral Hotel ☺ In the heart of the beach district, this five-story motel is a favorite with families. It has an indoor pool inside a glass pavilion, plus a deck. All units have a partial ocean view. Families can opt for six-person suites with a kitchen.

2 Baltimore Ave., Rehoboth Beach, DE 19971. www.admiralrehoboth.com. ✆ **888/882-4188** or 302/227-2103. 73 units. $168–$239 double. Supplementary charges apply on some peak or holiday weekends. Rates plummet in shoulder season. Children 12 and under stay free in parent's room. 2-night minimum stay required in summer. AE, DISC, MC, V. Free parking. Closed mid-Nov to mid-Mar. **Amenities:** Indoor pool; sun deck; whirlpool. *In room:* A/C, TV, fridge, hair dryer, microwave, free Wi-Fi.

Comfort Inn Rehoboth ★ Within sight of the Rehoboth outlets, this hotel is perfectly located for serious shoppers, and it's just 2 miles to the beach. Guest rooms are clean, comfortable, and spacious. Some have a microwave or whirlpool tub. The DART bus to the beach stops right outside.

4439 Hwy. 1, Rehoboth Beach, DE 19971. www.comfortinnrehoboth.com. ✆ **800/590-5451** or 302/226-1515. Fax 302/226-1550. 96 units. $130–$220 double. Rates include breakfast. 2-night minimum stay required on summer weekends. AE, DC, DISC, MC, V. Free parking. **Amenities:** Fitness room; outdoor pool. *In room:* A/C, TV, fridge, hair dryer, microwave, free Wi-Fi.

Heritage Inn Between Lewes and Rehoboth's beach—each is 3 miles away, this hotel has an American traditional theme. Rooms have red, white, and blue Early American decor; three units have whirlpools; and six are family suites.

Rte. 1 and Postal Lane (P.O. Box 699), Rehoboth Beach, DE 19971. www.rehobothheritage.com. ✆ **800/669-9399** or 302/644-0600. 86 units. $169–$229 double. Rates include continental breakfast. AE, DISC, MC, V. **Amenities:** Fitness center; outdoor pool. *In room:* A/C, TV w/free movies, fridge, hair dryer, free Wi-Fi.

Oceanus Motel This L-shaped, three-story motel—a classic mid-1960s design—lies 2 blocks from the beach and just off Rehoboth Avenue in a quiet neighborhood. Each room shares a porch overlooking the good-size pool.

6 2nd St. (P.O. Box 324), Rehoboth Beach, DE 19971. www.oceanusmotel.com. ✆ **800/852-5011** or 302/227-8200. 38 units. $169–$199 double. Supplementary charges of $10–$20 apply on certain weekends. Children 12 and under stay free in parent's room. DISC, MC, V. Free parking. Closed Nov to mid-Mar. **Amenities:** Outdoor pool. *In room:* A/C, TV, fridge, hair dryer, microwave, free Wi-Fi.

The Sandcastle Motel ★ You can't miss this motel, built in the shape of a sugary-white sand castle off the main thoroughfare. Its location, about 5 blocks from the beach, is ideal for shopping and walking to restaurants. Each large, well-laid-out room has a balcony. The pool has a lifeguard on duty.

123 2nd St. (off Rehoboth Ave.), Rehoboth Beach, DE 19971. www.thesandcastlemotel.com. ✆ **800/372-2112** or 302/227-0400. 60 units. $159–$249 double. 2- or 3-night minimum stay required on some weekends and holidays. AE, DISC, MC, V. Free parking in enclosed garage. Closed Nov–Mar. **Amenities:** Indoor pool; sun deck. *In room:* A/C, TV, fridge, hair dryer, free Wi-Fi.

DEWEY BEACH

Atlantic Oceanside Motel This modern three-story structure is on the main beach highway, equidistant from the bay and the ocean (which are about a block away). The rooms are of the standard motel variety, but its closeness to the beach and Dewey nightlife recommend it. Families (and those with pets) may prefer the **Oceanside Suites** at 21003 Coastal Hwy.—where they offer efficiencies and one-bedroom suites in a quieter area 2 blocks from Dewey.

1700 Coastal Hwy., Dewey Beach, DE 19971. www.atlanticoceanside.com. ✆ **800/422-0481** or 302/227-8811. 61 units. $35–$249 double; $45–$299 suites. 3-night minimum stay required on summer weekends. AE, DC, DISC, MC, V. Free parking. Motel closed mid-Nov to mid-Mar. Suites open year-round. Pets accepted in off season for fee at motel; year-round in suites. **Amenities:** Outdoor pool; sun deck. *In room:* A/C, TV w/free movies, fridge, microwave, free Wi-Fi.

The Bay Resort Motel ☺ It's a little out of the way in Dewey (read: quieter), but this three-story complex, set on a strip of land between the bay and the ocean, is the ideal place to watch the sun set on Rehoboth Bay. From the 250-foot pier on the bay, you can drop a fishing line or watch the sailboats drift by. Each unit has a balcony facing either the pool or the bay.

126 Bellevue St. (P.O. Box 461), Dewey Beach, DE 19971. www.bayresort.com. ✆ **800/922-9240** or 302/227-6400. 67 units. $159–$229 double. Children 15 and under stay free in parent's room. 2- or 3-night minimum stay required on summer weekends and holidays. DISC, MC, V. Free parking. Closed Nov–May. **Amenities:** Outdoor pool. *In room:* A/C, TV w/free movies, hair dryer, kitchenette, free Wi-Fi.

Best Western Gold Leaf ★ A block from both the beach and the bay, this four-story motel is across from the Ruddertowne complex and convenient to all of Dewey's attractions. Each comfortable room has a balcony and a view of the bay, ocean, or both. Four king rooms feature whirlpool tubs. A few rooms have three double beds. It has been completely renovated from the exterior walls to the bathroom counters to the French doors that let in the ocean breezes. If you like Dewey, this should be your hotel.

1400 Hwy. 1 (at Dickinson St.), Dewey Beach, DE 19971. www.bestwesterngoldleaf.com. ✆ **800/422-8566** or 302/226-1100. Fax 302/226-9785. 75 units. $89–$229 double. Ask about reduced-rate packages Nov–Mar. 2- or 3-night minimum stay required in summer and on holiday weekends. Children 16 and under stay free in parent's room. Rates include continental breakfast. AE, DC, DISC, MC, V. Free garage parking. Pets accepted in off season for fee. **Amenities:** Fitness center; rooftop pool; sun deck. *In room:* A/C, TV, fridge, hair dryer, Internet, microwave.

Where to Eat

REHOBOTH BEACH

Expensive

The Back Porch Café ★ INTERNATIONAL For more than 20 years, diners have enjoyed the Key West atmosphere in Delaware along with the fresh, creative fare. Flavors are global, though the food is local and seasonal: scallops, crab, and salmon paired with in-season fruits and vegetables. The sweetbreads are popular, and loin of rabbit is always on the menu. Everything but the baguettes is made in-house. The bartenders offer potent creations, including house coffee flamed tableside. Besides the cozy dining room, there are three outdoor decks. Live, mellow music brings in crowds Friday nights. The light *après*-surf menu is perfect with a cocktail before dinner.

59 Rehoboth Ave., Rehoboth, DE 19971. ✆ **302/227-3674.** www.backporchcafe.com. Reservations recommended Fri–Sat. Main courses $12–$16 lunch, $30–$36 dinner. DISC, MC, V. June–Sept daily 11am–10pm; early Oct Thurs–Sun 11am–10pm and Fri 5:30–10pm. Closed late Oct–May.

Blue Moon AMERICAN/INTERNATIONAL Off the main drag (so to speak), this restaurant is in a bright blue-and-mango cottage. The interior features curved banquettes and exotic flowers. The menu changes three times a year. You can count on rack of lamb, salmon, and duck—small plates are another option—but the presentations are unexpected. So is the entertainment, from drag karaoke to a jazz brunch.

35 Baltimore Ave., Rehoboth, DE 19971. ✆ **302/227-6515.** www.bluemoonrehoboth.com. Reservations recommended. Main courses $23–$32. AE, DC, DISC, MC, V. Mon–Sat 6–10pm; Sun 10:30am–2pm and 6–10pm. Closed Jan.

Nage ★★★ NEW AMERICAN A tiny delight tucked into the corner of the Shore Plaza shopping center on Route 1, Nage makes room for 100 clamoring for their seasonal menu filled with creative gems. *Nage,* French for "swims," specializes in seafood but has become known for—of all things—burgers. Sandwiches include the prime rib burger at lunch and dinner. At dinner, choose crab cakes, steak, or their signature seafood stew in a lobster and saffron broth. Or pair wines and starters for a small-plate feast. sandwiches and flatbreads are also available.

19730 Coastal Hwy., Rehoboth, DE 19971. ✆ **302/226-2037.** www.nage.bz. Reservations required for dinner. Main courses $9–$16 lunch, $11–$32 dinner. AE, MC, V. Lunch Tues–Sat 11:30am–2:30pm; dinner daily 5–9pm.

Moderate

Celsius ★ CONTINENTAL Leave the Delaware shore for an evening on the Mediterranean. Three small dining rooms are decorated with yellow walls, sun-splashed murals, and red-and-yellow tablecloths. But the tastes aren't confined to the Riviera. Entrees have sauces inspired by a variety of traditions, both European and Asian. So you can choose from ahi tuna, paella, or a crab cake. There's a wide choice of tapas/appetizers and a children's menu. For a great deal, try the three-course $25 prix-fixe menu from 5 to 8pm.

50 Wilmington Ave., Rehoboth, DE 19971. ✆ **302/227-5767.** Reservations recommended on Fri–Sat. Main courses $15–$26. MC, V. Mon–Sat 5–10pm; Sun 10am–2pm and 5–10pm.

Jake's Seafood House ★ SEAFOOD Both locations are spacious, with plenty of dining rooms, though still noisy. The seafood is fresh, prepared well, and can be paired with some affordable wines. Started by a Baltimore family, Jake's specializes in seafood the way locals like it. Grilled fish (including a delectable tuna), crab cakes (done Baltimore style), sandwiches, and a few beef dishes are straightforward. Petite portions are a welcome addition.

2 locations: 29 Baltimore Ave., Rehoboth, DE 19971 (✆ **302/227-6237**), and 19178 Coastal Hwy. Rehoboth, DE 19971 (✆ **302/644-7711**). www.jakesseafoodhouse.com. Reservations not accepted. Main courses $8–$14 lunch, $13–$45 dinner. AE, DC, DISC, MC, V. Daily 11:30am–9pm. Downtown location closed Oct–Mar.

Obie's by the Sea AMERICAN You can't dine any closer to the ocean than here beside the boardwalk. Obie's offers indoor and open-air dining. A casual atmosphere prevails, with an all-day menu of sandwiches, burgers, ribs, salads, and "clam bakes" (clams, shrimp, chicken, corn, and biscuits). There's DJ music and dancing on weekends.

On the boardwalk (btw. Virginia and Olive aves.), Rehoboth, DE 19971. ✆**302/227-6261.** Reservations not accepted. Main courses $4.95–$19. AE, MC, V. Mid-May to mid-Sept daily 11am–1am; Apr to mid-May and mid-Sept to early Nov Fri–Mon 11am–1am. Closed mid-Nov to Mar.

Porcini House Bistro NORTHERN ITALIAN Sit inside or, better yet, on the rooftop deck among the treetops. Relax with a cool drink while your pasta or entree is cooked. Look for pasta with seafood or Mama's comfort food. Try an Italian-style meat or seafood dish. Like mushrooms? They appear in the mac and cheese, signature soup, and a special appetizer.

210 2nd St., Rehoboth, DE 19971. ✆ **302/227-6494.** www.theporcinihouse.com. Reservations recommended. Main courses $7–$20. AE, DC, DISC, MC, V. Mon–Thurs 11am–9pm; Fri 11am–11pm; Sat 11am–1am; Sun 11am–9pm.

Inexpensive

Cafe Papillon FRENCH This little walk-up on "Penny Lane" has plenty of treats for breakfast or lunch: filled croissants, sweet or savory crepes, sandwiches, and cappuccino. The counter and tables are outside, so this is definitely a seasonal delight.

Penny Lane, 42 Rehoboth Ave., Rehoboth, DE 19971. ✆**302/227-7568.** Reservations not accepted. Crepes $4–$8; sandwiches $5–$8. No credit cards. June–Aug daily 8am–11pm; May and Sept–Oct Sat–Sun 8am–11pm.

Royal Treat ★ BREAKFAST/ICE CREAM The family-owned Royal Treat continues to fry up a hearty breakfast for the hungry sun worshipers who crowd into the three cheery dining rooms or the screened porch. Then they come back later for ice cream. This old-fashioned Rehoboth landmark near the boardwalk has been serving breakfast for 3 decades.

4 Wilmington Ave., Rehoboth, DE 19971. ✆**302/227-6277.** Reservations not accepted. All items $2–$10. No credit cards. May–Sept daily 8–11:30am and 1–11:30pm.

Summer House ★ ☺ SEAFOOD Expect the usual beach fare and you'll be happy but select one of the daily specials—sirloin topped with egg and béarnaise or crawfish étouffée—and you'll be surprised at how good they are. A comfortable space dominated by the bar is only the front room. If you bring the kids or grandma, ask for a booth in the other dining room. It's casual, friendly, and family-style—until the party begins after dinner hour.

228 Rehoboth Ave., Rehoboth, DE 19971. ✆ **302/227-3895.** www.summerhousesaloon.com. Reservations not accepted. Main courses $11–$24. AE, DC, DISC, MC, V. Daily 11:30am–1am.

DEWEY BEACH

Rusty Rudder AMERICAN/SEAFOOD This California-style restaurant on the bay has been a favorite of young beachgoers since 1979. It offers great views from its dining rooms, decks, and terraces. Dinner entrees include crab cakes, prime rib, and enormous seafood platters. A land-and-sea buffet is offered nightly in summer, Friday and Saturday in the off season. The star of dinner, however, is the overflowing salad bar. At lunch, choose from appetizers, sandwiches, and salads. There's entertainment most summer nights, weekends in the shoulder season.

113 Dickinson St. (on the bay). ✆**302/227-3888.** www.deweybeachlife.com. Main courses $8–$35 lunch, $15–$35 dinner. AE, DC, DISC, MC, V. Summer daily 11:30am–10pm (Sun brunch 10am–2pm); Oct–Apr Thurs–Sun 11:30am–9pm.

What to See & Do

Rehoboth and Dewey offer a quieter, more relaxed alternative to Ocean City, Maryland, but both have nightlife and shops that stay open past 5pm, which you won't find at Bethany, Lewes, or Fenwick Island. If the sandy beaches, good restaurants, and little shops don't interest you, maybe the outlets will.

INDOOR ATTRACTIONS

The **Rehoboth Art League,** 12 Dodds Lane (✆ **302/227-8408;** www.rehobothartleague.org), sponsors gallery exhibits, art classes, and community events including the cottage tour in July and art show in August.

The **Rehoboth Beach Museum** ★, 511 Rehoboth Ave. (✆ **302/227-7310**), home to the town's historical society, tells the town's story in a rehabbed ice house. Of particular interest are the bathing costumes, beach accessories, and beach photos from days gone by. It's open in season Monday through Friday 10am to 4pm and Saturday and Sunday 11am to 3pm. November through April, the museum is closed Tuesdays and Wednesdays. Admission is $5 for adults; $3 for students, military, and seniors; $3 for age 13 to 17; and free 12 and under.

The **Anna Hazzard Tent House,** 17 Christian St., off Rehoboth Avenue (✆ **302/226-1119**), is one of the original tiny tent buildings erected in the 19th century when Rehoboth was a summer retreat for Methodists. Admission is free. It's open on first Fridays June through October, for a 9am guided tour.

ESPECIALLY FOR KIDS

Funland, on the boardwalk between Delaware and Brooklyn avenues (✆ **302/227-1921;** www.funlandrehoboth.com), has rides and games. The rides for the preschool set are varied enough to keep the youngsters busy; rides for kids 8 and over are more limited. It's open from Mother's Day weekend to the weekend after Labor Day, the arcade from 10am, the rides from 1pm. It closes when everybody's ready to go home.

About 1½ miles north of town is **Jungle Jim's Adventure Land,** 36944 Country Club Rd. (✆ **302/227-8444;** www.funatjunglejims.com), which offers go-carts, miniature golf, bumper boats, a rock-climbing wall, outdoor rides, and a water park. It's open weekends in May and September and daily from Memorial Day to Labor Day from 10am to 11pm.

Pirate Adventures (✆ **302/539-5155;** www.pirateadventuresoceancity.com) takes off from the pier at Harpoon Hanna's, 142nd Street and the bay, seven times a day. There's treasure, sea chanteys, storytelling, and other pirate stuff during the hourlong voyage. Tickets are $20 for those over 3 and $10 for toddler pirates. Babies are free.

Rehoboth Summer Children's Theatre (✆ **302/227-6766;** www.rehobothchildrenstheatre.org) puts on shows for the kids at venues around the Rehoboth area, including the Theatre of the Arts, 20 Baltimore Ave., and the Bay Center in Ruddertowne. Favorites such as *Peter Pan* and *Snow White* are performed selected summer weeknights. Curtain time is 11am or 7pm. The theater also offers weeklong summer camps and acting workshops. Call for reservations.

SHOPPING THE OUTLETS & THE BOARDWALK

The **Tanger Outlet Centers** ★, stretching for 2 miles down Route 1 (✆ **800/4TANGER** [482-6437] or 302/226-9223; www.tangeroutlet.com), have become a destination in their own right. Clothing stores include Brooks Brothers, L.L.Bean, Coach, OshKosh, and DKNY. Some 150 outlet stores offer accessories, housewares,

THE life-saving STATIONS

Just south of Dewey and beside the Ocean City Inlet are two buildings that memorialize the men of the U.S. Life-Saving Service.

The pumpkin-and-brown **Indian River Life-Saving Station,** on Route 1, south of Dewey (✆ **302/227-6991;** www.destateparks.com/attractions/life-saving-station), has been restored to its 1905 appearance. Built in 1876 as an Atlantic-coast outpost to look for ships in distress, it was transferred to the U.S. Coast Guard in 1915, decommissioned in 1962, and restored in 1998. Listed on the National Register of Historic Places, its spare interior recalls the rescuers who saved sailors from sinking ships. Admission is $4 for adults, $3 for seniors, and $2 for children 6 to 12. Guided tours ($5) are available until a half-hour before closing. Or use your cellphone for an audio tour. From April through October, it's open daily from 8am to 4:30pm. Off season, it's open select weekends 8:30am to 4pm. Call ahead.

In Ocean City, the white-and-red **Ocean City Life-Saving Station Museum,** at the Inlet end of the boardwalk (✆ **410/289-4991;** www.ocmuseum.org), recalls the men who saved 4,500 sailors off these shores. Artifacts include a restored surf rescue boat and a pictorial history of storms that have raged here. Other exhibits focus on O.C. history, including bathing suits and lifeguards. Admission is $3 for adults, $1 for children 6 to 12. (Discount coupons online.) Hours are June through Labor Day daily from 10am to 10pm, and September, May, and October daily from 10am to 5pm. Call ahead for winter hours.

china and crystal, sneakers, and handbags. Two centers are on the western side of Route 1; the third stretches between them on the east. You can't walk from center to center—and you have to be dedicated if you want to hit all the shops in a single day. Get a map so you can plan the most efficient route. Parking can be a challenge on weekends or rainy days when Route 1 traffic can slow to a crawl. This place is so popular, New Jersey residents hop on the Cape May–Lewes Ferry to spend a day shopping in sales-tax-free Delaware. Hours are Monday through Saturday from 9am to 9pm and Sunday from 11am to 7pm. In summer, Sunday hours begin at 9am.

In downtown Rehoboth, there are a few shops on the boardwalk but the most interesting are along Rehoboth Avenue, which intersects the boardwalk at its midpoint. Most are open 10am to 6pm, with extended hours in summer.

Azura The owners design the stylish clothes sold here. Look for jewelry, furnishings, and accessories as well. 139 Rehoboth Ave. ✆**302/226-9650.**

Carlton's When you haven't packed your party dress or sport coat, stop here for something classic but stylish. 31 Rehoboth Ave. ✆**302/227-3590.**

Christmas Spirit You can always find Santas, angels, and ornaments in this festive shop. 161 Rehoboth Ave. ✆**302/227-6872.**

Heidi Lowe Jewelry This yellow cottage is home to Lowe's own creations with room for other jewelry artisans. 328 Rehoboth Ave. ✆**302/227-9203.** www.heidilowejewelry.com.

Ibach's Head here for chocolates: nonpareils, cashew turtles, cherry cordials. There's saltwater taffy, too. 9 Rehoboth Ave. ✆**877/270-9674** or 302/227-2870.

Peninsula Laminations The folks here dry-mount prints and posters and laminate them for a unique look. There are lots of great resort posters. 3 N. 1st St. ✆ **302/226-7510.** www.peninsulalaminations.com.

Scandinavian Occasion Sweet lace curtains, colored glass, and semiprecious stone jewelry are just the beginning of the treasures you'll find here. 125 Rehoboth Ave. ✆ **302/227-3945.**

Sea Shell Shop This is a treasure-trove of seashell art, lamps, and jewelry, as well as loose shells, sponges, and hermit crabs. Little hands, the owners say, are always welcome. 119 Rehoboth Ave. ✆ **302/227-6666.** www.seashellshop.com.

Tickled Pink Stop in for Lilly Pulitzer's pink-and-green country-club style. 235 Rehoboth Ave. ✆ **866/536-7456** or 302/227-7575. www.tickledpinkapparel.com.

Tiger Lili Trendy fashions and accessories are featured in this shop run by Mrs. Delaware 2008. 18 Rehoboth Ave. ✆ **302/226-0731.** www.tigerlilirehoboth.com.

SPAS

Rehoboth has become something of a spa resort, with plenty of places to choose from. **Avenue Apothecary & Spa,** 110A Rehoboth Ave. (✆ **302/227-5649;** www.avenuedayspa.com), offers European facials, waxing, makeup, and hair and nail care. It has a spa shop as well. The **Spa at the Bellmoor,** 6 Christian St. (✆ **800/425-2355** or 302/227-5800; www.thebellmoor.com), offers massage, facials, body treatments, waxing, and nail care. The **Spa by the Sea,** 19266 Coastal Hwy. (✆ **302/227-8640;** www.spa-by-the-sea.com), offers traditional massage, facials, manicures, and other treatments. Just need a massage? Call on **One Spirit Massage Studio,** 169 Rehoboth Ave. (✆ **302/226-3552;** www.onespiritmassage.com).

Outdoor Activities

BIKING With its flat terrain and shady streets, Rehoboth is ideal for bicycling. Bikes are allowed on the boardwalk between 5 and 10am from May 15 to September 15, and anytime off season.

A scenic 6-mile **Junction and Breakwater Trail** connects Rehoboth and Lewes via a crushed-stone trail suitable for walkers, joggers, bikers, and wheelchairs; motorized vehicles are prohibited. The 15-mile round-trip takes 2 hours or more, depending on where and how long you stop. Find the trail head behind the Tanger Outlets shopping area on the east side or Route 1. A map is available at **www.destateparks.com/Activities/trails.j-and-b-trail.pdf**.

Insider's note: If you stop by one of the bike shops, they can give you directions from downtown Rehoboth to the trail. It's an easy ride. Stop at **Atlantic Cycle** (18 Wilmington Ave.; ✆ **302/226-2543**), **Bob's Bikes** (1st and Maryland Ave.; ✆ **302/227-7966**), or **Bikes to Go** (174 Rehoboth Ave.; ✆ **302/227-7600**) and rent a bike for about $6 an hour or $12 to $16 a day. Bikes to Go has a really good map indicating seven interesting bike rides.

GOLF The number of public golf courses between Fenwick and Rehoboth has grown in recent years to include the **Rookery** (27052 Broadkill Rd., Milton, DE 19968; ✆ **302/313-GOLF** [4653]; www.rookerygolf.com), an 18-hole course off the Broadkill River; **Baywood Greens** (32267 Clubhouse Way, Long Neck, DE, 19966; ✆ **888/844-2254** or 302/947-9800; www.baywoodgreens.com), 18 holes among flowers, man-made ponds, two tunnels, and eight bridges; **Bear Trap Dunes** (11 Willow Oak Ave., Ocean View, DE 19970; ✆ **877/BEARTRAP** [232-7872] or

302/537-5600; www.beartrapdunes.com), 27 holes among wetlands and dunes; and **Bayside** (31806 Lakeview Dr., Selbyville, DE 19975; ✆ **302/436-3400,** ext.1; www.livebayside.com/golf), a Jack Nicklaus course with views of Assawoman Bay.

STAND-UP PADDLING The newest craze at the beach is stand-up paddling. Rent a board and paddle at **Delaware Paddle Sports** (✆ **302/645-7300**), **Delmarva Board Sport Adventures** (✆ **301/651-0542**), or **East of Maui** (✆ **302/227-4703**). Rentals run about $25 an hour to $45 a half-day.

TENNIS There are public courts at **Rehoboth City Courts,** on Surf Avenue between Rehoboth Beach and North Shores (✆ **302/227-3598**); near Rehoboth Elementary School, on State Street. Private courts may be rented at Rehoboth Beach Sailing Association (✆ **302/381-5685**) on the bay at McKinley Street in Dewey.

WATERSPORTS **Bay Sports,** 111 Dickinson St., Dewey Beach (✆ **302/227-7590**), rents kayaks, pedal boats, sailboats, Hobie catamarans, and jet skis by the half-hour, hour, or day. A kayak or pedal boat goes for $15 to $25 an hour. Hobie cats are $50 to $65. Stop by **Dewey Beach Parasailing,** Route 1 at Dickinson Street (✆ **302/227-9507;** www.flydewey.com), to go parasailing. Reservations are recommended; rides cost $65 to $75, depending on how high you want to go.

Rehoboth & Dewey Beaches After Dark

Sandwiched between the quiet family resorts of Bethany Beach and Fenwick Island to the south and Lewes to the north, Rehoboth and Dewey beaches offer the only consistent nightlife on the Delaware coast.

CLUBS & BARS

REHOBOTH BEACH Live acts are scheduled on weekends at **Dogfish Head Brewings and Eats,** 320 Rehoboth Ave. (✆ **302/226-2739**). In summer, **Irish Eyes,** 52 Rehoboth Ave. (✆ **302/227-5758**), schedules DJs on Saturday nights. There's a pool table and 16 TVs to catch all the football action in fall and winter. Feeling mellow? Try **Victoria's,** at Olive and the boardwalk (✆ **302/227-0615**), for jazz piano Friday and Saturday 6 to 10pm.

DEWEY BEACH Dewey Beach's rocking nightlife revolves around two mainstays: the **Rusty Rudder,** 113 Dickinson St., on the bay (✆ **302/227-3888**), and the **Bottle & Cork,** 1807 Hwy. 1 (✆ **302/227-7272**). The crowd tends to be 20- to 35-year-olds looking to party. The Rudder holds deck parties and has occasional bands or other activities; the cover varies. The Bottle & Cork, open only in spring and summer, is a surprisingly large rock club that hosts both local and nationally known bands; the cover varies. When Better Than Ezra or Joan Jett is in the house, expect a big crowd.

The **Starboard,** 2009 Hwy. 1 (✆ **302/227-4600;** www.thestarboard.com), is usually crowded with young people. It serves breakfast, lunch, and dinner in summer—the Bloody Marys are famous. Go to the website for special events. Closed November to April.

GAY & LESBIAN REHOBOTH

A number of Rehoboth nightspots cater to a GLBT clientele. Gay-owned **Aqua Grill,** 57 Baltimore Ave. (✆ **302/226-9001;** aquagrillrehoboth.com), draws a young crowd of mostly men for drinks and live entertainment. The **Blue Moon,** 35 Baltimore Ave. (✆ **302/227-6515**), has a happy hour popular with men. DJs and the mellow lounge in back at **Cloud 9,** 234 Rehoboth Ave. (✆ **302/226-1999;**

www.cloud9de.com), draw a mixed clientele. **Dogfish Head Brews & Eats,** 320 Rehoboth Ave. (✆ **302/226-2739**), is primarily straight but draws a mixed crowd for its craft beer and live entertainment. A lesbian crowd goes to the **Frogg Pond,** 3 S. First St. (✆ **302/227-2234;** www.thefroggpond.com) for live entertainment and games. Dancing and karaoke draw the crowd to **Purple Parrot,** 134 Rehoboth Ave. (✆ **302/226-1139**).

THE PERFORMING ARTS

The newly rebuilt open-air **Rehoboth Beach Memorial Bandstand,** at Rehoboth Avenue and the boardwalk (✆ **302/227-2233**), hosts more than 40 free concerts and other events on summer weekends, starting at 8pm. Check with the visitor center for an up-to-date schedule.

Clear Space Theatre Company, 20 Baltimore Ave. (✆ **302/227-2270;** www.clearspacetheatre.org), presents new shows February through November: lots of musicals, a little light comedy, and holiday favorites.

BETHANY BEACH & FENWICK ISLAND, DE ★

100 miles SE of Wilmington; 120 miles SE of Baltimore; 130 miles SE of Washington, DC

Nicknamed the "Quiet Resorts," Bethany Beach and Fenwick Island have the most laid-back atmosphere of the Maryland and Delaware beach resorts. They offer a calm alternative to the bustle of Ocean City and the sophistication and shopping of Rehoboth. This pleasant stretch of condominium communities, state parks, and beaches may be quiet at night, but it offers visitors—especially families—so much during the day: It's a great place to sit back and enjoy the beach, swim in the surf, bicycle along quiet roads, bird-watch in the dunes or coastal waterways, and stroll on the tiny Bethany Beach boardwalk.

Essentials

GETTING THERE **By Car** Whether you're approaching from points north or south, it is best to take Route 113 and to avoid crowded Route 1—particularly in July and August. To reach Bethany Beach, take Route 26 east at Dagsboro; to reach Fenwick Island from the north, take Route 20 south (just outside of Dagsboro); and to get to Fenwick from the south, turn west on Route 54 at Selbyville. From the west, take Route 50 across the Bay Bridge to Route 404 east, then turn south on Route 113 and follow the directions above.

By Plane Visitors arriving by plane can fly into the **Salisbury–Ocean City–Wicomico Regional Airport;** see p. 261 for details.

VISITOR INFORMATION The **Bethany–Fenwick Area Chamber of Commerce** (✆ **800/962-SURF** [7873] or 302/539-2100; www.bethany-fenwick.org) is on Route 1, adjacent to the Fenwick Island State Park. It publishes a booklet called *The Quiet Resorts* and stocks plenty of brochures. It's open year-round, Monday through Friday from 9am to 5pm, Saturday and Sunday from 10am to 4pm. Bethany's **Town Hall,** 214 Garfield Pkwy. (✆ **302/539-8011**), also has brochures and a small museum.

GETTING AROUND Since Bethany Beach and Fenwick Island are within 5 miles of each other, most people take a car, but bikes and inline skates are also useful. All motels provide free guest parking; most restaurants also have access to parking for customers. Many Bethany and Fenwick streets are subject to metered or permit parking at $1.50 an hour, and rules are strictly enforced. Bethany's meters are enforced May 15 to September 15 from 10am to 11pm. ***Tip:*** Skip the meters and stop at the kiosk for a parking permit. These run $20 a day or $137 a week and eliminate the need to keep the meters fed. The kiosk and change machines around town will also make change.

Once you park, get around Bethany Beach (but not to Sea Colony or South Bethany) via the **Beach Trolley.** It costs a quarter (exact change) to ride and runs from 9:30am to 7:30pm in summer. Flag it down and it will stop.

ORIENTATION If it weren't for the signs in the median on Route 1, you'd never know there were three different communities. But officially, there are Bethany Beach, South Bethany, and Fenwick Island. North of the town of Fenwick is the Fenwick Island State Park, all beach and parking lot with no restaurants, shops, or hotels. Fenwick Island is like a hyphen, connecting Ocean City to Delaware. Traveling north from O.C., you'll hardly know you've left the state.

Head north to find Bethany Beach and its quieter, all-residential neighbor, South Bethany. Bethany Beach is home to a small shopping area and boardwalk. Between the two is the huge condo resort called Sea Colony. Bethany and South Bethany have public beaches; Sea Colony's are private.

SPECIAL EVENTS The **Bethany Beach Boardwalk Arts Festival** (© **302/539-2100**), a juried festival of fine arts and crafts, is held the Saturday after Labor Day from 10am to 5pm. In late September, join in the **Make-a-Wish Triathlon at Sea Colony** (www.tricolumbia.org) or just cheer on the athletes. The **Fall Surf-Fishing Tournament** is held in October; the **Spring Surf-Fishing Tournament** takes place on a weekend in early May. For information, call © **302/539-2100.**

Where to Stay

Bethany Beach and Fenwick Island are packed in summer, with more and more people booking a week in a condominium unit or beach house. New developments are springing up on Route 24, a short drive from the beach, now that almost every oceanfront parcel has been developed.

Bethany has a variety of accommodations, from oceanfront mansions to houses in town, from duplexes and town houses to condos tucked under trees. The condo resort **Sea Colony ★★★** is an attractive option, with rental units in nine oceanfront high-rises and a variety of condos on the west side of Route 1. With 12 pools, one is close to every unit. Tennis villas are surrounded by 34 courts, four indoor. There are also walking and biking paths, a fitness center, and a children's center. Shuttles take Sea Colony West guests to the beach. Guests need a pass for the beach, pools, tennis courts, fitness centers, and shuttles; these cost $35 per person per week in season.

Look for your vacation rental early: Bookings are accepted up to a year in advance though you might still find a nice place a few weeks before you arrive. Rentals range from $500 per week for a small unit up to the thousands for oceanfront homes with room for extended family. Some good rental companies to call include **Coldwell Banker** (© 302/539-1777; www.cbvacations.com), **Tansey-Warner, Inc.** (© 302/539-3001; www.tanseywarner.com), **Tidewater Realty, Ltd.** (© 800/888-7501 or 302/539-7500; www.tidewaterrealty.com), and **Wilgus** (© 800/441-8118; www.wilgusassociates.com). **Resort Quest** (© **888/500-4254** or 302/537-8888; www.resortquestdelaware.com) specializes in Sea Colony units. All of them will send brochures describing their rental properties.

Hotel rooms for July and August are booked months in advance, have higher rates, and often require weekend surcharges and 2- or 3-night minimum stays. Get your beach fix at a budget rate by visiting in spring or especially the fall when the weather can be beautiful and the water is warm. Beaches are fairly quiet in early June and after mid-August when schools reopen.

BETHANY BEACH

The Addy Sea Bed & Breakfast ★ You'll find this Victorian jewel far from the Bethany-size crowds but right by the ocean. A century-old cedar-shake cottage with wraparound porch, the Addy Sea offers quiet comfort along with a grand view from most rooms. Corner rooms (nos. 6 and 7) are brighter and have the best vistas. Room no. 12 has a king-size bed, Jacuzzi, and TV, while room no. 10 has a niche with windows offering a 180-degree view.

99 Ocean View Pkwy. (at N. Atlantic Ave.), Bethany Beach, DE 19930. www.addysea.com. ✆ **800/418-6764** or 302/539-3707. Fax 302/539-7263. 13 units. $100–$375 double. Rates include full breakfast, afternoon tea, and lunch in summer. 2- or 3-night minimum required on weekends and holidays. AE, DISC, MC, V. Free parking. **Amenities:** Beach equipment; communal TV. *In room:* A/C, hair dryer, free Wi-Fi.

Bethany Arms Motel & Apartments ☺ Ideal for families who want to be close to the ocean, this five-building complex offers motel units with fridges and microwaves, as well as apartments with kitchens and ocean views. Two buildings are on the boardwalk, with three in back between the boardwalk and Atlantic Avenue. First-floor room views can be obscured by the dunes.

Atlantic Ave. and Hollywood St. (P.O. Box 1600), Bethany Beach, DE 19930. www.beach-net.com/bethanyarms.html. ✆ **302/539-9603.** 50 units. $75–$250 double. Surcharges may apply. 2- or 3-night minimum stay required on summer weekends and holidays. MC, V. Free parking. Closed late Oct to early Mar. *In room:* A/C, TV, fridge, microwave.

FENWICK ISLAND

Fenwick Islander Motel On the bay side of the highway, just north of the Maryland-Delaware state line, this three-story motel offers simple, clean accommodations. These efficiency units have kitchenettes; second- and third-floor rooms have balconies. Rooms in back are off the highway and quieter, with a view of the canal.

Rte. 1 and S. Carolina Ave. (btw. S. Carolina and W. Virginia aves.), Fenwick Island, DE 19944. www.fenwickislander.com. ✆ **800/346-4520** or 302/539-2333. Fax 302/537-1134. 63 units. $49–$189 double. Children 9 and under stay free in parent's room; children 10–16 stay for $5 each per night. Surcharges and minimum-stay requirements may apply on weekends and holidays. Weekly rates available. AE, DISC, MC, V. Free parking. Closed Nov–Mar. **Amenities:** Outdoor pool. *In room:* A/C, hair dryer (upon request), kitchenette.

Ric-Mar Apartments and Cottages ☺ These old-fashioned beach apartments and cottages, still family-owned, offer Fenwick's closest accommodations to the beach, 100 feet away. Guests can choose from studio efficiencies or one- and two-bedroom apartments. Three units that sleep six rent by the week in summer. The units are old, but clean and "beachy." Three cottages, which rent by the week, are good for families.

Delaware and Bunting aves., Fenwick Island, DE 19944. www.ricmarfenwick.com. ✆ **302/539-9613.** 14 units. $110–$145 efficiency; $125–$250 apt. 3-night minimum stay required in high season. Cottages $900–$2,500 a week. DISC, MC, V. Free parking. Closed mid-Sept to mid-May. **Amenities:** Patio and deck w/grills; outdoor pool. *In room:* A/C, TV, kitchenette.

Seaside Inn At this highway-side motel a half-block from the beach, rooms are simply furnished. Larger king and two-queen units have sleeper sofas and more room. A pool is behind the office. The only bad news: no water views.

1401 Coastal Hwy., Fenwick Island, DE 19944. www.seasideinnfenwick.com. ✆**800/417-1104** or 302/251-5000. 61 units. $49–$185 double. Surcharges and minimum-stay requirements on some weekends and holidays. Children 17 and under stay free in parents' room. AE, DISC, MC, V. Free parking. Closed mid-Oct to mid-May. **Amenities:** Outdoor pool. *In room:* A/C, TV, fridge, hair dryer (upon request), microwave.

Where to Eat

The restaurants of the Bethany Beach and Fenwick Island area provide a pleasant blend of waterside and inland dining, mostly at moderate prices. Family-oriented, lower-priced restaurants are mixed in with fine-dining establishments that offer quality, ambience, and creative food. Unless otherwise noted, most restaurants serve alcohol. (Note that in Bethany, alcoholic beverages are available only in restaurants—there are no bars.) ***Note:*** Hours in the "Quiet Resorts" can change as crowds diminish off season. Always call ahead if you're visiting in the off season—that is, before Memorial Day and after Labor Day. Fenwick stays a bit livelier until the greyhounds have left after Columbus Day weekend.

Since motels in Bethany and Fenwick do not serve breakfast, you may want to check out some of the following places, particularly Frog House and Warren's Station.

BETHANY BEACH

Baja Beach House GrillMEXICAN Fresh Mexican is on the menu at this *muy* casual eatery owned by a Bethany native. Burritos, tacos, and fajitas, as well as burgers and sandwiches, are cooked as soon as you order them at the counter. Angus burgers are another option. Breakfast is served daily. You can call ahead for carryout or stay to eat inside this sleek, California-style shop.

109 Garfield Pkwy., Bethany Beach, DE 19930. ✆ **302/537-9993.** www.bajabeachhouse.com. Reservations not accepted. Main courses $6–$12. AE, MC, V. Hours vary depending on season, but always open for breakfast, lunch, and dinner in summer, plus long weekends in the spring and fall off season; call ahead.

The Cottage Cafe RestaurantAMERICAN This homey place has updated its country-cottage look but kept the comfort foods that make it so popular. The menu offers everything from pot roast and meatloaf to seafood, soup-and-salad, and pastas.

Rte. 1 at Hickman Plaza, Bethany Beach, DE 19930. ✆ **302/539-8710.** www.cottagecafe.com. Reservations not accepted. Main courses $7–$25, lunch, $9–$28 dinner. AE, DC, MC, V. Daily 11am–1am.

Frog House ☺AMERICAN You can sleep in and still get breakfast at the Frog House, where it's served until 2pm. The 12 kinds of pancakes range from apple to chocolate chip. Lunchtime favorites include sandwiches, burgers, and salads; dinner brings fried chicken, steamed shrimp, and crab cakes. It's casual, friendly, and reasonably priced.

116 Garfield Pkwy., Bethany Beach, DE 19930. ✆**302/539-4500.** Reservations not accepted. Main courses $3–$10 breakfast, $3–$8 lunch, $7–$18 dinner. DISC, MC, V. Mar–May Fri–Sat only; Memorial Day to Labor Day daily 7am–9pm; Sept–Nov 8am–2pm. Closed Dec–Feb.

Grotto Pizza PIZZA The crowds keep coming to Grotto Pizza. There are outlets throughout Delaware, and Bethany has *two*—both packed at dinnertime. Enjoy the crispy crust, savory sauce, and cheese—and the perfect white pizza. The menu also has salads, subs, and pastas. Grotto has branches in Dewey and Rehoboth; delivery is available, too.

793 Garfield Pkwy., Bethany Beach, DE 19930 (✆ **302/537-3278**), and 8–10 York Beach Mall, South Bethany (✆ **302/537-6600**). www.grottopizza.com. Reservations not accepted. Pizza $9.75–$20. AE, DISC, MC, V. Summer Sun–Thurs 11am–11pm, Fri–Sat 11am–midnight; hours vary in off season, so call ahead. The York Beach Mall location closes in off season.

Mango Mike's SEAFOOD The beach vibe makes this casual place a lot of fun. Friendly waitstaff make it pleasant. And a seat on the deck overlooking the ocean makes it a place to linger (if there isn't a long line of hungry people waiting). Inside, the decor is beach-shack modern. The menu features fresh seafood and slightly Caribbean dishes, such as coco-loco-nut shrimp salad and jerk-chicken salad.

Garfield Pkwy. and the boardwalk, Bethany Beach, DE 19930. ✆ **302/537-6621.** www.mangomikes.com. Reservations accepted only for 5–6pm. Main dishes $15–$30. AE, MC, V. June–Sept daily 11:30am–11:30pm; Apr–May and Oct–Thanksgiving weekend Fri–Sat 11am–9pm, Sun 11am–3pm. Closed Dec–Mar.

McCabe's Gourmet Market DELI This deli and market is a local favorite for sandwiches, salads, and fresh-baked breads and pastries. ***Tip:*** Visitors in South Bethany walk from the beach to pick up sandwiches for their beachside picnic—it's that close. Call ahead and your order will be waiting.

Rte. 1, in the York Beach Mall (just north of Fenwick Island State Park), South Bethany. ✆ **302/539-8550.** www.mccabesgourmet.com. Reservations not accepted. Sandwiches $5–$10. AE, DISC, MC, V. Summer daily 7am–5pm (or later); fall and spring Tues–Sat 7am–5pm, Sun 7am–4pm. Closed Jan to mid-Mar.

Sedona ★ AMERICAN Offering welcome sophistication in Bethany Beach, Sedona is a great place to sneak away from the kids and have an adult meal (although well-behaved children are welcome). The sleek interior has room for 70; in summer, make a reservation or be prepared to wait. Traditional recipes get a contemporary accent here. Choices range from rack of lamb to seared tuna, and sometimes there's antelope. Tapas (three dishes for $20) is a new feature that's catching on.

26 Pennsylvania Ave., Bethany Beach, DE 19930. ✆ **302/539-1200.** www.sedona-bethany.com. Reservations recommended. Main courses $28–$39. AE, DISC, MC, V. Daily 5:30–9:30pm in summer; winter Fri–Sat 5–10pm. (Call to confirm off-season hours.) Closed Jan–Mar.

FENWICK ISLAND

David Twining's Nantuckets ★ SEAFOOD This is a place for grown-ups, with bright dining rooms, white tablecloths, and an innovative menu offering rich beef, garlicky mashed potatoes, famous quahog *chowdah,* and a lobster shepherd's pie that doesn't need a crust. If you like a more casual dining experience, try the adjacent bar, a cheerful place to grab a cold drink, appetizer, or whole meal. Service is top-notch. Early-bird specials are available before 5:45pm; there's happy hour in the taproom from 4 to 7pm.

Rte. 1 and Atlantic Ave. ✆ **800/362-3463** or 302/539-2607. www.nantucketsrestaurant.com. Reservations recommended. Main courses $9–$30. AE, DC, DISC, MC, V. Daily 4–10pm taproom; 5pm–midnight dining rooms (until 9pm in off season).

Harpoon Hanna's ★ ☺ SEAFOOD This bayside restaurant has its ups and downs, but you can always count on fresh fish, along with a crisp tropical salad with mandarin orange and tiny shrimp. What *really* draws the crowds are the warm breads—raisin, rye, and coconut muffins—and fresh fish prepared three ways. Food is surprisingly good in spite of the crowds, the hours, and the demands put on the young but eager waitstaff. In summer, arrive early—about 4:30pm or so—or plan on a wait. The Tiki Bar has nightly parties, sometimes with live entertainment. Children are welcome; docks available for diners arriving by boat. Brunch is served on Sunday.

142nd St. (at Rte. 54). ✆ **800/227-0525** or 302/539-3095. www.harpoonhannasrestaurant.com. Reservations not accepted. Main courses $8–$13 lunch, $10–$25 dinner. AE, DISC, MC, V. Mon–Sat 11am–1am; Sun 10am–1am.

Warren's Station AMERICAN Families have been coming here since the 1960s. The big, white restaurant, which resembles a lifesaving station, serves good-size portions of traditional foods, including a turkey dinner; beef, chicken, and seafood entrees; and a heavenly "crab cutlet," a big fluffy crab cake from an old Deal Island Church recipe. Not that hungry? Try a burger, sandwich, or salad. Leave room for homemade pie. No alcohol is served.

1406 Coastal Hwy., Fenwick Island, DE 19944. ✆ **302/539-7156.** www.warrensstation.com. Reservations not accepted. Main courses $2–$9 breakfast, $3–$9 lunch, $9–$18 dinner. DISC, MC, V. Mid-May to Labor Day daily 8am–9pm; Sept 4:30–8:30pm. Closed Oct to mid-May.

What to See & Do

The 1-mile-long **Bethany Beach Boardwalk** has only a few businesses on it. It's more of a promenade, perfect for a walk near the beach. Most of the shops and fast-food eateries are on **Garfield Parkway,** which intersects the boardwalk midway. **Fenwick Island** has no boardwalk between its hotels and its beach with gentle dunes. Shops and businesses are along Route 1.

To see sunken treasure, head to the **DiscoverSea Shipwreck Museum,** 708 Coastal Hwy., Fenwick Island (✆ **302/539-9366;** www.discoversea.com), a small museum above the Sea Shell City shop. The collection includes jewelry, coins, china, and a seashell display. Admission is free. Hours are Memorial Day through Labor Day daily from 11am to 8pm, September through December and April and May Saturday and Sunday from 11am to 4pm.

Built in 1859, the **Fenwick Island Lighthouse,** on the Transpeninsular Line, Route 54, a quarter-mile west of Route 1, is one of Delaware's oldest. The lighthouse is still in operation; its beams can be seen for 15 miles. Its grounds and ground floor are open to the public July and August, Friday through Monday 10am to 2pm, and May, June, and September, Saturday and Sunday 10am to 2pm. Find the gate on 146th Street in Ocean City. Admission is free.

Across from the lighthouse is the **Viking Golf Theme Park,** Routes 1 and 54, Fenwick Island (✆ **302/539-1644**), an amusement park with miniature golf, a water park, and go-carts. Hours vary according to weather. The water park is open from Memorial Day weekend to Labor Day, daily from 10am to 8pm. Miniature golf is open from Easter weekend to October, on warm weekends from 10am to 11pm, and in summer daily from 10am to midnight.

Outdoor Activities

BIKING The flatland along Route 1 in Bethany Beach and Fenwick Island is ideal for bicycling; however, caution is advised during peak traffic season in July and August. Bethany also has bike lanes through town.

Prefer a quiet ride under a canopy of loblolly pines? **Assawoman Wildlife Area** offers several bike-accessible roads that wind through tidal marshland and forests. To get here, take Route 26 west and turn left on Double Bridges Road, left to Camp Barnes Road, and follow signs to Assawoman. The park, which charges no admission, is open 7am to sunset.

Bethany Cycle and Fitness Shop, 792B Garfield Pkwy. (✆ **302/537-9982**), rents beach bicycles for $5 to $12 an hour or $20 per day.

FISHING Fishing, both in the bay and in the surf, is a major draw. Licenses are required if you're over 16. Details at the park office or at **www.dnrec.delaware.gov/fw/fisheries/pages/newfishinglicense.aspx**. Off-road vehicles must have a surf-fishing tag to be permitted on the beaches. Surf fishing is permitted when lifeguards are off duty. The Bethany–Fenwick Area Chamber of Commerce sponsors two surf-fishing tournaments a year, in early May and October; for information, call ✆ **302/539-2100.**

Fenwick Island State Park has 3 miles of ocean beach, most of which is open to surf fishing, and considerable tracts of open bay, ideal for both fishing and crabbing. There are also dune crossings for off-road vehicles; a surf-fishing vehicle permit is required. Call ✆ **302/227-3071** for vehicle permits and maps of fishing areas. Similar facilities are available at **Delaware Seashore State Park** (✆ **302/227-2800**). Admission is $8 for out-of-state visitors, $4 for Delawareans at both parks.

HIKING & BIRDING During the off season, **Fenwick Island** and **Delaware Seashore** state parks, both on Route 1, are great places for a walk along deserted beaches. In high season, however, when these beaches are covered with sunbathers, it's best to head out at sunrise or venture a little inland. ***Tip:*** Bring bug repellent.

Assawoman Wildlife Area (see "Biking," above) welcomes hikers on its few miles of dirt roads through tidal marsh and forests. An observation tower on the way to Mulberry Landing makes it easy to view a variety of shorebirds.

PADDLING & SAILING To tour the quieter waters of Assawoman Bay, a salt marsh, Assateague Island, or a nearby cypress stand, stop by **Coastal Kayak** (✆ **877/445-2925** or 302/539-7999; www.coastalkayak.com). It has a stand on the bay across from Fenwick Island State Park. Their outstanding tours cost $50 to $55 for adults and $10 less for children; they last 90 minutes to 2 hours. It also rents kayaks, stand-up paddleboards, sailing catamarans, and windsurfers—and it delivers. (Get a coupon from the website.)

TENNIS **Sea Colony** (p. 254) is the largest tennis resort on the East Coast, sporting 26 courts, including four outdoor lighted courts, four clay courts, and four indoor courts. If tennis is your game, contact a real-estate agent about renting a condo in Sea Colony's tennis villas.

Shopping

BETHANY BEACH Most of the shopping in Bethany Beach is along or near Garfield Parkway, with a few shops on the boardwalk. They're generally open daily from 10am to 5pm, with extended hours in summer.

Bethany Beach Books, 99 Garfield Pkwy. (✆ **302/539-2522**), is the place to pick up some beach reading. For your sweet tooth, head to the **Fudge Factory,** 3 Town Center (✆ **302/539-7502**), or follow the delectable aromas to **Fisher's Popcorn,** 108 Garfield Pkwy. (✆ **888/436-6388** or 302/539-8833).

Stop in **Alice H. Klein,** on Garfield Parkway (✆ **302/539-6992**), for delicate, handcrafted jewelry. Bethany's premier boutique is the eclectic **Japanesque,** 16 Pennsylvania Ave. (✆ **302/539-2311**), which carries a wide selection of Japanese jewelry, home furnishings, and books.

FENWICK ISLAND If you like country items, visit the **Seaside Country Store** (✆ **302/539-6110;** www.seasidecountrystore.com). This big, red store on Route 1, has room after room of merchandise with a country feel—from gifts and clothing to home decor to candy. It's closed December through February. **Pottery Place** (✆ **302/539-3603;** www.potteryplaceperks.com) has lots of beachy merchandise, but those in the know show up for their first cup of joe. The coffee bar in the back of the shop has wonderful coffee drinks. It's open at 7am for your caffeine fix year-round.

OCEAN CITY, MD ★★★

116 miles S of Wilmington; 144 miles SE of Baltimore; 130 miles SE of Washington, DC

For many Marylanders, heading "downy ocean" or "to the shore" means only one thing: a summer vacation in Ocean City, a 10-mile stretch of skinny barrier island. Ocean City hosts some four million summer visitors. So many visitors arrive that for 3 months of the year, Ocean City is the second-largest city in the state. Ocean City's entire beach is open to the public. They come for the 9 miles of **Atlantic beach,** 2.5-mile boardwalk, and diversions such as minigolf and Ferris wheels. The boardwalk, built in 1902, is crowded with hotels, some of them dating to the 1920s. Restaurants, ice-cream stands, and shops fill in the gaps. At its end, near the fishing pier, you'll find amusement rides and a Ferris wheel. On the **bayside,** watersports rule and dining comes with a sunset view. In **West Ocean City** are golf courses, fishing boats, and a horse-racing track and casino. For a more primitive experience, head to **Assateague,** home of wild ponies, undeveloped beaches, and basic necessities.

THINGS TO DO Ocean City has become a year-round destination. Sunning and jumping waves are tops in summer, but off season, the resort offers plenty to do: Kayak Assawoman Bay, hit a few balls on a waterfront golf course, bike along the flat terrain, or gamble in the Ocean Downs slots parlor. Sunsets and seafood bring everybody out to bayside restaurants each evening. Nearby **Berlin** boasts some good shopping and holiday cheer in December.

EATING & DRINKING Seafood, pizza, and ice cream are what everybody craves in Ocean City. The oldest eating establishments on the **boardwalk** are the ice-cream stands and pizza parlors lining **Coastal Highway.** At 5, the beaches empty out and the **bayside** seafood restaurants fill up. Reservations aren't necessary but expect to wait. Want a romantic dinner for two? A number of fine-dining spots offer creative menus and take reservations.

NATURE People aren't the only ones enjoying the beach. Observant sunbathers can watch pelicans and dolphins making their way up the coast, kids often dig for sand crabs, and late summer bathers know to watch for jellyfish. The quieter waters surrounding Ocean City—the bays of **Assawoman,** Sinepuxent, and Montego—attract fishermen, sailors, parasailers, and kayakers. For a closer, quieter look, nature lovers go to **Assateague,** or one of the nearby state parks.

Out on Coastal Highway, shopping centers, restaurants, hotels, and condos demand your attention and your money. Miniature-golf courses are popular: They're all crowded after dark, and there are some dandies (p. 275).

Essentials

GETTING THERE **By Car** Route 50 goes right to Ocean City. To reach the southern end of town, continue on Route 50 to the bridge that enters O.C. at Caroline Street. For those staying at 60th Street or above, take Route 90 and cross the bridge at 62nd Street. An alternative route (but only one lane each way) is to turn on Route 404 East past Queenstown; follow it into Delaware. Turn south onto Route 113 south. Route 26 east connects with Bethany. Turn south on Route 1 to Ocean City. Or take Route 54 to Fenwick to Route 1. However you get there, avoid Route 1 in Rehoboth—especially on weekends, when traffic slows to a crawl most of the day. ***Tip:*** Call ✆ **877/229-7726** on your way to the Bay Bridge for up-to-date traffic reports.

By Plane The **Salisbury–Ocean City–Wicomico Regional Airport,** 30 minutes west of Ocean City, near Salisbury (✆ **410/548-4827**), handles commuter flights to and from Baltimore, Washington, Philadelphia, and points south via **US Airways Express** (✆ **800/428-4322;** www.usairways.com). Private planes also fly into that airport, as well as **Ocean City Municipal Airport,** 3 miles west of town off Route 611 (✆ **410/520-5412**).

If you arrive via Baltimore/Washington International Thurgood Marshall Airport, then you can arrange to have the **BayRunner Shuttle** (✆ **410/912-6000;** www.bayrunners.com) pick you up; it makes five trips daily.

Car rentals are available from **Avis** (✆ **410/742-8566;** www.avis.com) and **Hertz** (✆ **410/749-2235;** www.hertz.com), both at the Wicomico Regional Airport. At the Ocean City airport, **Express** (✆ **410/213-7336**) rents cars.

By Bus **Greyhound** (✆ **800/231-2222;** www.greyhound.com) has daily service into Ocean City from points north and south, with nonstop buses from Baltimore, Washington, DC, and Salisbury. Buses stop at the **West Ocean City Park & Ride,** 12848 Ocean Gateway (✆ **410/289-9307**).

VISITOR INFORMATION The **Ocean City Convention and Visitors' Bureau** operates a visitor center in the Roland E. Powell Convention Center, 4001 Coastal Hwy., at 40th Street, bay side (✆ **800/626-6232** or 410/289-8181; www.ococean.com). It's open daily from 8:30am to 5pm in season, Monday to Friday 8:30am to 5pm off season.

If you're heading into town from Route 50, stop at the information center run by the **Greater Ocean City Chamber of Commerce,** Routes 707 and 50, 1½ miles from Ocean City (✆ **410/213-0552;** www.oceancity.org). It's a great place to pick up brochures and coupons. Open daily from 8:30am to 4:30pm except January and February, when it's closed on Sunday.

Tip: If you have only 1 night to stay at the beach, check with the staff at either center. Although most hotels advertise 2- or 3-night minimum stays on weekends, they can probably find you accommodations.

Look for coupons and event schedules in ***Ocean City Visitors' Guide, Sunny Day, Beachcomber,*** and ***Beach Guide,*** in restaurants, stores, and hotels.

GETTING AROUND **By Bus** In peak season, when parking is scarce, the bus is the most convenient way to get around. Buses run 24 hours a day. They follow one route, from the Delaware border south along Coastal Highway to the inlet, returning north along Baltimore Street and Coastal Highway. In summer, buses run every 10 minutes; from October 20 to Memorial Day, they run every half-hour. The fare is $1

North Ocean City

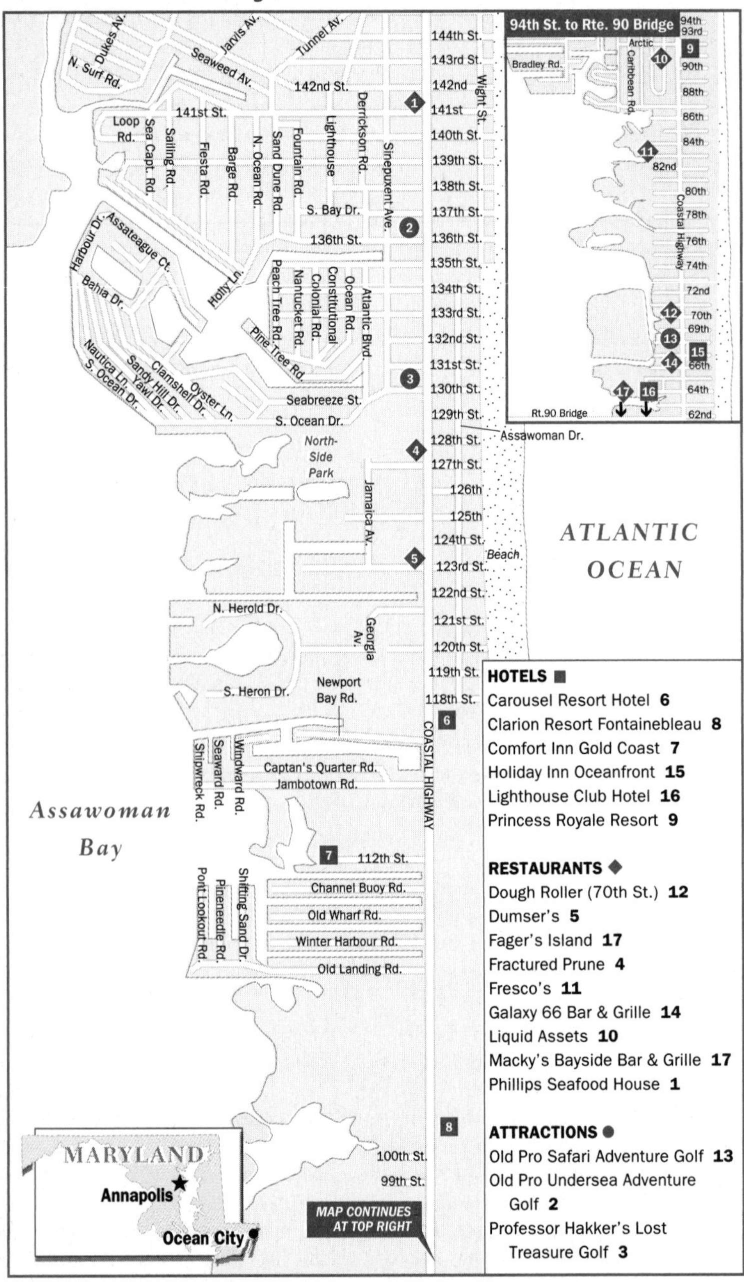

a ride or $3 to ride for 24 hours. For information, contact the **Ocean City Transportation Department,** 66th Street, bay side (✆ **410/723-1606**).

A **park-and-ride lot,** on Route 50 in West Ocean City (on the western side of the bridge), has free parking. Visitors can board a shuttle to South Division Street near the inlet to either spend the day there or catch a bus to other O.C. destinations. It costs $1.

By Boardwalk Tram ★ The tram travels 2½ miles between the inlet and 27th Street, stopping to pick up passengers who signal the driver. In summer, it runs every 10 minutes from 7am to midnight daily. On weekends from Easter to May, and in September and October, it runs every 15 minutes. To get off, raise your hand and the tram will stop. The fare is $3 one-way or $6 to ride all day. A frequent rider pass offers eight rides anytime for $20. It's great for parents with tired children—and a good way for first-time visitors to become familiar with the boardwalk.

By Taxi Taxi services are a good bet for late-night partiers and nondrivers, alike. These include **Sunset Taxi** (✆ **410/250-8294**), **Eastern Shore Taxi** (✆ **410/524-6647**), and **Ocean City Taxi** (✆ **443/912-2222**).

PARKING Parking is difficult at the height of the season. A majority of public facilities, such as shopping centers and restaurants, offer free parking. Eight public lots, mostly around the southern end of Ocean City, and most downtown streets have pay stations (change or credit card), which must be fed $1.50 an hour 24 hours a day April 15 through October 15. Parking is free off season. You can find change machines at several lots: Worcester Street; Somerset Street and Baltimore Avenue; Dorchester Street and Baltimore Avenue; North Division Street and Baltimore Avenue; and Fourth Street and Baltimore Avenue. The largest public lot is the Hugh T. Cropper parking lot at the inlet, with 1,200 paid spaces. The first 30 minutes here are free; then the rate is $2.50 an hour in season, $1.50 off season. If you plan to park here for nighttime activities, be aware that hundreds of other people will have the same idea—and the wait to get in the lot, and later to get out, can be long.

ORIENTATION Ocean City stretches for 10 miles, with one main north-south thoroughfare, Coastal Highway. It becomes two one-way streets on the southern end at around 32nd Street: Philadelphia goes south, Baltimore heads north. Cross streets are designated by numbers (from 1st to 145th), with numbers decreasing to the south. It's vital to know the cross street when looking for a shop or restaurant (though if you have a street address, the first two numbers usually tell you the cross street). Attractions and businesses on the cross streets are designated as either ocean side (east of Coastal Hwy.) or bay side (west of Coastal Hwy.). If you see an address that says Atlantic Avenue, it's oceanfront.

SPECIAL EVENTS Ocean City's party atmosphere is enhanced by festivals throughout the year; below is just a selection of the largest and most popular.

Everybody in O.C. is Irish on the Sunday closest to St. Patrick's Day for the **St. Patrick's Day Parade and Festival.** Every year, more and more people decide this is the place for the "wearin' of the green." The 4-day **Springfest,** held the first week of May, brings crafts, music, and food to the inlet parking lot. Lots of businesses open now, as O.C. prepares for summer.

On the **Fourth of July,** some 300,000 people crowd into Ocean City. Fireworks over Assawoman Bay top off the family-style picnic held at Northside Park beginning at 1pm. A second fireworks display takes place at North Division Street, at the south

Lower Ocean City

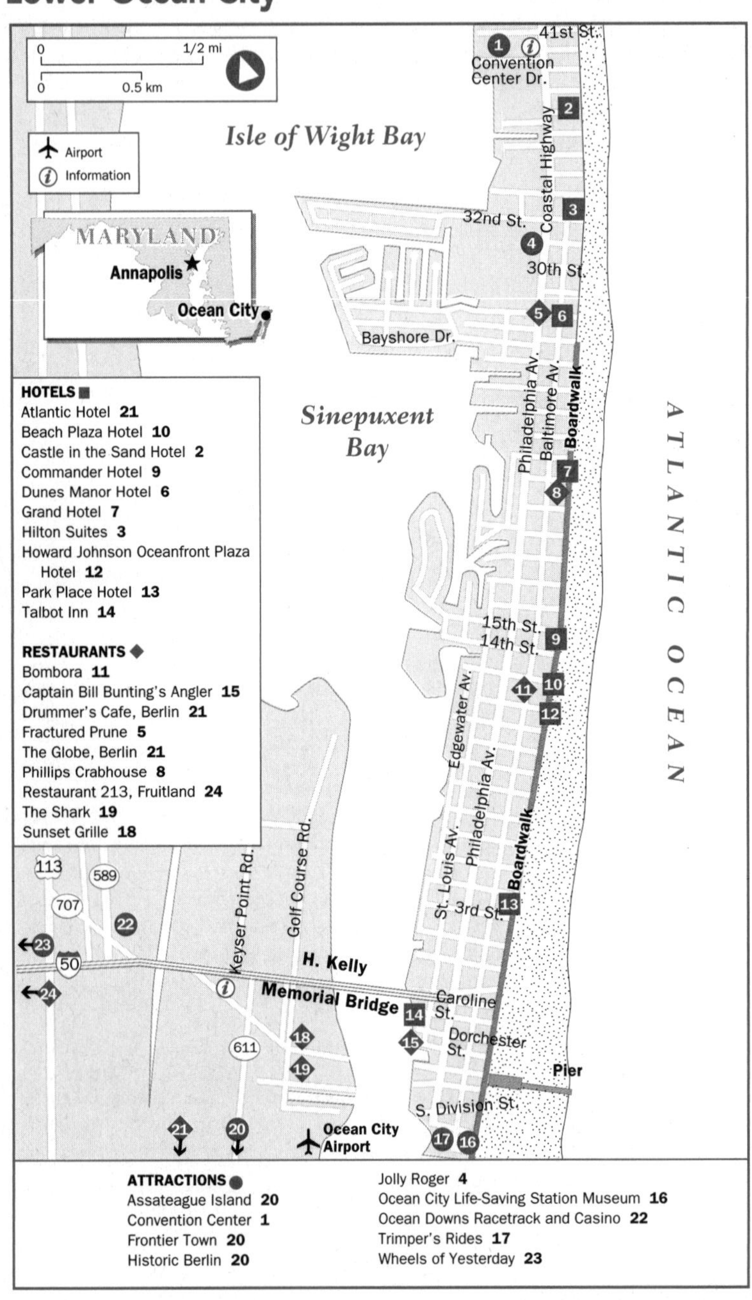

end of the boardwalk. Festivities begin with a concert at 8pm; fireworks begin at both locations at 9:30pm.

The **White Marlin Open ★** (www.whitemarlinopen.com) is held the first full week in August. Some 400 boats register for this annual fishing expedition. In 2011, prize money for the biggest white marlin, blue marlin, shark, and tuna totaled more than $2 million. Stop by the Harbor Island Marina on the bay side for the weigh-ins every night from 4 to 9pm. They reel in some whoppers. A 1,062-pound blue marlin broke a state record in 2009.

The **Sunfest** festival, the third week of September, officially ends the summer season with crafts, music, and food at the inlet. From mid-November to New Year's, holiday displays make up the **Winterfest of Lights ★★**. The first takes place at the inlet, where you can drive past the lit displays. The second takes place in Northside Park. For $3 for those 12 and older, you can ride the tram through the light displays and then stop to see Santa, have hot chocolate, and browse the gift shop.

Activities are scheduled nearly every summer evening on the beach or at North Side Park: Sundae Sundays, movies, concerts, and bonfires. Check with the visitor center.

[FastFACTS] OCEAN CITY

Area Code Ocean City's area codes are **410** and **443.**

Beach Wheelchairs Free beach-accessible chairs are available on a first-come, first-served basis from the beach patrol. Or reserve your chair at the convention center (✆ **410/289-2800**) or police department by calling ✆ **410/723-6610.**

Dentists Emergency work is provided at **Atlantic Dental Associates,** 12308 Ocean Gateway, at Route 50 (✆ **410/213-7575**).

Emergencies Dial ✆ **911** for fire, police, or ambulance.

Hospitals Go to the **75th Street Medical Center,** 7408 Coastal Hwy. (✆ **410/524-0075**); the **Atlantic General Hospital,** 9733 Healthway Dr., Berlin (✆ **877/641-1100** or 410/641-1100); or the **Peninsula Regional Medical Center,** 100 E. Carroll St., Salisbury (✆ **410/546-6400**).

Newspapers Ocean City's weekly newspaper is ***Ocean City Today.*** Dailies from Baltimore, Washington, and Philadelphia are also available.

Pharmacies Go to **Bailey's,** Eighth Street and Philadelphia Avenue (✆ **410/289-8191**), or **CVS,** 116 Philadelphia Ave. (✆ **410/289-6513**).

Police If it's not an emergency, dial ✆ **410/723-6600** for Ocean City police, ✆ **410/641-3101** for state police, or ✆ **410/289-7556** for beach patrol.

Post Office The main post office is at 71st Street and Coastal Highway, bay side (✆ **410/275-8777**). There's also one at the visitor center on Route 50 west of the bridge into Ocean City.

Public Restrooms On the boardwalk, restrooms are at Worcester, Caroline, 8th, and 27th streets. Other locations are at Third and St. Louis Avenue next to the Skate Park, the transit centers at South Division Street, and 144th Street, and the Park & Ride west of the Route 50 bridge.

Taxes The state sales tax is 6%.

Transit Information Dial ✆ **410/723-1606.**

Visitor Information Dial ✆ **800/OC-OCEAN** (626-2326) or 410/289-8181.

Weather Dial ✆ **800/OC-OCEAN** (626-2326) or 410/548-9262.

Where to Stay

More than in any other part of Maryland, lodgings here rely on a high season. Summer—especially July and early August—commands the highest rates, often with weekend supplements. In many cases, minimum stays of 2 or 3 nights are required. Reservations are essential for weekends. Most hotels have pools (ask if it's important to you), but those with indoor pools can fill up in the off season, especially on holiday weekends. Every hotel has rooms that are accessible for those with disabilities; nearly all have free parking.

Rates are a little lower on rooms without an ocean view or with a partial view. January rates are bargain basement (for good reason), but tariffs in spring and fall are also economical, and many hotels offer packages. Spring can be rainy, but September is terrific: The beach is nearly empty (except on weekends), lots of restaurants are still open, and the water is warm. Early June can also be a good time—as long as you're willing to put up with "June Bugs" (new high-school graduates celebrating their freedom). Valentine's Day and Christmas also draw a crowd; look for hotel packages and special menus for both holidays, as well as light displays and New Year's Eve parties.

For many families, renting a condo or town house is the only way to go. With several bedrooms and bathrooms, full kitchens, and living rooms, these offer a convenient way to take everybody to the beach. Most rent from Saturday to Saturday. Several real-estate companies offer hundreds of units on both the ocean and the bay; try **Coldwell Banker** (✆ **800/633-1000;** www.cbvacations.com) or **Long and Foster** (✆ **866/677-6937**) for rentals in Ocean City, as well as in the "suburbs" of west Ocean City. Rates start at $1,000 a week and take off from there. Every unit is different, so read the brochures and check the firms' websites. Generally, units are well kept, with fairly new furniture, appliances, and often a stash of paperbacks and board games. Bring your own paper products and linens. Just about everything else is usually provided. (Check the listings to be sure.) The best units—that is, the newest and closest to the beach—are snapped up by January or February, but if you decide in May to go to the beach, you'll still have plenty of choices.

EXPENSIVE

Carousel Resort Hotel ★★ The Carousel is an attractive choice for families and couples. One of the oldest of north Ocean City's high-rises, it offers plenty of amenities, including pools indoor and out, restaurants, a beach bar and grill, a playground, and pizza delivery. Rooms are well equipped, if small, and even have kitchenettes. If those 237 rooms aren't enough, 102 two- and three-bedroom oceanfront condo units are available in the 22-story tower. Carousel is a conference center and can be fully booked. Off season, the hotel offers some great values.

11700 Coastal Hwy., Ocean City, MD 21842. www.carouselhotel.com. ✆ **800/641-0011** or 410/524-1000. Fax 410/524-7766. 339 units. $59–$349 double; $179–$499 condo. Weekly rates available. AE, DC, DISC, MC, V. Free parking. **Amenities:** Oceanfront restaurant; outdoor restaurant; deli and coffee bar; 2 bars; fitness room; indoor ice rink (open to the public); Jacuzzi; indoor pool; outdoor pool; sauna; tennis court. *In room:* A/C, TV, DVD or VCR (in condos), fridge, hair dryer, Internet, microwave.

Clarion Resort Fontainebleau ★★ On the ocean, far from the boardwalk and in the midst of Condo Row in northern Ocean City, this hotel offers oversize rooms and suites, all with tiny balconies and views of the ocean and the bay. The seven two-story cabana suites, with sitting rooms and huge bedrooms, are spacious and fun. The

Clarion also rents 73 one-, two-, and three-bedroom units at the adjacent **Marigot Beach Condominiums.**

10100 Coastal Hwy. (at 101st St.), Ocean City, MD 21842. www.clarionoc.com. ✆**800/638-2100** or 410/524-3535. Fax 410/524-3834. 250 units. $99–$389 double; $119–$479 condos. AE, DC, DISC, MC, V. Free self- and valet parking. Pets okay in hotel for fee. **Amenities:** Restaurant; beach bar and grill; 2 lounges; beach-chair rental; fitness center; playground; indoor pool; spa; terrace. *In room:* A/C, TV, fridge, hair dryer, microwave, free Wi-Fi.

Dunes Manor Hotel ★ On 28th Street just beyond the boardwalk, this 11-story modern hotel tries its best to capture days gone by. The Victorian-style facade, cupolas, and wide porch with rocking chairs are just the beginning. Tea and crumpets are offered every summer afternoon. Each unit is up-to-date in every way, with an oceanfront view, a balcony, one king-size or two double beds, and a decor of light woods and floral fabrics. Rooms on upper floors have the best views; nine units have kitchenettes.

2800 Baltimore Ave., Ocean City, MD 21842. www.dunesmanor.com. ✆**800/523-2888** or 410/289-1100. Fax 410/289-4905. 170 units. $45–$304 double; $109–$359 efficiency. Weekly rates available. AE, DC, DISC, MC, V. Free parking. **Amenities:** Restaurant and lounge; fitness center; indoor/outdoor pool; sun deck; whirlpool. *In room:* A/C, TV, fridge, hair dryer, microwave, Wi-Fi.

Hilton Suites Ocean City Oceanfront ★★★ New on the oceanfront, you can't miss the blue-and-white 12-story tower dominating the skyline in O.C.'s midsection. And the Hilton offers spacious rooms and amenities such as a swim-up pool bar, a huge children's pool, an outdoor hot tub, and changing rooms for guests staying after check-out. The 225 suites feature sitting rooms with flatscreen TVs and pullout sofas, well-stocked kitchens, spacious bathrooms with jetted tubs, and bedrooms with two queen-size or one king-size bed. Specialty corner, terrace, and penthouse suites are available.

3200 Baltimore Ave., Ocean City, MD 21842. www.oceancityhilton.com. ✆ **866/729-3200** or 410/289-6444. 225 suites. $199–$499 suite. 3-night minimum in peak season. Weekly rates available. AE, DISC, MC, V. Free self- and valet parking. **Amenities:** Restaurant; lounge; swim-up pool bar; oceanfront grill; fitness room; outdoor hot tub; outdoor children's activity pool, indoor pool, and outdoor adult pool. *In room:* A/C, 2 TVs w/movies and video games, hair dryer, kitchen, MP3 docking station, free Wi-Fi.

Lighthouse Club Hotel ★★★ Empty your wallet and pamper yourself in this boutique hotel, on Isle of Wight Bay. You can't miss the inn, which resembles a gabled, red-roofed screw-pile lighthouse from the Route 90 bridge. Inside, the lobby soars to a skylight three stories up. A circular staircase takes guests to their rooms, which are decorated in white and rattan. Balconies overlook the bay or wetlands. Eight units have gas fireplaces and Jacuzzis. Light-keeper suites on the top level offer more spacious surroundings. A new paneled morning room with deck is set up with coffee all day, afternoon cookies, and games and puzzles for those rainy or cold afternoons.

The adjacent **Edge** (rates begin at $209 a night) may be even more luxurious, with two-story guest rooms, private Jacuzzis, sitting areas, gas fireplaces, and DVD players. Each unit has a balcony overlooking the pool. The Left Bank suite has a Jacuzzi next to picture windows overlooking the bay. Two penthouse suites top the hotel.

201 60th St. (on the bay), Ocean City, MD 21842. www.fagers.com. ✆**800/371-5400** or 410/524-5400. Fax 410/524-3928. 23 units in the Lighthouse; 12 units in the Edge. $79–$365 double. Off-season packages are a good deal in winter. Rates include continental breakfast. AE, DC, DISC, MC, V. Free parking. **Amenities:** Restaurant (see Fager's Island, under "Where to Eat," below); Jacuzzi; pool. *In room:* TV/DVD, fridge w/soda, hair dryer, Wi-Fi.

Princess Royale Resort ★ ☺ What makes this the place to stay is the Olympic-size indoor pool. Even if it rains, the pool is big enough for everybody. It's part of a recreation center, glassed in with a sauna, Jacuzzis, and a poolside cafe that will keep your kids happy. Rooms are rented in the lower five floors; the upper floors are condo units. One-bedroom suites sleep 2 to 6 people, two-bedrooms sleep 6 to 8, and three-bedrooms sleep up to 10.

9100 Coastal Hwy., Ocean City, MD 21842. www.princessroyale.com. ✆ **800/4-ROYALE** (476-9253) or 410/524-7777. Fax 410/524-1623. 310 units, 25 condos. Double $79–$349; condo $169–$565. AE, DISC, MC, V. Free parking. Children 11 and under stay free in parent's room. **Amenities:** 2 restaurants; bar; comedy club; fitness center; Jacuzzi; minigolf; indoor pool; sauna; tennis courts; beach volleyball court. *In room:* A/C, TV, hair dryer, kitchenette (full kitchen in condos), free Wi-Fi.

MODERATE

Beach Plaza Hotel Though it was updated in 2011, you'll still see the old hotel's Victorian chandeliers, wrought-iron fixtures, and fireplace. Cool blues and grays have been used to update the walls, furniture, and floors. Besides the 60 newly renovated standard guest rooms, there are 26 courtyard apartments with kitchenettes in the adjacent building and three-bedroom units with full kitchen behind the hotel. (They haven't been refurbished.) The big porch with rocking chairs remains a draw. So does the new **Bombora** restaurant (see p. 271).

1301 Atlantic Ave. (btw. 13th and 14th sts.), Ocean City, MD 21842. www.beachplazaoc.com. ✆ **800/492-5834** or 410/289-9121. Fax 410/289-3041. 96 units. $70–$209 double; $90–$309 apt. Weekly rates available. 2-night minimum stay required on weekends. AE, DC, DISC, MC, V. Free parking. Closed Nov to mid-Apr. **Amenities:** Restaurant. *In room:* A/C, hair dryer (on request), free Wi-Fi.

Castle in the Sand Hotel A good choice for families who don't want to break the bank, this modern hotel with a castlelike exterior is set on the beach at 37th Street, about 10 blocks from the boardwalk. Standard rooms have the usual amenities. Corner units are a bit bigger. For the most room, check into a condo or one of the quaint apartments in 36 beach cottages. Two-bed, two-bathroom condos go for about $2,000 a week; apartments run about $1,500. Outside is Ocean City's largest outdoor pool (at 25m [82 ft.]). A beachside restaurant offers live music daily mid-May to mid-September.

3701 Atlantic Ave., Ocean City, MD 21842. www.castleinthesand.com. ✆ **800/552-SAND** (7263) or 410/289-6846. Fax 410/289-9446. 180 units. $79–$319 double (standard, suites, and efficiencies). Weekly rates available. AE, DC, DISC, MC, V. Free parking. Closed mid-Nov to mid-Feb. **Amenities:** Restaurant; bar and grill; children's summer activities; outdoor pool. *In room:* A/C, TV/DVD w/movies, fridge, hair dryer, kitchen (in some), microwave (in some), free Wi-Fi.

Commander Hotel In the center of the boardwalk, this successor to one of O.C.'s oldest hotels offers lots of conveniences and comforts. A variety of accommodations—from efficiencies to suites—are available. The Promenade Suites lead onto the second-story deck and pool, while the corner Captain's Suites offer more room, with lots of windows overlooking the boardwalk and beach. Cabana Suites, though a good size, overlook Baltimore Avenue.

1401 Atlantic Ave., Ocean City, MD 21842. www.commanderhotel.com. ✆ **888/289-6166** or 410/289-6166. 110 units. $75–$309 double. Weekly rates available. Children 4 and under stay free with 2 parents. MC, V. Free parking. Closed Nov to mid-Mar. **Amenities:** Restaurant; lounge; outdoor and indoor pools; oceanfront sun deck. *In room:* A/C, TV, fridge, hair dryer, microwave (in most rooms).

Grand Hotel The higher you go in this 12-story hotel, the better the rooms get. Upgraded bedding and sliding glass doors to the balconies overlooking a wide swatch of beach make the top floor "signature rooms." The 12th floor has Jacuzzi rooms. Almost every room looks out on the ocean, and they are all big and comfortable with a kitchenette. Plus, it's right on the boardwalk, but at the quiet north end, with a variety of eateries and shops at the boardwalk level. Suites on the eighth floor have two bedrooms and bigger TVs.

2100 Baltimore Ave., Ocean City, MD 21842. www.grandhoteloceancity.com. ✆**800/447-6779** or 410/289-6191. Fax 410/289-7591. 251 units. $115–$329 double; $259–$600 suites. AE, DC, DISC, MC, V. Free parking. **Amenities:** Restaurant; lounge; pool bar; coffee shop; indoor and outdoor pools w/sun deck; sauna. *In room:* A/C, TV, fridge, hair dryer, microwave, free Wi-Fi (lower floors).

Holiday Inn Oceanfront ★★ In the center of O.C., on the beach, this eight-story hotel is convenient to everything. Its resort amenities make it a good choice for a weekend or a week. There are hammocks by the pool, a newly resurfaced tennis court, and a 10-person Jacuzzi. Each long, narrow room has a balcony and sitting area, sleeping area, and kitchenette. Units on the top three floors have fireplaces (electric—romantic, but not hot, in summertime). Room no. 813 has views of both ocean and bay.

6600 Coastal Hwy. (oceanfront at 67th St.), Ocean City, MD 21842. www.holidayinnoceanfront.com. ✆**800/837-3588** or 410/524-1600. Fax 410/524-1135. 216 units. $54–$334 double. Weekly rates available. AE, DC, DISC, MC, V. Free parking. **Amenities:** Restaurant; poolside bar and grill; children's summer programs; fitness center; outdoor and indoor pools; sauna; tennis; whirlpool. *In room:* A/C, TV/VCR w/movies, hair dryer, kitchenette, free Wi-Fi.

Howard Johnson Oceanfront Plaza Hotel ★ Beds and baths were upgraded in 2011, improving this moderately priced choice on the boardwalk. Guest rooms are decorated in soft colors and textures and most have a balcony with full or partial ocean views. Deluxe oceanfront units have sleeper sofas.

1109 Atlantic Ave., Ocean City, MD 21842. www.hjoceanfrontplaza.com. ✆**800/926-1122** or 410/289-7251. Fax 410/289-4901. 90 units. $59–$349 double. Children 17 and under stay free in parent's room. AE, DC, DISC, MC, V. Free parking. **Amenities:** Restaurant; bar; gift shop; Jacuzzi; indoor pool. *In room:* A/C, TV w/movies, fridge, hair dryer, microwave, free Wi-Fi.

INEXPENSIVE

Comfort Inn Gold Coast For value and location, this bayside hotel is a good choice. Set back from the highway, its bayside rooms boast a lovely view but only slightly higher rates. Even the king/whirlpool rooms are a bargain in a town where bargains are hard to find. Though not every room has a view, all are comfortable. Renovations in 2011 gave the rooms, decorated in tan and white, a sleeker look. The hotel's next door to the Gold Coast Mall, with shops, restaurants, and movie theaters.

11201 Coastal Hwy. (at 112th St.), Ocean City, MD 21842. www.comfortgoldcoast.com. ✆**800/228-5150** or 410/524-3000. Fax 410/524-8255. 202 units. $49–$219 double. Children 17 and under stay free in parent's room. AE, DISC, MC, V. Free parking. **Amenities:** Children's play area; health club; Jacuzzi; indoor pool; bayview sun deck. *In room:* A/C, TV w/movies, fridge, hair dryer, microwave, free Wi-Fi.

Park Place Hotel Owned by a longtime O.C. hotelier family, the hotel has standard rooms with space for all that beach paraphernalia. There are kitchenettes and pullout sofas; oceanfront rooms have balconies; bayview rooms are bigger. Bayview king rooms have Jacuzzis. The Park Place, built in 2000, has committed to eco-friendly practices, including a solar water heater.

2nd and 3rd sts., Ocean City, MD 21842. www.ocparkplacehotel.com. ✆ **888/212-7275** or 410/289-6440. Fax 410/289-3389. 89 units. $60–$285 double. Weekly rates available. Children 11 and under stay free in parent's room. AE, DC, DISC, MC, V. Free parking. Closed Dec–Jan but open New Year's Eve. **Amenities:** Outdoor bar and grill; DVD/VCR rental; pool w/sun deck. *In room:* A/C, TV, fridge, hair dryer, microwave, Wi-Fi.

Talbot Inn The Talbot Inn is a great spot for fishermen and those who love the boardwalk. It's an easy walk to the Talbot Street Pier (where you can find a fishing boat or take a ride on the O.C. *Rocket*), to the inlet and its rides and shops, and to the widest part of the beach. The inn has two three-story buildings, one bayfront and the other without a view. Choose from efficiencies and two-bedroom apartments. Rooms without a view are a few feet wider and can sleep up to six. Apartments have enclosed balconies. Though this is an older property, it's well maintained and has that fantastic location. **M.R. Ducks,** the bar and clothing shop, is next door.

Talbot St., on the bay (P.O. Box 548), Ocean City, MD 21842. www.talbotstreetpier.com. ✆ **800/659-7703** or 410/289-9125. Fax 410/289-6792. 36 units. $50–$170 double. Weekly rates available. 3- or 4-night minimum stay required on summer weekends and holidays. DISC, MC, V. Free parking. **Amenities:** Restaurant; bar; marina. *In room:* A/C, TV, kitchenette, free Wi-Fi.

Where to Eat

As you might expect, seafood rules here. For the most part, a casual atmosphere prevails—although for the better restaurants, it's wise to make reservations and check on the dress code. Casual places don't take reservations, and the wait to be seated can last an hour. In summer, some restaurants open as early as 5am and continue serving until 10 or 11pm. Most places have full bar facilities. It's quieter from Columbus Day to Valentine's Day, and some places close, but you'll always have someplace to go.

EXPENSIVE

Fager's Island ★ AMERICAN/PACIFIC RIM Fager's Island plays up its bayfront location, with lots of decks, a gazebo, a pavilion, and a pier. The "1812 Overture" celebrates every sunset—it's a tradition here. The menu has a few Asian-inspired dishes, such as the Chilean sea bass with plum glaze, but you can also get a strip steak, crab cakes, a burger, quesadillas, or a sandwich. There's a kids' menu, too. The bar is shorts-and-T-shirt casual; you can stay late and enjoy live entertainment there. Head upstairs for more formal dining. On Sunday, a jazz brunch is offered.

201 60th St. (on the bay). ✆ **410/524-5500.** www.fagers.com. Reservations recommended for dinner. Main courses $7–$20 lunch, $18–$40 dinner. AE, DC, DISC, MC, V. Daily 11am–2am.

Fresco's ★ ITALIAN Overlooking a scene of bayside grasses dancing amid the gentle waves, the dining room is great for a romantic dinner. A pianist in the bar adds to the ambience. The food is fresh and beautifully prepared. Start with the salty, sweet cream of crab soup, fresh tomatoes with mozzarella, or house-made pasta bathed in a simple sauce and studded with lump crab meat. The wine list features 50 choices, 20 by the glass. (There's also a children's menu.) **Jive,** the bayfront lounge behind Fresco's, is a good place to stop for a cocktail—though with the view, the flatbread and martini menu, and the live music on weekends, you may not make it into Fresco's.

8203 Coastal Hwy. (on the bay). ✆ **410/524-8202.** www.ocfrescos.com. Reservations recommended for dinner. Main courses $18–$36. AE, DC, DISC, MC, V. Sun–Thurs 4:30–10pm; Fri–Sat 4:30–10:30pm.

Galaxy 66 Bar & Grille INTERNATIONAL Although it can't claim ocean or bay views, this purple-and-gold restaurant offers a sleek interior and an innovative menu that mixes familiar and exotic flavors. The menu, which changes regularly, recently included filet mignon with truffle demi-glace and rockfish and grouper. Light fare, offered from lunchtime until midnight, features sandwiches, pizza, soups, and salads. The rooftop Skye Bar overlooks Coastal Highway but is a great place for night owls.

6601 Coastal Hwy. ✆ **410/723-6762.** www.galaxy66barandgrille.com. Reservations recommended for dinner. Main courses $11–$16 lunch, $22–$30 dinner. AE, DC, DISC, MC, V. Daily 11:30am–4pm and 5–10pm (light fare until midnight).

The Hobbit ★★ SEAFOOD Despite its *Lord of the Rings* name, the Hobbit is a sleek room with a modern menu. Seasonal favorites are featured alongside fish and beef dishes and the always-in-demand Veal Pistachio. The wine list is extensive. The room has an "energetic" noise level when there's a crowd, but the big picture windows look out on tranquil waters.

81st St. and the bay. ✆ **410/524-8100.** www.thehobbitrestaurant.com. Reservations necessary. Entrees $26–$35. AE, DISC, MC, V. Daily 5–10pm. Closed Jan–Mar.

Jules ★★ AMERICAN An unassuming dining room in a shopping center, Jules offers surprisingly creative takes on local food. And they have a great Early Bird deal: three courses with a glass of wine for about $30. Dishes celebrate local seafood, beef, and even tomatoes and corn with classic sauces and seasonings inspired by the world's cuisine. It's casual but the food makes it swank enough for a low-key celebration.

11805 Coastal Hwy. ✆ **410/524-3396.** www.julesoc.com. Reservations recommended on weekends. Entrees $24–$32. AE, DISC, MC, V. Daily 5–10pm Mar–Nov. Closed Mon Dec–Feb.

Liquid Assets ★★ TAPAS/WINE BAR Tucked behind a wine shop, this casual dining room offers wines, martinis, and plenty of small plates to pair with them. Choose from seafood appetizers, cheese plates, salads, or wings. If you prefer heartier fare, there are burgers, sandwiches, steaks, and seafood. The restaurant also offers lunch and carryout.

9301 Coastal Hwy. ✆ **410/524-7037.** www.ocliquidassets.com. Reservations not accepted. Entrees $9–$15 lunch, $10–$24 dinner. AE, DC, DISC, MC, V. Sun–Thurs 11:30am–11pm; Fri–Sat 11:30am–midnight.

MODERATE

Bombora LATIN/ASIAN Come for breakfast and you'll get your eggs or waffles or Cap'n Crunch–crusted French toast. Come for lunch (weekends only) or dinner and enjoy Latin or Asian flavors when you can choose from small plates, flatbreads, soups, and salads. Look for sandwiches and tacos at lunch and spicy dinner entrees such as Tikka Masala braised chicken, mojo marinated pork or skirt steak with chimichurri. Crab cakes are on the menu all day. Dining on the oceanfront veranda is a definite plus.

1300 Atlantic Ave. (in the Beach Plaza Hotel at the boardwalk). ✆ **410/289-9121.** www.bomboraoc.com. Reservations for dinner recommended on weekends. Entrees $14–$26 dinner, $9–$12 lunch, $8–$14 breakfast. AE, DISC, MC, V. Mon–Thurs 8am–noon and 5–9pm; Fri 8am–noon and 5–10pm; Sat-Sun 8am–3pm and 5–10pm. Free parking on-site.

Captain Bill Bunting's Angler AMERICAN This spacious restaurant, at the marina of Ocean City, has been a favorite since 1938. It features an air-conditioned dining room with nautical decor, plus a deck overlooking the bay—an ideal spot to see the fishermen bringing back their bounty. The menu revolves around daily fresh-fish specials, plus steaks and seafood platters. Spend $12 on food and you may come aboard for an evening ocean cruise for $2—a nice way to get out on the water. Lunch focuses on raw-bar selections, fish sandwiches, salads, and burgers. ***Note:*** For early risers, doors open at 6am for breakfast.

Talbot St., on the bay. ✆ **410/289-7424.** www.theangleroc.com. Reservations recommended for dinner. Main courses $7–$16 lunch, $17–$33 dinner. AE, DISC, MC, V. May–Oct daily 6am–11pm. Bar until 2am Sat–Sun. Closed Nov–Apr.

Macky's Bayside Bar & Grill AMERICAN/REGIONAL Watch the sun set (as Kate Smith sings "God Bless America") while you sit outside with a crab cake or steak. The restaurant is designed to resemble an old beach shack, but it's the tables on the "beach" that fill up first. The food's okay; the atmosphere is the real draw. The lunch menu includes sandwiches, pizza, and salads. A kids' menu is available. Or come late and stay for the party.

54th St. (on the bay). ✆ **410/723-5565.** www.mackys.com. Reservations not accepted. Main courses $8–$15 lunch, $14–$28 dinner. AE, DC, DISC, MC, V. Daily 11am–2am (dinner served until 10pm; light fare until 1am). Closed mid-Oct to Mar.

Phillips Seafood Restaurants SEAFOOD The Phillips family dynasty began with a small crab house at 21st Street and Philadelphia Avenue. This used to be Ocean City's finest restaurant. Four decades later, the two remaining outlets are still quite popular, even if the food is only okay. **Phillips Crabhouse,** at 21st Street, is casual, with white paper on the tables and a huge menu that emphasizes crab. A seafood buffet is also popular. It's open for lunch. **Phillips Seafood House,** at 141st and Coastal Highway, is along O.C.'s condo strip. It's designed to resemble the original and offers the same dinner menu. The lines look like the original's, too.

Phillips Crabhouse, 2004 Philadelphia Ave. (at 21st St.). ✆ **410/289-6821.** www.phillipsseafood.com. Reservations not accepted. Main courses $10–$20 lunch, $20–$40 dinner. AE, DISC, MC, V. Apr–Oct daily noon–10pm. **Phillips Seafood House,** 14101 Coastal Hwy. ✆ **800/799-2722** or 410/250-1200. Reservations not accepted. Main courses $20–$40 dinner. AE, DISC, MC, V. Mon–Fri 5–9:30pm; Sat–Sun 4–9:30pm. Closed Nov to Palm Sunday.

Seacrets ★★ BREAKFAST This may be the young singles' hangout after dark (okay, after 9am when the bar opens), but it's one of the best places in O.C. for breakfast on a summer morning. Palm trees shade diners as they sit into waterside booths. Caribbean music and a bay breeze—and a Bloody Mary (after 9am) or good cup of coffee—make this breakfast paradise. You can come for other meals or the nightlife, but it's good to start your day here.

117 W. 49th St. ✆ **410/524-4900.** www.seacrets.com. Reservations not accepted. Main courses $5–$13 breakfast, $8–$25 all-day menu. AE, DISC, MC, V. Breakfast daily in season 8–11am; Thurs–Sun mid-Sept to June 8–11am. (Regular hours daily 11am–11pm; bar until 2am.) Free parking.

The Shark ★ SEAFOOD Local seafood rules in this restaurant that rises above the fishing docks in West Ocean City. Small plates and entrees featuring seafood caught from that boat, along with local organic produce and dairy, rise above the usual, too. Steamed shellfish options are succulent; mako shark (of course) is a specialty. I order it every time I stop in. Another fun option is a wine flight with a few of the small plates. Lunch features $5 specials.

12933 Sunset Ave., West Ocean City. ✆ **410/723-5565.** www.ocshark.com. Reservations recommended. Main courses $7–$14 lunch, $17–$32 dinner. AE, DISC, MC, V. Daily 11:30am–10pm.

Sunset Grille SEAFOOD Across the street from The Shark, this waterfront eatery has a fine-dining side and a partying side at **Teasers Dockside Bar.** You can count on a good meal and a fun drink. I'm partial to the fruity Cheap Sunglasses. The menu is heavy on the seafood, with local fish, crabs, and oysters, depending on the season. The dining room is dimly lit and quiet, but there are outside tables in summer and all the friends you want at the dockside bar, where there is live music most nights in summer. Come by boat if you want. Lots of specials can make dining here a good deal.

2924 Sunset Ave., West Ocean City. ✆ **410/213-8110.** www.ocsunsetgrille.com. Reservations recommended. Main courses $8–$14 lunch, $22–$30 dinner. AE, DISC, MC, V. Daily 11am–9pm (later in season). Closed Sun mid-Oct to mid-Jan.

INEXPENSIVE

Dough Roller PIZZA Ocean City has some good pizza joints, but this one is also pretty, with each of the five locations decorated with carousel horses and gingerbread woodwork. Also on the menu are burgers, sandwiches, subs, New England grinders, and pasta. Pancakes are served all day.

2 boardwalk locations: S. Division St. (✆ **410/289-3501**) and 3rd St. (✆ **410/289-2599**). Coastal Hwy. locations: at 41st St. (✆ **410/524-9254**) and 70th St. (✆ **410/524-7981**). Reservations not accepted. Main courses $6–$24. AE, MC, V. Summer daily 7am–midnight; call for winter hours, which are much more limited (1 location is always open).

Dumser's ☺ AMERICAN/ICE CREAM An O.C. favorite since 1939, this eatery began as an ice-cream parlor but is now a popular restaurant. The atmosphere is homey, with comfort foods like fried chicken, roast turkey, and crab cakes. Breakfast is served in warmer weather. Lunch choices include sandwiches, salads, subs, and soups. There's a kids' menu but no liquor. Save room for dessert: Dumser's is still an ice-cream parlor at heart with more than 20 sundaes. A second location, **Dumser's Drive-In,** 49th Street and Coastal Highway (✆ **410/524-1588**), is also open year-round and has a similar menu but no breakfast. Three boardwalk locations serve ice cream only.

12305 Coastal Hwy. ✆ **410/250-5543.** Reservations not accepted. Main courses $4–$10 breakfast, $5–$11 lunch, $9–$22 dinner. MC, V. Mid-June to Labor Day daily 7am–11pm; Sept to mid-June daily 7am–9pm.

Fractured Prune ★ 🎁 DONUTS/LUNCH If you like donuts, don't come to O.C. without stopping at one of the three Prunes. Outrageous donuts are made to order, dipped in one of a variety of glazes, toppings, and sugars, and served hot. You can mix the cherry glaze with the chocolate chips, or top chocolate glaze with peanuts or coconut. Not a sugar fiend? They have breakfast sandwiches, too.

28th St. and Coastal Hwy. (✆ **410/289-4131**); 127th St. and Coastal Hwy. (✆ **410/250-4400**); and 9636 Stephen Decatur Hwy., West Ocean City (✆ **410/213-9899**). www.fracturedprune.com. Reservations not accepted. Donuts $12 a dozen. No credit cards. Daily 6am–1pm.

What to See & Do

A fascinating self-guided **Walking Tour of Historic Downtown Ocean City** is available at the visitor center on 40th Street.

Wheels of Yesterday Car enthusiasts will enjoy strolling through the rows of classic cars, plus a few kiddie cars and a replica of a 1950s service station. Curator Jack Jarvis will lead you through the exhibits, most of which are part of the private collection of Granville D. Trimper, owner of many of the amusements on the boardwalk. Favorites include a 1928 Lincoln, Jack Benny's Overland, cars used in the movies *Hoosiers* and *Tuck Everlasting,* and a shiny gold 1960 Studebaker Hawk.

12708 Ocean Gateway (Rte. 50). ✆ **410/213-7329.** Admission $5 adults, $3 children 12 and under. June–Sept Mon–Sat 9am–9pm, Sun 9am–5pm; Oct–May Sat–Sun 9am–5pm. Take the Rte. 50 bridge out of Ocean City. The museum is on the left, across from the shopping outlets.

ESPECIALLY FOR KIDS

Ocean City, which claims to be the number-one family resort on the East Coast, is home to several amusement parks and child-oriented activities. Before you head for the attractions, look for coupons for everything from miniature golf to go-carts, at either visitor center or in one of the local newspapers, such as *Sunny Day* or *Beachcomber.*

Frontier Town ★ ☺ Frontier Town has been stuck in Old West time for more than 50 years—it was a winner in 1959 and still is today. The cowboys and outlaws work hard to make you believe you're in the Old West, with train rides, pony rides, cancan shows, bank holdups, and gunfights. In a separate park (with separate admission), there's a water park and miniature golf. Campsites on Sinepuxent Bay are also available from April to October.

Rte. 611, 4 miles south of Rte. 50. Old West park ✆ **410/289-7877.** Water park ✆ **410/641-0693.** www.frontiertown.com. Combination admission for both parks $24 taller than 42 inches, $20 shorter than 42 inches. Children 3 and under are free for everything. For Old West park, $14 ages 11 and over and $12 ages 4–10. Water park and miniature golf $14 taller than 42 inches, $12 shorter. Golf day or night, $4 ages 11 and older, $2 ages 4–10. Mid-June to Labor Day daily 10am–6pm (miniature golf until 10pm). Free parking. Take Rte. 50 west and turn left on Rte. 611 toward Assateague.

Jolly Roger This is where you'll find Speedworld (the largest go-cart racing complex of its kind in the U.S.), two minigolf courses, a water park, and more than 30 other rides. Go-cart tracks have minimum-height requirements. A zip-line attraction is new at Speedworld.

30th St. and Coastal Hwy. ✆ **410/289-3477.** www.jollyrogerpark.com. Water park $35. Passport entrance fees $25–$100. Daily Memorial Day to Labor Day: rides noon–midnight; Speedworld 2pm–midnight; golf 9am–5pm; water park 10am–8pm. Speedworld and golf also Apr to Memorial Day, Sept, and weekends in Oct. Closed Oct–Mar. Free parking.

Ocean Bowl Skate Park Skateboards are forbidden from most of Ocean City, so skaters head over to the 17,000-square-foot concrete bowl on Third Street and St. Louis Avenue. The park, the country's oldest municipal skate park, has areas suitable for beginner to advanced. Pads and helmets, which are required, can be rented here.

3rd Street and St. Louis Ave. **410/289-BOWL** (2695). www.oceanbowl.com. Weekdays $12, weekend days $15, weekly pass $40. Daily in summer 9:30am–dark; Sept–Nov Mon–Fri 11:30am–dark, Sat–Sun 9:30am–dark; Dec–Feb Mon, Tues, Thurs, Fri 1:30pm–dark, Sat–Sun 9:30am–dark. Mar–May Mon–Fri 2:30–8:30pm, Sat–Sun 9:30am–dark.

Pier Rides Rides here appeal mostly to older kids and teens who like centrifugal force, but the Ferris wheel is a highlight for all ages. Rising high above everything else in old Ocean City, it offers spectacular views of the ocean, the beach, and the boardwalk. It's a wonderful place to be at sunset. The rest of the rides seem to change every season, although the Venetian double-decker carousel is always in its place.

On the inlet in downtown Ocean City. ✆ **410/289-3477.** Rides about $5 or so each. Easter to late Sept Sat–Sun 11am–midnight; summer daily noon–midnight.

Trimper's Rides & Amusements Established in 1887, this is the granddaddy of O.C. amusement areas. It has more than 100 indoor and outdoor rides, including

MINIGOLF mania IN O.C.

Ocean City may have the highest concentration of minigolf courses of any barrier island on earth. Here's a rundown of some of the best.

- **Jungle Golf,** Jolly Roger Park, 30th Street and Coastal Highway (✆ **410/289-3477**): Plastic lions and a rhino look on as you negotiate 18 holes that climb the sides of a series of man-made waterfalls. Although this course has one lame hole early on—a straight 10-foot putt—most are fun. Challenging holes on the back 9 ensure you'll end your round with a thrill. Open Memorial Day to Labor Day.
- **Lost Galaxy Golf,** 33rd Street and Coastal Highway (✆ **410/524-4FUN** [4386]): Here you can play golf in outer space. Sure, the special effects are cheesy and the water is the oddest blue, but you've got to love the spaceships, aliens, and fun maze of holes. It's open year-round.
- **Old Pro Golf,** 136th Street and Coastal Highway (✆ **888/OLD-PRO1** [653-7761]; www.oldprogolf.com): All six Old Pro courses are good, but this is the best. The newest course, which has a jungle theme, is enclosed in a hangarlike barn. Old Pro has another indoor course at 68th Street. Both get crowded when it's rainy or cold. If you *really* like minigolf, get the **Old Pro Pass** for $16, which lets you play every Old Pro course as much as you want for a day. If you're fast, you can do them in about 5 hours. Open year-round.
- **Professor Hakker's Lost Treasure Golf,** 139th Street and Coastal Highway (✆ **410/250-5678**): You can't miss this place—it's got an airplane in the roof. There are two courses: Gold and Diamond. The decor is reminiscent of the *Indiana Jones* movies, with water traps, caves, and even a bridge. Closed December through March.

a water flume and a 1902 merry-go-round with hand-carved animals. The indoor rides are open year-round, but only on weekends in cooler months.

Boardwalk near the inlet, btw. S. Division and S. 1st sts. ✆ **410/289-8617.** www.trimpersrides.com. Most rides $2–$8. A $23 wristband allows unlimited rides 1–7pm. Summer Sat–Sun noon–midnight, Mon–Fri 3pm–midnight; Mar–Apr and Oct–Nov Sat–Sun noon–closing; indoor rides hours vary Dec–Feb. Outdoor rides closed Nov–May.

Golf

Ocean City promotes itself as a major golfing destination; many courses offer vacation packages with O.C. hotels. The courses listed below welcome visitors and can be contacted directly or through the **Ocean City Golf Getaway Association,** 9935 Stephen Decatur Hwy. (✆ **800/4-OC-GOLF** [462-4653]; www.oceancitygolf.com).

All courses are open year-round from dawn to dusk. Most courses in the area use a multitiered system for greens fees, which means they vary from morning to afternoon to evening. However, fees generally range from $40 to $96, with cheaper rates in the off season and on summer afternoons. Fall rates are usually the highest; if you're a January golfer, you'll find bargains then. ***Tip:*** Consider starting a round at about 4pm; the rates often drop in the early evenings, and the temperatures go down, too.

Bay Club Eight miles from the boardwalk, the Bay Club offers two 18-hole par-72 courses. Features include a driving range, practice green, club rentals, and lessons.

9122 Libertytown Rd., Berlin. ✆ **800/229-2582** or 410/641-4081. www.thebayclub.com.

The Beach Club Golf Links A reserved tee time is recommended at this semi-private club, which has two 18-hole par-72 courses. It has a pro shop, club rentals, driving range, and putting green.

9715 Deer Park Dr., Berlin. ✆ **800/435-9223** or 410/641-GOLF (4653). www.beachclubgolflinks.com.

Deer Run Golf This 18-hole, par-70 course is off Route 50, before you reach the beach. It also has a driving range, putting green, and golf lessons. They also rent clubs.

8804 Logtown Rd., Berlin. ✆ **800/435-9223** or 410/629-0060. www.golfdeerrun.com.

Eagle's Landing Golf Course The scenery here may distract you from your game. This public 18-hole course also offers club rentals, lessons, a pro shop, practice facilities, and a clubhouse restaurant. Reservations are recommended.

12367 Eagle's Nest Rd., Berlin. ✆ **800/283-3846.** www.eagleslandinggolf.com.

Glen Riddle Golf Club Ocean City's newest course occupies the farmland where racehorses Man O'War and War Admiral were raised. The two courses are named for the horses. Man O'War resembles British links, and the historic training track is a cross hazard on 3 holes. War Admiral requires membership. A **Ruth's Chris Steakhouse** is on the premises.

11501 Maid at Arms Lane, Berlin. ✆ **888/632-4747** or 410/213-2325. www.glenriddlegolf.com.

Ocean City Golf Club Founded in 1959, this club has two USGA-rated 18-hole championship courses, a seaside par 72, and a bayside par 73. Facilities include a clubhouse with a restaurant, bar, and pro shop.

11401 Country Club Dr., Berlin. ✆ **800/442-3570** or 410/641-1779. www.oceancitygolfclub.com.

River Run A Gary Player 18-hole signature course, the par-71 River Run is a favorite in West O.C. Facilities include a pro shop, locker room, PGA golf pros, carts, a driving range, and putting greens. Reserving a tee time is recommended.

11605 Masters Lane, Berlin. ✆ **800/733-RRUN** (7786) or 410/641-7200. www.riverrungolf.com.

Rum Pointe Seaside Golf Links This 18-hole, par-72 championship course, designed by the father-son team of P. B. and Pete Dye, has 17 holes overlooking Sinepuxent Bay and Assateague Island. Facilities include a pro shop, driving range, and clubhouse with restaurant. Reserving a tee time is recommended.

7000 Rum Pointe Lane, Berlin. ✆ **888/809-4653** or 410/629/1414. www.rumpointe.com.

Other Nonbeach Activities

BIKING An early morning ride down the boardwalk is traditional for lots of families. Boardwalk biking is allowed between 2 and 10am in summer, and anytime in the off season. Cyclists on Coastal Highway share a lane with the buses. A headlight and rear reflector are required on all bikes after dark. Rental rates vary, but expect to pay $6 an hour for a two-wheeler, $12 an hour for a tandem, and $8 for "funcycles" (recumbent tricycles). Two good sources are **Continental Cycle,** 73rd Street and Coastal Highway (✆ **410/524-1313**), and **Mike's Bikes,** 10 N. Division St. (✆ **410/289-5404**).

COAST CRUISES For sightseeing at top speed and a splash, ***Sea Rocket,*** Dorchester Street at the bay (✆ **410/289-5887**), and the ***O.C. Rocket,*** Talbot Street Pier (✆ **410/289-3500**), offer a great diversion from the beach. Both are 70-foot 150-passenger open-top speedboats that zoom along the waters of Ocean City and beside Assateague Island. The trips last about 50 minutes; they cost about $17 for adults, $8 for children 7 to 10. Departures run every hour or two from late May to September. ***Tip:*** People in the back tend to get very wet. Save this ride for a warm day.

Assateague Adventure (✆ **410/289-3500;** www.assateagueadventure.com) offers nature cruises to Assateague Island three or four times a day. These 90-minute tours, which leave from Talbot Street Pier, include 30 minutes on the island, an opportunity to dredge for clams or put your hand in the touch tank. The cost is $8 to $16; everybody pays an additional $1 landing fee. Reservations are suggested. **Island Explorer** also offers similar cruises to Assateague at least three times a day summer and fall from the Dorchester Street pier. Call ✆ **410/289-0004.** The 80-minute cruise is $17 for adults, $13 for seniors, $9 for kids.

Duckaneer (✆ **410/289-3500**) departs the Talbot Street Pier on a pirate adventure several times a day. Daytime cruises are geared to the kiddies; adults might find the evening cruises more fun. Cruises cost $9 for ages 1 to 3 and $19 for everybody else. Reservations are not necessary (but a good idea).

FISHING Since Ocean City is surrounded by the Atlantic and four bays, fishing boats abound. Departures usually run from April to October. Rates range from $325 for make-up charters up to $2,400 for tuna, shark, or white marlin. Get a spot on the rail of a headboat for about $28. Trips leave as early as 5am. Rod rentals are available. Fishing licenses are required for both the ocean and coastal bays. For details, go to **www2.md.wildlifelicense.com**.

Most boats set sail from one of O.C.'s three main fishing marinas: the **Ocean City Fishing Center,** in West Ocean City (✆ **800/322-3065;** www.ocfishing.com); the **Bahia Marina,** on the bay at 22nd Street (✆ **410/289-7438;** www.bahiamarina.com); and the **Sunset Marina,** 12911 Sunset Ave. (✆ **877/514-3474;** www.ocsunsetmarina.com). Call them for information on the kinds of boats available, as well as their rates and departure times. The ***Angler*** (✆ **410/289-7424;** www.theangleroc.com), a reliable headboat, also takes 7:30am trips from the Talbot Street Pier on the bay. The ***Happy Hooker*** (✆ **410/289-3500;** www.fishhappyhooker.com) leaves at least twice a day from the Talbot Street Pier.

HORSE RACING ☺ Four miles west of Ocean City, **Ocean Downs,** 10218 Racetrack Rd. (Rte. 589), just off Route 50, in Berlin (✆ **410/641-0600;** www.oceandowns.com), features up to 10 harness races Wednesday through Sunday nights June through August. Live racing runs from 7 to about 11pm. Simulcast TV racing from other tracks begins daily at noon year-round. Admission and parking are free. Clubhouse admission is extra. The racetrack is very kid-friendly: Winning pacers and trotters are led to the winner's circle, where children gather around for a close look. A parade of horses starts each evening's races, with the lead horse getting close enough for the kids to pet. Many horses and their drivers are local, too. There's also a restaurant and lounge, as well as the slots parlor. See below.

KAYAKING **Assateague Explorer** runs kayaking tours off Assateague between Memorial Day and Columbus Day six times a day for $40 for adults, $36 for children. Call ✆ **757/336-5956** or visit www.assateagueisland.com/kayaktours.htm.

SEGWAYS Rent a Segway from **Boardwalk Segways,** 6 Somerset St. (✆ **410/289-1203**), for $20 a half-hour, $30 for an hour. Training sessions are complimentary before your rental begins. Open March through November. The company also rents strollers, mobility scooters, and wheelchairs. Segways must follow boardwalk rules for bikes (allowed until 10am in summer, anytime in the off season).

SLOTS The slots parlor usually has a crowd at **Casino Ocean Downs,** 10218 Racetrack Rd., Berlin (✆ **410/641-0600;** www.oceandowns.com). With 750 machines, there's room for one more whether you're interested in penny slots, or a virtual game of blackjack or roulette. (There are no true gaming tables—you have to go to Dover for them.) An evening of slots and the pacers outside is a good diversion from beach activities. Kids can come to the races but aren't allowed inside the casino. A fast-food cafeteria and bar will help keep up your strength. Open 8am to 2am daily.

SURF FISHING Surf fishing is permitted on all public beaches. However, between 9am and 6pm you cannot fish within 150 feet of swimmers or of anyone on the beach, which, in peak season, can be impossible. Fishing licenses are required for the ocean and coastal bays. For details, go to www2.md.wildlifelicense.com. **Public fishing piers** are at Inlet Park (this one charges a fee), as well as on the bay side at the Third Street Pier, Ninth Street Pier (which is lighted), and Northside Park (at 125th St.). For fishing supplies, visit **Bahia Marina,** on the bay at 22nd Street (✆ **410/289-7438**).

SURFING The beach between the fishing pier and the inlet has been set aside for surfers on summer weekdays. On weekends, different beaches rotate as surf beaches. Go to **www.ococean.com/ocbp** for each day's location. **K-Coast Surfshop,** on 35th Street (✆ **410/524-8500**), or on 78th Street (✆ **410/723-3330**), keeps an up-to-date schedule and offers lessons and rentals. **Malibu's Surf Shop** (✆ **410/289-3000;** www.malibus.com) offers a daily surf report on its website. The 24-hour surfing info line is ✆ **410/524-7685.**

TENNIS The town of Ocean City operates a **USTA Tennis Center** at 61st Street and the bay (✆ **410/524-8337**) with six courts and three fast-dry clay courts with tournaments, lessons, and camps. Other tennis courts are at Third and St. Louis Avenue, 94th Street and bayside, and Gorman Park at 136th.

WATERSPORTS From April through October, O.C. is a hotbed of sailing, parasailing, windsurfing, jet-skiing, power-boating, water-skiing, and more. For information on jet skis, contact **Bay Sports,** on the bay between 21st and 22nd streets (✆ **410/289-2144**). For skiff and pontoon-boat rentals, try **Bahia Marina,** on the bay at 22nd Street (✆ **410/289-7438**), or **O.C. Parasail,** Talbot Street Pier, near the inlet and at 54th Street and the bay (✆ **410/723-1464**). For pontoon boats, jetboats or tubing, call **Bayside Rentals** (✆ **410/289-7112**). Check the visitor center for up-to-date information. Visitors in North Ocean City might want to check out **Action Watercraft** (✆ **800/243-8938**), which rents powerboats and jet skis, and offers parasailing trips from the 142nd Street Marina in Fenwick.

Shopping

The shopping in Ocean City may not be high class, but there's a lot of it. The boardwalk, the outlet center, dozens of strip malls along Coastal Highway, and antiques in nearby Berlin are all happy to take visitors' money.

The Fish That Didn't Get Away

For 1 week in August, Ocean City is the center of the angling universe. Even if you didn't bring your 50-foot yacht and your $1,000 entry fee, you can join in the excitement of the **White Marlin Open,** where the winning fish can garner a prize worth $1.5 million or more. Head to the docks for the nightly weigh-in. The boats come in between 4 and 9pm—with most arriving around 7pm. See the fish that didn't get away: blue and white marlins, wahoo, and dolphin-fish (mahimahi), all of impressive size. Entrepreneurs set up booths for food, drink, and mementoes. The city provides a shuttle from the convention center, relieving visitors of the worries of where to park and where the heck this dock is.

If you enter town from the Route 50 bridge, you'll pass the **Ocean City Factory Outlets (www.ocfactoryoutlets.com),** a half-mile from the bridge at the intersection of Golf Course Road. The strip center is small but an okay diversion on a rainy day. The 20-plus outlets include Aerospostale, Jos. A. Bank, and Kitchen Collection. Serious shoppers head to Tanger in Rehoboth (see below). Parking is free and plentiful; a daily shuttle also stops at a variety of O.C. hotels from late July to mid-September (check the website for a schedule). The complex is open Sunday through Thursday from 10am to 6pm (until at least 8pm June–Aug), and Friday and Saturday from 10am to 9pm. ***Insider tip:*** If you've been dying for a piece of Smith Island cake, the state dessert, they sell them here at Smith Island Cakes by the slice or whole cake.

The **Tanger Outlet Centers,** in Rehoboth, have a much bigger selection—and Delaware charges no sales tax. Serious shoppers may want to head north. See p. 249.

The most popular shopping destination in O.C. is the boardwalk—27 blocks of souvenirs, candy, snack shacks, and, of course, T-shirts. You'll find much the same merchandise in all the souvenir shops, but there are a few places worth visiting. **Ocean Gallery World Center,** at Second Street (✆ **410/289-5300;** www.oceangallery.com), is a standout, with its facade of art from around the world. Its three stories are full of art posters, prints, and sofa-size oil paintings. The **Kite Loft,** at Fifth Street (✆ **410/289-6852;** www.kiteloft.com), has a selection of kites (from simple to really cool), flags, windsocks, and toys. There's also a location on 131st Street.

For something sweet, **Candy Kitchen** specializes in fudge and saltwater taffy and has numerous locations. If you're down near the inlet, stop in at **Wockenfuss Candy,** First Street and the boardwalk (✆ **410/289-7013**), for fine chocolates.

Ocean City After Dark

From people-watching on the boardwalk to a game of miniature golf to cocktails at the hundreds of beach and bayside bars, high-season Ocean City has almost as much nightlife as it has sand. There's something for everybody—certainly lots of places for singles to meet, as well as a few spots to relax with a beer. Many are open on weekends year-round—and you can count on a party for New Year's Eve and St. Patrick's Day. Below are a few fun places to try.

B.J.'s on the Water B.J.'s has live entertainment on Wednesdays and weekends at 9pm in high season, plus a sports bar, raw bar, and full menu. No cover charge. 75th St., on the bay. ✆ **410/524-7575.** www.bjsonthewater.com.

Fager's Island Fager's Island's bar is a popular watering hole for the well-heeled over-30 set, with summer deck parties in the summer and live music most nights spring through fall. 201 60th St., on the bay. ✆ **410/524-5500.** www.fagers.com.

The Greene Turtle DJs spin the tunes on weekends. A game's always on the TVs. There's a second location at 9616 Stephen Decatur Hwy. in west Ocean City and they're springing up in Rehoboth and Lewes, too (✆ **410/213-1500**). 11601 Coastal Hwy. ✆ **410/723-2120.** www.greeneturtle.com.

Jive A more mature crowd comes here for martinis, dancing, and the bayside view. Located behind Fresco's restaurant, it's a good place to stop before or after dinner. Or since they serve light fare, a good place to stop for snacks, wine, martinis, and "oldies" music on weekends. Open Wednesday through Sunday. 83rd St. and the bay. ✆ **410/524-1111.** www.ocjive.com. No cover.

Party Block Three clubs in 1 block—the Paddock, Big Kahuna's, and Rush—make this one of *the* places for the college-age crowd to meet and dance. Paddock features live music and bikini contests; Kahuna's the place for '80s, '90s, and dance music; with techno and hip-hop at Rush. And in summer, there's the Pool Bar. Cover usually charged after 10pm. 17th St. and Coastal Hwy. ✆ **410/289-6331.** www.partyblock.com.

Seacrets, Jamaica Seacrets is a Caribbean-themed mega beach bar and grill, decorated with palm trees, twinkling lights, and sand. In the large, covered dance area, crowds of young and old are treated to live reggae or party music every night. Seacrets also serves light fare, but it's best to come very early if you want to eat. Even kids are welcome early; they'll enjoy the theme-park decor. ***Tip:*** Much of Seacrets is outside, so it might not be the best choice if rain is in the forecast. 49th St., on the bay. ✆ **410/524-4900.** www.seacrets.com. Cover varies.

Food and Fun Nearby in Salisbury

Just a few minutes away is the small shore town of Salisbury, which hosts a museum and baseball team and is just a short drive or bus ride from O.C.

Delmarva Shorebirds The Class A South Atlantic League affiliate of the Baltimore Orioles were league champs in 1997 and 2000.

Arthur W. Perdue Stadium, Hobbs Rd., Salisbury. ✆ **410/219-3112** for tickets. www.theshorebirds.com. From O.C., take Rte. 50 west to Salisbury. Turn left on Hobbs Rd. after the Rte. 13 bypass.

Evolution Craft Brewing Company I first tasted the ales, porters, and stouts at Evolution's tasting room in Delmar, Delaware. But the company outgrew its home and opened a larger space in Salisbury in March 2012, complete with a new gastropub. The new place features a full-service restaurant and tasting room, along with more room for their brewery. So, though I can't tell you about the restaurant yet, I can encourage you to find the tasting room for a pint or a growler filled with one of their well-crafted brews.

200 Elmwood St., Salisbury, MD 21804. ✆ **443/260-BEER** (2337). www.evolutioncraftbrewing.com. Restaurant 11:30am–midnight Sun-Thurs, 11:30am-12:30am Fri–Sat. Tasting room daily 1–9pm. AE, DC, DISC, MC, V.

Restaurant 213 ★★★ 🎁 FRENCH Those who love good food may want to venture out to this tiny restaurant along an unassuming stretch of Business Route 13 in Fruitland, south of Salisbury. The chef-owner—who has cooked at the White House—has crammed 13 tables into a low space and topped them with white cloths and stylish white dishes. Those plates are filled with silky sauces, which pair with fish and meat in a most heavenly way. The wine list runs 50 pages and includes descriptions, pictures of the labels, and a chart listing which wines pair with the regular menu items. Dinner includes an *amuse bouche* and, at the end, a package with something for breakfast—a nice touch. Sunday's prix-fixe menu offers five courses for $35.

213 N. Fruitland Blvd. (Rte. 13 Business N.), Fruitland. ✆ **410/677-4880.** www.restaurant213.com. Reservations recommended on weekends. Main dishes $29–$36. AE, MC, V. Tues–Sat 5–9pm.

The Ward Museum of Wildfowl Art ★★ Named for Lem and Steve Ward, brothers from Crisfield who turned decoy carving into an art, this museum houses the world's largest collection of contemporary and classic wildfowl art, with works by the Ward brothers, and galleries tracing the history of decoy making, from Native American reed figures to the most recent winners of the Ward World Championship Carving Competition, held each spring in Ocean City. The museum has programs for children, workshops on carving for adults, and an exceptional gift shop.

909 Schumaker Dr., Salisbury. ✆ **410/742-4988.** www.wardmuseum.org. Admission $7 adults, $5 seniors, $3 students; $17 per family. Mon–Sat 10am–5pm; Sun noon–5pm. Closed Jan 1, Thanksgiving, and Dec 25. From Rte. 50, turn onto Rte. 13 south; turn left onto College Ave., which will veer left and become Beaglin Park Dr.; the museum is on the right.

ASSATEAGUE ISLAND NATIONAL SEASHORE, MD/VA ★★

161 miles S of Wilmington; 57 miles S of Ocean City; 174 miles SE of Baltimore; 177 miles SE of Washington, DC

Imagine yourself here on a sunny afternoon—enjoying the surf, ocean breezes, and warm sand with your family, your friends, and a fat white-and-brown pony. The famous wild horses of Assateague are not shy. The band of bachelor ponies isn't, anyway. Though the majority of the horses try to stay away from people, the rest hang around the parking lot, poke their noses in open car windows, pose for pictures along the highway, or stand completely still on the beach while the wind tosses their manes.

More than 2.5 million people come to Assateague Island each year to enjoy this pristine barrier island and those ponies. On the Maryland half of this 37-mile-long island, you can see some of the 150 ponies up close. They are harder to see on the Virginia side, where they tend to stay farther from the trails.

Heed the warnings and don't touch or feed the ponies. They are wild and can be unpredictable. They're pretty, but they do bite and kick.

Most visitors are drawn to the guarded beaches in front of the state park's store, refreshment stands, and restrooms, or the campgrounds. But you don't have to walk too far to find deserted beaches, inhabited only by the horses and a few sika deer and shorebirds, including the endangered piping plover.

Wherever you go, be aware of Assateague's second-most-famous inhabitants—mosquitoes. They really are as bad as the brochures, guidebooks, and park rangers tell you, so come prepared with bug spray, citronella candles, and long sleeves. Compared to nearby Ocean City, Assateague is still wild and primitive—no hotels, restaurants, convenience stores, or gas stations.

Assateague is part state park and part national seashore. The descriptions of rules, regulations, and activities that follow indicate which authority has jurisdiction over which parts. For specifics on the Virginia side of the island, see *Frommer's Virginia*.

Assateague Island & Chincoteague N.W.R.

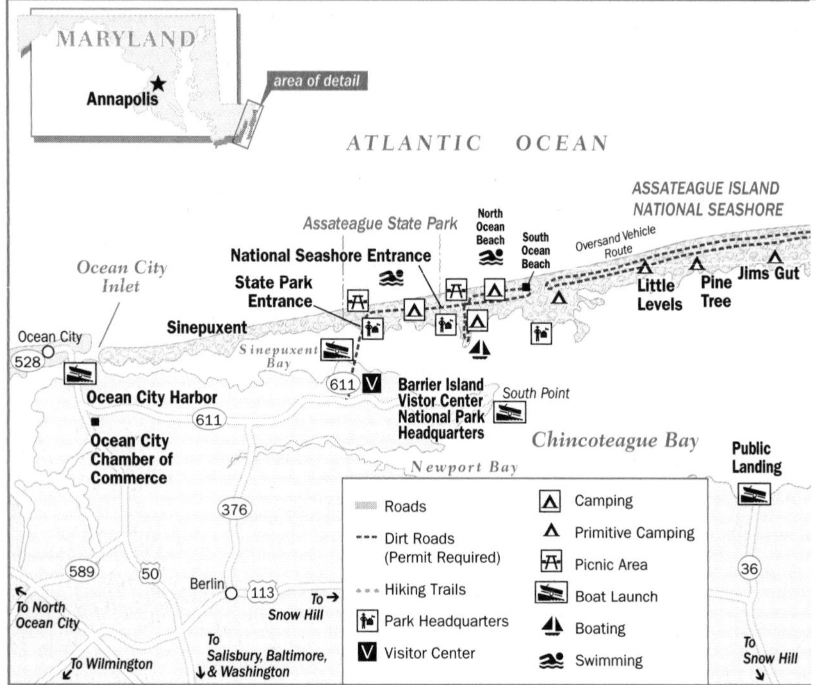

ACCESS In Maryland, take Route 611 south from Route 50 west from Ocean City. In Virginia, take Virginia Route 175 west across Chincoteague Island. The roads do not connect in the middle.

VISITOR CENTERS The National Park Service operates the **Barrier Island Visitor Center,** on Route 611 before you cross the bridge onto Assateague (✆ **410/641-1441**), and the **Campground Office,** in the park (✆ **410/641-3030**). The visitor center features exhibits, aquariums, videos, as well as the usual brochures and gift shop. It's open daily from 9am to 5pm. It's closed Easter and December 25. Maryland also operates **Assateague State Park** (✆ **410/641-2918**), at the northern end of the island. It connects to the national park but has its own amenities, regulations, and fees.

FEES & REGULATIONS **Assateague State Park** (✆ **410/641-2918**) charges an entry fee of $3 daily per state resident, $4 per out-of-state resident. Off season, it's $3 a vehicle.

Entry to the **Assateague Island National Seashore** is $15 per car year-round, good for a week. Walk-in and biking visitors are free. Most national-park regulations apply. Permits are required for backcountry camping and off-road vehicle use. Pets are allowed only in the Maryland side of the park and must be leashed. Alcohol use is prohibited in the state park. And ***don't feed the ponies.***

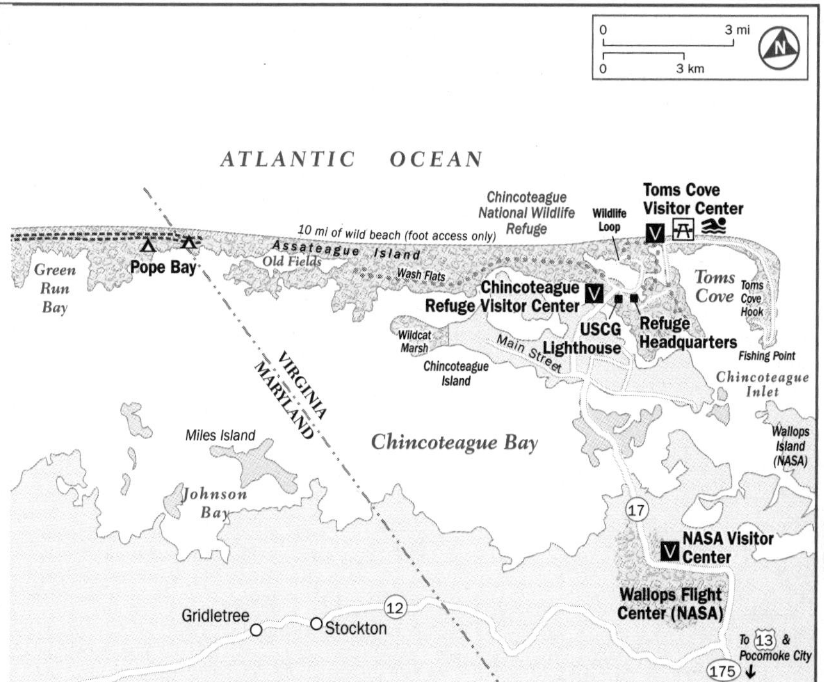

SEASONS Maryland's state park is open for day use from April 1 to December 1. Assateague Island National Seashore and Chincoteague National Wildlife Refuge are open year-round. There is no daily closing time on the Maryland side of the island, but only surf fishermen and campers staying in designated spots may stay overnight.

AVOIDING THE CROWDS & THE BUGS Weekends in summer are crowded. If you plan to camp, make reservations. The human population is not the biggest nuisance: Mosquitoes, biting flies, and ticks are abundant from April through September, and mosquitoes are especially a problem beginning at the end of July and following a heavy or steady rain. They're also much worse on the bay side of the island, so try to get an oceanside site if you're camping in the national park. Your best bet for avoiding the bugs is to wait until it gets cold enough to kill them all off. The good news is that sea breezes from the Atlantic keep the mosquitoes pretty much off the beach itself—so once you make it near the surf, you're safe.

RANGER PROGRAMS The National Park Service offers a wide variety of ranger-led programs throughout the summer, including nature hikes, surf-rescue demonstrations, canoe trips, campfire programs, and surf-fishing and shell-fishing demonstrations. For a rundown of activities, stop by the visitor centers or contact Assateague Island National Seashore, 7206 National Seashore Lane, Berlin (✆ **410/641-1441;** www.nps.gov/asis).

Seeing the Ponies

Finding and viewing the famed wild horses takes almost no effort, especially on the Maryland side of the island, where the ponies have free rein. In fact, you'll probably have to stop for a few begging ponies along the side of the road as you enter. (For your own safety, that of the ponies, and that of your car, roll up your windows and do not feed them.) When you're camping, you may hear a pack of horses stroll by your tent in the middle of the night or see the telltale signs in the morning. Stop by the beach in the evening after the crowds have left when the ponies roam the sand. ***Tip:*** Visitors in cars can pull over to watch the ponies or deer along 2 miles of Bayberry Drive between the state and national park entrances. Bikers are welcome, too.

In Virginia, the ponies are less accessible; you can generally see them—often in the distance—along the paved road called the Wildlife Tour, in the fenced marshes south of Beach Road, and from the observation platform on the Woodland Trail.

The annual **Pony Penning and Auction ★** (**© 866/PONYSWIM** [766-9794]; www.chincoteaguechamber.com/pony-swim), a unique exercise in population control, is held on Chincoteague Island, a barrier island adjoining Assateague, on the last Wednesday and Thursday of July. The Chincoteague "cowboys" round up the Virginia herd on Wednesday, and thousands of spectators watch as the horses swim from Assateague to Chincoteague, where the foals are auctioned off the next day. Campsites and hotel rooms (only available on Chincoteague and the mainland) fill up fast, so reserve well in advance. If you're staying in Ocean City, get up before dawn and drive the 60 miles to Chincoteague. You'll make it in time for the pony swim and be back in O.C. for dinner.

Although it's exciting to see the ponies swim across the channel, be aware that tens of thousands of people come to witness the annual event. You may only see the ponies as tiny dots as you wait along the shore shoulder-to-shoulder with hundreds of new friends. Traffic on the small island is almost too much to handle.

Outdoor Activities

Campfires are allowed in the national park, unlike the other ocean beaches in the area. They must be built below the high-tide mark. But don't bring firewood from out of state (it's illegal). A number of stands along Route 611 sell it. Fires must be extinguished until cold with water, not sand.

CRABBING, CLAMMING & FISHING Check with the staff at the visitor center for a map showing the best places to catch crabs, clams, and mussels. The best time to crab is late summer to early fall, in the morning or early evening. The most common approach is the string, bait, and net method: Attach a piece of bony chicken or a fish head to a string (chicken necks are the preferred bait) and cast out in shallow water. When you feel a tug, gently tow the line in. If there's a crab on the end, net it before you take it out of the water, then transfer it to a container and continue crabbing.

A single collapsible crab pot or trap may also be used, if it is attended at all times. You can purchase a crab pot at bait-and-tackle shops; they look like large chicken-wire boxes. Place bait in the center of the trap; drop it in clear, shallow water; and pull it up as soon as a crab walks in. All crabs must measure 5 inches point to point, and all egg-bearing females must be released. Limits are 1 bushel per person per day, or 2 bushels per boat per day. Crabbing is prohibited January through March.

Signing and raking are accepted methods for clamming. The mudflats at Virginia's Toms Cove are more suitable for signing. To sign for clams, walk along the mudflats at low tide and look for small openings, or "signs," indicating a clam. Then dig it out with a hand trowel or digging tool. Raking can be done at any tide level, but you need a clamming rake, which has a basket to catch the clams. Drag the rake through the mud until the tines scrape a shell; then dig up the mud, shake it loose, and catch the clam in the basket. Clams must be 1 inch wide; the limit is 1 bushel per person per day.

Mussels and oysters are rare in the waters surrounding the island. Oysters are rarely found off the private leased beds (and trespassing is prohibited). The park service asks that you take only what you will consume in mussels and oysters.

Bring your fishing license; both Maryland and Virginia law require them. Fishing is prohibited on guarded beaches and in designated surf zones.

HIKING & BIKING Conditions and trails for hiking and biking are better at the Virginia end of the island, but there are three .5-mile hiking trails on the Maryland end: Life of the Marsh, Life of the Forest, and Life of the Dunes. All are short, and all require bug repellent. Cyclists can use the 3-mile paved bike path along Bayberry Drive and the Oceanside campground.

In Virginia, about 5 of the 15 miles of trails are paved for cycling. The Wildlife Tour is closed to car traffic until 3pm each day, so hikers and bikers can have it all to themselves. The Woodland Trail, which leads to a pony observation platform, is also paved. These wooded paths are serene but exciting if you find the sought-after ponies.

OFF-ROAD VEHICLES The vast majority of Assateague is not accessible by car; however, off-road (or over-sand) vehicle routes stretch for 12 miles. Permits are required and are issued for a $90 to $150 annual fee. Call © **410/641-3030** or see **www.nps.gov/asis** for information and ORV regulations.

PADDLING & BOATING The only launch facility on the island is for canoes. It's at the end of Ferry Landing Road on the Maryland side. Larger boats can be launched for the day from the state park's marina just west of the bridge (across from the Barrier Island Visitor Center). The fee is $10.

Waters at the Maryland end of Chincoteague Bay are usually ideal for canoeing, though the tidal currents around Chincoteague Island are strong. The bay is generally shallow, so operators of larger boats should watch for sandbars. In summer, you can rent canoes from the concession at the end of Bayside Drive. Four backcountry canoe-in campsites are located in the national park. Permits are required and can be obtained at the ranger station in Maryland or at the Toms Cove Visitor Center in Virginia.

Coastal Kayak (© **877/44-KAYAK** [445-2925] or 302/539-7999; www.coastalkayak.com) offers eco-tours of the Assateague back bay. Tours cost about $50 for adults and $40 for children. (Discount coupons are on the website.) **Assateague Explorer** runs kayaking tours off Assateague between Memorial Day and Columbus Day six times a day for $40 for adults, $36 for children. Call © **757/336-5956** or check out www.assateagueisland.com/kayaktours.htm.

Super Fun Eco-Tours (© **410/656-9453;** www.superfunecotours.com/beer.htm) offers an Assateague kayak tour starting at Burley Oak Brewery in Berlin.

The park's **Coastal Bays Program** (© **410/726-3217**) offers canoe rentals for $40 a day, kayak rentals for $45, bicycles for $20, and clam rakes for $10. Hourly rentals as well as overnight and weekend are also available. Stand-up paddlers can also rent SUPs for $20 an hour or $75 for the day at the same site through **Delmarva Board Sports** (© **301/651-0542;** www.delmarvaboardsports.com).

SWIMMING Beaches are guarded from Memorial Day weekend through Labor Day weekend daily 10am to 5pm.

Camping

Accommodations on the island are limited to a state-run campground and two campgrounds and several backcountry campsites run by the National Park Service. ***Please note:*** No campfire wood from out of state is permitted in any park in Maryland.

The campground run by **Assateague State Park** (✆ **410/641-2120,** ext. 22, or 888/432-2267 for state camping reservations) is open April 1 through October 31. It has 311 sites on the ocean side of the island, with bathhouses (with flush toilets and hot showers), a camp store, and a snack bar. Reservations are accepted up to a year in advance. Sites are on the ocean side of the island and cost $32 to $42 per night.

The **National Park Service** (✆ **410/641-3030** for information, or 877/444-6777 for reservations) operates oceanside and bayside campgrounds that are slightly more primitive than the state-park facility. Both NPS campgrounds have chemical toilets, drinking water, and cold showers. There are also flush toilets and cold showers at the beach bathhouse. Reservations are recommended from April 15 to October 15—and are essential in warm weather. The rest of the year, campsites are available on a first-come, first-served basis. If possible, reserve a site at the oceanside campground for fewer pesky bugs. The cost is $20 per night from April 15 to October 15, $16 per night the rest of the year. There is no camping on the Virginia side.

In addition, the park has several backcountry or hike-in/paddle-in campsites along the Maryland end of the island. Each site has a chemical toilet and picnic table, but no drinking water. To use these sites, you must pick up a $5 backcountry permit from the ranger station during regular business hours.

Another camping and kayaking alternative is **Pocomoke River State Park** (✆ **410/632-2566**), about a 45-minute drive from the Virginia or Maryland end of Assateague, which is less crowded and more comfortable. It offers 230 improved campsites and 12 mini one-room cabins (some air-conditioned) in two wooded sites along both sides of the Pocomoke River. **Shad Landing** offers a marina, canoe, kayak, and boat rentals; a nature center; a swimming pool; and hiking and ORV trails. Its 201 campsites are available year-round: $31 for electric, $25 for nonelectric, and $56 for the eight cabins. Across the river, **Milburn Landing** is smaller, quieter, and open only from April to mid-December. Its 38 campsites cost $26 for electric, $21 for nonelectric; four cabins are $52.

To make reservations, call ✆ **888/432-2267,** or visit **http://reservations.dnr.state.md.us**. To get here, take Route 113 south. The park is 20 miles south of Berlin.

Paddling fans, once you see the Pocomoke, you're going to want to get out on it. Bring your own boat, rent one, or sign up for a tour with the **Pocomoke River Canoe Company** (✆ **410/632-3971;** www.atbeach.com/amuse/md/canoe). They're on the river in Snow Hill.

A Side Trip to Berlin, MD

Barely 20 minutes away from the Ocean City boardwalk is the historic town of Berlin. Its quaint stores and antiques shops have long been a favorite side trip for vacationers in Ocean City. It also has two charming places to stay, a good restaurant, and a little theater. These amenities and a location roughly equidistant from Assateague and Ocean City make Berlin a good diversion.

To get to Berlin from Ocean City, take the Route 50 bridge out of O.C. and follow Route 50; take a left on Route 113; Berlin is less than a mile away.

WHERE TO STAY

Atlantic Hotel ★ Richard Gere and Julia Roberts came here to film *Runaway Bride.* This three-story 1895 Victorian beauty features "new" antiques, feather beds and comforters, and flatscreen TV/DVD units. The Anna Suite includes sitting room and kitchen. Larger units are quite comfy while the smaller units can be a bit tight but are comfortable enough for the price. No. 20 is the Richard Gere Room (his room in the movie) but the corner No. 10 is larger and airier. For a bit of extra privacy, opt for the Gardener's Cottage behind the hotel with its sitting room and tiny front porch.

2 N. Main St., Berlin, MD 21811. www.atlantichotel.com. ✆ **800/814-7672** or 410/641-3589. Fax 410/641-4928. 17 units. July–Aug $140–$335 double; Apr–May and Sept–Oct $125–$295 double; Nov–Mar $55–$235 double. AE, DC, DISC, MC, V. Free parking. No children. **Amenities:** Restaurant; bar; outdoor porches. *In room:* A/C, TV/DVD, hair dryer.

Merry Sherwood Plantation ★ Drive through the gates and enter a hideaway filled with fragrant flowers, butterflies, and, at the end of the drive, an 1859 plantation house. Inside, the rooms are filled with antiques, sunshine streams through the porch windows, and breezes cool the high-ceilinged rooms. Front bedrooms are sunnier, but those in back are quieter. All but two units have private bathrooms; the two that share a bathroom are spacious and well appointed, and their claw-foot tub is equally charming. The honeymoon suite has a whirlpool tub, while the Stokes has a fireplace. And don't miss the cupola; it's a good place to catch a breeze—or ponder the universe.

8909 Worcester Hwy. (2½ miles south of Berlin on Rte. 113), Berlin, MD 21811. www.merrysherwood.com. ✆ **800/660-0358** or 410/641-2112. 8 units, 2 with shared bathroom. $100–$175 double off season; $125–$200 double in season. Rates include full breakfast. MC, V. Free parking. *In room:* A/C, free Wi-Fi.

WHERE TO EAT

For a sweet start or midafternoon pick-me-up, stop by **Baked Desserts,** 4C Bay St. (✆ **410/641-1800;** www.bakeddessertcafe.com), home of the peach dumpling (in season only), as well as gluten-free confections and other delights. The **Berlin Coffee House,** 17 Jefferson St. (✆ **410/629-1073**), features Chesapeake Bay Farms ice cream and Notting Hill coffee from Lewes.

Drummer's Cafe ★★ TRADITIONAL The Victorian-styled Drummer's Cafe is a local favorite and big with visitors, as well. A traditional lunch menu of soups, salads, sandwiches, and quiche of the day stay on the menu for dinner. Everything is fresh and local. Heartier entrees, crab cakes, catch of the day, and beef are available after 5pm. Appetizers are generous enough for light eaters. Diners prefer the screened porch in the summer but the paneled dining room is cozy. The bar fills with music Monday, Thursday, and Sunday.

At the Atlantic Hotel, 2 N. Main St. ✆ **410/641-3589.** www.atlantichotel.com. Reservations required for dinner. Main courses $18–$28; lunch $14–$15. AE, DC, DISC, MC, V. Daily 11am–10pm; Sun brunch 11am–3pm. From Ocean City, take Rte. 50 west 7 miles to Rte. 818 (Main St.).

The Globe AMERICAN A former movie theater, the Globe still uses its little stage for weekend jazz performances. Listen to the music up close with a drink and appetizer or take a table farther back to focus on the comfort-food entrees. There are all kinds of soup, sandwiches, and salads at lunch, and after 5pm entrees such as pasta, tuna, crab cakes, and steak. The **Balcony Art Gallery** upstairs features local artwork.

12 Broad St. ✆ **410/641-0784.** www.globetheater.com. Reservations recommended for dinner. Main courses $8–$13 lunch, .$10–$25 dinner. AE, DISC, MC, V. Sun 10am–10pm; Tues–Thurs 11am–10pm; Fri–Sat 11am–midnight.

WHAT TO SEE & DO

Berlin is featured in its own local museum. A new visitor center on Main Street will guide tourists to attractions around town. Berlin hosts a monthly **Art Stroll** on second Fridays from 5 to 8pm. The **Fiddlers Convention,** the last weekend in September, always draws a crowd. In early May, Main Street fills with the music of the **Berlin Blues and Jazz Fest.** Throughout December, shops celebrate a **Victorian Christmas,** with concerts the first weekend.

Berlin, MD Chamber of Commerce Visitor Center Stop for brochures and directions, to buy a T-shirt or visit the artists' galleries behind the lobby.

14 S. Main St. ✆ **410/641-4775.** www.berlinchamber.org. Mon–Fri 10am–4pm; Sat 10am–2pm.

Burley Oak Brewery Burley Oak sells its organic American, Belgian-inspired brews, crafted here and given names like Rude Boy and Seven Finger Farmer. **Super Fun Eco-Tours** (✆ **410/656-9453;** www.superfunecotours.com/beer.htm) offers an Assateague kayak tour here.

10016 Old Ocean City Blvd., Berlin, MD 21811. ✆ **443/513-4647.** www.burleyoak.com. Mon 4–10pm; Sun, Tues, Wed 11am–10pm; Thurs–Sat 11am–2pm.

Calvin B. Taylor House Museum Lovingly preserved, this Federal-style home features fine antiques and dazzling faux-finish woodwork, as well as exhibits recalling the life of the banker-owner and the town itself. Horse racing fans will want to see the portrait of War Admiral—he was raised on a farm nearby.

208 N. Main St. ✆ **410/641-1019.** www.taylorhousemuseum.org. Donations accepted. June–Oct Mon, Wed, and Fri–Sat 1–4pm.

Costa Ventosa Here's a good spot to visit on a bad beach day. The winery and tasting room showcase the locally produced merlot, chardonnay, and vidal blanc. If you'd like a taste, you have to stop here. It's the only place it is sold.

9031 Whaleyville Rd., Whaleyville 21872. ✆ **443/333-9867.** www.costaventosa.com. Fri–Sun noon–6pm. Closed Jan.

SHOPPING

Local arts and crafts take center stage at shops along Main Street and a few side streets. Most are open daily from 10am to 5pm, though on Sundays hours are limited mostly to 11am to 3pm with a few open until 4 or 5pm.

Local artists are featured at the **Worcester County Arts Council Gallery and Shop,** 6 Jefferson St. (✆ **410/641-0809**), open Tuesday to Friday 11am to 3pm, and at **Water's Edge Gallery,** 2 S. Main St. (✆ **410/629-1784**). Jeffrey Auxer displays his own traditional Venetian glass at his studio, 19 Jefferson St. (✆ **443/513-4210;** www.jeffreyauxer.com). Blair Parsons makes the jewelry at **TaDa,** 18 N. Main St., ✆ **410/641-4430;** www.blairelizabeth.com). **J.J. Fish Studio,** 14 N. Main St. (✆ **410/641-4805;** www.jjfishstudio.com), displays the owner's silver works and locally and American-made crafts from pottery to glass. **Bungalow Love,** 12 Williams St. (✆ **410/641-2781;** www.bungalowlove.net), mixes local crafts with fair-trade and vintage items. **Town Center Antiques** (✆ **410/629-1895**) has its wares at 1 N. Main St. and also at 113 N. Main St.

WILMINGTON

11

At first glance, Wilmington is all business, as it has been since the first Swedish settlers arrived in 1638. An industrial center since the American Revolution, it is now home to a number of large corporations, including banking, insurance, and pharmaceutical companies, as well as DuPont.

On weekends, the city trades the briefcase for play clothes. Parks and the Riverfront trail are filled with joggers and picnickers. It seems everyone heads for a restaurant. The museums, theaters, and Brandywine Valley beckon. Hotel deals are plentiful on weekends, and there's enough room in the restaurants, along the trails, and at any of the city's attractions.

ORIENTATION

Arriving

BY PLANE **Philadelphia International Airport** (✆ **800/745-4283;** www.phl.org) is about a half-hour from Wilmington. Car-rental agencies at the airport include **Avis** (✆ **800/331-1212**) and **Hertz** (✆ **800/654-3131**).

Delaware Express (✆ **800/648-5466** or 302/454-7800; www.delexpress.com) offers van service from the Philadelphia airport to Wilmington for about $40. Reserve by phone or online at least 24 hours in advance. Otherwise, look for their phone at baggage claim.

BY TRAIN **Amtrak** (✆ **800/USA-RAIL** [872-7245]; www.amtrak.com) serves Wilmington on its Northeast Corridor line, with Acela, Metroliner, and regional trains daily. The Amtrak station is at 100 S. French St. (at Martin Luther King, Jr., Blvd.), on the Riverfront. There's a taxi stand outside.

BY CAR I-95 cuts across the city's center. The **Delaware Memorial Bridge** (part of I-295) connects Wilmington to the New Jersey Turnpike and points north. From southern Delaware and the Eastern Shore, Route 13 will bring you into the city.

BY BUS **Greyhound** (✆ **800/231-2222;** www.greyhound.com) and **Peter Pan** (✆ **800/343-9999;** www.peterpanbus.com) provide daily bus service into the **Wilmington Transportation Center,** 101 N. French St. (✆ **302/655-6111**).

Visitor Information

Information on Wilmington, the Brandywine Valley, and New Castle is available from the **Greater Wilmington Convention and Visitors Bureau,** 100 W. 10th St., Ste. 20 (✆ **800/489-6664;** www.visitwilmingtonde.com). It's open Monday through Friday from 9am to 5pm. Motorists may want to stop first at the **I-95 Delaware Travel Plaza** visitor center, south of town between exits 1 and 3 (✆ **302/737-4059**) for maps, directions, and brochures. It's open daily, except December 25, from 8am to 8pm.

Special Events

For 10 days in June, music lovers turn out for free jazz at the **DuPont Clifford Brown Jazz Festival.** Visit **www.cliffordbrownjazzfest.com** for a schedule. Citizens turn out for **First Friday Art Loop** every month except January. Go to **www.wilmingtonde.gov/visitors/artloop** for details. The **Delaware Antiques Show** is held the first weekend in November. It is sponsored by Winterthur; go to **www.winterthur.org** for details.

City Layout

Three rivers run through Wilmington: the Brandywine, the Christina, and the Delaware. The **downtown** business area, between the Brandywine and Christina, is laid out in a grid system, less than 20 blocks wide and long. Though the downtown area is relatively small, attractions, restaurants, and hotels are spread out, with most south of downtown or in the northern suburbs. Aside from a few museums and shops along Market Street, you can't or wouldn't want to walk between major attractions.

Two areas of Wilmington also worth a visit are the **Riverfront** and the suburban north side. The Riverfront is about a 5-minute drive south of downtown between I-95 and the Christina River. To reach this home of arts venues, restaurants, offices, and condos, take Martin Luther King, Jr., Boulevard to Madison Street and follow the signs. Or head back to I-95 and take exit 6. Riverfront has lots of free parking.

The **north side** of Wilmington (north of Rte. 52 and northwest of I-95) features modest-to-lavish brick houses, parks, the **Trolley Square** neighborhood, and nearby **Little Italy,** with plenty of restaurants. The main thoroughfares are Delaware Avenue to Route 52 (also known as Pennsylvania Ave. and Kennett Pike); as you drive out Route 52, the cityscape soon gives way to rolling hills of the Brandywine Valley.

MAIN ARTERIES & STREETS Market Street runs north-south in downtown Wilmington. The east-west cross streets are numbered from 1st to 16th, with the lowest number on the southern end. The north-south streets bear the names of presidents and local heroes west of Market, and trees east of Market. Most streets are one-way, except for Fourth Street. I-95 enters Wilmington via two main avenues: Delaware (Rte. 52) at the north, and Martin Luther King, Jr., Boulevard at the south.

From I-95 and downtown, approach Wilmington's north side by using Route 52, which splits into Pennsylvania Avenue (Rte. 52) and Delaware Avenue about 2 blocks north of I-95. Both Routes 52 and 202 take you out to Brandywine Valley sites.

MAPS *Greater Wilmington and Brandywine Valley,* a booklet produced by the Greater Wilmington Convention and Visitors Bureau, has detailed maps of downtown and the Wilmington region with major attractions marked.

GETTING AROUND

BY BUS Wilmington is served by the **DART First State** (✆ **800/355-6066;** www.dartfirststate.com) bus system. Blue-and-white signs indicating stops are located throughout the city, and regular routes can take you to some hotels, museums, theaters, and parks, as well as to the malls and historic New Castle. Fares are based on a zone system; the minimum fare for one zone is $1.15. Exact change is

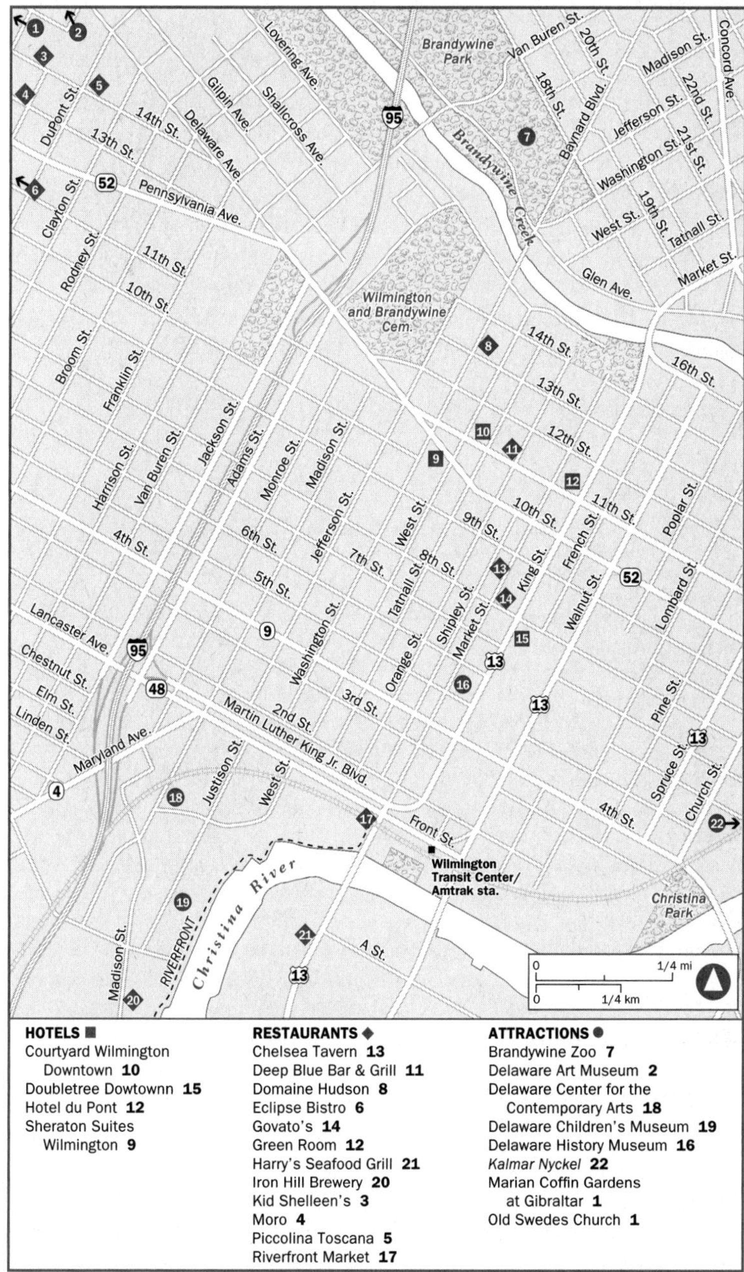
Brandywine Park
Van Buren St.
20th St.
Concord Ave.
Madison St.
18th St.
Baynard Blvd.
22nd St.
Jefferson St.
21st St.
Washington St.
19th St.
West St.
Tatnall St.
Glen Ave.
Market St.
Lovering Ave.
Gilpin Ave.
Shallcross Ave.
Brandywine Creek
DuPont St.
14th St.
13th St.
Delaware Ave.
Pennsylvania Ave.
Clayton St.
Rodney St.
11th St.
10th St.
Wilmington and Brandywine Cem.
14th St.
16th St.
13th St.
Broom St.
Franklin St.
12th St.
Jackson St.
Adams St.
Monroe St.
Madison St.
Harrison St.
Van Buren St.
10th St.
11th St.
Poplar St.
West St.
9th St.
Jefferson St.
French St.
4th St.
6th St.
7th St.
8th St.
King St.
5th St.
Tatnall St.
Shipley St.
Walnut St.
Lombard St.
Lancaster Ave.
Washington St.
Orange St.
Market St.
Chestnut St.
Elm St.
3rd St.
Pine St.
Linden St.
2nd St.
Martin Luther King Jr. Blvd.
Maryland Ave.
Justison St.
West St.
Spruce St.
Church St.
4th St.
Front St.
Wilmington Transit Center/ Amtrak sta.
Christina River
Christina Park
Madison St.
RIVERFRONT
A St.
0 1/4 mi
0 1/4 km
HOTELS ■
Courtyard Wilmington Downtown 10
Doubletree Dowtownn 15
Hotel du Pont 12
Sheraton Suites Wilmington 9
RESTAURANTS ◆
Chelsea Tavern 13
Deep Blue Bar & Grill 11
Domaine Hudson 8
Eclipse Bistro 6
Govato's 14
Green Room 12
Harry's Seafood Grill 21
Iron Hill Brewery 20
Kid Shelleen's 3
Moro 4
Piccolina Toscana 5
Riverfront Market 17
ATTRACTIONS ●
Brandywine Zoo 7
Delaware Art Museum 2
Delaware Center for the Contemporary Arts 18
Delaware Children's Museum 19
Delaware History Museum 16
Kalmar Nyckel 22
Marian Coffin Gardens at Gibraltar 1
Old Swedes Church 1

required. For schedule and fare information, call or visit the website. Fare cards are available online.

BY SHUTTLE DART also operates the **Trolley,** which for $1.15 (exact change required) takes visitors from Rodney Square to the Amtrak station to the Riverfront. The route goes up Walnut Street north via Rodney Square and West Street to 13th Street and down Market Street and King Street. Service is provided every 30 minutes. The whole ride takes about 15 minutes. Shuttles run Monday through Saturday from 7:30am to 7:30pm. Get a schedule from the visitor center or DART.

BY CAR Because Wilmington's attractions are scattered around town—and because so many pair a visit to the city with Brandywine Valley attractions—a car is necessary. If you aren't driving, rent a car from either **Enterprise,** 520 S. Walnut St. (✆ **302/656-5464**), or **Budget,** 100 S. French St. (✆ **302/652-0629**).

BY TAXI There's a taxi stand at the Amtrak station, across the street from the bus station. To order a taxi, call **Yellow Cab** (✆ **302/658-4340**).

[Fast FACTS] WILMINGTON

Area Code Wilmington's area code is **302.**

Emergencies Dial **911**).

Hospitals Downtown: **St. Francis Hospital,** 701 N. Clayton St. (✆ **302/421-4100**), and **Wilmington Hospital,** 501 W. 14th St. (✆ **302/733-1000**).

Newspapers & Magazines The city's daily newspaper is the ***News Journal.*** The best monthly magazine is ***Delaware Today.***

Pharmacies **Happy Harry's/Walgreens** has locations at 839 N. Market St., at Ninth Street (✆ **302/654-1834**), and at 1 Trolley Sq., Delaware Avenue and DuPont Street (✆ **302/655-6397**).

Police For nonemergencies, call ✆ **302/576-3940.** For emergencies, dial ✆ **911.**

Post Office The main downtown post office is at 500 Delaware Ave., Ste. 1 (✆ **302/656-0228**).

Taxes There is no sales tax in Delaware, but an 8% to 10% lodging tax applies to stays at city hotels.

WHERE TO STAY

Because Wilmington is a major destination for business travelers, numerous downtown hotels cater to them. That said, no matter where you go in Delaware, when you hear people refer to "The Hotel," they mean the Hotel du Pont in Wilmington. For more than 80 years, this hotel has dominated the Delaware lodging scene. Most hotels charge top prices Sunday through Thursday—spiking in late spring and early fall—but on weekends, rates drop. Summer is low season, and prices plummet, even at the Hotel du Pont. Look for packages combining accommodations with tickets to area attractions.

Tip: The suburbs offer additional choices—including the area's finest hotel. See chapter 12 for options in the Brandywine Valley.

Downtown

EXPENSIVE

Hotel du Pont ★★★ Opened in 1913 and owned by E. I. du Pont de Nemours and Company, this is the grandest accommodation in town. The 12-story Italian Renaissance structure is a showcase of marble, coffered ceilings, carved walnut, and genteel service. Each unit features DuPont's latest fibers and modern fixtures. Rooms are spacious and luxurious. Corner suites are grander, with living and dining rooms. Two floors are decorated in a more contemporary style. Weekenders will find various packages, and good deals.

11th and Market sts., Wilmington, DE 19801. www.hoteldupont.com. ✆ **800/441-9019** or 302/594-3100. Fax 302/549-3108. 217 units. $199–$499 double; $899–$1,249 suite. Weekend packages available. AE, DC, DISC, MC, V. Valet parking $22; self-parking $16. Pets under 20 lb. accepted with fee. **Amenities:** 2 restaurants; lobby lounge for cocktails and afternoon tea; coffee shop; airport limousine service; concierge; fitness center; golf course nearby; room service; tennis nearby. *In room:* A/C, flatscreen TV w/pay movies, hair dryer, minibar, MP3 docking station, Wi-Fi (fee).

Sheraton Suites Wilmington ★★ In Wilmington's financial section but convenient to Route 52, this contemporary 16-story hotel offers spacious suites with two queens or one king-size bed. Each has a full bedroom with dressing area and a living room with large-screen TV, wet bar, and desk. Furniture and white bedding were updated in 2007. **Basil's** serves breakfast, lunch, and dinner and has live jazz on Thursday evenings.

422 Delaware Ave., Wilmington, DE 19801. www.starwoodhotels.com/sheraton/suiteswilmington. ✆ **800/325-3535** or 302/654-8300. Fax 302/654-6036. 223 units. $125–$349 double. Weekend rates available. AE, DC, DISC, MC, V. Parking Sun–Thurs $16, Fri–Sat $12. **Amenities:** Restaurant; lounge; concierge-level rooms; fitness room; indoor pool; room service; sauna. *In room:* A/C, 2 TVs, hair dryer, kitchenette, Wi-Fi (free).

MODERATE

Courtyard Wilmington Downtown This hotel offers good value for downtown. Three room styles are available, with 80 king-bed rooms, 25 two-queen, and 18 spa rooms with a king-size bed and whirlpool tubs. All have contemporary furniture and most have sleeper sofas.

1102 West St., Wilmington, DE 19801. www.marriott.com. ✆ **800/321-2211** or 302/429-7600. Fax 302/429-9167. 126 units. $124–$224 double. AE, DC, DISC, MC, V. Self-parking $9.50; free parking Fri–Sat nights. **Amenities:** Restaurant; lounge; fitness center; room service. *In room:* A/C, TV, fridge, hair dryer, microwave, free Wi-Fi.

Suburbs

EXPENSIVE

Hilton Wilmington/Christiana ★ This hotel, nestled amid grassy grounds off exit 4B of I-95, is a good choice in the 'burbs—near the University of Delaware and surrounded by shopping malls. The brick building surrounds a courtyard with gazebo and pool. In front is a pond that's home to a family of swans (public feedings scheduled daily). Rooms are typical size and style for Hilton with contemporary furnishings and Brandywine artwork. An executive level includes continental breakfast, evening reception, and bigger rooms.

100 Continental Dr., Newark, DE 19713. www.hiltonchristiana.com. ✆ **877/696-8671** or 302/454-1500. Fax 302/454-0233. 266 units. $139–$284 double. Lower weekend rates available. AE, DC, DISC, MC, V. Free parking. Pets welcome for a fee. **Amenities:** Restaurant; lounge; concierge; fitness center; outdoor pool; room service; free shuttle to downtown and UDel. *In room:* A/C, flatscreen TV w/movies, fridge, hair dryer, MP3docking station, Wi-Fi (fee).

The Inn at Montchanin Village ★★★ Why sleep in a hotel room when you can wake up in a historic village surrounded by fragrant gardens? A few miles from downtown Wilmington, among the Brandywine châteaux, Montchanin Village is part of du Pont family history: It was once home to workers in the black powder mills and factories along the Brandywine. The whole village is listed on the National Register of Historic Places. Eleven buildings, completed between 1870 and 1910, became the

Inn at Montchanin Village in 1996. Nine of them, once the workers' residences, have been converted into 28 guest rooms, including one- and two-level suites. Six superior suites have king-size beds, marble bathrooms with oversize tubs, and gas fireplaces. All rooms open onto an outdoor sitting area, and first-level rooms and suites have gardens. The blacksmith shop houses **Krazy Kat's** (see "Where to Eat," below), while the health club and spa can be found in the Dilwyn Barn.

Rte. 100 and Kirk Rd. (P.O. Box 130), Montchanin, DE 19710. www.montchanin.com. ✆ **800/269-2473** or 302/888-2133. Fax 302/888-0389. 28 units (11 with shower only). $192–$244 double; $290–$399 suite. AE, DC, DISC, MC, V. Free parking. **Amenities:** Restaurant; lounge; health club; room service; spa. *In room:* A/C, TV/VCR or DVD, hair dryer, kitchenette, free Wi-Fi.

MODERATE

Best Western Plus Brandywine Valley Inn ★ Though very much a motor lodge, the innkeepers have gone to great lengths to make guests forget that fact once they step inside. Court units serve business travelers with queen-size or two double beds, high-speed Internet, Wi-Fi, desks with printers and cordless phones, and limousine service. The Country French Boudoirs, in contrast, are cozy, smaller rooms with romantic wall coverings and linens for a real bed-and-breakfast feel. (Blue rooms are a bit roomier than the red rooms.) Ask for one of the three Winterthur rooms, outfitted with rich fabrics and Winterthur reproduction furniture—over-the-top in decor and comfort. The location is perfect for Brandywine tourists, on Route 202 near Nemours.

1807 Concord Pike (Rte. 202), Wilmington, DE 19803. www.brandywineinn.com. ✆ **800/537-7772** or 302/656-9436. Fax 302/656-8564. 96 units. $119–$130 double; $325–$425 Winterthur chambers and suite. Packages available. Rates include bagel breakfast in lobby. Children 18 and under stay free in parent's room. AE, DC, DISC, MC, V. Free parking. **Amenities:** Fitness center; hot tub; outdoor pool, complimentary shuttle to nearby offices. *In room:* A/C, TV/DVD, fridge, hair dryer, free Wi-Fi.

Doubletree Hotel Wilmington Popular with business travelers and weekend tourists, this seven-story hotel on the Route 202 corridor is about halfway between Wilmington and the Brandywine museums and gardens. Guest rooms feature white duvets, marble-top chests, and flatscreen TVs. Corner rooms have bigger bathrooms and a bit more space. "Green" features are designed to save energy. Joggers may use the track at Widener University next door. For shoppers, Concord Mall is on the other side of the hotel. Doubletree fans visiting Wilmington on business may prefer the **Doubletree Downtown,** 700 N. King St. (✆ **302/655-0400**). It has 218 rooms on nine floors, an indoor pool, restaurant, lounge, and free Wi-Fi. It's 9 blocks to the train station.

4727 Concord Pike (Rte. 202), Wilmington, DE 19803. www.doubletreehotels.com. ✆ **800/222-TREE** (8733) or 302/478-6000. Fax 302/477-1492. 244 units (48 with shower only). $109–$350 double. Weekend packages available. AE, DC, DISC, MC, V. Free parking. **Amenities:** Restaurant; lounge; fitness center; hot tub; indoor pool; courtesy shuttle service within 5-mile radius, including downtown Wilmington. *In room:* A/C, TV or TV/VCR, hair dryer, MP3 docking station, Wi-Fi (fee).

WHERE TO EAT

Downtown

EXPENSIVE

Deep Blue Bar and Grill ★ SEAFOOD How do you like your seafood: sashimi, raw bar, traditional, or Pacific Rim style? Deep Blue's got it all. Set in a parking garage, of all things, this restaurant draws a crowd of 30-somethings to its popular bar.

(In this sleek modern setting, nothing can muffle the noise—quieter tables are across the room from the bar.) The menu is filled with interesting options, from the grilled yellowfin tuna to the caramelized sea scallops. A well-stocked wine cellar is certain to have something wonderful to go with all this great seafood.

111 W. 11th St. ✆ **302/777-2040.** www.deepbluebarandgrill.com. Reservations recommended for dinner. Main courses $12–$21 lunch, $22–$28 dinner. AE, DC, DISC, MC, V. Mon–Fri 11:30am–2pm; Mon–Sat 5:30–10pm.

Green Room ★★ FRENCH When you want to treat yourself to a night on the town, make reservations at the Green Room. The surroundings—carved ceilings, paneled walls, soaring windows, and grand chandeliers—are luxurious. You'll be reminded of that when you see the menu, too. Prices soar as high as the ceilings, but the food is exquisite. Some may find the atmosphere a little stiff; others may call it refined. The meals are perfect, with rich sauces and artful desserts. Brunch is served on Sunday. Buffets at lunch and dinner may appeal to those who want to taste everything. Or try the chef's three- and six-course tasting menus. Got theater tickets? The prix-fixe theater menu at $48 will get you in your seats in plenty of time.

At the Hotel du Pont, 11th and Market sts. ✆ **302/594-3154.** www.hoteldupont.com. Reservations required. Jackets required for men Fri–Sat. Main courses $12–$24 lunch, $27–$45 dinner. AE, DC, MC, V. Mon–Sat 6:30–11am, 11:30am–2pm, and 6–9pm; Sun 7am–10:30am, 11:30am–1pm, and 5–9pm.

Harry's Seafood Grill SEAFOOD The soaring dark-blue dining room of this Riverfront restaurant is dominated by a sea of stars on the ceiling; the windows overlook the Christina River. The menu changes daily to reflect the fresh seafood available—everything from lobster in the rough to fish and chips, ceviche to raw oysters. Rather than focus on Chesapeake-style seafood, the chef has gone global, with recipes from the Far East, Portugal, and regional American cuisine. The impressive wine list is designed to help those looking for something to pair with the great seafood—tasting flights are available.

101 S. Market St. ✆ **302/777-1500.** www.harrysseafoodgrill.com. Reservations recommended, even for lunch. Main courses $11–$20 lunch, $12–$60 dinner. AE, DC, DISC, MC, V. Mon–Thurs 11am–10pm; Fri–Sat 11am–11pm; Sun noon–9pm.

Moro ★★★ ITALIAN Just around the corner from rowdy Kid Shelleen's, this is a grown-up's restaurant, with sophisticated tastes served in a sophisticated dining room of curved banquettes and earth tones. The menu focuses on seafood with some meat dishes and of course pasta, with tasting menus, small plates, and half-portions. Pasta is house-made and sides are as tempting as the protein beside them. The wine list is extensive.

1307 N. Scott St., Wilmington, DE 19806. ✆ **302/777-1800.** www.mororestaurant.net. Reservations recommended. Main courses $11–$28; $45–$65 4- to 6-course tasting menu. AE, DC, DISC, MC, V. Tues–Sat 5–11pm.

MODERATE

Chelsea Tavern GASTROPUB This upscale eatery across from the DuPont Theatre is a natural for theatergoers. The food and atmosphere make it a good stopping spot anytime. The menu—flexible for those heading across the street—has a variety of appetizers, including mussels four ways, sandwiches, pizzas, and entrees, many from locally grown ingredients. An interesting late-night menu is served after 10pm. Did you hear theater fans rejoicing?

833 Market St., Wilmington, DE 19801. ✆ **302/482-3333.** www.chelseatavern.com. Reservations recommended, especially on theater nights. Main courses $10–$23 dinner, $10–$18 lunch and late fare. AE, DC, DISC, MC, V. Mon–Wed 11:30am–10pm; Thurs–Fri 11:30am–1am; Sat 4pm–1am; Sun 10am–2pm.

Domaine Hudson ★★ WINE BAR Come for the wine, from a list 400 bottles long, and selections you won't find anywhere else in Delaware. But stay for the food: The chef has created dishes to pair with your wines, which come in tastes (1½ oz.) and 3- or 5-ounce servings. Cheese plates feature artisanal choices from around the world. The menu and wine list change seasonally. Half-portions give you the opportunity to pair a few outstanding dishes with different wines. The servers are helpful without being overbearing. This wine bar is cozy and a little noisy if there's a crowd, but it's always fresh and fun. The place has new owners, who didn't mess with a good thing, and who have kept the name and the menu.

1314 N. Washington St., Wilmington, DE 19801. ✆ **302/655-WINE** (9463). www.domainehudson.com. Reservations recommended. Small plates $8–$15; main courses $15–$27. AE, DISC, MC, V. Tues–Sun 4:30–10:30pm.

Eclipse Bistro ★ ITALIAN They had me at the pesto-flavored dipping oil. A simple little thing, it was indicative of the care the kitchen takes with its food. Warm brown tables and leafy green walls, Sinatra crooning in the background, it's a good place to sit and relax with friends, knowing you'll have a good time. And the food is delightful: sandwiches on hearty rolls, salads, and entrees that have flavors from around the globe, Cajun, Asian, and of course Italian. Pasta is made on-site—always a plus.

1020 N. Union St., Wilmington, DE 19805. ✆ **302/658-1588.** www.platinumdininggroup.com. Reservations recommended. Main courses $8–$18 lunch, $11–$26 dinner. AE, DISC, MC, V. Mon–Fri 11:30am–2pm and 5:30–10pm; Sat 5:30–10pm; Sun 5–9pm.

Kid Shelleen's AMERICAN In a residential area on the city's north side, just above Trolley Square, this indoor/outdoor restaurant is always hopping. Inside, you'll find a pub atmosphere: exposed brick, dark wood, open charcoal grill, and sports on TV. But the food is better and the offerings more extensive than your average pub fare. Grilled food is featured, from their burgers to grilled salmon, blackened fish tacos, and steaks. Sandwiches, salads, and pasta are available, too. A friendly open bar area in the middle of the restaurant is dominated by a large-screen TV. It's always loud and fun.

1801 W. 14th St. (at Scott St.). ✆ **302/658-4600.** www.kidshelleens.com. Reservations recommended. Main courses $10–$21. AE, DC, DISC, MC, V. Mon–Sat 11am–1am; Sun 10am–2pm and 3pm–1am. Live music Wed at 9pm and DJ on Thurs at 10pm.

Piccolina Toscana ITALIAN TAPAS Toscana Kitchen offers small plates of Italian delights. Regular entrees are available for the heartier appetites but the small plates—grilled octopus, meatballs, crab and corn fritters, for example—give adventurous diners more to taste. Pizzettes, pastas, and meat entrees are still available. Panini and small plates are on the lunch menu.

1412 N. DuPont St. ✆ **302/654-8001.** www.piccolinatoscana.com. Reservations advised. Main courses $6–$23 lunch; $6–$12 small plates; $13–$28 entrees. AE, DC, DISC, MC, V. Mon–Fri 11:30am–2pm; Mon–Wed 5–10pm; Thurs–Sat 5pm–midnight; Sun 11:30am–2pm and 5–9pm.

INEXPENSIVE

Govatos AMERICAN Established in 1894, this Wilmington tradition makes an ideal midcity choice for breakfast or lunch. The menu offers sandwiches, burgers, salads, and home-style favorites. The main attractions are the desserts, because this place produces Delaware's largest selection of homemade chocolates and candies.

800 Market St. ✆ **302/652-4082.** www.govatoschocolates.com. Breakfast items $4–$8; lunch items $6–$12. MC, V. Mon–Fri 8:30am–3pm.

Suburbs

EXPENSIVE

Celebrity Kitchens ★ CONTEMPORARY/REGIONAL This is dining as entertainment—and a Food TV fan's dream come true. Local celebrity chefs prepare the night's feast, demonstrating as they go, answering questions, and debating the merits of food fads or TV chefs. For 2½ hours, fresh ingredients get sliced, sautéed, beaten, and baked into a four-course meal served with wine. Fun for foodies! As for the meal, expect fine ingredients expertly prepared, with a mix of flavors to savor. The nightly menus are online; you'll see a featured ingredient, cuisine, or chef.

1601 Concord Pike, Independence Mall. ✆ **302/427-2665.** www.celebritykitchens.com. Reservations required. 4-course dinners $60–$75. AE, DISC, MC, V. Mon–Sat 6–8:30pm.

Krazy Kat's ★★★ NEW AMERICAN The candlelit dining room in the old blacksmith shop at the Inn at Montchanin Village has a funny name, and even funnier animal "portraits" adorning its walls. But the real reason to come is the serious food. The seasonal menu is filled with creative combinations: silky crab bisque with Meyer-lemon crème fraîche, or cocoa nib–crusted antelope. The wine list is extensive and the service is polished and relaxed. The dessert menu is as interesting as the dinner menu. Half-size plates are a nice option.

At Montchanin Village, Rte. 100 and Kirk Rd. ✆ **302/888-4200.** www.montchanin.com/dining.html. Reservations recommended. Jackets suggested for men at dinner. Main courses $8–$18 lunch, $16–$32 dinner. AE, DC, DISC, MC, V. Mon–Fri 7–10am, 11:30am–2pm, and 5:30–9:30pm; Sat–Sun 8–11am and 5:30–9:30pm; Sun brunch 11am–2pm.

ATTRACTIONS

Though many visitors to Wilmington head out to the Brandywine Valley attractions, the city itself has several museums and sites of interest.

Blue Ball Barn ☺ This restored 1914 barn houses the only state-run folk-art museum in the country. In two barn-size rooms, you'll find 120 works by 50 artists, including flowers made from horseshoes, quilts reflecting African-American history, salvage and "Outsider" art, as well as paintings and collages, decoys, and sculpture. Amish, Native American, and early European cultures are also represented. The park also has a "Can-Do" playground, designed to be usable by children of all abilities.

Alapocas Run State Park, 1914 W. Park Dr., off Rte. 202, Wilmington. ✆ **302/577-1164.** www.destateparks.com/blueball. Admission to park May–Oct $6 per vehicle ($3 discount for DE residents); Nov–Apr free. Daily 9am–4pm. Closed Thanksgiving and Dec 25.

Brandywine Zoo ☺ This is a 12-acre place with 150 animals, but the petting zoo, the Siberian tiger, and the cute binturongs make it a good diversion for children. Visit with the curious little monkeys, most of them tamarins, that are as interested in the humans as the humans are in them. Set in Brandywine Park, a 180-acre urban oasis just off Van Buren Street, it's a good way to get away from the noise and heat of the city, too.

1001 N. Park Dr. ✆ **302/571-7747.** www.brandywinezoo.org. Admission $5 adults, $4 seniors, $3 ages 3–11. Daily 10am–4pm. Free parking.

Delaware Art Museum ★★ The Delaware Art Museum, home of 12,000 works, marks its centenary in 2012. It's best known for its collection of pre-Raphaelite art. The entrance, overlooking the sculpture garden, is crowned with a Dale Chihuly glass sculpture. First-floor galleries are devoted to the pre-Raphael works, local artist Howard Pyle and his fellow illustrators of the Brandywine school, and John Sloan and Early American modernism. A second-floor bridge lets visitors get a closer look at the Chihuly as they head to galleries filled with contemporary art, including works by Jacob Lawrence, Edward Hopper, and Jamie Wyeth. There is a 9-acre sculpture garden with a path leading to a labyrinth, a children's area, a cafe, and museum store.

2301 Kentmere Pkwy., Wilmington, DE 19806. ✆ **302/571-9590.** www.delart.org. Admission Wed–Sat $12 adults, $10 seniors, $6 college students, $6 children 7–18; Sun free. Wed–Sat 10am–4pm; Sun noon–4pm.

Delaware Center for the Contemporary Arts In an impressive building on Wilmington's Riverfront, this seven-gallery space focuses on contemporary visual arts by local and national artists. As a noncollecting museum, exhibits are always changing, with about 30 each year. Also featured are the works of the 26 artists who have studios here. A gift shop features handcrafted items.

200 S. Madison St., Wilmington, DE 19801. ✆ **302/656-6466.** www.thedcca.org. Free admission. Tues and Thurs–Sat 10am–5pm; Wed and Sun noon–5pm.

Delaware Children's Museum ☺ You'd think exhibits focusing on the environment, transportation, and—well, banking would be dry and unappealing to kids. Wrong! With something new at every turn, places to climb, activities, and lots of bright colors, children are crawling all over this place. And don't tell them, but the exhibits focus on science, technology, engineering, and math and are designed for preschool through about age 10. Older siblings have been seen enjoying the place with their younger brothers and sisters. It takes a good 2 to 3 hours to see and do everything.

550 Justison St. ✆ **302/654-2340.** www.delawarechildrensmuseum.org. $12 everyone over 12 months. Daily 9am–4:30pm. Closed Thanksgiving, Dec 25.

Delaware History Museum ★ ☺ In bright displays with lots of artifacts at toddler level, the "Distinctly Delaware" exhibit tells about 200-plus years of Delaware history. DuPont is heavily featured, but visitors will also learn about agriculture, the state's role in the Underground Railroad, and the famous Delawareans portrayed in wax, including civil-rights attorney Louis Redding and Emily Bissell, who created Christmas Seals. Grandma's Attic is a delightful place for kids to play. Children's programs are offered, too.

504 Market St. (near south end of Market St. Mall). ✆ **302/655-7161.** www.hsd.org. Admission $6 adults, $5 students and seniors, $4 children 3–18. Free 1st Fri. Wed–Fri 11am–4pm; Sat 10am–4pm.

Kalmar Nyckel A grand ship brought the first 24 Swedish settlers to the Delaware Valley in 1638. Now, on the shores of the Christina River near Old Swedes Church and Fort Christina Park, the *Kalmar Nyckel* Foundation has re-created the three-masted ship with its fine carvings and richly appointed captain's cabin. When it's in port, visitors can tour the 139-foot-long electric-blue ship and take a look at its guns, 7,500 square feet of sail, and 10-story-high main mast. The best time to find the *Kalmar Nyckel* at home is September through April. It sails along Delaware's coast—with 1 month each summer in Lewes—May through October. Ninety-minute excursions are offered when it is docked at Riverfront Park downtown (even pirate sails!). Three-hour sails are offered from Lewes in summer. See website for schedule and fees. The Sail Loft Museum has displays about shipbuilding and sailing the *Kalmar Nyckel*. The education center was newly constructed in late 2011. Off season, visitors may see the crew repairing sails and lines for the next sailing season.

1124 E. 7th St. ✆ **302/429-7447.** www.kalmarnyckel.org. Free admission to the museum. Cruises $20–$60. Sat–Sun 10am–4pm. To get to shipyard, take 4th St. east to Church St. Turn left on Church St.; turn right on 7th St.

Marian Coffin Gardens This 6-acre preserved du Pont green spot is off busy Route 52 near downtown Wilmington. A project of Preservation Delaware, the gardens feature a formal garden, reflecting pool, wooded paths, and a teahouse with seating (but no tea). Walk up to the stone terrace for a bird's-eye view of the layout. Bridal photographers often use the garden as a backdrop. The 1840s Gibraltar mansion is closed as it undergoes restoration.

1405 Greenhill Ave. (off Rte. 52). ✆ **302/651-9617.** Free admission. Daily dawn–dusk. Limited parking available on-site. DART bus stops nearby.

Old Swedes Church ★ Formally known as Holy Trinity Episcopal Church, this stone-and-brick building overlooking the Christina River is the oldest church in continuous use in the U.S. It was built in 1699 as part of the Swedish Lutheran Church. Today, artifacts tell of the parish's vibrant history. Parishioners donated the black-walnut pulpit; the king of Sweden presented the altar candles in 1988; Tiffany created one of the luminous stained-glass windows; and the church chest dates from 1713. Hendrickson House, moved here and restored in 1958, contains artifacts of rural Delaware from 1690 to 1800. A labyrinth is located here, as well.

606 Church St. (at 7th St.). ✆ **302/652-5629.** www.oldswedes.org. Tour admission $4 adults, $2 ages 6–12. Guided tours Wed–Fri 1–4pm, Sat 11am–4pm. Take 4th St.; turn left on Church St.

Riverfront Wilmington ★★★ On a bend in the Christina River, Wilmington has built brick-and-board walkways with views urban and wild. Beginning at the train station and ending at the Russell W. Peterson Urban Wildlife Refuge, this 1⅓-mile path takes visitors past shops, museums, and a series of signs illustrating Wilmington's history. Watch a rowing team glide by, discover a Canada goose on the shore, or catch a ride on the River Taxi.

Start at the **Tubman–Garrett Riverfront Park,** at Water and South French streets. Twenty-one placards spaced along the walkway tell the history of the Christina River and the city, beginning with the development of industry, shipbuilding, and other transportation here. The Underground Railroad, which ran through Wilmington, is remembered as well, as are efforts to restore wetlands and excavate archaeological sites. Sometimes you can also see the ***Kalmar Nyckel***. **Dravo Plaza,** lined with huge cranes, recalls the city's shipbuilding history and its contributions to World War II.

Hungry yet? The number of restaurants just keeps going up. Among them are **Harry's Seafood Grill,** 101 S. Market St. (**✆ 302/777-1500**), p. 295, and **Iron Hill Brewery,** 710 Justison St. (**✆ 302/472-2739**). If you just want a snack, stop at the **Riverfront Market,** 3 S. Orange St. (**✆ 302/425-4454**), where you can also pick up meats, fish, and produce to take home. It's open Monday through Friday from 9am to 6pm, Saturday from 9am to 4pm.

The **Delaware Theatre Company** and **Delaware Center for the Contemporary Arts** are headquartered here. The Riverfront also hosts festivals and concerts at

Dravo Plaza and along the walkway. Sports fans can see the Blue Rocks play minor-league baseball at **Frawley Stadium,** a short walk off the Riverfront.

If you get tired of walking, the **River Taxi** (✆ **302/530-5069**) will take you to your next stop for $6. From April to November, the 40-passenger pontoon boat shuttles passengers along a 30-minute loop. Call in cooler weather if you don't see the taxi.

Visitors who make it to the end will reach the **Russell W. Peterson Urban Wildlife Refuge.** The 225 acres of marshland are home to many birds and other creatures. The **DuPont Environmental Education Center ★★** (www.delawarenaturesociety.org) brings natural delights into the city center with touch-screen exhibits, free weekend nature activities, a boardwalk across the freshwater tidal pond, and a colorful garden path. The center is open Tuesday through Saturday 10am to 5pm, and Sunday noon to 4pm. The park is open dawn to dusk every day. Admission is free.

From the Riverfront, you can walk to **Frawley Stadium,** home of the Wilmington Blue Rocks minor-league baseball team. See below.

Madison St. (on the west) and Water St. (on the north) are the closest to the park. ✆ **302/425-4890.** www.riverfrontwilm.com. Plentiful parking at free lots near the Shipyard Shops, 900 S. Madison St., the Chase Center on the Riverfront, 800 S. Madison St., and near the Riverfront Market, 1 S. Market St. Some paid parking available near the Amtrak station, 100 S. French St. (at Martin Luther King, Jr., Blvd.).

Rockwood Museum ★★ This rural Gothic mansion, furnished with 17th-, 18th-, and 19th-century decorative arts, is a treasure. Built in 1850 by Joseph Shipley and set on 72 acres, it was expanded by the home's only other occupants, the Bringhursts, who lived here from 1891 to 1965. Rockwood boasts a pink parlor with gilded fireplace and moldings, a conservatory, and spacious bedrooms, decorated as they might have been in the Bringhursts' time. A highlight is the changing displays of beaded, brocade, and velvet Victorian clothing. Decorative painting in many of the rooms adds a touch of whimsy, especially in the charming kitchen. Rockwood is the centerpiece of a New Castle County–owned park with hiking trails, many of them paved and lighted. Get a trail map at the museum or download one from the website. Lots of events are scheduled, from lectures to ghost tours; listings are online. Thousands of tiny lights illuminate trees around the house in December.

610 Shipley Rd. ✆ **302/761-4340.** www.rockwood.org. Free admission to park; tours $5 ages 13 and older, $2 ages 2–12. Gardens and park daily dawn–dusk; house tours on the hour Wed–Sun 10am–2pm. I-95 north, take exit 9 (Marsh Rd.); follow the signs.

SPECTATOR SPORTS & OUTDOOR ACTIVITIES

BASEBALL The **Wilmington Blue Rocks** (✆ **302/888-BLUE** [2583]; www.bluerocks.com), a Class A Kansas City farm team, play at the 5,900-seat Daniel S. Frawley Stadium, off I-95 near the Riverfront. Tickets cost about $10. Parking is free. Frawley Stadium is also home of the **Delaware Sports Museum and Hall of Fame** (✆ **302/425-3263;** www.desports.org), open April through October, Tuesday through Friday from noon to 5pm. Admission is $4 for adults, $3 for seniors, and $2 for youths 12 to 19.

GOLF The rolling hills around Wilmington make for challenging golf. The following courses welcome visitors.

The **Delcastle Golf Course & Restaurant,** 801 McKennan's Church Rd. (✆ **302/998-9505;** www.delcastlegc.com), near Delaware Park, offers a par-72 18-hole championship course, pro shop, and restaurant open from 7am to dark, a driving range, and miniature golf. Greens fees range from $20 to $50.

The **Ed Oliver Golf Club,** 800 N. DuPont Rd. (✆ **302/571-9041;** www.edolivergolfclub.com), off Route 52 (Pennsylvania Ave.), has a par-69 18-hole championship course, driving range, pro shop, and restaurant; it also offers lessons and group clinics. Greens fees range from $24 to $45.

Rock Manor Golf Course, 1319 Carruthers Lane (✆ **302/295-1400;** www.rockmanorgolf.com), a public course that's been around since 1921, and updated in 2009 has 18 holes and newly designed boxes, greens, bunkers, and fairways. It's adjacent to Alapocas Park on Route 202. Rates run $30 to $59.

The **Three Little Bakers Golf Course & Country Club,** 3540 Three Little Bakers Blvd. (✆ **302/737-1877**), in the Pike Creek Valley southwest of Wilmington, has a par-71 18-hole course open daily to the public, except after 3pm on Thursday and Friday. Facilities include a pro shop, club rental, golf lessons, and bag storage. Greens fees range from $29 to $59.

HORSE RACING & CASINO For half a century, racing fans have placed their bets at **Delaware Park,** 4½ miles south of Wilmington, off I-95 exit 4B, Stanton (✆ **800/417-5687** or 302/994-2521; www.delawarepark.com). Thoroughbred racing is offered April through October Saturday and Monday to Wednesday; post time is 1:15pm. Simulcast racing is offered year-round. Slot machines are available 24 hours a day and gaming tables are open Monday through Thursday from 10am to 4am and continuously from Friday at 10am to Monday at 4am. There are restaurants and weekend entertainment.

PUBLIC PARKS Wilmington's playground is **Bellevue State Park,** 800 Carr Rd. (✆ **302/761-6963;** www.destateparks.com), on the northeast perimeter of the city. This 328-acre park was once the estate of the William du Pont family. Facilities include picnic areas, paths for walking, fitness trails, clay tennis courts, and an equestrian facility, plus ice-skating in winter.

Southwest of Wilmington is **Lums Pond State Park,** 1068 Howell School Rd., off Route 71, Bear (✆ **302/368-6989;** www.destateparks.com). Stretching along the Chesapeake & Delaware Canal, this 1,790-acre park contains the state's largest freshwater pond and is home to beaver colonies and waterfowl. The pond offers sunbathing (no swimming), fishing, and boating. Bring your own boat or rent a rowboat, canoe, paddleboat, or sailboat during the summer and on weekends in May and September; rates range from $7 to $14 per hour. The surrounding parklands include hiking and walking trails; a nature center; picnic areas; football, soccer, and baseball fields; basketball and tennis courts; and campsites.

Entry fees to Delaware state parks are seasonal, with no admission charged from November through April. Otherwise, the fee is $6 per out-of-state vehicle and $3 per Delaware-registered car. Both parks are open from 8am to sunset year-round.

A Side Trip to Fort Delaware State Park ★

Fort Delaware State Park, on Pea Patch Island, in Delaware City (✆ **302/834-7941;** www.destateparks.com), is 16 miles south of Wilmington, in the Delaware River. Take Route 13 or I-95 south from Wilmington to Route 9 (turn left), which will take you to Delaware City. A 5-minute ferry ride will take you to the park, which surrounds a five-sided granite fortress where prisoners of war were held during the Civil

War. Serious business went on here, but it doesn't stop a costumed reenactor from using a little humor as he greets visitors just before they enter through the sally port and explains the fort's role in 1864. Presentations throughout the day include guided tours and musketry and blacksmithing demonstrations. Not to be missed are the armory, the re-created laundry, kitchen, and offices, and the view of the Delaware River from the battlements. Nature lovers should save time to walk the trails beyond the fort and visit the observation tower to see the nesting birds and other wildlife. The ferry departs from Battery Park in Delaware City about every hour. Once on the island, a trolley will take you from the dock to the fort.

The ferry fare, which includes admission to the park, is $11 for adults, $10 for those 62 and over, and $6 for children ages 2 to 12. The site is open May through Labor Day; call for exact hours, the ferry schedule, and the schedule of events. Reenactments and living-history demonstrations are held throughout the summer. The witty guided tours by Confederate and Union reenactors and the very loud musket, artillery, and cannon demonstrations are great for both children and adults. Ghost tours and paranormal investigations have added a spooky dimension after Labor Day. Tickets are about $40.

Visiting the Historic Houses of Odessa

Historic Odessa, home to some fine examples of 18th- and 19th-century architecture, is only 30 minutes south of Wilmington—a good option for a side trip when visiting Wilmington. For more information, see p. 322.

SHOPPING

Two of the Wilmington area's biggest shopping malls are **Concord Mall,** 4737 Concord Pike (✆ **302/478-9271**), and **Christiana Mall,** 435 Christiana Mall Rd., I-95 exit 4A (✆ **302/731-9815**).

The downtown area offers some shopping, mostly on Ninth Street and along Market Street. **Govatos,** 800 Market St. (✆ **302/652-5252;** www.govatoschocolates.com), has made its own chocolates and candies since 1894. The shop is open Monday through Friday from 8am to 5pm though in summer it closes daily at 3pm. Their second shop in the Talleyville Shopping Center, 4105 Concord Pike (✆ **302/478-5324**), opens on Saturdays June through September.

On the Riverfront, the **Riverfront Market,** 3 S. Orange St. (✆ **302/322-9500;** www.riverfrontwilm.com), is a great place to stop for a sandwich or soup. Fresh seafood, meat, and produce are also available. It's open Monday through Friday from 9am to 6pm, Saturday from 9am to 4pm. Some places open early for breakfast.

WILMINGTON AFTER DARK

Consult the *News Journal*'s entertainment guide, ***Spark.*** It's available free around town or online at **www.sparkweekly.com**. Or check out ***Out & About*** magazine online at www.outandaboutnow.com.

The Performing Arts

CLASSICAL MUSIC & OPERA

For such a small city, Wilmington has a lively performing-arts scene. In the center of it is the **Grand Opera House ★**, 818 N. Market St. (✆ **302/658-7897** for information, 800/374-7263 or 302/652-5577 for tickets; www.grandopera.org), in the heart of downtown. Built in 1871 as part of a Masonic temple, this restored Victorian showplace is one of the finest examples of cast-iron architecture in America. The auditorium seats 1,190 and is home to the Delaware Symphony Orchestra and Opera Delaware. It also offers ballet, jazz, chamber music, pop music, and theater.

The **Delaware Symphony Orchestra** (✆ **302/656-7442** for info, 800/374-7263 or 302/652-5577 for tickets; www.delawaresymphony.org) is led by David Amado. The DSO's 90-plus performances a year range from classical to pops. Performances are held in the Grand Opera House, with chamber-music concerts in the Hotel du Pont ballroom. Tickets run $27 to $57.

Opera Delaware (✆ **302/658-8063** for info, 800/374-7263 for box office; www.operade.org) offers three operas a year with supertitles; offerings range from grand, to operetta, to children's programs. Ticket range from $25 to $70.

THEATER & DANCE

The **DuPont Theatre,** at 10th and Market streets (✆ **800/338-0881** or 302/656-4401; www.duponttheatre.com), has brought touring shows to downtown Wilmington for more than 80 years. In the Hotel du Pont, it has a 1,239-seat capacity amid vintage Victorian decor. In addition, local companies often stage performances here—including the First State Ballet's *Nutcracker.*

City Theater Company Professional productions are staged in the black-box theater of Opera Delaware Studios. Often the humor is as black as the theater. You can count on something from a little Sondheim to world premieres by local writers. Buy tickets online or with cash only at the door. 4 S. Poplar St. ✆ **302/220-8285.** www.city-theater.org.

Delaware Theatre Company 🎁 At the foot of Orange Street on the Riverfront, this 389-seat facility has no seat more than 12 rows from the stage. The theater is home to Delaware's only resident professional company, which presents classic and contemporary plays. 200 Water St. ✆ **302/594-1100** for box office. www.delawaretheatre.org.

The New Candlelight Theatre A big red barn in the northern suburb of Ardentown has been home to this dinner theater for more than 25 years. Admission includes a buffet dinner. On Thursday, Friday, and Saturday, the show is at 8pm; the Sunday show is at 3pm; Wednesday's matinee begins at 1pm. The house opens 2 hours earlier for the buffet. 2208 Millers Rd. (signposted off Harvey Rd.), Ardentown. ✆ **302/475-2313.** www.newcandlelighttheatre.com. Tickets $56 adults, $33 children.

The Club & Music Scene

Dravo Plaza, on Wilmington's Riverfront, features live music—jazz, reggae, classical, and blues—Thursdays in summer. The nightlife elsewhere is pretty mellow, dominated by folk music, blues, and hotel piano bars.

Basil's The restaurant/lounge in the Sheraton Suites Hotel presents jazz Thursdays from 8 to 11pm. 422 Delaware Ave. ✆ **302/654-8300.** Cover $5 for nonhotel guests.

Catherine Rooney's Set in Trolley Square, just down the street from Kelly's Logan House, CR is three venues in one. The original space focuses on food (Jameson's wings and Guinness, natch). **Hummingbird to Mars** has a speakeasy vibe atop the original CR. Sports fans gather for the big game at **CR Hooligan's.** All three have contemporary bands or DJs on weekends with other fun on weekdays. 1616 Delaware Ave. ✆ **302/654-9700.** www.catherinerooneys.com. Cover varies.

Kelly's Logan House An open-mic on Wednesdays and acoustic bands on Saturdays add to the friendly atmosphere of this old tavern. Built in 1864, Kelly's has been drawing characters from Al Capone to Wild Bill Hickok since it opened. Good pub fare is a plus. 1701 Delaware Ave. ✆ **302/652-9493.** www.loganhouse.com. Cover varies.

Kid Shelleen's This Trolley Square tavern features acoustic music on Wednesdays and DJ dance parties on Thursdays. 1801 W. 14th St. ✆ **302/658-4600.** www.kidshelleens.com. Cover varies.

Public House If karaoke or open-mic is your thing, stop here on Tuesday evenings. Live entertainment is scheduled some weekends. 900 N. Market St. ✆ **302/661-7920.** www.publichousewilmington.com. Cover varies.

World Cafe Live at the Queen In the refurbished Queen Theatre, the World has music and other live shows on Friday and Saturday nights—and serves lunch and dinner every day. 500 N. Market St. ✆ **302/994-1400.** www.queen.worldcafelive.com. Cover varies.

Film

Theatre N at Nemours This 221-seat theater shows independent and foreign films, plus the occasional football game or broadcast of live opera, several times a month. The schedule is online. Tickets are available an hour before showtime, online or by calling ✆ **302/571-4699.** Nemours Bldg., 1007 Orange St. ✆ **302/658-6070.** www.theatren.org.

Especially for Kids

Delaware Children's Theatre, 1014 Delaware Ave. (✆ **302/655-1014;** www.dechildrenstheatre.org), presents plays based on fairy tales and other stories. Tickets are $12, with performances on select Saturdays and Sundays at 2pm. ***Note:*** Adult visitors will enjoy visiting this ornate building for its historic and architectural value. Listed on the National Register of Historic Places, it was designed in 1892 by a woman as a women's club—which continues to own and operate the building. Parking for performances is free.

THE BRANDYWINE VALLEY & HISTORIC NEW CASTLE

12

The Brandywine Valley combines natural beauty with the best in art and craftsmanship. Its hills, rivers, and forests are dotted with mansions, gardens, and museums. Here, between Wilmington and across the Pennsylvania line, you'll find the homes and gardens of the du Pont family—which give the Brandywine the nickname "Château Valley"—and the rolling hills and woodlands where three generations of the Wyeth family have lived and found inspiration for their art.

South of Wilmington, New Castle, Delaware's original capital, recalls the First State's early days. The town has preserved its 18th-century past with cobblestone streets, brick sidewalks, and 200-year-old homes.

THE BRANDYWINE VALLEY

10 miles N of Wilmington; 35 miles W of Philadelphia; 73 miles N of Baltimore

Meandering north from Wilmington, the Brandywine River has a storied history. The river and its valley provided for early settlers, powered the first du Pont industry, and inspired a school of art. To the Native Americans, the river was the Wawset or Suspecoughwit, cherished as a bountiful shad-fishing source. The Swedes and Danes called it the Fishkill. Quakers and other English settlers renamed it the Brandywine and made it an important mill center in the 18th and 19th centuries. At its peak, more than 100 water-powered mills produced everything from flour, paper, and textiles to snuff and black powder, on which the American du Ponts first made their fortune. In more recent times, the valley has been home to a school of artists and illustrators, beginning with Howard Pyle and Frank Schoonover and including the Wyeth family—N. C.; Andrew, who lived and painted here until his death in 2009; and Jamie.

The Brandywine Valley begins near Wilmington and stretches into Pennsylvania. Those who wish to see Winterthur and Longwood Gardens can do both in a day, since they're only a 20-minute drive apart. The Pennsylvania side is also explored in *Frommer's Philadelphia & the Amish*

Country. Two main arteries, Routes 52 and 100, comprise the Brandywine Valley Scenic Byway—see **www.byways.org** for a map that works well with this chapter.

Essentials

GETTING THERE The valley's Delaware attractions are north of Wilmington, mostly along Route 52. By car, take I-95 into Wilmington to Delaware Route 52 North. The main Pennsylvania attractions are along U.S. Route 1. From Wilmington, Routes 52 and 100 both lead to U.S. Route 1. Alternate routes from I-95 are U.S. Route 202, which goes all the way to U.S. Route 1, and Route 141 to Route 52.

Bus service from Wilmington is available through **DART** (✆ **800/355-6066;** www.dartfirststate.com). See p. 325 for information on rail and air transportation.

VISITOR INFORMATION Contact or stop by the **Greater Wilmington Convention and Visitors Bureau,** 100 W. 10th St., Ste. 20, Wilmington (✆ **800/652-4088;** www.visitwilmingtonde.com), open Monday through Friday from 9am to 5pm; or stop by the branch at the **I-95 Delaware Travel Plaza,** between exits 1 and 3 near Newark, Delaware, open daily from 8am to 8pm. The **Chester County Visitor Center** is on U.S. Route 1 at the entrance to Longwood Gardens, Kennett Square, Pennsylvania (✆ **800/228-9933** or 610/388-2900; www.brandywinevalley.com), open Monday to Saturday from 11am to 5pm and Sunday noon to 5pm.

AREA CODE Brandywine Valley attractions in the Wilmington suburbs use the 302 area code. For Pennsylvania sights, inns, and restaurants dial 610.

SPECIAL EVENTS **Longwood Gardens** (✆ **610/388-1000**) has seasonal displays, including the **Christmas Display ★★★**, featuring hundreds of poinsettias and a lighted outdoor display. **Yuletide at Winterthur** (✆ **800/448-3883**) is always a sensation, with rooms decorated according to customs from throughout history. The **Battle of Brandywine Reenactment** (✆ **610/459-3342**), held in September, recalls local American Revolution history. In May, the **Winterthur Point to Point Races** (✆ **800/448-3883**) is a good place to see horses and to *be* seen.

Where to Stay

Wilmington area hotels are convenient bases from which to tour the Brandywine Valley, so check p. 292 for more places to stay. For a full DuPont experience, you may want to consider the Inn at Montchanin Village, originally part of the DuPont powder mills; see p. 293. Below are several inns and hotels in nearby Pennsylvania. Ask about packages that include entrance to area attractions when you make reservations.

Brandywine River Hotel ★ This hotel, on a hillside in the heart of the valley, is one of the area's best values—lots of amenities, good location, and well-decorated rooms for the price of an average chain hotel. With a facade of brick and cedar shingle, it is set among shops, restaurants, and galleries. Decorated with traditional furnishings, accommodations include standard doubles and executive units with sofa beds. The best rooms are the premium suites with fireplaces; both roomy and cozy.

Routes 1 and 100 (P.O. Box 1058), Chadds Ford, PA 19317. www.brandywineriverhotel.com. ✆ **800/274-9644** or 610/388-1200. 40 units. $129–$199 double; $159–$199 suite. Rates include continental breakfast and afternoon tea. AE, DC, DISC, MC, V. Free parking. Pets under 20 lb. accepted for $20 per day; must be crated when unattended. **Amenities:** Lobby bar; fitness center; room service. *In room:* A/C, flatscreen TV, hair dryer, free Wi-Fi.

Fairville Inn Bed & Breakfast This gracious 1857 inn, listed on the National Register of Historic Places, is set on 5 leafy acres near Winterthur. Its Colonial-style

The Brandywine Valley

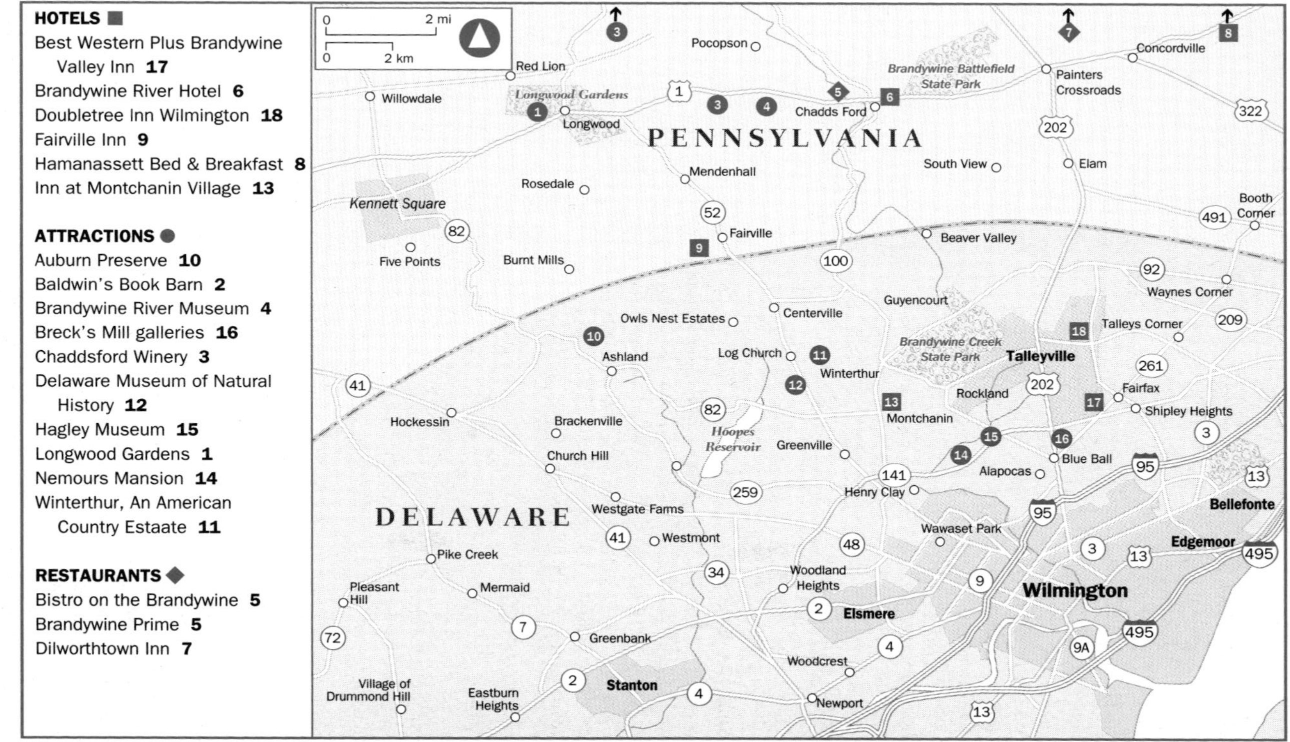

decor is warm and welcoming. The main house has five bedrooms; if you'd like more space, privacy, a private porch (or even a fireplace), ask for a room in the Springhouse or the Carriage House. Eight rooms have fireplaces.

506 Kennett Pike (Rte. 52), Chadds Ford, PA 19317. www.fairvilleinn.com. ✆ **877/285-7772** or 610/388-5900. 15 units. $170–$290 double. Rates include full breakfast and afternoon tea. 2-night minimum Apr–Dec weekends. AE, DISC, MC, V. Free parking. *In room:* A/C, TV, hair dryer, free Wi-Fi.

Hamanassett Bed & Breakfast ★★ This romantic 1856 country house with Palladian windows and a wide porch has long been a B&B. Owners Ashley and Glenn Mon have worked to make it luxurious. Brandywine attractions are only about 20 minutes away. Trees and flowers line the walking trails; nearby horses beg for a treat; a waterfall spills into the koi pond. The inn offers a casual solarium, a library, and bedrooms decorated with antiques and luxurious beds. Two cottages are available for families or pet owners. Cooking school packages are also available.

725 Darlington Rd., Media, PA 19063. www.hamanassett.com. ✆ **877/836-8212** for reservations, or 610/459-3000. 9 units. $180–$240 double; $245–$275 suite; $325–$475 cottage. Rates include full breakfast. AE, DISC, MC, V. Free parking. Pets accepted for a fee. Children 12 and under accepted in cottages. **Amenities:** Billiards; movie library. *In room:* A/C, TV/DVD, MP3 docking station, free Wi-Fi.

Where to Eat

Bistro on the Brandywine ★★ FRENCH/AMERICAN This casual bistro has diners waiting in line on weekends. Try the French onion soup, the inventive salads, the panini, and main courses such as cassoulet. Locally grown mushrooms are often featured in the dishes. Sharing plates for both lunch and dinner are a great way to try something new. Leave room for homemade ice cream, crème brûlée, or crepes.

1623 Baltimore Pike (Rtes. 1 and 100), Chadds Ford, PA 19317. ✆ **610/388-8090.** www.bistroonthebrandywine.com. Reservations recommended. Main courses $10–$16 lunch, $12–$21 dinner. AE, MC, V. Mon–Sat 11:30am–9pm; Sun 4–8pm.

Brandywine Prime Seafood & Chops at Chadds Ford Inn AMERICAN Old farmhouse meets contemporary style and cuisine at this stylish chophouse. The focus here is dry-aged beef, seafood, and a raw bar. The wine list includes local vintages, but if you have a favorite, feel free to bring it along. Sunday brunch is offered, and the bar has its own selection of burgers and small plates to go with a cocktail.

Corner of Rtes. 1 and Old 100, Chadds Ford, PA 19317. ✆ **610/388-8088.** www.brandywineprime.com. Reservations recommended. Main courses $20–$39. AE, MC, V. Mon–Thurs 5am–10pm; Fri–Sat 5–11pm; Sun 10am–2pm and 4–9pm.

Dilworthtown Inn ★ CONTINENTAL Along the road that was once the principal connection between Wilmington and West Chester, this establishment was built in 1758. The 15 dining rooms include the original kitchen and an outside stable area for warm-weather dining. Colonial furniture, wood beams, 11 fireplaces, gas lamps and candlelight, and Andrew Wyeth paintings set the mood. The menu includes an array of fine-dining options. Start with Dilworthtown mushroom soup or escargot; move on to rack of lamb or sea scallops. Pair with an offering from the 800-bottle wine cellar.

1390 Old Wilmington Pike and Brinton Bridge Rd. (off Rte. 202), West Chester, PA. ✆ **610/399-1390.** www.dilworthtown.com. Reservations required; jackets for men recommended. Main courses $25–$34. AE, DC, DISC, MC, V. Mon–Fri 5:30–9:30pm; Sat 5–9:30pm; Sun 3–8:30pm. Closed Wed before Labor Day to the following Tues.

The Du Pont Homes & Gardens

Each of the famous mansions reflects the personality of its owners and their lifestyles. For sheer splendor, visit the **Nemours Mansion.** If your tastes are more of a "garden" variety, **Longwood Gardens** has the most varied grounds. Even if you skip the house itself, don't miss the conservatories. If you have time for only one garden in the Brandywine Valley, go to Longwood. The famous **Winterthur** is more museum than home. The room with the Chinese wallpaper has earned its world-class reputation; this house tells more about the decorative arts than about the personality who gathered them here. (Marylanders should check out the Chestertown room and the Baltimore alcove.) Leave time for the gardens, especially the Enchanted Woods. The **Hagley Museum** is worth visiting to see how regular Americans lived and worked when the country was new. Its grounds offer a spectacular display of foliage in autumn.

Hagley Museum and Library ★★★ ☺ French émigré Eleuthère Irénée du Pont de Nemours built the first of his gunpowder mills here in 1802, and the first du Pont home in 1803. The mills grew in number and size, later to include workers' homes and a school. A visit to the 235-acre site can take a couple of hours or an entire day. Just the walk along the river, past the ruins of the old roll mills, will keep kids busy. The **visitor center** features an exhibit demonstrating how mills work, as well as the DuPont Science and Discovery display (including a NASCAR car and a spacesuit). Kids will love the adjacent **Hydroelectric Plant,** where they can learn about simple machinery at the "Easy Does It!" exhibit. Walk along the river and millrace to see the roll mills, the narrow-gauge railroad, and the dangerous steps it took to make gunpowder in the 1800s. Visit what remains of one of the workers' communities, the Gibbons House, the Sunday school, and the **Belin House Organic Cafe** (Mar–Dec daily 11:30am–4pm; closed Jan–Feb). The **Millwright Shop** dioramas and live demonstration explain how gunpowder was made. The exhibit on a 1920 explosion, along the path of the powder yards, serves as a bit of archaeological dig while highlighting the importance of safety.

Visitors to the family house, **Eleutherian Mills,** can catch a bus that offers a narrated tour through the powder yards to the Georgian-style residence where five generations of du Ponts lived. Rooms reflect the periods of the house's history from the 1800s to the 1920s. The French gardens, barn, and First Office are also worth a look. Hagley's Family Fun Events include dollar days, the Invention Convention in January, and bike and hike days; check the website for details.

Rte. 141, Wilmington, DE 19807. ✆ **302/658-2400.** www.hagley.org. Admission $11 adults, $9 students and seniors, $4 children 6–14. Visitor center daily 9:30am–4:30pm. Tours Mar 15–Dec daily 9:30am–4:30pm; Jan–Mar 14 Mon–Fri at 10:30am and 1:30pm and Sat–Sun 9:30am–4:30pm. Closed Thanksgiving, Dec 25. From Wilmington, take I-95 to Rte. 52 N. Turn right on Rte. 141; museum entrance is on the left.

Longwood Gardens ★★★ ☺ One of the world's most celebrated horticultural displays, Longwood Gardens showcases more than 11,000 different types of plants and flowers amid 1,050 acres of outdoor gardens and woodlands. The ever-blooming displays throughout the grounds and conservatory are both creative and delightful, thanks to Pierre S. du Pont, who purchased the existing farm and arboretum in 1906, and from 1907 to 1954 designed most of what is enjoyed today. Everybody has a favorite spot: the tropical paradise of the **Conservatory;** the eye-popping seasonal displays; the flower-garden walk that explodes in seasonal color; the **Chimes Tower** (with carillon); the **Idea Garden** to inspire home gardeners; the **Flower Garden Fountains;** the **Italian Water Garden;** or the **Main Fountain Garden,** whose 380 fountains and spouts rise over 130 feet high during one of the 5-minute displays throughout the day. There are also illuminated displays in the fountain garden on Tuesday, Thursday, and Saturday evenings June through September, plus fireworks displays on several evenings in summer (check the website for a schedule). The **East Conservatory** is filled with water features among the plantings (serious gardeners will enjoy the audio-wand tours). Behind the ballroom is an organ museum with interactive displays for children. The **Indoor Children's Garden** delights children and adults alike with its whimsical fountains and garden paths. Three fanciful **tree-houses** scattered among the gardens outside offer a bird's-eye view of the gardens.

Longwood's attractions also include seasonal plant displays (Christmas and Easter gardens are noteworthy) and hundreds of performances—even ice-skating in December; check the website for a schedule. Facilities include the **Peirce–du Pont House;** a large museum shop; and the **Terrace Restaurant,** which has both a cafe and full-service dining room. Reservations are recommended for the dining room. Electric scooters, wheelchairs, and strollers are available for rental.

Rte. 1 (just north of Rte. 52), Kennett Square, PA 19348. ✆ **610/388-1000.** www.longwoodgardens.org. Admission $18 adults, $15 seniors, $8 ages 5–18. AE, DC, DISC, MC, V. Mid-Jan to Mar daily 9am–5pm; Apr–May daily 9am–6pm; Memorial Day to Labor Day Mon–Wed and Sun 9am–6pm, Thurs–Sat 9am–10pm; Sept–Nov daily 9am–5pm; Thanksgiving to early Jan daily 9am–9pm.

Nemours Mansion & Gardens ★★★ It took 4 years and $39 million—and finally the restoration of this 1909 47,000-square-foot château was completed in 2009. The home of Alfred I. du Pont and his family, named after the du Pont ancestral home in France, the 102-room Louis XVI–style château is a model of extravagance. It boasts acres of marble, chandeliers, paintings from 4 centuries, a clock that once belonged to Marie Antoinette, and gates from palaces of Henry VIII and Catherine the Great. Just as dazzling as the house are the 100 acres of European-style gardens: a maze, sunken gardens, a reflecting pool, a colonnade, and wonderful sculptures. Tour reservations are a must. Tours begin at the visitor center; arrive 15 minutes before tour time.

850 Alapocas Rd., Wilmington, DE 19803. ✆ **800/651-6912** or 302/651-6912. www.nemoursmansion.org. Admission ages over 12 $15. Tours Tues–Sat 9am, noon, 3pm; Sun noon, 3pm. Closed Jan 1–Apr 30.

Winterthur Museum, An American Country Estate ★★★ ☺ Named after a town in Switzerland and pronounced "win-ter-tour," this eight-story mansion and country estate features one of the world's premier collections of American antiques and decorative arts. The estate was the country home of Henry Francis du Pont, a collector of furniture, who in 1951 turned it into a museum for American decorative arts. The 85,000 objects made or used in America, including Chippendale furniture, silver tankards by Paul Revere, and a dinner service made for George Washington, are displayed in the 175 period rooms. The galleries include exhibits of furniture styles, life at Winterthur, Early American craftsmen, and the Campbell Soup tureen collection. It takes more than one visit to see it all. General admission tickets include a 1-hour introductory tour. You can add a 1-hour or 2-hour tour for an in-depth exploration. Gardeners should take a 20-minute garden tram tour. Parents may want to take this from the visitor center to the Enchanted Woods children's gardens. Reservations are required for the in-depth tours. The **Yuletide Tour** is included in the general admission price and is offered from mid-November to December 31.

Children 8 and under are permitted on some tours, including the Yuletide Tour. Kids (and adults, too) will love the **Enchanted Woods,** a 3-acre fairy-tale garden filled with places to play, including a Faerie Cottage and Troll Bridge. Other facilities include two restaurants, an expansive museum store, and a bookshop.

5105 Kennett Pike (Rte. 52), Winterthur, DE 19735. ✆ **800/448-3883** or 302/888-4600. www.winterthur.org. General admission $18 adults, $16 students and seniors, $5 children 2–5. 1-hour reserved tour added to general admission $30 adults, $28 seniors and students, $17 ages 8–11. 2-hour reserved tour $40 adults, $38 seniors and students, $27 ages 8–11. AE, DISC, MC, V. Tues–Sun 10am–5pm (last tour at 3:30pm). Open Mon during Yuletide. Closed Thanksgiving and Dec 25. Call for other winter closings. Located on Rte. 52, 6 miles northwest of Wilmington and 5 miles south of Rte. 1.

Other Attractions

Auburn Heights Preserve ☺ Fans of trains and antique cars have visited this collection of Stanley Steamer cars and a miniature train for special events for years. A state park historic site since 2008, it opens to tourists eight Sundays a year and the Friday and Saturday after Thanksgiving. Visitors can look over the pristine Stanley Steamer automobiles lovingly collected by the Marshall family, ride the one-eighth-scale steam engine train around the property, enjoy performances, bring a picnic, and tour the 1897 granite Victorian home. The 200 wooded acres are lovely and peaceful.

3000 Creek Rd., Yorklyn, DE 19736. ✆ **800/349-2134.** www.auburnheights.org or www.destateparks.com/attractions. Admission $12 adults, $7 ages 2–12; house tour $12 additional. See website for opening times. Also by appointment. From Rte. 52 North, take Campbell Rd. to New London Rd. to Pyles Ford Rd. to Creek Rd.

Baldwin's Book Barn 🎁 With five floors of 300,000 rare and used books, maps, and prints in an 1822 stone barn, it's easy to while away hours getting lost among the stacks or perusing a book in the cozy reading room. There's no admission, but just try to get out of here without spending any money.

865 Lenape Rd. (Rtes. 100 and 52), West Chester, PA. ✆ **610/696-0816.** www.bookbarn.com. Daily 10am–6pm. Closed Jan 1, Thanksgiving, Dec 25. From Rte. 1, take Rte. 52 north. The barn is 6 miles past Rte. 1 on the left.

Brandywine Battlefield Historic Site On these rolling hills, George Washington's troops fought with the British for control of strategic territory near Philadelphia. On September 11, 1777, the Marquis de Lafayette saw his first military action here, and while the Colonial troops were defeated and had to withdraw to Philadelphia, he witnessed the courage and determination of the Americans, and convinced the French to form an alliance with the colonists. House tours of two Quaker farmhouses, which served as Washington's headquarters and Lafayette's quarters, are offered on the hour March to November. On-site are picnic areas and a visitor center with exhibits and a museum shop. Check the website for three driving tours. Call ahead to visit in spring.

1491 Baltimore Pike (Rte. 1), Chadds Ford, PA 91317. ✆ **610/459-3342.** www.ushistory.org/BRANDYWINE/. Admission $6 adults, $3 children 6–17, free 5 and under. Wed–Sat 9am–4pm; Sun noon–4pm. Mar–Dec.

Brandywine River Museum ★★★ This Civil War–era gristmill in a wooded setting—near the home and studio of three generations of Wyeth artists—has been converted into a museum that embraces the art of the Brandywine School and the setting that inspired it. Huge windows overlook the valley and river below. Inside are the paintings of Howard Pyle and artists he taught, including N. C. Wyeth, Frank Schoonover, and Maxfield Parrish. Works by N. C.'s children Andrew, Henriette, and Caroline hang here, as well as paintings by Jamie Wyeth, Andrew's son. Andrew has a gallery all his own, with his comments accompanying most pieces. Tours of N. C. Wyeth's house and studio are Tuesday through Sunday from April to November. The studio is worth seeing: Wyeth's paint-splattered smock hangs near his palette and the painting he was working on at the time of his death. The Kuerner Farm, inspiration for many of Andrew Wyeth's works, is open for tours Thursday through Sunday from April through November. The museum shop and restaurant have great views, too.

Rte. 1 and Pa. Rte. 100, Chadds Ford, PA 91317. ✆ **610/388-2700.** www.brandywinemuseum.org. Admission $10 adults, $6 seniors and students; studio or farm tour $5; audio tour $3. Daily 9:30am–4:30pm. Closed Dec 25. Just south of Rte. 100 on the Brandywine River.

Breck's Mill Galleries Two fascinating galleries are in this 1814 stone mill building downstream from the Hagley Museum. The **Somerville Manning Gallery** is devoted to 20th- and 21st-century art, including works by the Wyeth family and other artists trained in the Brandywine School tradition. The **André Harvey Studio** displays more than 40 of Harvey's realistic bronze sculptures of people and animals and sculptural gold jewelry. Call ahead for individual attention and to double-check hours.

Andre Harvey Studio: 101 Stone Block Row, Greenville, DE 19732. ✆ **302/656-7955.** www.andreharvey.com. Free admission. Mon–Sat 10am–4:30pm and by appointment. **Somerville-Manning Gallery:** 101 Stone Block Row, Greenville, DE 19732. ✆ **302/652-0271.** www.somervillemanning.com. Free admission. Tues–Sat 10am–5pm (vary in summer).

Chaddsford Winery You can sample the wine made in Pennsylvania's largest winery in a restored barn. Take a self-guided tour any day or half-hour guided tour Saturday at 2 or 4pm. For $8, buy a glass and try a variety of regional wines. Check the website for classes and festivals. This is also a good place to start on the Brandywine Valley Wine Trail, a collection of area wineries and vineyards. Get a map at Chaddsford or go to **www.bvwinetrail.com**. (Bring your GPS; the map's just a guide.)

632 Baltimore Pike (U.S. 1), Chadds Ford, PA 19317. ✆ **610/388-6221.** www.chaddsford.com. Free admission; full tasting session $8. Tours daily noon–6pm. Located 5 miles south of Rte. 202, just past the Brandywine River Museum. Closed Jan 1, Easter, Thanksgiving, and Dec 25.

Delaware Museum of Natural History ☺ Visitors are greeted by a giant squid "swimming" overhead in the glass entrance—perfect for a museum known for its mollusk and bird collections. (Did you know a squid is a mollusk?) Following a loop, visitors can look up at an allosaurus, one of Delaware's only dinosaurs, or tiptoe over the Great Barrier Reef exhibit located under the Plexiglas floor. The shell, gemstone, and mineral cases glitter with color and light. In warm weather, take a break on the patio by the butterfly garden. The museum is bound to intrigue the kids.

4840 Kennett Pike (Rte. 52), Wilmington, DE 19807. ✆ **302/658-9111.** www.delmnh.org. Admission $7 adults, $5 seniors, $6 children 3–17. Mon–Sat 9:30am–4:30pm; Sun noon–4:30pm. Located 5 miles northwest of Wilmington on Rte. 52. Closed Jan 1, Easter, July 4, Thanksgiving, and Dec 25.

HISTORIC NEW CASTLE

7 miles S of Wilmington; 40 miles SW of Philadelphia; 70 miles NE of Baltimore

New Castle, Delaware's original capital, was a major Colonial seaport. Peter Stuyvesant, who established a Dutch settlement named Fort Casimir, purchased the area from Native Americans in 1651. (It's said Stuyvesant designed the town's green by "pegging it off" with his wooden leg.) Later captured by the Swedes, reclaimed by the Dutch, who renamed it New Amstel, and then the English, who renamed it New Castle, this stretch of land along the west bank of the Delaware River remains much the way it was in the 17th and 18th centuries. Original houses and public buildings have been restored and preserved, along with brick sidewalks and cobblestone streets.

WILMINGTON & THE brandywine VALLEY FOR KIDS

Wilmington and its suburbs are home to palatial residences, elegant hotels, and immense gardens, not places you'd think of as kid-friendly. Several sites do welcome kids. The following are described in detail in this chapter and chapter 11, "Wilmington."

Brandywine Zoo (p. 297) A tiny zoo in the Brandywine Park has just 150 animals, but pint-size goats willing to be petted and little monkeys make this a child's delight.

Delaware Children's Museum (p. 298) Kids can set up a campsite, ring the train bell, or build a tower...while they're learning about ecology, physics, and biology.

Delaware History Museum (p. 298) This museum of First State history, housed in an old Woolworth's store in Wilmington, is bright and colorful, and has fun exhibits. Its hands-on Discovery Room lets kids touch artifacts and hear stories.

Delaware Museum of Natural History (p. 312) Children can enjoy the dinosaur fossils, lots of shells, special exhibits, and their own Discovery Room.

Fort Delaware State Park (p. 301) Kids will love this Civil War fort. Not only is there a boat ride to the island and a trolley ride to the fort, but reenactors lead guided tours laced with humor and give LOUD artillery demonstrations in summer.

Hagley Museum (p. 309) The family-friendly museum, set on the shady banks of the Brandywine River, tells the story of the du Pont family's early gunpowder mill. Kids love the gunpowder testing demonstration.

Longwood Gardens (p. 309) This is a sprawling landscape with fountains, animal-shaped hedges, and conservatories. Little ones shouldn't miss the children's indoor garden or whimsical treehouses.

Winterthur's Enchanted Woods (p. 310) These 3 acres will delight the young ones with a labyrinth, fountains, and a kid-size cottage.

Park your car (no meters here) and stroll past old homes and churches that line six streets near the water. Stop into the tiny shops and restaurants, mostly along Delaware Street. Everything is close by—even Battery Park by the river. Cool breezes, green places, and playground equipment make the park a nice break for children and adults.

Essentials

GETTING THERE From Wilmington, either take U.S. Route 13 south to Delaware Route 273 east to New Castle, or follow Delaware Route 9 south directly to New Castle. From the south, take Route 301 to Route 13 North. (It's a good day trip from Baltimore or Annapolis, too.)

VISITOR INFORMATION For information, contact the **New Castle Historical Society** (© **302/322-2794;** www.newcastlehistory.org) or stop by the Court House for a map and brochure outlining a walking tour of the town.

SPECIAL EVENTS **A Day in Old New Castle** (© **877/496-9498;** www.dayinoldnewcastle.org), the third Saturday in May, gives visitors a chance to tour the town's private homes and gardens, as well as public buildings, gardens, and museums. The **Historic New Castle Antiques Show** is held in Battery Park the last Sunday in August. **A New Castle Spirit of Christmas** features house tours, carolers, and carriage rides in mid-December; contact the **New Castle Historical Society** (© **302/322-2794;** www.newcastlehistory.org) for details.

Where to Stay

I suggest you base yourself in Wilmington, 7 miles away, since New Castle has few accommodations, though there is a recommendable B&B (listed below).

The Terry House Bed and Breakfast This 1860 brick town house's six guest rooms have queen-size or double beds and en suite bathrooms. Porches along the back of the house overlook Battery Park and the Delaware River. Rooms are spacious with antiques and chandeliers, though bathrooms are merely serviceable. Suite no. 7, on the third floor, has enough room for a family of four, and a spacious attic room looks over the trees to the park and river below. Lined with books, it's a bit like living in a library. The house is filled with collections from china to kitchen tools, and the walls are covered with portraits, photos, and prints. Once you meet the scholarly, charming innkeeper, you might feel you've arrived for a visit at your grandmother's house.

130 Delaware St., New Castle, DE 19720. www.terryhouse.com. ✆ **302/322-2505.** 4 units. $90–$110 double. Rates include full or continental breakfast. No credit cards. On-street parking. **Amenities:** Porch and garden w/access to Battery Park. *In room:* A/C, TV, free Wi-Fi.

Where to Eat

Jessop's Tavern COLONIAL Don't miss this tiny tavern in a 1724 building. The atmosphere and menu's Dutch, Swedish, and old English flavors are designed to reflect the area's history, with Colonial potpie (a delight), pot roast, fresh seafood, and English pub fare. At lunchtime, the salads, soups, and sandwiches on hearth-baked breads will keep you happy. Sweet-potato fries are a specialty. It's a casual place, a reminder of the town's seafaring days. Just need a quick bite? Stop next door at the **Dutch West Indies Company** (✆ **302/322-6111**) for a snack or ice cream.

114 Delaware St., New Castle, DE 19720. ✆ **302/322-6111.** www.jessops-tavern.com. Reservations not accepted, except for large parties. Main courses $7–$15 lunch, $10–$24 dinner. AE, DC, DISC, MC, V. Mon–Thurs 11:30am–10pm; Fri–Sat 11:30am–11pm; Sun 11:30am–8pm.

Trader's Cove CAFE Behind the showroom of Penn's Place is this delightful coffee shop. You can get your coffee, open up your laptop, get a Dana's dessert or a sandwich, or order up a glass of wine. A frothy latte is their signature beverage. Breakfast and lunch are served all day. There's a dining room and outside patio.

206 Delaware St., New Castle, DE 19720. ✆ **302/322-6334.** www.pennsplace.net. No reservations. Main courses $2–$13. AE, DISC, MC, V. Tues–Thurs 8am–7pm; Fri–Sat 8am–8pm; Sun 10am–6pm.

What to See & Do

Many historic buildings in New Castle are privately owned and not open to the public. Stop by the Court House to pick up a map and guide to the town's historic buildings, which points out the ones you can visit. ***Note:*** Almost everything (except a few restaurants and shops) is closed on Mondays and weekdays in winter.

A notable building is the 1820 **Immanuel Episcopal Church on the Green,** at Second and Harmony streets, which was the first parish of the Church of England in Delaware. Extensively damaged by fire in 1980, it has been carefully restored. The adjoining cemetery is the resting place of many prominent Delawareans, including George Read I, signer of the Declaration of Independence. Another is the **New Castle–Frenchtown Railroad Ticket Office,** a tiny white building and a stretch of track in Battery Park that recalls the 1820s horse-drawn railway.

The historic district has only a few shops. The most interesting is **Penn's Place,** 206 Delaware Ave. (✆ **302/322-6334;** www.pennsplace.net), a "menagerie" of artisans, set in the 1682 town house where William Penn is said to have slept his first night in America. You can see the room and shop for handcrafted items. For country items, stop by **Almost History,** 302 Delaware St. (✆ **302/322-6434**). Crafters will find **Two Morrow's Stitches That Count,** 306 Delaware St. (✆ **302/328-7888**), useful.

Amstel House ★★ This house is a fine example of Georgian architecture. It was likely the most elegant home in town when constructed in the 1730s. Today, it's furnished with antiques and decorative arts of the period. Look for the inscription in the hearth, commemorating when George Washington was a wedding guest here.

2 E. 4th St., New Castle, DE 19720. ✆ **302/322-2794.** www.newcastlehistory.org. Admission $5 adults, $2 children; combination ticket with the Dutch House $9 adults, $3 children. Apr–Dec Wed–Sat 11am–4pm; Sun 1–4pm. Closed holidays.

Dutch House One of the oldest brick houses in Delaware, this building has remained almost unchanged since its construction around 1700. Dutch antiques, from ice skates and wooden shoes to an enormous *kas* (wardrobe) and dining set are displayed. On nice days, take a walk in the kitchen garden outside.

32 E. 3rd St., on the green, New Castle, DE 19720. ✆ **302/322-2794.** www.newcastlehistory.org. Admission $5 adults, $2 children; combination ticket with the Amstel House $9 adults, $3 children. Apr–Dec Tues–Sat 11am–4pm; Sun 1–4pm.

Old Library Museum This fanciful hexagonal building, erected in 1892 by the New Castle Library Society, holds exhibits by the New Castle Historical Society. Its Victorian styling is attributed to the architectural firm of Frank Furness of Philadelphia.

40 E. 3rd St., New Castle, DE 19720. ✆ **302/322-2794.** www.newcastlehistory.org. Free admission. May–Dec Sat–Sun 1–4pm. Closed Jan to mid-May.

Old New Castle Court House ★ This building was Delaware's Colonial capital and the meeting place of the state assembly until 1777. Built in 1732 on the fire-charred remains of an earlier courthouse, it's been restored and modified over the years, though always maintaining its role as the focal point of town. You'll find portraits of men important to Delaware's early history, the original speaker's chair, and excavated artifacts. An exhibit on the Underground Railroad tells the thrilling story of a runaway slave and her family who were jailed here. Free guided tours are available.

211 Delaware St., on the green, New Castle, DE 19720. ✆ **302/323-4453.** www.history.delaware.gov. Free admission. Wed–Sat 10am–3:30pm; Sun 1:30–4:30pm.

Read House & Gardens ★★★ A walk through this 22-room Federal-style house is a walk through New Castle history. Originally the home of George Read II, son of a signer of the Declaration of Independence, it had only two other owners. Rooms from each "period" pay homage to them all. The Palladian windows and intricate composition-work moldings were part of the original design. Don't miss Mr. Read's law office or the second-floor bathing room, to which servants carried hot water. The second owner added formal gardens in the mid-1800s, now the oldest surviving gardens in Delaware—admission to them is free and worth the stop. The third owner's contributions included the European-style rathskeller in the basement installed during Prohibition; it's a hoot.

42 The Strand, New Castle, DE 19720. ✆ **302/322-8411.** www.hsd.org/read.htm. Admission $7 adults; $6 seniors, military, and students; $4 children. Apr–Dec Sun and Wed–Fri 11am–4pm, Sat 10am–4pm. Last tour is at 3:30pm. Gardens open to the public, no admission charged.

DOVER & CENTRAL DELAWARE

13

To race-car fans, Dover means NASCAR. To gamblers, it's a place to take a couple of chances. To history buffs, this town is where the U.S. Constitution got its first "yea" vote. Set in the middle of the state, Delaware's capital has its share of museums and attractions. Problem is, too many people fail to slow down on their way to the beach! What a shame.

At least the wildlife is smart enough to stop: Bombay Hook National Wildlife Refuge offers migrating visitors 16,000 acres of marsh and wetlands. The wild scenery makes it a good stop for humans, too.

DOVER

45 miles S of Wilmington; 84 miles E of Baltimore; 43 miles N of Rehoboth

Plotted in 1717 according to a charter by William Penn, Dover was originally designed as the Kent County seat. By 1777, this rich grain-farming community's importance had increased, and the state legislature, seeking a safe inland location as an alternative to the old capital of New Castle, relocated to the more central Dover. Delaware became the "first state" on December 7, 1787, when its delegates assembled at Dover's Golden Fleece Tavern to ratify the Constitution of the United States.

Today, Dover continues to be a hub of state government and business. Its history is showcased at a sprawling agricultural museum, a museum of American art stocked with lavish works donated by Delaware art collectors, and the Old State House. On the city's southern edge, Dover Air Force Base, the largest airport on the East Coast, is home to its own museum of aircraft.

Essentials

GETTING THERE From the north, take I-95 to Wilmington and head south on Route 1 or Route 13 (also known as the DuPont Hwy.) to Dover. Route 13, which runs the length of Delaware, is also the best way to approach Dover from the south. From Washington, DC, and west, take Route 50 across the Bay Bridge to Route 301 North. Follow 301 to 302 east, then take Route 454. From 454, take Route 8 into Dover.

Bus service to Dover is available through **Greyhound** (**© 800/231-2222;** www.greyhound.com), which stops at 716 S. Governors Ave. (**© 302/736-5183**).

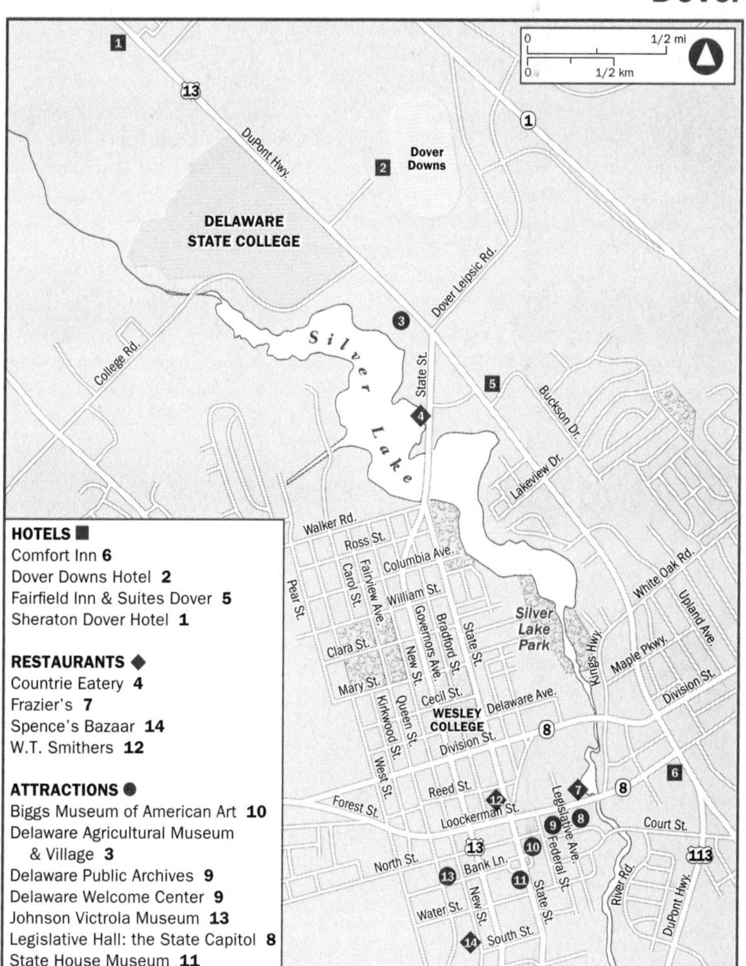

VISITOR INFORMATION Head first to the **Welcome Center,** 121 Duke of York St., Dover, DE 19901 (✆ **302/744-5055**). It offers information, exhibits, restrooms, and a gift shop, and is open Monday through Friday from 8am to 4:30pm, Saturday 9am to 4:30pm, and Sunday from 1:30 to 4:30pm. Sign up here for one of the informative 30-minute tours around the Green—a good introduction to Dover history—offered Monday through Saturday. If you are traveling from the north, you can also stop by the **Smyrna Visitor Center,** 5500 DuPont Hwy., Dover, DE 19901, 11 miles north of the capital on Route 13 (✆ **302/653-8910**).

GETTING AROUND You'll need a car. To rent one, contact **Avis** (✆ **302/734-5550**) or **Hertz** (✆ **302/678-0700**). For reliable 24-hour taxi service, call **City Cab of Dover** (✆ **302/734-5968**). ***Note:*** Amish buggies are common on the area's highways and byways, usually on the shoulders. Please drive with care and pass them slowly.

SPECIAL EVENTS Everything seems to stop for the two **"Monster Mile"** NASCAR weekends, in June and September, at Dover International Speedway (✆ **302/883-6500;** www.doverspeedway.com). Make your hotel reservations up to a year in advance. In late April or early May, several privately owned historic homes and gardens open to the public for **Dover Days** (✆ **800/233-5368;** www.doverdaysfestival.com). Costumed guides, maypole dancing, and crafts demonstrations take place on the Green. Cyclists come for the **Amish Country Bike Tour** (✆ **800/233-5368;** www.visitdover.com), held the Saturday after Labor Day. **Christmas in Odessa** (✆ **302/378-4900;** www.christmasinodessa.com) is held the first Saturday in December, with house tours, music, and crafts. Every first Saturday is special in Dover—programs and events are always scheduled then.

Where to Stay

Generally, Dover accommodations are moderately priced—but don't go looking for hotel rooms close to NASCAR weekends. Then, you'll have to look for lodging about an hour away: at the beach resorts, Wilmington, or on Maryland's Eastern Shore. Local hotels also tend to book up on summer weekends. Most of Dover's hotels are on Route 13 (DuPont Hwy.); these are largely modern chains with ample free parking.

Comfort Inn Businessmen and families head for this Comfort Inn, just off Route 13 at Loockerman Street. The closest motel to the historic district, this brick-fronted inn has two separate two-story buildings set behind an office building and off the busy highway. The plain but tidy decor and furnishings are typical of the chain.

222 S. DuPont Hwy. (Rte. 13), Dover, DE 19901. www.choicehotels.com. ✆ **800/424-6423** or 302/674-3300. 94 units. $110–$300 double. Rates include continental breakfast. AE, DC, DISC, MC, V. Pets accepted. **Amenities:** Fitness room; outdoor pool. *In room:* A/C, fridge, hair dryer, microwave, free Wi-Fi.

Dover Downs Hotel ★ This luxury hotel adjacent to the casino and racetracks offers trackview rooms and plenty of pampering. The hotel is Delaware's largest. Most units are spacious, with standard furnishings. Spa suites with Jacuzzi tubs, wet bars, and sitting rooms are available. Other suites feature billiard tables or fireplaces.

1131 N. DuPont Hwy., Dover, DE 19901. www.doverdownshotel.com. ✆ **866/4-RESERV** (473-7378) or 302/674-4600. 500 units. $125–$250 double; $175–$300 suite. Children 18 and under stay free in parent's room. AE, DISC, MC, V. **Amenities:** 6 restaurants; 2 coffee shops; lounge; fitness center; indoor pool; room service; shuttle service to downtown Dover; spa. *In room:* A/C, TV, fridge, Wi-Fi (fee).

Fairfield Inn & Suites Dover ★ This Marriott franchise has room for families and amenities for business travelers. Decorated in greens, orange, and navy, each suite has a pullout sofa, second TV, CD player, fridge, and microwave. Standard rooms are almost as spacious (double-doubles are biggest), though the fitness center is small.

655 N. DuPont Hwy., Dover, DE 19901. www.marriott.com/dovfi. ✆ **302/677-0900.** 77 units. $95–$159 double; $119–$189 suite. Rates include hot breakfast. AE, DC, DISC, MC, V. **Amenities:** Fitness center; indoor pool; spa. *In room:* A/C, flatscreen TV, CD player (in suites), fridge, microwave, free Wi-Fi.

Sheraton Dover Hotel ★ A favorite spot for business executives and conference attendees, this seven-story hotel is the most complete facility along the north-south corridor. Guest rooms are traditionally furnished, with mahogany reproduction furniture and rich jewel tones.

1570 N. DuPont Hwy. (Rte. 13), Dover, DE 19901. www.sheratondover.com. ✆ **302/678-8500.** Fax 302/678-9073. 156 units. $99–$199 double; $119–$535 suite. AE, DC, DISC, MC, V. **Amenities:**

Restaurant; lounge; club-level rooms; fitness center; indoor pool. *In room:* A/C, TV w/movies and games, fridge and microwave on request, free Wi-Fi.

Where to Eat

Chain restaurants line DuPont Highway. For something local, a few options are:

Countrie Eatery AMERICAN One thing draws the locals here: breakfast. They come for the omelets, the pancakes, and the bottomless cup of joe. Lunch and dinner are served, too, with home-style meatloaf, hot turkey sandwiches, and country dinners.

950 N. State St. ✆ **302/674-8310.** www.countrieeatery.com. Reservations not accepted. Main courses $4–$9 breakfast, $4–$10 lunch, $7–$16 dinner. No credit cards. Mon–Thurs 6:30am–8pm; Fri–Sat 6:30am–9pm; Sun 6:30am–4pm.

Frazier's PUB FARE Frazier's is within walking distance of the historic district and on a small pond. The decor is casual with paneling, wood ceiling beams, and long wood tables. There are 14 kinds of wings, seven cheese steaks, as well as soups, salads, wraps, sandwiches, and 15 burger choices. Prices are reasonable and the cream of crab and shrimp soup is worth a visit. Entertainment is scheduled most weekday evenings.

9 E. Loockerman St., Dover, DE 19901. ✆ **302/741-2420.** Fax 302/742-2563. Reservations accepted. Main courses $7–$20. AE, DISC, MC, V. Mon–Sat 11am–1am. Sun noon–1am.

Sambo's Tavern ★ SEAFOOD About 7 miles northeast of Dover Downs, this family-owned tavern has seafood delivered fresh from the Delaware Bay and produce from local farms every day. The rooms are rustic with wood-paneled walls, big picture windows overlooking the Leipsic River, and local newspapers covering the tables. Try the crab cakes, fried golden brown, or dig into a mound of steamed hard-shell clams. Sandwiches, salads, soups, and seafood platters round out the all-day menu. Boat docking is available. Patrons must be 21 or older to enter.

283 Front St., Leipsic, DE 19901. ✆ **302/674-9724.** Reservations recommended. Main courses $5–$31. DISC, MC, V. Mon–Sat 11am–10pm. Bar Mon–Sat 9am–11pm. Closed Nov–Mar.

Spence's Bazaar MARKET This old-time market has plenty of options for carryout: tasty pies and breads, sandwiches, hot pretzels, and candies, all made by members of Mennonite and Amish communities. Hours can vary, so it's best to call ahead if you have your heart set on shoofly pie. Don't get lost among the huge number of stalls that make up the flea market and auction business surrounding the market.

550 S. New St. ✆ **302/734-3441.** Tues and Fri 7:30am–5:30pm; Sat 7:30am–3pm.

W. T. Smithers AMERICAN This Victorian-style eatery is dainty enough for a girls' night out, but the bar is big enough for all your friends. Stop for lunch and enjoy overstuffed sandwiches (skip the crab cake though), a luscious cream of crab soup, or a salad. The dinner menu runs the gamut from fish and steak to a wide array of shrimp, scallops, fish, and crab dishes. Or come for the party: a DJ on Mondays, Wednesdays, and Thursdays, bands or DJs on Saturdays, and karaoke on Fridays.

140 S. State St., Dover, DE 19901. ✆ **302/674-8875.** Reservations recommended. Main courses $7–$10 lunch, $7–$22 dinner. AE, DC, DISC, MC, V. Daily 11am–1am.

What to See & Do

The major museums of Dover, as well as Legislative Hall and the state archives, have been designated the **First State Heritage Park at Dover.** A "park without boundaries," the various sites, nevertheless, have hours. Start your visit at the **Green,** where Delaware became the first state to ratify the U.S. Constitution in 1787. Most of

Dover's historic sites, government buildings, and museums are around or within walking distance of here. From Route 13, follow signs for the historic district and take State Street, which goes through the center of the Green. Other attractions, along with Dover's hotels and motels, are east of the historic district, along Route 13, also known as DuPont Highway. You'll need a car to get around this strip, home to Dover Downs, the Delaware Agricultural Museum and Village, and the Dover Air Force Base.

MUSEUMS & HISTORIC SITES

Biggs Museum of American Art Two floors of galleries are filled with antique furniture; silver tea services produced locally; and the works of the Hudson River School, the Peales, and local painters and sculptors. The collection of Sewell C. Biggs, a Delaware art patron, spans 2 centuries and includes 20th-century Impressionism.

406 Federal St. ✆ **302/674-2111.** www.biggsmuseum.org. Free admission. Wed–Fri 9am–4:30pm; Sat 9am–5pm; Sun 1:30–4:30pm.

Delaware Agricultural Museum & Village A huge barn right on DuPont Highway houses an enormous collection of tractors and other farm equipment—including a 1930s farm kitchen, log cabin, and crop-dusting plane. Outside, you'll find an 1890s village, complete with barn, farmhouses, train station, windmill, and church.

866 N. DuPont Hwy., Dover, DE 19901. ✆ **302/734-1618.** www.agriculturalmuseum.org. Admission $6 adults, $4 seniors, and $3 children 4–17. Tues–Sat 10am–4pm. Across from Dover Downs on Rte. 13.

Delaware Public Archives For part of every year, Delaware's copy of the Bill of Rights goes on display here. The document is one of seven extant from the first official imprint. The exhibit is open December 7 (Delaware Day) to July 4; the rest of the year it returns to the National Archives. In an agreement with the National Archives, the Bill of Rights will return to Delaware for half of each year for the next 20 years.

121 Duke of York St., Dover, DE 19901. ✆ **302/744-5000.** www.archives.delaware.gov. Free admission. Mon–Sat 9am–4:30pm; Sun 1:30–4:30pm.

First State Heritage Park ★★ Historic buildings around Dover's Green celebrate the accomplishments of Delawareans—and admission is free. Start at the **Welcome Center,** 121 Duke of York St. (in the Public Archives; ✆ **302/44-5055;** www.history.delaware.gov/museums), to get a map and see its exhibits. Nearby, the **Green,** the English-style town square at Bank Lane and State Street, was designed by William Penn more than 300 years ago. It was here that soldiers gathered to join the Revolutionary War troops. Look for the sign remembering the Golden Fleece Tavern, where Delaware's legislators voted to ratify the U.S. Constitution.

The **John Bell House,** the oldest surviving wooden structure in town, is at 43 The Green. Home of a 19th-century tavern owner, it's undergoing restoration. It's worth a look and it's where walking tours begin. The house is open Monday through Friday 10am to 3pm and first Saturdays 9:30am to 4:30pm.

The **Johnson Victrola Museum ★**, at New Street and Bank Lane, is packed with old records and antique phonographs that pay tribute to the man who made the Victrola a must-have in the early 1900s. Eldridge R. Johnson, a Delaware boy who founded the Victor Talking Machine Company, invented a way to make the original phonograph more compact and to control its volume. His invention made the machine popular—and made him a millionaire. Open Wednesday through Saturday from 9am to 3:30pm.

The **Old State House,** on the Green, dates to 1792. To mark the U.S. bicentennial in 1976, the Georgian-style Court House, with its 18th-century courtroom, legislative chambers, and deeds office where freed slaves filed their manumission papers, was restored to its original appearance. Although the state's General Assembly moved to the Legislative Hall in 1933, the State House continues to be used for ceremonial events. Stop by Monday through Saturday 4am to 4:30pm or Sunday 1:30 to 4:30pm.

Legislative Hall: The State Capitol This Georgian-style building, which houses the state's General Assembly, is open to visitors (bring photo ID). Tours are available Monday through Friday 9am to 4:30pm and first Saturdays 9am to 4:30pm.

152 Legislative Ave., Dover, DE 19901. ✆ **302/739-9194.** www.delaware.gov. Free admission. Mon–Fri 9am–3pm when Assembly is not in session; Mon–Fri 9am–noon on General Assembly session days.

NEARBY ATTRACTIONS

Air Mobility Command Museum (Dover Air Force Base) ★★ ☺ The name of this museum, in a restored World War II hangar listed on the National Register of Historic Places, doesn't describe the depth of this collection of aircraft. The planes and artifacts reflect the history of Dover Air Force Base since World War II, through the Berlin airlift and the Vietnam War and remind us of the brave men who flew and serviced these craft. Not only will you see the museum's first plane, a C-47A used in the 1944 D-Day paratroop drop over Normandy, but you also may have a chance to walk inside it. Several of the planes are usually open for tours. Cargo planes, air refueling planes, and jets that broke the sound barrier are here. You can also take a look at Air Force Two, the plane that carried vice presidents, first ladies, and sometimes the president until 2011. Tours are offered third Saturdays from 10am to 2pm.

1301 Heritage Rd. (off Rte. 113), Dover, DE 19902. ✆ **302/677-5938.** www.amcmuseum.org. Free admission. Tues–Sat 9am–4pm. Closed federal holidays. Take Rte. 9 (left from Dover) and look for signs.

Dover Downs Casino Dover Downs's slots casino draws busloads of gamblers. The 80,000-square-foot facility, adjacent to the racetrack, has live games, from baccarat to poker to roulette, as well as 2,800 slot machines. You must be 21 to play.

1131 N. DuPont Hwy., DE 19901. ✆ **800/711-5882** or 302/674-4600. www.doverdowns.com. Daily 24 hr. Closed Easter and Dec 25.

John Dickinson Plantation The home of John Dickinson, one of Delaware's foremost statesmen of the Revolutionary and Federal periods, was originally built in 1740. Destroyed by fire in 1804, the brick house was rebuilt in 1896. Guides dressed in period clothing give visitors a glimpse of the daily life of the Dickinson family, tenants, and slaves. It's located near the Air Mobility Command Museum.

340 Kitts Hummock Rd., Dover, DE 19901. ✆ **302/739-3277.** www.history.delaware.gov. Free admission. Wed–Sat 10am–3:30pm. Arrive at least 30 min. before closing time. Take Rte. 113 south from Dover to Kitts Hummock Rd., past the Dover Air Force Base.

Spectator Sports & Outdoor Activities

HARNESS RACING **Dover Downs** (✆ **800/711-5882;** www.doverdowns.com) offers harness racing November through April. Races run Monday through Thursday at 4:30pm, Saturday and Sunday at 5:30pm. Simulcast racing is offered year-round, daily from noon to midnight. **Harrington Raceway,** Route 13, Harrington (✆ **302/398-7223;** www.harringtonraceway.com), has 90 race days from April through June and

HISTORIC HOUSES OF ODESSA

The quiet town of Odessa, which dates back to the 18th century when it was called Cantwell's Bridge, was once a thriving crossroads. When trains and highways bypassed the town, it became a sleepy place. Now declared a historic district, Odessa features Georgian homes built just before the American Revolution by William Corbit and David Wilson—the centerpieces of the **Historic Houses of Odessa** (✆ **302/378-4119;** www.historicodessa.org). These two houses—along with a wood-sided working family's home and a 19th-century bank and hotel—are open to the public March through December. Original furnishings, a great Underground Railroad story, and the opportunity to walk through the Old Town make this a worthwhile stop. The Underground Railroad stop is getting new attention with a program "Freedom Seekers: The Odessa Story." The Corbit Sharp House is now part of the National Underground Railroad Network to Freedom. Tours are offered Thursday through Saturday 10am to 4:30pm, Sunday 1 to 4:30pm. The last tour begins at 3pm. Tickets are $10 adults, $8 seniors and students over age 12.

The quiet town comes to life on the first Saturday of December, when 30 historic houses spanning 3 centuries open for the Women's Club of Odessa's **Christmas in Odessa** (✆ **302/378-4900;** www.christmasinodessa.com). Public buildings and private homes are open for daytime and candlelight tours. Music, carriage rides, food, and a crafts shop are also available. Tickets are sold that day at the Old Academy, at Fourth and Main streets, for $20.

Odessa is 23 miles north of Dover and 22 miles south of Wilmington. To get here, take Route 13 and follow the signs to the historic district.

August through October, Sunday through Thursday with post time at 5:30pm. Simulcast is available daily from noon to midnight. Harrington has a 24-hour casino (closed Easter and Dec 25). The track is about 15 miles south of Dover.

STOCK-CAR RACING Twice a year, NASCAR fans flock to **Dover International Speedway,** 1131 N. DuPont Hwy. (Rte. 13 at Dover Downs), Dover, DE 19901 (✆ **800/411-3219;** www.doverspeedway.com). These two major race weekends in June and September draw some of the world's top drivers to Dover's 135,000-seat track. Tickets for adults start at $47 for general admission. Reserved seating for Sunday's race runs about $100; order online or call ✆ **800/441-7223.** Tickets go on sale 10 months prior to each race.

Catch the **Race Express Bus** from Blue Hen Corporate Center 3 miles south of the racetrack. Tickets are $20 a carload and include parking and round-trip shuttle. Race fans traveling from the Wilmington area can catch the bus at Christiana Mall. Tickets are $15 a person from the mall. Look for details at www.doverspeedway.com.

Silver Lake & Killens Pond State Park

Dover's beautiful **Silver Lake** is the core of a 182-acre recreation area in the heart of the city. Biking, swimming, and picnicking draw most people, and there's a boat ramp, exercise circuit, volleyball court, and walking/jogging trail. The park has entrances on Washington Street and Kings Highway; it's open year-round from sunrise to sunset. Contact the **Dover Parks and Recreation Department** (✆ **302/736-7050**) for info.

Some 13 miles south of Dover, about a half-mile east of Route 13, is **Killens Pond State Park ★**, 5025 Killens Pond Rd., Felton, DE 19943 (✆ **302/284-4526;**

www.destateparks.com/park/killens-pond). Covering 1,444 acres, with a 66-acre mill-pond, Killens Pond is a natural inland haven with picnic areas, shuffleboard courts, horseshoe pits, biking and hiking trails, volleyball courts, boat rentals, pond fishing, and camping. The **Killens Pond Water Park** has lap lanes, a mushroom fountain, and a lily-pad fun walk. Park entry fees daily May through October are $3 for Delaware-registered cars and $6 for out-of-state vehicles. Water-park admission is an additional $3 per person. The park is open year-round; the water park is open Memorial Day through Labor Day.

Also at the park are 77 campsites, with 10 cabins, 17 tent-only sites, and one pond-view cottage, open year-round. Reservations are taken up to 7 months in advance; call ✆ **877/987-2757.** Fees are $19 to $23 for tent sites and $25 to $29 for sites with water and electric hookup. ***Note:*** NASCAR fans fill the campsites quickly on race weekends in June and September. Be sure to reserve 7 months in advance.

Put Yourself in the Driver's Seat

Want to ride in a Sprint Cup car? Maybe even drive it yourself? **Monster Racing Driving School** (✆ **800/468-6946;** www.monsterracing.com) will let you get behind the wheel to "tame the monster" at Dover Speedway. For $99, you can ride the course for four laps with an instructor. Packages range from $389 to $949 to drive a race car for 30 laps, with shorter and less expensive alternatives in between.

The Performing Arts

Schwartz Center for the Arts This performing-arts venue, the beloved 1904 Dover Opera House, plays host to a wide variety of performers, from the Second City comedy troupe to the Preservation Hall Jazz Band. Film, plays, and ballet are also on the schedule, which is posted online. Children's programming is quite extensive. 226 S. State St., Dover, DE 19903. ✆ **302/678-3583.** www.schwartzcenter.com.

BOMBAY HOOK NATIONAL WILDLIFE REFUGE ★

45 miles S of Wilmington; 107 miles E of Baltimore; 53 miles N of Rehoboth

Bombay Hook, established in 1937 as part of a chain of refuges extending from Canada to the Gulf of Mexico, is Delaware's largest. Though its primary (and loudest) inhabitants and visitors are wintering ducks and geese, Bombay Hook also hosts herons, egrets, sandpipers, willets, and the occasional bald eagle, as well as a more permanent mammal, amphibian, and reptile population. If you've visited Maryland's Blackwater National Wildlife Refuge, Bombay Hook will be quite a contrast. The facilities are considerably more primitive—roads aren't paved, the trails are well marked but not well worn, and there are fewer programs and visitor services. There are also fewer visitors, so you may have the place to yourself, especially in the off season.

Essentials

GETTING THERE Take Route 13 north of Dover to Route 42; travel east (left) on Route 42 to Route 9, and then north on Route 9 for 1½ miles; turn right onto White-hall Neck Road, which leads to the visitor center.

VISITOR CENTER The visitor center/ranger station (✆ **302/653-9345;** http://bombayhook.fws.gov) is open year-round, Monday through Friday from 8am to 4pm, plus spring and fall weekends from 9am to 5pm. The park is open daily from sunrise to sunset.

FEES & REGULATIONS Entrance fees are $4 per car or $2 per person 16 and older on bike or on foot. Admission is free on hunting days—but access is limited, too. Deer, snow goose, and Canada goose hunting are permitted under special regulations in designated portions of the refuge during the regular Delaware hunting season.

Seeing the Highlights

Much of Bombay Hook is not accessible to the public. However, the 12-mile round-trip auto route, several nature trails, and three observation towers offer opportunities to see birds and other wildlife. The driving tour, which can also be biked, begins and ends at the visitor center and takes you by the three major wetland pools: Raymond Pool, Shearness Pool, and Bear Swamp Pool. Cyclists should note that the roads are dirt and gravel—though they are flat. The visitor center has binoculars for visitors' use. To see the most birds, come in May or June, when the shorebird population hits its peak. Or visit in October or November, when the ducks and geese can number 150,000.

BIRD-WATCHING Birds can be seen all along the auto tour, but for the best vantage point, hike to one of the three 30-foot observation towers, one overlooking each of the pools. Part of the trail to Bear Swamp Observation Tower is accessible; an observation platform at ground level below the tower provides a good view, and a viewing scope at wheelchair level has been installed on the dock.

The best times to see migratory birds are October through November and mid-February through March. Some 256 species have been counted. **Canada, tundra,** and **snow geese** begin arriving in early October, while **ducks**—pintail, mallard, American widgeon, and others—increase through November. **Shorebird** migration begins in April; their populations in the refuge peak in May and June.

The refuge is the year-round home to **bald eagles,** though they can be difficult to spot. Eggs begin hatching in April; the baby eagles begin to leave their nests in June. Shearness Pool serves as their roosting and nesting area. Parson Point Trail will take you to the back of the pool for a closer look. During mating and nesting season (Nov–June), however, this trail may be closed. Bring binoculars or stop at the observation tower along the auto route to get a glimpse of the eagles.

HIKING Hiking in the refuge is primarily a means of observing and photographing wildlife, so the nature trails aren't terribly strenuous or long. All the trails are flat and range from .25 mile to 1 mile long. Bring insect repellent and wear long sleeves from July through September. The Bear Swamp Trail is partially wheelchair accessible; the Parson Point Trail is the longest option. The Boardwalk Trail offers visitors a look at four different refuge habitats—woodland, freshwater pond, brackish pond, and salt marsh. Another trail leads to the Raymond Tower, set in a meadow.

PLANNING YOUR TRIP TO MARYLAND & DELAWARE

14

Maryland and Delaware, two of the smaller states, contain a wide variety of terrain, weather, and topography as well as both urban and rural areas. So a little advance planning can make your trip run more smoothly. This chapter will answer many questions you may have as you plan your trip.

GETTING THERE

By Plane

The gateway to Maryland is **Baltimore/Washington International Thurgood Marshall Airport (BWI),** 10 miles south of Baltimore and 20 miles north of Annapolis. Hundreds of domestic and international flights arrive daily, and it's a hub for several airlines. Most cities and towns are also convenient to **Washington Dulles International Airport** and **Ronald Reagan Washington National Airport,** both major international airports but deep in the heart of many DC traffic jams.

Most major airlines fly into BWI, including **Air Tran** (✆ 800/247-8726), **American** (✆ 800/433-7300), **British Airways** (✆ 800/247-9297), **Continental** (✆ 800/525-0280), **Delta** (✆ 800/221-1212), **Southwest** (✆ 800/435-9792), **United** (✆ 800/241-6522), and **US Airways** (✆ 800/428-4322).

Commuter flights fly into **Salisbury–Ocean City–Wicomico Regional Airport,** near Ocean City, Maryland.

Delaware does not have its own major airport. Located within easy reach are **Philadelphia International Airport,** 30 minutes from downtown Wilmington and 1½ hours from Dover; **BWI,** approximately 1½ to 2½ hours to most points in Delaware; and **Washington Dulles International Airport** and **Ronald Reagan Washington National Airport,** approximately 2½ to 3 hours to most points in Delaware. In addition, **New Castle County Airport,** about 5 miles south of Wilmington, serves private craft.

By Bus

Greyhound (✆ **800/231-2222;** www.greyhound.com) serves major points in Maryland and Delaware, including Wilmington and Dover, Annapolis, Baltimore, Ocean City, Easton, and Frederick, with express service from New York City to Baltimore (at South Baltimore and East Baltimore's Travel Plaza).

Two discount bus lines have stops in Baltimore. **Bolt Bus** (✆ **877/265-8287;** www.boltbus.com) stops near Penn Station, 1610 St. Paul St. **Megabus** (✆ **877/462-6342;** http://us.megabus.com) makes stops in White Marsh, a suburb on I-95 north of Baltimore City. New York buses stop on the south side of the White Marsh Park and Ride Lot near White Marsh and Honeygo boulevards. MTA buses operate between this lot and downtown. Mega Buses serving Buffalo, Toronto, Boston, Philadelphia, Washington, DC, and Richmond and Hampton, Virginia, stop on the southern side of the White Marsh Mall parking lot adjacent to Honeygo Boulevard.

By Car

The Eastern Seaboard's major north-south link from Maine to Florida, **I-95,** passes through Wilmington and Newark in Delaware as well as Baltimore and central Maryland. Construction on a toll road is ongoing north of Baltimore City, but it only accounts for part of the endless traffic tie-ups on this thoroughfare, especially at rush hour and on holiday weekends.

Other interstate highways that traverse Maryland are **I-83,** which connects Baltimore with Harrisburg and points north, and **I-70** and **I-68,** which connect Western Maryland to the rest of the state and to Pennsylvania, West Virginia, and Ohio. There are no other interstates in Delaware, but to access the state from Maryland and points south, use U.S. **Route 13** or **Route 113. Route 404** from Route 50 near Denton is another way to cross the Eastern Shore to the beaches.

Maps and brochures are available at visitor information centers on I-95 and I-70. Most are open from 9am to 5pm. Some locations even offer hotel reservation services.

For information on car rentals and gasoline (petrol) in Maryland and Delaware, see "Getting Around by Car," later in this section.

By Train

Amtrak (✆ **800/USA-RAIL** [872-7245]; www.amtrak.com) offers frequent daily service to Baltimore, at both Pennsylvania Station (downtown) and BWI Airport Rail Station, and to the Wilmington station at 100 S. French St. (at Martin Luther King, Jr., Blvd.). Penn Station is a quick cab ride to the Inner Harbor; BWI's rail station is not actually at the airport but nearby. Shuttle buses go to the airport; plenty of taxis wait to take travelers anywhere else. In Wilmington, the station is right on the Riverfront, a short cab ride to downtown hotels, about a half-hour or so to Brandywine destinations. There's also daily service to Newark, Delaware; and Aberdeen and New Carrollton, Maryland. Amtrak has limited service to and from the west at Cumberland and Rockville, Maryland. The high-speed Acela train runs along the Northeast Corridor.

International visitors can buy a **USA Rail Pass,** good for 15, 30, or 45 days of unlimited travel on **Amtrak** (✆ **800/USA-RAIL** [872-7245] in the U.S. or Canada, or 001/215-856-7953 outside the U.S.; www.amtrak.com). The pass is available online or through many overseas travel agents. See Amtrak's website for the cost of travel within the western, eastern, or northwestern United States. Reservations are generally required and should be made as early as possible. Regional rail passes are also available.

BY FERRY

The **Cape May–Lewes Ferry** travels daily between southern New Jersey and the lower Delaware coast. This 70-minute crossing is operated on a drive-on, drive-off basis and can accommodate up to 800 passengers and 100 cars. Full details on the ferry are given on p. 231.

BY BOAT

Cruise vessels depart from the Port of Baltimore's **South Locust Point Marine Terminal,** 2001 E. McComas St., about 5 miles from the Inner Harbor, where many of the best attractions and hotels are located. To get to Baltimore, follow I-195 west to Route 295 north, which will take you into downtown. **Taxis** to downtown attractions run about $22; they'll be waiting when the cruise ship docks.

GETTING AROUND

By Plane

Maryland and Delaware are two compact states; you probably won't need to fly from one point to the other. Commuter flights within Maryland do fly from Baltimore and Philadelphia airports to **Salisbury–Ocean City–Wicomico Regional Airport** (✆ **410/548-4827**), 40 minutes west of Ocean City, on the outskirts of Salisbury.

By Car

The most practical way to see both Maryland and Delaware is by car. Depending on traffic, it takes approximately 2 hours to get from Wilmington to Lewes; from 75 minutes to 2 hours, also depending on traffic, from Wilmington to Baltimore; 1 hour from Baltimore to Annapolis; 90 minutes from Baltimore to Washington, DC; 90 minutes from Baltimore to Frederick; 2½ hours from Frederick to Cumberland; and 2½ hours from Annapolis to Ocean City.

If you're planning to drive on the **Baltimore Beltway** (I-695), try to avoid rush hour. Congestion, particularly at the junctions to I-95, is terrible. Road widening is underway in some areas, but traffic is at its heaviest from 7 to 10am and 3 to 6pm.

The **I-95 Corridor Coalition** posts updates on lane closings and traffic delays online for both Maryland and Delaware (and all the other states along the highway) at **www.i95coalition.org**.

The tourism agencies in Maryland and Delaware both produce good free maps. However, if you plan to do any extensive driving on Maryland's Eastern Shore, you'll need more detail than the state maps provide. Contact the county tourism agencies (especially Somerset, Dorchester, and Talbot) for free county maps. There are a couple of special-interest maps, too. The best is the **Maryland Scenic Byways** map and guide, which offers some off-the-beaten-path routes with scenic stops. (Get them just so you can see what the black-eyed Susan signs along the road are referring to.) The state also puts out an excellent bicycle map.

Maryland and Delaware gas prices tend to be at or below the national average. Gas taxes are included in the printed price—and most gas stations post prices for all the grades, including diesel. One U.S. gallon equals 3.8 liters or .85 imperial gallons.

International visitors should note that insurance and taxes are almost never included in quoted rental car rates in the U.S. Be sure to ask your rental agency about additional fees for these. They can add a significant cost to your car rental.

If you're visiting from abroad and plan to rent a car in the United States, keep in mind that foreign driver's licenses are usually recognized in the U.S., but you may want to consider obtaining an international driver's license.

By Train

Amtrak has limited service to and from the west at Cumberland and Rockville, Maryland. The high-speed Acela train runs along the Northeast Corridor, connecting Maryland and Delaware.

MARC (✆ **800/325-RAIL** [7245]) commuter service runs between Washington, DC, and Baltimore during the week. MARC also serves Western Maryland in Brunswick and Frederick.

By Bus

Greyhound (✆ **800/231-2222** in the U.S., or 001/214-849-8100 outside the U.S. with toll-free access; www.greyhound.com) is the sole nationwide bus line. International visitors can obtain information about the **Greyhound North American Discovery Pass.** The pass, which offers unlimited travel and stopovers in the U.S. and Canada, can be obtained outside the United States from travel agents or through www.discoverypass.com. Passes can be activated at the downtown Baltimore bus terminal, 2110 Haines St. (✆ **410/752-7682**). It is open 24 hours.

You can travel in Baltimore on the Metro, Light Rail, or bus, all operated by the **Maryland Transit Administration** (**MTA;** ✆ **410/539-5000;** www.mtamaryland.com). The **Charm City Circulator** (www.charmcitycirculator.com) provides free transportation throughout the downtown Baltimore region.

In Wilmington and the Brandywine Valley, **DART First State** (✆ **302/577-3278;** www.dartfirststate.com) runs buses between the downtown business section and suburbs and tourist attractions.

TIPS ON ACCOMMODATIONS

Accommodations in both Maryland and Delaware can be found for everyone from the rock star to the budget traveler.

In Baltimore or Wilmington, you can find good packages at the big hotels in the tourist and business sections of town on nonholiday weekends, and shoulder/low seasons (fall, winter). These are pricier than the motels outside of town, but you'll be closer to major attractions.

Baltimore has three Marriotts, a Hyatt, a Sheraton, and a few independent hotels offering comfortable accommodations near the Inner Harbor.

If you prefer the suburbs, you can find chain hotels and motels near BWI, along Route 40 and I-95, and around the Beltway that circles Baltimore City. Two hotels near the airport are within walking distance of the Light Rail—with stops in downtown Baltimore. That's a good way to avoid the hassle of renting a car, driving in an unfamiliar city, and finding/paying for parking. The suburbs are home to several Sheratons, a Hilton, and an Embassy Suites. You can count on a clean, comfortable room at a Holiday Inn or Best Western, often with a simple continental breakfast included. In most cases, children stay in a parent's room at no extra charge.

Wilmington has a number of chain hotels in its business district; these usually have plenty of room on the weekends, often with free or reduced-price parking. There are some comfortable hotels on the outskirts of town, convenient to Wilmington and the Brandywine Valley. Chains include Holiday Inn, Embassy Suites, Quality Inn, and the Hilton.

For bed-and-breakfasts, head for Annapolis, Frederick, or Western Maryland. These areas are rich in B&Bs. Because they are old and often have delicate furnishings, innkeepers require children to be well behaved, if they are welcome at all. There may be no TV or hair dryer—but the bread will be fresh from the oven, and the furnishings usually reflect the locale. In addition, many B&Bs have made their accommodations as accessible as possible. Call ahead and check to see what can be done for you. Some innkeepers admit they haven't figured out how to accommodate a wheelchair while preserving a fine old house, but others are fully accessible.

Smokers should be aware that their cigarettes are usually not welcome in the house, not even on the porches.

If you're going to a beach resort in Delaware or Maryland, you've got lots of choices: chains, local hotels, or home and condo rentals. The chains offer predictable accommodations, while the local hotels range from clean and comfy to dazzling. What makes resort destinations really comfortable and economical for families are house and condo rentals. Real-estate agents in each resort (listed in specific chapters) can help you find a place big enough for a family reunion or cozy enough for newlyweds. At the beach, you'll have to pack linens, towels, and paper products, as these aren't provided. But you can count on a pretty well-equipped kitchen, living areas with TVs—and often VCRs—sleeping space, and bathrooms. House rentals have become more popular in Deep Creek Lake as well. Firms in both Annapolis and on the Eastern Shore have lined up an impressive array of homes available to the tourist, as well. In every place, there are lots of choices, many with hot tubs, boat piers, or beach access. Here linens are provided, so just bring paper products.

[FastFACTS] MARYLAND & DELAWARE

Area Codes The area code for all of Delaware is 302. Some Brandywine Valley attractions are in Pennsylvania; their area code is 610. Maryland has four area codes: 301 and 240 in the western half of the state, 410 and 443 in the eastern half, including Baltimore and Annapolis. In Maryland, you must always dial the area code first.

Business Hours Most businesses are open every day. Store operating hours are usually 10am to 5pm or later. Mall stores close at 9pm or later. Many tourist attractions, however, have had to cut back their hours and quite a few have eliminated opening hours on Monday, Tuesday, and sometimes Wednesday. Winter hours at the beach may be even more limited, Saturday and Sunday, if they open at all.

Customs Baltimore/Washington International Thurgood Marshall Airport is the only place visitors could have to go through customs. Agents arrive as the few international flights land at the airport so you don't have to worry about long lines or extensive waits. Customs is located in the nearly empty international wing near the Light Rail station—convenient for getting into Baltimore City.

Disabled Travelers Hotels, restaurants, and attractions—as well as public transportation and even sidewalks—have added ramps, elevators, audio description and Braille, and other amenities to enable travelers with disabilities to visit. It's been a challenge for some historic sites, though most have at least some access for all visitors. Some older B&Bs and inns have not been able to update their accommodations to make them accessible but even that is beginning to change.

Doctors In downtown Baltimore, one option for finding a doctor is **Mercy Medical Center**'s doctor referral, ✆ **800/636-3729.** Both Baltimore and Wilmington have world-class hospitals with top-notch emergency rooms. Your hotel should be able to provide referrals for doctors, as well.

Drinking Laws The legal age for purchase and consumption of alcoholic beverages is 21; proof of age is required and often requested at bars, nightclubs, and restaurants, so bring ID when you go out. Do not carry open containers of alcohol in your car or any public area that isn't zoned for alcohol consumption. The police can fine you on the spot. Don't even think about driving while intoxicated.

Beer, wine, and liquor are available only in licensed liquor stores in Maryland and Delaware. In Ocean City, beer and wine are sold more widely than hard liquor, which is available only from a county-run outlet. In most areas, alcohol sales are permitted on Sunday though in Bethany Beach, Delaware; Baltimore County; Cambridge, Maryland; and Garrett County, Maryland, Sunday sales are restricted to those drinking alcohol with a meal. There are no package sales on Sunday in Cambridge and Garrett County. Bars may not sell alcohol in Maryland and Delaware after 2am.

Electricity Like Canada, the United States uses 110 to 120 volts AC (60 cycles), compared to 220 to 240 volts AC (50 cycles) in most of Europe, Australia, and New Zealand. Downward converters that change 220–240 volts to 110–120 volts are difficult to find in the United States, so bring one with you.

Embassies & Consulates All embassies are in the nation's capital, Washington, DC. Some consulates are in major U.S. cities. For information of your country's consulate or embassy, check **www.embassy.org/embassies**.

Emergencies Dial ✆ **911** for any emergency requiring police, firefighters, or ambulance.

Health **Bugs, Bites & Other Wildlife Concerns** Maryland and Delaware don't pose any unusual health risks to the average visitor. If you're hiking or camping, be aware that this is deer-tick country, and deer ticks can carry Lyme disease. Wear long sleeves and pants tucked into your socks, cover your head, and inspect yourself for ticks later. Insect repellent containing DEET also helps repel ticks. After your trip, watch for a bull's-eye-shaped rash that can appear 3 days to a month following infection (but be aware that not everyone who is infected will get the rash). There is now a vaccine available for Lyme disease; consult your doctor if you're planning to take an extensive trip to deer tick–infested areas.

Respiratory Illnesses Baltimore's air quality can be hard on people with asthma or other lung ailments, especially in the hot, humid summer. Weather reports provide alerts whenever the air quality index is so poor that people are advised to stay inside.

Sun/Elements/Extreme Weather Exposure If you will be out in the sun or near the water or snow, remember your sunscreen and a hat. Maryland and Delaware enjoy mostly moderate weather, otherwise.

Insurance For information on traveler's insurance, trip cancellation insurance, and medical insurance while traveling, please visit **www.frommers.com/tips**.

Internet & Wi-Fi Wi-Fi is everywhere just about in both Maryland and Delaware. Many hotels offer free service; the more expensive hotels charge to connect although even they have free Wi-Fi in their lobby or lounge. BWI airport offers Wi-Fi for a fee, and it is also available at the Amtrak rail stations.

Legal Aid While driving, if you are pulled over for a minor infraction (such as speeding), never attempt to pay the fine directly to a police officer; this could be construed as attempted bribery, a much more serious crime. Pay fines by mail, or directly into the hands of the clerk of the court. If accused of a more serious offense, say and do nothing before consulting a lawyer. In the U.S., the burden is on the state to prove a person's guilt beyond a reasonable doubt, and everyone has the right to remain silent, whether he or she is suspected of a crime or actually arrested. Once arrested, a person can make one telephone call to a party of his or her choice. The international visitor should call his or her embassy or consulate.

LGBT Travelers In Baltimore, the main resource for gay men and lesbians is the **Gay and Lesbian Community Center of Baltimore,** 241 W. Chase St. (✆ **410/837-5445**). The center also produces the ***Baltimore Gay Paper*** (www.glccb.org), available free at area restaurants, nightclubs, bars, and bookstores. In Delaware, Rehoboth Beach is a popular destination for gay and lesbian travelers. Information is posted on **www.camprehoboth.com** or look for the *Letters from Camp Rehoboth* newsletter.

WHAT THINGS COST IN MARYLAND & DELAWARE	US$
Taxi from BWI Airport to downtown Baltimore	30.00
Double room, harbor view, Baltimore Hyatt in May	369.00
Double room, Holiday Inn Inner Harbor in May	129.00
Double room, Tidewater Inn, Easton, in May	189.00
Double room, Sheraton Suites, Wilmington in May	119.00
Double room, Holiday Inn Ocean City, MD, high season	245.00
Three-course dinner without wine, Sabatino's, Baltimore	25.00
Three-course dinner without wine, Green Room, Wilmington	65.00
Four-course dinner without wine, Volt, Frederick	80.00
Three-course dinner without wine, Bill Bunting's Angler, Ocean City	42.00
Bottle of beer at Max's Taphouse, Fells Point, Baltimore	5.25
Leinenkugel draft at Leinenkugel's Power Plant Live, Baltimore	5.25
Dogfish Head pint at Dogfish Head Brewings & Eats, Rehoboth	5.50
Glass of wine Domaine Hudson wine bar, Wilmington	10.00
Hawaiian martini, Roy's Restaurant, Baltimore	12.00
Cup of coffee	2.00–4.00
1 gallon of regular gas	3.60
Admission to most museums	Free–12.00
Admission to Fort McHenry	7.00
Round of mini-golf in Ocean City	8.00

Mail At press time, domestic postage rates were 32¢ for a postcard and 45¢ for a letter. For international mail, a first-class letter of up to 1 ounce costs $1.05 (85¢ to Canada and to Mexico); a first-class postcard costs the same as a letter. For more information, go to **www.usps.com**.

If you aren't sure what your address will be in the United States, mail can be sent to you, in your name, c/o General Delivery at the main post office of the city or region where you expect to be. (Call ✆ **800/275-8777** for information on the nearest post office.) The addressee must pick up mail in person and must produce proof of identity (driver's license, passport). Most post offices will hold mail for up to 1 month, and are open Monday to Friday from 8am to 6pm, and Saturday from 9am to 3pm.

Always include zip codes when mailing items in the U.S. If you don't know your zip code, visit www.usps.com/zip4.

Medical Requirements Unless you're arriving from an area known to be suffering from an epidemic (particularly cholera or yellow fever), inoculations or vaccinations are not required for entry into the United States.

Money & Costs Frommer's lists exact prices in the local currency. The currency conversions provided were correct at press time. However, rates fluctuate, so before departing consult a currency exchange website such as **www.oanda.com/currency/converter** to check up-to-the-minute rates.

THE VALUE OF THE U.S. DOLLAR VS. OTHER POPULAR CURRENCIES

US$	Can$	UK£	Euro (€)	Aus$	NZ$
1.00	1.00	0.65	0.78	.96	1.24

Beware of hidden credit card fees while traveling. Check with your credit or debit card issuer to see what fees, if any, will be charged for overseas transactions. Recent reform legislation in the U.S., for example, has curbed some exploitative lending practices. But many banks have responded by increasing fees in other areas, including fees for customers who use credit and debit cards while out of the country—even if those charges were made in U.S. dollars. Fees can amount to 3% or more of the purchase price. Check with your bank before departing to avoid any surprise charges on your statement.

For help with currency conversions, tip calculations, and more, download Frommer's convenient Travel Tools app for your mobile device. Go to **www.frommers.com/go/mobile** and tap on the Travel Tools icon.

Newspapers & Magazines The *Sun* and the *Washington Post* are Maryland's major newspapers. In Annapolis, look for the *Capital*, and in the Mid-Shore, the *Star Democrat*. You'll find the Wilmington *News-Journal* and the Philadelphia *Inquirer* in Delaware.

Packing Weather can be variable in the mid-Atlantic, making it important to dress in layers. Bring a hat and sunscreen if you'll be on the water or the beach. Even in summer, the ocean beaches can be chilly in the evening. And so can the hotels, shops, and restaurants. Pack a light sweater or light shawl. If you will be boating, make sure to have soft-soled shoes; sneakers will do.

For more helpful information on packing for your trip, download our convenient Travel Tools app for your mobile device. Go to **www.frommers.com/go/mobile** and tap on the Travel Tools icon.

Passports Virtually every traveler entering the U.S. is required to show a passport. All persons, including U.S. citizens, traveling by air between the United States and Canada, Mexico, Central and South America, the Caribbean, and Bermuda are required to present a valid passport. ***Note:*** U.S. and Canadian citizens entering the U.S. at land and sea ports of entry from within the Western Hemisphere must now also present a passport or other documents compliant with the Western Hemisphere Travel Initiative (WHTI; see www.getyouhome.gov for details). Children 15 and under may continue entering with only a U.S. birth certificate, or other proof of U.S. citizenship.

Police Dial ✆ **911** in an emergency anywhere in either Maryland or Delaware.

Safety While most of Maryland and Delaware enjoy relatively low crime rates, Baltimore has a nagging problem with property and violent crime—although it's nowhere near as bad as on the TV show, *The Wire*. Wilmington also has neighborhoods where visitors are advised not to go. The major tourist areas of both cities are fairly well policed, but be alert and follow common-sense precautions.

If you're using public transport, it's best to travel during the day and to keep valuables out of sight. It is safer and smarter to drive or take a cab between neighborhoods (unless otherwise noted) than to walk, even when the distance is not too great. Keep a good city map at hand to help you out if you're lost. Neighborhoods can go from safe to scary in a matter of a few blocks. It's best to keep on the main routes and turn around if anything looks worrisome.

Smoking Smoking in restaurants, bars, and other public places is illegal in Maryland and Delaware. A few Delaware hotels offer rooms for smokers—but the majority of bed-and-breakfasts do not.

Taxes The United States has no value-added tax (VAT) or other indirect tax at the national level. Delaware has no sales tax but does have an 8% to 10% **lodging tax.**

Maryland's **sales tax** is 6% on everything except groceries, and **lodging taxes** range from 4.5% to 7.5%. These taxes will not appear on price tags or quoted prices.

Telephones Many stores sell **prepaid calling cards** in denominations up to $50. Many public pay phones at airports now accept American Express, MasterCard, and Visa. **Local calls** made from most pay phones cost either 25¢ or 35¢. Most long-distance and international calls can be dialed directly from any phone. **To make calls within the United States and to Canada,** dial 1 followed by the area code and the seven-digit number. **For other international calls,** dial 011 followed by the country code, city code, and the number you are calling.

For **directory assistance** ("Information"), dial ✆ **411** for local numbers and national numbers in the U.S. and Canada. For dedicated long-distance information, dial 1, then the appropriate area code plus 555-1212.

Time The continental United States is divided into **four time zones:** Eastern Standard Time (EST)—in which Maryland and Delaware are situated, Central Standard Time (CST), Mountain Standard Time (MST), and Pacific Standard Time (PST). Alaska and Hawaii have their own zones. For example, when it's 9am in Los Angeles (PST), it's 7am in Honolulu (HST),10am in Denver (MST), 11am in Chicago (CST), noon in New York City (EST), 5pm in London (GMT), and 2am the next day in Sydney.

Daylight saving time is in effect from 1am on the second Sunday in March to 1am on the first Sunday in November, except in Arizona, Hawaii, the U.S. Virgin Islands, and Puerto Rico. Daylight saving time moves the clock 1 hour ahead of standard time.

For help with time translations, and more, download our convenient Travel Tools app for your mobile device. Go to **www.frommers.com/go/mobile** and tap on the Travel Tools icon.

Tipping In hotels, tip **bellhops** at least $1 per bag ($2–$3 if you have a lot of luggage) and tip the **chamber staff** $1 to $2 per day (more if you've left a big mess for him or her to clean up). Tip the **doorman** or **concierge** only if he or she has provided you with some specific service (for example, calling a cab for you or obtaining difficult-to-get theater tickets). Tip the **valet-parking attendant** $1 every time you get your car.

In restaurants, bars, and nightclubs, tip **service staff** and **bartenders** 15% to 20% of the check, tip **checkroom attendants** $1 per garment, and tip **valet-parking attendants** $1 per vehicle.

As for other service personnel, tip **cab drivers** 15% of the fare; tip **skycaps** at airports at least $1 per bag ($2–$3 if you have a lot of luggage); and tip **hairdressers** and **barbers** 15% to 20%.

For help with tip calculations, currency conversions, and more, download our convenient Travel Tools app for your mobile device. Go to **www.frommers.com/go/mobile** and tap on the Travel Tools icon.

Toilets You won't find public toilets or "restrooms" on the streets in most U.S. cities, but they can be found in hotel lobbies, bars, restaurants, museums, department stores, railway and bus stations, and service stations. Large hotels and fast-food restaurants are often the best bets for clean facilities. Restaurants and bars in resorts or heavily visited areas may reserve their restrooms for patrons.

Visas The U.S. State Department has a **Visa Waiver Program (VWP)** allowing citizens of the following countries to enter the United States without a visa for stays of up to 90 days: Andorra, Australia, Austria, Belgium, Brunei, Czech Republic, Denmark, Estonia, Finland, France, Germany, Greece, Hungary, Iceland, Ireland, Italy, Japan, Latvia, Liechtenstein, Lithuania, Luxembourg, Malta, Monaco, the Netherlands, New Zealand, Norway, Portugal, San Marino, Singapore, Slovakia, Slovenia, South Korea, Spain, Sweden, Switzerland, and the United Kingdom. (***Note:*** This list was accurate at press time; for the most up-to-date list of countries in the VWP, consult www.travel.state.gov/visa.) Even though a visa isn't necessary, in an effort to help U.S. officials check travelers against terror watch lists before they arrive at U.S. borders, visitors from VWP countries must register online through the Electronic System for Travel Authorization (ESTA) before boarding a plane or a boat to the U.S. Travelers must complete an electronic application providing basic personal and travel eligibility information. The Department of Homeland Security recommends filling out the form at least 3 days before traveling. Authorizations will be valid for up to 2 years or until the traveler's passport expires, whichever comes first. Currently, there is a US$14 fee for the online application. Existing ESTA registrations remain valid through their expiration dates. ***Note:*** Any passport issued on or after October 26, 2006, by a VWP country must be an **e-Passport** for VWP travelers to be eligible to enter the U.S. without a visa. Citizens of these nations also need to present a round-trip air or cruise ticket upon arrival. E-Passports contain computer chips capable of storing biometric information, such as the required digital photograph of the holder. If your passport doesn't have this feature, you can still travel without a visa if the valid passport was issued before October 26, 2005, and includes a machine-readable zone; or if the valid passport was issued between October 26, 2005, and October 25, 2006, and includes a digital photograph. For more information, go to **www.travel.state.gov/visa**. Canadian citizens may enter the United States without visas, but will need to show passports and proof of residence.

Citizens of all other countries must have (1) a valid passport that expires at least 6 months later than the scheduled end of their visit to the U.S.; and (2) a tourist visa.

For information about U.S. visas go to **www.travel.state.gov** and click on "Visas." Or go to one of the following websites:

Australian citizens can obtain up-to-date visa information from the **U.S. Embassy Canberra,** Moonah Place, Yarralumla, ACT 2600 (✆ **02/6214-5600**) or by checking the U.S. Diplomatic Mission's website at **http://canberra.usembassy.gov/visas.html**.

British subjects can obtain up-to-date visa information by calling the **U.S. Embassy Visa Information Line** (✆ **09042-450-100** from within the U.K. at £1.20 per minute; or ✆ **866/382-3589** from within the U.S. at a flat rate of $16, payable by credit card only) or by visiting the "Visas to the U.S." section of the American Embassy London's website at **http://london.usembassy.gov/visas.html**.

Irish citizens can obtain up-to-date visa information through the **U.S. Embassy Dublin,** 42 Elgin Rd., Ballsbridge, Dublin 4 (✆ **1580-47-VISA** [8472] from within the Republic of Ireland at €2.40 per minute; **http://dublin.usembassy.gov**).

Citizens of **New Zealand** can obtain up-to-date visa information by contacting the **U.S. Embassy New Zealand,** 29 Fitzherbert Terrace, Thorndon, Wellington (✆ **644/462-6000; http://newzealand.usembassy.gov**).

Visitor Information In Maryland, contact the **Maryland Office of Tourism Development** (✆ **866/639-3526;** www.visitmaryland.org). Its website has links to county websites as well. For information on Baltimore, contact **Visit Baltimore** (✆ **877/BALTIMORE** [225-8466] or 410/659-7300; www.baltimore.org). **Annapolis** visitors should contact the Annapolis and Anne Arundel County Conference and Visitors Bureau (✆ **888/302-2852** or 410/280-0445; www.visitannapolis.org).

For information on parks, forests, and wildlife refuges, contact the **Maryland Department of Natural Resources** (✆ **877/620-8DNR** [8367] or 410/260-8DNR [8367]; www.dnr.maryland.gov).

In Delaware, contact **Delaware Tourism Office** (✆ **866/2VISITDE** [284-7483] or 302/672-6834; www.visitdelaware.com). For beach and Dover information, contact **Southern Delaware Tourism** (✆ **800/357-1818** or 302/856-1818; www.visitsoutherndelaware.com). For information on Wilmington and the Brandywine Valley, contact the **Greater Wilmington Convention and Visitors Bureau** (✆ **800/489-6664** or 302/652-4088; www.visitwilmingtonde.com).

Weather and Traffic In Wilmington, dial ✆ **302/429-9000** for weather, time, and a few ads. Baltimore's phone forecast number has been discontinued. Both Maryland and Delaware have adopted the ✆ **511** traffic information line. Dial the three-digit code for local traffic updates and other info.

Index

G

H